Spoken Cree

Level I

Spoken Cree

Level I

West Coast of James Bay

C. Douglas Ellis

Original Informants

John Wynne
Anne Scott
Xavier Sutherland

The University of Alberta Press

Published by

The University of Alberta Press
Ring House 2
Edmonton, Alberta, Canada T6G 2E1

ISBN 0–88864–347–0

Canadian Cataloguing in Publication Data

Ellis, C.D. (Clarence Douglas), 1923–
Spoken Cree, level I, west coast of James Bay

Includes bibliographical references and index.
ISBN 0–88864–347–0

1. Cree language—Grammar. 2. Cree language—Conversation and phrase books. 3. Cree language—Dialects—James Bay Region (Ont. and Quebec) 4. Cree language—Spoken Cree. I. Wynne, John. II. Scott, Anne. III. Sutherland, Xavier. IV. Title.
PM986.E55 2000 497'.3 C–00910958–7

Printed on acid-free paper. ∞

Printed and bound in Canada by Hignell Book Printing Ltd., Winnipeg, Manitoba.

The University of Alberta Press gratefully acknowledges the support received for its publishing program from The Canada Council for the Arts. In addition, we also gratefully acknowledge the financial support of the Government of Canada through the Book Publishing Industry Development Program for our publishing activities.

Canada

CONTENTS

ᐸᑳᓇᐢᑌᐤ ᐆᒪ ᒪᓯᓇᐃᑲᓐ
ᐁ ᑭᐢᑭᓯᑐᑕᐚᑲᓂᐏᐟ
ᑳ ᑮ ᓃᑳᓇᑭᓱᐢᐸᓐ ᑭᒋᐊᔭᒥᐁᐏᑭᒫᐤ
ᑵᐱᕐᐟ ᒛᓐ ᓓᓂᓴᓐ

ᑳ ᑮ ᑭᐢᑕᑭᓱᐟ ᒣᒁᒡ ᐁ ᐑᒋᐱᒫᑎᓰᒥᑕᐠ
ᐊᓄᒡ ᒫᑲ ᐲᓕᐢ ᐁ ᑭᐢᑭᓯᑐᑕᐚᐠ

To the Memory
of
Robert John Renison
Archbishop

Great while he lived among us
he remains great in our memory

PREFACE

The present volume forms Level One of a three-part Cree language course. The second edition of *Spoken Cree*, published in 1983, pointed to the need for materials at a higher level and of a length more closely tailored to the academic year. The more advanced materials have now been developed and the entire treatment organized into three parts to form a three-year course in spoken Cree. Levels Two and Three will follow.

Each lesson unit begins with a basic conversation (§A), comprising new grammatical features and vocabulary in context. This is followed by a discussion of the grammar (§B), a drill section (§C), conversation practice (§D), a further conversation for listening and comprehension (§E), a reference list of new vocabulary items (§F), and a review section of questions and answers (§G). Level One is self-contained requiring no supplementary material. Current plans are to omit the final glossary from Levels Two and Three and to issue instead a Cree Learner's Dictionary, containing lexical items occurring in all three parts of the text.

The length of the basic conversation calls for comment. Certain redundancies still remaining in the 1983 edition have been pruned and longer dialogues broken into shorter sections that can be more easily managed one at a time. Excessive abridgement of earlier materials, however, or undue brevity in new conversations have been avoided. So-called poly–synthetic languages such as Cree which belong, moreover, to a different genetic stock, differ in many ways from the Standard Average European model. One result of this is that there is less transfer from language to language to assist the English speaking learner. Where access to native speakers is especially limited, experience has supported the value of ample exposure to the language to reinforce the models. Similar reasoning suggests a corresponding value in allowing §E of each unit, Listening In, to extend to sometimes considerable length, especially later in the course.

Supplementary Conversations I and II are not integral to the sequence of lessons. They were added (particularly Conversation I) at the express desire of students working in a typical campus setting and away from a Cree cultural milieu to enable them to discuss topics of local interest. Their omission will not disrupt the graduated flow of lesson material. The focus throughout is essentially pedagogical; but it is hoped that the grammatical sections, supplemented by the topical index, may be of some use as a reference grammar.

I am deeply grateful to the many persons who have helped with the production, checking and recording of new and sometimes earlier Cree materials. In particular mention should be made of the late Mr. James Wesley, Mr. Silas Wesley, Mr. and Mrs. Simon Friday and Mrs. Emily Wynne, all of Kashechewan, Ontario; the late Mr. Andrew Faries and Mrs. Emily Chilton of Moose Factory; Mrs. Mary Bird, Mrs. Agnes Hunter, Mrs. Mary Lou Iahtail, Mr. Gregory Spence, Mr. William Louttit, Mr. Matthew Sutherland, Mr. M. Metat, and many others who have on occasion provided help and information and whose assistance, though not individually mentioned, is recalled with the deepest appreciation. For the illuminating illustrations which accompany the lesson units, sincerest thanks are due to Mrs. Claire Wharmby and for the evocative line drawings in Unit 10, Drill 1, to my former neighbour, the late Mr. Fred Todds. The permission of Harcourt, Brace and Co., to quote the passage on p. 252 from *Language* by the late Edward Sapir is hereby gratefully acknowledged, as is that of the editors of the *International Journal of American Linguistics* to use materials from Vol. 37, no. 2, p. 83, in Appendix 1, and of the University of Manitoba Press to use Text 24 from *âtalôhkâna nêsta tipâcimôwina/Cree Legends and Narratives*, here printed as a reading selection in syllabics (Unit 18.D. pp. 471–72).

The sincerest appreciation is also due to Ms. Mary Mahoney-Robson of the University of Alberta Press for her meticulous editorial attention to detail, her valuable suggestions for improvement in layout and type selection and, perhaps, most of all, for her unremitting patience with an overcautious technophobe. Lastly, I owe the deepest gratitude to Ms. Eiko Emori of Eiko Emori, Inc., of Ottawa, whose timely intervention and most generous assistance rescued the organisation of a whole computer facility for imminent collapse.

Much of the field work and grammatical analysis for the 1983 edition of *Spoken Cree* were made possible through a sabbatical fellowship from the Canada Council, a study leave from McGill University and the allocation of office space by McGill's Centre for Northern Studies and Research. Field work and production of the advanced sections of *Spoken Cree* and the necessary reworking of Level One to fit the new three level format were made possible by a grant from the Multiculturalism Programs of the Department of Canadian Heritage. To all the above I tender the sincerest thanks as well as to colleagues who, as always, with tact and understanding have drawn to my attention errors they never should have had to.

C.D.E.

HOW TO USE THIS BOOK

PRELIMINARY MATERIAL

The preliminary sections, "Cree Sound System" and "Cree Grammar", provide information on the Cree sound system and an overview of certain grammatical features. They may be read as a helpful orientation before beginning Unit One. A "Pronunciation Drill" follows and will aid the reader in proper pronunciation of the Cree language.

A. BASIC CONVERSATION

The basic conversation should ideally be listened to several times, with particular attention being given to the rhythm and intonation of the Cree, before any attempt is made to learn it. "Learning" the basic conversation does not imply memorizing the text so as to be able to repeat the whole conversation by heart. It means being able to look at the English column and to reproduce the Cree equivalent without hesitation. It is strongly suggested that this be done for at least the first ten lesson units.

B. DISCUSSION OF GRAMMAR

When the basic conversation has been "overlearned" it is time to study Section B carefully. Questions you may have had when learning Section A will normally be answered in Section B, where the grammar is discussed. Your next step is to move on to Section C, where the various grammatical models are drilled.

C. DRILLS

The purpose of the drills is to enable you to "overlearn" the grammatical patterns to the point where your response becomes automatic. Unlike basic conversations, drills are practice routines. They differ in length and value. If a grammatical point is thoroughly mastered before the end of a drill (or the beginning!) it is better to proceed directly ahead. Keep in mind, however: mastery in this context means the ability to use the grammatical feature correctly and without undue hesitation. It does not mean merely understanding the explanation.

D. CONVERSATION PRACTICE
When the first three sections of each unit have been thoroughly covered, Section D provides a check routine for review as well as guidelines to help you develop a free conversation. Note the illustrations at the beginning of each unit. They recall the theme of the basic conversation and may be used as visual aids to developing further dialogue.

E. LISTENING IN
Listen to the "Listening In's" several times, or until you can follow the Cree with ease. If you find it necessary to follow the written text, do so until everything is clear; then close your book and follow the spoken line, just listening.

F. REFERENCE LIST
The Reference List is not a vocabulary to be memorized out of context. It is provided as a convenient reference and, in some units, includes earlier materials which may have been forgotten.

G. REVIEW
If time is short this section may be systematically omitted. As a review and refresher, however, it is helpful whether used by oneself or with a drill partner.

APPENDICES
Appendix I provides a synoptic view of the organisation of the Cree verb. Reference to this from time to time will help you keep a sense of where you are in the system. Appendix II shows the inflectional paradigm for each part of the verb taught in Level One. This will be expanded in Levels Two and Three as more of the verb system is introduced.

GLOSSARY
The glossary contains all the vocabulary items taught in Level One. Before using it, read the note about Stem-Class Codes and Abbreviations on p. 492.

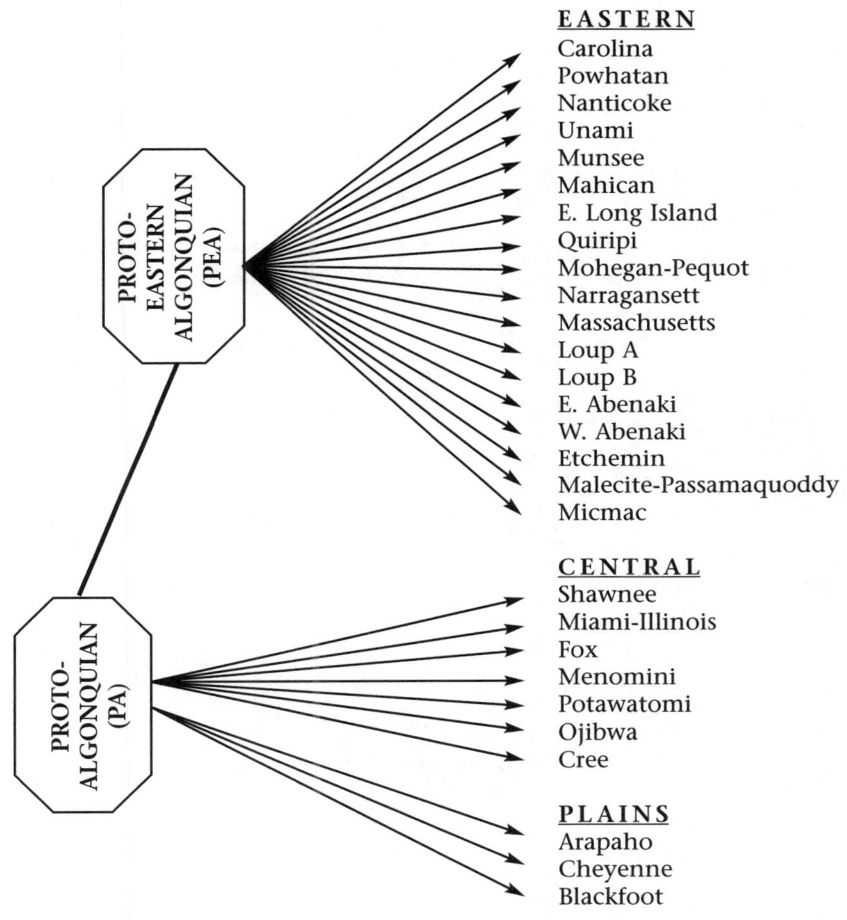

FAMILY TREE DIAGRAM OF ALGONQUIAN LANGUAGES

Adapted from Karl Teeter, "Genetic Classification in Algonquian," National Museum of Canada, Bulletin 214, Ottawa, 1967, p. 3.

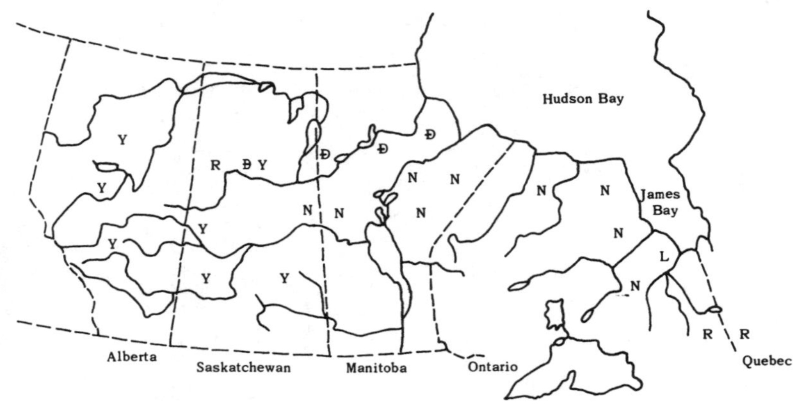

Major Cree Dialects

L — Moose Cree

N — Swampy Cree

Y — Plains Cree

D — Woods Cree

R — "R" Cree

INTRODUCTION

Cree is a member of the Algonquian family of languages (see diagram, p. xix) and is the most widely spoken of the Algonquian languages of Canada. Used all the way from Northern Quebec in the East to the foothills of the Rocky Mountains in the West, it covers an area extending from the trans-continental railway line in the South as far northward as Churchill and several hundred miles north of Prince Albert. While Cree shows dialect differences, it is recognizably the same language whether on the western plains, in the northern woodlands or on the shores of James Bay. The two most widespread dialects are Plains and Swampy Cree. It is Swampy and Moose Cree, spoken to the southeast of the Swampy Cree area, with which the present course is concerned.

Swampy Cree, sometimes known as the N-Dialect, is heard from Manitoba eastward through the muskeg and the forest covered lands of Northern Ontario to the shores of Hudson's and James Bay. To the south and slightly eastward is spoken the closely allied Moose Cree which has preserved the sound represented in English spelling by "l", now lost in Swampy Cree and replaced by "n": *e.g.,*

Moose Cree	milwêlihtam	he likes it
Swampy Cree	minwênihtam	he likes it.

Certain other minor differences exist, but speakers of different dialects, certainly of Moose and Swampy Cree, understand each other readily and are no more inconvenienced in conversation than two English speakers would be, one of whom spoke a British and the other a North American type of English. Dialects are often designated by the letter name of the sound with which the historic /l/ has merged: *e.g.,* the Y Dialect, N-Dialect, etc. The map of "Major Cree Dialects" gives a general indication of their geographic distribution.

The form of the first person, singular pronoun illustrates the relationship:

Moose Cree	nîla	L Dialect
Swampy Cree	nîna	N Dialect
Plains Cree	nîya	Y Dialect
Woods Cree	nî∂a (∂ as in English *th*en)	D Dialect
"R" Cree	nîra	R Dialect

This project was originally undertaken with the needs of Anglican missionary personnel in mind. Although Swampy Cree covers a wider area than that of the Moose Dialect, most of the Anglican literature used in both areas is published in Moose Cree. A compromise was adopted for this text. While it was decided to use Swampy Cree as the standard, the transcription regularly shows "l" where this appears in Moose Cree. Those who wish to learn the Moose Cree form are thus enabled to do so. The recordings, however, unless otherwise specified, reflect the N-Dialect usage where "l" is simply to be read as "n".

The Cree used in this course represents the accepted, conversational standard of the village of Kashechewan, formerly Albany Post, Ontario. This settlement of several hundred speakers is situated about eight kilometres / five miles up the Albany River from James Bay, and is on the fringe of Swampy Cree country. The voices recorded in Cree are those of speakers who have this as their first language and the material itself has been checked by native speakers throughout for idiomatic and formal accuracy.

The organisation of the lesson material is based on the concept of language as rule governed behaviour, where the rules generate what are perceived as a set of language patterns or behaviour habits. Emphasis is deliberately placed on two features:

1) the learning of "chunks" of language material in a natural setting, and
2) the pattern-drill type of exercise, rather than translation.

The approach is straightforwardly in the "stimulus-response" tradition, intended to promote an automatic control of the language patterns, rather than to present the student with a set of grammatical puzzles to be solved. Rote learning has often been disparaged as a mindless exercise. Admittedly it can be. There are, however, areas of experience, particularly in the development of certain skills, where rote learning, leading to instant and correct response without the necessity of laboured thought, has a certain social, and even survival, value. Perhaps most people, given time, can untangle the intricacies of a foreign grammar; but it is difficult to sustain running, verbal communication where this has to be done repeatedly. The basic conversations are built around situations in a Cree community and feature basic language materials which would be useful in such a cultural context. They are designed to be "learned" in the sense that the student, looking at any part of the English column, should be able unhesitatingly to produce the corresponding Cree. Grammatical points are then discussed in Section B and drilled in Section C of each lesson unit. The intention is that "overlearning", not merely passive understanding, of the basic conversational models, active mimicry of pronunciation and drill of grammatical patterns to the point of automatic response will culminate in an ability to "talk Cree" naturally and without undue effort.

Level One of the present course will develop a familiarity with typical day-to-day situations and, at the structural level, introduce the three orders of the Cree verb: independent, imperative and conjunct. Where morphology is concerned, the primary emphasis is on inflection. Once a basic familiarity with the language is acquired the syllabic system can be quickly learned, while reversing the procedure slows learning appreciably. Hence, introduction of the Cree syllabary is reserved until Unit Eighteen. In Level Two syllabic spelling is introduced in Sections A and E and, in Level Three, reading selections and review are finally in syllabic spelling only. Levels Two and Three of the course build further control of the language with important and more complex grammatical forms.

Substantive material of particular interest to medical, business, teaching and mission personnel is introduced throughout the text. An appreciation of local culture, however, is felt to be a necessary preliminary to any effective communication of values framed in terms of a different cultural setting.

CREE SOUND SYSTEM

Language may be regarded as a kind of signal code. Like any other communications code it is composed essentially of two things: a) the stuff out of which the signals are made: *e.g.,* light, sound, diagrams, types of motion, etc., and b) the agreed system of using this basic material so that it can convey messages. In the case of language the basic "stuff" which we perceive is sound produced by the human speech tract. The agreed system by which we employ this sound in a carefully patterned way to convey messages is called, in a general sense, grammatical structure or grammar. The sound substance of language might be compared to the building materials in a house; the grammar, to the plan by which the materials are put together. Clearly, much has to go on in the brain by way of organizing both the sound system and the various levels of grammatical structure. In our present state of knowledge, this level of organization must be inferred since it cannot be directly perceived. For the practical purposes of learning, however, we shall consider the area of language which we perceive as broadly structured on two immediately apparent levels:

grammar
sound-system

Let us first briefly consider the Cree sound system.

An unfamiliar language often seems to the listener to display a wide variety of unusual sounds. The fact is that every language makes use of a fairly limited selection of *key* sounds or sound types, in comparison with the total range possible to the human speech tract. The thing to note about these *key* or *distinctive* sounds is that each one is recognizably different from every other key sound in the same language even though it may itself show a certain range of phonetic variation.

Phonetic Variation of Distinctive Sounds

For an example of phonetic variation within a key sound range, consider the English words, "keel" and "cool". We can tell by a little experimentation that the initial consonant in "cool" is made further back in the mouth than the initial consonant in "keel". (Try pronouncing them one after the other and feel the difference.) What is happening is that the vowel in each case changes the position of the k sound which immediately precedes it, as the tongue gets into a position more suitable to the enunciation of the vowel itself. Yet, ordinarily, if a speaker made the initial sound in "kill" and that in "cool", without saying the remainder of either word, the average English speaker would consider them as essentially the same sound. Of course, if we listen carefully there actually *is* a difference between the two k's; but it is nothing like as important as the difference between k and p. Substitution of one k-sound for another does not do anything to change the message; whereas the substitution of p for either will give us a completely different word: "peel" or "pool". In short, where the difference is automatically conditioned by surrounding sounds, as with the different types of k, we learn to disregard the difference and hear all the variants of k as just one distinctive sound. The only contrasts to which we really attend are those of the k versus p variety, since they make a difference in the meaning for us.

The point of all this is that a distinctive sound occurring in any one language may be slightly altered phonetically by surrounding sounds and yet be recognizable as maintaining its own identity which makes it different from every other distinctive sound in that language. One might regard each *key* or *distinctive* sound as, in fact, a small range of sound. This will be particularly apparent from the vowel diagram below. Within each range the proper variants of each distinctive sound are then combined into larger units (*i.e.,* parts of words or words) which convey meaning to users of that particular code.

There are in every language a limited number of these recognizably *distinctive* sounds, vowels as well as consonants. We may conveniently refer to them as *phonemes*. A *phonetic* transcription would take account of every minute sound difference which the transcriber could perceive (*e.g.,* the two k's above) whether they made a difference to the meaning or not. A *phonemic* spelling notes only the sound contrasts which make a difference to the meaning. Therefore a phonemic spelling would write all the k sounds in English with one letter. The convention is to use slant bars to mark a phonemic transcription, thus: /k/, when we wish to show that it is distinctive differences only which we are marking, such as the contrast between k and p. The Cree which we are studying (Moose Cree) has twelve such distinctive consonantal sounds and seven vowels. These are the sounds represented by the letters in the sections in Roman transcription throughout the text. The following diagram illustrates the point of articulation in the mouth of the consonantal sounds.

Consonants

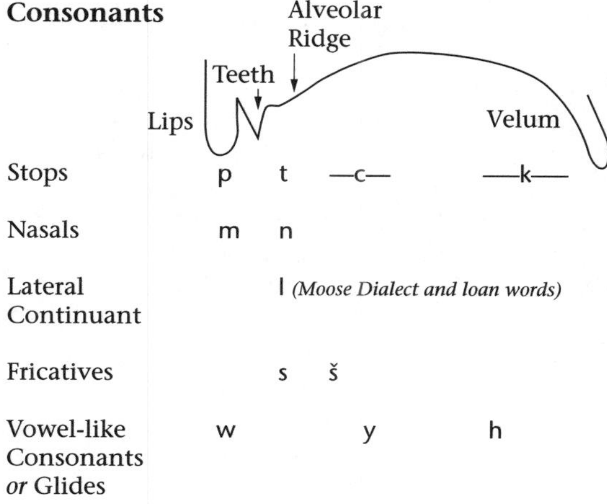

Voicing is not distinctive (*i.e.*, phonemic) in Cree, but it often occurs on stops medially when preceded by a stressed long vowel or a nasal, as well as in certain other places: *e.g.*,

	mâci-	[ma·dži]
but	măci-	[mʌtʃi].

/h/, where it occurs between vowels, sometimes undergoes a carry-over of voicing producing almost the effect of a glottal stop: *e.g.*, êhêpik "spider" > ê'êpik. At other times it may be replaced by /y/: *e.g.*, ayamihêw "she speaks to him" may be heard as ayamiyêw.

Pre-aspiration of Stops

A puff of air before a stop consonant marks a phonemic distinction: *e.g.*,

pêtâw	he brings it	pêhtâw	he waits for it
akocin	he hangs	akohcin	he floats
pakân	nut	pahkân	separately

(The pre-aspiration is very light in Moose Cree and up the west coast of James Bay. It becomes somewhat easier to distinguish as one moves inland to the West.)

A feature to note about the occurrence of aspiration is that the emphatic utterance of an initial vowel is often preceded by [h] which, in this position, is merely an indication of heavy stress. Similarly, utterances ending in a vowel often drift off in a kind of soft aspiration which, however, signals no difference in meaning.

/s/ varies all the way from apico-alveolar position to that of lamino-alveopalatal.

/c/ and /š/ are often more fronted than English "ch" in "church". This sometimes makes it difficult for the English speaker to distinguish the positional variants, or *allophones,* of /s/ from /š/. /š/, however, appears always to be characterized by some measure of retroflexion. In initial position (šîpî stretch), between vowels (iši thus, so) or finally (wayêš about, approximately), it is almost identical with English /š/ as in "hush". Note the distinction between

	môla n'tôsihtân	I'm hard of hearing
and	môla n'tôšihtân	I'm not making it,
or	nakiskaw	a little while
and	nakiškaw	meet him.

To the north and west of the Moose area pre-aspirated stops are easier to hear, but the distinction between /s/ and /š/ is more difficult to catch. In Western (Plains) Cree, /s/ and /š/ fall together and no contrast remains between the two.

/n/. When the dropping of a short vowel leaves /n/ immediately adjacent to a following stop, assimilation of the nasal to the same position of articulation takes place: *e.g.,*

nipâskisikan	my gun	> m'pâskisikan
nitêm	my dog	> n'têm (with light voicing on /t/)
nicîmân	my canoe	> n'cîmân (with light voicing on /c/)
nikotwâs	six	> [ŋkʊtɔ˞s].

Two or three interesting usages in the Fort Albany-Kashechewan area may be due to Ojibwa contact:

šâŋkwêš	a quarter	Cf. Ojibwa šânkwêššiw	mink
šâkitât	nine (Moose Cree)	šâŋkitât *or* šâŋk (Kashechewan)	
		Cf. Ojibwa šânkwasswi	nine[1]
mîkwêc	thank you	> [mîŋkwêc] (*with some speakers*).	

/w/ is pronounced with lips held straighter, *i.e.,* less rounded, than in English.

[1] Piggott, G.L. and A. Grafstein, *An Ojibwa Lexicon* (Ottawa: National Museums of Canada, 1983), p. 151.

Vowels

Cree has seven vowel phonemes: four long, three short. Long vowels are transcribed in this text with a circumflex accent, < ˆ >, over the letter. In the Cree syllabic writing system a super-imposed dot is used to indicate vowel length, except in the case of /ê/ (syllabic ᐁ), which is always long. The vowels are

LONG	SHORT
î	
	i
ê	
ô	o
â	a

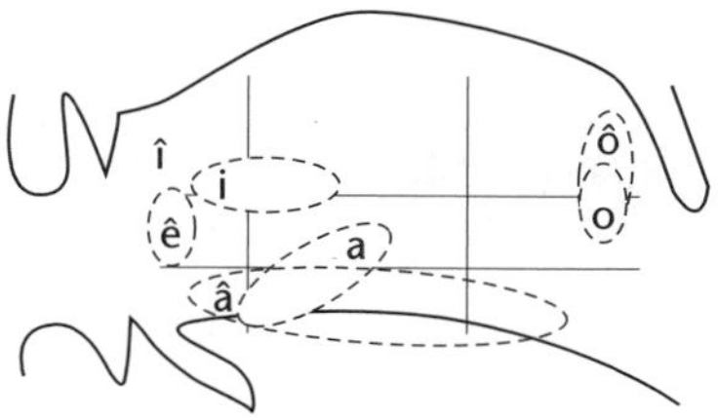

The mid-to-high back vowels are accompanied by a greater degree of lip-rounding, the low-back by a lesser degree, the front by none at all.

î is pronounced approximately as in English "seen".

ê is produced at the front of the mouth and is open, as in German Mädchen, or is close to the vowel of English "they", without the final 'y'-glide.

ô varies all the way from "o", as in English "bone" to "oo", as in English "boon".

â ranges in quality all the way from a vowel much like that in English "mash", through the "a" in "hall".

ĭ varies all the way from the "i" in English "pin", to "e", as in English "get". It is made with the tongue surface lower and is more central than Cree /î/.

ŏ ranges roughly from the "o", as in "more", to the vowel in "foot".

ă covers the range from the vowel in English "hat" to that in "hut". Immediately before /y/, it may sound almost like /ê/: *e.g.,* âšay [a·žɛy].

Vowel length makes an important difference. Compare nimaskisin "my shoe" with nimâskisin "I am lame", or sakihikan "screw", with sâkihikan "lake".

CAUTION: The foregoing comparisons to English vowels are only rough approximations. The type of English referred to is that spoken in the area of Montreal and much of central Canada. The comparisons will be completely invalid for many English speakers from other dialect areas and are, in any case, offered only as rough indications rather than adequate descriptions in terms of articulatory phonetics. The key to an authentic, native pronunciation lies in mimicry of a native speaker.

CREE GRAMMAR

The "Cree Sound System" dealt with the basic sound signals with which the Cree language code operates. (Remember: sound *in itself* does not convey meaning. The basic function of the sound signals is to keep meanings apart.) In the following section we will take a quick look at features of the system by which the meaning elements of the code are put together to transmit more complex messages. Attention is focussed particularly on certain features in which Cree differs markedly from English.

This description might be compared to a rapid survey flight over unknown country to gain a general idea of surface conditions before beginning a journey overland. From the air one could see whether the country was flat or mountainous, well watered or dry, heavily forested or otherwise. In the same way a quick glance at some outstanding structural characteristics of a new language is often helpful in suggesting the kind of thing one may expect to meet as learning proceeds.

Word Order and Word Form

How do we know which words are closely connected with which others in any utterance?

In many languages the *arrangement* of words in a sentence is of basic importance in conveying meaning. "John hit Bill" and "Bill hit John" are statements indicating a reversal in the relationship of the persons under discussion. In some languages, however, a change in word order might alter the emphasis of the statement, but not the basic meaning which would be indicated not so much by the word order as by the form of the words themselves. Consider the two sentences, "I love thee" and "Thee love I". Obviously the meaning is the same even though the word order is different. By contrast, "Thee love I" and "Thou lovest me" have retained the same word order for the pronouns, but the *form* of the words themselves indicates a change in the direction of the action. Perhaps we would write "Thee love I" only under pressure of versification; but the point is that in these two sentences we signal who the doer of the action is and who the recipient by the *form* of the words, not by their *order*. Note how not only the pronouns, but the verb as well, signalled by its form what the subject was: *love-lovest*. This is a form of *agreement* or *concord*.

A violation of our accepted speech habits in this connection sounds odd to us; but if the distortion is not too great we are still able to discern meaning. For example, in a one-time popular ballad occur the words, "Daylight come, an' me wan' go home". Standard English usage would require, "Daylight comes, and I want to go home"—yet everyone understands the dialect form. The *form* of the words (or *morphology*) has been distorted, but the word *order* (*syntax*) has remained by and large intact. Since English relies heavily on word order rather than word form to show the relation of words to each other, and since the word order has been maintained, we are still able to grasp the message.

In Cree the balance is the other way around. Much more meaning is signalled by the *form* of the words themselves than is the case in English. Verbs, for example, show extensive concord for gender and number with nouns and pronouns which stand as their subject or object. Just as an English speaker will observe English habits of word order rather carefully, so a Cree speaker will be just as attentive to word form since this is of basic importance to him in conveying meaning. Word endings (and beginnings) are just as vital in Cree as the dictionary meaning of the word itself. Without them it is impossible to talk Cree. Because of the relative importance of word form, the grammar of the Basic Conversations has been controlled to allow greater concentration in this area and the drills have been designed to stress this feature. The goal is to encourage production of the right form automatically without undue strain or hesitation. It is possible to do this in conversation only if the forms have been drilled to the point of becoming automatic.

Preference for Verbal Constructions

Another general sort of feature which stands out in Cree is a preference for saying a thing with verbs, where English would lean more heavily on nouns. An English speaker might remark, "It's time for lunch now". Note the empty subject, "it", plus two nouns, "time" and "lunch". In Cree it would be more natural to say, "Now (it) so goes that (one) eat": "âšay ispaliw kici-mîcisonâniwahk". Neither the "it" nor the "one" is separately expressed in Cree. Both are included in the verb form.

Again, describing words in Cree are not adjectives. They are normally intransitive verb forms. It is as though, instead of saying "She is slender", "He is strong", "It is funny", one were to say, "She slenders", "He strongs", "It funnies". Similarly, "It is a fine day", might be paraphrased from Cree as, "It-fine-days", a single verb form! This preference for verbal constructions brings us to another feature of Cree: the combining of various different elements to make up words.

Word Building

Under this heading we shall look briefly at three major mechanisms of word building: *inflection, derivation* and *(stem) composition.*

Inflection

It was noted above that Cree depends heavily on changes in the form of its words to convey meaning. As an example consider the following:

cîmân	canoe	cîmânihk	in the canoe
ocîmâniwâw	their canoe	ocîmâniwâhk	in their canoe

Such changes are called *inflections* (literally, "bendings") of the word at one or both ends. Cree uses inflection to signal a number of categories: possessor, number, case, etc. We shall study these as the course proceeds. When the inflectional material is removed, what remains is the stem of the word. Inflection is the outermost layer of word building.[1]

Derivation

Derivation is the mechanism by which stems are built. Many common stems are quite simple, like cîmân—canoe, or nâpêw—man, each of which consists of a root and a final element. (The hyphen after the stem indicates that this is the point at which any further material such as an inflectional ending may be added.) Other stems, both nouns and verbs, are more complex and consist of several recognizable elements put together to form a single stem. This stem is then furnished with such inflectional endings as may be required to form a complete word. For example, in English one "has a headache". The Cree têwistikwânê- might be paraphrased as "ache...head...icate-", or some such word. The pattern is a neat and regular one, and any number of other things may be substituted for ...stikwân-, head: *e.g.,* têwi...sit...ê- have an aching foot, têw...âpit...ê- have a toothache. In the composite form the first member signals the action, the second, the focus of the action and the third, the appropriate stem ending to which the inflectional material is added. The result is an intransitive verb with easily recognizable parts. "She takes off (her) hat", "He visits (his) nets", admit of corresponding treatment. This combination of elements into one form on a specific pattern is a common feature of Cree. Once the patterns are learned, it should be no more difficult to say this kind of thing in one word in Cree than to say the equivalent in a sentence of several words in English. Cree, and other so-called *polysynthetic* languages, often transact as much business in a word as a language like English

[1] Cf. Wolfart, H.C. and Janet F. Carroll, *Meet Cree,* 2nd. ed. (Edmonton: University of Alberta Press, 1981), pp. 33–52.

does in a whole sentence. These regular patterns of combination are used not only with verbs, but extend to other types of stems as well: *e.g.,* cîkah...ikan—chop instrument, axe; cîkah...ikan...âhtik(w)—axe handle. Derivation builds stems by adding elements to a root (or some similar base) or to another stem.

Composition or *Compounding of Stems*
In addition to changing the endings on stems (*inflection*) and building them up internally (*derivation*), a third device for word construction is to put stems together to form compounds. In composition one or more prior members are prefixed to a noun stem, a verb stem or a particle.[2] This involves prefixing elements to nouns or verbs rather than adding them on after some initial segment as in derivation. We do something like this in English. A kennel may alternatively be called a dog-house. "Dog" is prefixed to qualify "house". A small canine may be called a house-dog. Here "house" is prefixed to qualify "dog".The several major ways of doing this in Cree are illustrated in the following examples:

1) Particle + Noun. Particle stems are commonly prefixed to a noun stem to form a compound stem: ayawaši fresh + wîyâs- meat, combine to form ayawaši-wîyâs- fresh meat; kayâši old + âlahkonâw- bread, form kayâši-âlahkonâw stale bread. These particle prefixes are not adjectives. They behave more like English prefixes "sub-", as in subcommittee, sublet, or "pre-", as in preview and many may also be prefixed to verb stems.

2) Noun + Noun. One noun stem may be prefixed to another to form a compound. From nâpêw- man + âpatisîwin- work, may be generated a typical compound, nâpêwi-âpatisîwin- man's work. nisk- goose + pîsim(w)- moon, month, combine to form the compound, niski-pîsim(w)- goose moon, April. (Note connective i- between stems.)

3) Verb + Noun. A verb stem may occur as the prior member in stem composition: makošê- feast + kîšikâw- day, yield the compound stem makošêwi-kîšikâw- feast day (used in some areas for Christmas). (Note connective wi- between verb stem and noun.)

4) Particle + Verb. Prefixed particles are particularly common with verbs. For example, pêci movement towards speaker + nîmi- dance, combine to produce pêci-nîmi- come to dance. Add the further prefix, kî completed action, and ...w, third person singular actor, and one has kî-pêci-nîmiw he came to dance.

[2] Bloomfield, L., 1946, p. 103.

5) Verb + Verb. Examples of a verb stem prefixed to another verb stem may be seen in forms such as mâtinawê-kîšikâ- be Saturday (distribution day at the old Hudson's Bay posts) < mâtinawê- distribute + kîšikâ- be day.

Other variations occur and will be studied in the units ahead. Note that the members of a compound form are written with connecting hyphens.

Stem Classes

Words in Cree fall into one of three stem classes or parts of speech. They are

1) *Substantives—i.e.,* noun-like words, including pronouns.
   a) Nouns—both independent stems and dependent stems which can occur only in non-initial combination with other elements. Nouns belong to one of two genders: animate or inanimate.
   b) Pronouns—personal, demonstrative, etc.

2) *Verbs*—In addition to independent verb stems, there are also a number of *stem finals* which carry concrete meaning: *e.g.,* walk, go, fly, etc., but which require a preceding, initial element to form a full stem: *e.g.,* ...pali- go preceded by pimi... along, yields pimipali- go along. Verbs fall into four basic types: intransitive, further subdivided for animate or inanimate subject (VAI and VII respectively) and transitive, with animate or inanimate object (VTA and VTI respectively).

3) *Particles*—forms which are never inflected: ohci for, from; wîskâc ever; iši so, etc.

Gender

Gender means a classification of nouns such that certain closely associated words show a specific type of concord for the class of noun with which they are constructed. In many Indo-European languages adjectives change their shape to show the gender of the noun they modify. In Algonquian languages it is verbs which show concord for the gender class of noun.

Cree nouns belong to one of two genders: *animate* or *inanimate.* It happens that the names of all living creatures are contained in the animate class; but so are the names of a good many lifeless objects like socks, kettles, stones, paddles, flour, etc. No living creatures are represented in the second, the *inanimate* group. So for purposes of convenience, one class of nouns is called *animate* and the other, *inanimate*. Verbs which go with these nouns show by their form to which class the noun with which they are constructed belongs. Pronouns (except for personal pronouns and one intensive), display the same two-way classification.

Among English speakers, popular thinking about gender often confuses it with sex. While there is obviously a connection as far as the use of the personal pronouns, he-she, him-her(s), it-its, is concerned, this is about the only trace of such a distinction which is left in English. In Cree, the grammatical dividing line is not drawn between masculine and feminine at all but, as we have seen, between animate and inanimate. Gender, in short, is a purely grammatical classification denoting what kinds of words require certain grammatical treatment. Its relation, if any, to biology is often quite incidental.[3]

Number

Nouns, pronouns and verbs show forms for two numbers: *singular* and *plural*.

Case

Three separate cases may be formally distinguished for nouns and at least one pronominal form:[4]

1) the *mention case* or *nominative*. This is the form in which a noun appears when it is the subject or object of a verb, or in citation form.
2) the *oblique case* or *locative*. This is the form displayed when nouns are used to indicate a point of location or with certain particles denoting spatial or temporal relationships often expressed by a prepositional phrase in English:

e.g.,	cîmân	a canoe
	cîmânihk	in a/the canoe
	cîmânihk ohci	from a/the canoe.

3) the *address case* or *vocative*. This is used when addressing someone, as: *e.g.,* nôhtâ (My) Father. Formal distinction between this and the nominative, however, exists in only a few words and in some areas the nominative is used for purposes of address.

[3] Some languages, *e.g.,* Inuktitut, have no gender classification.
[4] kotakiy the other one, shows a locative form, kotakîhk. It is the only pronominal form in which this has been noted.

Obviative or Further Third Person

In the English sentence, "Bill saw George as he went down the street", there is no way of knowing with certainty to whom the "he" refers unless further elaboration is added: *e.g.,* he (Bill) or he (George). Cree, however, leaves no doubt since a further third (or "fourth") person can be quite clearly indicated. In what follows, 3 will represent the first third person mentioned and 3′, the further third person.

	cwân	wâpamêw	mêriwa	ê-kihtohtêt
	John (3)	sees (her: 3′)	Mary (3′)	as - 3 goes away (John is going away)
but,	cwân	wâpamêw	mêriwa	ê-kihtohtêlici
	John	sees (her: 3′)	Mary (3′)	as - 3′ goes away (Mary is going away)

This mechanism, known as *obviation* and so useful for maintaining clarity, extends throughout Cree for all nouns, demonstrative and certain other pronouns, and verbs. The first third person is known as the *proximate,* the second as the *obviative*. It is actually possible, where a noun is possessed by a further third person, to distinguish a further obviative or fifth position.

Cf. cwân ostêsa
John (3) his (3) older brother (3′): *i.e.,* John's older brother

and cwân ostêsa otôtêmilîw
John (3) his (3) older brother (3′) his (3′) friend (3″)
i.e., John's older brother's friend.

The foregoing sketch outlines certain major features of Cree grammar which differ considerably from what we are used to in English. The material in the course has been arranged and graded to present the structure of Cree in a convenient learning order. The lesson material in any one unit should be learned thoroughly before proceeding to the next. The student is urged to make use of every opportunity to talk with Cree speakers from the very outset of the course. Listening and speaking are much more important, in that order, than reading and writing. In learning your own language listening came first, then speaking. Reading and writing followed much later. By the time the course is completed there should have been established a good, basic control of the Cree language and, it is hoped, a reliable foundation on which to build further competence and control.

Pronunciation Drills

You are eager to learn a few expressions that might be useful on your first arrival in a village where Cree is spoken. Before doing this, however, practise the pronunciation of the following words, imitating the recording or your Cree teacher as closely as you can. "He" is used for convenience as the third person, singular subject; but the same forms would be used for the subject "she". Remember, gender in Cree distinguishes between *animate* and *inanimate* and does not parallel the *male, female* sex distinction the way it may do to some extent in other languages.

a.i /â/

âpaham	he *or* she opens it
kâsow	he *or* she hides
âhcipitêw	he *or* she moves it by pulling

The quality of the /â/ vowel is much like that in English "bad, lad, sad".

a.ii /w/ + /â/ Note the change in the quality of the /â/ when preceded by /w/. Think of the English "wash, want, wasp, Walter".

wânaw	far, far away	kwâpaham	he dips it
ê'kwâni	then (*emphatic*)	wâciyê	hello, good-bye
ospwâkan	pipe (for smoking)	awâšiš	child

a.iii Consonant + /w/ + /â/: *e.g.,* /-lwâ-/, /-nwâ-/, /-šwâ-/:

milwâšin	it is fine, it is nice
kinwâw	it is long
šwâp	store, shop

Note how the sound represented by /w/ disappears entirely or almost entirely, but it still conditions the quality of the /â/, so that milwâšin sounds much like "milawshin" and šwâp much like "shop" in English. (Do not let yourself pronounce it as "shwop".)

Note: Words used to illustrate pronunciation are not included in the Reference List unless they also occur in Section A, Basic Conversation, or Sections C, D or E.

a.iv /â/ + /w/. Listen to the vowel in the final syllable in each of the following words:

ay'hâw	well, uh...	niwâpamâw	I see him / her
kîšikâw	day	okimâw	manager, boss
nitêpwâtâw	I call him/her	nipâw	he sleeps

Note how the final /w/ makes the /â/ just before it sound somewhat like the vowel in English "how" or "now". It is not as deep or far back in the mouth as the first vowel in "Walter" or "swallow".

a.v Now contrast the /â/ in the words of the left hand column with the /â/ in those on the right. Mimic the Cree pronunciation.

ay'hâw	well, uh...	cîmân	canoe
ihtâw	he is (somewhere)	nitihtânân	we are (somewhere)
nikiskêlimâw	I know her	nikiskêlimânân	we know her
kîšikâw	day	ê-kîšikâk	that it is day
okimâw	manager, boss	nitokimâm	my boss
nîšo šwâpa	two stores	nîšošâp	twelve

a.vi From time to time words have been borrowed from English. Among them are

šwâp	shop
kwâpiy	coffee
cwân	John
wâciyê	*From English greeting,* "What cheer!"
wâpašîšin	free trader, *from English* "opposition": *i.e.,* to the Hudson's Bay Company.

Where the vowel in the source word sounds much like the o in "shop", this is represented in Cree by the vowel /â/. The feeling, however, that an /â/ of this type requires a preceding /w/ is so strong among Cree speakers, that one sometimes notices the suspicion of a /w/ just before the vowel is spoken.

b. /i/ + /w/

In the following words, note how the vowel /i/ is affected when followed by /w/: *e.g.,* pôsiw "he embarks, he departs by vehicle" sounds much like what we might write as *poosoo* in conventional, English spelling.

nipôsin	I embark	*but*	pôsiw	he embarks
ninôkosin	I appear	*but*	nôkosiw	he appears
nitâpatisin	I work	*but*	âpatisiw	he works
niwâpin	I see	*but*	wâpiw	he sees
nitôtakikomin	I have a cold	*but*	otakikomiw	he has a cold
nimihcilawêsin	I am sorry	*but*	mihcilawêsiw	he is sorry

c.i Consonant + /w/ + /êw/. Contrast the following:

itêw	he says to him	
itwêw	he says	
pîhtokêw	he enters	(*alternate*
pîhtokwêw	he enters	*forms*)

c.ii Now listen to the pronunciation of the following and imitate each word several times.

itwêw	he says
pîhtokwêw	he enters
âhtokwêw	he moves camp
kîsiswêw	he cooks him
pâskiswêw	he shoots him
otâmahwêw	he hits him

Note how the effect of a consonant + /w/ before the /ê/ of the final syllable is to make it sound much like the /o/, in kâsow (Drill a.i., above).

d. Elision of /i/ and /a/

The two short vowels, /i/ and /a/, are frequently elided in the course of rapid speech, as may be observed in the complete sentences of the Basic Conversation and in the following.

Cree writes	but says
nika-wâpamâw	ŋ'ka-wâpamâw
nikiskêlihtên	ŋ'kiskê'ltên
nitôkimâm	n'tôkimâm
nitapin	n'tapin
natawêlihtam	n'tawêl'tam
nitapwoy	n'tapwoy
nicîmân	n'cîmân

What do you notice about the point of articulation of the consonants which are adjacent to each other after the elision of the vowel? Do you notice any other elision? /h/ before syllables beginning with p, t, c and k is not usually written in Moose Cree syllabic spelling, although it is regularly shown in transliteration in this text.

As you mimic the pronunciation, imitate any short cuts or contractions. Actual language is the **spoken**, not the written word. Spelling is, for the most part, only a more or less imperfect attempt to represent the distinctive sounds of the language. To force the spoken language into line with some supposed standard of correctness in the written word is to put the cart before the horse. We are all aware of the anomalies of English spelling. While standard Cree orthography is not nearly as inexact or out of date as its English counterpart, it still falls somewhat short of representing the spoken word with one hundred percent accuracy. So take the voice of the living speaker as your guide and the spoken word as your model.

UNIT ONE

HUDSON BAY
COMPANY

A. BASIC CONVERSATION

Greetings and Useful Expressions

A visitor has just arrived at a Cree village. Several canoes can be seen moored along the river bank. By the path up to the village, the visitor asks a local resident for directions.

Visitor:	wâciyê!	Hello!
Resident:	wâciyê.	Hello.
Visitor:	tântê	where ?
	tântê šwâp?	Where (is) the store?
	[Pronounce as "shop".]	
Resident:	nêtê	yonder, over there
	mêskanaw	path
	mêskanâhk	on the path
	nêtê piko, mêskanâhk.	Just over there, down the path.
Visitor:	okimâw	manager, "boss"
	mâka	but
	tântê mâka okimâw?	But where's the manager?
Resident:	ihtâw	he / she is (at a place)
	šwâpihk ihtâw	he is at the store
	mâškôc	perhaps, maybe
	mâškôc šwâpihk ihtâw.	Perhaps he's at the store.
Visitor:	nâ	"question marker"
	ôtê	hither
	ôtê nâ? *or* ôtê nâ itêhkê?[1]	This way?

1 ôtê "hither, this way"; itêhkê "-wards, on the side": ôtê itêhkê "hitherwards, on the hither side": *i.e.,* this way.

Resident:	êkotê![2]	That's the way! That's right!
Visitor:	nimawâpin piko	I'm only visiting
	nimawâpin piko ôta.	I'm only visiting here.
	kimawâpin nâ *kîla*?	Are *you* just visiting?
Resident:	môla	no, not
	môla, nitasîhkân ôta.	No, I live here.
Visitor:	môla ninisitohtên.	I don't understand.
	itwê	say [Imperative]
	mîna itwê.	Say (it) again.
	pêhkâc itwê.	Say (it) slowly.
	pêhkâc mîna itwê.	Say (it) again slowly.
Resident:	nitašîhkân ôta.	I live here.
Visitor:	âšay ninisitohtên.	Now I understand.
	kââ!	oh!
	kââ, ôta mâka kitašîhkân!	Oh, you live here, then!
Resident:	ihtâwin	village, settlement
	êkôma[2]	this one [emphatic]
	êhê, êkôma n'tihtâwin.	Yes, this (is) my village.
	nâspic	very, very much
	nâspic milwâšin ôta.	It's very nice here.

Study Section B, Discussion of Grammar, carefully, then proceed to Drills 1 through 6.

[2] êkotê: contraction of êwako "the selfsame, the very" + itê a particle meaning "at a place" > êkotê "this very way"; êwako + ôma "this one" > êkôma "this very one".

B. DISCUSSION OF GRAMMAR

1. Verbs: Animate Intransitive—VAI

1.1 Subject Prefixes

Cree verbs show what the subject is by a set of prefixes and verb endings. For example, nipâ means "sleep".[1] If the speaker is the subject: *i.e.,* **I** sleep, the prefix is ni... and the ending ...n giving the full form, ninipân—I sleep, I am sleeping. Where the subject is the addressee: *i.e.,* **you**, the prefix is ki... with the same ending: kinipân—you sleep, you are sleeping. In other words, with the prefix ni... the speaker is involved in the action: *i.e.,* is the subject; ki... means the addressee is involved. Where neither 1st nor 2nd person is involved, *i.e.,* where the subject is a 3rd person, there is no prefix.

ni...nipâ...n	I sleep
ki...nipâ...n	you sleep
nipâ...w	he *or* she sleeps

The endings are used to show whether the subjects are singular or plural. These forms will be learned later but may be illustrated as follows:

ni...nipâ...n	I sleep	ni...nipâ...nân	we sleep
ki...nipâ...n	you (sg.) sleep	ki...nipâ...nâwâw	you (pl.) sleep
nipâ...w	he *or* she sleeps	nipâ...wak	they sleep

For the moment we shall focus our attention on the singular only. Also, since prefixes and suffixes are not really separate words, we shall write each form as a single unit: ninipân, nipâw, etc.

1.2 Imperative

In Section 1.1, the meaning given for nipâ was "sleep". This represents the simplest form of the verb, stripped of any prefixes or suffixes: the so-called

[1] Entries in the Reference List and the Glossary are listed by stems. A hyphen indicates the point at which inflectional material may be added to the stem. The triple point ... is used to separate elements in inflected forms and to show inflectional (and later, derivational) elements when cited alone: *e.g.,* ni... or ...ihk.

stem. In the Basic Conversation section you also learned another stem, itwê "say". The stem alone expresses the imperative or command form: nipâ—sleep, itwê—say. (Caution: verbs like itwê, with a stem ending in ê, change the ê to â with the prefixes ni... and ki...: *e.g.,* nit...itwân—I say; and nit... is just the form of ni... before a vowel. Apart from that, everything is regular.)

1.3 Gender and Verbs

Gender is a grammatical category and simply means classes of nouns reflected in the behaviour of associated words.[2] Cree has two such classes of nouns or genders: *animate* and *inanimate*. Verbs that accompany nouns must show by their form to which gender the nouns belong. At the moment we are dealing only with verbs that do not take an object: *i.e.,* intransitive verbs. Where the **subject** is animate, *e.g.,* nipâw—**he/she** sleeps, we speak of Animate Intransitive Verbs, listed as VAI in the Reference List and Glossary. Where the subject is inanimate: *e.g.,* milwâšin—**it** is nice, they are listed as Inanimate Intransitive Verbs or VII.

2. Nouns

2.1 Gender of Nouns

Cree nouns (as noted in Unit 1.B.1.3) belong to one of two genders, *animate* or *inanimate*. This means that nouns require certain grammatical agreement on the part of other words with which they are associated. Gender classification does not necessarily follow biological lines: *e.g.,* âšokwan—wharf, is an animate noun as shown by the agreement of the demonstrative pronoun, awa—this one, whereas cîmân—canoe requires the inanimate form of the pronoun, ôma. Animate nouns are listed NA and inanimate as NI in the Reference List and Glossary.

awa âšokwan	this wharf
ôma cîmân	this canoe

2.2 Personal Possessor Prefixes

The possessor prefixes on a word are like the subject prefixes, part of the whole word: *e.g.,* kitâšokwan—your dock, ocîmân—his canoe. The possessor prefix pattern is as follows:

[2] Hockett, C.F., 1958; p. 231.

	NA		NI	
1	nitâšokwan	my dock	nicîmân	my canoe
2	kitâšokwan	your dock	kicîmân	your canoe
3	otâšokwana	his/her dock	ocîmân	his/her canoe

Note the form of the possessor prefix with t before a vowel, and the final a on otâšokwana. This final a occurs regularly when an animate noun is possessed by a third person.

When you come to the drills you will notice an m on the end of some possessed forms. Certain nouns always take an **…ιm**[3] suffix when possessed. Learn the forms as they stand so that you automatically add the suffix every time you use this noun with a possessor prefix.

2.3 Locative Case

Nouns also have a neat little suffix, …**ιhk**,[3] which means "in, at, on *or* to". Nouns with this suffix attached, which shows location, are said to be in the *locative* case. So,

âšokwan	dock, wharf	>	âšokwanιhk[3]	at *or* on the wharf
cîmân	canoe	>	cîmânιhk	in the canoe
šwâp	store	>	šwâpιhk	at, in *or* to the store

Words ending in w or y show a contraction:

mêskanaw	path + …ιhk	>	mêskanâhk	on the path, on the trail
sîpiy	river + …ιhk	>	sîpîhk	on *or* in the river

(Cree has no word for *the* or *a(n)*. In English translation one or the other is normally supplied from the context.)

3. Particles

Particles, unlike nouns or verbs, are stems that do not take any inflection. They perform a number of functions, some adverbial, indicating time, place and manner. They are listed, for the most part, as IPC: *i.e.,* Indeclinable Particle.

[3] From time to time you will notice certain inflectional and derivational suffixes spelled with an initial ι when introduced in Section B, but spelled with an ordinary i elsewhere. Treat them both in pronunciation as being the same /i/ vowel. The different spelling has to do with certain very old sound changes that still affect the forms of modern Cree. These will be discussed periodically (*v.* Units 7, 11, 13, 16) and the spelling will help identify where the changes take place. *See also* Ellis, C. Douglas, 1957; §2.1, p. 78.
[4] âšokwan: variant of âšokan.

3.1 Time

Only one such particle has occurred so far: âšay now, by now; already:

âšay ninisitohtên	now I understand (it)

If waiting for a signal to start, you might ask:

âšay nâ?	now?

3.2 Place

Among those that you have met are:

ôta	here	ôtê	hither	nêtê	over there, yonder
		êkotê	that way	nêtê piko	just over there
		tântê	where?		

3.3 Manner

A whole range of particles falls into this group:

mîna	again
pêhkâc	slowly
nâspic	very, very much

and others, which you will meet.

3.3.1 Negative Particle

The negative particle used by itself can simply mean "no":

môla, nitašîhkân ôta	No, I live here.

It also functions as a negator with verbs, negating an affirmative statement:

môla nitašîhkân ôta	I do not live here;
môla ninisitohtên	I do not understand.

3.3.2 Question Marker

Simple questions which can be answered by "yes" or "no" (sometimes called Yes-No or Y.N. questions) are formed by adding the question marker, nâ, after the first, full word of the sentence: *e.g.,*

kimawâpin nâ?	Are you visiting?
šwâpihk nâ kitihtân?	Are you at the store?

Where the question is a single word, the rule still holds:

cwâniy nâ?	Johnny?
tâpwê nâ?	Really?

C. DRILLS

It is obviously useful to know a fairly large number of words in a language; but any extended communication becomes possible only through knowing the patterns by which words and parts of words (for example, plural endings on nouns or past tense markings on verbs) are combined into meaningful utterances. The secret of rapid and effortless conversation is to practise these patterns until they become second nature, automatic responses.

Each language has its own formulae for assembling the parts. For example, in English the formula, I see (a)..., can be used with any number of different nouns neatly fitted into the slot at the end. Some of the drills which follow are designed to help you drop easily and naturally into the various speech patterns of Cree. By practising them you will begin, right from the start, to treat Cree as a language to be spoken rather than as a puzzle to be solved. Occasional deviations from the accustomed patterns may appear from time to time in the Basic Conversations or Drills with little or no comment. Learn them as they come, just as you did in your own language. If they require extended explanation, this will be found under Section B, Discussion of Grammar. There is normally no point in asking the native speaker of any language, just because he or she is a native speaker, *why* something is said this way or that. This is especially the case if the language is one in which grammatical instruction is not generally given in school. Pressing grammatical queries this way will probably be seen as asking awkward questions to the point of embarrassment and will likely result in a loss of interest in any attempt to help you learn the language. If a usage puzzles you, it is legitimate to ask *when* a given thing is said or *how* you would say such and such; but you must then be prepared to draw your own conclusions. This is particularly important if you are working with a speaker alone; but even in the classroom deferring grammatical problems to the appropriate period saves time.

1. Repeat after the recording, first down each column noting what is the same, then across each row noting what is different.

I	you	he/she	
ni|mawâpin	ki|mawâpin	mawâpiw	visit
nit|ihtân	kit|ihtân	ihtâw	be at a place
nit|itohtân	kit|itohtân	itohtêw	go to a place (by foot)
ni|tašîhkân	ki|tašîhkân	tašîhkêw	dwell
nit|išinihkâson	kit|išinihkâson	išinihkâsow	be named, be called

Note how the prefix forms, ni... and ki..., take the forms, nit... and kit... before a vowel (Unit 1.B.2.2)

2. Expand the simple statement, ihtâw, by prefacing it with the locating expression given on the recording (and in the left hand column). Then mimic the full form after the recording.

Model: šwâpihk ihtâw
Response: šwâpihk ihtâw

šwâpihk ihtâw
sîpîhk
ôta
nêtê
nêtê piko
mêskanâhk
nêtê piko mêskanâhk

3. Complete each of the following fragments with the appropriate word from the list given.

milwâšin, kimawâpin, nitihtâwin, itwê, ihtâw, môla, êkotê, mêskanâhk

	(Cover this column)
1. êhê, êkôma ___________.	nitihtâwin
2. šwâpihk mâškôc _________.	ihtâw
3. pêhkâc mîna _______.	itwê
4. nâspic __________ ôta.	milwâšin
5. ___________ nâ kîla?	kimawâpin
6. _______ ninisitohtên.	môla
7. nêtê piko ___________.	mêskanâhk
8. ôtê nâ itêhkê? êhê, _________.	êkotê

4. Put the following sentences into Cree on the pattern:

šwâpihk n'titohtân. I'm going to the store.

	(Cover this column)
1. I'm going to the store.	šwâpihk n'titohtân.
2. I am here.	ôta n'tihtân.
3. You live in the village.	ihtâwinihk kitašîhkân.
4. She is at the store.	šwâpihk ihtâw.
5. He is on the path.	mêskanâhk ihtâw.
6. He is over there on the path.	nêtê mêskanâhk ihtâw.
7. She is just over there on the path.	nêtê piko mêskanâhk ihtâw.
8. You are in the village now.	âšay ihtâwinihk kitihtân.
9. It's very nice here.	nâspic milwâšin ôta.
10. Are *you* just visiting?	kimawâpin nâ kîla?

5.1 Answer the following questions with êhê, followed by a full statement: *e.g.*,

Question:	kitašîhkân nâ ôta?	Do you live here?
Reply:	êhê, nitašîhkân ôta.	Yes, I live here.

The recording will check you and allow space to repeat the correct reply.

	(Cover this column)
1. kitašîhkân nâ ôta?	êhê, n'tašîhkân ôta.
2. kimawâpin nâ ôta?	êhê, nimawâpin ôta.
3. kitihtân nâ ôta?	êhê, n'tihtân ôta.
4. âšay nâ šwâpihk kititohtân?	êhê, âšay šwâpihk n'titohtân.
5. mîna nâ šwâpihk kitihtân?	êhê, mîna šwâpihk n'tihtân.
6. âšay nâ kinisitohtên?	êhê, âšay ninisitohtên.

5.2 Drill the following on the same pattern, but answer in the negative: *e.g.*,

Question: tašîhkêw nâ ôta?
Reply: môla, môla tašîhkêw ôta.

1. tašîhkêw nâ ôta?	môla, môla tašîhkêw ôta.
2. mawâpiw nâ ôta?	môla, môla mawâpiw ôta.
3. ihtâw nâ ôta?	môla, môla ihtâw ôta.
4. itohtêw nâ anta?	môla, môla itohtêw anta.
5. âšay nâ kihtohtêw [is going away]?	môla, môla âšay kihtohtêw.
6. milwâšin nâ ôta?	môla, môla milwâšin ôta.

6. Transform the following sentences into questions by adding the question marker, nâ, in the right place.

1. šwâpihk kititohtân.	šwâpihk nâ kititohtân?
2. ôta ihtâw.	ôta nâ ihtâw?
3. kinisitohtên.	kinisitohtên nâ?
4. nâspic milwâšin ôta.	nâspic nâ milwâšin ôta?
5. ôtê itêhkê.	ôtê nâ itêhkê?
6. ôta mâka tašîhkêw.	ôta nâ mâka tašîhkêw?
7. âšay pêhkâc nititwân.	âšay nâ pêhkâc n'titwân?
8. mawâpiw piko ihtâwinihk.	mawâpiw nâ piko ihtâwinihk?

D. CONVERSATION PRACTICE

1. Cover the Cree column in the Basic Conversation and, looking at the English only, try to say aloud the corresponding word or expression in Cree. If there are any points at which you get stuck, mark them and keep going. Go back and drill the sections you have marked. When you think you have learned them, repeat the whole conversation in Cree, looking at the English column only. (Tip: This seems difficult at first, because the Cree words bear little, if any, resemblance to words in English; but as you get more and more used to the sound and shape of Cree words they gradually become easier to remember.)

Do not proceed to Unit 2 until you can repeat the Cree column in the conversation without hesitation from looking at the English.

2. Check the drills for difficulties. Be sure you can make the correct responses without hesitating.

3. Strike up a conversation with your teacher or a fellow student in which you enact a meeting with someone on your first arrival in a village. Ask where the store is and where the Manager is. Look a little puzzled and say you cannot understand and would he or she say it again more slowly. Then make polite inquiry as to whether the other person lives in the village or (**nêstapiko**) is just visiting. Remark on what a pleasant place it is; then say "Good-bye" (which is also **wâciyê**).

At first you may have difficulty recognizing words which you actually know; but don't give up. Use your Cree with native speakers at every opportunity; and gradually you will find yourself more and more at home as you get used to the sound of the language.

E. LISTENING IN

In learning a language it is much more important to hear the same thing twenty times than to hear twenty new things once.

Listen while John, a newcomer, asks where to find the store Manager. (ililiw means "person" or, in particular, an Indian person.) Listen several times until you are able to follow the conversation without looking at the text.

Cwân:	wâciyê.
Ililiw:	wâciyê.
Cwân:	tântê okimâw?
Ililiw	nêtê piko, âšokwanihk.[1]
Cwân:	tântê mâka âšokwan? nêtê nâ?
Ililiw:	êhê, nêtê piko sîpîhk.[2] ôta nâ kitašîhkân?
Cwân:	môla, nimawâpin piko.
Ililiw:	nâspic milwâšin ôta.
Cwân:	môla ninisitohtên. pêhkâc mîna itwê.
Ililiw:	nâspic milwâšin ôta.
Cwân:	tâpwê![3] âšay ninisitohtên.
Ililiw:	tân' êšinihkâsoyin[4] mâka kîla?
Cwân:	cwân n'tišinihkâson, cwân mitât n'tišinihkâson.
Ililiw:	âšay mâka âšokwanihk nititohtân.
Cwân:	tâpwê nâ? nêsta nîla.[5] âšokwanihk nititohtân. tântê mâka šwâp?
Ililiw:	nêtê piko, mêskanahk.
Cwân:	ôtê nâ itêhkê?
Ililiw:	êkotê! môla mâškôc âšokwanihk ihtâw okimâw. šwâpihk mâskôc ihtâw.
Cwân:	ay'hâw[6]—šwâpihk mâškôc n'ka-itohtân.[7] wâciyê.
Ililiw:	wâciyê.

1 at the wharf
2 at the river
3 yes indeed: *lit.*, truly, really
4 what is your name?
5 I also, me too
6 well, uh
7 I shall go, I'll be going

F. REFERENCE LIST

The Reference List is not intended as a vocabulary to be memorized. As the name suggests, it is a list for convenient reference when the meaning or some other aspect of a word slips your mind. Everything in it has already been learned in the context of either the Basic Conversation or in the Drills. The symbols for parts of speech have already been explained in Unit 1.B.1.3, B.2.1 and B.3. To these we add PR for Pronoun. Others will be added as the course proceeds. A hyphen after an entry indicates a stem that may be inflected and the point at which any inflectional material would follow. The triple point, ..., is used to indicate inflectional or derivational elements when cited alone or to mark off such when they are components of full, grammatical forms.

anta	IPC	there [*not as far away as* nêtê]
âšay	IPC	now, by now; already
âšokwan-	NA	wharf, dock, jetty
êhê	IPC	yes
êkotê	IPC	the very way, that('s) the way
êkôma	PR intensive	this very one [inanimate singular]
ihtâ-	VAI	be (at a place, *as opposed to* be, exist)
ihtâwin-	NI	village
iliiliw-	NA	person, *usually* Indian person
išinihkâso-	VAI	be so named, be called
itêhkê	IPC	...wards, on the... side
itohtê-	VAI	go (to a given place)
itwê-	VAI	say
kââ	IPC	oh!
ki(t)...	Prefix	2nd person possessor *or* subject marker: your, you
kihtohtê-	VAI	go away
kîla	PR [2nd pers. sing.]	you
kinisitohtên	VTI	you understand it [This class of verbs will be learned later.]

mawâpi-	VAI	visit
mâka	IPC	but, however; and
mâškôc	IPC	perhaps, maybe
mêskanaw-	NI	path, trail, road
milwâšin-	VII	be nice, be fine, be pleasant
mîna	IPC	again
môla	IPC	no; not
nâ	IPC	question marker
nâspic	IPC	very, very much
nêsta	IPC	and; also, too
nêstapiko	IPC	or
nêtê	IPC	yonder, over there [*further away than* anta]
ni(t)...	Prefix	1st person possessor *or* subject marker: my, I
ninisitohtên	VTI	I understand it [This class of verbs will be learned later.]
nîla	PR [1st pers. sing.]	I
o(t)...	Prefix	3rd person possessor: his, her
okimâw-	NA	manager, boss
ôta	IPC	here
ôtê	IPC	hither, to here, this way, in this direction
pêhkâc	IPC	slowly, carefully
piko	IPC	only
sîpiy-	NI	river
šwâp-	NI	shop, store
tašîhkê-	VAI	dwell, live
tântê	IPC	where?
tâpwê	IPC	truly, really
wâciyê*	IPC	Hello; Good-bye

* Further to the west of James Bay wâciyê is used as a parting salute only. The usual greeting is tânis' êkwa? How then?, or its contraction, tân'si?

G. REVIEW

Use your imagination in this section and in every review section which follows. Many of the questions and answers are directly related to the conversation topics covered. Some are not. In either case, try to imagine a situation in which the question or answer could be used, and follow the instructions.

1.A Kakwêcihkêmôwina—Questions

Answer the following questions using material from the Basic Conversation. Do not reply merely "êhê" or "môla".

1. âšay nâ šwâpihk ihtâw okimâw?
2. tântê šwâp?
3. âšokanihk nâ itohtêw cwân?
4. ôma nâ kitihtâwin?
5. kitašîhkân nâ ôta?
6. cwân nâ kitišinihkâson?
7. âšay nâ kikihtohtân?
8. kimawâpin nâ piko ôta ihtâwinihk?
9. milwâšin nâ ôta ihtâwinihk?
10. âšay nâ kinisitohtên?

1.B Naškwêwašihtwâwina—Answers

From the Basic Conversation or Drill section make up questions that might be answered by the following statements.

1. nêtê piko, mêskanâhk.
2. êhê, tašîhkêw ôta.
3. môla, môla nâspic milwâšin ôta.
4. âšay šwâpihk n'titohtân.
5. âšay mâškôc šwâpihk ihtâw.
6. êhê, cwân n'tišinihkâson.
7. tâpwê, nâspic milwâšin ôta!
8. môla ninisitohtên.
9. môla, nimawâpin piko nîla.
10. ôtê itêhkê.

UNIT TWO

A. BASIC CONVERSATION

1. Inquiries: Who and What?

While at the river bank the visitor asks another woman the Cree term for various objects, and identifies herself.

Visitor:	ôma	this one *(inan.)*
	kêkwân	what?
	kêkwân ôma?	What is this?
Resident:	nôhtâwiy	my father
	cîmân	canoe, boat
	cîmân ôma,	This (is) a canoe,
	nôhtâwiy ocîmân.	my father's canoe.
	âpatisiw	he works
	âskaw	sometimes
	âskaw âpatisiw ôta.	Sometimes he works here.
	otamîw	she is busy, she is occupied
	iši-otamîw	she is busy there, she is thus-busy
	nikâwiy	my mother
	nikâwiy mâka šwâpihk iši-otamîw.	But my mother is busy at the store.
	âšokwanihk ta-ihtâw	she will be at the wharf
	wîpac mâškôc	soon perhaps
	wîpac mâškôc âšokwanihk ta-ihtâw.	Perhaps she'll soon be at the wharf.
Visitor:	nêsta ôma? kêkwân ôma?	And this? What is this?
Resident:	awa	this one *(anim.)*
	apwoy awa.	This (is) a paddle.
	nistês otapwoya.	My (older) brother's paddle.
	tân' êšinihkâsoyin mâka kîla?	But what's your name?
Visitor:	nîla	I, me
	iskwêw	woman
	natóhkolon-iskwêw	nurse ('doctor-woman')

	sôsan n'tišinihkâson.	My name is Susan.
	n'tohkolon-iskwêw nîla.	I'm a/the nurse.
	anohc	(right) now (âšay = by now)
	tânt' êtohtêyan mâka anohc?	Where are you going now?
Resident:	n'ka-itohtân	I'll be going
	ay'hâw	well, uh...
	ay'hâw,—wîpac šwâpihk	Well,—I'll be going to
	n'ka-itohtân.	the store presently.
Visitor:	mîkwêc. wâciyê.	Thank you. Good-bye.
Resident:	wâciyê.	Good-bye.

2. Kinship Terms: Not John, But His Father

Two more people, Annie and Emily, arrive at the dock, and the following conversation takes place.

Êmiliy:	kâ-kîšikâk	which is day
	anohc kâ-kîšikâk	today
	tân' êhtiyan anohc kâ-kîšikâk?	How are you (faring) today?
Âniy:	nimilopalin	I'm getting along well
	nâspic nimilopalin.	Very well.
	ihtâw nâ cwân ôta?	Is John here?
Êmiliy:	ôhtâwiya	his father
	môla. ôhtâwiya mâka	No; but his father
	wîpac ôta ta-ihtâliwa.	will soon be here.
Âniy:	tâpwê	really, truly
	tâpwê nâ? tašîhkêliwa nâ	Really? Does his
	ôhtâwiya ôta anohc?	father live here now?
Êmiliy:	nititêlihtên	I think (it)
	âpatisiliwa	he (3') works
	âskaw	sometimes
	nikiskêlihtên	I know (it)
	môla nikiskêlihtên. âskaw mâka	I don't know (it). Sometimes he
	âpatisiliwa ôta, n'titêl'tên.	works here though, I think.

	ostêsa	his older brother
	ostêsa mâka mawâpiliwa ôta.	His older brother is visiting here, though.
	pîta išinihkâsoliwa.	His name is Peter.
Âniy:	ta-kîwêw	he 'll be going home/returning
	wîpac mâškôc ta-kîwêw cwân.	Perhaps John will be going home soon.
Êmiliy:	ošîma nêsta mâka omisa	his (younger) sibling and his older sister
	nôkosiliwa	they (3') appear, they can be seen
	pêci-nôkosiliwa	they can be seen coming
	âšay pêci-nôkosliwa ošîma nêsta mâka omisa.	You can see his young brother and his older sister coming this way.
	ohtohtêliwa	they (3') are coming from
	šwâpihk ohtohtêliwa	They are coming from the store.

B. DISCUSSION OF GRAMMAR

1. Verbs

1.1 Proximate and Obviative (Nearer and Further Third Person) Subjects

From the section on "Cree Grammar", you will recall that Cree distinguishes between two third persons in a narrative: the first mentioned, or *proximate,* and any further third person *grammatically dependent* on the first and known as the *obviative.* The first mentioned third person is often designated in paradigms and grammatical notations as 3, the further third person as 3′, "three prime": *e.g.,*

cwân (3) itohtêw	John (3) is going (there)
cwân (3) ôhtâwiya (3′) itohtê**liwa**	John's father is going (there)

First (1) and second (2) persons may be thought of as occupying a single position, and anything possessed by either then falls into the 3 slot. Anything possessed by 3 is then in further third position, 3′, as illustrated in the diagram:

ni...
______ 3 _ _ _ _ _ _ _ 3′
ki...

In this case the grammatical dependency is one of possession: cwân, in third person position is the possessor of ôhtâwiya, which is then pushed out into the further or more remote third person position. (The example in "Cree Grammar", p. xxxvii, showed another kind of grammatical dependency: 3′ was the object of a verb of which 3 was the subject.) If, however, both persons are in the **same** grammatical slot: *e.g.,* The boy and the dog ran away, the two nouns are jointly the subject of the verb and could together be replaced by "they": They ran away. In this case both third persons are treated as proximate (nearer).

——DRILLS 1 AND 2——

1.2 Preverbs

In Unit 1.C.3, particles were described as stems that do not take any inflection. Many of these particles are small, independent words: *e.g.*, ôta, âšay, etc. Some particle stems, however, are normally prefixed to other stems: verbs, nouns or other particles. Since they are all separate stems, we show this by joining them with a hyphen. Particle prefixes that you have met are the following:

1.2.1 Future Marker

The future marker with ni... and ki... subject prefixes is **ka**-, immediately following the personal subject prefixes, and **ta**-, future marker with a third person subject. Both ka- and ta-, as particle stems themselves, are joined to any other stem by a hyphen: *e.g.*,

ni**ka** - itohtân	I shall go (there
ki**ka** - nipân	you will sleep
ta - kihtohtêw	he will go away
ta - kîwêliwa ostêsa	his (older) brother will go home

——DRILLS 3 AND 4——

1.2.2 Preverbs ιši, **pêci**

ι**ši**- so, thus, there (*referring back to a preceding expression of* place *or* manner of doing something, so-called *anaphoric reference*) and **pêci**- towards speaker, this way.

ι**ši**. You have met several expressions using a locating particle or a noun in the locative case: âšokwanihk ihtâw—He is at the wharf; šwâpihk n'titohtân—I am going to the store; ihtâwinihk nâ kitašîhkân?—Do you live in the village? In each of these the locating expression occurred first and one of three verbs followed: ihtâ-, itohtê- or tašîhkê-. All three of these verbs have a built-in element meaning "there" or "thus", which refers back to the locating expression: *i.e.*, at the wharf he there-is, to the store I thus-go *or* there-go, in the village do you there-live?

Other Cree verbs that do not have any such built in element require a grammatical marker to refer back to the locating expression if it comes before the verb. So where šwâpihk precedes otamîw, Cree requires the preverb, ι**ši**- so, thus:

šwâpihk ι**ši**-otamîw	she is busy at the store
ôta ι**ši**-âpatisiw	he works here
êkotêni ê-ι**ši**-milwâšihk	that's a good way

pêci is a particle that, when prefixed to a verb, means that the action expressed by the verb takes place "coming towards" the speaker. For example:

âpatisiw—he works,	pêci-âpatisiw—he comes to work
nôkosiw—he appears, he comes into sight	pêci-nôkosiw—he comes into sight as he approaches
kîwê—return, go back, go home	pêci-kîwê—come back, come home

When particle stems such as iši and pêci are joined to other stems this is marked by a hyphen and they form a *compound* stem. The future marker then precedes the whole compound stem; and, as a particle stem, it also is joined by a hyphen to what follows: *e.g.*,

ta-pêci-nôkosiw.	she will come into view
šwâpihk nâ ka-iši-âpatisin?	will you work at the store?

NOTE: In rapid speech kika-, as in kika-âpatisin, is often contracted to ka-âpatisin.You will also often hear a 'y'-glide between ka- and a following vowel, as in kay-ihtân. This is a common transition feature and should be mimicked wherever it occurs.

1.3 Verbs with Question Words: **tâni, tântê**

We have seen how to form Yes-No questions in Cree with the question marker, nâ. Other questions, however, require something more than a mere Yes or No for an answer. They are designed to elicit specific information and usually begin with a so-called question word: how, where, when, etc. These are known as Content Questions and in Cree they take a special form of the verb which you will learn later. In the meantime, to help further conversation, the occasional content question is introduced, such as

tân' êšinihkâsoyin?	What is your name?
tânt' êtohtêyan?	Where are you going?
tân' êhtiyan?	How are you (faring)?

Learn these as chunks—they are not very long; and at the appropriate point the forms of the verb regularly used for this type of query will be presented and discussed in full.

2. Nouns

2.1 Dependent Stems

A group of nouns, including the names of relatives, body parts and what are regarded in Algonquian tradition as highly personal possessions, are always possessed in their most ordinary form of occurrence: *e.g.*,

ôhtâwiya	his father
kîpit	your tooth
nîwat	my hunting bag

These are known as *dependent* stems since, unlike cîmân and other nouns that can be used without a possessor prefix, these must have a personal possessor prefix or some other prior element to form a full word. For the present do not try to use them in unpossessed form or you run the risk of developing non-Cree speech habits. They are listed as NDA or NDI and throughout Level One will be cited in the Reference List (§F) in possessed form.

3. Pronouns

3.1 Personal Pronouns

You have noted that possessors are indicated by prefixes, the so-called *allocational* prefixes, ni(t)..., ki(t)..., o(t)..., (Unit 1.B.2.2) and not by possessive adjectives such as my, your, etc., as in English. Apart from the prefixes, however, there are separate pronouns, often used to lend emphasis or point up a contrast:

nîla	I, me
kîla	you (sg.)
wîla	he, she; him, her

ta-kihtohtêw nâ wîla? môla, nîla mâka n'ka-kihtohtân.
Will he be going away? No, but I'll be going.

Note carefully that Cree distinguishes between *living* and *lifeless*, rather than *masculine, feminine* and *neuter*. Where an English speaker keeps "he" and "she" apart, Cree speakers are used to no such distinction in their own language. They may sometimes be heard speaking of a man as "she" or a woman as "he" until they acquire greater familiarity with English usage. ocîmân, for example, may mean either "his" or "her" canoe. The context, or a slight elaboration, can clarify meaning further.

——DRILL 6——

3.2 Demonstrative Pronouns

In the discussion of gender (Unit 1.B.2.1) two forms of the demonstrative pronoun were shown: awa—this (animate) one , and ôma—this (inanimate) one. Nouns *belong* to one of the two genders, demonstrative pronouns *select the appropriate form* to show the gender of the noun with which they are associated:

awa apwoy	this paddle
ana apwoy	that paddle
ôma cîmân	this canoe
anima cîmân	that canoe

Just as verbs and nouns show forms for the obviative or further third person, so demonstrative pronouns display a form for the obviative.

awa / **ana** nâ kitapwoy?	Is this (one) / that your paddle?
ôho / **anihi** nâ otapwoya?	Is this (one) / that his paddle?
ôma / **anima** nâ kicîmân?	Is this (one) / that your canoe?
ômêliw / **animêliw** nâ ocîmân?	Is this (one) his canoe?

Where apwoy and cîmân are possessed by a third person and so are in the *further* third person slot, the pronoun also takes a form for further third person or obviative.

——DRILL 7——

4. Word Building and Word Order

4.1 Word Building

A series of forms such as

taŝîhkêw
nitaŝîhkân
nika-taŝîhkân

leads one to realize that a single Cree word may express as much as a whole English sentence. Furthermore, within the word the order of the various components is normally fixed: *i.e.*, ka must precede -taŝîhkân but must follow the personal prefix ni.... Where a preverb such as pêci is involved, the order required is nika-pêci-taŝîhkân.

4.2 Word Order

While word order is to some extent freer in Cree than in English a preferred order is normally observed in certain sequences, especially sequences of particles. The Basic Conversation illustrates the position of a number of particles that occur in a fixed order. The frequent occurrence of stock phrases, wîpac mâŝkôc—soon probably, âŝay nâ—now?, quickly makes this order familiar. Note however the following points.

4.2.i mâŝkôc ordinarily falls into *second* place in the sequence of particles:

âŝay mâŝkôc perhaps now
mîna mâŝkôc again perhaps.

4.2.ii mâka fits into second place in a sentence. Where mâka and mâŝkôc occur in sequence with nothing preceding, mâŝkôc moves forward leaving second place to mâka:

mâŝkôc mâka ta-kihtohtêw But perhaps he will go away.

4.2.iii Both mâka and mâŝkôc yield second place to nâ: *e.g.*,

kîla nâ mâka ka-pêci-âpatisin ôta?
But will *you* be coming to work here?

4.2.iv Where all three occur, the order is nâ ... mâka ... mâškôc:

kîla nâ mâka mâškôc ka-pêci-âpatisin ôta?
But will you perhaps be coming to work here?

—DRILL 8—

4.3 Verbless Questions and Statements

Questions in Cree of the *equational* type: *i.e.*, What *is* this? Whose *is* that?, etc., do not normally contain a verb: *e.g.*, kêkwân ôma? tântê šwâp? If this seems odd, remember that we also have verbless questions in English: Why the fuss? Whither away? What now?, and so on.

Corresponding to verbless questions, verbless statements are also common:

cîmân ôma	this (is) a canoe
âšokwan awa	this (is) a wharf

In each of these *equational* sentences (*i.e.*, this = a canoe; this = a wharf) the complement comes in first position.

—DRILL 10—

C. DRILLS

1. Repeat after the recording, down each column then across each row.

3	3′
mawâpi...w	mawâpi...liwa
âpatisi...w	âpatisi...liwa
ihtâ...w	ihtâ...liwa
itohtê...w	itohtê...liwa
kihtohtê...w	kihtohtê...liwa
tašîhkê...w	tašîhkê...liwa
otamî...w	otamî...liwa
išinihkâso...w	išinihkâso...liwa

2.1 In each of the following, replace the third person subject with ôhtâwiya mâka (in the last three exchanges just ôhtâwiya) and complete the sentence with the appropriate verb form.

	(Cover this column)
cwân šwâpihk ta-ihtâw	ôhtâwiya mâka šwâpihk ta-ihtâliwa
cwân šwâpihk ta-itohtêw	..... šwâpihk ta-itohtêliwa
cwân šwâpihk ta-iši-âpatisiw	..... šwâpihk ta-iši-âpatisiliwa
pîta išinihkâsow	..... pîta išinihkâsoliwa
nistês ôta tašîhkêw	..... ôta tašîhkêliwa
âšay nâ šwâpihk ihtâw âlik?	âšay nâ šwâpihk ihtâliwa ôhtâwiya?
âšay nâ kitohtêw âlik?	âšay nâ kitohtêliwa ôhtâwiya?
âšay nâ otamîw kimis?	âšay nâ otamîliwa ôhtâwiya?

2.2 Answer the following questions on the pattern:

Question: ta-itohtêw nâ wîla?
Reply: môla, ostêsa mâka ta-itohtêliwa.

Mimic the correct version after the recording.

	(Cover this column)
ta-itohtêw nâ wîla?	môla, ostêsa mâka ta-itohtêliwa.
nêtê nâ ta-ihtâw?	môla, ostêsa mâka nêtê ta-ihtâliwa.

ta-mawâpiw nâ wîla?	môla, ostêsa mâka ta-mawâpiliwa.
tašîhkêw nâ ôta?	môla, ostêsa mâka ta-tašîhkêliwa ôta.
âšay nâ otamîw wîla?	môla, ostêsa mâka ta-otamîliwa.
ta-câhcâmow [sneeze] nâ wîla?	môla, ostêsa mâka ta-câhcâmoliwa.
cwân nâ išinihkâsow wîla?	môla, ostêsa mâka cwân išinihkâsoliwa.
cîmânihk nâ iši-pêhow [wait]?	môla, ostêsa mâka cîmânihk iši-pêholiwa.

3. Show that you can distinguish between present and future reference in the verb. Repeat each sentence. Where reference is to present time, add anohc; where it is to the future preface the sentence with wîpac.

Model: tânt' êtohtêyan mâka kîla?
Response: tânt' êtohtêyan mâka kîla anohc?

		(Cover this column)
1.	tânt' êtohtêyan mâka kîla?	anohc
2.	mâškôc ta-kîwêw cwân.	wîpac
3.	tašîhkêliwa nâ ôhtâwiya ôta?	anohc
4.	šwâpihk nâ kitihtân?	anohc
5.	âšokwanihk n'ka-ihtân.	wîpac
6.	mâškôc ka-nisitohtên.	wîpac
7.	kimilopalin nâ?	anohc
8.	šwâpihk n'ka-itohtân.	wîpac

———DRILLS 4, 5, 6 AND 7 ARE NOT RECORDED———

4. Given either anohc or wîpac and a verb stem, complete each sentence with the correct present or future form of the verb.

Model: wîpac mâškôc ni... (âpatisi-)
Response: wîpac mâškôc nika-âpatisin.

1.	wîpac mâškôc ni... (âpatisi-).	nika-âpatisin
2.	anohc nâ ki... (mawâpi-)?	kimawâpin
3.	anohc mâka sîpîhk (itohtê-) emiliy.	itohtêw
4.	wîpac ni... (kihtohtê-).	nika-kihtohtân
5.	wîpac mâškôc ostêsa ôta (ihtâ-).	ta-ihtâliwa
6.	anohc mâškôc šwâpihk iši- (otamî-) cwân.	otamîw
7.	wîpac nâ ki... (kîwê)?	kika-kîwân
8.	wîla mâka wîpac (pêci-nôkosi-).	ta-pêci-nôkosiw

5. From the list of words immediately below, fill in the blanks in the following paragraph.

natohkolon-iskwêw	ôho	pêci-nôkosiliwa
ta-kîwêw	tašîhkêliwa	ihtâw
êhtiyan	âskaw	wîpac
ocîmân		

wâciyê! tân' ____________ anohc kâ-kîšikâk? tântê ______________ - ________? šwâpihk nâ ________? ______ mâškôc ihtâwinihk n'ka-itohtân. âšay ôta _____________ cwân ostêsa. ômêliw cwân _________ ; _____ nêsta wîla otapwoya. ________ ôta iši-âpatisiw, n'titêl'tên. wîpac mâka mâškôc __ - ______. âšay _____ - ____________ ošîma nêsta mâka omisa.

6.1 With each of the nouns in the left hand column below there is provided a personal pronoun: *e.g.,* cîmân : nîla. Repeat the pronoun, nîla, and put the noun into the corresponding possessed form: *e.g.,* nîla nicîmân.

		(Cover this column.)
cîmân:	nîla	nîla nicîmân
cîmân:	kîla	kîla kicîmân
cîmân:	wîla	wîla ocîmân
mêskanaw:	nîla	nîla nimêskanaw
mêskanaw:	kîla	kîla kimêskanaw
mêskanaw:	wîla	wîla omêskanaw
âšokwan:	nîla	nîla nitâšokwan
âšokwan:	kîla	kîla kitâšokwan
âšokwan:	wîla	wîla otâšokwan**a**
ôhtâwiya:	nîla	nîla nôhtâwiy
ôhtâwiya:	kîla	kîla kôhtâwiy
ôhtâwiya:	wîla	wîla ôhtâwiy**a**

What do you notice about âšokwan and ôhtâwiya, both animate nouns, when they are possessed by a third person?

Note that the next three nouns are a little different: the possessed form ends in ...**(ɩ)m** and okimâw, like other animate nouns, adds ...**a** when possessed by a third person possessor.

		(Cover this column.)
sîpiy:	nîla	nîla nisîpî**m**
sîpiy:	kîla	kîla kisîpî**m**
sîpiy:	wîla	wîla osîpî**m**
šwâp:	nîla	nîla nišwâpi**m**

šwâp:	kîla	kîla kišwâpi**m**
šwâp:	wîla	wîla ošwâpi**m**
okimâw:	nîla	nîla nitôkimâ**m**
okimâw:	kîla	kîla kitôkimâ**m**
okimâw:	wîla	wîla otôkimâ**ma**

6.2 The nouns and pronouns below are in random order. Uncover the right hand column line by line to check your answer and drill as in 6.1 until you can produce the corresponding possessed form correctly and without hesitation.

		(Cover this column)
mêskanaw:	nîla	nîla nimêskanaw
cîmân:	kîla	kîla kicîmân
âšokwan:	nîla	nîla nitâšokwan
âšokwan:	wîla	wîla otâšokwana
mêskanaw:	wîla	wîla omêskanaw
sîpiy:	nîla	nîla nisîpîm
ôhtâwiya:	nîla	nîla nôhtâwiy
sîpiy:	wîla	wîla osîpîm
âšokwan:	kîla	kîla kitâšokwan
okimâw:	wîla	wîla otôkimâma
okimâw:	kîla	kîla kitôkimâm
ôhtâwiya:	kîla	kîla kôhtâwiy
mêskanaw:	kîla	kîla kimêskanaw
cîmân:	wîla	wîla ocîmân
cîmân:	nîla	nîla nicîmân
ôhtâwiya:	wîla	wîla ôhtâwiya
sîpiy:	kîla	kîla kisîpîm
šwâp:	kîla	kîla kišwâpim
šwâp:	wîla	wîla ošwâpim
okimâw:	nîla	nîla nitôkimâm
šwâp:	nîla	nîla nišwâpim

7. awa (*animate*) = this one; ôma (*inanimate*) = this one.

7.1 The following frame means, "This is a ...". Mimic each item after the recording or repeat aloud until you are sure which nouns take awa and which ôma.

cîmân ôma
sîpiy ôma
šwâp ôma

šwâp ôma
okimâw awa
kikâwiy awa

mêskanaw ôma	sîpiy ôma
iskwêw awa	cîmân ôma
âšokwan awa	mêskanaw ôma
nôhtâwiy awa	apwoy awa

7.2 Now test yourself by putting the correct form, awa or ôma, after the noun. Cover the the right hand column, checking your answers line by line.

	(Cover this column)	
âšokwan	awa	ana
mêskanaw	ôma	anima
sîpiy	ôma	anima
okimâw	awa	ana
kistês	awa	ana
cîmân	ôma	anima
šwâp	ôma	anima
apwoy	awa	ana

Repeat the above drill, replacing awa with ana and ôma with anima.

7.3 When the possessed noun is in the further third person slot (*i.e.,* obviative) the demonstrative pronoun must show agreement. The following frame means, "Is this his...?" Repeat aloud as in 7.1, above.

ôho nâ ošîma?	ômêliw nâ ocîmân?
ôho nâ omisa?	ômêliw nâ otihtâwin?
ôho nâ otapwoya?	ômêliw nâ omêskanaw?
ôho nâ otâšokwana?	ômêliw nâ ošwâpim?
ôho nâ okâwiya?	ômêliw nâ omîcim [his food]?

7.4 Drill as in 7.2, above, checking your answers with those in the right hand column.

	(Cover this column)
omîcim	ômêliw nâ omîcim?
ocîmân	ômêliw, etc.
ostêsa	ôho
omêskanaw	ômêliw
otâšokwana	ôho
otapwoya	ôho
otihtâwin	ômêliw
omisa	ôho
ôhtâwiya	ôho
ošwâpim	ômêliw

Repeat the above drill, replacing ôho with anihi and ômêliw with animêliw.

8.1 Drill the position of the following modifying particles by mimicking the recording or repeating aloud, line by line.

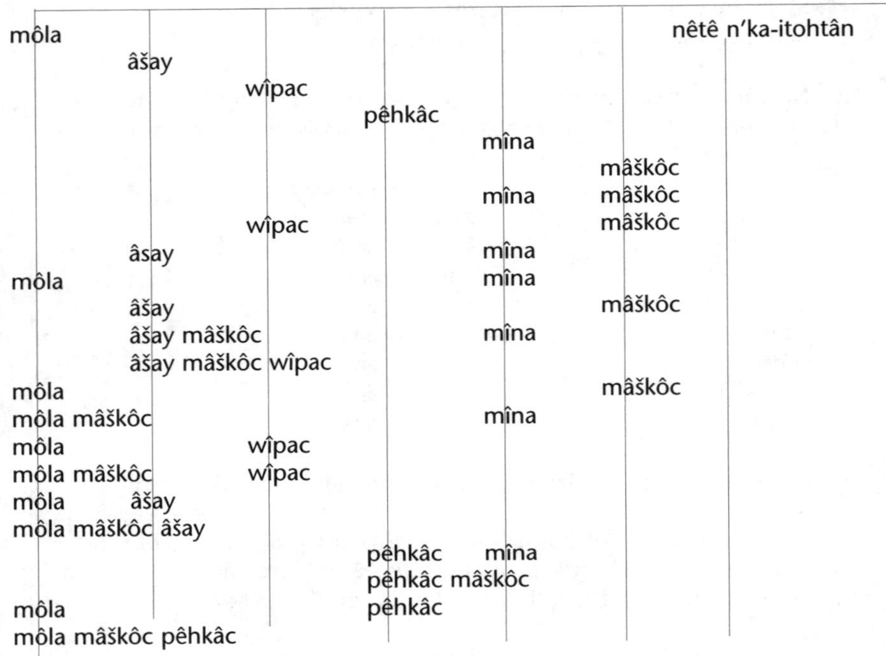

môla						nêtê n'ka-itohtân
	âšay					
		wîpac				
			pêhkâc			
				mîna		
					mâškôc	
				mîna	mâškôc	
		wîpac			mâškôc	
	âsay			mîna		
môla				mîna		
	âšay				mâškôc	
	âšay mâškôc			mîna		
	âšay mâškôc	wîpac				
môla					mâškôc	
môla mâškôc				mîna		
môla		wîpac				
môla mâškôc		wîpac				
môla	âšay					
môla mâškôc	âšay					
			pêhkâc	mîna		
			pêhkâc mâškôc			
môla			pêhkâc			
môla mâškôc	pêhkâc					

What do you notice about the position of mâškôc?

What do you notice about the position of the other particles?

8.2 The following sets of particles are in random order. Re-arrange them in the correct order within each set, adding nêtê n'ka-tašîhkân or nêtê ta-ito-htêw. Cover the right hand columns.

		(Cover this column)
1.	âšay mîna	âšay mîna
2.	mâškôc wîpac	wîpac mâškôc
3.	môla âšay	môla âšay
4.	mîna môla	môla mîna
5.	mâškôc âšay	âšay mâškôc
6.	wîpac âšay	âšay wîpac
7.	pêhkâc mîna	pêhkâc mîna
8.	mâškôc âšay môla	môla mâškôc âšay
9.	wîpac mîna âšay	âšay wîpac mîna

		(Cover this column)
10.	môla wîpac mâškôc	môla mâškôc wîpac
11.	mîna âšay mâškôc	âšay mâškôc mîna
12.	âšay wîpac mâškôc	âšay mâškôc wîpac
13.	mâškôc môla pêhkâc mîna	môla mâškôc pêhkâc mîna
14.	âšay mâškôc môla pêhkâc	môla mâškôc âšay pêhkâc
15.	mîna wîpac pêhkâc âšay	âšay wîpac pêhkâc mîna

9. Quick review. Turn the statements below into simple questions by using nâ after the first word in the sentence.

1.	šwâpihk kititohtân.	7.	nâspic kimilwêlihtên ôta.
2.	wîpac mîna ta-mawâpiw.	8.	âšay kikihtohtân.
3.	âšay kinisitohtên.	9.	âšay wîpac ta-kihtohtêw, wîla.
4.	pêhkâc ta-itwêw.	10.	ka-otamîn šwâpihk.
5.	cwân išinihkâsow.	11.	ôta tašîhkêliwa ostêsa.
6.	kimawâpin piko, kîla.	12.	wîpac âšokwanihk ta-ihtâw.

10. Verbless questions and statements (not recorded). Drill the questions below with the various answers suggested or others that provide a satisfactory reply.

		Answers
1.	tântê šwâp?	nêtê piko, mêskanâhk.
2.	tântê kôhtâwiy?	nêtê, šwâpihk.
3.	tântê mâka kicîmân?	nêtê, âšokwanihk.
4.	tântê mêskanaw?	ôta piko.
5.	ôtê nâ itêhkê?	êkotê.
6.	tântê âlik mitât?	nêtê ocîmânihk.
7.	kêkwân ôma?	cîmân ôma.
8.	kêkwân mâka ôma?	apwoy awa.

D. CONVERSATION PRACTICE

1. Cover the Cree column in the Basic Conversation and, reading the English column line by line, give the Cree equivalents aloud. If you get stuck, note the place and keep going.

Go back to the beginning and drill the sections you have marked; then repeat the whole conversation as above. Do not proceed to Unit Three until you can repeat the Cree column unhesitatingly from looking at the English.

2. Check the drills for difficulties. Be sure you can make the correct responses with little or no hesitation.

3. Hold a conversation with your teacher, a fellow student or, if you are working alone, an imaginary friend. Introduce yourself, inquire about various objects lying around and discuss where various members of the other person's family are, where they work and where they live. Note that one or another may be going home soon and that so-and-so can be seen coming from the store, the wharf, the village, etc. Use the illustration at the beginning of the unit for ideas.

4. You have just arrived as Nurse or Post Manager (nitôkimâwin I am [the] Manager). Someone thinks that perhaps you are only visiting; so put him right. He asks where your canoe is and mentions that he is going to the store shortly. You remark that it is nice here and that maybe you will come and live in the village.

Recall the various expressions you have learned and remember to work them into the conversation at every opportunity.

E. LISTENING IN

Annie looks up as Emily arrives at the wharf, looking a little glum.

Âniy:	wâciyê! tân' êhtiyan anohc kâ-kîšikâk?
Êmiliy:	nâspic nimilopalin anohc. môla mâka nâspic milopaliw ôta.
Âniy:	tâpwê nâ?
Êmiliy:	êhê. môla âpatisiw nôhtâwiy, môla nêsta âpatisiw nistês.
Âniy:	tâpwê, môla milwâšin. ka-ihtân nâ ôta kîla, nêstapiko ka-âhtakwân[1] nâ?
Êmiliy:	ay'hâw,—môla mâškôc n'ka-kihtohtânân.[2] šwâpihk iši-âpatisiw nišîm; wîpac nêsta mâškôc môsonîhk[3] ta-pêci-ohtohtêw nimis.
Âniy:	kââ! nâspic milwâšin nêtê môsonîhk. tašîhkêw anta nistês. okosisa[4] mâka ôta ta-pêci-mawâpiliwa, nititêlihtên.
Êmiliy:	tântê mâka kicîmân? âšokanihk[5] nâ?
Âniy:	êhê, nêtê piko sîpîhk.
Êmiliy:	ôtê nâ itêhkê?
Âniy:	êkotê! wîpac mâškôc ta-pêci-itohtêw okimâw. kihci-[6] otamîw nêtê âšokanihk anohc. nîla mâka, nipêhon piko ôta. ihtâwinihk iši-mawâpiw nitânis.[7]
Êmiliy:	tânt' êtohtêyan mâka anohc?
Âniy:	wîpac mâškôc n'ka-kîwânân. [See note 2.] âšay mâka mâškôc âšokanihk n'ka-itohtân.
Êmiliy:	wâciyê.
Âniy:	wâciyê.

[1] move away

[2] we *subject*

[3] Moosonee, on Moose River near James Bay

[4] his son

[5] âšokan: *regional variant of* âšokwan. *v.* Unit 1.B.2.3, fn.4.

[6] greatly

[7] my daughter

F. REFERENCE LIST

Nouns with dependent stems (Unit 1.B.2) are listed under the form for third person singular possessor: *e.g.,* okâwiya, ostêsa, etc. Isolated verb forms to be learned by rote now but presented in full later are listed under the form in which they occur: *e.g.,* ninisitohtên, nimilwêlihtên.

ana	PR dem. anim. prox.	that one
anihi	PR dem. anim. obv.	that one
anima	PR dem. inan. prox.	that one
animêliw	PR dem. inan. obv.	that one
anohc	IPC	now
anohc kâ-kîšikâk		today (*lit.,* now when-it-is-day)
apwoy-	NA	paddle
awa	PR dem. anim. prox.	this one
ay'hâw	IPC [pause word]	well, uh...
âhtokwê-	VAI	move camp, move away
âniy-	NA [proper name]	Annie
âpatisi-	VAI	work
âskaw	IPC	sometimes
âšokan-	NA	wharf, jetty, dock: *regional variant of* âšokwan-.
câhcâmo-	VAI	sneeze
cîmân-	NI	canoe, boat
êhtiyan	VAI conj. indic.	that you are faring: *v.* ihti-.
êmiliy-	NA [proper name]	Emily
êtohtêyan	VAI conj. indic.	that you are going: *v.* itohtê-.
ihti-	VAI	fare (in health); be ailing
isa	IPC	to be sure, of course
iskwêw-	NA	woman
iši	IPV	so, thus
ka	IPV future marker with ni... and ki... subject prefixes	shall, will
kêkwân	PR interrog.	what?

(kêkwân-	NI	thing)
kihci	IPV / N	great, greatly
kimilwêlihtên	VTI	you (sg.) like it [This class of verbs will be learned later.]
kîla	PR personal	you (sg.)
milopali-	VA/II	go well, get along well
mîcim-	NI	food
mîkwêc	IPC	thank you
môsoniy-	NI [proper name]	Moosonee: townsite eight kms. up Moose River at SW corner of James Bay, Ontario
natohkolon-iskwêw-	NA	nurse
nawac	IPC	quite, pretty much
nâpêw-	NA	man
nimilwêlihtên	VTI	I like it [This class of verbs will be learned later.]
nititêlihtên	VTI	I know (it) [This class of verbs will be learned later.]
nîla	PR personal	I
nôkosi-	VAI	appear, be visible
ohtohtê-	VAI	come from (not in sense of 'originate from')
okâwiya	NDA	his/her mother: kikâwiy-, nikâwiy-, etc.
okimâwi-	VAI	be manager
okosisa	NDA	his/her son: kikosis-, nikosis-, etc.
omisa	NDA	his/her (older) sister: kimis-, nimis-, etc.
ostêsa	NDA	his/her (older) brother: kistês-, nistês-, etc.
ošîma	NDA	his/her younger sibling (*no distinction as to sex*) kišîm-, nišîm-, etc.
otamî-	VAI	be busy
otânisa	NDA	his/her daughter: kitânis-, nitânis-, etc.
ôho	PR dem. anim. obv.	this one
ôma	PR dem. inan. prox.	this one
ômêliw	PR dem. inan. obv.	this one
pêci	IPV	in this direction, towards speaker
pêho-	VAI	wait
ta	IPV future marker with 3 and 3' subjects	shall, will
tâni	IPC	how?
wîla	PR personal	he, she
wîpac	IPC	soon, shortly
wîwat-	NDI	his (hunting) bag: nîwat-, kîwat-, etc.

G. REVIEW

2.A Kakwêcihkêmôwina—Questions

Answer the following questions with full sentences. Do not reply merely "êhê" or "môla".

1. šwâpihk nâ itohtêw cwân?
2. ômêliw nâ cwân ocîmân?
3. tašîhkêw nâ ôta kistês?
4. tân' êhtiyan anohc kâ-kîšikâk?
5. šwâpihk nâ kititohtân?
6. kîla nâ kicîmân ôma?
7. ôho nâ âlik otapwoya?
8. mawâpiw nâ kikâwiy ôta?
9. šwâpihk nâ iši-âpatisiw?
10. wîpac nâ mâškôc âšokanihk ta-ihtâw?
11. kitôkimâwin nâ kîla ôta?
12. okimâwiw nâ kôhtâwiy ôta?
13. âšay nâ ihtâwinihk pêci-ohtohtêliwa cwân ošîma nêsta mâka omisa?
14. tânt' êtohtêyan mâka kîla?
15. kimilwêlihtên nâ [do you like it] kîla ôta?

2.B Naškwêwašihtwâwina—Answers

Formulate questions to which the following would be appropriate answers.

1. môla nâspic nimilwêlihtên ôta.
2. êhê, wîpac mâškôc âšokanihk n'ka-itohtân.
3. tâpwê, nîla nicîmân ôma.
4. môla, nistês mâka okimâwiw.
5. âšay šwâpihk pêci-ohtohtêliwa.
6. êmiliy n'tišinihkâson.
7. êkotê, ôtê itêhkê.
8. êhê, ôhtâwiya nêsta âšay tašîhkêliwa ôta.
9. môla, okâwiya mâka âšokanihk iši-pêholiwa.
10. wîpac nawac [quite] n'ka-âhtokwân.

11. êhê, âšay ninisitohtên.
12. kââ, ôta mâka kitašîhkân.
13. tâpwê, nâspic milwâšin ôta.
14. môla, âskaw mâka n'tâpatisin ôta.
15. ay'hâw, âšay pêci-nôkosiliwa ošîma. wîpac mâškôc ta-kîwêw.

UNIT THREE

A. BASIC CONVERSATION

1. Calling in at the Camp Trade[1]

Caller:	nipîhtokwân	I enter
	kî [verbal prefix]	can, may
	wâciyê. n'ka-kî-pîhtokwân nâ?	Hello. May I come in?
Camp Trader:	wâciyê. pêci-pîhtokwê.	Hello. Come in.
	kipimâtisin	you are living
	milo [prefix]	good
	kimilo-pimâtisin nâ?	Are you keeping well?
Caller:	nimilomahcihon	I feel well
	êhê, nâspic nimilomahcihon.	Yes, I feel very well.
	êtamahcihoyan	that you feel so
	tân' êtamahcihoyan kîla?	How do you yourself feel?
Camp Trader:	wayêš	about, approximately
	môla wayêš.	All right.
	kêkwân [NI]	something
	kinatawêlihtên nâ?	do you want it?
	kin'tawêl'tên nâ kêkwân?	Do you want something?
Caller:	masinahikan	book
	ninatawêlihtên	I want it
	ninatawêlihtên masinahikan.	I want a book.
Camp Trader:	kêko	which (one)?
	kêko masinahikan? ôma nâ?	Which book? This one?

[1] A smaller, auxiliary post nearer the trapping grounds where trapping gear, provisions and sometimes a few medicines and books are kept.

Caller:	tôwihkân	kind, sort
	mayêw	that's not it
	êkwânima	that (is the) one
	mayêw tôwihkân.	That's not the kind.
	êkwânima tôwihkân.	That's the kind.
Camp Trader:	walawîtimihk	outside
	awênihkân	somebody, a person
	niwâpamâw	I see him
	niwâpamâw awênihkân walawîtimihk.	I see somebody outside.
Caller:	ana	that one
	nikosis ana.	That's my son.
Camp Trader:	pîhtokwêw	he enters
	wîpac mâškôc ta-pîhtokwêw.	Maybe he'll come in shortly.
	walawîw	he'll go out
	wîpac mâškôc ta-walawîw.	Maybe he'll soon go out.
	manâ	isn't it
	kîšikâw	it is day
	milo-kîšikâw	it is a fine day
	milo-kîšikâw, manâ?	It's a fine day, isn't it?
	tahkâyâw	it is cold
	kimiwan	it is raining
	môla âšay kimiwan, tahkâyâw mâka.	It's not raining now, but it's cold.
Caller:	otakikomiw	she has a cold
	êliwêhk	especially, ... ever!
	êliwêhk tahkâyâw! nikâwiy otakikomiw.	Is it ever cold! My mother has a cold.
	kwayask	properly
	môla kwayask kî-nipâw.	She can't sleep properly.
Camp Trader:	môla wîlâhpahk	that's too bad, that's a pity
	nimihcilawêsin	I'm sorry
	nimihcilawêsin. môla wîlâhpahk.	I'm sorry. That's too bad.
	mâcika	look here, behold
	...âpoy [suffix]	liquid

	ostostocikanâpoy	cough syrup
	natohkolon *as* NI	medicine
	mâcik' ôma n'tohkolon, ostostocikanâpoy.	Here's some medicine, some cough syrup.
	êkwâni	so then [emphatic]
	êkwâni nâ?	Is that all? That's it, then?
Caller:	êkwâni.	That's all. That's it.
	êko, êkwa	then, so then
	êko wâs' âni ...	that's that, then ...
	êko wâs' âni. âšay n'ka-kihtohtân. n'ka-âpatisin.	Well, that's that. I'll be going now. I have to work.

2. Other People's Canoes and Things

A:	animêliw	that one (obv. sg.)
	animêliw nâ cwân ocîmân?	Is that John's canoe?
B:	ohcistiniliw	it (0') leaks, it lets in water
	êhê, ohcistiniliw mâka.	Yes, it leaks though
A:	milwâšiniliw	it (0') is good
	tâpwê nâ? môla nâspic milwâšiniliw.	Really? It's not very good.
B:	milwâšišiliwa	he (3') is good
	nawac mâka milwâšišiliwa wîla otâšokana.	Yes, but his wharf is in fairly good condition.
A:	mayêliwa	he (3') is not (the one)
	mayêliwa wîla otâšokana.	That's not his wharf.
	mayêliw	it (0') is not (the one)
	mayêliw nêsta wîla ocîmân.	That's not his canoe either.
B:	ihtakwaniliw	it (0') is (there)
	niwanêlihtên	I'm thinking wrongly
	êhê, niwanêl'tên, —mêskanâhk ihtakwaniliw.	Right, I'm mistaken, —it's on the path.

B. DISCUSSION OF GRAMMAR

1. Verbs

1.1 Inanimate Intransitive Verbs—VII

Verbs with an animate subject (VAI) are matched by parallel forms for an inanimate subject, the verbs which are designated as VII:

kikosis âšokanihk ihtâw	your son is at the wharf
kicîmân âšokanihk ihtakwan	your canoe is at the wharf

Inanimate intransitive verbs often represent the construction which, in English, begins with the empty subject, "it": *e.g.*, **it** is raining, **it** is cold, **it** is strange, etc. The word following "it is..." usually denotes a quality such as rainy, cold, strange,—or acts as a complement: it is day, ...night, ...home.

In Cree the same kind of notion is expressed by using an inanimate intransitive verb consisting of an element which contains the basic idea: *i.e.*, good, strange, day, coupled with a verbal ending. So we have

mil$^{W}/_{O}$	good	milwâšin	it is good, it is fine
tahk	cold	tahkâyâw	it is cold
tipisk	night	tipiskâw	it is night
kîšik	day	kîšikâw	it is day

Many elements such as tahk... do not stand alone unless they are full words in their own right. Otherwise they must occur in combination with some noun-forming or verb-forming element. (We have a usage something like this in English with *aero-*, as in *aero*car, or *tele-*, as in *tele*gram, *tele*phone, *tele*vision, and so on; so Cree usage is perhaps not without certain near parallels in English.)

As one would expect, inanimate intransitive verbs do not occur with subject prefixes ni... and ki..., but only with third person, inanimate subjects which we write as 0 for nearer third person (*i.e.*, proximate) and 0′ for further third person (obviative).

All VII with 0 subject end in either w or n. (Actually, the subject ending is ...w for *all* VII, including those with stems ending in ...n like milwâšin. Hence, one would expect milwâšinw and, in fact, the /w/ appears in the plural form, milwâšinwa. This is because of a rule which requires that the sound /w/ be dropped whenever it occurs in final position *after a consonant*. Thus milwâšinw in the singular becomes milwâšin, and the same thing happens to all other verb stems ending in ...n. (See §2.1.2 below.)

0	milwâšin -	it is good	kîšikâw -	it is day
	ihtakwan -	it is (there)	kišitêw -	it is hot
	milopaliw -	it is going well		
0′	milwâšin...ɩliw		kîšikâ...liw	(< kîšikâ...ɩliw
	ihtakwan...ɩliw		kišitê...liw	< kišitê...ɩliw
			milopali...liw	< milopali...ɩliw)

Remember: Intransitive Verbs show agreement for the gender of the **subject**:

milwâšišiw âšokan	the wharf is good
milwâšin cîmân	the canoe is good
awênihkân anta ihtâw	someone is there
kêkwân anta ihtakwan	something is there
šwâpihk nâ ihtâw kitânis?	is your daughter at the store?
masinahikan ôta ihtakwan	the book is here

——DRILL 1——

1.2 Obviative of Inanimate Intransitive Verbs

Unit 2.B.1.1 and 2.B.3.2 pointed up the distinction in Cree between a more immediate third person (okimâw, kôhtâwiy, cwân) and a more remote third person (ôhtâwiya, otôkimâma, etc.). Anything possessed by 3 must be in the further third person position, or obviative (*v.* p. xxxvii and diagram, p. 24). Just as *animate* intransitive verbs provide for a further third person *animate* subject, so *inanimate* intransitive verbs provide for a further third person *inanimate* subject, 0′:

ohcistiniliw nêsta cwân ocîmân — John's canoe is leaking too.

Like VAI stems (*v.* §1.4.1 below) VII stems also end in either a vowel or /n/. Unlike VAI, however, all VII have a distinct form for obviative *plural*, 0'p. These are included in the set below but will be learned in full later. (V in the following paradigm stands for "vowel".)

VII

Vowel Stems			n-Stems
0	V...w		n...w̶
0p	V...wa		n...wa
0'	V...liw	(< V...łliw)	n...ɩliw
0'p	V...liwa	(< V...łliwa)	n...ɩliwa

NOTE. The cross bar through a letter denotes dropping or assimilation of the sound represented.

——DRILL 2——

1.3 kî: Potential Prefix

The potential prefix, kî, "can, be able to", is one of a series which precedes the verb stem but follows time markers and / or personal subject markers: *e.g.,*

môla n'ka-kî-pêci-itohtân	I shall not be able to come.
n'ka-kî-pîhtokwân nâ?	May I come in?

——DRILL 3——

1.4 Stem Vowels

1.4.1 VAI Stem Vowels

All animate intransitive verbs (VAI) take the same endings after the stem vowel:

api...w	i-stem	he sits
nipâ...w	â-stem	he sleeps
itohtê...w	ê-stem	he goes (to a place)
pêho...w	o-stem	he waits
walawî...w	î-stem	he goes out
takošin...w̶[1]	n-stem	he arrives

[1] VAI n-stems are studied fully in Unit 12.

(You have met several verbs, ninisitohtên, nikiskêlihtên, kinatawêlihtên, which are translated by English intransitive verbs, "I understand, I know, you want". In Cree they are a kind of regular, transitive verb, even though sometimes listed in older dictionaries as intransitives. We shall meet them later. Meanwhile learn the occasional form which occurs in the conversations.)

1.4.2 ê-stems

Note the stem vowel in the following forms:

	nip **â** w ———>	ninip **â** n
but	itoht **ê** w ———>	nititoht **â** n

ê-stems regularly change the stem vowel to /â/ for ni... and ki... subjects. The change is easily remembered by learning new verbs in the form for third person singular subject which always shows the /ê/ stem vowel.

——DRILL 4——

1.5 ιši, *continued*

The prefix particle, ιši always refers back to or relates to something which *precedes* it in the phrase (Unit 2.B.1.2.2). Hence, locating expressions, when they precede the verb require it to be prefixed by ιši: *e.g.,*

walawîtimihk iši-âpatisiw.	He works outside.

This is always the case for 3(p) or 3' subjects; but in some localities, even where a locating expression precedes the verb, you may notice that ιši is omitted with a ni... or ki... subject: *e.g.,*

walawîtamihk nâ kitâpatisin?	Do you work outside?

Follow the use of the area in which you are located.

——DRILL 5——

2. Nouns

2.1 Possessed Theme Suffix: ...ιm-

You have already noted (Unit 2.C.6.1) forms such as

nišwâpim	*from*	šwâp
nisîpîm	*from*	sîpiy
nitôkimâm	*from*	okimâw

The basic form of this possessed theme suffix is ...ιm, added to the noun stem: *e.g.,*

šwâp- ————> nišwâpim

This stem formation with ...ιm, is referred to as a *possessed theme.* The ...ιm suffix commonly appears with loan words used in possessed form: *e.g.,*

šwâp-	>	nišwâpim
šôliyân- (money)	>	nišôliyânim
kwâpiy- (coffee)	>	nikwâpîm.

2.1.1 Stems in Vowel + /w/ or /y/

Where the noun stem ending in /w/ takes the possessed theme suffix, a regular contraction takes place: *e.g.*

nitôkimâw- + ...ιm	>	nitôkimâm
nitiskwêw- + ...ιm	>	nitiskwêm
nitililiw- + ...ιm	>	nitililîm

Nouns ending in a vowel + /y/ do not show quite the same predictability, for example, apwoy but nitapwoy. Most nouns, however, ending in /iy/ show the same contraction as above:

nisîpiy- + ...ιm	>	nisîpîm, osîpîm, etc.

Many nouns, including most nouns with dependent stems,do not take the possessed theme suffix. As variants occur, the possessed forms will be taught.

2.1.2 Stems in Consonant + /w/

Certain stems, verbs as well as nouns (*v.* §1.1. and §1.4.1 above: takošin...w) end in a consonant followed by /w/:

mistikw-	tree (NA), stick (NI)
môsw-	moose

The /w/ is dropped from the singular in the mention case,

môs anta ihtâw	a moose is there

because of the same sound law which deletes the final /w/ in milwâšin (§1.1 above): *i.e.,* a final /w/ after a consonant is dropped.

When ...ɩm follows the /w/, however, in a possessed form, the /w/ is then no longer in final position. The sequence of /w + ɩ/ results in the single sound, /o/: *i.e.,*

nimistikw- + ...ɩm	>	nimistikom
nimôsw- + ...ɩm	>	nimôsom.

In localities where ...ɩm is not used with the stem mistikw-, the possessed form in the singular would be nimistik, no final /w/.

2.2 Stems in /aw/ or /ay/

Where stems end in /aw/ or /ay/ the possessed theme does not ordinarily occur: *e.g.,*

mêskanaw-	>	nimêskanaw

——DRILL 6——

3. Pronouns: Demonstrative, *a further note*

In Unit 2.B.3.2 you met the various forms for "this one" and "that one". Sometimes related forms which look different on the surface show a surprising resemblance at an underlying level. The negative particle, môla, for example, is actually a contraction of namawila. The initial syllable is dropped and the remainder, mawila, contracted to môla. If awa originally paralleled ana in all its forms, then the same type of contraction would give us

ôma *from a hypothetical* *awima (*matching* anima)

ômêliw *from a hypothetical* *awimêliw (*matching* animêliw)

and ôhi (the form occurring in several dialects) *from a form,* *awihi.

The apparent differences in form may then be seen simply as examples of a regular contraction.

[* marks hypothetical, underlying shapes which do not appear as actual grammatical forms.]

4. Intonation

4.1 Yes-No Questions

All languages show certain characteristics of rhythm, stress, intonation and so on. As we know from our own language, meaning beyond the bald, dictionary value of the words themselves can often be critically altered by the tone of voice. For example:

He is cóming,

with the voice rising in pitch to the syllable, *com-*, then falling, is clearly a statement. If the pitch continues to rise, with the highest pitch on the *-ing*, the utterance will normally be interpreted as a question. Try it.

In Cree the intonation contour of an utterance is perhaps more fixed and does not condition meaning in quite the same way as in English. An incorrect intonation pattern, however, can still be confusing and even irritating to the listener. In any case it marks the speaker as an "outsider' to the group.

Listen carefully to the pitch level of the voice in the questions of Intonation Drill 1. Play the recording several times (or ask your teacher to repeat) while you draw a pencil line to indicate the rise and fall of the voice (*i.e.,* the intonation contour) for each utterance. Ask yourself: Do short pauses affect the contour? How? Finally, repeat each utterance several times yourself. Mimic the voice of the Cree speaker as faithfully as you can. Do not confuse *pitch* with *stress*. Their relation is somewhat different in Cree and in English. Be sure you hear what the Cree speaker is actually saying, and not what your English speech habits trick you into thinking he is saying!

——INTONATION DRILL 1——

4.2 Declarative Statements

The intonation contour of an utterance in Cree as a rule shows less of a roller coaster pattern than we often find in English. A fairly long utterance may be continued on one pitch level until broken by a pause. Three main pitch levels may be discerned:

1. an initial or low level from which the voice ordinarily begins, and on which it comes to rest at a final pause.

2. a higher or mid-level, used to carry the bulk of any utterance. It may

show a glide upwards, as in the case of a simple question or, in terms of absolute pitch, be lower in a second and dependent clause. [Note the example below.]

3. a high level used for emphasis, in excitement and to make the voice carry.

A typical contour for a declarative statement at Kashechewan on the west coast of James Bay might be drawn as follows:

minwên'tam ê-takwâkininik, ê-pâminân'ci niska.
He likes it in the Fall as the geese are flying.

The comma marks a pause, and this is accompanied by a dip in the contour.

——INTONATION DRILL 2——

a) Check your mimicry of the Cree speaker's intonation on the foregoing. What favourite type of contour would you draw for a simple statement? —for a simple question?

b) To develop a speech habit through mimicry is more useful than trying to speak through conscious observance of a set of rules. Nonetheless, overt awareness of a pattern both helps in hearing it and is a useful check on one's own chance carelessness.

In Cree, as in English, different speech habits prevail in different areas. If you have a model from the area where you expect to use Cree, this is obviously your goal in mimicry. Otherwise mimic the tape, even if you know it represents the habits of a dialect area other than your own. It is always better to speak some kind of authentic sounding Cree, than a hodge-podge which is nobody's native language. You can adjust to local usage somewhere else with a little practice.

Two main types of intonation contour have been studied:

1. that for a simple question, with nâ;
2. that for a declarative statement.

The simplest type of contour for a question with nâ, may be represented by a line beginning at the low pitch level and gliding up for the length of the utterance, with the up-sweep more marked towards the end. (The mid-level is here drawn just above the line of print for greater legibility.)

âšay nâ?

milopaliw nâ?

âšay nâ kikihtohtân?

A short break or pause has the effect of putting a dent in the contour: *e.g.*,

kitôkimâwin nâ kîla ôta?

ê'ko nâ ôtê itêhkê šwâpihk?

(*v.* also Intonation Drill 1, Nos. 6, 7, 12, 16, 18, 19)

A declarative statement, on the other hand, shows a different type of contour: *e.g.*,

šwâpihk n'titohtân.

môla ninisitohtên.

wîpac mâškôc ta-pêci-pîhtokwêw.

Once the voice rises from the low, initial pitch it is almost as though the question contour had been turned upside down. Where a longer pause occurs, as in the two complex sentences which follow, the contour also breaks sharply: *e.g.*,

môla, cîmân n'kî-wâpahtên.

êhê, nawac nimilwêl'tên ôta.

In the compound sentence below each half displays its own contour:

âšay môla kimiwan, tahkâyâw mâka.
[*v.* Intonation Drill 2, No. 15]

When you have finished the intonation drills, proceed to the pronunciation drill.

C. DRILLS

I. PATTERN DRILLS

1. Inanimate Intransitive Verb—VII

1.1 Mimicry Drill

Mimic the recording, repeating down the column for each set, then across each row to contrast the endings. Note what formal feature the members of each set have in common and in what formal feature they contrast.

kîšikâ...w	it is day	ihtakwan...~~w~~	it is (at a place)
tipiskâ...w	it is night	kimiwan...~~w~~	it is raining
tahkâyâ...w	it is cold		
kišitê...w	it is hot	milwâšin...~~w~~	it is good, it is fine
mayê...w	there is not	otâkošin...~~w~~	it is evening
milopali...w	it is going well		

1.2 ihtâw : : ihtakwan

Follow the model:

Recording:	awênihkân ...	*or*	sîpiy ...
Reply:	awênihkân nêtê ihtâw		sîpiy nêtê ihtakwan

	(Cover this column.)
sîpiy	ihtakwan
nikosis	ihtâw
âšokan	ihtâw
mêskanaw	ihtakwan
šwâp	ihtakwan
nikâwiy	ihtâw
masinahikan	ihtakwan

natohkolon [medicine NI *v.* natohkoliy.]	ihtakwan
awênihkân	ihtâw
okimâw	ihtâw
kêkwân	ihtakwan
nôhtâwiy	ihtâw
nitânis	ihtâw
cîmân	ihtakwan

2. Obviative of VII

2.1 Mimicry Drill

Mimic the recording, first down each column then across each row.

0 Subject (3rd person inanimate)	0′ Subject (Further 3rd person inanimate)
milwâšin	milwâšiniliw
ohcistin	ohcistiniliw
otâkošin	otâkošiniliw
ihtakwan	ihtakwaniliw
kimiwan	kimiwaniliw
kišitêw	kišitêliw
mayêw	mayêliw
milopaliw	milopaliliw
kêšikâw	kîšikâliw
tipiskâw	tipiskâliw
tahkâyâw	tahkâyâliw

2.2 Change the 0-Subject (*e.g.*, cîmân) to 0′ (*e.g.*, ocîmân) and alter the verb form accordingly.

Cue:	**(Uncover this column line by line to check your response)**
milwâšin kicîmân.	milwâšiniliw ocîmân.
ohcistin kicîmân.	ohcistiniliw ocîmân.
ihtakwan nâ kicîmân sîpîhk?	ihtakwaniliw nâ ocîmân sîpîhk?
mayêw nîla nicîmân.	mayêliw wîla ocîmân.

milopaliw nâ kicîmân?	milopaliliw nâ ocîmân?
milwâšin ninatohkolonim.	milwâšiniliw onatohkolonim.
mayêw kîla kitôstostocikanâpôm.	mayêliw wîla otôstostocikanâpôm.

3. **kî** can, be able; may. Expand each frame by the insertion of kî in the proper position on the model

Cue:	môla mâškôc ka-ihtân anta. You probably won't be there.
Expansion:	môla mâškôc ka-kî-ihtân anta. You probably won't be able to be there.

		(Use this column as a check)
1.	môla mâškôc ka-ihtân anta.	môla mâškôc ka-kî-ihtân anta.
2.	ta-apiw nâ okimâw âšokanihk?	ta-kî-apiw nâ okimâw âšokanihk?
3.	wîpac mâškôc n'ka-walawîn.	wîpac mâškôc n'ka-kî-walawîn.
4.	šwâpihk ta-itohtêw kitânis.	šwâpihk ta-kî-itohtêw kitânis.
5.	âšay môla ka-kihtohtân.	âšay môla ka-kî-kihtohtân.
6.	mîna nâ ka-âpatisin anta?	mîna nâ ka-kî-âpatisin anta?
7.	môla nipâw kwayask.	môla kî-nipâw kwayask.
8.	n'ka-pîhtokwân nâ?	n'ka-kî-pîhtokwân nâ?
9.	ta-tašîhkêw nâ ôta?	ta-kî-tašîhkêw nâ ôta?
10.	môla âšay ta-okimâwiw ôta.	môla âšay ta-kî-okimâwiw ôta.

4. In the following conversation complete each partial sentence by filling in the blank with an appropriate word from the list given. Each word should be used once only.

tahkâyâw, ohcistiniliw, n'kî-nipân, pêci-pîhtokwê, kêko, ihtakwaniliw, tôwihkân, êkwâni, nimilomahcihon, awênihkân, ostostocikanâpoy, n'ka-kihtohtân, êkwânimêliw, otakikomiw

âniy:	wâciyê! n'ka-kî-pîhtokwân nâ?
okimâw:	êhê, ____________________. tân' êtamahcihoyan?
âniy:	nâspic ____________________. tân êhtiyan mâka kîla?
okimâw:	apišîš mâškôc n'tôtakikomin. __________ nêsta nîwa [my wife]. êliwêhk __________ anohc kâ-kîšikâk.
âniy:	tâpwê! kitayân nâ [do you have] ____________________?
okimâw:	môla n'tayân. môla kwayask ________________.
âniy:	nimihcilawêsin. ay'hâw, nin'tawêl'tên masinahikan.
okimâw:	mâcik' ôma masinahikan. __________ nâ?

âniy:	êkwânima ______________. __________________ nâ âlik ocîmân?
okimâw:	môla. nêtê mêskanâhk ________________.
âniy:	__________________, n'titêl'tên.
okimâw:	tâpwê. kââ, niwâpamâw _______________ walawîtimihk.
âniy:	nikosis ana. âšay ___________________.
okimâw:	wâciyê.
âniy:	wâciyê.

5. AI Stem Vowels. Drill the following on the model:

Cue: ta-apiw nâ?
Reply: môla mâškôc. nîla mâka n'ka-apin.

		(Check column)
1.	ta-apiw nâ?	... n'ka-apin.
2.	ta-mihcilawêsiw nâ?	... n'ka-mihcilawêsin.
3.	ta-ihtâw nâ ôta?	... n'ka-ihtân ôta.
4.	ta-nipâw nâ ôta?	... n'ka-nipân ôta.
5.	ta-itohtêw nâ?	... n'ka-itohtân.
6.	ta-tašîhkêw nâ ôta?	... n'ka-tašîhkân ôta.
7.	ta-milomahcihow nâ?	... n'ka-milomahcihon.
8.	ta-walawîw nâ?	... n'ka-walawîn.

6. ıši so, thus

6.1 On the model,

Cue: šwâpihk nâ kitiši-âpatisin?
Reply: êhê, šwâpihk nitiši-âpatisin.

Replace šwâpihk with each of the successive items:

šwâpihk nâ kitiši-âpatisin?
âšokanihk
mêskanâhk
ôta
nêtê
nêtê nâ âsokanihk [Reply: êhê, nêtê âšokanihk, *etc.*]
nêtê nâ mêskanâhk
nêtê nâ šwâpihk
nîhci [downstairs, below]
walawîtimihk
pîhtokwamihk [inside, indoors]
išpimihk [upstairs, aloft]

6.2 Put the locating expression before the verb and add ιši in its appropriate position.

Cue: âšay nâ kitâpatisin šwâpihk?
Response: tâpwê, šwâpihk n'tiši-âpatisin.

		(Check column)
1.	âšay nâ kitâpatisin šwâpihk?	tâpwê, šwâpihk n'tiši-âpatisin.
2.	âšay nâ kinipân nêtê âšokanihk?	... nêtê âšokanihk n'tiši-nipân.
3.	âšay nâ n'ka-kî-apin mêskanâhk?	... mêskanâhk ka-kî-iši-apin.
4.	âšay nâ âpatisiw nêtê âšokanihk?	... nêtê âšokanihk iši-âpatisiw.
5.	âšay nâ kitâpatisin nêtê?	... nêtê n'tiši-âpatisin.
6.	âšay nâ âpatisiw ôta?	... ôta iši-âpatisiw.
7.	âšay nâ apiw âšokanihk?	... âšokanihk iši-apiw.
8.	âšay nâ kit-âpatisin nêtê mêskanâhk?	... nêtê mêskanâhk n'tiši-âpatisin.

7. Possessed nouns. Given a noun and a personal pronoun, produce the corresponding possessed form of the noun, on the model:

7.1 Cue: masinahikan :: nîla
Response: nîla nimasinahikan

		(Check column)
1.	masinahikan :: nîla	nîla nimasinahikan
2.	otânisa :: nîla	nîla nitânis
3.	natohkolon :: nîla	nîla nin'tohkolonim
4.	kitânis :: wîla	wîla otânisa
5.	kikosis :: wîla	wîla okosisa
6.	kikâwiy :: wîla	wîla okâwiya
7.	masinahikan :: wîla	wîla omasinahikan
8.	natohkolon :: wîla	wîla onatohkolonim

7.2 Proceed as in 7.1 above, with the following random set.

1.	masinahikan :: kîla	kîla kimasinahikan
2.	nitânis :: wîla	wîla otânisa
3.	natohkolon :: nîla	nîla ninatohkolonim
4.	kikosis :: kîla	kîla kikosis
5.	kikâwiy :: wîla	wîla okâwiya
6.	ôhtâwiya :: wîla	wîla ôhtâwiya
7.	cîmân :: kîla	kîla kicîmân
8.	okimâw :: nîla	nîla nitôkimâm

II. INTONATION DRILLS

1. Repeat the following sentences after the recording. Mimic the rise and fall of the speaker's voice as closely as you can. (You might draw in the intonation contours as on p. 58)

1. milopaliw nâ?
2. âpatisiw nâ?
3. kimilo-'mâtisin nâ?
4. ôma nâ?
5. n'ka-pêci-pîhtokwân nâ?
6. kitôkimâwin nâ kîla?
7. kitôkimâwin nâ kîla ôta?
8. kitihtân nâ ôta?
9. kitašîhkân nâ ôta?
10. kin'tawêlimâw nâ ôta?
11. âšay nâ?
12. ôta nâ iši-ayamihâwikimâwiw wîla? [Is *he* the clergyman here?]
13. šwâpihk nâ itohtêw?
14. âšay nâ kikihtohtân?
15. kin'tawêl'tên nâ kêkwân?
16. kiwâpamâw nâ âšokan nêtê?
17. kîla nâ okimâw?
18. môšak nâ tašîhkêw ôta?
19. ê'ko nâ ôtê itêhkê šwâpihk?

2. Drill the following statements as you did the questions above. Concentrate on mimicking the Cree as you hear it.

1. šwâpihk n'titohtân.
2. wâpamêw okosisa.
3. êhê, šwâpihk iši-âpatisiw.
4. môla ninisitohtên.
5. nêtê piko mêskanâhk.
6. môla, cîmân mâka n'kî-wâpahtên.
7. wîpac mâškôc ta-pêci-pîhtokwêw.
8. nimawâpin piko.
9. n'tôkimâwin, nîla.
10. n'tayamihêwikimâwin, nîla.
11. cwân nâkociy n'tišinihkâson.
12. niwâpamâw kikosis.
13. awasitê 'pišîš nimâhkîmihk.
14. êhê, nawac nimilwêl'tên ôta.
15. âšay môla kimiwan, tahkâyâw mâka.
16. môla kikiskêlimitin [I don't know you]
17. âšokanihk ihtâw.
18. môla kî-nipâw.
19. môla kwayask kî-nipâw.
20. wîpac mâškôc n'ka-milo-'mâtisin.

III. PRONUNCIATION DRILL

This is not so much a pattern as a "patter" drill. Practise the following question-answer exchanges until you can repeat the Cree effortlessly at normal conversational speed.

a.	šwâpihk nâ itohtêw kitânis?	môla, nîla mâka šwâpihk n'titohtân.
	apiw nâ ôta?	môla, nîla mâka n'tapin ôta.
	otakikomiw nâ cwân?	môla, nîla mâka n'tôtakikomin.
	âpatisiw nâ?	môla, nîla mâka n'tâpatisin.
	cwân nâ išinihkâsow wîla?	môla, nîla mâka cwân n'tišinihkâson.
b.	šwâpihk nâ kititohtân?	êhê, šwâpihk n'titohtân.
	kitapin nâ ôta?	tâpwê, n'tapin ôta.
	kitôtakikomin nâ?	tâpwê, n'tôtakikomin.
	kitâpatisin nâ?	tâpwê, n'tapâtisin.
	cwân nâ kitišinihkâson kîla?	tâpwê, cwân n'tišinihkâson.

NOTE that before a vowel the personal prefixes always end in /t/ : nit..., kit..., ot..., and the t̲ is always written in standard Cree spelling. This is not the case with /y/ glides heard between vowels as in kay̲-âpatisin. These intervocalic glides should, nonetheless, be mimicked carefully after the recording, even though they are not written.

NOTE also: after the personal prefixes ending in the sound, /t/, the short /o/ is regularly lengthened to /ô/: otakikomiw, but kitôtakikomin.

D. CONVERSATION PRACTICE

1. Considerable stress has been laid on mimicry. Remember, however, that this means mimicry not only of the sounds represented by the spelling, but also careful imitation of the rise and fall of the voice, pause and stress.

When you have learned the Basic Conversations, close your book and play the tape again, this time concentrating on the intonation contours, pause points and the placing of stress.

2.1 Imagine that you are the new post manager (okimâw), nurse (natohkolon-iskwêw), teacher (okiskinohamâkêsiw) or clergyman (ayamihêwikimâw:[1] *pronounce this as* ayamihêyokimâw). Someone has just come to see you and you extend a cordial invitation to come in and sit down (api anta sit there). Inquire about your visitor's son, daughter or any other member of the family. Find out what your visitor wants and ask whether he / she has a cold, express regret if this is so and ask whether he / she needs any medicine and what kind (kêko tôwi-natohkolon what kind of medicine?). Make a few casual remarks about the weather, conclude the conversation and say Good-bye.

2.2 Someone travelling through your settlement wants to know exactly where you live, where you work and whether you are the post manager, forestry agent (amiskokimâw) and whether you like it in this part of the country. Develop a conversation along these lines with someone else in the class.

3. Cover the Cree column in the Basic Conversations and be sure you can give the Cree equivalent of the English without hesitation.

Useful Expressions

maci-kîšikâw	it is a bad day, bad weather
mil'-otâkošin	it is a fine evening
milo-tipiskâw	it is a fine night
kimiwan	it is raining

[1] *i.e.,* "prayer leader," the Anglican term for "priest," used in the village where much of the present material was developed. The Roman Catholic term is mêhkotêwihkonayêw, "black robe."

E. LISTENING IN

Listen to your teacher or to the recording as the following dialogue is read. During the first reading, LOOK AT YOUR TEACHER'S mouth but do not interrupt the reading. Follow the text as the passage is read for the second time, marking the sections which require special attention. Ask for a repetition of these passages at conversational speed. Note enunciation, speech-rhythm and intonation carefully.

If you are using a recording, listen to the following dialogue with your book closed. When you have heard the recording several times, open your book and follow the text, checking off and learning any expressions you may have missed. Then practise repeating the dialogue, carefully mimicking the voice recorded on the tape. Pay special attention to enunciation, speech-rhythm and intonation.

Natohkolon:[1] wâciyê. pêci-pîhtokwê. nâspic milo-kîšikâw, manâ?

Cwân: tâpwê milwâšin. tahkâyâw mâka.

Natohkolon: êliwêhk tahkâyâw! môla kikiskêlimitin [I don't know you] tân' êšinihkâsoyin.

Cwân: cwân wâpanow n'tišinihkâson.

Natohkolon: kââ! âšay kikiskêlimitin. tân' êtamahcihoyin?

Cwân: môla wayêš.

Natohkolon: tântê mâka kikosis? môla niwâpamâw walawîtimihk.

Cwân: wîpac mâškôc walawîtimihk ta-ihtâw. šwâpihk iši- âpatisiw. kin'tawêlimâw nâ ôta?

Natohkolon: êhê, môla nâspic milo-pimâtisiw. otakikomiw n'titêlimâw.

Cwân: tâpwê! nêsta nitânis otakikomiw, nêsta wîla. môla kwayask kî-nipâw.

Natohkolon: kin'tawêl'tên nâ natohkolon?[2] ostostocikanâpoy mâškôc? nâspic milwâšin.

Cwân: êhê, n'kiskêl'tên. âšay mâka nawac milomahcihow. môla n'tawêl'tam[3] n'tohkoloniliw.

[1] natohkolon, as an animate noun = "doctor" around western James Bay.

[2] Used as NI by some speakers in place of standard natohkoliy- NI medicine: *obv.* natohkolîliw.

[3] she doesn't want (it), she doesn't need (it).

Natohkolon:	ê'kwâni. ka-ihtân nâ kîla ôta?
Cwân:	êhê, nêtê piko mêskanâhk. nêsta kîla?
Natohkolon:	êhê, mâškôc n'ka-tašîhkân ôta. nâspic nimilwêl'tên.
Cwân:	tâpwê! nêsta nîla nawac nimilwêl'tên. kiwâpamâw nâ âšokan nêtê?
Natohkolon:	tântê? kââ! âšay niwâpamâw.
Cwân:	ay'hâw, ê'kwâna nîla n'tâšokan. ê'kwânimêliw mâka nistês ocîmân. nistês nêsta ôta tašîhkêw.
Natohkolon:	môla n'kiskêlimâw. milwâšiniliw mâka wîla ocîmân. wîpac mâškôc ta-pêci-mawâpiw.
Cwân:	êhê, mâškôc. êko wâs' âni, âšay n'ka-kihtohtân.
Natohkolon:	wâciyê.
Cwân:	wâciyê.

F. REFERENCE LIST

amiskokimâw-	NA	'beaver boss', Lands and Forests officer
ana	PR dem. anim. prox. sg.	that one
anima	PR dem. inan. prox. sg.	that one
animêliw	PR dem. inan. obv. sg.	that one
api-	VAI	sit
awênihkân-	NA	somebody, someone
ayamihêwikimâw-	NA	clergyman
âpatisi-	VAI	work
êko (*further west,* êkwa)	IPC	so, well then,
êko wâs' âni		well, that's that (*concluding a conversation*)
ê'kwâni	PR dem. inan. intensive	that (is it) [êwako that very one + ani emphatic ptcl.]
ê'kwânima	PR dem. inan. prox.	that very one
êliwêhk	IPC	especially, very much so
êtamahcihoyin	VAI conj. indic.	that you feel (health-wise). *v.* itamahciho-.
ihtakwan-	VII	be (at a place)
išpimihk	IPC	above, aloft; upstairs
itamahciho-	VAI	feel so (health-wise)
kêko	PR interrog.	which (one)?
kêkwân-	NI	thing, something
kêyâpac	IPC	still, yet; more
kikiskêlimitin	VTA 1 → 2	I know you (*sg.*)
kimiwan-	VII	rain
kinatawêlimâw	VTA 2 → 3	you (*sg.*) want him / her
kišitê-	VII	be hot
kiwâpamâw	VTA 2 → 3	you (*sg.*) see him / her
kî	IPV	potential prefix, can, be able to
kîšikâ-	VII	be day
kwayask	IPC	properly, correctly
maci	IPN / V	bad: *e,g.,* maci-kîšikâw
maci-kîšikâ-	VII	be a bad day
manâ	IPC	is it not? n'est-ce pas [nama not + nâ]

masinahikan-	NI	book
mayê-	VAI / VII	not be
mâcik'	IPC	lo, behold; look!
mêhkotêwihkonayêw-	NA	priest (*Roman Catholic*): *lit.*, 'black robe'
mihcilawêsi-	VAI	be sorry
milo	IPN / V	good: *e.g.*, milo-kîšikâw
milo-kîšikâ-	VII	be a fine day
milomahciho-	VAI	feel well
milo-pimâtisi-	VAI	be well, be in good health
milo-tipiskâ-	VII	be a fine night
mil'-otâkošin-	VII	be a fine evening *or* late afternoon
milwâšiši-	VAI	be good, be fine
môla wîlâhpahk		that's too bad, that's a pity
natawêlihtam	VTI 3 → 0	he wants it
natohkoliy-	NI	medicine: *obv.* natohkolîliw.
natohkolon-	NA	doctor:
natohkolon-	NI	medicine: *used by some speakers at* Kêšîciwan *for MC* natohkoliy-, *q.v.*
nipâ-	VAI	sleep
nititêlimâw	VTA 1 → 3	I think (him)
niwanêlihtên	VTI	I'm thinking wrongly, I'm mistaken, I'm wrong
nîhci	IPC	below; downstairs
ohcistin-	VII	leak, let in water
ostostocikanâpoy-	NI	cough medicine
otakikomi-	VAI	have a cold: lit., have mucus
otâkošin-	VII	be evening
pimâtisi-	VAI	live, be living
pîhtokwamihk	IPC	indoors, inside
pîhtokê- } pîhtokwê- }	VAI	enter
tahkâyâ-	VII	be cold
tipiskâ-	VII	be night, be dark
tôwi	IPN	kind of ...
tôwihkân-	NI	kind, type, sort
walawî-	VAI	go outside
walawîtimihk	IPC	outside
wayêš	IPC	about, approximately

G. REVIEW

3.A Kakwêcihkêmôwina—Questions

Answer the following questions with full sentences. Avoid replying merely "êhê" or "môla".

1. wâciyê! n'ka-kî-pîhtokwân nâ?
2. tân' êtamahcihoyin?
3. kimilo-pimâtisin nâ?
4. kinatawêlihtên nâ masinahikan?
5. kêko tôwi-masinahikan?
6. kiwâpamâw nâ nikosis walawîtimihk?
7. âpatisiw nâ kitânis?
8. ta-apiw nâ okimâw âšokanihk?
9. milwâšin nâ nêtê kitihtâwinihk?
10. šwâpihk nâ iši-âpatisiw cwân?
11. ta-pîhtokwêw nâ?
12. kimawâpin nâ piko, nêstapiko ka-ihtân ôta?
13. milo-kîšikâw nâ anohc kâ-kîšikâk?
14. natawêlihtam nâ kikosis kêkwâliw?
15. tahkâyâw manâ?
16. kêyâpac [still] nâ otakikomiw kikâwiy?
17. nipâw nâ kwayask?
18. ihtâw nâ nikosis ôta?
19. kêkwân ôma?
20. šwâpihk nâ iši-âpatisiliwa okimâw okosisa?
21. kêyâpac nâ kitôstostotên?
22. ohcistiniliw nâ cwân ocîmân?
23. mâškôc niwanêlihtên. ômêliw nâ cwân ocîmân?
24. kišitêw nâ anta šwâpihk?

3.B Naškwêwašihtwâwina—Answers

Formulate questions to which the following would be appropriate answers.

1. êhê, nâspic milo-kîšikâw anohc kâ-kîšikâk.
2. môla wayêš.
3. êhê, n'ka-âpatisin ôta âšokanihk.
4. tâpwê, milo-kîšikâw.
5. âšay môla kimiwan, tahkâyâw mâka.
6. kââ! âšay niwâpamâw walawîtimihk.
7. êhê, nâspic mil'-otâkošin.
8. êliwêhk tahkâyâw!
9. tâpwê milwâšin.
10. êhê, môla ninipân kwayask.
11. nâspic ostostotam.
12. ostostocikanâpoy piko ninatawêlihtên.
13. êhê, êkwâni.
14. môla. wîpac mâškôc n'ka-kihtohtân.
15. môla nâspic otakikomiw. môla mâka nâspic milomahcihow.
16. mayêw tôwihkân.
17. tâpwê, ohcistiniliw nêsta cwân ocîmân.
18. môla nikiskêlihtên.
19. âšay šwâpihk iši-âpatisiw.
20. mayêliw wîla otâšokana.
21. mâškôc niwanêlihtên.
22. môla, nimawâpin piko.
23. wâciyê. pêci-pîhtokwê.
24. nawac mâka milwâšišiliwa wîla otâšokana.

UNIT FOUR

A. BASIC CONVERSATION

1. Finding the Way; the Taste of Fresh Baking

Visitor:	ê'ko nâ ôtê itêhkê šwâpihk?	Is this the way to the store?
	antê	there, thither
	ê'ko nâ antê itêhkê šwâpihk?	Is that the way to the store?
Cwân:	ka-wâpahtên	you will see it
	at'-îtohtê	start to go along
	môla. ôtê piko at'-îtohtê	No, just go along this path
	mêskanâhk, ka-wâpahtên mâka.	and you will see it.
	mâhkiy	tent
	nimâhkîmihk	to, at, in my tent
	awasitê	more (*of degree*)
	nêtê, awasitê itêhkê nimâhkîmihk.	Over there, past my tent.
	âstamitê	to this side, facing side
	nêtê, âstamitê nimâhkîmihk.	Over there, to this side of my tent.
Visitor:	awênihkân?	who?
	awênihkân ana wîla?	Who is that person?
	natawêlihtam kêkwâliw	he / she wants something
	nititêlimâw	I think him
	n'tawêl'tâm kêkwâliw n'titêlimâw.	I think he wants something.
Cwân:	niwîkimâkan	my wife
	nistês. awa mâka niwîkimâkan.	My older brother. And this (is) my wife.
	âlahkonâwa NA *obviative*	bread
	kîsiswêw	she is baking (*animate object*)
	kîsiswêw âlahkonâwa.	She's baking bread.
Visitor:	oški[1] [prefix form]	new, fresh
	nimilwêlimâw	I like him (*any animate object*)
	nâspic nimilwêlimâw oški-âlahkonâw.	I'm very fond of fresh bread.

[1] In the Moose area and east of James Bay ayawaši often replaces oški in the sense of "fresh".

	wîhkacišiw	it (*animate*) is delicious
	šâkoc	sure! (*emphatic*)
	šâkoc wîhkacišiw!	It sure is delicious!
Cwân:	kayâši [prefix form]	old, stale
	ispîš	than
	tâpwê! awasitê wîhkacišiw ispîš wîla kayâši-âlahkonâw.	Yes, Sir! It tastes better than stale bread.
	wîyâs	meat, flesh
	nêsta oški-wîyâs nimilwêl'tên.	I like fresh meat too.
Visitor:	môs	moose
	mâwac	most (*of degree*)
	mâwac nimil'wêl'tên môso-wîyâs	I like moose-meat most
	kotak	other, another
	ispîš wîla kotak mîcim	than (all) other food
	šâkoc wîhkašin	it sure is delicious!
	šâkoc wîhkašin! mâwac nimilwêl'tên môs'-wîyâs ispîš wîla kotak mîcim.	It sure tastes good! I like moose-meat most of all food.

2. How Long Have You Been Speaking Cree?

Cwân:	pitamâ	first
	âstam	come here
	awa mâka nišîm. êtiy, âstam pitamâ!	And this is my younger brother. Eddie, come here a minute!
Visitor:	môšak nâ tašîhkêw ôta?	Does he always live here?
Cwân:	nakiskaw	a little while
	môla, nimis mâka nakiskaw ta-tašîhkêw.	No, but my older sister will be staying for a little while.
	matêw	she is not (at a place)
	kotak	another, the other
	itâpicîw	she is away
	itâpicîw kotak anohc. matêw ôta.	The other one is away just now. she is not here.
Visitor:	ki...kiskêlimâw	you know him
	kikiskêlimâw nâ ayamihêwikimâw ôta?	Do you know the clergyman here?

Cwân:	šôliyân	money
	šôliyânikimâw	"paymaster", Indian Agent[2]
	kiskêlimêw	he knows him
	môla. nistês mâka kiskêlimêw šôliyânikimâwa.	No, but my older brother knows the Indian Agent.
Visitor:	ayâwêw	he has him
	otêma	his dog
	ayâw	he has it
	ayâw ocîmân anta. ayâwêw nêsta otêma anta.	He has his canoe there. He also has his dog there.
Cwân:	ta-pôsiw	he will go away (by vehicle)
	êhê, n'kiskêl'tên. wîpac mâka mâškôc ta-pôsiw.	Yes, I know. I imagine he'll soon be off though.
	kit...ililîmon	you speak Cree
	kitililîmon, manâ?	You speak Cree, eh?
Visitor:	apišîš piko.	Only a little.
	išinihkâtêw	it is called
	ê-'lilîmoyin	as you speak Cree
	tân' êšinihkâtêk?	how is it called?
	tân' êšinihkâtêk anima kêkwân ê-'lilîmoyin?	What is that thing called in Cree?
Cwân:	mîšahwêw	he repairs it (*animate*)
	apwoy išinihkâsow. nistês mâka mîšahwêw otapwoya.	It's called a paddle; and my older brother's repairing his paddle.
	kit...ôhci-ililîmon	you have been speaking Cree
	kinwêš	a long time
	kinwêš nâ kitôhci-ililîmon?	Have you been speaking Cree long?
Visitor:	ni...kiskinohamâson	I'm learning
	môla nâspic kinwêš. nikiskinohamâson mâka.	Not very long. I'm learning, though.
Cwân:	ni...wêmistikôšîmon	I speak English.
	apišîš niwêmistikôšîmon	I speak English a little
	nêsta nîla. apišîš piko niwêmistikôšîmon.	So am I. I speak English only a little.

[2] The rôle of Indian Agent no longer exists but the term may still be heard in other contexts: *e.g.,* bank manager.

B. DISCUSSION OF GRAMMAR

1. Verbs: Transitive Verbs

This unit is mainly about *transitive* verbs: *i.e.,* verbs which take an object. Just as there are two sets of *intransitive* verbs in Cree, depending on whether the subject is animate or inanimate, so there are two sets of *transitive* verbs. These take different endings, and often a different stem,[1] to show whether the object is animate or inanimate. Since transitive verbs show this change for *object* rather than for subject, the letters "A" and "I" are written *after* the "T": *viz.,* VTA and VTI. Examples of the two types of transitive verb are

niwâpam...âw	VTA	I see him, her (*any animate object*)
niwâpaht...ên	VTI	I see it (*any inanimate object*)

Note the different inflectional endings; and just after the root, wâp..., which means "see; light; bright" the different stem finals mark the gender of the object, ...am- for animate and ...aht- for inanimate.

1.1 Transitive Animate Verbs—VTA

We normally use "him" or "her" to translate the object of a transitive animate verb; and the object is represented in the glossary as "s.o."': *i.e.,* "someone". Remember, however, that *any animate noun* may properly stand as the object of a VTA. Study the following examples:

1.	wîpac ka-wâpamâw âšokan.	You'll soon see the wharf.
2.	nikiskêlimâw okimâhkân.	I know the Chief.
3.	mîšahwêw apwoya.	He's repairing the paddle.
4.	kiwâpamâw nâ nistês?	Do you see my (older) brother?
5.	môla nimilwêlimâw ana atim.	I don't like that dog.
6.	ayamihêw iskwêwa.	She's talking to the woman
7.	kinatawêlimâw nâ kotak apwoy?	Do you want the other paddle?
8.	n'ka-kîsiswâw nâ âlahkonâw?	Shall I bake (some) bread?
9.	ayâwêw šôliyâna.	He has (some) money.

———DRILLS 1.1 THROUGH 1.6———

[1] The *stem* is that part of the word which is left when inflectional material has been stripped away: *e.g.,* âpatisi-, nipâ-, wâpam-, kiskêliht-.

1.2 Transitive Inanimate Verbs—VTI

Transitive Inanimate verbs fall into two types: Type 1, where the stem ends in a consonant:

wâpaht...am	he sees it
kiwâpaht...ên	you see it
kîsis...am	he cooks it
nikîsis...ên	I cook it

Type 2 verbs are those where the VTI member of the VTA-VTI pair displays a stem ending in a vowel and takes the same endings as animate intransitive verbs such as ihtâ...w, nipâ...w, etc.

ayâ...w	she has it
nitayamihtâ...n	I read it (*v.* nitayamih...âw VTA I speak to him)

These are sometimes called "pseudo-transitive" verbs and will be listed as VAI-T. Although they take the same inflectional endings as animate intransitive verbs, they function as VTI stems in taking an object. Study the following examples:

10.	kikîsisên nâ môs'-wîyâs?	Are you cooking moose meat?
11.	nikiskêlihtên kêkwân.	I know something.
12.	wâpahtam sîpîliw.	She sees the river.
13.	âšay kitayân cîmân.	Now you have a canoe.
14.	n'ka-kî-wâpahtên mâhkiy ôta ohci.	I'll be able to see the tent from here.
15.	ta-ayamihtâw nâ masinahikaniliw?	Will he read the book?
16.	kinatawêlihtên nâ kêkwân?	Do you want something?
17.	nawac nimilwêlihtên anta.	I like it pretty well there.
18.	ayâw mîcimiliw.	He has (some) food.

1.3 VAI, VTA, VTI

Some verbs show forms extending through the three sets: VAI, VTA and VTI:

VAI		VTA		VTI	
wâpiw	he sees	wâpamêw	he sees him	wâpahtam	he sees it
niwâpin	I see	niwâpamâw	I see him	niwâpahtên	I see it

From time to time you will meet a verb which is translated as an intransitive, but which is transitive in form: *e.g.,*

itêlihtam	he thinks (it)
ostostotam	he coughs (it)

Both of these take a formal object, although we translate them into English as intransitives. This has sometimes led to their being classed as a kind of intransitive verb in older glossaries or dictionaries.

———DRILLS 2.1 THROUGH 2.6———

1.4 Transitive Verbs and the Obviative

1.4.1 Obviative and Further Obviative

In the Basic Conversation to the last unit there occurred the word, kêkwân, and in the Basic Conversation to this unit, the form, kêkwâliw, both with the same lexical meaning, "something". Similarly, âšokan and âšokana both mean "wharf, dock". The first one of each pair occurs when the word stands in third person position, the second when it occurs in further third person position, or obviative, as in the following diagram.

ni... and ki...	3, 0 (3rd person position)	3', 0' (4th position)	3", 0" (5th position)
niwâpahtên kiwâpamâw	kêkwân âšokan		
	wâpahtam wâpamêw	kêkwâliw âšokana	
		(wâpahtamiliwa wâpamiliwa	kêkwâliw âšokana)

Where the subject occupies first or second person position (*i.e.,* is ni... or ki...), the object of the verb is in third position. Where the actor occupies third position, the object immediately moves out to further third, bracketed above as 4th. All nouns and most pronouns show by a regular change of form whether they stand in third (*i.e.,* proximate) or fourth (*i.e.,* obviative) position. (Note that the obviative form for an *unpossessed* noun: *e.g.,* cîmâniliw, is the same whether the position is fourth or fifth, and this holds for both genders. The fifth position is known as *further obviative* or *surobviative.* More details will be introduced later on. Meanwhile, it is important to get used to the idea of the obviative and the mechanisms which mark it.

1.4.2ni..., ki... subjects with 3′, 0′ object

You will note in the drills that an "I" or "you" (*i.e.,* a ni... or ki...) subject is never used in the same sentence as an object possessed by a 3rd person as, for example:

> *I* see *her* brother.
> *I* see *his* canoe.

"Brother" and "canoe" are objects of the verb, "see"; but since "his" and "her" mark third persons possessors, "brother" and "canoe" are automatically one position further out in Cree grammar: *i.e.,* in the obviative or 4th position. When a verb with ni... or ki... subject takes an object in the obviative, there is a special form of the verb to show that a position has been "jumped", so to speak. This will be learned later (Units 13 and 14). For the present, restrict yourself to the patterns in the drills; otherwise you risk introducing non-Cree speech patterns into your new set of language habits.

———DRILLS 3.1 THROUGH 3.4———

1.5 Degrees of Comparison

awasitê, mâwac; ispîš

The marker of the comparative degree in Cree is awasitê, 'more', that of the superlative, mâwac, 'most'. In each case, the particle may be used to modify a verb: *e.g.,*

milwâšin	VII	it is nice, it is good
awasitê milwâšin		it is nicer, it is better
mâwac milwâšin		it is (the) nicest, it is (the) best

It may also be used to modify another particle: *e.g.,*

wîpac soon — awasitê wîpac sooner

The compared item is then introduced by ispîš 'than': *e.g.,*

awasitê nimilwêlihtên ôta ispîš wîla mâmihk.
I like it more here than down-river.

The use of ispîš, however, unlike that of its English counterpart, is extended to the superlative degree: *e.g.,*

mâwac nimilwêlimâw ispîš kotakiyak ililiwak ôta.
I like him best of all (the) people here.

Both awasitê and mâwac may be used with any one of the four types of verbs:

VAI	wîhkacišiw	awasitê wîhkacišiw	mâwac wîhkacišiw
VII	tahkâyâw	awasitê tahkâyâw	mâwac tahkâyâw
VTA	milwêlimêw	awasitê milwêlimêw	mâwac milwêlimêw
VTI	milwêlihtam	awasitê milwêlihtam	mâwac milwêlihtam

———DRILLS 4 THROUGH 5.4———

1.6 matêw : : matakwan

The forms, ihtâ- VAI "he is (at a place)"' and ihtakwan- VII "it is (at a place)", were learned in Units 1 and 3, respectively. The negative forms of each are matêw VAI "he / there is not" and matakwan VII "it / there is not", respectively.

The two negative forms are based on the verb, têw VAI "he is", and takwan VII "it is". The forms occur where existence, not location at a point, is affirmed. têw is heard in affirmative statement on the east coast of James Bay, but occurs only in the contracted negative, matêw (from nama têw) on the west shore. matakwan is the contracted form of nama takwan.

———DRILL 6———

2. Nouns: Proximate and Obviative

2.1 Obviative

In Unit 2.B.1.1 (and also Unit 3.B.1.2) the Obviative was described as a further third person. This does not mean just any other third person beyond the first one mentioned. In the sentence,

niwâpamâw	âšokan, -	nêsta atim.
I see	(a) wharf, -	and (a) dog.

âšokan and atim are actually in the same grammatical slot, as objects of the verb with ni... subject; and, as such, both are proximate in form. The fact that atim is added as an afterthought makes it another third person but does not push it out to the obviative, since both nouns are objects of the same verb with the same first person subject, ni.... Consider, however, the following two sentences:

iskwêw wâpamêw atimwa.	The woman sees the dog.
okimâw natawêlihtam cîmâniliw.	The manager wants the canoe.

In each case the subject is already a third person, proximate; so the object of the verb must now be in *further* third, or obviative, position.

You have now met two conditions which require a noun to be in the obviative:

1. when it is possessed by a third person possessor; and
2. when it is the object of a verb with a third person subject.

2.2 Obviative of Possessed Nouns

In the obviative form of unpossessed nouns, the sign marking the obviative position for animate nouns is ...**a**: *e.g.*, ililiw**a**, âšokan**a**, atimw**a**. For inanimate nouns the marker is the suffix, ...**ɩliw**, as in cîmân**iliw**, sîpî**liw**, (< sîpiy...**ɩliw**), wîyâs**iliw**. It may happen, however, that a noun possessed by first or second person stands as object of a verb with third person subject and, as such, must go into the obviative position. In such cases the ni... and ki... personal possessor prefixes occur as usual at the beginning of the word and the obviative marker appears at the end: *e.g.*,

wâpahtam nicîmâniliw. He (3) sees my canoe (0′).
kiskêlimêw kôhtâwiya. He (3) knows your father (3′).

Where he (3rd person) sees his own canoe,

wâpahtam ocîmân,

ocîmân is already marked as obviative by the o... possessor prefix and does not require the suffix, ...ɩliw.

DRILL 7

2.3 Possessed Theme, *continued*

The possessed theme has already been discussed (Unit 3.B.2.1). Use of the suffix is sometimes subject to regional variation but other considerations also determine its use. *Cf.* omîcim his food, but omîcim*ima* (pl.) his supplies. This is perhaps related to a further use which distinguishes between innate and acquired possession: *e.g.*, oskan NDI his bone (*i.e.*, part of his body) and otôskanim his bone (*i.e.*, an animal bone which belongs to someone), or ostikwân his head, and otôstikwânim his flywheel (as on an outboard motor).

3. Demonstrative Pronouns

Demonstrative pronouns that have occurred up to this point are

awa	this one (*anim.*)	ôma	this one (*inan.*)
ana	that one (*anim.*)	anima	that one (*inan.*) *with variant* ani
ê'ko (< êwako)	this, that, the very one (*anim.*)	ê'ko (< êwako)	this, that, the very one (*inan.*)
kotak	other one (*anim.*)	kotak	other one (*inan.*)

Used in close apposition with a noun, the demonstrative pronoun carries out much the same function as a demonstrative adjective in English: *e.g.,*

awa ililiw	this person	ôma mîcim	this food
ana atim	that dog	anima cîmân	that canoe

ê'ko (êwako), the intensive pronoun, is regularly coupled in emphatic use with awa or ôma, as ê'kwâwa this one, or ê'kôma that one. When used alone, it shows no difference in form for gender or number (Unit 7.B.6). Apart from an infrequently encountered obviative, êwakwêliw (Unit 5.B.4), it is uninflected.

4. Syntax

Sentence Models (for optional study).

One of the basic sentence models studied to date centres on the intransitive verb with animate subject (1.B.1). This may be represented by the formula +S... +P, where S = subject slot, filled by a personal prefix, and P, the predicate slot, filled by a verb. ("+" = an obligatory element, "±" = an optional element, "..." = a form which must be bound to something else)

The present unit introduces a further sentence model which centres on a transitive verb, showing ni..., ki..., and Ø (3rd person) prefixes, followed by the stem proper, with stem final often showing selection for gender of the object (*v.* 4.B.1 above): *e.g.,*

ni...milw...êlim...âw	I - good - by thought: anim. stem final - 3 sing. obj. *i.e.,* I like him / her.
ki...milw...êliht...ên	you - good - by thought: inan. stem final - 0 object *i.e.,* you like it
(Ø)...kîs...is...am	3 - cook - by heat: inan. stem final - 0 object *i.e.,* he / she cooks it

Note how the inflectional ending shows concord for person (and number: 6.B.1) of the subject for both transitive animate and transitive inanimate verbs. For VTA, concord in the inflectional suffix also denotes gender, number and proximate or obviative status of the object. For VTI only gender and proximate or obviative status are marked. The above sentence model may be expressed in its baldest form by the formula:

+S... +P +...O ("O" in the sentence formula = object.)

The verb form has reference *within itself* to both subject and object. The above sentence model may be expanded or transformed, or elements may be substituted within the frame to produce the different sentences common to Cree. A simple expansion is to name either the subject or object, or both: *e.g.,*

kiwâpahtên mâhkiy You-see-it (the) tent.

Here mâhkiy stands in cross reference to the object marked by the inflectional ending. The relationship may be expressed by the formula: +S... +P +...O ±xO, where "±" = optional, and "xO" = external object. You have also already met the type:

nîla, nikîsisên Me, I-cook-it.

This, in turn, may be represented by the formula: ±xS +S... +P +...O. A combination of the two would yield

nîla, nikîsisên wîyâs Me, I-cook-it (the) meat: *i.e.,*
±xS +S...+P +...O ±xO.

A further typical expansion might well be

wîpac ta-mîšahwêw kistês otâšokana Your brother will soon repair his wharf.

Using "M" to symbolize a modifier and "F" for future marker, the structure of the last sentence may be expressed as

±M +S... ±F... +P +...O ±xS ±xO

Keep in mind that +S..., when it is a third person subject, is realised as Ø: *i.e.,* no personal prefix. Obligatory elements are signalled by "+" and optional by "±". Study the examples in grammatical sections 1.1 and 1.2 of this unit and note how one or more modifying particles at the beginning of a sentence affects the preferred word order for subject and object in cross reference.

C. DRILLS

1. Transitive Animate Verbs: ni..., ki..., 3 Subject

1.1 Mimic the recording, first down each column, then across each row.

ni..., ki...	3
niwâpam...âw kiwâpam...âw	wâpam...êw
nikiskêlim...âw kikiskêlim...âw	kiskêlim...êw
nititêlim...âw kititêlim...âw	itêlim...êw
nitayamih...âw kitayamih...âw	ayamih...êw
nikîsisw...âw kikîsisw...âw	kîsisw...êw
nitayâw...âw kitayâw...âw	ayâw...êw

1.2 Given a form of the verb and a personal pronoun to indicate the subject, supply the appropriate verb form: *e.g.,*

Cue: wâpamêw :: nîla
Response: niwâpamâw

	(Check column)
wâpamêw :: nîla	niwâpamâw
natawêlimêw :: kîla	kinatawêlimâw
itêlimêw :: wîla	itêlimêw
ayâwêw :: kîla	kitayâwâw
nitayamihâw :: wîla	ayamihêw
kiskêlimêw :: nîla	nikiskêlimâw

ayamihêw :: kîla	kitayamihâw
kîsiswêw :: nîla	nikîsiswâw
natawêlimêw :: nîla	ninatawêlimâw
nikîsiswâw :: wîla	kîsiswêw
wâpamêw :: kîla	kiwâpamâw
kikiskêlimâw :: wîla	kiskêlimêw

1.3 Mimic the recording, first down, then across.

niwâpamâw âšokan kiwâpamâw âšokan	wâpamêw âšokana
nikiskêlimâw okimâw kikiskêlimâw okimâw	kiskêlimêw okimâwa
nimilwêlimâw atim kimilwêlimâw atim	milwêlimêw atimwa
nikîsiswâw âlahkonâw kikîsiswâw âlahkonâw	kîsiswêw âlahkonâwa
nitayâwâw šôliyân kitayâwâw šôliyân	ayâwêw šôliyâna
nitayamihâw šôliyânikimâw kitayamihâw šôliyânikimâw	ayamihêw šôliyânikimâwa

1.4 Given a noun and a form of the verb, reverse their order and put the noun in the form required for the object of the verb: *e.g.,*

Cue: âlahkonâw :: nikîsiswâw
Response: nikîsiswâw âlahkonâw.

	(Check column)
âlahkonâw : nikîsiswâw	nikîsiswâw âlahkonâw
atimwa : wapamêw	wâpamêw atimwa
okimâw : milwêlimêw	milwêlimêw okimâwa
âšokana : nitayâwâw	nitayâwâw âšokan
âlahkonâw : kîsiswêw	kîsiswêw âlahkonâwa
okimâw : kiskêlimêw	kiskêlimêw okimâwa
âlahkonâwa : ninatawêlimâw	ninatawêlimâw âlahkonâw
šôliyâna : kitayâwâw	kitayâwâw šôliyân
apwoy : kinatawêlimâw	kinatawêlimâw apwoy

âšokan : kiwâpamâw	kiwâpamâw âšokan
kikâwiy : nitayamihâw	nitayamihâw kikâwiy
okimâwa : kitayamihâw	kitayamihâw okimâw

1.5 Answer the following questions on the model,

Question: kikiskêlimâw nâ nikosis?
Answer: môla, môla n'kiskêlimâw kikosis.

		(Check column)
1.	kikiskêlimâw nâ nikosis?	môla, môla nikiskêlimâw kikosis.
2.	kiwâpamâw nâ nitânis?	môla, môla niwâpamâw kitânis.
3.	kiwâpamâw nâ nôhtâwiy?	môla, môla niwâpamâw kôhtâwiy.
4.	kimilwêlimâw nâ nitâšokan?	môla, môla nimilwêlimâw kitâšokan.
5.	kikîsiswâw nâ nitâlahkonâm?	môla, môla nikîsiswâw kitâlahkonam.
6.	kimîšahwâw nâ nitapwoy?	môla, môla nimîšahwâw kitapwoy.
7.	kitayâwâw nâ nišôliyânim?	môla, môla nitayâwâw kišôliyânim.
8.	kitayâwâw nâ nitêm?	môla, môla nitayâwâw kitêm.

1.6 Answer the following questions on the model.

Question: ka-wâpamâw nâ kikosis?
Answer: môla, cwân mâka ta-wâpamêw okosisa.

1.	ka-wâpamâw nâ kikosis?	môla, cwân mâka ta-wâpamêw okosisa.
2.	ka-wâpamâw nâ kikâwiy?	môla, cwân mâka ta-wâpamêw okâwiya.
3.	ka-ayamihâw nâ kitânis?	môla, cwân mâka ta-ayamihêw otânisa.
4.	ka-ayamihâw nâ kôhtâwiy?	môla, cwân mâka ta-ayamihêw ôhtâwiya.
5.	ka-kiskêlimâw nâ okimâw?	môla, cwân mâka ta-kiskêlimêw okimâwa.
6.	ka-kîsiswâw nâ âlahkonâw?	môla, cwân mâka ta-kîsiswêw âlahkonâwa.
7.	ka-ayâwâw nâ šôliyân?	môla, cwân mâka ta-ayâwêw šôliyâna.
8.	ka-natawêlimâw nâ atim?	môla, cwân mâka ta-natawêlimêw atimwa.

2. Transitive Inanimate Verbs: ni..., ki..., 3 Subject

2.1 Mimic the recording, first down each column, then across each row.

niwâpaht...**ên**	wâpaht...**am**
kiwâpaht...**ên**	
nikiskêliht...**ên**	kiskêliht...**am**
kikiskêliht...**ên**	

nititêliht...**ên** itêliht...**am**
kititêliht...**ên**

nikîsis...**ên** kîsis...**am**
kikîsis...**ên**

nitayâ...**n** [VAI-T] ayâ...**w**
kitayâ...**n**

niwawêšihtâ...**n** [VAI-T] wawêšihtâ...**w** (fix up, decorate)
kiwawêšihtâ...**n**

2.2 Given the personal pronoun to indicate the subject, supply the appropriate verb form: *e.g.,*

Cue: nîla :: wâpahtam
Response: niwâpahtên

	(Check column)
nîla :: wâpahtam	niwâpahtên
kîla :: natawêlihtam	kinatawêlihtên
wîla :: itêlihtam	itêlihtam
kîla :: ayâw	kitayân
wîla :: milwêlihtam	milwêlihtam
nîla :: kiskêlihtam	nikiskêlihtên
kîla :: itêlihtam	kititêlihtên
nîla :: kîsisam	nikîsisên
nîla :: natawêlihtam	ninatawêlihtên
wîla :: nitayân	ayâw
wîla :: kinatawêlihtên	natawêlihtam
kîla :: niwawêšihtân	kiwawêšihtân

2.3 Mimic the recording, first down, then across.

niwâpahtên cîmân wâpahtam cîmâniliw
kiwâpahtên cîmân

nimilwêlihtên môso-wîyâs milwêlihtam môso-wîyâsiliw
kimilwêlihtên môso-wîyâs

ninatawêlihtên mîcim natawêlihtam mîcimiliw
kinatawêlihtên mîcim

nikîsisên kêkwân kikîsisên kêkwân	kîsisam kêkwâliw
nitayân masinahikan kitayân masinahikan	ayâw masinahikániliw
niwawêšihtân mâhkiy kiwawêšihtân mâhkiy	wawêšihtâw mâhkîliw

2.4 Given a noun and a verb form, reverse their order and put the noun in the form required for the object of the verb: *e.g.*,

Cue: cîmân : wawêšihtâw
Response: wawêšihtâw cîmâniliw

	(Check column)
cîmân : wawêšihtâw	wawêšihtâw cîmâniliw
môso-wîyâs : nikîsisên	nikîsisên môso-wîyâs
sîpiy : kiskêklihtam	kiskêlihtam sîpîliw
mâhkiy : wâpahtam	wâpahtam mâhkîliw
kêkwâliw : kitayân	kitayân kêkwân
sîpiy : nikiskêlihtên	nikiskêlihtên sîpiy
mâhkiy : niwawêšihtân	niwawêšihtân mâhkiy
môs'-wîyâs : milwêlihtam	milwêlihtam môs'-wîyâsiliw
cîmâniliw : niwâpahtên	niwâpahtên cîmân
mîcim : ayâw	ayâw mîcimiliw

2.5 Answer the following questions on the model,

Question: kiwâpahtên nâ nicîmân?
Answer: môla, môla niwâpahtên kicîmân.

1.	kiwâpahtên nâ nicîmân?	môla, môla niwâpahtên kicîmân.
2.	kiwâpahtên nâ nimâhkîm?	môla, môla niwâpahtên kimâhkîm.
3.	kikîsisên nâ niwîyâsim?	môla, môla nikîsisên kiwîyâsim.
4.	kimilwêlihtên nâ nimôs'-wîyâsim?	môla, môla nimilwêlihtên kimôs'-wîyâsim.
5.	kiwawêšihtân nâ nicîmân?	môla, môla niwawêšihtân kicîmân.
6.	kinatawêlihtên nâ nimîcim?	môla, môla ninatawêlihtên kimîcim.
7.	kitayân nâ nimasinahikan?	môla, môla nitayân kimasinahikan.
8.	kikîsisên nâ nimîcim?	môla, môla nikîsisên kimîcim.

2.6 Answer the following questions on the model,

Question: ka-wâpahtên nâ sîpiy?
Answer: môla, wîla mâka ta-wâpahtam sîpîliw.

		(Check column)
1.	ka-wâpahtên nâ sîpiy?	môla, wîla mâka ta-wâpahtam sîpîliw.
2.	ka-wâpahtên nâ cîmân?	... -ta-wâpahtam cîmâniliw.
3.	ka-milwêlihtên nâ mâhkiy?	... -ta-milwêlihtam mâhkîliw.
4.	ka-kiskêlihtên nâ sîpiy?	... -ta-kiskêlihtam sîpîliw.
5.	ka-ayân nâ natohkolon?	... -ta-ayâw natohkoloniliw.
6.	ka-kîsisên nâ môs'-wîyâs?	... -ta-kîsisam môs'-wîyâsiliw.
7.	ka-wawêšihtân nâ cîmân?	... -ta-wawêšihtâw cîmâniliw.
8.	ka-natawêlihtên nâ mîcim?	... -ta-natawêlihtam mîcimiliw.

3. Complete the following sentences by selecting the noun of the gender required by the verb. The recording will give you two nouns and the fragment to be completed. Mimic the correct form from the recording. If you are not using a recording, uncover the right hand column line by line to check your answer.

3.1

1.	niwâpahtên ...... (sîpiy - âšokan).	sîpiy
2.	kinatawêlimâw nâ ...... (mîcim - atim)?	atim
3.	wîpac mâškôc mîna ka-ayâwâw ...... (šôliyân - cîmân).	šôliyân
4.	wîpac nâ ka-kî-wawêšihtân ...... (cîmân - apwoy)?	cîmân
5.	awasitê nimilwêlihtên ...... (âlahkonâw - môs'-wîyâs).	môs'-wîyâs
6.	môla mâškôc nâspic kimilwêlimâw awa ...... (âlahkonâw - mîcim).	âlahkonâw
7.	âšay nâ kikiskêlihtên ...... (okimâw - sîpiy)?	sîpiy
8.	môla kwayask nikiskêlimâw ...... (kôhtâwiy - masinahikan).	kôhtâwiy
9.	môla mâškôc ka-kî-ayân ...... (môs - mîcim).	mîcim
10.	apišîš piko ninatawêlihtên ...... (šôliyân - natohkolon).	natohkolon
11.	âšay niwâpamâw ...... (ililiw - mâhkiy).	ililiw
12.	šâkoc mâka n'ka-kîsisên ...... (kêkwân - âlahkonâw).	kêkwân

3.2 Complete the following, as above.

1.	âšay mîna ayâwêw ...... (mîcimiliw - šôliyâna).	šôliyâna
2.	môla natawêlihtam ...... (kêkwâliw - otêma).	kêkwâliw
3.	wîpac nâ ta-kî-wawêšihtâw ...... (apwoya - cîmâniliw)?	cîmâniliw
4.	môla kiskêlimêw ...... (sîpîliw - okimâwa).	okimâwa
5.	awasitê milwêlimêw ...... (môso-wîyâsiliw - šôliyânikimâwa).	šôliyânikimâwa
6.	môla mâškôc ta-wâpamêw ...... (môswa - mâhkîliw).	môswa

7.	mîna mâškôc ta-kîsisam ...... (mîcimiliw - âlahkonâwa).	mîcimiliw
8.	âšay nâ ayâw ...... (atimwa - masinahikaniliw)?	masinahikaniliw
9.	wîpac mâškôc ta-kî-wawêšihêw ...... (apwoya - cîmâniliw).	apwoya
10.	môla milwêlihtam ...... (atimwa - mâhkîliw).	mâhkîliw
11	môla nêsta kiskêlihtam ...... (sîpîliw - ililiwa).	sîpîliw
12.	ta-kîsiswêw nâ ..... (môso-wîyâsiliw - âlahkonâwa)?	âlahkonâwa

What do you notice about the object of every verb in 3.2?

3.3 The cue will give you a noun and a choice of two verb forms. Select the verb form proper to the gender of the noun, as follows:

Cue: sîpiy: niwâpamâw - niwâpahtên
Response: niwâpahtên sîpiy

			(Check column)
1.	sîpiy:	niwâpamâw - niwâpahtên	niwâpahtên sîpiy
2.	âšokan:	kiwawêšihtân - kiwawêšihâw	kiwawêšihâw âšokan
3.	cîmân:	kinatawêlihtên nâ - kinatawêlimâw nâ	kinatawêlihtên nâ cîmân
4.	okimâw:	kiwâpahtên - kiwâpamâw	kiwâpamâw okimâw
5.	âlahkonâw:	n'ka-kîsiswâw - n'ka-kîsisên	n'ka-kîsiswâw âlahkonâw
6.	ililiw:	kimilwêlimâw nâ - kimilwêlihtên nâ	kimilwêlimâw nâ ililiw
7.	mîcim:	n'tayâwâw - n'tayân	n'tayân mîcim
8.	šôliyân:	ninatawêlimâw - ninatawêlihtên	ninatawêlimâw šôliyân
9.	mâhkiy:	kimilwêlimâw - kimilwêlihtên	kimilwêlihtên mâhkiy
10.	kêkwân:	kikîsisên nâ - kikîsiswâw nâ	kikîsisên nâ kêkwân

3.4 In the following, select the verb form proper to the obviation or non-obviation of the noun.

1.	wîyâsiliw:	môla n'tayân - môla ayâw	môla ayâw wîyâsiliw
2.	natohkoliy:	natawêlihtam - ninatawêlihtên	ninatawêlihtên natohkoliy
3.	môswa:	wîpac ta-wâpamew - wîpac n'ka-wâpamaw	wîpac ta-wâpamêw môswa
4.	apwoya:	ka-wawêšihâw - ta-wawêšihêw	ta-wawêšihêw apwoya
5.	mîcimiliw:	nâspic nimilwêlihtên - nâspic milwêlihtam	nâspic milwêlihtam mîcimiliw
6.	okimâw:	kiskêlimêw - nikiskêlimâw	nikiskêlimâw okimâw
7.	âlahkonâwa:	ka-kîsiswâw - ta-kîsiswêw	ta-kîsiswêw âlahkonâwa

4. Complete each partial sentence of the following conversation by filling in the blank with an appropriate word or phrase from the list given. Each word should be used once only.

kinwêš, âstamitê, kîsiswêw, ôtê itêhkê, kêkwâliw, nimilwêlihtên, êtohtêyan, kitôhci-ililîmon, at'-îtohtê, niwîkimâkan, wîhkacišiw, ispîš, šwâpihk, êšinihkâtêk, išinihkâsow, nimilwêlimâw.

cwân: kinwêš nâ ____________?

âlik: môla nâspic ________ . ê'ko nâ ____________ šwâpihk?

cwân: êhê. ôtê piko ________ mêskanâhk. wîpac mâškôc ka-wâpahtên: nêtê, ________ nimâhkîmihk.

âlik: mîkwêc. awênihkân mâka ana wîla? natawêlihtam ________ n'titêlimâw.

cwân: nišîm. awa mâka ____________. ________ âlahkonâwa.

âlik: kââ! šâkoc __________! nâspic ________ oški-âlahkonâw. awasitê mâka __________ môs'-wîyâs. mâwac nimilwêlihtên ______ wîla kotak mîcim. tân' __________ anima kêkwân ê-ililîmonâniwahk [in one's speaking Cree]?

cwân: apwoy __________, nîla n'tapwoy. tânt' __________ mâka anohc?

âlik: ay'hâw, ________ n'ka-itohtân.

cwân: wâciyê.

âlik: wâciyê.

5. Degrees of Comparison: awasitê ~ mâwac.

5.1 Cue: apišîš piko kitâpatisin, manâ?
Response: awasitê mâškôc n'tâpatisin ispîš kîla.

apišîš piko kitâpatisin, manâ?	awasitê mâškôc n'tâpatisin ...
" " kitâhkosin, manâ?	awasitê mâškôc n'tâhkosin ...
" " kitôtakikomin, manâ?	awasitê mâškôc n'tôtakikomin ...
" " kitililîmon, manâ?	awasitê mâškôc n'tililîmon ...
" " kimilo-pimâtisin, manâ?	awasitê mâškôc nimilo-pimâtisin ...
" " kiwêmistikôšîmon, manâ?	awasitê mâškôc niwêmistikôšîmon ...
" " kinipân, manâ?	awasitê mâškôc ninipân ...
" " kimilopalin, manâ?	awasitê mâškôc nimilopalin ...
" " kimihcilawêsin, manâ?	awasitê mâškôc nimihcilawêsin ...

5.2 Cue: awasitê nâ kimiwan ôta ispîš anta?
Response: môla. mâwac kimiwan anta n'titêl'tên.

awasitê	nâ	kimiwan	ôta	ispîš	anta	?	môla. mâwac kimiwan ...
"	"	tahkâyâw	"	"	"	?	môla. mâwac tahkâyâw ...
"	"	kišitêw	"	"	"	?	môla. mâwac kišitêw ...
"	"	milo-kîšikâw	"	"	"	?	môla. mâwac milo-kîšikâw ...
"	"	milwâšin	"	"	"	?	môla. mâwac milwâšin ...
"	"	mil'-otâkošin	"	"	"	?	môla. mâwac mil'-otâkošin ...
"	"	pîkopaliw	"	"	"	?	môla. mâwac pîkopaliw ...

5.3 Cue: kimilwêlihtên nâ ôma cîmân?
Response: tâpwê! awasitê nimilwêlihtên ispîš wîla kotakiy.
[kotakiy = "the" other]

kimilwêlihtên nâ ôma cîmân?	tâpwê! awasitê nimilwêlihtên ...
kikiskêlihtên nâ ôma sîpiy?	tâpwê! awasitê nikiskêlihtên ...
kinatawêlihtên nâ ôma mîcim?	tâpwê! awasitê ninatawêlihtên ...
kiwawêšihtân nâ ôma mâhkiy?	tâpwê! awasitê niwawêšihtân ...
kimilwêlihtên nâ anima masinahikan?	tâpwê! awasitê nimilwêlihtên ...
kikîsisên nâ anima môs'-wîyâs?	tâpwê! awasitê nikîsisên ...
kiwâpahtên nâ anima kêkwân?	tâpwê! awasitê niwâpahtên ...

5.4 Cue: kimilwêlimâw nâ awa apwoy?
Response: êhê. mâwac mâka nimilwêlimâw kotakiy apwoy.

kimilwêlimâw nâ awa apwoy?	êhê. mâwac mâka nimilwêlimâw ...
kikiskêlimâw nâ awa okimâw?	êhê. mâwac mâka nikiskêlimâw ...
kinatawêlimâw nâ awa atim?	êhê. mâwac mâka ninatawêlimâw ...
kimilwêlimâw nâ awa âlahkonâw?	êhê. mâwac mâka nimilwêlimâw ...
kikiskêlimâw nâ awa atim?	êhê. mâwac mâka nikiskêlimâw ...
kinatawêlimâw nâ awa âšokan?	êhê. mâwac mâka ninatawĕlimâw ...

6. matêw :: matakwan, negative of ihtâw : ihtakwan, respectively.

6.1 Cue: šwâpihk nâ ihtâw kikosis?
Response: matêw nikosis šwâpihk anohc.

šwâpihk nâ ihtâw kikosis?	matêw nikosis šwâpihk anohc.
cîmânihk nâ ihtâw kitânis?	matêw nitânis cîmânihk ...
âšokanihk nâ ihtâw kitêm?	matêw nitêm âšokanihk ...
mâhkîhk nâ ihtâw kicawâšimiš?	matêw nicawâšimiš mâhkîhk ...

sîpihk nâ ihtâw kitapwoy?	matêw nitapwoy sîpîhk ...
nêtê nâ ihtâw kitâlahkonâm?	matêw nitâlahkonâm nêtê ...
šwâpihk nâ ihtâw kôhtâwiy?	matêw nôhtâwiy šwâpihk ...
ôta nâ ihtâw kistês?	matêw nistês ôta anohc.

6.2 Cue: âšokanihk nâ ihtakwan kicîmân?
Response: matakwan n'cîmân âšokanihk anohc.

âšokanihk nâ ihtakwan kicîmân?	matakwan n'cîmân âšokanihk anohc.
cîmânihk nâ ihtakwan kimasinahikan?	matakwan nimasinahikan cîmânihk ...
nêtê nâ ihtakwan kimâhkîm?	matakwan nimâhkîm nêtê anohc.
šwâpihk nâ ihtakwan kimîcim?	matakwan nimîcim šwâpihk anohc.
mâhkîhk nâ ihtakwan kinatohkolonim?	matakwan ninatohkolonim mâhkîhk ...
ôta nâ ihtakwan kimôs'-wîyâsim?	matakwan nimôs'-wîyâsim ôta ...
nêtê nâ ihtakwan kišwâpim?	matakwan nišwâpim nêtê anohc.

7. Obviative of Possessed Nouns. In each of the following, complete the second sentence by selecting the correct one of the two forms enclosed in brackets. If you are using a recording, mimic the correct response. Correct forms are given at the end of the drill.

1. niwâpamâw kitâšokan. wîla mâka môla wâpamêw (kitâšokan ~ kitâšokana).
2. nimilwêlimâw kitâlahkonâm. cwân mâka môla milwêlimêw (kitâlahkonâm ~ kitâlahkonâma).
3. mâškôc kinatawêlimâw nišôliyânim. nimis nêsta natawêlimêw (nišôliyânima ~ nišôliyânim).
4. kinatawêlihtên nicîmân. cwân mâka môla natawêlihtam (nicîmâniliw ~ nicîmân).
5. âšay n'ka-kîsisên kimîcim. môla ta-kî-kîsisam kikâwiy (kimîcim ~ kimîcimiliw).
6. wîpac mâškôc ka-wâpahtên nišwâpim. wîpac mâškôc kôhtâwiy nêsta ta-wâpahtam (nišwâpim ~ nišwâpimiliw).
7. âšay mîna n'ka-wawêšihtân kimasinahikan. âšay nistês nêsta ta-wawêsihtâw (nimasinahikan ~ nimasinahikaniliw).
8. wîpac mâškôc n'ka-wâpamâw kôhtâwiy. wîpac mâškôc ta-wâpamêw nêsta cwân (kôhtâwiy ~ kôhtâwiya).
9. âšay n'kiskêlimâw kistês. môla mâka kiskêlimêw cwân (kistês ~ kistêsa).
10. kiwâpahtên nâ nimâhkîm? wâpahtam nâ (nimâhkîmiliw ~ nimâhkîm)?

1. kitâšokana
2. kitâlahkonâma
3. nišôliyânima
4. nicîmâniliw
5. kimîcimiliw
6. nišwâpimiliw
7. nimasinahikaniliw
8. kôhtâwiya
9. kistêsa
10. nimâhkîmiliw

D. CONVERSATION PRACTICE

1. Cover the Cree columns of the Basic Conversation and make sure that you can give the Cree equivalent of the English without hesitation. Mark any features which cause you difficulty and drill them individually. Repeat the above process through the whole of the Basic Conversation.

2. Imagine a situation in which you introduce members of your family to a friend. Tell the friend that you have a canoe at the wharf, but that you are going to the store. You want some fresh meat, fresh bread, etc. There is no moose meat at the store; but you like it best of all food. Discuss various preferences in food (maškwašiya NI pl. vegetables), people you know in the village (ihtâwinihk), and indicate that you must go away soon and that you have to work.

3. Ask whether a friend has known the post manager, forestry agent (amiskokimâw NA), nurse, clergyman or priest a long time, and whether you or the person in question speaks Cree or English better.

E. LISTENING IN

Visitor: wâciyê, wâciyê. tântê âlik?
Cwân: môla n'kiskêl'tên. matêw ôta wîla anohc.
Visitor: tâpwê nâ? wîpac mâškôc ta-pêc'-îtohtêw šôliyânikimâw. âšay ayâw ocîmân nêtê âšokanihk. n'tawêl'tam kêkwâliw n'titêlimâw; môla mâka ililîmow.
Cwân: kinwêš nâ ohci-ihtâw ôta?
Visitor: môla mâškôc. šwâpihk mâškôc ta-itohtêw pitamâ.
Cwân: ay'hâw, kiwî[1]-ayamihâw nâ niwîkimâkan? nêtê ihtâw, apišîš awasitê itêhkê nimâhkîmihk. âpatisiw wîla anohc; apišîš mâka wêmistikôšîmow. ôta piko at'-îtohtê mêskanâhk, ka-wâpamâw mâka.
Visitor: âšay nâ âpatisiw?
Cwân: êhê, âšay kîsiswêw âlahkonâwa.
Visitor: milwâšin. mâwac nimilwêlimâw oški-âlahkonâw ispîš wîla kotak mîcim.
Cwân: awasitê nâ ispîš wîla môso-wîyâs?
Visitor: ay'hâw, môla mâškôc. šâkoc mâka wîhkacišiw.
Cwân: âšay pêc'-îtohtêw niwîkimâkan. sopâya, âstam pitamâ! šôliyânikimâw âšokanihk ihtâw. âšay šwâpihk itohtêw; wîpac mâka mâškôc ta-pôsiw. ka-kî-ayamihâw nâ?
Visitor: šôliyânikimâw wîla,—âšay ayamihêw awênihkâna. ayâwêw nêsta otêma anta cîmânihk.
Cwân: nakiskaw mâškôc ta-ihtâw ôta.
Visitor: môla n'titêl'tên. wî-wâpamêw ayamihêwikimâwa.
Cwân: môla wîlâhpahk. ay'hâw, wîpac ta-ihtâw ôta niwîkimâkan. ta-kî ayamihêw nêsta.
Visitor: êko wâs' âni,[2]—wâciyê.
Cwân: wâciyê.

[1] wî IPV want to
[2] *i.e.,* êko wâsa ani so that's it then, so that's that

F. REFERENCE LIST

antê	IPC	thither
apišîš	IPC	a little, a bit
ati	IPV	begin (to)
atimw-	NA	dog *v.* otêma.
at'-îtohtê	VAI imperative	begin to go (there): *contraction of* ati-itohtê
awasitê	IPC	more (*of degree*) *v.* itêhkê.
awasitê itêhkê	IPC	on the far side of, beyond
awênihkân-	PR interrog. anim. prox. sg.	who
ayamih-	VTA	speak to s.o., address s.o.
ayamihtâ-	VAI-T	read s.t., *lit.,* address s.t.
ayawiši	IPN	fresh (as of food) sometimes as ayawaši; *cf.* p. 75, n. 1 *v.* oški.
ayâ-	VAI-T	have s.t.
ayâw-	VTA	have s.o.
âlahkonâw-	NA	bread
âstam	IPC	come here, *lit.,* 'facing this way' (*functions as verbal imperative to which* ...ik *may be added to form plural*)
âstamitê	IPC	to this side (of): *opposite of* awasitê itêhkê
ê	IPV	as (doing), in (doing): *subordinating particle used with conjunct order of the verb: e.g.,* ê-ililîmonâniwahk in (one's) speaking Cree, as one speaks Cree.
ê'ko	PR intensive, anim. / inan.	the very one, the selfsame one: *contraction of* êwako (*marked as indeclinable, but occurs in obviative form,* êwakwêliw)
ililîmo-	VAI	speak Cree
ispîš	IPC	than
išinihkâso-	VAI	be called, be named
išinihkâtê-	VII	be called, be named
itâpicî-	VAI	be away, be absent
itêliht-	VTI	think (s.t.)
itêlim-	VTA	think ([about] s.o.)

kayâši	IPN	old, stale
kinwêš	IPC	a long time
kiskêliht-	VTI	know s.t.
kiskêlim-	VTA	know s.o.
kiskinohamâso-	VAI	learn
kîsis-	VTI	cook s.t., bake s.t.
kîsisw-	VTA	cook s.o., bake s.o.
kotak-	PR anim. / inan. prox. sing.	other, another one
kotakiy-	PR anim. / inan.	the other, the other one *v.* kotakîliw.
kotakîliw	PR inan. obv. sg.	the other, the other one
maškwašiy-	NI	grass: *pl.* vegetables
matakwan-	VII	not be (at a place) *v.* matê-.
matê-	VAI	not be (at a place) *v.* matakwan-.
mâhkiy-	NI	tent (rectangular base)
mâwac	IPC	most (*of degree*)
milwêliht	VTI	like s.t.
milwêlim-	VTA	like s.o.
mîcim-	NI	food
mîšah-	VTI	mend s.t., repair s.t.
mîšahw-	VTA	mend s.o., repair s.o.
môsw-	NA	moose
môso-wîyâs-	NI	moose meat
môšak	IPC	always
nakiskaw	IPC	a little while
ohci	IPC	from, for
ohci	IPV	from, as of: *e.g.*, kinwêš ohci-ililîmow he has been speaking Cree for a long time (*lit.*, he speaks Cree from a long time)
okimâhkân-	NA	chief
oški	IPC / IPV	new *v.* ayawiši.
otêma	NDA (*poss'd form*)	his dog *v.* atimw-.
pitamâ	IPC	first (before doing anything else)
pôsi-	VAI	depart by vehicle, embark

šâkoc	IPC	sure thing! certainly!
šôliyân-	NA	money *Cf.* "shilling".
šôliyânikimâw-	NA	Indian Agent, *lit.*, "paymaster" (former government representative in dealings with Indian band)
wâpaht-	VTI	see s.t.
wêmistikôšîmo-	VAI	speak English
wî	IPV	want (to)
wîhkaciši-	VAI	taste good, be delicious
wîhkašin-	VII	taste good, be delicious
wîkimâkan-	NA	wife
wîyâs-	NI	flesh, meat

G. REVIEW

4.A Kakwêcihkêmôwina—Questions

Answer the following questions with full sentences. Avoid replying merely "êhê" or "môla".

1. ê'ko nâ ôtê itêhkê kimâhkîmihk?
2. tântê âšokan?
3. ê'ko n' ântê itêhkê sîpîhk?
4. awênihkân ana wîla?
5. kikâwiy, mawâpiw nâ ôta nêsta wîla?
6. âšay nâ mâhkîhk ihtâw kikosis?
7. tântê cwân okosisa otêmilîw?
8. tân' êšinihkâtêk ôma kêkwân ê-'lilîmonâniwahk?
9. ôma nâ kîla kimasinahikan?
10. kitayâwâw nâ n'tapwoy?
11. awasitê nâ wîhkašin ôma mîcim ispîš wîla môso-wîyâs?
12. âšay nâ itâpicîw kišîm?
13. ta-mîšahwêw nâ kistês otâšokana?
14. nâspic milo-kîšikâw manâ?
15. ayâwêliwa nâ âlik okosisa otêmilîw ôta?
16. kôhtâwiy nâ nêsta ôta ihtâw?
17. pîkopaliliw nâ cwân ocîmân?
18. kiskêlimêw nâ kistês amiskokimâwa?
19. kinwêš nâ kitôhci-ililîmon?
20. wêmistikôšîmow nâ kiwîkimâkan?
21. ê'ko nâ awa kistês?
22. natawêlihtam nâ natohkolon-iskwêw kêkwâliw?
23. kinwêš nâ kitôhci-tašîhkân ôta?

4.B Naškwêwašihtwâwina—Answers

Formulate questions to which the following would be appropriate answers.

1. nakiskaw piko n'ka-ihtân ôta.
2. êhê, nâspic nimilwêlimâw oški-âlahkonâw.
3. ôtê piko at'-îtohtê mêskanâhk, ka-wâpahtên mâka.
4. apwoy išinihkâsow.
5. matêw ôta. šwâpihk mâškôc ta-ihtâw.
6. nikiskinohamâson piko.
7. nicîmân mâškôc.
8. êhê, nîla n'tapwoy awa.
9. saylas išinihkâsow.
10. kîsiswêw âlahkonâwa.
11. wîpac mâka mâškôc ta-pôsiw.
12. nistês otapwoya.
13. môla. nitânis mâka nakiskaw ta-tašîhkêw.
14. šâkoc nimilwêlihtên môso-wîyâs.
15. apišîš piko n'tililîmon.
16. âšokanihk n'ka-itohtân pitamâ.
17. kinatawêlihtên nâ kêkwân?
18. mâwac nâ kimilwêlihtên môso-wîyâs ispîš wîla kotak mîcim?
19. mâškôc âšokanihk âpatisiliwa.
20. tâpwê, nêsta ayawiši-wîyâs nawac nimilwêlihtên.
21. wîpac mâškôc n'ka-kî-wawêšihtân.
22. âšokanihk ihtakwaniliw; môla mâka nâspic milwâšiniliw.
23. môla mâka nâspic kinwêš n'tôhci-kiskêlimâw ana ililiw.

UNIT FIVE

A. BASIC CONVERSATION

1. Village Activities

Alec:	môso-wîyâs*iliw*	moose meat (0′)
	kîsis*amiliwa*	she (3′) is cooking it
	cwân owîkimâkana kîsisamiliwa môso-wîyâsiliw.	John's wife is cooking some moose meat.
Visitor:	kîsisw*êliwa*	she (3′) is baking it (anim.)
	owîkimâkana kîsiswêliwa nêsta âlahkonâwa.	His wife is baking some bread too.
	otâlahkonâm*ilîw*	her (3′) bread (3″)
	wîhkaciši*liwa*	it (3″) is delicious
	wîhkacišiliwa wîla otâlahkonâmilîw.	Her bread is delicious.
Alec:	milwêliht*amiliwa*	he (3″) likes it
	ošîmilîw nâspic milwêlihtamiliwa môso-wîyâsiliw.	He younger brother is very fond of moose meat.
	cîmân*iliw*	canoe (0′)
	ayâ*liwa*	he (3″) has it
	âšay ayâliwa cîmâniliw âšokanihk.	He already has a canoe at the wharf.
Visitor:	ômêliw	this one (0′)
	mayê*liw*	it (0′) is not
	n'kiskêl'tên. mayêliw mâka ômêliw cwân ocîmân.	I know, but this one is not John's canoe.
	ocîmân*ilîw*	his (3′) canoe
	animêliw	that one (0′)
	mayêliw nêsta animêliw ocîmân.	That's not his canoe either.
	ošîma wîla ocîmânilîw.	It's his younger brother's canoe.

	ôho	this one (3′)
	awênihkân ôho otâšokana?	Whose wharf is this?
	anihi	that one (3′)
	awênihkân anihi otâšokana?	Whose wharf is that?
Alec:	otâšokan*ilîw*	his (3′) wharf
	cwân ostêsa otâšokanilîw.	John's older brother's wharf.

2. Useful Queries

You have learned how to transform a simple statement into a question by using the question marker, nâ. Questions which require something other than a yes-no answer, however, and which begin with a question word: *e.g.*, how, when, why, etc., use a special set of verb forms called the *conjunct order*. These *content questions* will be studied in detail before much longer. Meanwhile, learn to recognize and use some of these useful and frequently heard queries.

Etiy:	tân′ êhtiyin?	How are you? What's ailing you?
	awâšiš	child
	tân′ êhtit	what's ailing him?
	tân′ êhtit mâka awâšiš?	And what's wrong with the child?
Saylas:	ostostotam	he coughs
	âhkosiw	he is sick
	âhkosiw. môšak ostostotam.	He's sick. He's always coughing.
Etiy:	tânt′ êtohtêyin?	Where are you going?
	tânt′ êtohtêt?	Where is he going?
Saylas:	âhkosîwikamik	hospital
	âhkosîwikamik*ohk*	to the hospital
	âhkosîwikamikohk n′titohtân.	I'm going to the hospital.
	kââ!	Oh!
Etiy:	wîyâpahtaman (*with question word*)	that you see (it)
	kêkwân wîyâpahtaman?	What (is it) that you see?
	cîmân nâ?	A canoe?
Saylas:	wêpâstan	it is drifting
	wâlaw	far off
	mâmihk	down river

	êhê. nêtê wâlaw mâmihk iši-wêpâstan.	Yes. It's drifting away off down river.
Etiy:	šâ!	tsk, tsk!
	wîyâpamat *(with question word)*	that you see (him/her)
	šâ! awênihkân wîyâpamat anta?	Tsk, tsk! Who (is it) that you see there?
Saylas:	tân' êšinihkâsot?	what is his name?
	akâmihk	across (the water)
	ililiw piko. môla mâka n'kiskêlimâw tân' êšinihkâsot. akâmihk mâškôc iši-âpatisiw.	Just (some) person. I don't know what his name is though. He probably works across (the water).
Etiy:	nêtawêlihtahk *(with question word)*	that he wants (it)
	kêkwâliw n'tawêl'tahk?	What (is it) that he wants?
Saylas:	môla kêkwâliw n'tawêl'tam.	He doesn't want anything.
Etiy:	êhtôtaman *(with question word)*	that you are so-doing (it)
	tân' êhtôtaman anta?	What (is it) that you are doing there?
	tân' êhtôtahk?	what (is it) that he is doing?
	tân' êhtôtahk mâka wîla kistês?	And what is your older brother doing?
Saylas:	pîkopaliw	it is broken
	mîšaham cîmâniliw. apišîš pîkopaliliw.	He's repairing a canoe. It's slightly broken.

B. DISCUSSION OF GRAMMAR

1. Verbs: VTA and VTI 3 and 3′ Subject

To the inflectional suffixes already learned for transitive verbs may now be added those for the *obviative*: *i.e.,* 3′ subject. They are

VTA ...	...êliwa
VTI ...	...amiliwa
VAI-T...	...ɩliwa

Compare the following.

She sees him.	wâpamêw.
Her younger brother sees him.	ošîma wâpamêliwa.
He coughs.	ostostotam.
His younger brother coughs.	ošîma ostostotamiliwa.
He has it.	ayâw.
His younger brother has it.	ošîma ayâliwa.

Study the following examples.

1.	môla ayâwêw kišîm apwoya.	Your younger brother doesn't have a paddle.
2.	ostêsa ayâwêliwa atimwa anta.	His older brother has the dog there.
3.	kî-miskawêw okosisa akâmihk.	She found her son across the water.
4.	âsay nâ kî-ayamihêw kôhtâwiya?	Has he spoken to your father already?
5.	âšay kîsiswêw nimis otâlahkonâma.	By now my older sister is baking her bread.
6.	okâwiya kî-wanihêliwa ošôliyânimilîw.	His mother has lost her money.
7.	nâspic âhkosiliwa otânisa.	Her daughter is very ill.
8.	wîpac mâškôc ta-miskam ocîmân.	Maybe he'll soon find his canoe.
9.	mîna kî-kîsisamiliwa otânisa omîcimilîw.	His daughter cooked her food again.
10.	môla ta-mîšaham cîmâniliw.	He won't repair the canoe.
11.	otêma natawêlihtamiliwa owîyâsimilîw.	His dog wants his (own) meat.
12.	cwân ayâw omâhkîm nêtê mâmihk.	John has his tent yonder down river.

———DRILLS 1.1 THROUGH 2.5———

2. Nouns

2.1 3′ Possessor

In Cree a careful distinction in form is made between nouns possessed by a third person (3) and those possessed by a further third person (3″). This distinction is made for both animate and inanimate genders: *e.g.,*

John's	wharf	John's	older brother's	wharf
3	3′	3	3	3″
Cwân	otâšokana	Cwân	ostêsa	otâšokanilîw
John's	canoe	John's	young brother's	canoe
3	0′	3	3′	0″
Cwân	ocîmân	Cwân	ošîma	ocîmânilîw

(The recordings have been made by speakers of Eastern Swampy Cree. In their speech the further obviative (3″) or *surobviative* marker occurs in the form, /…inîw/. Further west this occurs under the form, /…iniw/: *i.e.,* the same as the ending for the unpossessed NI obviative.)

2.2 Locative in /…ohk/

Turn back to Unit 3.B.2.1.2 and note how the suffix …ιm changes to …om after stems like mistikw-, môsw-, which end in a consonant + /w/, designated as **Cw**. Across a boundary between word components such as mistikw- + …ιm, /w/ + /ι/ > /o/. The locative ending, …ιhk follows the same rule. So we have

âhkosîwikamik — hospital	âhkosâwikamikohk — at the hospital
mistik — tree	mistikohk — in *or* on the tree

———DRILL 4———

3. Pronouns

3.1 Obviative of Demonstratives

In Unit 2.B.3.2 you were introduced to the obviative forms of awa and ôma. To these we now add the obviative forms of êwako and kotak, the *alternative* pronoun.

ôho	this one (*anim.*)	**ômêliw**	this one (*inan.*)
anihi	that one (*anim.*)	**animêliw**	that one (*inan.*)
		(**anihêliw** may be heard in the Moose area.)	
kotakiya an/the other one (*anim.*)		**kotakîliw** an/the other one (*inan.*)	

êwako rarely occurs in obviative form, usually appearing in combination with some form of awa or ôma. An inanimate obviative form, **êwakwêliw,** occurs alone.

3.2 kotak :: kotakiy

The form, kotakiy (the other one of two) is distinct from kotak (another one). Both forms occur for both genders. In the obviative both kotak and kotakiy show the animate kotakiya and inanimate kotakîliw.

kotakiy (the other one), unlike the demonstratives, awa, ôma, etc., also occurs in a locative form, kotakîhk. One ordinarily hears—

ôta cîmânihk - in this canoe (*i.e.,* here in the canoe),
nêtê cîmânihk - in that far canoe (*i.e.,* yonder in the canoe),
anta wayêš cîmânihk - in another canoe (*i.e.,* elsewhere in a canoe),

but kotakîhk cîmânihk - in *the* other canoe.

———DRILL 5———

3.3 Personal Pronouns

There is no obviative form for the personal pronouns.

4. Syntax: Content Questions and the Conjunct Order

A few very common content questions were introduced in Unit 2.B.1.2 and you observed that the verbs took a different set of endings from those used in ordinary statements or in questions with nâ (Unit 1.B:1.1): *e.g.,*

	šwâpihk nâ kititohtâ**n**?	Are you going to the store?
but	tântê êtohtê**yan**?	Where are you going?
	cwân itohtê**w**.	John is going (there).
but	tântê êtohtê**t**?	Where is he going?

The inflectional endings which you first learned belong to the *independent order* of the verb. The independent order of endings is used in main clauses and "yes-no" questions. Sometimes, however, the verb is in another clause which is joined to a main clause: for example, I saw him *when he passed by*. The second clause is joined to the first by the conjunction, "when". Where we have this (con)joining of clauses, the verb in the conjoined, or dependent, clause goes into the conjoining, *i.e.,* the *conjunct* order and shows the *conjunct* endings.

The conjunct order is also used with question words: where? how? who?, etc. In Cree these carry the force of 'where (is it) ...?', 'how (is it) ...?', 'who (is it)...?', as though they were full sentences in themselves: that is, they are used predicatively. In the Basic Conversation wîyâpahtaman was glossed as '*that* you see (it)' and êhtôtaman, '*that* you are so-doing (it)'. The content questions, then, would mean:

	tân' êhtôtahk?	What [*lit.,* how] (is it) that he is doing?
	kêkwân wîyâpahtaman?	What (is it) that you see?
and	tânt' êtohtêyan?	Where (is it) that you are going?

Common use in English is, What is he doing?, Where are you going?, and so on. For now, learn the handful of new questions by rote. They will help in conversation and can all be answered with verbs in the independent order, which you know. The conjunct order will be studied in detail later, both the inflectional endings and the vowel changes which occur in the first syllable. For quick reference, the following table shows the conjunct endings presented so far with the corresponding endings of the independent order, for second and third person singular subjects.

	Independent		Conjunct	
VAI	2 ...**n**	[kititohtân]	...**yan** *or* ...**yin**	[êtohtêyan]
	3 ...**w**	[išinihkâsow]	...**t**	[êšinihkâsot]
VTA	2 ...**âw**	[kiwâpamâw]	...**at** (*short* /a/)	[wîyâpamat]
	3 ...**êw**	[wâpamêw]	...**ât** (*long* /a/)	[wîyâpamât]
VTI	2 ...**ên**	[kinatawêlihtên)	...**aman**	[nêtawêlihtaman]
	3 ...**am**	[natawêlihtam]	...**ahk**	[nêtawêlihtahk]

C. DRILLS

I. INTONATION DRILL

Drill the following content questions with the recording. Listen first to the rhythm and intonation of the speaker's voice. With a pencil mark the intonation contour over each question. Finally, mimic the intonation of the Cree speaker as faithfully as you can while repeating the questions yourself. Practise the drill until you can reproduce the intonation pattern without effort. (Since intonation may vary somewhat from area to area, the questions are also spelled in syllabics so that a Cree speaker, if available, can read them for you.)

1.	tântê šwâp?	ᑖᐣᑌ ᐧᔖᑊ ?
2.	tântê mâka šwâp?	ᑖᐣᑌ ᒫᑲ ᐧᔖᑊ ?
3.	tântê sîpiy?	ᑖᐣᑌ ᓰᐲ ?
4.	tântê mâka sîpiy?	ᑖᐣᑌ ᒫᑲ ᓰᐲ ?
5.	tân' êtamahcihoyin?	ᑖᐣ ᐁᑕᒪᐦᒋᐦᐅᔨᐣ ?
6.	tân' êtamahcihoyin mâka kîla?	ᑖᐣ ᐁᑕᒪᐦᒋᐦᐅᔨᐣ ᒫᑲ ᑮᓚ ?
7.	tânt' êtohtêyin?	ᑖᐣᐟ ᐁᑐᐦᑌᔨᐣ ?
8.	tân' êhtiyin?	ᑖᐣ ᐁᐦᑎᔨᐣ ?
9.	tân' êhtôtaman?	ᑖᐣ ᐁᐦᑑᑕᒪᐣ ?
10.	tân' êhtôtaman anta walawîtimihk?	ᑖᐣ ᐁᐦᑑᑕᒪᐣ ᐊᐣᑕ ᐧᐊᓚᐧᐄᑎᒥᐦᐠ ?
11.	tân' êhtôtahk mâka wîla kiwîkimâkan?	ᑖᐣ ᐁᐦᑑᑕᐦᐠ ᒫᑲ ᐧᐄᓚ ᑭ ᐧᐄᑭᒫᑲᐣ ?
12.	tân' êhtit an' awâšiš?	ᑖᐣ ᐁᐦᑎᐟ ᐊᐣ ᐊᐧᐋᔑᔥ ?

13. kêkwân wîyâpahtaman? ᑫᐧᑳᐣ ᐧᐄᔮᐸᐦᑕᒪᐣ ?

14. kêkwân n'tawêl'taman? ᑫᐧᑳᐣ ᐣᑕᐧᐁᓪᑕᒪᐣ ?

15. awênihkân wîyâpamat? ᐊᐧᐁᓂᐦᑳᐣ ᐧᐄᔮᐸᒪᐟ ?

16. awênihkân ana wîla? ᐊᐧᐁᓂᐦᑳᐣ ᐊᓇ ᐧᐄᓚ ?

17. tân' êšinihkâsoyin kîla? ᑖᐣ ᐁᔑᓂᐦᑳᓱᔨᐣ ᑮᓚ ?

18. tân' êšinihkâsoyin mâka kîla? ᑖᐣ ᐁᔑᓂᐦᑳᓱᔨᐣ ᒫᑲ ᑮᓚ ?

19. kêko tôwi-masinahikan?* ᑫᑯ ᑑᐧᐃ ᒪᓯᓇᐦᐃᑲᐣ ?

20. kêko paski-masinahikan?** ᑫᑯ ᐸᐢᑭ ᒪᓯᓇᐦᐃᑲᐣ ?

II. PATTERN DRILLS

1. Transitive Animate Verbs: 3 and 3′ Subjects

1.1 Mimic the recording, first down each column, then across each row.

3-	3′-
wâpamêw	wâpamêliwa
kiskêlimêw	kiskêlimêliwa
milwêlimêw	milwêlimêliwa
natawêlimêw	natawêlimêliwa
itêlimêw	itêlimêliwa
mîšahwêw	mîšahwêliwa
kîsiswêw	kîsiswêliwa
ayâwêw	ayâwêliwa

* Which kind (of) book? ** Which part (of the) book?

1.2 From the bracketed forms supply the correct *subject* for the verb. Mimic the correct form as given on the recording.

		(Check column)
1.	(nikosis ~ okosisa) wâpamêw.	nikosis
2.	(nikosis ~ okosisa) wâpamêliwa.	okosisa
3.	(ôhtâwiya ~ kôhtâwiy) kiskêlimêw.	kôhtâwiy
4.	(ôhtâwiya ~ kôhtâwiy) kiskêlimêliwa.	ôhtâwiya
5.	(otêma ~ nitêm) natawêlimêliwa.	otêma
6.	(okimâw ~ ošîma) itêlimêw.	okimâw
7.	(niwîkimâkan ~ owîkimâkana) kîsiswêliwa.	owîkimâkana
8.	(šôliyânikimâw ~ okosisa) ayâwêw.	šôliyânikimâw
9.	(ošîma ~ nišîm) kîsiswêw.	nišîm
10.	(ililiw ~ otêma) ayâwêliwa.	otêma

1.3 Select the form of the verb required by the subject.

1.	nitêm (wâpamêw ~ wâpamêliwa).	wâpamêw
2.	otânisa (milwêlimêliwa ~ milwêlimêw).	milwêlimêliwa
3.	cwân ošîma (kiskêlimêw ~ kiskêlimêliwa).	kiskêlimêliwa
4.	nistês (natawêlimêliwa ~ natawêlimêw).	natawêlimêw
5.	okimâw (wawêšihêw ~ wawêšihêliwa).	wawêšihêw
6.	cwân okâwiya (ayâwêliwa ~ ayâwêw).	ayâwêliwa
7.	owîkimâkana (kîsiswêliwa ~ kîsiswêw).	owîkimâkana
8.	atim (ayâwêliwa ~ ayâwêw).	atim

1.4 Expand each of the following by selecting the correct form of the object. Assume in each case that the subject of the verb is also the possessor of the object.

1.	nâspic milwêlimêw (otêma ~ otêmilîw).	otêma
2.	mâškôc ta-natawêlimêw (otapwôlîw ~ otapwoya).	otapwoya
3.	âšay nâ kîsiswêliwa otânisa (otâlahkonâmilîw ~ otâlahkonâma)?	otâlahkonâmilîw
4.	ôhtâwiya âšay wâpamêliwa (ošôliyânima ~ ošôliyânimilîw).	ošôliyânimilîw
5.	ošîma môla ta-ayâwêliwa (otêmilîw ~ otêma).	otêmilîw
6.	môla mâškôc ta-kîsiswêw (otâlahkonâma ~ otâlahkonâmilîw).	otâlahkonâma
7.	nišîm môla ayâwêw (otapwoya ~ otapwôlîw).	otapwoya
8.	pêhkâc mîna ošîma wawêšihêliwa (otâšokana ~otâšokanilîw).	otâšokanilîw

1.5 Answer the following questions on the model:

Recording: wâpamêw nâ okosisa?
Reply: môla, ošîma mâka wâpamêliwa okosisilîw.

1. wâpamêw nâ okosisa? ... wâpamêliwa okosisilîw
2. kiskêlimêw nâ ôhtâwiya? ... kiskêlimêliwa ôhtâwîlîw
3. milwêlimêw nâ otâšokana? ... milwêlimêliwa otâšokanilîw
4. natawêlimêw nâ ošôliyânima? ... natawêlimêliwa ošôliyânimilîw
5. kîsiswêw nâ otâlahkonâma? ... kîsiswêliwa otâlahkonâmilîw
6. ayâwêw nâ otêma? ... ayâwêliwa otêmilîw
7. kîsiswêw nâ omôsoma? ... kîsiswêliwa omôsomilîw
8. natawêlimêw nâ otapwoya? ... natawêlimêliwa otapwôlîw

2. Transitive Inanimate Verbs: 3, 3′ Subjects

2.1 Mimic the recording, first down each column, then across each row.

3 -	3′-
wâpahtam	wâpahtamiliwa
kiskêlihtam	kiskêlihtamiliwa
milwêlihtam	milwêlihtamiliwa
natawêlihtam	natawêlihtamiliwa
itêlihtam	itêlihtamiliwa
mîšaham	mîšahamiliwa
kîsisam	kîsisamiliwa
ayâw	ayâliwa
ayamihtâw	ayamihtâliwa

Of which set of verb endings do those on the last two verbs above remind you?

2.2 From the brackets supply the correct form to stand as subject to the verb. Mimic the correct form as given on the recording.

		(Check column)
1.	(ôhtâwiya ~ kôhtâwiy) wâpahtam.	kôhtâwiy
2.	(nikosis ~ okosisa) wâpahtamiliwa.	okosisa
3.	(cwân ~ cwân otânisa) milwêlihtam.	cwân
4.	(ôhtâwiya ~ kôhtâwiy) milwêlihtamiliwa.	ôhtâwiya
5.	(okimâw ~ ošîma) natawêlihtamiliwa.	ošîma
6.	(otêma ~ nitêm) natawêlihtam.	nitêm
7.	(kitânis ~ otânisa) kiskêlihtamiliwa.	otânisa
8.	(ošîma ~ nišîm) wawêšihtâw.	nišîm.

2.3 Select the form of the verb required by the subject.

1.	cwân (kiskêlihtam ~ kiskêlihtamiliwa).	kiskêlihtam
2.	owîkimâkana (ayâw ~ ayâliwa).	ayâliwa
3.	atim (wâpahtamiliwa ~ wâpahtam).	wâpahtam
4.	okâwiya (kîsisamiliwa ~ kîsisam).	kîsisamiliwa
5.	otânisa (itêlihtam ~ itêlihtamiliwa).	itêlihtamiliwa
6.	nitêm (ayâw ~ ayâliwa).	ayâw
7.	nistês (kîsisamiliwa ~ kîsisam).	kîsisam
8.	cwân okâwiya (ta-milwêlihtamiliwa ~ ta-milwêlihtam).	ta-milwêlihtamiliwa

2.4 Answer the following questions on the model:

Recording: wâpahtam nâ ocîmân?
Reply: môla, ošîma mâka wâpahtamiliwa ocîmânilîw.

		(Check column)
1.	wâpahtam nâ ocîmân?	... wâpahtamiliwa ocîmânilîw
2.	kiskêlihtam nâ osîpîm?	... kiskêlihtamiliwa osîpîmilîw
3.	milwêlihtam nâ omâhkîm?	... milwêlihtamiliwa omâhkîmilîw
4.	natawêlihtam nâ owîyâsim?	... natawêlihtamiliwa owîyâsimilîw
5.	kîsisam nâ omîcim?	... kîsisamiliwa omîcimimilîw
6.	wawêšihtâw nâ omasinahikan?	... wawêšihtâliwa omasinahikanilîw
7.	ayâw nâ onatohkolonim?	... ayâliwa onatohkolonimilîw
8.	itêlihtam nâ kêkwâliw?	... itêlihtamiliwa kêkwâliw.

2.5 Complete each sentence with the correct one of the two bracketed items. Correct responses are listed below.

1. mâškôc okosisa ta-wâpahtamiliwa (otêmilîw ~ ocîmânilîw).
2. âlik okosisa môla ayâwêliwa (otapwôlîw ~ omâhkîmilîw).
3. wîpac ta-kî-wawêšihtâliwa ošîma (omâhkîmilîw ~ otapwôlîw).
4. ostêsa nâ âšay wâpamêliwa (omîcimimilîw ~ otôkimâmilîw)?
5. okâwiya natawêlimêliwa (otâlahkonâmilîw ~ omîcimimilîw).
6. ta—kîsisamiliwa nâ otânisa (otâlahkonâmilîw ~ omîcimimilîw)?
7. êhê, šâkoc kiskêlimêliwa okosisa (ôhtâwîlîw ~ osîpîmilîw).
8. tâpwê kiskêlihtamiliwa ošîma (otêmilîw ~ ocîmânilîw).

1. ocîmânilîw
2. otapwôlîw
3. omâhkîmilîw
4. otôkimâmilîw
5. otâlahkonâmilîw
6. omîcimimilîw
7. ôhtâwîlîw
8. ocîmânilîw

3. Complete each of the following partial sentences by filling in the blank with an appropriate word or phrase from the list below. Use each 'filler' once only.

mîšaham, êhtôtahk, ocîmânilîw, iši-âpatisiliwa, ka-pêci-kîwân, ocîmân, kotak, wîyâpahtaman, ostostotam, milo-kîšikâw, mâmihk, kîsisamiliwa, âhkosîwikamikohk, pîkopaliliw

Etiy:	tân' ____________ wîla kistês? môšak otamîw, manâ!
Alik:	êhê, ___________ cîmâniliw. apišîš _____________.
	nêtê wâlaw __________ kî [past] -iši-wêpâstaniliw.
Etiy:	šâ! wîpac mâškôc ____________________ n'ka-itohtân nîla.
	âhkosiw awâšiš. môšak ______________.
Alik:	___-________-__________ nâ anohc kâ-kîšikâk?
Etiy:	môla nikiskêl'tên. mâškôc ta-kimiwan. môla nâspic
	_______-____________.
Alik:	tâpwê! kêkwân ______________ nêtê âšokanihk? awênihkân wîla ocîmân?
Etiy:	mayêliw cwân ___________. mâškôc ošîma________________.
	akâmihk mâškôc ____________________ ošîma. owîkimâkana
	mâka âšay __________________ môs'-wîyâsiliw. mâwac
	nimilwêl'tên môs'-wîyâs ispîš wîla ________ mîcim.

4. The Locative, *continued*

Answer the following questions, putting the noun into the locative, on the model:

Cue:	tântê cîmân?
	Where is the canoe?
Response:	âstamitê piko, apišîš ôtê itêhkê pil <u>ocîmânihk</u>.
	Just to this side, a little this side of Bill's canoe.

		(Check column)
1.	tântê cîmân?	... pil ocîmânihk
2.	tântê âšokan?	... pil otâšokanihk
3.	tântê masinahikan?	... pil omasinahikanihk
4.	tântê mêskanaw?	... pil omêskanâhk
5.	tântê šwâp?	... pil ošwâpimihk
6.	tântê mâhkiy?	... pil omâhkîmihk
7.	tântê sîpiy?	... pil osîpîmihk
8.	tântê âhkosîwikamik?	... pil otâhkosîwikamikohk
9.	tântê n'tohkolonikamik [dispensary]?	... pil on'tohkolonikamikohk

5. Obviative of awa, ôma;
ana, anima;
kotak.

The recording will give two forms of the pronoun, followed by a sentence with a pause before the last word. Repeat the sentence, filling in the pause with the correct form of the pronoun. The recording will check you.

5.1

			(Check column)
1.	(awa ~ ôho)	kiwâpamâw nâ ..... okimâw?	awa
2.	(awa ~ ôho)	kiskêlimêw nâ ..... ililiwa?	ôho
3.	(awa ~ ôho)	natawêlimêw nâ ..... šôliyâna?	ôho
4.	(awa ~ ôho)	kikîsiswâw nâ ..... âlahkonâw?	awa
5.	(ana ~ anihi)	âšay mâka ayâwêw ..... atimwa.	anihi
6.	(ana ~ anihi)	wîpac ka-kî-kîsiswâw ..... âlahkonâw.	ana
7.	(ana ~ anihi)	awasitê nimilwêlimâw ..... âšokan.	ana
8.	(ana ~ anihi)	mâškôc kiskêlimêw ..... ililiwa.	anihi
9.	(ana ~ anihi)	âšay natawêlimêw ..... apwoya.	anihi
10.	(awa ~ ôho)	âšay wâpamêw ..... atimwa.	ôho
11.	(ana ~ anihi)	mîna n'ka-wawêšihâw ..... âšokan.	ana
12.	(awa ~ ôho)	šâkoc mâka kikiskêlimâw ..... ililiw.	awa

5.2

1.	(ôma ~ ômêliw)	wâpahtam nâ ..... kêkwâliw?	ômêliw
2.	(ôma ~ ômêliw)	kikiskêlihtên nâ ..... sîpiy?	ôma
3.	(ôma ~ ômêliw)	kinatawêlihtên nâ ..... mâhkiy?	ôma
4.	(ôma ~ ômêliw)	kîsisam nâ ..... mîcimiliw?	ômêliw
5.	(anima ~ animêliw)	âšay mâka kitayân ..... masinahikan.	anima
6.	(anima ~ animêliw)	wîpac ta-kî-wawêšihtâw ..... mâhkîliw.	animêliw
7.	(anima ~ animêliw)	nâspic nimilwêlihtên ..... môso-wîyâs.	anima
8.	(anima ~ animêliw)	šâkoc mâka natawêlihtam ..... kêkwâliw.	animêliw
9.	(ôma ~ ômêliw)	wîpac ta-wâpahtam ..... sîpîliw.	ômêliw
10.	(anima ~ animêliw)	kinatawêlihtên nâ ..... masinahikan?	anima
11.	(ôma ~ ômêliw)	môla mâškôc n'ka-kîsisên ..... mîcim.	ôma
12.	(anima ~ animêliw)	wîpac mâškôc ta-ayâw ..... natohkoloniliw.	animêliw

5.3

1.	(kotak ~ kotakiya)	kiwâpamâw nâ ..... môs?	kotak
2.	(kotak ~ kotakiya)	kiskêlimêw nâ ..... ililiwa?	kotakiya
3.	(kotak ~ kotakiya)	natawêlimêw nâ ..... šôliyâna?	kotakiya
4.	(kotak ~ kotakiya)	kitayâwâw nâ ..... atim?	kotak
5.	(kotak ~ kotakîliw)	âšay mâškôc kitayân ..... masinahikan.	kotak
6.	(kotak ~ kotakîliw)	âšay mâškôc ayâw ..... masinahikaniliw.	kotakîliw
7.	(kotak ~ kotakîliw)	tâpwê nâ kinatawêlihtên ..... kêkwân?	kotak
8.	(kotak ~ kotakîliw)	awasitê natawêlihtam ..... natohkoloniliw.	kotakîliw
9.	(kotak ~ kotakîliw)	tâpwê, wîpac n'ka-ayân ..... cîmân.	kotak
10.	(kotak ~ kotakiya)	âšay nâ wâpamêw ..... âšokana?	kotakiya
11.	(kotak ~ kotakîliw)	âšay mâka ayâw ..... masinahikaniliw.	kotakîliw
12.	(kotak ~ kotakiya)	apišîš piko nimilwêlimâw ..... ililiw.	kotak

D. CONVERSATION PRACTICE

1. Cover the Cree columns of the Basic Conversation and make sure that you can give the Cree equivalent of the English without hesitation. Drill difficult points as in earlier units by placing a tick at any point where you get stuck, then drilling each of these until you can produce it without hesitation. Finally, go through the section again without stopping.

2. Tell about a friend of yours (nitôtêm 'my friend') whose brother, sister, husband (onâpêma) or wife is ill and will be going to hospital. Your friend's canoe is broken, however, and his son is repairing (mîšaham) it. His son knows the river well. Right now (mwêhci anohc) his daughter is baking bread and your friend is very fond of it, especially fresh bread. Later on (nâkê) she will probably be cooking some moose meat. Her mother is very ill, however, and needs some medicine, etc., etc.

3. Make up other conversations in which you use 3′ as subject, until you find you can call up the forms without undue hesitation. It helps to sketch out a few conversational exchanges on paper first, noting verbs which you want to use. Then practise with a friend, real or imaginary!

E. LISTENING IN

Saylas:	tânt' êtohtêyin kîla?
Cwân:	šwâpihk piko n'titohtân. šôliyânikimâw anta ihtâw n'titêlimâw. mâškôc n'ka-kî-ayamihâw. ayâwêw šôliyâna nîla ohci.[1] ê'ko nâ ôtê itêhkê?
Saylas:	môla,—nêtê itêhkê. ôtê piko at'-îtohtê mêskanâhk.
Cwân:	mîkwêc.
Saylas:	âstam pitamâ! kiwâpahtên nâ kêkwân anta?
Cwân:	môla. môla kêkwân niwâpahtên. kêkwân wîyâpahtaman kîla?
Saylas:	tâpwê, môla nikiskêl'tên. môla n'kî-wâpahtên kwayask. awasitê itêhkê mâka nimâhkîmihk ihtakwan.
Cwân:	kââ! cîmân manâ? mâškôc wêpâstan.
Saylas:	môla mâškôc. pîkopaliw n'titêl'tên.
Cwân:	šâ! môla wîlâhpahk. awênihkân ocîmân?
Saylas:	ay'hâw, âlik ošîma ayâliwa cîmâniliw âšokanihk. mayêliw mâka ômêliw wîla ošîma ocîmânilîw. âšay kinwêš ohci-ihtakwaniliw[2] âšokanihk.
Cwân:	awênihkân mâka otâšokana anihi?
Saylas:	nistês otâšokana. apišîš pîkopaliliwa nêsta wîla. wîpac mâka mâškôc ta-kî-mîšahwêw.[3]
Cwân:	ta-milwâšin. ay'hâw, tântê šwâp?
Saylas:	nêtê piko, âstamitê âšokanihk. kêkwân n'tawêl'taman šwâpihk?
Cwân:	n'tawêl'tam n'tohkoloniliw niwîkimâkan. môšak ostostotam. otakikomiw n'titêlimâw. tahkâyâw nâspic nimâhkîmihk.
Saylas:	êliwêhk tahkâyâw! môla nâspic milo-kîšikâw.
Cwân:	êhê, wîpac mâškôc ta-kimiwan.
Saylas:	tâpwê! ka-wâpamâw nâ nêsta okimâw?
Cwân:	môla mâškôc. matêw šwâpihk. âpatisiw nêtê âšokanihk anohc wîla. šôliyânikimâw piko niwî[4]-wâpamâw.
Saylas:	ayâw ocîmân nêtê sîpîhk.
Cwân:	nistês ocîmân animêliw.

[1] ohci IPC for

[2] ohci *as* IPV from: kinwêš ohci-ihtakwaniliw it is there (as) from a long time (ago)

[3] repair it: *recording has* wawêšihêw fix it up, decorate, spruce up

[4] wî IPV want (to)

Saylas:	milwêl'tam nâ kistês ôta?
Cwân:	tâpwê, nawac milwêl'tam ôta. awasitê milwâšin ôta ispîš wîla mâmihk sîpîhk. tântê mâka wîla kikosis?
Saylas:	âhkosîwikamikohk iši-âpatisiw, - nitânis mâka nêsta.
Cwân:	kiwîkimâkan nâ nêsta?
Saylas:	môla. nimâhkîmihk ihtâw. âšay kîsiswêw âlahkonâwa. apišîš mâka otakikomiw nêsta wîla.
Cwân:	kitayân nâ ostostocikanâpoy?
Saylas:	apišîš piko ostostotam. môla nâspic âhkosiw. wîpac mâškôc awasitê ta-milopaliw.
Cwân:	milwâšin.
Saylas:	êko wâs' âni; âšay n'ka-kihtohtân. wâciyê.
Cwân:	wâciyê.

F. REFERENCE LIST

akâmihk	IPC	across (the water)
anihi	PR dem. anim. obv.	that one
awâšiš-	NA	child
âhkosi-	VAI	be sick, be ill
âhkosîwikamikw-	NI	hospital
êhtit	VAI chgd. conj. indic. < ihti-	that he is faring, that he is ailing [*with question words and dependent clauses*]
êhtiyan, ...yin	VAI chgd. conj. indic. < ihti-	that you are faring, that you are ailing [*with question words and dependent clauses*]
êhtôtahk	VTI chgd. conj. indic. < ihtôt-	that he is (so-) doing [*with question words and dependent clauses*]
êhtôtaman	VTI chgd. conj. indic. < ihtôt-	that you are (so-) doing [*with question words and dependent clauses*]
êšinihkâsot	VAI chgd. conj. indic. < išinihkâso-	that his name is, that he is called [*with question words and dependent clauses*]
êtiy-	NA [proper name]	Eddie
êtohtêt	VAI chgd. conj. indic. < itohtê-	that he is going [*with question words and dependent clauses*]
êtohtêyan, ...yin	VAI chgd. conj. indic. < itohtê-	that you are going [*with question words and dependent clauses*]
ihti-	VAI	ail, fare, be in such and such a state of health
ihtôt-	VTI	so do (it)
mâmihk	IPC	down river
mwêhci	IPC	exactly. *v.* mwêhci anohc.
mwêhci anohc		right now
natohkolonikamikw-	NI	dispensary
nâkê	IPC	later, later on
nêtawêlihtahk	VTI chgd. conj. indic. < natawêliht-	that he wants [*with question words and dependent clauses*]

nêtawêlihtaman	VTI chgd. conj. indic. < natawêliht-	that you want [*with question words and dependent clauses*]
nitôtêm-	NDA	my friend *v.* otôtêmimâw-.
ohci	IPC	for [*with mention case*]
ohci	IPV	from, as of: kinwêš ohci-ihtakwan it is there as of a long time, it has been there a long time
ostostot-	VTI	cough (it)
otôtêmimâw-	NA	friend: (*unpossessed form*)
pîkopali-	VAI / VII	be broken
saylas-	NA [proper name]	Silas
šâ!	IPC	tch, tch!, tsk, tsk!
wâlaw	IPC	far away
wêpâstan-	VII	drift, drift away
wêpâši-	VAI	drift, drift away
wîyâpahtaman	VTI chgd. conj. indic. < wâpaht-	that you see s.t. [*with question words and dependent clauses*]
wîyâpamat	VTA chgd. conj. indic. < wâpam-	that you see s.o. [*with question words and dependent clauses*]
wîyâpamât	VTA chgd. conj. indic. < wâpam-	that he sees s.o. [*with question words and dependent clauses*]

G. REVIEW

5.A Kakwêcihkêmôwina—Questions

Answer the following questions avoiding single word answers where possible.

1. tânt' êtohtêyin?
2. tân' êhtôtahk mâka wîla kiwîkimâkan?
3. awênihkân otapwoya ôho?
4. ômêliw nâ saylas ocîmân?
5. milwêlihtamiliwa nâ cwân ošîma môso-wîyâsiliw?
6. kêkwân wîyâpahtaman nêtê mâmihk sîpîhk?
7. awênihkân mâka anihi otâšokana?
8. wêpâstan nâ kicîmân nêtê mâmihk sîpîhk?
9. tân' êhtit mâka awâšiš?
10. tân' êhtiyan nêsta kîla?
11. masinahikan nâ? kêko tôwihkân nêtawêlihtaman?
12. tân' êhtit mâka kôhtâwiy?
13. awênihkân wîyâpamat anta?
14. tân' êhtôtaman?
15. âhkosîwikamikohk nâ kititohtân?
16. cwân nâ ostêsa otâšokanilîw ôho?
17. kêkwâliw nêtawêlihtahk wîla kiwîkimâkan?
18. mîšaham nâ kistês cîmâniliw?
19. môšak nâ ostostotamiliwa owîkimâkana?
20. ta-pêci-mawâpiliwa nâ cwân ostêsa?
21. otânisa nâ ta-kî-kîsiswêliwa âlahkonâwa?
22. ôhtâwiya nâ mîna ta-kî-mîšahwêliwa otâšokanilîw?

5.B Naškwêwašihtwâwina—Answers

Make up questions to which the statements below would be suitable answers

1. âšay ninatawêlimâw n'tapwoy?
2. môla kêkwâliw natawêlihtam.
3. êhê, nâspic wîhkacišiliwa otâlahkonâmilîw.
4. mayêliw mâka animêliw cwân omâhkîm.
5. cwân ostêsa ôho otâšokanilîw.
6. âlik owîkimâkana kîsisamiliwa môso-wîyâsiliw.
7. nicîmân mâškôc. nêtê wâlaw mâmihk iši-wêpâstan.
8. môšak âpatisiw wîla. âšay wawêšihtâw ocîmân.
9. ostêsa nêsta. âšay wawêšihtâliwa ocîmânilîw.
10. môla mwêhci ninisitohtên. apišîš piko nitililîmon.
11. êhê, otakikomiliwa nêsta wîla owîkimâkana.
12. nêsta sopâya [Sophia] otânisa ostostotamiliwa.
13. ostostocikanâpôliw natawêlihtam âlik.
14. êhê, êkotê! ôtê piko âstamitê nimâhkîmihk.
15. nâspic nimilopalin. âskaw piko apišîš n'tostostotên.
16. âšay niwâpahtên kimâhkîm.
17. pîkopaliw n'titêl'tên.
18. môla. môla nâspic milwâšiniliw. kotakîliw natawêlihtam.
19. apišîš âhkosiliwa ocawâšimiša [her child].
20. tâpwê kiskêlihtamiliwa. âšay âšokanihk ihtâliwa.

UNIT SIX

A. BASIC CONVERSATION

1. "One, Two, Three..."

John approaches his friend, David, who seems to be counting something.

Cwân:	ê-'lilîmoyan	in (your) talking Cree
	kitakihtâson	you are counting
	kitakihtâson nâ ê-'lilîmoyan?	Are you counting in Cree?
Têpit:	nikocihtân	I'm trying (it).
	ohci	*completed aspect marker with negative*
	wîskâc	ever
	môla. môla wîskâc n'tôhci-kocihtân.	No, I never tried it.
Cwân:	akihtâson	numeral
	kici (+ Conjunct)	in order that
	'ci-kiskêl'taman	in order that you know (it)
	âpatan	it is useful
	ay'hâw, nâspic âpatan 'ci-kiskêl'taman akihtâsona.	Well, it's very useful to know the numbers.
	nâspitohtawêw	he imitates him, he mimics him
	nâspitohtawin	say after me, mimic me
	n'ka-itwân	I will say
	nîla n'ka-itwân.	I will say (them).
	nâspitohtawin kîla.	You repeat after me.
	pêyak	one
	nîšo	two
	nisto	three
	nêw	four
	niyâlan	five
	n'kotwâs	six
	nîswâs	seven
	niyânânêw	eight
	šân'k *or* šâkitât	nine
	mitâht *or* mitâtaht	ten

2. How Many Canoes?

Têpit:	ki...cîmân...inaw	our canoe (yours and mine)
	wîhtamawin	tell me
	wîhtamawin: kiwâpahtên nâ kicîmâninaw?	Tell me: do you see our canoe (yours and mine)?
Cwân:	nêma	yonder one (*distant*)
	nêma nâ, wâlaw mâmihk sîpîhk?	That one, away off down-river?
Têpit:	pâhkwâhk	on the dry part, on shore
	kî	*completed action marker with affirmative*
	n'kî-sêskipitên	I beached it
	lâlatin[1]	on the bank (close to water level)
	môla, ôma piko lâlatin. n'kî-sêskipitên pâhkwâhk.	No, the one just over on the bank. I pulled it up on the shore.
Cwân:	tânitahto	how many ...
	cîmâna	canoes
	tânitahto-cîmâna wiyâpahtaman?	How many canoes do you see?
Têpit:	kitakihtên	you are counting it *or* them
	nêstapiko	or
	nisto, nêstapiko mâškôc nêw. ka-kî-akihtên nâ, kîla?	Three, or maybe four. Can *you* count them?
Cwân:	kîkiwâw	your (2p) home
	nêta	over thereabouts
	êhê, âšay niwâpahtên. nêta nâ ihtakwan kîkiwâw?	Yes, I see them now. Is your home over there?
Têpit:	n'kî-âhtakwânân	we (excluding you) moved away
	môla n'tôhci-sâpêlihtênân	we weren't keen on it
	môla wîla anohc. n'kî-âhtakwânân. niwîkimâkan nêsta nîla môla n'tôhci-sâpêlihtênân.	Not *now*. We moved away. My wife and I weren't keen on it.

[1] nânâmatin heard in area of Lake Winnipeg (N-Dialect).

3. It's Better Upstream

Cwân:	kitihtânâwâw	you (2p) are (at a place)
	sîpîhk natimihk	upstream, upriver
	âšay sîpîhk n'timihk kitihtânâwâw, tâpwê nâ?	You live upstream now, —is that right?
Têpit:	nôhcimihk	in the bush
	n'kî-cimatânân	we (excluding you) set it up
	n'kî-kawinênân	we (excl. you) knocked it down
	wâskâhikan	house (*orig.*, stockade)
	n'kî-nakatênân	we left it
	êhê. n'kî-nakatênân wâskâhikan. n'kî-kawinênân nimâhkîminân.	Yes. We left the house. We broke camp.
	n'kî-cimatânân nimâhkîminân nôhcimihk.	We pitched our tent in the woods.
	ihtâwak	they are (at a place)
	kiyâpic, kêyâpac	still, yet; more
	nitôtêminânak	our (not your) friends
	misiwê	all
	misiwê n'tôtêminânak kiyâpic nêtê ihtâwak.	All our friends are still over there.
Cwân:	omâhkîmiwâw	their camp (*lit.*, their tents)
	šišôtêw	(at) the shore (-line)
	tântê omâhkîmiwâw? nêtê nâ šišôtêw?	Where is their camp? Down by the shore?
Têpit:	ohci	for
	namêsak	fish
	êhê, kêyâpac anta ihtâwak. awasitê milwâšin namêsak ohci.	Yes, they're still there. It's better for fish.
Cwân:	nipiy	water
	awasitê mâka šâkoc milwâšin nipiy n'timihk sîpîhk.	The water sure is better upstream though.
Têpit:	pâhkwatinâw	the bank, the land is dry
	nêsta pâhkwatinâw anta.	And the bank's dry there too.

B. DISCUSSION OF GRAMMAR

1. Verbs

1.1 Plural Subjects: Prefixes and Suffixes

Up to this point only singular subjects have been studied. In this unit you will meet the corresponding plural forms. Remember that the personal prefixes tell whether the subject is first, second or third person (ni..., ki..., or Ø: *i.e.,* no prefix). Whether the subject is singular or plural, however, (*i.e.,* whether ni... means "I" or "we") is shown by the suffix (Cf. Unit 1.B.1.1):

ninipâ...n	I am sleeping
ninipâ...nân	we are sleeping.

The following notation is used to distinguish personal subjects:

3 = he, she
3p = they
1 = I
1p = we (*i.e.,* ni... is pluralized)
2 = you, singular, "thou"
2p = you, plural (*i.e.,* ki... is pluralized)

	VAI	VTA	VTI
3	... w	... w	... am
3p	... wak	... êwak	... amwak
1	ni(t) ... n	ni(t) ... âw	ni(t) ... ên
2	ki(t) ... n	ki(t) ... âw	ki(t) ... ên
1p	ni(t) ... nân	ni(t) ... ânân	ni(t) ... ênân
2p	ki(t) ... nâwâw	ki(t) ... âwâw	ki(t) ... ênâwâw

Verbs listed as VAI-T show inflectional features identical with those of the VAI Class: *e.g.,*

ninipâ...n	I sleep	nikocihtâ...n	I try it
		nimîci...n	I eat it
nipâ...w	he *or* she sleeps	kocihtâ...w	he *or* she tries it
		mîci...w	he *or* she eats it

Transitive verbs display stems for both animate and inanimate *objects,* as you have seen: *e.g.,* wâpam- VTA, wâpaht- VTI; kîsisw- VTA, kîsis- VTI, etc. Verbs of the VAI-T type with stem ending in /...htâ-/ commonly show the corresponding VTA member with stem-final in /...h-/: *e.g.,*

	VAI-T	VTA
	koci**htâ**...w	koci**h**...êw
	wani**htâ**...w	wani**h**...êw
	wawêši**htâ**...w	wawêši**h**...êw
but note:	ayâ...w	ayâw...êw

These forms with prefixes for the personal subject belong to the *independent* order of the verb: that is, the set of verb forms used in main clauses, as contrasted with the *conjunct* order, the set of verb endings used in dependent clauses (Unit 2.B.1.3; Unit 5.B.4) The tense you have been learning is the *present* or so-called *neutral* tense. Study the following examples.

1.	nikîsiswânân âlahkonâw.	We're baking bread.
2.	kiyâpic nâ kitakihtênâwâw cîmâna?	Are you (2p) still counting the canoes?
3.	wîpac mâškôc n'ka-kihtohtânân.	We'll probably soon go away.
4.	n'kî-nakatênân kêkwân kîkihk.	We left something at your place.
5.	namêsa kî-ayâwêwak.	They had (some) fish.
6.	kitâhtakwânâwâw nâ mâmihk sîpîhk?	Are you (2p) moving away downriver?
7.	môla wîla anohc. nitôtêminânak mâka kiyâpic natimihk sîpîhk ihtâwak.	Not right now. Our friends are still upriver though.
8.	môla sâpêlihtamwak.	They are not keen on it.
9.	mîna kinâspitohtâwâw okimâw.	You (2p) are mimicking the boss again.

———DRILLS 1.1 THROUGH 3.7———

If part way through a drill you find that you can easily cope, proceed to the next one at that point rather than letting the drills become tedious.

1.2 Completed Aspect Marker

The completed aspect marker is the prefix particle, **kî-**, where a statement is in the affirmative. It marks completed events and actions. Consequently its reference is normally to the past: *e.g.,*

itohtêw	he goes (there)
kî-itohtêw	he went (there).

In a negative statement the full form of the completed action marker is **kî-ohci-**: *e.g.,*

môla kî-ohci-itohtêw he did not go (there).

In colloquial use, however, negative statements normally drop the kî- and retain ohci- alone. Common usage is môla ohci-itohtêw he did not go, he has not gone (there).

NOTE that the completed aspect marker, kî-, and the potential prefix, kî- (Unit 3.B.1.3) sound alike in Cree of this area. The potential prefix, how ever, even in the negative, retains the shape kî-.

———DRILLS 4.1 AND 4.2———

2. Nouns

2.1 Plural Possessors: Prefixes and Suffixes for 1p, 2p and 3p.

Where the personal possessor of a noun is plural this is shown by a set of inflectional suffixes. (The pattern closely parallels that of personal prefixes and suffixes with verbs.)

Where a noun forms a possessed theme with ...ιm, the inflectional suffixes are placed immediately after: *e.g.,*

nicîmâninân our canoe,
but nišôliyânιminân our money.

The pattern for possessed nouns is as follows. ...(ιm), in the paradigm represents the possessed theme wherever it occurs.

	NA	NI
1	ni(t) .... (ιm)	ni(t) .... (ιm)
2	ki(t) .... (ιm)	ki(t) .... (ιm)
3	o(t) .... (ιm)...a	o(t) .... (ιm)
1p	ni(t) .... (ιm)...ιnân	ni(t) .... (ιm)...ιnân
2p	ki(t) .... (ιm)...ιwâw	ki(t) .... (ιm)...ιwâw
3p	o(t) .... (ιm)...ιwâw...a	o(t) .... (ιm)...ιwâw

NOTE particularly the force of the personal prefixes, both subject and possessor. ni...is used where the actor or possessor is speaker and the addressee is *excluded.* ki... is used wherever the actor or possessor *includes* the addressee. (Note kicîmâninaw [A.2 above], further discussed in Unit 7) Where ni... and ki... stand for a plural subject or possessor, this is shown by inflectional suffixes.

3. Personal Pronouns: Plural

In the following paradigm note the relation in form between the singular and plural forms of the personal pronouns. They are as follows:

1	nîla	I	1p	nîlanân	we (*excluding addressee[s]*)
2	kîla	you (sg.)	2p	kîlawâw	you (pl.)
3	wîla	he, she; it	3p	wîlawâw	they

———DRILLS 5 AND 6———

4. Syntax

4.1 Subjects and Objects

In Unit 4.B.4 the inflectional endings for the verb were described as showing concord for person, number and obviation of the subject for transitive verbs. In addition, inflectional suffixes to transitive verb stems were noted as displaying concord for gender as well as certain other features of the object. This has been further illustrated by the inflectional suffixes introduced in this unit. A piece-by-piece break down of a specimen sentence will make this clear:

ni...wâp...am...ânân atim We see the dog.

ni..., speaker (addressee excluded); wâp..., see (*also* bright; white); ...am-, VTA stem final; ...ânân, fused form consisting of ...â..., direction signal indicating action from subject to object and ...nân, pluralizer of ni... subject prefix, and atim, dog NA.

4.2 Sentence Models (for optional study)

The earlier formula for the above verb form may now be modified to indicate that the inflectional suffix displays certain concord with the subject and object rather than saying it simply *includes* the object. For sentences of the type nimilwêlimâw atim or kiwâpahtên mâhkiy, the formula was written as

+ S... + P + ...O : ±O

The formula implies that statement of the object within the verb form, a sentence word, is obligatory, and that it may be optionally repeated separately on an expansion of the sentence. In the light of the function of the suffixes introduced in the present unit, we may now write instead

+ S... + P o-s ±O

where "o-s" denotes concord for object and subject without specifying further details. No longer is the object included in a verb form of this kind. The inflectional suffix simply displays concord. The simplest expansion of the basic kernel sentence may involve separate statement of the object, but this is optional. For VAI and VII we may correspondingly write + S... + Ps. Thus the formulae for the two types of kernel sentence consisting respectively of an intransitive and a transitive verb form in the independent order may be stated as

+ S... + Ps	*e.g.,* niwâpin	I see	VAI
+ S... + Po-s	*e.g.,* kiwâpamâw	you (sg.) see him	VTA
	kiwâpahtên	you (sg.) see it	VTI

C. DRILLS

I. PRONUNCIATION DRILLS

When the sound, /c/: *i.e.*,[tš] as in church, occurs in word final position, Cree speakers may often be heard making an unreleased [t] in its place. One would expect to hear wîpac nawac, instead of which one often hears wîpat nawat. This tendency is especially strong when /c/ is followed by another sound made close to the same point of articulation, as in the above example, where assimilation takes place. (Cf. Diagram in the "Cree Sound System", p. xxvi.)

Practice the following with the tape recording:

môl' êškwâ wîskâ**t** ___ **n**'tôhci-wâpahtên anima.

wîpa**t** ___ **n**awa**t** ___ **n**'ka-pêc'-îtohtân.

nâspi**t** ___ **n**imilwêl'tên ôma masinahikan.

wêsâ pêhkâ**t** ___ **n**'tayamin,

and even wîpa**t** ___ **m**âškô**t** ___ **t**a-kihtohtêw.

This is not an unvarying rule since, especially in slower speech, the /c/ in final position is often clearly enunciated as [tš]. Where the assimilation takes place in more rapid speech a useful practise is to note the instance carefully and imitate it (to yourself) so as to develop natural Cree speaking habits as closely as possible.

II. PATTERN DRILLS

The sequences in this section should be drilled fairly rapidly. They are designed to help you recognize the relation in shape between verb (and later, noun) endings and to respond deftly to straightforward "we - you : : you - we" type questions. If you make an incorrect response, note it but do not stop the drill. Keep moving and repeat the section to correct the error. If you do not need a drill in its entirety, move on quickly to the next.

1. Animate Intransitive Verbs (VAI) with 1p, 2p and 3p subjects. Drill across each pair of columns: *i.e.,* 1 and 1p, then 2 and 2p. Keep in mind that the ni...subject excludes the person addressed, even when ni... is plural. So nitililîmonân means "we, but not you" speak Cree. "We, including you", is a slightly different form which we shall soon meet; but learn the following first.

1.1

1	1p	2	2p
nimawâpin	nimawâpinân	kimawâpin	kimawâpinâwâw
ninipân	ninipânân	kinipân	kinipânâwâw
nitašîhkân	nitašîhkânân	kitašîhkân	kitašîhkânâwâw
nitililîmon	nitililîmonân	kitililîmon	kitililîmonâwâw
niwalawîn	niwalawînân	kiwalawîn	kiwalawînâwâw

1.2

3	3p	
mawâpiw	mawâpiwak	
nipâw	nipâwak	
tašîhkêw	tašîhkêwak	(Note the change of the stem vowel from
itwêw	itwêwak	nitašîhkâ̲n and nititwâ̲n.)
ililîmow	ililîmowak	
walawîw	walawîwak	

1.3 Show that you recognize the subject of the following verbs by citing the appropriate pronoun after the verb form: *e.g.,*

Cue: nimawâpinân
Response: nimawâpinân, nîlanân

	(Check column)
nimawâpinân	nimawâpinân, nîlanân
nitâhkosinân	nîlanân
kitâpatisinâwâw	kîlawâw
pimâtisiwak	wîlawâw
nicimatânân	nîlanân
kinipânâwăw	kîlawâw
itohtêwak	wîlawâw
nititohtânân	nîlanân
mawâpiwak	wîlawâw
kikihtohtânâwâw	kîlawâw
âhkosiwak	wîlawâw
niwalawînân	nîlanân
kitâhtakwânâwâw	kîlawâw

1.4 Given the personal pronouns to indicate the subject, supply the appropriate verb form: *e.g.,*

Cue: âpatisiw :: kîlawâw
Response: kitâpatisinâwâw

akihtâsow	::	nîlanân	nitakihtâsonân
pîhtokwêw	::	nîlanân	nipîhtokwânân
itwêw	::	kîlawâw	kititwânâwâw
ihtâw	::	kîlawâw	kitihtânâwâw
pimâtisiw	::	wîlawâw	pimâtisiwak
walawîw	::	wîlawâw	walawîwak
išinihkâsow	::	nîlanân	nitišinihkâsonân
mawâpiw	::	kîlawâw	kimawâpinâwâw
itohtêw	::	kîlawâw	kititohtânâwâw
kihtohtêw	::	wîlawâw	kihtohtêwak
okimâwiw	::	nîlanân	nitôkimâwinân
pimâtisiw	::	wîlawâw	pimâtisiwak
walawîw	::	kîlawâw	kiwalawînâwâw
âhtakwêw	::	nîlanân	nitâhtakwânân
akihtâsow	::	wîlawâw	akihtâsowak

1.5 Substitution Drill. In the following drill answer the ni… subject with ki…, and vice versa: *e.g.,*

Cue: âšay nâ kinipânâwâw?
Response: êhê, âšay ninipânân.

or

Cue: âšay nâ n'ka-kî-nipânân?
Response: êhê, âšay ka-kî-nipânâwâw.

âšay nâ kinipânâwâw?	êhê, âšay ninipânân.
âšay nâ n'ka-walawînân?	êhê, âšay ka-walawînâwâw.
ka-tašîhkânâwâw nâ ôta?	êhê, n'ka-tašîhkânân ôta.
n'ka-tašîhkânân nâ ôta?	êhê, ka-tašîhkânâwâw ôta.
n'ka-pîhtokwânân nâ mâhkîhk?	êhê, ka-pîhtokwânâwâw mâhkîhk.
nâspic nâ kî-âhkosinâwâw?	êhê, nâspic n'kî-âhkosinân.
âšay nâ n'ka-apinân anta?	êhê, âšay ka-apinâwâw anta.
pêhkâc nâ ka-kî-ililîmonâwâw?	êhê, pêhkâc n'ka-kî-ililîmonân.
n'ka-kî-âhtakwânân nâ?	êhê, ka-kî-âhtakwânâwâw.

1.6 When the subject of the verb in the question is 3, reply with a 3p subject and vice versa: *e.g.,*

Cue:	âpatisiw nâ kistês?
Response:	môla, kotakiyak mâka âpatisiwak.

or

Cue:	âpatisiwak nâ kotakiyak?
Response:	môla, nistês mâka âpatisiw.

âpatisiwak nâ kotakiyak?	môla, nistês mâka âpatisiw.
nipâwak nâ kotakiyak?	nipâw
itohtêwak nâ kotakiyak?	itohtêw
akihtâsowak nâ kotakiyak?	akihtâsow
walawîwak nâ kotakiyak?	walawîw
ililîmow nâ kistês?	môla, kotakiyak mâka ililîmowak.
pîhtokwêw nâ kistês?	pîhtokwêwak
âhkosiw nâ kistês?	âhkosiwak
cimatâw nâ kistês?	cimatâwak
âhtakwêwak nâ kotakiyak?	âhtakwêw
wêmistikôšîmow nâ kistěs?	wêmistokôšîmowak
pimâtisiwak nâ kotakiyak?	pimâtisiw
ihtâw nâ kistês âšokanihk?	ihtâwak
šwâpihk nâ iši-âpatisiwak kotakiyak?	iši-âpatisiw

2. Transitive Inanimate Verbs (VTI + two VAI-T) with 1p, 2p and 3p subjects. Drill across each pair of columns. If you are using a recording, repeat after each recorded item.

2.1

1	1p	2	2p
niwâpahtên	niwâpahtênân	kiwâpahtên	kiwâpahtênâwâw
nikiskêlihtên	nikiskêlihtênân	kikiskêlihtên	kikiskêlihtênâwâw
nikîsisên	nikîsisênân	kikîsisên	kikîsisênâwâw
nikawinên	nikawinênân	kikawinên	kikawinênâwâw
ninakatên	ninakatênân	kinakatên	kinakatênâwâw
ninisitohtên	ninisitohtênân	kinisitohtên	kinisitohtênâwâw
nitayân	nitayânân	kitayân	kitayânâwâw
niwanihtân	niwanihtânân	kiwanihtân	kiwanihtânâwâw

2.2

3	3p
kiskêlihtam	kiskêlihtamwak
milwêlihtam	milwêlihtamwak
kîsisam	kîsisamwak
kawinam	kawinamwak
sêskipitam	sêskipitamwak
ayâw	ayâwak
wanihtâw	wanihtâwak

2.3 Show that you recognize the subject of the following verbs by citing the appropriate pronoun after the verb form: *e.g.,*

Cue: niwâpahtênân
Response: niwâpahtênân, nîlanân

	(Check column)
niwâpahtênân	niwâpahtênân, nîlanân
nakatamwak	wîlawâw
kikîsisênâwâw	kîlawâw
nikawinênân	nîlanân
milwêlihtamwak	wîlawâw
kinatawêlihtênâwâw	kîlawâw
nikîsisênân	nîlanân
kiwâpahtênâwâw	kîlawâw
ninisitohtênân	nîlanân
kiskêlihtamwak	wîlawâw
wâpahtamwak	wîlawâw
kikiskêlihtênâwâw	kîlawâw

2.4 Given the personal pronoun to indicate the subject, supply the appropriate verb form: *e.g.,*

Cue: kawinam :: nîlanân
Response: nikawinênân

			(Check column)
kawinam	::	wîlawâw	kawinamwak
kîsisam	::	wîlawâw	kîsisamwak
natawêlihtam	::	kîlawâw	kinatawêlihtênâwâw
milwêlihtam	::	kîlawâw	kimilwêlihtênâwâw
kiskêlihtam	::	nîlanân	nikiskêlihtênân
wâpahtam	::	nîlanân	niwâpahtênân
kîsisam	::	kîlawâw	kikîsisênâwâw

kawinam	::	nîlanân	nikawinênân
milwêlihtam	::	wîlawâw	milwêlihtamwak
nakatam	::	nîlanân	ninakatênân
sêskipitam	::	kîlawâw	kisêskipitênâwâw
nakatam	::	wîlawâw	nakatamwak

2.5 Substitution Drill. In the following drill, answer the ki... subject with ni... and vice-versa: e.g.,

Cue: âšay nâ kiwâpahtênâwâw?
Response: êhê, âšay niwâpahtênân.

or

Cue: âšay nâ n'ka-wâpahtênân?
Response: êhê, âšay ka-wâpahtênâwâw.

	(Check column)
âšay nâ kiwâpahtênâwâw?	êhê, âšay niwâpahtênân.
wîpac nâ ka-kawinênâwâw?	êhê, wîpac n'ka-kawinênân.
âšay nâ n'ka-nisitohtênân?	êhê, âšay ka-nisitohtênâwâw.
âšay nâ n'ka-kîsisênân mîcim?	êhê, âšay ka-kîsisênâwâw mîcim.
môla nâ kisâpêlihtênâwâw anta?	êhê, môla nisâpêlihtênân anta.
n'ka-nakatênân nâ anima cîman?	êhê, ka-nakatênâwâw anima cîmân.
nâspic nâ n'ka-milwêlihtênân ôma?	êhê, nâspic ka-milwêlihtênâwâw ôma.
mîna nâ ka-natawêlihtênâwâw nipiy?	êhê, mîna n'ka-natawêlihtênân nipiy.
pêhkâc nâ kî-sêskipitênâwâw cîmân?	êhê, pêhkâc n'kî-sêskipitênân cîmân.

2.6 Complete the fragment using the correct form of whatever verb occurs in the initial section. If you are using a recording, it will repeat the fragment twice, then give the correct response.

Cue: môla mâškôc n'ka-wâpahtênân, wîlawâw mâka ...
Response: ... wîlawâw mâka ta-wâpahtamwak.

		(Check column)
1.	môla mâškôc n'ka-wâpahtênân, wîlawâw mâka ...	ta-wâpahtamwak
2.	âšay ka-kî-kawinên mâhkiy. wîlawâw nêsta ...	ta-kî-kawinamwak
3.	mîna n'ka-kî-nakatênân cîmân anta. wîlawâw nêsta ...	ta-kî-nakatamwak
4.	mâškôc ka-milwêlihtên. wîlawâw mâka. môla ...	ta-milwêlihtamwak
5.	wîpac mâškôc n'ka-natawêlihtên kicîmân. kotakiyak nêsta ...	ta-natawêlihtamwak
6.	môla mâškôc kisâpêlihtênâwâw anta. kotakiyak nêsta môla nâspic ...	sâpêlihtamwak
7.	âšay n'ka-kîsisênân mîcim. wîlawâw nêsta ...	ta-kîsisamwak
8.	môla mâškôc ninisitohtênân. wîlawâw mâka ...	nisitohtamwak

3. Transitive Animate Verbs (VTA) with 1p, 2p and 3p subjects. Drill across each pair of columns. If you are using a recording, repeat after each recorded item.

3.1

1	1p	2	2p
niwâpamâw	niwâpamânân	kiwâpamâw	kiwâpamâwâw
nikîsiswâw	nikîsiswânân	kikîsiswâw	kikîsiswâwâw
nikawinâw	nikawinânân	kikawinâw	kikawinâwâw
ninakatâw	ninakatânân	kinakatâw	kinakatâwâw
nitayâwâw	nitayâwânân	kitayâwâw	kitayâwâwâw
niwanihâw	niwanihânân	kiwanihâw	kiwanihâwâw
ninisitohtawâw	ninisitohtawânân	kinisitohtawâw	kinisitohtawâwâw
nimiskawâw	nimiskawânân	kimiskawâw	kimiskawâwâw

3.2

3	3p
wâpamêw	wâpamêwak
kîsiswêw	kîsiswêwak
kawinêw	kawinêwak
sêskipitêw	sêskipitêwak
ayâwêw	ayâwêwak
miskawêw	miskawêwak
wanihêw	wanihêwak
nisitohtawêw	nisitohtawêwak

3.3 Show that you recognize the subject of the following verbs by citing the appropriate pronoun after the verb form: *e.g.,*

Cue: kikîsiswâwâw
Response: kikîsiswâwâw, kîlawâw

	(Check column)
niwâpamânân	niwâpamânân, nîlanân
kikîsiswâwâw	kîlawâw
nakatêwak	wîlawâw
nikiskêlimânân	nîlanân
kiwawêšihâwâw	kîlawâw
ayâwêwak	wîlawâw
nitayâwânân	nîlanân
kiwanihâwâw	kîlawâw
ninakatânân	nîlanân
nisitohtawêwak	wîlawâw
kimiskawâwâw	kîlawâw
nitayamihânân	nîlanân

3.4 Given the personal pronoun to indicate the subject, supply the appropriate verb form: *e.g.,*

Cue:	wâpamêw :: nîlanân
Response:	niwâpamânân

wâpamêw	::	wîlawâw	wâpamêwak
nakatêw	::	kîlawâw	kinakatâwâw
kîsiswêw	::	nîlanân	nikîsiswânân
kawinêw	::	wîlawâw	kawinêwak
ayâwêw	::	kîlawâw	kitayâwâwâw
wanihêw	::	nîlanân	niwanihânân
nisitohtawêw	::	wîlawâw	nisitohtawêwak
wâpamêw	::	nîlanân	niwâpamânân
nisitohtawêw	::	kîlawâw	kinisitohtawâwâw
wanihêw	::	kîlawâw	kiwanihâwâw
kiskêlimêw	::	wîlawâw	kiskêlimêwak
kawinêw	::	nîlanân	nikawinênân

3.5 In the following drill answer the ni… subject with ki…, and vice-versa: *e.g.,*

	Cue:	wîpac nâ n'ka-wâpamânân?
	Response:	êhê, wîpac ka-wâpamâwâw.
or	Cue:	wîpac nâ ka-wâpamâwâw?
	Response:	êhê, wîpac n'ka-wâpamânân.

	(Check column)
wîpac nâ ka-wâpamâwâw?	êhê, wîpac n'ka-wâpamânân.
mîna nâ ka-kiskêlimâwâw awa?	êhê, mîna n'ka-kiskêlimânân awa.
âšay nâ n'ka-nakatânân apwoy?	êhê, âšay ka-nakatâwâw apwoy.
nâspic nâ kimilwêlimâwâw atim?	êhê, nâspic nimilwêlimânân atim.
pêhkâc nâ n'ka-sêskipitânân?	êhê, pêhkâc ka-sêskipitâwâw.
mîna nâ n'ka-kiskêlimânân?	êhê, mîna ka-kiskêlimâwâw.
môla nâ kisâpêlimâwâw ana ililiw?	êhê, môla nisâpêlimânân ana ililiw.
âšay nâ kinakatâwâw âšokan?	êhê, âšay ninakatânân âšokan.
nâspic nâ n'ka-milwêlimânân okimâw?	êhê, nâspic ka-milwêlimâwâw okimâw.
môla nâ n'ka-kî-miskawânân awa?	êhê, môla ka-kî-miskawâwâw awa.
pêhkâc nâ ka-sêskipitâwâw?	êhê, pêhkâc n'ka-sêskipitânân.

3.6 Complete the fragment, using the correct form of whatever verb occurs in the initial section. If you are using a recording, it will provide the fragment twice, then give the correct response.

Cue: môla mâškôc ninisitohtawânân; wîlawâw mâka ...
Response: ... wîlawâw mâka nisitohtawêwak.

1.	môla mâškôc ninisitohtawânân; wîlawâw mâkâ ...	nisitohtawêwak
2.	tâpwê, môla n'kiskêlimânân; wîlawâw mâka ...	kiskêlimêwak
3.	môla mâškôc kisâpêlimâwâw; wîlawâw nêsta môla ...	sâpêlimêwak
4.	mâškôc n'ka-milwêlimânân; wîlawâw mâka môla ...	ta-milwêlimêwak
5.	âšay ka-kî-kawinâwâw; wîlawâw nêsta ...	ta-kî-kawinêwak
6.	wîpac mâškôc ka-kî-nisitohtawâwâw; wîlawâw mâka, môla ...	ta-kî-nisitohtawêwak
7.	môla mâškôc n'ka-kîsiswânân namês; wîlawâw mâka ...	ta-kîsiswêwak
8.	wîpac mâškôc ka-wâpamâwâw okimâw; wîlawâw mâka,môla ...	môla ta-wâpamêwak
9.	âšay niwawêšihânân âšokan; wîlawâw nêsta ...	wawêšihêwak
10.	kinwêš kitôhci-nakatâwâw šôliyân anta; wîlawâw mâka, môla kinwês ...	ohci-nakatêwak

4. Completed Aspect Marker

4.1 Drill the following questions, answering the first time through in the affirmative, the second time through in the negative. Only the negative replies are tabulated in the check column.

Cue: šwâpihk nâ kî-itohtêw?
Did he go to the store?
Response: (1st time) êhê, šwâpihk kî-itohtêw.
(2nd time) môla šwâpihk ohci-itohtêw.

		(Check column)
1.	šwâpihk nâ kî-itohtêw?	môla šwâpihk ohci-itohtêw.
2.	kî-wâpahtam nâ cîmâniliw?	môla ohci-wâpahtam cîmâniliw.
3.	kî-âhtakwêw nâ mâškôc?	môla mâškôc ohci-âhtakwêw.
4.	kî-wâpahtênâwâw nâ anima?	môla n't-ôhci-wâpahtênân anima.
5.	âšokanihk nâ n'kî-pêc'-îtohtânân?	môla âšokanihk kitôhci-pêc'-îtohtânâwâw.
6.	nâspic nâ kî-nipîwan anta?	môla nâspic ohci-nipîwan anta.
7.	kî-pôsiw nâ?	môla ohci-pôsiw.
8.	kî-nisitohtam nâ?	môla ohci-nisitohtam.

9. kî-pâhkwatinâw nâ? — môla ohci-pâhkwatinâw.
10. kî-âpatan nâ? — môla ohci-âpatan.

4.2 Drill the following negative questions with affirmative answers: *e.g.*,

Cue: môla nâ kitôhci-kiskêlimâw êntiriy?
Didn't you know Henry?
Response: tâpwê n'kî-kiskêlimâw êntiriy.
Certainly I knew Henry.

		(Check column)
1.	môla nâ kitôhci-kiskêlimâw êntiriy?	tâpwê n'kî-kiskêlimâw êntiriy.
2.	môla nâ kitôhci-kiskêlimâwâw êntiriy?	tâpwê n'kî-kiskêlimânân êntiriy.
3.	môla nâ ohci-kiskêlimêw ênt'rîwa?	tâpwê kî-kiskêlimêw ênt'rîwa.
4.	môla nâ n'tôhci-kiskêlimânân êntiriy?	tâpwê kî-kiskêlimâwâw êntiriy.
5.	môla nâ ohci-kiskêlimêwak ênt'rîwa?	tâpwê kî-kiskêlimêwak ênt'rîwa.
6.	môla nâ n'tôhci-kiskêlimâw êntiriy?	tâpwê kî-kiskêlimâw êntiriy.
7.	môla nâ n'tôhci-kiskêl'tên sîpiy?	tâpwê kî-kiskêl'tên sîpiy.
8.	môla nâ n'tôhci-kiskêl'tênân sîpiy?	tâpwê kî-kiskêl'tênâwâw sîpiy.
9.	môla nâ ohci-kiskêl'tam sîpîliw?	tâpwê kî-kiskêl'tam sîpîliw.
10.	môla nâ kitôhci-kiskêl'tên sîpiy?	tâpwê n'kî-kiskêl'tên sîpiy.
11.	môla nâ kitôhci-kiskêl'tênâwâw sîpiy?	tâpwê n'kî-kiskêl'tênân sîpiy.
12.	môla nâ ohci-kiskêl'tamwak sîpîliw?	tâpwê kî-kiskêl'tamwak sîpîliw.

5. Possessed Nouns: 1p, 2p and 3p personal possessors. As you practise the following drills note how the personal possessor prefixes and suffixes used with the noun resemble the verbal inflections. Also, note how animate nouns possessed by a third person add an /a/ to the suffix. Drill down each column, then across each row.

5.1 Animate Nouns

"our"	"your (pl.)"	"their"
nitâšokaninân	kitâšokaniwâw	otâšokaniwâwa
nišôliyâniminân	kišôliyânimiwâw	ošôliyânimiwâwa
ninamêsiminân	kinamêsimiwâw	onamêsimiwâwa
nitôkomâminân	kitôkimâmiwâw	otôkimâmiwâwa
nitâlahkonâminân	kitâlahkonâmiwâw	otâlahkonâmiwâwa
nimôsominân	kimôsomiwâw	omôsomiwâwa

nitêminân	kitêmiwâw	otêmiwâwa
nicawâšimišinân	kicawâšimišiwâw	ocawâšimišiwâwa
nitapwônân	kitapwôwâw	otapwôwâwa
nôhtâwînân	kôhtâwîwâw	ôhtâwîwâwa
nikâwînân	kikâwîwâw	okâwîwâwa
nistêsinân	kistêsiwâw	ostêsiwâwa

5.2 Inanimate Nouns

nicîmâninân	kicîmâniwâw	ocîmâniwâw
nimasinahikaninân	kimasinahikaniwâw	omasinahikaniwâw
nišwâpiminân	kišwâpimiwâw	ošwâpimiwâw
nimîcimiminân	kimîcimimiwâw	omîcimimiwâw
niwîyâsiminân	kiwîyâsimiwâw	owîyâsimiwâw
nisîpîminân	kisîpîmiwâw	osîpîmiwâw
nimâhkîminân	kimâhkîmiwâw	omâhkîmiwâw
ninipîminân	kinipîmiwâw	onipîmiwâw
nimêskanânân	kimêskanâwâw	omêskanâwâw
nîkinân	kîkiwâw	wîkiwâw

5.3 The recording will give you a series of nouns, each followed by a personal pronoun. Put the noun into the form required by the personal possessor denoted by the pronoun: *e.g.,*

Cue: cîmân :: nîlanân
Response: nicîmâninân

			(Check column)
cîmân	::	nîlanân	nicîmâninân
âšokan	::	kîlawâw	kitâšokaniwâw
namês	::	wîlawâw	onamêsimiwâwa
apwoy	::	nîlanân	nitapwônân
mîcim	::	kîlawâw	kimîcimimiwâw
mâhkiy	::	wîlawâw	omâhkîmiwâw
masinahikan	:	kîlawâw	kimasinahikaniwâw
mîcim	::	wîlawâw	omîcimimiwâw
ôhtâwiya	::	nîlanân	nôhtâwînân
wîki	::	kîlawâw	kîkiwâw
nipiy	::	nîlanân	ninipîminân

mêskanaw	::	wîlawâw	omêskanâwâw
šôliyân	::	kîlawâw	kišôliyânimiwâw
môs	::	wîlawâw	omôsomiwâwa
awâšiš	::	nîlanân	nicawâšimišinân

5.4 Reply to questions containing a ni... subject and / or personal possessor with ki... and vice-versa: *e.g.,*

Cue: n'ka-wâpamânân nâ n'kosisinân?
Response: tâpwê, âšay ka-wâpamâwâw kikosisiwâw.

		(Check column)
1.	n'ka-wâpamânân nâ n'kosisinân?	tâpwê, âšay ka-wâpamâwâw kikosisiwâw.
2.	kinatawêlimâwâw nâ kitapwôwâw?	... ninatawêlimânân ... nitapwônân
3.	kiwâpamâwâw nâ nitâšokaninân?	... niwâpamânân ... kitâšokaniwâw
4.	n'ka-miskawânân nâ kitêmiwâw?	... ka-miskawâwâw ... nitêminân
5.	ka-kawinâwâw nâ nitâšokaninân?	... n'ka-kawinânân ... kitâšokaniwâw
6.	n'ka-kî-ayâwânân nâ kitêmiwâw?	... ka-kî-ayâwâwâw ... nitêminân
7.	n'ka-nakatânân nâ kitapwôwâw anta?	... ka-nakatâwâw ... nitapwônân
8.	kî-wanihâwâw nâ nišôliyâniminân?	... n'kî-wanihânân ... kišôliyânimiwâw
9.	n'ka-kiskêlimânân nâ kitôkimâmiwâw?	... ka-kiskêlimâwâw ... nitôkimâminân

5.5. Answer the following questions on the model:

Cue: kiwâpamâwâw nâ kikosisiwâw?
Response: môla, kotakiyak mâka wâpamêwak okosisiwâwa.

1.	kiwâpamâwâw nâ kikosisiwâw?	môla, ... wâpamêwak okosisiwâwa
2.	kimilwêlimâwâw nâ kinamêsimiwâw?	... milwêlimêwak onamêsimiwâwa
3.	kikîsiswâwâw nâ kitâlahkonâmiwâw?	... kîsiswêwak otâlahkonâmiwâwa
4.	ka-kawinâwâw nâ kitâšokaniwâw?	... ta-kawinêwak otâšokaniwâwa
5.	ka-kî-miskawâwâw nâ kitêmiwâw?	... ta-kî-miskawêwak otêmiwâwa
6.	âšay nâ kitayâwâwâw kišôliyânimiwâw?	... ayâwêwak ošôliyânimiwâwa
7.	kî-wanihâwâw nâ kicawâšimišiwâw?	... kî-wanihêwak ocawâšimišiwâwa
8.	kinisitohtawâwâw nâ kistêsiwâw?	... nisitohtawêwak ostêsiwâwa
9.	mîna nâ ka-wâpamâwâw kôhtâwîwâw?	... ta-wâpamêwak ôhtâwîwâwa
10.	kiwâpahtênâwâw nâ kîkiwâw?	... wâpahtamwak wîkiwâw
11.	kikawinênâwâw nâ kimâhkîmiwâw?	... kawinamwak omâhkîmiwâw
12.	ka-kîsisênâwâw nâ kimîcimimiwâw?	... ta-kîsisamwak omîcimimiwâw

6. Complete the sentence with the object of the gender required by the verb.

			(Check column)
1.	(atim ~ mîcim)	âšay nâ kitayâwâwâw ....?	atim
2.	(wâskâhikan ~ ililiw)	môla niwâpahtênân	wâskâhikan
3.	(šôliyâna ~ wîyâsiliw)	mâškôc ta-natawêlihtam	wîyâsiliw
4.	(âšokana ~ wîki)	wîpac nâ ta-mîšahwêw ....?	âšokana
5.	(apwoy ~ cîmân)	môla mâškôc ka-kî-sêskipitênâwâw	cîmân
6.	(masinahikan ~ okimâw)	môšak ninâspitohtawânân	okimâw
7.	(cîmâniliw ~ apwoya)	âšokanihk iši-nakatam	cîmâniliw
8.	(nipiy ~ awâšiš)	âšay nâ n'ka-wâpamânân ....?	awâšiš
9.	(môso-wîyâs ~ âlahkonâw)	mîna nâ ka-kîsisênâwâw ....?	môso-wîyâs
10.	(namês ~ mîcim)	môla nâspic nimilwêlimânân	namês

D. CONVERSATION PRACTICE

1. Cover the Cree columns in the Basic Conversation and, looking at the English, be sure you can give the Cree equivalent without hesitation. Uncover the Cree line by line. Go through the whole conversation without stopping and mark difficult passages. Learn these thoroughly; then drill the conversation again as above. N.B.—Learn all new words in context. The list at the end of the unit is for reference only and is not to be memorized.

2. Review the drills, putting a check against items which still cause hesitation. Drill until you can handle each sequence smoothly.

3.a. Discuss the relative merits of upriver and downriver for fishing, fresh water, pitching a tent and why you decided to move camp.

3.b. Teach somebody how to count in Cree. Then discuss how many canoes the other person sees on the river and how many at the wharf. Ask where his or her friends are staying (tânt' êhtâcik? Where are they?) and whether they have been there a long time.

3.c. Talk about a child who is very sick and has been coughing and sneezing a great deal. You think that you know what is wrong, but you have no medicine. So tell your friend that you will take the child to the dispensary, that you will leave your canoe at the wharf and go to the store for some medicine. It is just past your tent, down the path (išiwil- VTA take him / her somewhere; išiwitâ- VAI-T take it somewhere; natohkolonikamikw- NI dispensary).

E. LISTENING IN

"Something's Going On"

Cwân:	kêkwân wîyâpahtaman anta?
Âniy:	môla n'kiskêl'tên. mâškôc matakwan kêkwân.
Cwân:	šâkoc mâka kitakihtâson.
Âniy:	êhê. âšay niwâpahtên kêkwân nêtê wâlaw, mâmihk sîpîhk.
Cwân:	cîmân mâškôc, êh?
Âniy:	môla. ihtakwan mâka piko kêkwân.
Cwân:	ihtâwak mâka šišôtêw sîmyan nêsta owîkimâkana.
Âniy:	šišôtêw nâ kî-iši-cimatâwak omâhkîmiwâw?
Cwân:	êhê, nôhcimihk kî-iši-âhtakwêwak.
Âniy:	môla nâspic milwâšin anta.
Cwân:	misiwê otêmiwâwa mâka kiyâpic nêtê kî-iši-nakatêwak.
Âniy:	tâpwê nâ? awasitê mâškôc milwâšin namêsak ohci.
Cwân:	tântê,—mâmihk nâ nêstapiko n'timihk?
Âniy:	namêsak ohci, mâmihk awasitê iši-milwâšin.
Cwân:	tân' êhtiyin? nâspic kitostostotên!
Âniy:	apišîš mâškôc n'tôtakikomin.
Cwân:	kin'tawêl'tên nâ ostostocikanâpoy? n'tayân nimâhkîmihk.
Âniy:	mîkwêc. wîpac mâškôc awasitê ta-milopaliw. n'ka-kawinênân nimâhkîminân. môla nâspic pâhkwatinâw ôta. n'timihk n'ka-iši-cimatânân.
Cwân:	awasitê ta-milwâšin n'titêl'tên. môla nâspic nisâpêl'tên nîla ôta astamitê šwâpihk.

F. REFERENCE LIST

akiht-	VTI	count s.t.
akihtâso-	VAI	count
akihtâson-	NI	number, numeral
akihtâsowin-	NI	number, numbering
akim-	VTA	count s.o.
âhtakwê-	VAI	move camp
âpatan-	VII	be useful
cimatâ-	VAI-T	erect s.t., pitch it (a tent), build it (a house)
êhtâcik	VAI chgd. conj. indic. < ihtâ-	that they are (there) [*with question words and dependent clauses:* tânt' êhtâcik? Where are they?]
išiwil-	VTA	take s.o. (somewhere)
išiwitâ-	VAI-T	take s.t. (somewhere)
...îk-	NDI	home, dwelling, *v.* kîki, nîki, wîki
kawin-	VTA / VTI	knock s.o./ s.t. down; *with* mâhkiy- break camp
kici	IPV + conjunct	so that, in order that
kitôtêm	NDA	your (2) friend v. nitôtêm-, otôtêma
kiyâpic	IPC	more, more of; still, yet. *v. alternate* kêyâpac
kî	IPV	*completed aspect or past time marker w. affirmative*
kîki	NDI	your (2) home *v.* nîki, wîki (<...îk-)
kîlawâw	PR [2nd pers. pl.]	you
lâlatin	IPC	on the bank (near water level)
misiwê	IPC	all
mitâhtw	IPC	ten: *variant of* mitâtaht, *q.v.*
mitâtaht	IPC	ten

nakat-	VTA / VTI	leave s.o./ s.t. behind
namês-	NA	fish
namêsak	NA pl.	fish
nanâmatin	IPC	on the bank (near water level) *Lake Winnipeg, N Dialect: v.* lâlâtin.
natimihk	IPC	upstream. *v.* mâmihk, U5.
nâspitoht-	VTI	imitate s.t.
nâspitohtaw-	VTA	imitate s.o.
nâspitohtawin	VTA imperative 2 - 1	say after me, imitate me
nêma	PR dem. inan prox.	yonder one, yon one (*more distant than* anima)
nêta	IPC	over yonder, yonder thereabouts
nêw	IPC	four
nikotwâsw	IPC	six
nipiy-	NI	water
nisto	IPC	three
nitôtêm-	NDA	my friend *v.* kitôtêm-, otôtêma
niyâlanw	IPC	five
niyânânêw	IPC	eight
nîki	NDI	my home *v.* kîki, wîki (<...îk-)
nîswâsw	IPC	seven
nîšo	IPC	two
nôhcimihk	IPC	in the bush, inland
ohci	IPV	*completed aspect or past time marker with negative v.* kî *and* ohci, Unit 4.
otôtêma	NDA	his / her friend: nitôtêm, kitôtêm, etc.
pâhkwatinâ-	VII	be dry ground, be a dry bank
pâhkwâ-	VII	be dry
pâhkwâhk	IPC	on the dry (part)
pêyakw	IPC	one
sâpêliht-	VTI	*with negative:* not be keen about s.t.
sâpêlim-	VTA	*with negative:* not be keen about s.o.
sêskipit-	VTA / VTI	pull s.o./ s.t. ashore, beach s.o./ s.t.
šâkitâtw	IPC	nine. *Cf.* šânkw.
šânkw	IPC	nine. *Cf.* šâkitâtw.
šišôtêw	NI and IPC	the shore, at the shore; edge of a plain
tânitahto	IPC	how many ...?

wîhtamaw-	VTA	tell s.o.
wîhtamawin	VTA imperative 2 - 1	tell me
wîki	NDI	his / her home: nîki, kîki, *etc.* (< ...îk-).
wîla	PR [3rd pers. sg.]	he, she; it
wîla	IPC intensive	*e.g.,* môla wîla anohc not NOW
wîlawâw	PR [3rd pers. pl.]	they
wîskâc	IPC	ever, at any time

G. REVIEW

6.A Kakwêcihkêmôwina—Questions

Answer the following questions using material from the Conversations and Drills. Do not reply merely, "êhê" or "môla".

1. tântê omâhkîmiwâw kitôtêmiwâwak?
2. tân'tahto-mâhkiya wiyâpahtaman?
3. awasitê nâ milwâšin anta namêsak ohci?
4. kikiskêlihtên nâ kitakihtâsowina?
5. kitililîmon nâ?
6. kiwâpahtên nâ nimâhkîminân?
7. wîskâc nâ kitakihtâson ê-'lilîmoyin?
8. tântê kimâhkîmiwâw?
9. kî-sêskipitên nâ nicîmâninân lâlatin?
10. kêkwân wiyâpahtaman âšokanihk?
11. nêtê nâ ihtakwan kîki?
12. kîla,—itwê kitakihtâsowina.
13. kî-wâpamâwak nâ nitêminânak?
14. n'ka-kawinên nâ kimâhkîmiwâw?
15. awasitê nâ milwêl'tamwak kitôtêmak n'timihk sîpîhk?
16. kêko cîmân mêlwêlihtaman, ôma nêstapiko kôhtâwiy ocîmân?
17. kî-nakatâw nâ n'tapwoy lâlatin?
18. môšak nâ kitakimâwak kicawâšimišak?
19. kî-miskên nâ nimasinahikan?
20. âšay nâ sîpîhk n'timihk kitihtânâwâw?

6.B Naskwêwašihtwâwina—Answers

Make up questions which may be answered by the following statements.

1. kî-sêskipitam pâhkwâhk.
2. môla wîskâc n'tôhci-kocihtân.
3. êhê, lâlatin ihtakwan.
4. âšay sîpîhk n'timihk ihtakwan.
5. misiwê n'cawâšimišak kêyâpac nêtê ihtâwak.
6. môla wîla milwâšin.
7. šâkoc niwâpahtên wâlaw mâmihk sîpîhk.
8. niwawêšihtân cîmân.
9. nôhcimihk ihtâwak.
10. êliwêhk tahkâyâw ôta!
11. tâpwê, n'kî-nakatênân wâskâhikan.
12. nikosis kêyâpac nêtê ihtâw.
13. môla. kî-nakatamwak šišôtêw.
14. nêtê piko.
15. êhê, n'kiskêl'tên.
16. apišîš piko n'tililîmon. n'kiskinohamâson mâka.
17. môla mwêhci n'kiskêl'tên. cîmân mâškôc.
18. môla mâškôc n'ka-kî-miskên.
19. môla. šwâpihk n'kî-iši-nakatâw.
20. môla šwâpihk n'tôhci-iši-nakatâw.
21. awasitê nimilwêl'tên kotakiy.

UNIT SEVEN

A. BASIC CONVERSATION

The Elusive Inclusive

Several short conversations between John and his wife, Annie.

1. Dripping Wet

Cwân:	pêtâpan	it is daybreak, dawn is coming
	âšay nâ pêtâpan?	Is it daybreak yet?
Âniy:	ati	(gradually) begin to—
	êhê, âšay ati-kîšikâw.	Yes, it's beginning to be day.
Cwân:	lipâci-kîšikâw	it's a drizzly day,—a dirty day
	kišâstaw	Gosh!
	kišâstaw! tâpwê lipâci-kîšikâw!	Gosh! What a drizzly day!
	môla kî-nipâw awênihkân ôta.	A fellow can't sleep here.
	kiwâpwayâninaw	our blanket (yours and mine)
	nipîwan	it is wet
	ohcikawin	it leaks (by dripping)
	ohcikawin nêsta kimâhkîminaw nêsta mâka nipîwan kiwâpwayâninaw.	Our tent is leaking and our blanket is wet.
Âniy:	wî	want to—
	kiwî-ati-ayamin	you want to begin talking
	kwantaw	pointlessly, trivially, at random
	âšay mîna kwantaw kiwî-ati-ayamin!	There you go, starting an argument!

2. How Many "We's"?

Âniy:	iškotêw ohci	for a fire
	kic'-îspaliyahk	that we (*you and I*) may so go, [that we may so get along
	mihta	logs
	kitayânânaw nâ mâka mihta kic'-îspaliyahk iškotêw ohci?[1]	Have we enough wood for a fire?
Cwân:	têpiskâk	last night
	n'kî-pâhpin	I laughed
	mihtihkân	woodpile
	kitayânânaw nîšo mihtihkâna. n'kî-pâhpin têpiskâk.	We (21) have two cords. I laughed last night.
Âniy:	wîyatwêw	he is joking
	kî-wîyatwânâwâw nâ misiwê âšokanihk?	Were you all joking at the wharf?
Cwân:	môla, môla kwantaw n'tôhci-wîyatwânân.	No, we weren't just fooling around telling jokes.
	okipahowêsiw	the policeman
	šôliyânikimâw nêsta anta kî-ihtâw nêsta mâka okipahowêsiw. pêci-mawâpiwak.	Both the Indian Agent and the policeman were there. They are visiting.
Âniy:	wîyatêlihtâkwan	it is funny
	ay'hâw, môla nâspic wîyatêlihtâkwan.	Well, that's not very funny!
Cwân:	walašawêwin	the law
	nâkacihtâw	he observes it, he attends to it
	êhê, okipahowêsiw mâka kî-itwêw, "awasitê n'ka-nâkacihtânân walašawêwin".	No, but the policeman said, "We (1p) must obey the law better".

[1] An alternative to kic'-îspaliyahk iškotêw ohci would be kê-pônihkâkêyahk "that we will make a fire using them". The construction will be introduced later when the conjunct order is discussed fully.

Âniy:	môla ohci-awêpaliw	he didn't make sense
	môla wayêš ohci-iši-awêpaliw.	He didn't make much sense.
	pîkonamwak	they break it
	okipahowêsiwak mâka šâkoc	Policemen don't break it.
	môla pîkonamwak.	
Cwân:	n'ka-nâkacihtânân	we (*excluding you*) must obey it
	ka-nâkacihtânânaw	we (*including you*) must obey it
	ispîš wîla	instead of it
	n'kiskêl'tên. okipahowêsiw	I know. But the policeman said,
	mâka kî-itwêw,	"We (*not you*) must obey it",
	"n'ka-nâkacihtânân", mâka,	instead of
	ispîš wîla, "ka-nâkacihtânânaw".	"We (*all of us*) must obey it".
Âniy:	kî(la)nânaw	we (*including you*)
	ayamiwiniliw	word
	(w)êmistikôšiwak	Englishmen
	kêkwân ohci	what for, why
	kikiskêl'tên nâ mâka kêkwân	Do you know why, though?
	ohci? êmistikôšiwak mâka	The English have only
	ayâwak pêyak piko	one word
	ayamiwiniliw "kî(la)nânaw"	for *you and us*
	ohci nêsta "nîlanân".	and *us, but not you.*
Cwân:	ê-wêmistikôšîmonâniwahk	in one's talking English
	pêyakwan	it is one, it is the same
	ê'ko n' âni?	is that it?
	ê'ko n' âni mâka pêyakwan	—and it's the same thing in
	ê-wêmistikôšîmonâniwahk:	English:
	"kî(la)nânaw"	*you-and-I* and
	nêsta "nîlanân"?	*we-but-not-you*?

3. (Mis)communication

Âniy:	macihtwâwin	sin, wickedness
	kî-tôtênânaw	we (*you and I*) have done it
	ayamihê'-kîšikâw	it is Sunday
	kâ	which (*relative*)
	kâ-kî-ayamihê'-kîšikâk	which was Sunday
	mâhcic	last
	mâhcic kâ-kî-ayamihê'-kîšikâk	last Sunday

	kikiskisin nâ mâhcic kâ-kî-ayamihê'-kîšikâk, ayamihêwikimâw kî-wî-itwêw: "misiwê kî-tôtênânaw macihtwâwin"?	Do you remember last Sunday, the parson wanted to say, "We (*including you*) have sinned"?
	kotakiyak kî-itwêw mâka, "n'kî-tôtênân", wîla nêsta mâškôc kotakiyak ayamihêwikimâwak.	the others But he said, "We (*not you*) have done it", —himself and perhaps some other clergy.
	itam âskaw itwêw, "nôhtâwînân"; tâpwê mâka wî-itam, "kôhtâwînaw".	he says it Sometimes he says, "Our (*not* *your*) Father", when he really means "Our (*and your*) Father".
Cwân:	kî-wani-tôtam.	He made a mistake, *lit.,* he mis-did it.
Âniy:	cikêmânima cikêmânima, kî-wanitôtam.	of course, naturally Of course, he made a mistake.
Cwân:	pîtoš wîhtamwak môla nâ kî-wîhtamwak pîtoš "kî(la)nânaw" nêsta "nîlanân"?	differently they tell it Can't they tell the difference between "us (*including you*)" and "us (*but not you*)"?
	nisitohtâtowak ayamihítowak šâkoc ayamihitowak. kî-nisitohtâtowak nâ mâka?	they understand each other they talk to each other They certainly talk to each other. But can they understand each other?
Âniy:	nikêhcinâhon êhê, mâškôc; môla mâka n'kêhcinâhon.	I am sure Yes, perhaps; but I'm not sure.

B. DISCUSSION OF GRAMMAR

1. Verbs

1.1 Contrast Between 1p and 21 Subjects

Cree, unlike English, makes a distinction between "we", excluding "you", and "we", including "you". Compare the two forms,

	nimawâpinân	we (*but not you*) are visiting
and	**kimawâpinânaw**	we (*including you*) are visiting.

In the first the prefix, ni... denotes that the the addressee is excluded. In the second, ki... indicates inclusion of the person(s) addressed in the "we". 2p "you pl." and 21 both include the addressee, and so share the prefix, ki... The contrast between 2p and 21 is maintained by different inflectional suffixes:

	kimawâpinânaw	we (21) are visiting,
vs.	**kimawâpinâwâw**	you (2p) are visiting.

The paradigm for all eight personal animate subjects is as follows:

	VAI		VTI			VTA		
3		...w		...am	[0′]		...êw	[3′]
3p		...wak		...amwak	[0′]		...êwak	[3′]
3′		...ɩliwa[1]		...amiliwa	[0″]		...êliwa	[3″]
1	ni(t)	...n	ni(t)	...ên	[0]	ni(t)	...âw	[3]
2	ki(t)	...n	ki(t)	...ên	["]	ki(t)	...âw	["]
1p	ni(t)	...nân	ni(t)	...ênân	["]	ni(t)	...ânân	["]
21	ki(t)	...nânaw	ki(t)	...ênânaw	["]	ki(t)	...ânaw	["]
2p	ki(t)	...nâwâw	ki(t)	...ênâwâw	["]	ki(t)	...âwâw	["]

(Objects for VTI and VTA are listed in square brackets after each form.)

[1]...ɩliwa >...liwa after vowel. *v.* Appendix 2, fn. 3.

Study the following examples:

1.	n'kî-wîyatwânân piko.	We (*but not you*) were only joking.
2.	têpiskâk kî-ayamihitonânaw.	We (*you and I*) spoke to each other last night.
3.	tâpwê nâ ka-itâpicînâwâw?	Is it true that you (2p) will be away?
4.	âšay mâka niwâpahtênân mêskanaw nîlanân.	But now we (*not you*) see the path.
5.	môla mâškôc kwayask kî-sêskipitênâwâw kîlawâw.	Perhaps you (2p) didn't beach it properly.
6.	môla kiwî-wani-tôtênânaw kîlanânaw.	We (*you and I*) don't want to make a mistake.
7.	n'kî-wanihânân atim nêtê akâmihk.	We (*not you*) lost the dog over across the water.
8.	kišâstaw! kî-pîkonânaw apwoy.	Gosh! We (*you and I*) 've broken the paddle.
9.	âšay kitati-nisitohtawâwâw.	Now you (2p) are beginning to understand him.
10.	wîpac n'ka-kawinênân mâhkiy.	We (*not you*) 'll soon break camp (*lit.,* knock the tent down).
11.	šwâpihk nâ kitiši-nakatânaw awâšiš?	Are we (*you and I*) leaving the child at the store?
12.	tâpwê mâka kî-kîsiswâwâw ana môs!	You (2p) certainly cooked that moose!

———DRILLS 1.1 THROUGH 1.5———

1.2 Verbal Prefixes: **ati, wî**

The prefix particle, ati, is used to indicate gradual onset rather than a sudden beginning: *e.g.,*

kimiwan	it is raining
ati-kimiwan	it is beginning to rain

ati precedes the main verb stem and follows the subject prefixes, ni..., ki..., if any. It also follows the various aspect markers, ka / ta; kî / ohci, etc.: *e.g.,*

wîpac mâškôc n'ka-ati-itohtân.	I shall probably soon begin to go (there).
ta-ati-kimiwan.	It will begin to rain.
âšay ati-milo-kîšikâw.	It's already beginning to be a good day.

wî, like **ati**, precedes the main verb stem and follows subject prefixes and / or aspect markers. It denotes intended or desired action and is translated "want to..., going to...": *e.g.,*

nipâw	he sleeps
wî-nipâw	he wants to sleep
ta-wî-nipâw	he will want to sleep.

It also covers the same area of meaning as the English "going to... ": *e.g.,*

wî-kimiwan	it is going to rain.

These prefixes, which may be added to what is already a full verb form, are known as *preverbs*. Their occurrence is extremely common: *e.g.,*

ati-âpatisiw	he is (gradually) beginning to work
wî-âpatisiw	he wants to work
iši-âpatisiw	he so works (*referring back to a locating expression*).

In Cree syllabic spelling preverbs are often written as separate words, even though they function somewhat like forms such as "sub-" in English "sub-committee", or "mis-" in "misspell". Indeed, a partial analogy to the use of preverbs is the use of certain English prefixes with an otherwise independent verb form of which they then become an integral part: *viz.,*

meditated
premeditated
unpremeditated

Other particles such as pêci (*v.* pêci-mawâpiwak) are also preverb forms, as are the aspect markers. Order of occurrence, including that of the personal prefixes, may be charted as follows:

ni... ki...	ka / ta kî / ohci	wî	ıši	kakwê pêci ati	Base Verb Stem	Inflectional Suffix(es)

Some preverbs, like pêci, ati, kakwê, display a greater freedom of position in relation to other preverb components. The meaning of the total form will usually determine this without ambiguity.

Personal prefixes and *inflectional suffixes* belong to an outer layer of word building. A noun or verb stem can remain very much the same in shape and function while *inflectional* prefixes and suffixes are added at will to denote different subjects or possessors (and, in the case of transitive verbs, objects). *Preverb particles*, however, belong to a more internal layer of word building and operate as an integral part of the compound stem which they help form. In standard Roman transcription, elements forming compound stems (*e.g.*, a particle prefix and a verb stem) are joined by hyphens. (See "Cree Grammar," *Composition*, p. xxxiv) Inflectional and derivational elements are normally written without any linking device: nicîkahikanâhtik my axe-handle. In citation form or when separated to make recognition easier, they are preceded or followed in this book by the triple point, ... : *e.g.*, ni..., ...âhtik.

———DRILLS 2.1 AND 2.2———

1.3 Reciprocal Construction

The reciprocal form of the verb is obtained by adding to the VTA stem the reciprocal stem builder, ...ιto... plus the regular VAI inflectional suffixes: *e.g.*,

wâpamêwak	they see him
wâpamι**to**wak	they see each other
nitayamihâw	I speak to him
nitayamihι**to**nân	we (1p) speak to each other

When a VTA stem ending in /aw/ and the reciprocal stem with initial /ι/ come together to produce the sequence, /awι/, this is contracted to /â/: *e.g.*, nisitoht**aw**ιtowak contracts to nisitoht**â**towak they understand each other.

———DRILL 3———

2. Nouns

2.1 Contrast Between 1p and 21 Possessors

The distinction in Cree between "we - *exclusive*" (1p) and "we - *inclusive*" (21) holds for personal possessors as well as for verb-subjects. One must specify in Cree whether the addressee is included or not in the "we" or "our". (The distinction is an obligatory one, imposed by the structure of the language, and provides an interesting example of how linguistic structures lead us to make certain forced observations.)

The following paradigm is the pattern for a possessed noun, independent stem, both NA and NI.

ni(t)	Noun Stem	(...ιm)	...ø ...ιnân
ki(t)			...ø ...ιnaw ...ιwâw
o(t)			...ø[NI], ...a[NA] ...ιwâw, ...ιwâwa ...ιlîw

(Obviative markers are shown for o(t)... possessor only. Locative suffix is not included.)

3. Pronouns

3.1 Personal Pronouns

To the personal pronouns introduced in the last unit must now be added kîlanânaw, we (*including you*). Throughout most of the N-Dialect area, the form heard is the contracted kînânaw, as on the recording.

———DRILLS 4.1 AND 4.2———

3.2 Intensive **êwako** + Demonstratives

êwako (ê'ko), coupled with the demonstratives which you have already learned, awa and ôma, creates the intensive use: "this *or* that very (one)", "this *or* that selfsame (one)". The translation may sound archaic in English, but is of regular occurrence in Cree where emphasis is required. Apart from an infrequently occurring obviative, êwako by itself is indeclinable.

	Animate		Inanimate
Proximate:	ê'kwâwa ê'kwâna	(êwakwâwa) etc.	ê'kôma ê'kwânima *or* ê'kwâni
Obviative:	ê'kôho ê'kwânihi		ê'kômêliw ê'kwânimêliw

Obviative forms such as ê'kwânimêliw are formed on the pattern of the simple demonstratives. Where the complex forms are used predicatively: *e.g.*, ê'kwânima "That is the one", the corresponding question is normally

êwako nâ awa?
ôko?
ôho?
etc.

The reply is then êhê, ê'kwâwa..., and so for the other forms.

4. Particles: Affirmative, êhê; Negative, môla

Frequent confusion arises between speakers of Cree and English over the difference in use between êhê, "yes" and môla, "no". Study the following exchanges.

i.	Question:	ta-milo-kîšikâw nâ?	Will it be a fine day?
	Reply:	*êhê,* nâspic ta-milo-kîšikâw.	*Yes,* it will be a very fine day.
		môla, môla ta-milo-kîšikâw.	*No,* it will not be a fine day.

To a straightforward query requiring a simple affirmative or negative answer the Cree speaker replies êhê, or môla, much as an English speaker would answer "yes" or "no". Now, contrast the next two exchanges with the one above.

ii.	Question:	môla nâspic milo-kîšikâw, manâ?	It's not a very good day, is it?
	Reply:	*êhê,* môla nâspic milo-kîšikâw.	*No,* it's not a very good day.
	Question:	môla mâškôc ta-milo-kîšikâw, manâ?	It probably won't be a fine day, will it?
	Reply:	*môla,* nâspic ta-milo-kîšikâw.	*Yes,* it will be a very fine day.

In Example ii., êhê and môla are better thought of as the rough equivalents of the English "Right" or "Wrong", indicating agreement or disagreement with the statement submitted by the first speaker. The last exchange above might be reworded in English:

Question:	It probably won't be a fine day, will it?
Reply:	*Wrong,* it will be a very fine day.

———DRILLS 6.1 THROUGH 6.3———

êhê is normally heard under much the same form in Moose (L-Dialect) and Swampy Cree (N-Dialect). môla, however, is a contraction of namawila, the form under which it is encountered in the written language or occasionally in solemn speech. Colloquial use ranges through nam', nama, nam'wac, namawila to môla (môna, *i.e.,* contracted namawina, in the N-Dialect) depending on the area.

C. DRILLS

1. Contrast between 1p and 21 Subjects

1.1 Mimic the recording, first down each column, then across each row.

	1p (we—but not you)	**21** (we—including you)
VAI	nitayami**nân**	kitayami**nânaw**
	nipâhpinân	kipâhpinânaw
	niwîyatwânân	kiwîyatwânânaw
	nitayamihitonân	kitayamihitonânaw
	niwalawînân	kiwalawînânaw
VTI	niwâpaht**ênân**	kiwâpaht**ênânaw**
	nikîsisênân	kikîsisênânaw
	nipîkonênân	kipîkonênânaw
	ninakatênân	kinakatênânaw
	nimiskênân	kimiskênânaw
VTA	niwâpam**ânân**	kiwâpam**ânaw**
	nikîsiswânân	kikîsiswânaw
	nikawinânân	kikawinânaw
	nimiskawânân	kimiskawânaw
	nitayâwânân	kitayâwânaw

1.2 Drill the following question-answer series, contrasting the 1p and 21 subjects, on the model:

Question: n'ka-âpatisinân nâ, nîlanân piko?
Reply: môla. misiwê ka-âpatisinânaw.

The recording will check you. The check column contains the correct form of the verb.

	(Check column)
n'ka-âpatisin nâ, nîlanân piko?	ka-âpatisinânaw
n'ka-nipânân nâ, nîlanân piko?	ka-nipânânaw
n'ka-ililîmonân nâ, nîlanân piko?	ka-ililîmonânaw
n'ka-pîhtokwânân nâ, nîlanân piko?	ka-pîhtokwânânaw
n'ka-walawînân nâ, nîlanân piko?	ka-walawînânaw
n'ka-ayamihitonân nâ, nîlanân piko?	ka-ayamihitonânaw
n'ka-âhtakwânân nâ, nîlanân piko?	ka-âhtakwânânaw
n'ka-kihtohtânân nâ, nîlanân piko?	ka-kihtohtânânaw

1.3 Drill as above, on the model:

Question: âšay nâ n'ka-wâpahtên?
Reply: êhê, tâpiskôc (together) ka-wâpahtênânaw.

âšay nâ n'ka-wâpahtên?	ka-wâpahtênânaw
âšay nâ n'ka-miskên?	ka-miskênânaw
âšay nâ n'ka-sêskipitên?	ka-sêskipitênânaw
âšay nâ n'ka-nakatên?	ka-nakatênânaw
âšay nâ n'ka-pîkonên?	ka-pîkonênânaw
âšay nâ n'ka-kawinên?	ka-kawinênânaw
âsay nâ n'ka-wani-tôtên?	ka-wani-tôtênânaw
âšay nâ n'ka-kîsisên?	ka-kîsisênânaw

1.4 Continue as above, but on the model,

Question: wîpac nâ n'ka-ayamihânân?
Reply: êhê, kîlawâw nêsta nîla, ka-ayamihânaw.

wîpac nâ n'ka-ayamihânân?	ka-ayamihânaw
wîpac nâ n'ka-miskawânân?	ka-miskawânaw
wîpac nâ n'ka-wâpamânân?	ka-wâpamânaw
wîpac nâ n'ka-wawêšihânân?	ka-wawêšihânaw
wîpac nâ n'ka-kîsiswânân?	ka-kîsiswânaw
wîpac nâ n'ka-kiskêlimânân?	ka-kiskêlimânaw
wîpac nâ n'ka-kawinânân?	ka-kawinânaw
wîpac nâ n'ka-wanihânân?	ka-wanihânaw

1.5 Repeat and complete the fragment with the proper form from the bracket. The correct form is both on the recording and in the check column.

		(Check column)
1.	kîlanânaw, wîpac tâpiskôc (n'ka-itohtânân ~ ka-itohtânânaw)	ka-itohtânânaw
2.	nîla nêsta niwîkimâkan, môla mâškôc (ka-âhtakwânânaw ~ n'ka-âhtakwânân)	n'ka-âhtakwânân
3.	nîlanân piko (nikiskêlimânân ~ kikiskêlimânaw)......	nikiskêlimânân
4.	nêsta kîlanânaw (ka-kî-sêskipitênânaw ~ n'ka-kî-sêskipitênân)......	ka-kî-sêskipitênânaw
5.	kîla nêsta mâka nîla, tâpiskôc (n'kî-miskênân ~ kî-miskênânaw)......	kî-miskênânaw
6.	nimis nêsta nîla, wîpac (ka-kîsiswânaw ~ n'ka-kîsiswânân)......	n'ka-kîsiswânân
7.	môla wîskâc ka-wanihâw; nîlanân mâka (ka-wanihânaw ~ n'ka-wanihânân)......	n'ka-wanihânân
8.	âšay nâ kinatawêlihtên ôma mâhkiy? niwîkimâkan nêsta nîla môla (kitôhci-sâpêlihtênânaw ~ nitôhci-sâpêlihtênân)......	nitôhci-sâpêlihtênân

2. Prefix Particles: **ati, iši**

2.1 **ati** "begin to -". Drill the following question-answer series on the model,

Question: âšay nâ ohcistin?
Reply: môla. wîpac mâka ta-ati-ohcistin.

	(Check column)
âšay nâ ohcistin?	môla. wîpac mâka ta-ati-ohcistin.
âšay nâ otâkošin?	...... ta-ati-otâkošin.
âšay nâ lipâci-kîšikâw?	...... ta-ati-lipâci-kîšikâw.
âšay nâ tipiskâw?	...... ta-ati-tipiskâw.
âšay nâ tahkâyâw?	...... ta-ati-tahkâyâw.
âšay nâ maci-kîšikâw?	...... ta-ati-maci-kîšikâw.
âšay nâ kimiwan?	...... ta-ati-kimiwan.
âšay nâ pêtâpan?	...... ta-ati-pêtâpan.

2.2 **iši** with a preceding, locating particle. You will remember that when a locating particle precedes the verb, the verb takes the prefix iši, referring back to the particle. The following drill is not recorded but the check column provides the correct verb form.

Question: kiwâpamâw nâ nitêm anta?
Reply: êhê, anta n'tiši-wâpamâw kitêm.

		(Check column)
1.	kiwâpamâw nâ nitên anta?	êhê, anta n'tiši-wâpamâw kitêm.
2.	wâpamêw nâ otêma anta?	iši-wâpamêw
3.	wâpamêliwa nâ ostêsa otêmilîw anta?	iši-wâpamêliwa
4.	n'ka-âpatisin nâ ôta?	êhê, ôta ka-iši-âpatisin.
5.	ka-âpatisinânaw nâ ôta?	ka-iši-âpatisinânaw
6.	kî-nakatamwak nâ ocîmâniwâw nêtê?	êhê, nêtê kî-iši-nakatamwak ocîmâniwâw.
7.	kî-nakatênâwâw nâ nicîmân nêtê?	n'kî-iši-nakatênân
8.	n'ka-nakatênân nâ kicîmân nêtê?	ka-iši-nakatênâwâw

3. Reciprocal formation with ...ıto-. In your reply make the appropriate change of subject for the reciprocal form: *e.g.,*

Question: kiskêlimêw nâ?
Does she know him?
Reply: tâpwê, kiskêlimitowak.
Certainly, they know each other.

1. kiskêlimêw nâ? — tâpwê, kiskêlimitowak.
2. n'ka-milwêlimânân nâ? — tâpwê, ka-milwêlimitonâwâw.
3. kî-ayamihâw nâ? — tâpwê, n'kî-ayamihitonân.
4. ka-kî-wâpamitin [I...see you] nâ? — tâpwê, ka-kî-wâpamitonânaw.
5. ka-kî-miskâtin [I...find you] nâ? — tâpwê, ka-kî-miskâtonânaw.
6. kî-nâspitohtawâw nâ? — tâpwê, n'kî-nâspitohtâtonân.
7. nisitohtawêw nâ? — tâpwê, nisitohtâtowak.
8. n'ka-kî-nisitohtawânân nâ? — tâpwê, ka-kî-nisitohtâtonâwâw.

4. Contrast between 1p and 21 possessors

4.1 Mimic the recording, first down each column, then across each row.

1p (ours, but not yours)	**21** (ours, yours and mine)
nicîmâninân	kicîmâninaw
nitâšokaninân	kitâšokaninaw
nitiškotêminân	kitiškotêminaw
nicawâšimišinân	kicawâšimišinaw
nitêminân	kitêminaw
nîkinân	kîkinaw
nikâwînân	kikâwînaw
nimêskanânân	kimêskanânaw

4.2 Drill the following question-answer exchanges, contrasting the 1p and 21 possessors, on the following model. Where the subject in the question is 21, answer with a 1p subject and vice-versa: *e.g.,*

Question: kîlanânaw nâ kicîmâninaw ôma?
Answer: môla; nîlanân piko nicîmâninân.

		(Check column)
1.	kîlanânaw nâ kicîmâninân ôma?	nicîmâninân
2.	kîlanânaw nâ kitâšokaninaw awa?	nitâšokaninân
3.	nîlanân nâ nitêminân awa?	kitêminaw
4.	nîlanân nâ nimêskanânân ôma?	kimêskanânaw
5.	kîlanânaw kimâhkîminâw ôma?	nimâhkîminân
6.	nîlanân nâ nitôkimâminân awa?	kitôkimâminaw
7.	kîlanânaw nâ kîkinaw ôma?	nîkinân
8.	nîlanân nâ niwâskâhikaniminân ôma?	kiwâskâhikaniminaw

5. Complete each partial sentence by filling in the blank with an appropriate word from the following list:

lipâci-kîšikâw, n'kî-pâhpinân, wîyatêlihtâkwan, kîlanânaw, nikêhcinâhon, ohcikawin, ê'kwâni pêyakwan, kitayânânaw, n'ka-nâkacihtânân, kî-nisitohtâtowak.

Cwân: kišâstaw! tâpwê __________-___________! ______________ nêsta kimâhkîminaw.
Âniy: ______________ nâ mâka mihta kic'-îspaliyahk iškotêw ohci?
Cwân: êhê. ______________ misiwê âšokanihk têpiskâk. okipahowêsiw kî-itwêw, "________________" walašawêwin, ispîš wîla "ka-nâkacihtânânaw".

Âniy:	tâpwê ______________. pêyak piko ayamiwiniliw ayâwak wêmistikôšiwak, "__________" ohci, nêsta "nîlanân".
Cwân:	môla nâ kî-wîhtamwak pîtoš "kîlanânaw" nêsta "nîlanân"?
Âniy:	_______ _______ ê-wêmistikôšîmonâniwahk.
Cwân:	šâkoc ayamihitowak. ___________ nâ mâka?
Âniy:	êhê, mâškôc; môla mâka ___________.

6. **êhê** versus **môla**

6.1. In B.4.ii, p. 170, êhê is translated as "no" and môla as "yes". Drill the following question-answer sequence on the model given. Note that you are *agreeing* with the speaker in each case; so the answer will be êhê, with repetition of the statement.

Question: môla nâspic milo-kîšikâw, manâ?
Reply: êhê, môla nâspic milo-kîšikâw.

môla nâspic milo-kîšikâw, manâ?
môla nâspic kimiwan, manâ?
môla nâspic tahkâyâw, manâ?
môla nâspic nipîwan, manâ?
môla nâspic lipâci-kîšikâw, manâ?
môla nâspic natawêlihtâkwan [necessary], manâ?
môla nâspic wîyatêlihtâkwan, manâ?
môla nâspic milwâšin, manâ,?

How would you translate êhê into English in this drill?

6.2 When you have drilled the above set, repeat the sequence on the model below, expressing *disagreement* with the basic assumption of the speaker. Think of the meaning as you drill.

Question: môla mâškôc ta-milo-kîšikâw, mana?
Reply: môla. nâspic ta-milo-kîšikâw.

môla mâškôc ta-milo-kîšikâw, manâ?
môla mâškôc ta-ohcistin, manâ?
môla mâškôc ta-kišitêw, manâ?
môla mâškôc ta-kimiwan, manâ?
môla mâškôc ta-pâhkwatinâw, manâ?
môla mâškôc ta-milwâšin, manâ?
môla mâškôc ta-tahkâyâw, manâ?
môla mâškôc ta-âpatan, manâ?

How would you translate môla into English in the above?

6.3 Reply to each question, indicating agreement or disagreement with the speaker's initial statement, as shown in the brackets. The recording will give the correct reply. êhê and môla only are shown in the check column.

Cue:	môla nâspic kišitêw, manâ?	
Response:	êhê, môla nâspic kišitěw.	
		(Check column)
(Agree)	môla nâspic kišitêw, manâ?	êhê
(Agree)	môla nâspic nipîwan, manâ?	êhê
(Disagree)	môla mâškôc ta-milo-kîšikâw, manâ?	môla
(Disagree)	môla mâškôc ta-âpatan, manâ?	môla
(Agree)	môla nâspic ohci-šâpopêkan [ground was wet], manâ?	êhê
(Disagree)	môla nâspic ohci-pîkopaliw, manâ?	môla
(Disagree)	môla mâškôc mîna ka-kî-wawêšihâw, manâ?	môla
(Agree)	môla kiyâpic ka-natawêlihtênâwâw, manâ?	êhê
(Agree)	môla wîskâc n'tôhci-wâpahtên, manâ?	êhê
(Disagree)	môla mâškôc šwâpihk ka-itohtân, manâ?	môla
(Agree)	môla nâspic ohcistin, manâ?	êhê
(Agree)	môla mâškôc nâspic ta-milwâšin, manâ?	êhê
(Disagree)	môla âšay nâspic n'tawêl'tâkwan, manâ?	môla
(Agree)	môla mâškôc mîna ka-wâpamânaw, manâ?	êhê
(Disagree)	môla mâškôc ta-pâhkwatinâw, manâ?	môla
(Disagree)	môla wîskâc ohci-ayâwêw šôliyâna, manâ?	môla

D. CONVERSATION PRACTICE

1. Cover the Cree column in the Basic Conversation and, looking only at the English column, say the corresponding Cree line aloud. Uncover the Cree, line by line, to check yourself. If there are any points at which you get stuck, mark them and keep going.
Then go back and drill the sections you have marked until you can look at the English and give the Cree equivalent.
Return to the beginning and repeat the whole conversation as above.

2. Check the drills for difficulties. Practise with another person if possible or with the recording; but be sure you can make the correct responses without hesitation.

3.1 Discuss your favourite spot for a campsite: upstream *vs.* downstream and why you prefer one (awasitê niminwêlihtên) to the other.

3.2 Grumble about the weather, the leaking tent, the spot you selected for your tent and why. Discuss the English speakers who can't distinguish between "us (*you and me*)" and "us (*but not you*)".

> they get it wrong - wani-tôtamwak;
> they (don't) include themselves - (môla) ašitakimowak;
> they say (things) backwards when they first talk Cree -
> naspâc [back to front] itwêwak ê-ililîmocik oskac [at first].

Recall the mistake made by the policeman. He said, "We (*but not you*) must obey the law." But he was talking nonsense: policemen don't break it. - môla pîkonamwak. Perhaps they understand each other, but you're not sure.

3.3 Compare someone else's tent, canoe, etc., with your own or with a friend's. Talk about the number of canoes, dogs, paddles, etc., which you have.

E. LISTENING IN

Côsipîn: âšay pêci-nôkosiw kišîm.[1] nâspic wîyatêl'tâkosiw.
Pâtniy: tâpwê. môšak wîyatwêw.
Côsipîn: niwî-mîlâw[2] masinahikaniliw. nawac wîyatêl'tâkwan ôma masinahikan.
Pâtniy: môla mâškôc ta-ayamihtâw,[3] n'titêl'tên. wîpac wî-kihtohtêw.
Côsipîn: tâpwê, môla wîlâhpahk. môla nêsta nîla nâspic nisâpêl'tên ôma masinahikan.
Pâtniy: ka-itohtânânaw šwâpihk. môla manâ wîlâta[4] ka-âpatisin, manâ?
Côsipîn: êhê, êškwâ[5] nakiskaw mâka. niwî-têpwâtâw[6] pitamâ ninâpêm.[7] "êtiy, šwâpihk n'titohtân. kin'tawêl'tên nâ kêkwân anta ohci?
Etiy: môla wîla anohc mwêhci. ohcikawin mâhkiy, niwî-mîšahên mâka. êliwêhk mâka lipâci-kîšikâw. môšak ohcikawin ôma mâhkiy, môla nêsta pâhkwatinâw......
Pâtniy: tâpwê êlikohk[8] ayamiw kwantaw.
Côsipîn: kwantaw piko wîyatwêw, môla tâpwê.[9] nâspic milwêl'tam ôta. tântê mâka kîla kicîmân? ka-kî-âpacihtânânaw nâ?
Pâtniy: cikêmanima. kî-nakatam lâlatin ninâpêm.
Côsipîn: kî-ihtâw ôta šôliyânikimâw.
Pâtniy: kêkwân ohci?
Côsipîn: wîla nêsta okipahowêsiw kî-pêci-mawâpiwak.
Pâtniy: kiskinohamâsow kici-ililîmot.[10]
Côsipîn: n'kiskêl'tên. âskaw môla kwayask kî-itwêw ê-ayamit. êmistikôšiwak môla kî-wîhtamwak pîtoš kî'nânaw nêsta nîlanân.
Pâtniy: ê-wêmistikôšîmonâniwahk pêyak ê'ko ihtakwan ayamiwin.

[1] pêci-nôkosiw—he's coming into view
[2] niwî-mîlâw—I want to give him
[3] ayamihtâw—VAI-T he reads it, "addresses" it
[4] wîlâta—nonetheless
[5] êškwâ—yet
[6] niwî-têpwâtâw—I want to call him
[7] ninâpêm—my husband. *v.* nâpêw.
[8] êlikohk—vigorously, a great deal
[9] môla tâpwê—not seriously
[10] kici-ililîmot—that he speak Cree: *i.e.* to speak Cree

Côsipîn:	okipahowêsiw kî-itwêw, "n'ka-nîkacihtânân walašawêwin", ispîš wîla, "ka-nâkacihtânânaw".
Pâtniy:	kocihtâw wîlâta. ê'kwâni milwâšin.
Côsipîn:	êmistikôšiwak môšak otânâhk itêhkê[11] âpacihtâwak ê-ayamicik oskac, tâpiskôc[12] ê-wêmistikôšîmonâniwahk.
Pâtniy:	môla n'kiskêl'tên kêkwân ohci.
Côsipîn:	otânâhk itêhkê itêl'tamwak. ê'kwâni ohci.
Pâtniy:	ayamihitowak mâka, šâkoc!
Côsipîn:	tâpwê! šâkoc mâka otânâhk itêhkê ka-itêl'tên 'ci-nisitohtaman.

[11] Other speakers preferred naspâc for, "back to front, backwards, wrong way to"

[12] tâpiskôc—as, like

F. REFERENCE LIST

ašitakimo-	VAI	count oneself in, include oneself
ati	IPV	(gradually) begin to. *e.g.*, ati-kimiwan it is beginning to rain
ayami-	VAI	speak
ayamihê'-kîšikâ-	VII	be Sunday: kâ-kî-ayamihê'-kîšikâk which was Sunday
ayamihito-	VAI reciprocal	speak to each other
ayamihtâ-	VAI-T	read s.t., "address" s.t., *v.* ayamih-, Unit 4.
ayamiwin-	NI	word
âwêpali-	VAI	*w. negative:* môla âwêpaliw he doesn't talk sense
cikêmânima	IPC	naturally! of course!
êlikohk	IPC	a great deal, vigorously
êmistikôšiw-	NA	Englishman, White-man. *v.* wêmistikôšiw-.
êškwâ	IPC	yet
êwako	PR intensive	the very one, the selfsame one
ê-wêmistikôšîminâniwahk	VAI, indf. subject conj. indic.	in one's speaking English *v.* wêmistikôšîmo-.
ispali-	VAI / VII	get along so, go so. *v.* kici-ispaliyahk.
iškotêw-	NI	fire
itêhkê	IPC	-wards, on the side of (*with preceding particle and locative)*: *v.* otânâhk itêhkê.
kâ	IPV restrictive, relative + conj. indic.	who (*of persons*), which (*of things*), when (*of time*), *with conj. indic.* where (*with* iši, *of place*).
kêhcinâho-	VAI	be sure
kici-ispaliyahk	VAI 21 conj. indic.	so that we may get by: *i.e.,*(A.2) so that we may have enough
kišâstaw	IPC	Gosh! My, but...!
kîlanânaw	PR personal	(*L-Dialect*)—we (*inclusive*)
kînânaw	PR personal	(*N-Dialect*)—we (*inclusive*)

kotakiyak	PR dem. anim. prox. pl.	others, the others
kwantaw	IPC	to no purpose, at random; offhand, not seriously; *contraction of* pakwantaw, *q.v.*
lipâci-kîšikâ-	VII	be a drizzly day
macihtwâwin-	NI	sin
mâhcic	IPC	at last, last
miht-	NI	log, stick of chopped wood. *sg.* mihti, *pl.* mihta
mihtihkân-	NI	woodpile, cord (of wood)
mîl-	VTA	give s.o.: mîlêw he gives him
naspâc	IPC	back to front, wrong way to, wrongly
nâkacihtâ-	VAI-T	attend to s.t., observe s.t.
nipîwan-	VII	be wet
ohcikawin-	VII	be dripping, be leaking (as a house *or* tent)
okipahowêsiw-	NA	policeman: *i.e.,* the one who shuts away
oskac	IPC	at first
otânâhk	IPC	back, behind
otânâhk itêhkê	IPC	toward the back, behind, backwards
pakwantaw	IPC	to no purpose, idly, offhand, at random *v.* kwantaw.
pâhpi-	VAI	laugh
pêci-nôkosi-	VAI	come into view, appear
pêtâpan-	VII	be daybreak, be dawn, come the dawn
pîkon-	VTA / VTI	break s.o./ s.t.
pônihkê-	VAI	make a fire (in a stove)
pônihkâkê-	VAI	make a fire out of s.t.; use s.t., to make a fire
šâpopêkan-	VII	be soaking (of the ground)
tâpiskôc	IPC	as, like; both
têpiskâk	VII changed conj.	last night
têpwât-	VTA	call s.o.
walašawêwin-	NI	law
wani-tôt-	VTI	do s.t. wrongly, misdo s.t.
wanîhkê-	VAI	forget

wâpwayân-	NI	blanket
wâskâhikan-	NI	house (*originally* stockade, palisade)
wêmistikôšiw-	NA	Englishman, White-man: *often as.* êmistikôšiw
wî	IPV	want to, be going to
wîlâta	IPC	nonetheless
wîyatêlihtâkosi-	VAI	be funny
wîyatêlihtâkwan-	VII	be funny
wîyatwê-	VAI	joke

G. REVIEW

7.A Kakwêcihkêmôwina—Questions

Answer the following questions with full sentences. Do not reply merely "êhê" or "môla".

1. šwâpihk nâ kî-iši-âpatisinâwâw têpiskâk?
2. awênihkânak wîlawâw?
3. mîna nâ kwantaw kiwî-ati-ayamin?
4. tântê mihtâ iškotêw ohci?
5. môšak nâ kinâkacihtân walašawêwin?
6. kêyâpac nâ ohcikawin kimâhkîm?
7. ka-kî-miskên nâ niwâpwayâninân?
8. tân'tahto-mihtihkâna wiyâpahtaman walawîtimihk?
9. wîpac nâ ta-pêci-mawâpiwak okipahowêsiw nêsta šôliyânikimâw?
10. nâspic nâ wîyatêl'tâkwan ôma masinahikan?
11. môla wayêš ohci-iši-âwêpaliw, manâ?
12. âšay nâ ati-ililîmow?
13. ayamiw nâ kwayask, nêstapiko âskaw wani-tôtam?
14. kî-nisitohtâtowak nâ ayamihêwikimâw nêsta ililiwak?
15. môšak nâ âpacihtâwak wêmistikôšiwak *nîlanân* ispîš wîla *kîlanânaw?*
16. môla nâ kiskêl'tamwak pîtoš ôho nîšo?
17. ka-kî-wâpamânaw nâ kitâšokan ôta ohci?
18. ka-têpwâtaw nâ kinâpêm?
19. kimilwêl'tên nâ ê-wêmistikôšîmonâniwahk?
20. naspâc nâ kititwân ê-'lilîmoyin?
21. môšak kinâkacihtânâwâw walašawêwin, manâ?
22. ôta nâ kî-ihtâw amiskokimâw [Lands and Forests Agent]?
23. môšak nâ wîyatwêw wîla kišîm?
24. kiwî-mîlâw nâ masinahikaniliw?
25. kî-ašitakimow nâ nêsta wîla nêsta kîlanânaw?

7.B Naškwêwašihtwâwina—Answers

Formulate questions that might be answered by the following statements.

1. tâpwê lipâci-kîšikâw.
2. walawîtimihk ihtâw.
3. môla n'tôhci-kawinênân.
4. šôliyânikimâw mâškôc nêsta ayamihêwikimâw.
5. nistês wîla.
6. tâpwê, môšak pâhpiw.
7. môla mwêhci n'kiskêl'tên, n'kotwâs mâškôc.
8. kitayânânaw nisto mihtihkâna.
9. môla kitôhci-wîyatwânânaw.
10. êhê, wîyatêl'tâkwan nawac.
11. môla niwî-têpwâtâw. nipâw mâškôc.
12. mâškôc kî-nisitohtâtowak; môla mâka n'kêhcinâhon.
13. pêyak ayamiwiniliw piko ayâwak wêmistikôšiwak *kîlanânaw* ohci nêsta *nîlanân.*
14. êhê. môla wayêš ohci-iši-âwêpaliw.
15. tâpwê. misiwê kî-tôtênânaw macihtwâwin, kî-itwêw.
16. êhê, âšay n'kiskisin.
17. môla wîla âšay niwî-mîlâw masinahikaniliw.
18. tâpwê, êlikohk ayamiw kwantaw. môla tâpwê mâka.
19. cikêmânima. kî-nakatam lâlatin ninâpêm.
20. môla nin'tawêl'tên kêkwân anta ohci.
21. âšokanihk n'kî-iši-nakatên.
22. âskaw môla kwayask kî-itwêw ê-ayamit.
23. môla. pêci-mawâpiwak piko.
24. šâkoc kocihtâw. otânâhk itêhkê mâka itêl'tam.
25. apišîš piko. kocihtâw mâka.

UNIT EIGHT

A. BASIC CONVERSATION

1. Just Window Shopping

Twâmas:	palacîs-	(pair of) trousers
	nin'tawêlimâw oški-palacîs.	I need new trousers.
	itakisow	he so amounts, he costs
	tân' êtakisot?	How much do they cost?
Tik:	kayâši	old
	kayâši-ayahâw NA *or* NI	old thing
	tân' êhtit kikayâši-ay'âw?	What's wrong with your old ones?
Twâmas:	mêscipaliw	he / it is worn out
	âšay pîkopaliw nêsta mêscipaliw.	They're torn and worn out now.
Tik:	wîlâhcikana	clothes, "wearables"
	astotina	hats
	kâ-atâwêt	the trader
	kâ-atâwêt ayâw astotina nêsta kotakiya wîlâhcikana.	The trader has (some) hats and other clothes.
Twâmas:	n'ka-kanawâpahtên	I shall look at it
	n'ka-natawi-kanawâpahtên	I shall go (to) look at it
	n'tawâc	just as well
	n'tawâc mwêhci n'ka-n'tawi-kanawâpahtên.	I might as well go right along and look at them.
Tik:	nitêmak	my dogs
	nitašamâwak	I feed them
	pitamâ	first (in time)
	pitamâ n'ka-n'tawi-ašamâwak n'têmak.	I have to go and feed my dogs first.
	mikisimowak	they are barking
	ôlowak	they are howling

	âsay ôlowak nêsta mikisimowak mâka.	They're already howling and barking.
Twâmas:	acimošiš	a pup
	kitayâwâwak nâ acimošišak?	Have you any pups?
Tik:	n'kî-akimâwak	I counted them
	otâkošîhk	yesterday
	êhê, otâkošîhk n'kî-akimâwak.	Yes, I counted them yesterday.
	âpihkow	he is loose (an animal)
	n'ka-sakahpitâwak	I'll tie them up, I'll tether them
	âpihkowak; wîpac mâka âšay n'ka-sakahpitâwak.	They're loose; but I'll soon be tying them up now.
Twâmas:	n'ka-otinâw	I"ll take him
	ka-kanawêlimâw nâ?	will you keep him?
	ka-kanawêlimâw nâ pêyak nîla ohci? nâkê mâškôc n'ka-otinâw.	Will you keep one for me? I'll probably take him later.
	niwâpamâw sopâya nêtê. niwî-ayamihâw kêkwâliw ohci.	I see Sophia over there. I want to talk to her about something.

2. Geese and Ducks

Thomas passes a tent on the riverbank. Standing nearby with a group of children is Sophia looking out over the river.

Twâmas:	kêkwân? tân' êhkihk?	What is it? What's happening?
Sopâya:	sâkahikanihk	on the lake
	šîšîpak	ducks
	ihkin	it happens
	môla wayêš ihkin. n'takimâwak šîšîpak anta sâkahikanihk.	Nothing's happening. I'm counting the ducks there on the lake.
Twâmas:	koškwêlihtamwak	they are surprised
	têpwêwak	they are shouting
	misiwê awâšišak	all the children
	misiwê awâšišak têpwêwak.	All the children are shouting.
	koškwêl'tamwak nâ?	Are they surprised?

Sopâya:	pilêsiwak	birds
	nipâskiswânânak (*or* ...ik)	we (1p) are shooting them
	mâškôc n'ka-pâskiswânânik pilêsiwak.	Perhaps we'll shoot (some) birds.
Twâmas:	môla niwâpamâwak.	I don't see any.
Sopâya:	asiškiy	mud
	anta, ašiškîhk.	There, on the mud.
Twâmas:	kê-wâpahk	tomorrow
	ka-pêšiwâwâwak	you (pl.) will bring them
	ê'kwân' êkoši	never mind
	ê'kwân' êkoši! mâškôc ka-pêšiwâwâwak pilêsiwak kê-wâpahk.	Never mind! Perhaps you'll bring in some birds tomorrow.
Sopâya:	pâpihlâwak	they fly in this direction
	niskak ôtê pâpihlâwak	geese are flying this way
	natohta!	listen!
	n'tohta! niskak ôtê pâpihlâwak.	Listen! Some geese are flying this way.
	kipêhtawâwak nâ?	do you (sg.) hear them?
	wîstâsihtâkosiwak	they are noisy
	kišâstaw, wî-wîstâs'tâkosiwak!	Gosh, but they're noisy!
	kipêhtawâwak nâ?	Do you hear them?
Twâmas:	pimihlâwak	they're flying (along)
	capašîš	low
	wêsâ	too much
	wêsâ wîpac niskak ohci, manâ?	(It's) too early for geese, isn't it?
	capašîš nêsta pimihlâwak.	They're flying low too.
	ê-takwâkihk	in the Fall
	mihcêt	many
	mihcêt nawac kitayâwânawak ê-takwâkihk. ka-wâpamâwak.	We (*including you*) get a good many in the Fall. You'll see them.
	âhkikwak	seals
	kikâhcitinânawak	we (*including you*) catch them
	âskaw mâškôc ka-kâhcitinânawak âhkikwak sîpîhk.	Sometimes perhaps we'll catch seals in the river.

Twâmas:	kostâciwak	they are afraid
	ta-kostâciwak nâ niskak ôta?	Will the geese be frightened here?
Sopâya:	ispakocinwak	they are flying (*lit.*, hanging) high
	môla, âšay wêsâ ispakocinwak.	No, they're flying too high now.
	nipêhtawâwak âšay kêyâpac pilêsiwak.	I already hear more birds.
Twâmas:	pâskisikan	a gun
	êko isa	so then ...
	êko isa. n'ka-n'tawâpahtên pâskisikan.	Righto! I'm going to get a gun.

B. DISCUSSION OF GRAMMAR

1. Nouns

1.1 Plural Formation of Nouns

1.1.1 Unpossessed Nouns

The plural of unpossessed, nouns is formed by adding to animate stems the plural suffix, ...**ak**, or to inanimate, ...**a**. Where the noun stem ends in a consonant + /w/: *e.g.,* môsw-, atimw-, âhkikw-, mistikw-, the /w/ is dropped in the singular (Unit 3.B.2.1.2, p. 54) but reappears when further inflectional or derivational material is added to the stem: *e.g.,*

Singular		Plural
môs	*but*	môswak (moose)
atim		atimwak
âhkik		âhkikwak
mistik		mistikwa

This gives the plural suffixes the appearance of having the alternate forms, ...**wak** and ...**wa**. At first it may be helpful to learn the plural as a base form from which the singular can be predicted. In this way one automatically learns which stems terminate in /w/ and which do not; and, incidentally, knowing the plural form is a helpful device for remembering the gender of nouns.

Where the noun stem does not end in a consonant + /w/ the addition of ...ak forms the plural: *e.g.,*

âšokan	âšokanak
namês	namêsak
ililiw	ililiwak
cîmân	cîmâna
sîpiy	sîpiya

With nouns of the type, niska, maskwa (a bear), the plural is formed by the addition of ...**k**: *e.g.,*

niska	niskak
maskwa	maskwak

1.1.2 Possessed Nouns

When a noun occurs with a personal possessor, the noun stem is followed by the plural indicator (if any) for the person possessor and this is followed by the plural indicator for the noun: *e.g.,*

nikosis...ak	my sons
nikosis...inân...ak	our sons
kitâšokan...ak	your (2) wharves
kitâsokan...iwâw...ak	your (2p) wharves
ocîmân...a	his / her canoes
ocîmân...iwâw...a	their canoes

The possesed theme, ...**ιm**-, where it occurs to form a possessed stem, comes immediately after the noun and before any possessor plural or noun plural indicator: *e.g.,*

kinisk...im	your (2) goose
kinisk...im...ak	your (2) geese
kinisk...im...iwâw...ak	your (2p) geese
nimistik...om (< nimistikw...ιm)	my stick
nimistikom...a	my sticks
nimistikom...inân...a	our (1p) sticks.

The chart from Unit 7.B.2, p. 169, may now be expanded by the addition of the plural suffix. Obviative endings to accompany each personal possessor have also been included.

ni(t)	Noun Stem	(...ιm)	...Ø	...ak^{NA} ...a^{NI}	...a$^{NAobv.}$...ιliw$^{NIobv.}$	
			...ιnân		...Ø	
ki(t)			...Ø		...ιliw	
			...ιnaw		...Ø	
			...ιwâw		...Ø	
						NA, NI surobv.
o(t)			...Ø		...Ø	
			...ιwâw		...Ø	...ιlîw

Plural and obviative markers are mutually exclusive and are to be read down the column for each personal possessor as appropriate. The locative suffix is not included.

1.1.3 Number with the Obviative

1.1.3.1 Difference Between Animate and Inanimate Nouns
In Drill 2.1 you will observe that môswa, apwoya, atimwa, etc., display the same form for both singular and plural. To focus attention on this is, of course, the purpose of the drill. In the obviative, *animate* nouns *give no indication by their form* as to whether the noun is singular or plural. Drill 2.2, however, shows a series of *inanimate* nouns displaying formal contrast between singular and plural: cîmâniliw *vs.* cîmâna.

1.1.3.2 Possessed Animate Nouns
Animate nouns possessed by 3 or 3p give no indication by their ending whether the noun itself is singular or plural: *e.g.,*

okosisa	his son *or* sons
okosisiwâwa	their son *or* sons

1.1.3.3 Possessed Inanimate Nouns
Inanimate nouns possessed by 3 or 3p *do* show whether the noun itself is singular or plural: *e.g.,*

ocîmân	his canoe
ocîmâna	his canoes
ocîmâniwâw	their canoe
ocîmâniwâwa	their canoes

In the case of 3′ possessor, all formal distinction as to number for both possessor and noun possessed, whether animate or inanimate, disappears: *e.g.,*

okosisilîw	his *or* their son *or* sons
ocîmânilîw	his *or* their canoe *or* canoes.

———DRILLS 1 THROUGH 2.2———

2. Verbs

2.1 Transitive Verbs with Animate Object—VTA

Transitive animate verbs (VTA), whenever the subject is ni... or ki..., show by the plural suffix, ...ak, that the *object* is plural. Where the subject is 3 or 3p, the ...ak ending indicates that the *subject* is plural: *e.g.,*

	kiwâpamâw	you (2) see him
	kiwâpamâwak	you (2) see them
but	wâpamêw	3 sees him *or* them
	wâpamêwak	3p see him *or* them.

Remember that when the subject is a third person, the object is in the obviative and so is unspecified as to number. The chart of VTA forms in Unit 7.B.1, p. 165, may now be expanded as follows:

		-3	-3p	-3′	-3″
1	ni(t)	...âw	...âwak		
2	ki(t)	...âw	...âwak		
1p	ni(t)	...ânân	...ânân<u>ak</u> (*or* ...<u>ik</u>)		
21	ki(t)	...ânaw	...ânawak		
2p	ki(t)	...âwâw	...âwâwak		
3				...êw	
3p				...êwak	
3′					...êliwa

Where the subject is 3′ and object 3″ no formal distinction in number is made for either.

The hyphen precedes each number on the top line of the chart to show that the person-number denotes the object.

NOTE: ...ak ~ ...ik.

You will note in A.2 (Geese and Ducks, p. 192), for example, that where the subject is 1p, the animate plural suffix occurs as ...ik. In the N-Dialect around the area of Kashechewan this variant appears to be restricted to use with the 1p subject in the independent order, although freer fluctuation between ...ak and ...ik is reported elsewhere.

2.2 Transitive Verbs with Inanimate Object—VTI

Transitive inanimate verbs (VTI) display the same inflectional endings for both singular and plural objects. (*v.* paradigm, Unit 7.B.1, p. 165.) Note that *all* verbs, transitive and intransitive alike, show by their endings whether the *subject* (unless it is obviative) is singular or plural.

Study the following sentences:

1.	kiwî-ašamâwak nâ acimošišak anohc?	Do you want to feed the pups right now?
2.	n'ka-kanawêlimânânak nîšo pilêsiwak kîla ohci.	We'll keep two birds for you.
3.	môla wîla oniskima ôho. nîla n'kî-pâskiswâwak.	These are not *his* geese. *I* shot them.
4.	otâkošîhk kî-sakahpitêwak otêmiwâwa.	They tied their dogs up yesterday.
5.	kiyâpac nâ kî-otinâwâwak namêsak cîmânihk ohci?	Have you taken the fish from the boat yet?
6.	wîpac mâškôc ka-pêhtawânawak niskak.	We'll probably soon hear some geese.
7.	môl' êškwâ ohci-pêšiwêw šîšîpa ôtê.	He hasn't brought any ducks here yet.
8.	âniy onâpêma kî-wanihêliwa otêmilîw.	Annie's husband lost his dog(s).
9.	ninatawêlihtên oški-astotin; ninatawêlihtên oški-wîlâhcikana nêsta.	I need a new hat; I need new clothes too.
10.	kiwî-kanawâpahtênâwâw nâ ôma wâpwayân? môla, âšay nisto wâpwayâna n'tayânân.	Do you (2p) want to look at this blanket? No, we (1p) have three blankets already.
11.	kî-natawâpahtam pâskisikaniliw. tâpwê mâka, nîšo pâskisikana ta-pêtâw.	He has gone to fetch a gun. In fact, he'll bring two guns.
12.	cwân okosisa kî-wanihtâliwa ocîmânilîw. kî-nakatamiliwa misiwê otayânilîw nêtê mâmihk.	John's son(s) lost his/their canoe(s). He/they left all his/their things yonder downstream.

2.3 Preverbs and Derived Stems

You have already met certain verbal prefixes or "preverbs" (Unit 7.B.1.2, p. 166) used to qualify an otherwise full verb form. This is not unlike a familiar mechanism in English:

n'kî-tôtên	I did it	n'kî-*wani* -tôtên	I *mis*did it
nikiskisin	I remember	ni*wani* -kiskisin	I *mis*remember: *i.e.,* it slips my mind.

In addition to the use of preverbs, Cree builds other descriptive stems by combining an initial root and a final element, the minimum required to form a verb stem. These final suffixes often resemble a full word stem in shape and so are called *deverbal* suffixes. For example, the common stems, wâpam-, wâpaht-, are paralleled by the suffixes, ...âpam-, ...âpaht-. The root, nataw... "tend to, seek to" + VTI deverbal suffix, ...âpaht- form a stem, natawâpaht-. Added inflectional material yields the full form,

natawâpahtam	he goes to fetch it
n'ka-natawâpahtên	I'll go get it.

The combination of root, kanaw... "focus on, retain" + VTI deverbal suffix, ...âpaht- + inflectional material, yields the form,

kanawâpahtam	he looks at it
n'ka-kanawâpahtên	I shall look at it.

kanawâpaht- is now a full stem. Roots such as kanaw..., nataw..., if required to precede the stem to clarify or add to meaning, may be turned into preverbs by the addition of /i/: thus,

n'ka-natawi-kanawâpahtên	I'll go take a look at it.

The same two roots have appeared in the Basic Conversation with the suffix, ...êlim-, êliht-, "by thought": *e.g.,*

natawêlimêw	he wants him, he needs him
kanawêlimêw	he keeps him, he takes care of him

and, of course, itêlimêw he thinks (him), itêlihtam he thinks (it), from the root, it...,"so, thus" + ...êlim- + inflectional suffix.

Hyphens are not used between the components of a "derived" stem such as nataw + êlim-, or kanaw + âpaht-. Once the stem has reached its minimum complete form necessary for inflection, then any preceding stems linked to form a compound stem are joined by a hyphen: *e.g.,* kî-, pêci-, natawi-, etc. Further drill and study of this type of grammatical mechanism will be provided as we proceed.

3. Syntax

3.1 Concord for Plural Objects

In Unit 6.B.4.2, p. 137, concord is illustrated between the inflectional ending of a transitive verb and both subject and object. This kind of agreement is one way of showing a relationship between words which stand in some kind of construction with each other. In English the relation between words in a sentence is perhaps most often signalled by word order. In Cree the form of the word more often provides the useful signal (*v.* "Cree Grammar", Word Order and Word Form, p. xxxi).

It is important to note that both transitive *animate* (VTA) and transitive *inanimate* (VTI) verbs show concord for gender, person and number of the **subject**, except where the subject is obviative. For the **object**, transitive *animate* verbs (VTA) display concord for both gender and number, except where the object is obviative. Transitive *inanimate* verbs (VTI) express concord for gender only: *e.g.,*

VTA	ki...wâpam...âwâw...ak	you...see (VTA stem)... (3 obj. + pl. subj)...(anim. pl.) obj.
	Ø...wâpam...êliwa	3...see (VTA stem) ...(3'. subj. + 3" obj.)
VTI	ni...wâpaht...ênân	I...see (VTI stem) ...(0 obj. + pl. subj.)
	Ø...wâpaht...amw...ak	3...see (VTI stem) ...(0' obj. + pl. subj.)

———DRILL 6———

C. DRILLS

1. Plural of Unpossessed Nouns

1.1 When given the singular of the following animate nouns reply with the plural, on the model:

Recording: pêyak âšokan
Reply: nîšo âšokanak

		(Check column)
1.	pêyak âšokan	nîšo âšokanak
2.	" apwoy	" apwoyak
3.	" ililiw	" ililiwak
4.	" awâšiš	" awâšišak
5.	" namês	" namêsak
6.	" šîšîp	" šîšîpak
7.	" âhkik	" âhkikwak
8.	" môs	" môswak
9.	" atim	" atimwak

1.2 Drill the following inanimate nouns from singular to plural, as in 1.1 above.

1.	pêyak cîmân	nîšo cîmâna
2.	" ayamiwin	" ayamiwina
3.	" mâhkiy	" mâhkiya
4.	" wâskâhikan	" wâskâhikana
5.	" wâpwayân	" wâpwayâna
6.	" sîpiy	" sîpiya
7.	" mêskanaw	" mêskanawa
8.	" âhkosîwikamik	" âhkosîwikamikwa
9.	" natohkolonikamik	" natohkolonikamikwa
10.	" mihti	" mihta
11.	" wâwi (egg)	" wâwa

1.3 Drill as above.

		(Check column)
1.	pêyak âsokan	nîšo âsokanak
2.	" namês	" namêsak
3.	" cîmân	" cîmâna
4.	" pilêsiw	" pilêsiwak
5.	" mâhkiy	" mâhkiya
6.	" ayamiwin	" ayamiwina
7.	" atim	" atimwak
8.	" astotin	" astotina
9.	" âhkik	" âhkikwak
10.	" šîšîp	" šîšîpak
11.	" šwâp	" šwâpa
12.	" niska	" niskak

2. Obviative Object

2.1 Animate Nouns, Obviative: no distinction as to number

Reply to the following questions on the pattern:

Question: âšay nâ wâpamêw (pêyak) môswa?
Does he see (one) moose?
Reply: êhê, âšay nîšo wâpamêw môswa.
Yes, now he sees two moose.

(Check column)
nîšo … môswa,
(and so for all animate nouns in the obviative)

1. âšay nâ wâpamêw pêyak môswa?
2. âšay nâ nakatêw pêyak apwoya?
3. âšay nâ sakahpitêw pêyak atimwa?
4. âšay nâ kanawêlimêw pêyak awâšiša?
5. âšay nâ otinêw pêyak namêsa?
6. âšay nâ kî-nâspitohtawêw pêyak ililiwa?
7. âšay nâ kîsiswêw šîšîpa?
8. âšay nâ kiskêlimêw awênihkâna?

What change, if any, do you observe in the *animate* nouns above to signal a plural in the obviative?

2.2 Inanimate Nouns, Obviative: Note the distinction as to number

Reply to the following questions on the pattern:

Question: âšay nâ kawinam mâhkîliw?
Is he taking down the tent now?
Reply: tâpwê, âšay misiwê kawinam mâhkiya.
Certainly, he's taking all the tents down now.

		(Check column)	
1.	âšay nâ kawinam mâhkîliw?	...misiwê	... mâhkiya
2.	âšay nâ kîsisam kêkwâliw?		kêkwâna
3.	âšay nâ otinam cîmâniliw?		cîmâna
4.	âšay nâ ayâw masinahikaniliw?		masinahikana
5.	âšay nâ wâpahtam wâpwayâniliw?		wâpwayâna
6.	âšay nâ nisitohtam itwêwiniliw?		itwêwina
7.	âšay nâ ta-kî-miskam sâkahikaniliw?		sâkahikana
8.	âšay nâ kî-nakatam iškotêliw?		iškotêwa

What indication of number is displayed by the inanimate nouns in the obviative?

3. Concord Shown by the Verb for Number with Animate Object

3.1 Proximate Object

Drill the following question-answer series on the model:

Recording: kitayâwâw nâ atim?
Have you a dog?
Reply: tâpwê, n'tayâwâwak âtiht atimwak.
Certainly, I have several dogs.

The recording will check you and allow time to repeat the correct answer

		(Check column)
1.	kitayâwâw nâ atim?	... âtiht atimwak
2.	kitayâwâw nâ âhkik?	âhkikwak
3.	kitayâwâw nâ apwoy?	apwoyak
4.	kitayâwâw nâ namês?	namêsak
5.	kitayâwâw nâ šôliyân?	šôliyânak
		[Plural means "some change"]
6.	kitayâwâw nâ šîšîp?	šîšîpak
7.	kitayâwâw nâ awâšiš?	awâšišak

8. kitayâwâw nâ acimošiš? — acimošišak
9. kitayâwâw nâ pilêsiw? — pilêsiwak
10. kitayâwâw nâ niska? — niskak

3.2 Complete the fragment by selecting the correct object for the verb. You will hear the fragment *twice* on the recording, followed by a pause in which you repeat and complete it. Mimic the full form as recorded. The correct replies are given below.

1. kiwî-ayamihâw nâ (awâšiš ~ awâšišak) _____________?
2. môla wîskâc kitôhci-akimâwak (apwoy ~ apwoyak) ___________.
3. wîpac n'ka-sakahpitânân (acimošišak ~ acimošiš) _________.
4. wîskâc nâ kî-wanihâwâwak (atimwak ~ atim) __________?
5. âšay mîna n'tayâwâw (šôliyânak ~ šôliyân) __________.
6. âšay nâ kipîkonâwâw (âsokan ~ âšokanak) __________?
7. môla mâškôc ka-wâpamânawak (niskak ~ niska) _________.
8. n'ka-kî-pâskiswânânik nâ (pilêsiw ~ pilêsiwak) ___________?
9. ka-kî-kanawêlimânaw nâ (namêsak ~ namês) _________?
10. tâpwê, môla nipêhtawâwak (šîšîpak ~ šîšîp) __________?

1. awâšiš
2. apwoyak
3. acimošiš
4. atimwak
5. šôliyân
6. âšokan
7. niskak
8. pilêsiwak
9. namês
10. šîšîpak

3.3 Complete the fragment by selecting the correct one of the bracketed forms, on the model:

Recording: (kî-wâpamâw ~ kî-wâpamâwak). âšay nâ _______ okipahowêsiw?
Reply: âšay nâ kî-wâpamâw okipahowêsiw?

1. âšay nâ (kî-wâpamâw ~ kî-wâpamâwak) ______________ okipahowêsiw?
2. wîpac mâškôc (ka-pêhtawânawak ~ ka-pêhtawânaw) _____________ môs.
3. môla wîskâc (n'tôhci-pêšiwânân ~ n'tôhci-pêšiwânânik) ____________ âhkikwak.
4. mâškôc (ka-pâskiswâwâwak ~ ka-pâskiswâwâw) ______________ pilêsiwak.

5. mihcêt nawac (kitayâwânawak ~ kitayâwânaw) ____________ namêsak.
6. anohc mwêhci (niwî-ayamihâwak ~ niwî-ayamihâw) ______ niwîkimâkan.
7. môla wîskâc (nisakahpitânânak ~ nisakahpitânân) _________ acimošišak.
8. môl' êškwâ (kitôhci-pîkonâwâw ~ kitôhci-pîkonâwâwak) _________ apwoy.
9. mîna mâškôc (n'ka-ayâwânânik ~ n'ka-ayâwânân) ____________ šôliyân.
10. wîpac mâškôc (ka-kî-pâskiswâw ~ ka-kî-pâskiswâwak) _________ šîšîpak.
11. tâpwê, môla (niwâpamâwak ~ niwâpamâw) _____________ niskak ôta.
12. môla nâspic (kisâpêlimâwak ~ kisâpêlimâw) _________ ana ililiw, manâ?

1. kiwâpamâw
2. ka-pêhtawânaw
3. n'tôhci-pêšiwânânik
4. ka-pâskiswâwâwak
5. kitayâwânawak
6. niwî-ayamihâw
7. nisakahpitânânak
8. kitôhci-pîkonâwâw
9. n'ka-ayâwânân
10. ka-kî-pâskiswâwak
11. niwâpamâwak
12. kisâpêlimâw

4. Verb with Proximate, Inanimate Object, Singular and Plural

Drill the following exchanges on the model:

Question: kiwâpahtên nâ cîmân?
Do you see a canoe?
Reply: tâpwê, niwâpahtên âtiht cîmâna.
Certainly, I see several canoes.

		(Check column)	
1.	kiwâpahtên nâ cîmân?	tâpwê,	niwâpahtên âtiht cîmâna.
2.	kin'tawêl'tên nâ astotin?	"	nin'tawêl'tên ... astotina
3.	kitôtinên nâ wâpwayân?	"	n'tôtinên ... wâpwayâna
4.	kikîsisên nâ kêkwân?	"	n'kîsisên ... kêkwâna
5.	kinakatên nâ pâskisikan?	"	ninakatên ... pâskisikana
6.	kitayamihtân nâ masinahikan?	"	n'tayamihtân ... masinahikana
7.	kiwâpahtên nâ atâwêwikamik?	"	niwâpahtên ... atâwêwikamikwa
8.	kitayân nâ mihti?	"	n'tayân ... mihta

What change do you note in the verb to show concord for the plural of an *inanimate* object?

5. Complete each of the following fragments by choosing the noun of correct gender to stand as object to the verb. The checklist of correct responses follows the drill.

1. âšay nâ kiwâpahtên ___________ (âšokan ~ mâhkiy)?
2. mîna mâškôc nipêhtawâwak _____________ (atimwak ~ pâskisikana).
3. wîpac mâškôc ta-miskawêw _____________ (cîmâna ~ apwoya).
4. ka-kî-wâpamânawak nâ _____________ (cîmâna ~ âhkikwak)?
5. môla nâ kitakihtên ____________ (šîšîpak ~ cîmâna)?
6. kikiskêlimâwak nâ ________________ (kitôtêmiwâwak ~ kitakihtâsona)?
7. môl' êškwâ wâpahtam _____________ (nipîliw ~ niska).
8. môla ohci-wâpamêw _____________ (sîpîliw ~ âhkikwa).
9. niwî-ayamihânân _______________ (masinahikan ~ sopâya).
10. âšay mîna kawinamwak _____________ (âšokan ~ mâhkîliw).
11. môla ayâwêwak ______________ (šôliyâna ~ mîcimiliw).
12. môla kiskêlihtamwak _____________ (akihtâsona ~ ililiwa).

1. mâhkiy
2. atimwak
3. apwoya
4. âhkikwak
5. cîmâna
6. kitôtêmiwâwak
7. nipîliw
8. âhkikwa
9. sopâya
10. mâhkîliw
11. šôliyâna
12. akihtâsona

6. Complete each partial sentence by filling in the blank with the appropriate word or phrase from the list. You may find an either-or choice; but use each word or phrase only once.

n'ka-pêšiwâwak, wîstâs'tâkosiwak, niska, šîšîpak, êliwêhk, anohc kâ-takwâkihk, n'ka-n'tawâpahtên, atâwêwikamikohk, pilêsiwak, oški-palacîs, ka-kî-pêhtawâwak, n'ka-n'tawi-ašamâwak, mîcimiliw, ispakocinwak.

Twâmas: kišâstaw, _____________ atimwak.

Aysâya: tâpwê! _____________ wâlaw ohci. ___________ n'tawêl'tamwak. kî-wâpamâwak nâ âšay ______________ ?

Twâmas: môla. awâšišak piko kî-wâpamêwak ________ otâkošîhk. ___________ kî-koškwêl'tamwak! mâškôc _________________ kê-wâpahk. âšay wêsâ _____________. mâškôc ka-pâskiswânawak ________ __________. anohc mwêhci ___________________ n'ka-itohtân.

	nin'tawêlimâw _____-__________. pitamâ ______________ n'têmak.		
Aysâya:	nipêhtawâwak âšay kêyâpac ______________.		
Twâmas:	êko isa. ________________ pâskisikan.		

7. Possessed Nouns: Animate and Inanimate, Singular and Plural
(Not recorded)

The purpose of this drill is to provide practice in switching grammatical forms from question to answer, quickly and correctly. Where a question has a ki... subject or possessor, the answer should contain a ni... subject or possessor, and vice-versa, in the corresponding place: *e.g.*,

Question:	kî-miskawâw nâ nišôliyânim?
	Did *you* find *my* money?
Reply:	tâpwê, n'kî-miskawâw kišôliyânim.
	Certainly, *I* found *your* money.

Where ki... represents kîlanânaw or where there is a 3rd person subject or possessor, obviously no change of subject or possessor is needed in the reply. The check column will give the relevant changes of form.

		(Check column)
1.	kî-miskawâw nâ nišôliyânim?	tâpwê, n'kî-miskawâw kišôliyânim.
2.	ka-ašamâwâwak nâ nitêminânak?	... n'ka-ašamânânak kitêmiwâwak
3.	kimilwêl'tênâwâw nâ niwâpwayâninâna?	... nimilwêl'tênân kiwâpwayâniwâwa
4.	ka-pêtânânaw nâ kipâskisikanínawa?	... ka-pêtânânaw kipâskisikanínawa
5.	ka-akimâwâwak nâ n'tapwônânak?	... n'ka-akimânânak kitapwôwâwak
6.	kî-otinam nâ omasinahikana?	... kî-otinam omasinahikana
7.	kikîsiswânaw nâ kiniskiminaw ôta?	... kikîsiswânaw kiniskiminaw ôta
8.	ka-sêskipitênânaw nâ kicîmânínawa?	... ka-sêskipitênânaw kicîmânínawa
9.	kî-pîkonâw nâ n'tapwoy?	... n'kî-pîkonâw kitapwoy
10.	ta-kî-miskawêw nâ otapwoya?	... ta-kî-miskawêw otapwoya
11.	kikawinênâwâw nâ nimâhkîminâna?	... nikawinênân kimâhkîmiwâwa
12.	n'ka-ašamâw nâ kitêm?	... ka-ašamâw nitêm
13.	n'ka-mîšahwânân nâ kipalacîs?	... ka-mîšahwâwâw nipalacîs
14.	ka-kiskêlihtênânaw nâ kimêskanânawa?	... ka-kiskêlihtênânaw kimêskanânawa
15.	ta-kî-sakahpitêwak nâ otêmiwâwa?	... ta-kî-sakahpitêwak otêmiwâwa
16.	n'ka-ašitakimânânak nâ kikosisiwâwak?	... ka-ašitakimâwâwak nikosisinânak

D. CONVERSATION PRACTICE

1. Review the Basic Conversation carefully, making sure as you uncover each line of Cree that there is no hesitancy in your responses. If you find items requiring further work, mark them but continue your review without stopping. Go back and master the difficult sections; then drill the Basic Conversation right through once more.

2. Check all the drills carefully, making sure everything has been mastered before proceeding to new material.

3. Develop a conversation about new clothes which you need. Your old things are all worn out and you must go shopping soon. Right now, however, you have to feed your dogs, mend your canoe, go fetch some firewood and, perhaps, go look at some things in the store.

Discuss goose-hunting. People can hear the geese. They are flying high, but are making an awful racket. Ask whether any other animals (awiyâšîšak) or birds are ever caught.

Practise any further topics of conversation you can think of, using only vocabulary and constructions which you have had to date.

4. After you have heard the Listening In (Section E) and are sure that you understand everything, close your book and strike up a conversation as nearly like the Listening In as possible, with another member of the class. If studying alone, try an imaginary conversation or monologue. In either case, imitate as authentically as you can the intonation contours of the recorded version.

E. LISTENING IN

Twâmas: kišâstaw, wîstâs'tâkosiwak atimwak!
Aysâya: tâpwê! niwâpamâwak kicêmišišak antê.
Twâmas: âšay êlikohk ôlowak.
Aysâya: n'kiskêl'tên. ka-kî-pêhtawâwak wâlaw ohci. âpihkowak anohc wîla; wîpac mâka âšay n'ka-sakahpitâwak.
Twâmas: tân' êhtit mâka wîla nâha[1] kotak atim?
Aysâya: âhkosiw. wîpac mâka mâškôc pîtoš ta-ihtiw.
Twâmas: cîmis[2] kî-ayâw oški-pîskâkaniliw[3] otâkošîhk.
Aysâya: kî-ayâw nâ atâwêwikamikohk ohci?
Twâmas: êhê. misiwê mêscipaliwa nîla niwîlâhcikana.
Aysâya: kâ-atâwêt kî-ayâwêw nêsta oški-apwoya, manâ? nîšo mâka kanawêlimêw nîla ohci.
Twâmas: nêsta nîla n'ka-wâpamâw pêyak kêkwâliw ohci.
Aysâya: kêkwân ohci? tân' êhkihk?
Twâmas: môla wayêš ihkin. pâskisikan piko nin'tawêl'tên.
Aysâya: kî-wâpamâwak nâ âšay niskak?
Twâmas: awâšišak piko kî-wâpamêwak otâkošîhk. êliwêhk kî-koškwêl'tamwak.
Aysâya: mâškôc ka-pâskiswânawak âtiht anohc kâ-takwâkihk. n'kî-wâpamâwak âtiht šîšîpak ašiškîhk otâkošîhk.
Twâmas: nêsta nîla, n'kî-pêhtawâwak niskak; nâspic mâka wêsâ kî-ispakocinwak.
Aysâya: ê'kwân' êkoši, wêsâ misawâc[4] wîpac niskak ohci. šâkoc mâka mihcêt kâhcitinêwak ililiwak ê-takwâkinilik.[5]
Twâmas: awasitê niwî-kâhcitinâwak ispîš wîla niyâlan piko anohc kâ-takwâkihk.
Aysâya: niyâlan nâ piko kî-ayâwâwak?
Twâmas: êhê. kî-pîkopaliw m'pâskisikan; môla mâka mîna n'tôhci-pâskisikân.

[1] nâha that one yonder [PR dem. an. prox. sg.]
[2] James
[3] pîskâkan NI jacket: *contraction of* pîsiskâkan
[4] misawâc IPC anyway, anyhow
[5] Obviative in dependent clause where subject of verb in main clause is 3rd person, animate.

F. REFERENCE LIST

acimošiš-	NA	puppy
astotin-	NI	hat
ašam-	VTA	feed s.o.
ašiškiy-	NI	mud
awiyâšîš-	NA	animal, beast
atâwêwikamikw-	NI	store
ayân-	NI	thing (possessed), possession
âhkikw-	NA	seal (sea animal)
âpihko-	VAI	be loose(d), be untethered
capašîš	IPC	low, low down; below
cîmis-	NA [proper name]	James
êko isa	IPC [phrase]	So then...!, Well, then...! (Conversation concluder prior to departing)
ê'kwân' êkoši	IPC [phrase]	Never mind!
ê-takwâkihk	VII conj. indic.	in the Fall. *v.* takwâkin-.
ihkin-	VII	happen; fare, ail
ispakocin-	VAI	fly high: *lit.,* hang high
itwêwin-	NI	something said, word, utterance
kanawâpaht-	VTI	look at s.t.
kanawâpam-	VTA	look at s.o.
kanawêliht-	VTI	keep s.t.
kanawêlim-	VTA	keep s.o.
kâ-atâwêt	Nom. A [VAI conj.]	trader: *lit.,* (one) who trades
kâhcitin-	VTA / VTI	catch s.o./ s.t.
kê-wâpahk	VII [fut. ptcl. prefix + conj. indic.]	tomorrow: *lit.,* when it will dawn
kicêmišiš-	NDA	your puppy. *v.* nicêmišiš-, ocêmišiša.
kiskisi-	VAI	remember
kitêm-	NDA	your dog. *v.* nitêm-, otêma.
kostâci-	VAI	be afraid
koškwêliht-	VTI	be surprised (at s.t.)

maskw-	NA	bear: *sg.* maskwa, *pl.* maskwak
mêscipali-	VAI / VII	be worn out
mihcêt	IPC	many, much
mikisimo-	VAI	bark
misawâc	IPC	anyway, anyhow
natawâpaht-	VTI	go to see s.t., go to fetch s.t.
natawâpam-	VTA	go to see s.o., go to fetch s.o.
natawi-	IPV	go to (do s.t.)
natawi-ašam-	VTA	go to feed s.o.
natawi-kanawâpaht-	VTI	go to look at s.t.
natawi-kanawâpam-	VTA	go to look at s.o.
natoht-	VTI	listen to s.t.
natohta	VTI 2 imperative	listen (to s.t.)
nâha	PR dem. anim. prox. sg.	that one (more distant), yonder one
nicêmišiš-	NA	my puppy. *v.* kicêmišiš-, ocêmišiša.
nipah-	VTA	kill s.o.
nisk-	NA	goose: *sg.* niska, *pl.* niskak
nitêm-	NDA	my dog. *v.* kitêm- otêma, etc.
n'tawâc	IPC	just as well
ocêmišiša	NDA	his puppy. *v.* nicêmišiš-, kicêmišiš-, etc.
otâkošîhk	IPC	yesterday
otêma	NDA	his dog: *v.* nitêm-, kitêm-.
otin-	VTA / VTI	take s.o./ s.t.
ôlo-	VAI	howl
palacîs-	NA	trousers, pants (*from English* breeches)
pâpihlâ-	VAI	fly hither, fly this way
pâskis-	VTI	shoot s.t.
pâskisikan-	NI	gun
pâskisw-	VTA	shoot s.o.
pêht-	VTI	hear s.t.
pêhtaw-	VTA	hear s.o.
pêšiw-	VTA	bring s.o.
pêtâ-	VAI-T	bring s.t.
pêyak	IPC	one; a certain ...
pilêsiw-	NA	bird
pimihlâ-	VAI	fly
pîskâkan-	NI	jacket: *contraction of* pîsiskâkan-

sakahpit-	VTA / VTI	tie s.o./ s.t. (to s.t.), tether s.o.
sâkahikan-	NI	lake
sopâya-	NA [proper name]	Sophia
šîšîp-	NA	duck
takwâkin-	VII	be Autumn, be Fall. *v.* ê-takwâkihk.
têpwê-	VAI	shout, proclaim
wani-kiskisi-	VAI	misremember, forget
wêsâ	IPC	too (much)
wîlâhcikan-	NI	a wearable, article of clothing: *usu. in pl.*, wîlâhcikana.
wîlâht-	VTI	wear s.t.
wîlâm-	VTA	wear anim. obj., *e.g.*, palacîs-.
wîstâsihtâkosi-	VAI	be noisy
wîstâsihtâkwan-	VII	be noisy

G. REVIEW

8.A Kakwêcihkêmôwina—Questions

Answer each question with a full sentence. Avoid replying merely "êhê" or "môla".

1. mêscipaliw nâ kipalacîs?
2. tân'tahtw-astotina nêtawêl'taman?
3. ayâw nâ kotakiya wîlâhcikana kâ-atâwêt?
4. ka-at'-îtohtân nâ mwêhci anohc?
5. kî-sakahpitêw nâ otêma?
6. kiwî-ayamihâw nâ sopâya kêkwâliw ohci?
7. âšay nâ ka-n'tawi-ašamâwak kitêmak?
8. môšak nâ mikisimowak aniki atimwak?
9. tân' êhkihk ôta?
10. ta-koškwêl'tamwak nâ awâšišak, kititêl'tên?
11. ka-kî-wâpamânawak nâ kotakiyak šîšîpak?
12. môla nâ kiwâpamâwak pilêsiwak?
13. môla nâ kî-wî-pâskiswâwâwak?
14. kêyâpac nâ kipêhtawâwâwak pilêsiwak?
15. ta-pêšiwêw nâ pilêsiwa kê-wâpanilik[1] mâškôc?
16. capašîš nâ pimihlâwak niskak?
17. âskaw nâ kiwâpamâwâwak šîšîpak ôta?
18. ka-kî-pêhtawânawak nâ awâšišak?
19. ta-kî-akimêw nâ pilêsiwa anta sâkahikanihk?
20. apišîš wîpac niskak ohci, manâ?
21. wîskâc nâ kî-nipahâwâw [kill] âhkik?
22. ôtê nâ pâpihlâwak niskak?

[1] kê-wâpanilik: obviative in dependent clause, "when it will be dawn", since subject of verb in main clause is 3rd person, animate.

8.B Naškwêwašihtwâwina—Answers

Formulate questions for which the following statements would be suitable answers.

1. nin'tawêlimâwak kâ-pîsisicik šôliyânak.[1]
2. mitoni mêscipaliw.
3. môla wîla anohc. nâspic ispakocinwak.
4. môla mâškôc. âšay pimihlâwak.
5. šâkoc nipêhtawâwak. âšay n'ka-n'tawâpahtên pâskisikan.
6. akimêw šîšîpa sâkahikanihk.
7. êhê, wêsâ wîpac mâškôc.
8. âskaw n'kâhcitinânân âhkik ê-takwâkihk.
9. mwêhci anohc n'ka-at'-îtohtân.
10. nin'tawi-ašamânânak nitêminânak.
11. awâšišak piko koškwêl'tamwak.
12. êhê. têpwêwak misiwê.
13. môla nâspic nisâpêl'tên ôta.
14. nôhtâwiy mâškôc. môla mwêhci n'kiskêlimâw
15. anta, ašiškîhk.
16. ê'kwân' êkoši! mâškôc ta-pêšiwêw pilêsiwa kê-wâpanilik.[2]
17. mikisimowak n'cêmišišak piko.
18. êhê. mihcêt nawac kinipahânawak ê-takwâkihk.
19. môla ta-kostâciwak.
20. tâpwê, wîstâs'tâkosiwak.
21. nâspic ta-koškwêl'tamwak.
22. môla mwêhci n'kiskêl'tên. pêyak piko mâškôc.
23. môla. otâkošîhk n'kî-sakahpitâwak.
24. cikêmânima! môšak n'tawêl'tamwak mîcimiliw.

[1] kâ-pîsisicik šôliyânak small change

[2] kê-wâpanilik: obviative in dependent clause, "when it will be dawn", since subject of verb in main clause is 3rd person, animate.

UNIT NINE

A. BASIC CONVERSATION

School Days

1. On the Way to School

Wîliy:	kâ-kiskinohamâkêt	the teacher
	kî-matwêhcicikêw	she rang the bell
	âstam!	come!
	âstam! âšay kî-matwêhcicikêw kâ-kiskinohamâkêt.	Come on! The teacher's already rung the bell.
Cwâniy:	iskôliwiw	he goes to school
	kici-iskôliwiyân	that I go to school
	môla nimilwêl'htên 'ci-iskôliwiyân.	I don't like going to school.
	pwâstaw	late
	pwâstaw ka-kî-pîhtokwânânaw. môla kâ-kiskêlimikonaw.[1]	We can go in late. She won't notice us (*lit.*, know us).
Wîliy:	n'kî-kisiwâsîstâk	she got mad at me yesterday.
	nâspic n'kî-kisiwâsîstâk otâkošîhk.	She got very mad at me yesterday.
Cwâniy:	kêkišêp	this morning
	kî-waniškân	you got up
	kî-pwâstawi-waniškân	you got up late
	kî-pwâstawi-waniškân kêkišêp, manâ?	You got up late this morning, eh?
Wîliy:	n'tôsâmihkwâmin	I sleep in
	môla n'tôhci-osâmihkwâmin. wîpac n'kî-waniškân.	I didn't sleep in. I got up early.
Cwâniy:	ka-kitotik	she will scold you, rebuke you
	môla mâškôc ka-kitotik.	She probably won't scold you.

[1] *i.e.*, know us (who we are). An adult speaker would probably prefer môla ka-pisiskâpamikonaw, "she will not notice us".

	'ci-kîwêyin	that you go home
	ka-tôtâk	she will do to you
	mâškôc ka-tôtâk 'ci-kîwêyin.	Maybe she'll make you go home.

2. At School

Wîliy:	niwêpinik	he throws me (away)
	n'kâhci-wêpinik	he pushes me, he shoves me
	'wênihkân n'kâhci-wêpinik!	Hey, somebody's shoving me!
Iskwêšiš:	ohcitaw	purposely, on purpose
	êkâ kito!	don't bellow, don't cry out!
	awas!	Away! Off with you!
	awas! 'kâ kito! môla ohcitaw n'tôhci-tôtên.	Aw g'wan! Shut up! I didn't do it on purpose.
Kâ-kiskinohamâkêt:	tân' êhtiyêk?	What's wrong with you?
Cwâniy:	kî-otâmahwêw	he (3) hit her (3')
	kî-kâhci-wêpinikow	he (3) was pushed by her (3')
	kî-pihci-kâhci-wêpinikow	he was accidentally pushed by her
	aylîna kî-pihci-kâhci-wêpinikow.	He got pushed accidentally by Eileen.
	kî-otâmahwêw mâka.	He hit her though.
Aylîn:	n'kî-pihci-tôtawâw	I did it to him accidentally
	mâtow	she cries
	(ê-mâtot) môla ohcitaw n'tôhci-kâhci-wêpinâw.	(Crying) I didn't push him on purpose.
	n'kî-pihci-tôtawâw.	I did it to him accidentally.
Kâ-kiskinohamâkêt:	kotakiya (3') pâhpihikow[2]	the others (3') are laughing at him (3)
	kiwî-môhik	he wants to make you cry
	êkwâni	there now, that'll do
	'kwâni, 'kwâni. môla kiwî-môhik. kotakiya pâhpihikow.	There now, there now! He doesn't want to make you cry. The others are laughing at him.

[2] Speaker on recording says: kotakiyak pâhpihikowak the others are being laughed at.

Wîliy:	mîsîw	he defecates
	mîsîwikamik	outhouse (normal term)
	niwî-šikin	I'm going to *or* want to urinate
	kišâstaw, niwî-n'tawi-šikin mîsîwikamikohk.	Gee, I need to go to the toilet.
Kâ-kiskinohamâkêt:		
	walawîwikamik	outhouse (polite term)
	ka-išiwilikoliwa	he (3') will take you
	cwâniy ostêsa ka-išiwilikoliwa walawîwikamikohk.[3]	Johnnie's big brother will take you to the outhouse.
	(Turning to the class)	
	otinamok [VTI 2p imperative]	take them
	awâšišak, otinamok kimasinahikaniwâwa.	Children, take your books.
Cwâniy:	n'kî-ayamihtân	I can read it
	môla n'kî-ayamihtân ôma.	I can't read this.
Kâ-kiskinohamâkêt:		
	papâmohtahikow	he is taken by 3' for a walk (about)
	kî-papâmohtahikow omisa	his big sister took him for a walk
	ê-ayamihtâyan	in your reading it
	tôta [VTI imperative sg.]	do it
	ôtê tôta ê-ayamihtâyan: kî-papâmohtahikow cwân omisa.	Read it this way: John's big sister took him for a walk.
Cwâniy:	otâpânâsk NA	sled
	kî-pimipalihêw otâpânâskwa	he made the sled go
	ocâpânišîš NI	snowmobile
	kî-pimipalihtwâw ocâpânišîšiliw.	He drove the snowmobile.
	kî-pimipalihêw otâpânâskwa.	He made the sled go.
Kâ-kiskinohamâkêt:		
	ka-kî-natawê[4]-mêtawânâwâw	you (2p) may go to play
	kikisisawisîn	you (2) are clever
	tâpwê kikisisawisîn. âšay misiwê ka-kî-n'tawê-mêtawânâwâw.	You're a very smart boy. Now you may all go out and play.

[3] Note /w + i/ > [o]. The speaker says [wʌnʌwiyokʌmikohk].

[4] natawê, rather than natawi, is also heard.

3. After Recess

Âniy:	kitêpwâtikonaw	she is calling us (21)
	âšay kitêpwâtikonaw kâ-kiskinohamâkêt.	The teacher is calling us now.
Kâ-kiskinohamâkêt:	masinahwânêkinwâna	papers
	nâpêšišak	boys
	kî-mîlikowâwak	they gave you (2p)
	misiwê nâ kî-mîlikowâwak nâpêšišak masinahwânêkinwâna?	Did the boys give you all some papers?
Âniy:	n'kî-mîlikonânik	they gave us (1p)
	masinahikanâhtikwa	pencils
	êhê. nêsta masinahikanâhtikwa n'kî-mîlikonânik.	Yes. They gave us pencils too.
Kâ-kiskinohamâkêt:	ka-tôtênânaw akihtâsowina. âniy, tân'tahto ani nîšo nêsta nisto?	We'll do some arithmetic. Annie, how much is two and three?
Âniy:	nîšo nêsta nisto, nîswâs.	Two and three are seven.
Kâ-kiskinohamâkêt:	ka-nôcihtânânaw	we (21)'ll have to work at it
	mitoni	entirely, altogether
	môla mitoni kwayask. êškwâ kwayask ka-nôcihtânânaw.	That's not quite right. We'll have to correct it.
	tân'îlikohk	(up to) how much?
	otina [VTI imperative sg.]	take it (*Cf.* English "take away".)
	nêšta niyâlan, otina mâka nîšo, tân'îlikohk mâka?	And five, minus two, is how much?
Âniy:	tâpask	probably not, it is unlikely that
	niwanâhikon	I get confused, I get disturbed
	âskaw apišîš niwanâhikon. tâpask kwayask n'kî-tôtên.	Sometimes I get mixed up. I probably didn't do it right.
Kâ-kiskinohamâkêt:	kici-mîcisonâniwahk	in order that one may eat
	ispaliw	it so goes
	êhê. âšay mâka ispaliw 'ci-mîcisonâniwahk.	Right, but it's time for lunch now.

B. DISCUSSION OF GRAMMAR

1. Inverse of Transitive Animate Verbs: VTA

1.1 ...ι**kw**...

As your knowledge of transitive animate verbs, VTA, has expanded you have learned how to say "I saw him *or* them", but not "he *or* they saw me". In short, you can work from the nearer person to the farther but not in the inverse direction. Consider the situation in English briefly. Whether we say

i. He sees me (where *"sees"* is active)
or ii. I am seen by him (where *"am seen"* is passive)

the situation is the same: *i.e.,* the direction of the action is from third person back to first person: 1 ← 3. Contrast both of these with "I see him", where the direction of action is from first to third person: 1 → 3. To express this change of direction in English requires one of two things:

(*in* i. above) an exchange of subject and object with change of shape in the pronouns: *I* to *me* and *him* to *he,* plus a change of *see* to *sees.*

(*or in* ii.) a still more sweeping transformation which alters an active to a passive construction with a change in the verb form and specification of the agent by a preposition.

In Cree the change from *direct* (1 → 3) to *inverse* (1 ← 3) is effected by a simple change of direction signals, ...**â**... for direct, ...ι**kw**... for inverse:

niwâpam...**â**...w	I see him *or* her. (direct)
niwâpam...ι**kw**...w	He *or* she sees me. (inverse)

The /w/'s merge; and since /w/ in final position after a consonant is dropped, the two contrasting forms end up as

niwâpamâw	I see him *or* her
niwâpamik	He *or* she sees me.

Other underlying forms also follow the regular sound changes. *niwâpam...ιkw...ιnân, for example, surfaces in actual speech as niwâpamikonân, he sees us *or* we are seen by him. The paradigm, paralleling that in Unit 8.B.2.1, p. 198, is as follows:

	3-	3p-	3′-	3″-
-3			...ιkow	
-3p			...ιkowak	
-3′				...ιkoliwa
-1	ni(t)...ιk	...ιkwak	[...ιkoliwa]	
-2	ki)t)...ιk	...ιkwak	[...ιkoliwa]	
-1p	ni(t)...ιkonân	...ιkonânak	[...ιkonâna]	
-21	ki(t)...ιkonaw	...ιkonawak	[...ιkonawa]	
-2p	ki(t)...ιkowâw	...ιkowâwak	[...ιkowâwa]	

NOTE. The dashes *following* the persons at the top of the chart and *preceding* those at the side show that in a form such as niwâpamik, although the person prefixes remain in the same position, the direction of traffic has changed. In other words, in Cree the grammatical subject remains the same, but what was formerly the goal of verb action has now become the actor.

1.2 Stem Finals /...hw-, ...sw-/

Certain VTA stems end in /hw/ or /sw/: *e.g.,* otâmahw- hit s.o., pâskisw- shoot s.o. In the inverse forms this leads to the sequence, /w + ι/ as in *otâmahw...ιkw..., *pâsk...ιsw...ιkw.... Since /w + ι/ > /o/ across a morpheme boundary (Unit 3.B.2.1.2), we would expect, and regularly get, forms such as n′tôtâmahok he hits me, from *n′tôtâmahwιkw; and from *kipâskiswιkw... ιnawak comes the regularly occurring form, kipâskisokonawak they are shooting (at) us.

1.3 Stem Final in /...aw-/

Forms such as kitôtawâw you do it to *or* for her, nikisiwâsîstawâw I get angry with him, kiwîhtamawânawak we (21) tell them, have stems ending in /...aw/. When followed by the inverse signal, ...ιkw, regular contraction takes place:

*kitôtaw...ιkw > kitôtâk	she does it to *or* for you
*nikisiwâsîstaw...ιkw > nikisiwâsîstâk	he gets angry with me
*kiwîhtamaw...ιkw...ιnawak > kiwîhtamâkonawak	they tell us.

The form, niwanâhikon I am confused by it (A.3), may appear momentarily puzzling. It belongs to a set of 1 ← 0 (not 1 ← 3) endings and will be studied later.

Study the following sentences.

1.	môl' êškwâ n'tôhci-wâpamik kâ-kiskinohamâkêt.	The teacher hasn't seen me yet.
2.	ohcitaw nikâhci-wêpinikonân.	He's shoving us on purpose.
	vs. n'kî-pihci-kâhci-wêpinikonân.	He shoved us accidentally.
3.	yâkwâ! ka-otâmahok.	Look out! He'll hit you.
4.	môs kî-kîsisokow nikâwiya.	The moose was cooked by my mother.
5.	tâpwê ka-kisiwâsîstâkowâw.	She'll be angry with you (pl.) for sure.
6.	môla kitôhci-wanâhikonawak kêkišêp.	They didn't disturb us (21) this morning.
7.	ka-tôtâkwak 'ci-iskôliwiyan.	They'll make you go to school.
8.	môla 'wênihkân ka-wîhtamâkonaw.	Nobody will tell us (21).
9.	awâšišak kî-môhikowak atimwa.	The children were made to cry by the dog.
10.	kî-ayamihêw mêrîwa, môla mâka ohci-wî-ayamihikow.	He spoke to Mary, but she wouldn't speak to him.
11.	misiwê ka-mîlikowâwak nâpêšišak masinahikana.	You will all be given books by the boys.
12.	môla ka-kî-pîhtokwânânaw pwâstaw. kâ-kiskinohamâkêt ka-akimikonaw.	We can't go in late. The teacher will count us.

———DRILLS 1.1 THROUGH 1.6———

2. The Causative

2.1 You have probably noticed a patterned relationship between certain verbs occurring in this unit and others which you have already learned:

pimipaliw	he goes along	pimipali**hêw**	he causes him to go along
papâmohtêw	he walks about	papâmohta**hêw**	he takes him for a walk
itohtêw	he goes there	itohta**hêw**	he takes him there

This causative formation normally appears with matching stem finals: VTA ...**h**- and VAI-T ...**htâ**-, with some verbs showing ...**tâ**- or ...**htwâ**-:

itohta**h**êw	itohta**htâ**w
pimipali**h**êw	pimipali**htwâ**w

Several other verbs which show the same formation show an interesting shift in meaning:

ayamiw	he speaks	ayami**hêw**	he speaks to him
		ayami**htâw**	he reads it (*i.e.*, addresses it)
pâhpiw	he laughs	pâhpi**hêw**	he laughs at him
		pâhpi**htâw**	he laughs at it
âpatisiw	he works	âpaci**hêw**	he works for him
		âpaci**htâw**	he uses it

———DRILLS 2.1 AND 2.2———

2.2 Note the last sentence in A.1 above: mâškôc ka-tôtâk 'ci-kîwêyin, Maybe she'll make you go home. The VTA kîwêhtah- occurs, meaning, "*take* s.o. back, *take* s.o. home", as contrasted with "*make* s.o. go home", with tôtaw-kici- [+ conjunct indicative].

3. Particles and Compound Stems

In the last unit (8.B.2.3) the formation of compound stems by prefixing certain preverb particle stems to a verb stem was briefly noted. In this unit further particles are introduced:

ohcitaw purposely,—with the contrasting preverb,
pihci accidentally;
wîpac early, soon,—with contrasting independent particle,
pwâstaw and preverb form, pwâstawi, both meaning late.

Note that while ohcitaw and wîpac always occur as independent particles, pihci is invariably a preverb forming a compound stem. pwâstaw is used as an independent particle with some verbs, but with others as a prefixed form, pwâstawi. Study the following:

1. ohcitaw kî-tôtên.	You did it on purpose.
2. n'kî-pihci-tôtawâw.	I did it to him accidentally.
3. wîpac n'kî-waniškânân.	We got up early
4. pwâstaw ka-kî-pîhtokwânâwâw.	You can go in late.
5. kî-pwâstawi-waniškâw.	She got up late.

4. **nêsta "+"; otina "-"**

When adding and subtracting, nêsta means "and, plus". otina take it, is the VTI 2 sg. imperative of otinam: *e.g.,* nîswâs, otina mâka nîšo, niyâlan 7 - 2 = 5. Think of the primary grade formula: "Seven, take away two ..."

From the VTI stems natoht- and otin- you have met the 2 (singular) imperative forms, natohta and otina, respectively, and the 2p imperative, otinamok. Does this suggest any regular pattern of forming VTI imperatives? Think about it.

5. **...yân**

In addition to the conjunct endings listed in Unit 5.B.4 you have now met the VAI 1st person, singular conjunct ending, ...**yân**: kici-iskôliwi**yân** that **I** go to school.

Contrast this with 2nd person, singular, kici-iskôliwi**yan** that **you** go to school.

This will serve as one more instance of the importance of vowel length in Cree.

6. **Contraction—A Reminder**

Remember that ki..., 2nd person prefix + ka, future marker, contract in normal speech to ka:

kika-wâpahtên > ka-wâpahtên   you will see it.

C. DRILLS

1. Inverse of Transitive Animate Verbs (VTA) with Independent Order

Drill the following question-answer series until you can respond correctly and without hesitation. Uncover the check column line by line to confirm your answers.

1.1 Cue: âšay nâ kiwâpamik iskwêw?
Does the woman see you now?
Response: môl' êškwâ n'tôhci-wâpamik.
She hasn't seen me yet.

		(Check column)
1.	âšay nâ kiwâpamik iskwêw?	môl' êškwâ n'tôhci-wâpamik.
2.	" kitayamihik iskwêw?	" n'tôhci-ayamihik.
3.	" kikitotikowâw iskwêw?	" n'tôhci-kitotikonân.
4.	" kikâhci-wêpinikowâw iskwêw?	" n'tôhci-kâhci-wêpinikonân.
5.	" kiwanâhikwak awâšišak?	" n'tôhci-wanâhikwak.
6.	" kikiskêlimikwak awâšišak?	" n'tôhci-kiskêlimikwak.
7.	" nipâhpihikonânak aniki?	" kitôhci-pâhpihikowâwak.
8.	" kitêpwâtikonawak aniki?	" kitôhci-têpwâtikonawak.
9.	" kikisiwâsîstâkowâw okimâw?	" n'tôhci-kisiwâsîstâkonân.
10.	" kipêhtâkwak nâpêšišak?	" n'tôhci-pêhtâkwak.
11.	" kitôtâmahokowâw kâ-kiskinohamâkêt?	" n'tôhci-otâmahokonân.
12.	" nipâskisokonânak aniki?	" kitôhci-pâskisokowâwak.

1.2 Cue: kî-ayamihikow nâ anihi iskwêšiša?
Was he / she spoken to by that / those girls?
Response: tâpwê, tâpiskôc kî-ayamihikowak anihi.
Certainly, they were both spoken to by that / those (girls).

		(Check column)
1.	kî-ayamihikow nâ anihi iskwêšiša?	tâpwê, tâpiskôc kî-ayamihikowak anihi.
2.	kî-mîlikow nâ "	" kî-mîlikowak "
3.	kî-kitotikow nâ "	" kî-kitotikowak "
4.	kî-wanâhikow nâ "	" kî-wanâhikowak "

5. kî-pêhtâkow nâ " " kî-pêhtâkowak "
6. kî-kisiwâsîstâkow nâ " " kî-kisiwâsîstâkowak "
7. kî-otâmahokow nâ " " kî-otâmahokowak "
8. kî-pâskisokow nâ " " kî-pâskisokowak "

1.3 From the brackets select the form required by the verb. Correct responses are listed below.

Recording: ________ kî-ayamihikowak okimâwa. (nâpêw ~ nâpêwak)
Reply: nâpêwak kî-ayamihikowak okimâwa.

1. ________ kî-ayamihikowak okimâwa. (nâpêw ~ nâpêwak)
2. ________ kî-têpwâtikonaw. (kimosôm ~ omosôma)
3. ________ kî-pâhpihikow wîwa. (okimâw ~ okimâwak)
4. nâspic n'kî-wanâhik ________ otâkosîhk. (natohkolon ~ natohkolona)
5. kî-mîlikwak nâ ________ omasinahikaniwâwa? (awâšiša ~ awâšišak)
6. kiwî-wîhtamâkowâwak kêkwâliw ________. (ililiwak ~ ililiwa)
7. tâpask ka-kitotikonaw ________. (ana iskwêw ~ aniki iskwêwak)
8. awâšišak kî-mîlikowak otastotiniwâwa ________. (iskwêšišak ~ iskwêšiša)
9. mêriy okosisa kî-kîhkâmikoliwa ________. (wîwa ~ wîwilîw)
10. ________ âšay têpwâtikow kišê-ililiwa. (nâpêw ~ nâpêwak)
11. kiwîhtamâkowâwak nâ ________? (kikosisak ~ okosisa)
12. mâškôc n'kî-pêhtâkonânak ________ . (atimwak ~ atimwa)

1. nâpêwak
2. kimošôm
3. okimâw
4. natohkolon
5. awâšišak
6. ililiwak
7. ana iskwêw
8. iskwêšiša
9. wîwilîw
10. nâpêw
11. kikosisak
12. atimwak

1.4 Select the form of the verb required by the actor.

Recording: (ka-ayamihik ~ ka-ayamihikwak) ________ nikosis.
Reply: ka-ayamihik nikosis.

1. (ka-ayamihik ~ ka-ayamihikwak) ____________ nikosis.
2. âniy (kî-kâhci-wêpinikow ~ kî-kâhci-wêpinikoliwa) ________ anihi nâpêšiša.
3. (kî-papâmohtahikowâw ~ kî-papâmohtahikowâwak) nâ _________ kikâwîwâw?
4. (ka-kanawêlimíkonaw ~ ka-kanawêlimikónawak) __________ kinîkihikonawak.
5. (kî-miskâkow ~ kî-miskâkowak) _____________ cwân nôhcimihk nâpêwa.
6. (n'kî-otâmahok ~ n'kî-otâmahokoliwa) ______________ nišîm.
7. (niwanâhikonânak ~ niwanâhikonân) ______________ ana iskwêšiš.
8. misiwê (kî-mîlikoliwa ~ kî-mîlikowak) ____________ wîlâhcikana okimâwa.
9. (niwâpamikonân ~ niwâpamikonânak) ______________ atimwak.
10. (kî-milwêlimikowak ~ kî-milwêlimikwak) ____________ kêkât misiwê ililiwa.
11. (n'ka-pâhpihik ~ n'ka-pâhpihikwak) ______________ kotakiyak.
12. môla (ka-pâskisókonaw ~ ka-pâskisokónawak) ____________ okimâw.

1. ka-ayamihik
2. kî-kâhci-wêpinikow
3. kî-papâmohtahikowâw
4. ka-kanawêlimikonawak
5. kî-miskâkow
6. n'kî-otâmahok
7. niwanâhikonân
8. kî-mîlikowak
9. n'ka-wâpamikonânak
10. kî-milwêlimikowak
11. n'ka-pâhpihikwak
12. ka-pâskisokonaw

1.5 Turn the following from Inverse to Direct.

Recording: môla mâškôc n'ka-têpwâtik nišîm.
Response: môla mâškôc n'ka-têpwâtâw nišîm.

		(Check column)
1.	môla mâškôc n'ka-têpwâtik nišîm.	n'ka-têpwâtâw
2.	ka-wanâhikónawak nâ ililiwak?	ka-wanâhânawak
3.	n'ka-kitotikonân nikâwiy?	n'ka-kitotânân
4.	nâpêšišak kî-otâmahokowak iskwêšiša.	kî-otâmahwêwak
5.	tâpask ka-natawêlimikowâwak awâšišak.	ka-natawêlimâwâwak
6.	ocawâšimišiwâwa kî-pêhtâkoliwa otêmilîw.	kî-pêhtawêliwa
7.	kî-pâhpihikwak nâ ililiwak?	kî-pâhpihâwak
8.	kî-mowikow âhkik atimwa.	kî-mowêw
9.	saylas osisima ta-kanawâpamikoliwa okâwîlîw.	ta-kanawâpamêliwa

10. âšay kitayamihikowâw okimâw. — kitayamihâwâw
11. n'ka-nisitohtâkonânak nâ? — n'ka-nisitohtawânânak
12. môla wîškâc n'tayamihikwak awâšišak. — n'tayamihâwak

1.6 Turn the following from Direct to Inverse.

Recording: n'ka-mîlâw nikâwiy.
Response: n'ka-mîlik nikâway.

1. ka-mîlâw nâ kôhtâwiy? — ka-mîlik
2. kî-wanihânaw [lose] kistês ê-kîwêt? — kî-wanihikonaw
3. niwî-kanawêlimâwak awâšišak. — niwî-kanawêlimikwak
4. tâpask n'ka-nisitohtawâw. — n'ka-nisitohtâk
5. n'kî-têpwâtânân kâ-kiskinohamâkêt. — n'kî-têpwâtikonân
6. âšay wîpac ta-kisiwâsîstawêw. — ta-kisiwâsîstâkow
7. ka-môhâwâwak nâ iskwêšišak? — ka-môhikowâwak
8. pitamâ niwî-natawâpamâw šôliyânikimâw. — niwî-natawâpamik
9. misiwê 'wênihkânak kî-pâhpihêwak. — kî-pâhpihikowak.
10. tâpwê n'ka-milo-tôtawâw. — n'ka-milo-tôtâk
11. wîskâc nâ kî-pêhtawâw amisk? — kî-pêhtâk
12. mâškôc ka-kiskêlimâwâwak awâšišak. — ka-kiskêlimikowâwak

2. Causative Formation

2.1 Replace the VTA or VTI forms with the corresponding VAI from which they are derived. Use the same subject.

Recording: šwâpihk itohtahêw.
She's taking him to the store.
Response: šwâpihk itohtêw.
He's going to the store.

1. šwâpihk itohtahêw. — šwâpihk itohtêw.
2. mîna mâškôc n'ka-ayamihâw. — mîna mâškôc n'ka-ayamin.
3. âšay nâ kiwî-pim'palihtwânâwâw? — âšay nâ kiwî-pim'palinâwâw?
4. môšak nipâhpihikonânak. — môšak nipâhpinân.
5. wîpac mâškôc ta-âpacihêwak. — wîpac mâškôc ta-âpatisiwak.
6. apišîš piko ka-mîcisohik. — apišîš piko ka-mîcison.
7. otâkošîhk kî-papâmohtahânawak. — otâkošîhk kî-papâmohtânânaw.
8. môla ta-kiskêlihtamohikow. — môla ta-kiskêlihtam.

2.2 Complete the sentence with the derived VTA or VTI form required, using the same subject.

Recording: âšay niwî-ayamin. sopâya ______________.
Response: sopâya niwî-ayamihâw.

1.	âšay niwî-ayamin. sopâya ______________.	sopâya niwî-ayamihâw.
2.	môla wîskâc kitâpatisin. cîmân môla __________.	cîmân môla kitâpacihtân.
3.	mêskanâhk itohtêw. awâšiša ____________.	awâšiša itohtahêw.
4.	têpiskâk n'kî-pâhpinân. okimâw ____________.	okimâw n'kî-pâhpihânân.
5.	anohc mâka ka-kî-papâmohtânânaw. awâšišak nêsta ______________.	awâšišak nêsta ka-kî-papâmohtahânawak.
6.	âskaw ayamiwak. âskaw masinahikaniliw ____________.	âskaw masinahikaniliw ayamihtâwak.
7.	otâpânâskohk kipimipalinâwâw. kêyâpac nâ otâpânâsk ______________?	kêyâpac nâ otâpânâsk kipimipalihâwâw?

3. Fill in the blanks in the following passage with an appropriate word from the list given.

Each word should be used once only.

kotakiyak, 'wênihkân, êhê, ka-tôtênânaw, 'ci-iskôliwiyan, kêkišêp, ispaliw, n'kî-kisiwâsîstâkonân, mwêhci, kitêpwâtikonaw, kwayask, niwanâhikon, ohcitaw, âpatisîwiniliw, kâ-kiskinohamâkêt, êhkihk.

Cwân:	n'kî-pwâstawi-waniškân _________. apišîš n'kî-osâmihkwâmin.
Wîliy:	môla mâškôc kimilwêl'tên ______________.
Cwân:	____, môla nimilwêl'tên. âstam mâka,—âšay kî-matwêhcicikêw __________________. nâspic __________________ otâkošîhk.
Wîliy:	tâpwê nâ? tân' ________?
Cwân:	___________ n'kî-kâhci-wêpinik; n'kî-otâmahwâw mâka.
Wîliy:	__________ nâ kî-tôtawâw, nêstapiko kî-pihci-âhkohâw [hurt]?
Cwân:	môla _______ n'kiskisin. n'kî-kitotikonân mâka kâ-kiskinohamâkêt.
Wîliy:	ta-kî-pêci-mêtawêwak nâ __________, kititêl'tên?
Cwân:	môla n'kiskêl'tên. kêyâpac mâškôc ka-mîlíkonaw ____________ kâ-kiskinohamâkêt. ______________ akihtâsona nêsta. âskaw môla _________ n'tôtên. apišîš ___________.
Wîliy:	âstam! âšay ______________ kâ-kiskinohamâkêt. âšay mâškôc _________ 'ci-pîhtokwêyahk.

D. CONVERSATION PRACTICE

1. Cover the left hand column of the Basic Conversation and be sure you are able to give the Cree equivalent to each English word and sentence. Uncover the right hand column line by line to check yourself.

2. Imagine that you have just arrived in the village. Ask for the school (kiskinohamâtôwikamik), the name of the person who gives you directions and whether he knows the teacher and how many children are in the school. Comment on the number of tents and of people, exactly six, breaking camp. That will leave only three tents. Perhaps some people will move up or downriver looking for moose or geese. Discuss which you prefer to eat.

3. You always sleep in and arrive late at school. You dislike school, but your father makes you go. You're good at reading (nihtâ-ayamihtâ- VAI-T) but don't like arithmetic. Sometimes 3 + 3 = 6, sometimes not. You get mixed up and the teacher gets annoyed with you.

4. Think up any other topics for free discussion or soliloquy. Try to develop maximum facility in using the vocabulary you have learned rather than continually looking up new words.

E. LISTENING IN

We pick up a conversation between the teacher and one of Jimmy's parents.

Teacher: —ay'hâw, môla mâka wayêš ihkin.[1] wêsâ pwâstaw pîhtokwêw kiskinohamâtôwikamikohk.

Parent: cikêmânima! mitoni kwayask kititwân. môšak wî-osâmihkwâmiw ana cîpâš,[2] môla nêsta wî-waniškâw. môla mâka milwâšiniliw pwâstaw 'ci-iskôliwit.

Teacher: kiwî-wâpahtên nâ n'tôški-kiskinohamâtôwikamikonân? âskaw niwanâhikon kwayask 'ci-miskamân[3] mêskanaw.

Parent: cîmiy nâ kî-mîlik masinahikaniliw otâkošîhk? môla kwayask kî-ohci-nôcihtâw otakihtâsona.

Teacher: êhê, n'kî-mîlik. mîna mâka pwâstaw kî-pêci-iskôliwiw.

Parent: êlikohk kî-kitotikow ôhtâwiya. kî-tôtâkow 'ci-iskôliwit.

Teacher: êko mâka. âšay kiwâpahtên kitôški-kiskinohamâtôwikamikonaw. nâspic mâka kata-milwâšin, n'titêl'tên. âšay ka-pîhtokwânânaw. niwî-n'tawi-matwêhcicikân.

Cîmiy: âstam! âšay kî-matwêhcicikêw kâ-kiskinohamâkêt.

Âniy: awênihkân n'kâhci-wêpinik.

Kâ-kiskinohamâkêt:
'kwâni, 'kwâni! môla ohcitaw kitôhci-wî-tôtâk. kipâhpihikwak kotakiyak iskwêšišak.

Âniy: n'kî-otâmahok mâka.

Kâ-kiskinohamâkêt:
kî-pisci[4]-tôtâk piko. êko awâšišak, apik. âšay mîna ispaliw 'ci-âpatisinâniwahk. ay'hâw, kî-mîlikowâw nâ 'wênihkân masinahwânêkinwâna?

Âniy: môl' êškwâ n'tayânân.

[1] it doesn't matter, it makes no difference
[2] cîpâš NA scamp, rascal
[3] finding: *lit.*, that I find it
[4] pisci: alternative form of pihci

Kâ-kiskinohamâkêt:
misiwê nâ kitihtâwak ôta? tântê wîliy? 'wênihkân nâ âšay kî-wâpamêw wîliwa?

Âniy: tâpask ihtâw wîkihk. kî-wâpamikow nisto nâpêšiša, nêtê piko mêskanâhk. mâškôc kî-n'tawi-mêtawêw.

Kâ-kiskinohamâkêt:
tâpwê ta-kitotikow okâwiya. ay'hâw, otinamok kimasinahikaniwâwa. kâ-tôtênânaw akihtâsona. tân'tahto ani niyâlan nêsta niyâlan?

Cîmiy: nîla n'kiskêl'tên ... mitâht.

Kâ-kiskinohamâkêt:
êkot' âni. nâspic kikisisawisîn. môla wîskâc kiwanâhikon. kinihtâ-ayamihtân nêsta.

Âniy: môla kisisawisîw. kakêpâtisiw.

Kâ-kiskinohamâkêt:
'kwâni, 'kwâni. âšay kêkât ispaliw 'ci-mîcisonâniwahk. nakiskaw ka-kî-n'tawi-mêtawânâwâw. ê'kwâni mâka.

F. REFERENCE LIST

awás!	IPC	away with you! be off! go away!
awihâsom-	VTA	borrow (from) s.o.
ayamihtâ-	VAI-T	read s.t. *v.* ayamih-.
aylîn-	NA [proper name]	Eileen
âhkoh-	VTA	hurt s.o.
cîpâš-	NA	scamp, silly rascal
cîstahw-	VTA	prick s.o., puncture s.o. give s.o. an injection
êkâ	IPV	not (*with imperative and conjunct*)
ilikohk	IPC	as much as, up to: tân'îlikohk how much?
iskôliwi-	VAI	go to school, attend school
kakêpâtisi-	VAI	be stupid
kâhci	IPV	shove, push
kâhci-wêpin-	VTA / VTI	shove s.o./ s.t., push s.o./ s.t.
kâ-kiskinohamâkêt	Nom. A	teacher *v.* kiskinohamâkê-.
kêkišêp	IPC	this morning
kisisawisî-	VAI	be smart, be clever
kisiwâsi-	VAI	be angry
kisiwâsîstaw-	VTA	become angry at s.o.
kiskinohamâkê-	VAI	teach
kiskinohamâtôwikamikw-	NI	school
kišiwâh-	VTA	anger s.o.
kito-	VAI	bellow: 'kâ kito keep quiet! shut up!
kitot-	VTA	scold s.o. severely, bawl s.o. out *v.* kîhkâm-.
kîhkâm-	VTA	scold s.o. mildly, chide s.o. *v.* kitot-.
kîwê-	VAI	return, go home
masinahwânêkinwân-	NI	paper
matwêhcicikê-	VAI	ring the bell
mâna	IPC	repeatedly, frequently
mâto-	VAI	cry *v.* môh-.
mêriy-	NA [proper name]	Mary

misk-	VTI	find s.t.
miskaw-	VTA	find s.o.
mitoni	IPC	entirely, very much so, altogether
mîci-	VAI-T	eat s.t. *v.* mow-.
mîciso-	VAI	eat
mîpit-	NDI	tooth
mîpiti-natohkolon-	NA	dentist
mîsî-	VAI	defecate
mîsîwikamikw-	NI	outdoor toilet *v.* walawîwikamikw-.
mow-	VTA	eat s.o. *v.* mîci-.
môh-	VTA	make s.o. cry *v.* mâto-.
nanâskom-	VTA	thank s.o., be obliged to s.o.
nâpêšiš-	NA	boy
nihtâ	IPV	be good at (doing) s.t., be given to (doing) s.t.
nôcih-	VTA	work at s.o.
nôcihtâ-	VAI-T	work at s.t.
ocâpânišîš-	NI	snowmobile
ohcitaw	IPC	purposely
ohpin-	VTA / VTI	lift s.o. / s.t. up
osâmihkwâmi-	VAI	sleep in, oversleep
otâmah-	VTI	hit s.t.
otâmahw-	VTA	hit s.o.
otâpânâskw-	NA	sled
otina	VTI 2 imperative	take it, take them
otinamok	VTI 2p imperative	take it, take them
papâmohtah-	VTA	take s.o. for a walk
papâmohtê-	VAI	walk about
papâ-wîcêw-	VTA	accompany s.o. around
pâhpih-	VTA	laugh at s.o.
pihci	IPV	accidentally. .
pimipali-	VAI	go along
pimipalih-	VTA	make s.o. go, drive s.o.
pimipalihtwâ-	VAI-T	make s.t. go, drive s.t.
pisci	IPV	accidentally: *alternate form of* pihci, *q.v.* *Cf.* root in pistahw- (√ pist...)
pisiskâpaht-	VTI	notice s.t.
pisiskâpam-	VTA	notice s.o.
pistah-	VTI	hit s.t. accidentally *v.* otâmah-.
pistahw-	VTA	hit s.o. accidentally *v.* otâmahw-.

pwâstaw	IPC	late
pwâstawi	IPV	late
sîmiyan-	NA [proper name]	Simeon
šiki-	VAI	urinate
tânîlikohk	IPC	(up to) how much
tâpask	IPC	it is unlikely that, probably not (*with independent*)
têpit-	NA [proper name]	David
tôt-	VTI	do s.t.
tôta	VTI 2 imperative	do it
tôtaw-	VTA	do to s.o., do for s.o.
walawîwikamikw-	NI	outhouse (*more polite word*) *v.* mîsîwikamikw.
wanâh-	VTA	disturb s.o., interrupt s.o., confuse s.o. *v.* niwanâhikon (A.3 above) I get mixed up, **it** confuses me
waniškâ-	VAI	get up (from sleeping)
wêpin-	VTA / VTI	throw s.o./ s.t. out *v.* kâhci-wêpin-.

G. REVIEW

9.A Kakwêcihkêmôwina—Questions

Answer each question with a full sentence. Avoid replying merely "êhê" or "môla". It may help if you imagine you are attending elementary school.

1. wîpac nâ kikâwiy kî-pêšiwik iskôlihk kêkišêp?
2. kikisiwâsîstâk nâ mâna kâ-kiskinohamâkêt?
3. kî-pistahokowâw nâ okimâw nêstapiko ohcitaw?
4. ta-âhkohikow nâ natohkolona, kititêl'tên?
5. wîliy, kôhtâwiy nâ kitayamihik?
6. ohcitaw nâ kî-tôtâk?
7. n'ka-âhkohik nâ mîpiti-n'tohkolon [dentist]?
8. môla tâpwê kitôhci-kitotik, manâ?
9. kî-kâhci-wêpinikwak nâ nêstapiko kî-kâhci-wêpinâwak?
10. ohpinikow nâ okâwiya awâšiš?
11. kikišiwâhikwak [anger] nâ mâna?
12. môla nâ kiwî-ayamihikwak?
13. ka-kî-wâpamikonawa nâ sîmiyan ôhtâwiya?
14. kî-nakatikwak nâ âšokanihk?
15. n'ka-cîstahokonân [give an injection] nâ n'tohkolon?
16. ka-kî-wîcihikwak nâ?
17. ta-kî-wîcêwikow nâ âniy omisa?
18. ka-ašitakimikonaw nâ?
19. kî-pêhtâkonawak nâ kwayask?
20. môla kitôhci-wîhtamâk, manâ?

9.B Naskwêwasihtwâwina—Answers

Formulate questions to which the following might be appropriate answers.

1. môla, môla ka-môhik wîlâta.
2. êhê, ošîma nêsta kî-papâ-wîcêwikow [accompany around].
3. n'kî-kišiwâhik ohcitaw.
4. n'kî-nanâskomikwak [thanked] mîcimiliw ohci otâkošîhk.
5. môla nâspic niwanâhikwak êkâ nâspic ê-wîstâsihtâkosicik.
6. cîmânihk ka-pôsihikowâw.
7. wîpac mâškôc ka-tôtâkonaw 'ci-kîwêyahk.
8. kî-wîhtamâkowak anihi iskwêwa wêskac.
9. môla ohci-pâskisokow môs ililiwa.
10. kî-mâmîšahokowak astisak omisa.
11. môla n'tôhci-cîstahok natohkolon-iskwêw.
12. niska kî-kîsisokow okâwiya.
13. n'kî-natohtâkonânak okipahowêsiwak.
14. mâškôc nistês ka-wîcêwikowâw.
15. nîla n'kiskêl'tên ... niyânânêw.
16. têpit ostêsa môla niwî-išiwilikonâna.
17. 'kâ kito! môla ohcitaw n'tôhci-tôtên.
18. okâwiya ka-ayamihikonawa.
19. môla âpatan. môla ninisitohtâkonânak.
20. saylas ostêsa kî-awihâsomikow [borrowed] ocîmân.

UNIT TEN

A. BASIC CONVERSATION

At the Store: Sizes and Prices

Twâmas:	niwî-masinahikân	I want to write, I want to sign
	tântê okimâw? niwî-masinahikân.	Where's the Manager? I want to sign (for credit).[1]
Okimâšiš:	n'ka-nanâtawâpamâw	I shall look for him
	matêw ôta. n'ka-nanâtawâpamâw nâ?	He's not here. Shall I look for him?
Twâmas:	môla. môl' âpatan.	No. It's not worth the trouble.
Okimâšiš:	kiwî-šwâpihkân nâ?	Do you want to shop?
	kiwî-šwâpihkân nâ kêkwân?	Do you want to shop (for) something?
Twâmas:	ašikanak	socks
	pakwayâna	shirts
	nîšo pakwayâna nêsta ašikanak.	Two shirts and some socks.
Okimâšiš:	nîšošâp	twelve
	pêyakošâp	eleven
	mâškôc piko pêyakošâp nêstapiko nîšošâp pakwayâna n'tayân anohc kâ-kîšikâk.	I think I have only eleven or twelve shirts today.
	ôma mâškôc ka-nahiškên n'titêl'tên.	I think this one will probably fit you.
Twâmas:	ispihcâw[2]	it is size...
	tân' êspihcâk?	What size is it?
Okimâšiš:	nikotwâsošâp	sixteen
	n'kotwâsošâp ispihcâw.	It's size sixteen.

[1] When a trapper was getting his gear together, preparatory to going out to the trapline, he normally signed for credit, or "debt". The amount granted was commonly felt to be a mark of confidence in his performance.

[2] Alternate form, ispîhcâw. *Cf.* ispîhcikiti-.

Twâmas:	kîhkêhtakâhk	in the corner
	niyâlošâp	fifteen
	nêsta palacîs nin'tawêlimâw.	I need trousers too.
	kitayâwâwak wayêš niyâlošâp palacîsak kîhkêhtakâhk.	You have about fifteen trousers in the corner there.
Okimâšiš:	tân' êspîhcikitit?	What size is it (anim.)?
Twâmas:	itikitiw	it (anim.) is of such a size
	nistomitana nîšo	thirty-two
	nîšitana nîšo	twenty-two
	nîsitana nîšo nêstapiko nistomitana nîšo itikitiw.	It's size twenty-two or thirty-two.
Okimâšiš:	pîsiskâkan	coat, jacket
	askihk	kettle
	kotak nâ kêkwân, oški-askihk nêstapiko pîsiskâkan.	Anything else, a new kettle or a coat?
Twâmas:	milwâšišiwak	they are fine looking
	aniki	those ones
	n'kî-wâpamâwak aniki askihkwak. milwâšišiwak. tânîlikohk mâka?	I saw those kettles. They're fine looking. How much are they though?
Okimâšiš:	sêns	cent(s)
	nêmitana	forty
	ahtay NA	dollar; fur
	nistw-ahtay	three dollars
	ôko nâ? nistw-ahtay mîna nêmitana sêns.	These ones? Three dollars and forty cents.
	šânkw-ahtay	nine dollars
	nimihcilawêsin,—šânkw-ahtay.	Sorry!—nine dollars.
Twâmas:	maskisin	shoe
	n'ka-otinâw askihk. n'ka-otinên nêsta maskisina.	I'll take a kettle. I'll take some shoes too.
Okimâšiš:	ôho	these ones
	ka-tipahên	you'll pay (for) it *or* them
	ka-kî-tipahên nâ mâka anohc ôho?	Will you be able to pay for these now?

Twâmas:	walahpicikan	a (wrapped up) parcel
	ka-kî-tahkonên nâ?	will you be able to hold it?
	êhê. ka-kî-tahkonên nâ ôma walahpicikan?	Yes. Can you hold this parcel?
	šôliyânak	monies, change
	kâ-pîsisicik šôliyânak	small change
	ninanâtawâpamâwak[3] kâ-pîsisicik šôliyânak.	I'm looking for some small change.
Twâmas:	n'ka-kociškên	I'll try it *or* them on
	anihi	those ones
	n'ka-kî-kociškên nâ anihi maskisina?	May I try those shoes on?
Okimâšiš:	kiwî-kociškawâw nâ?	do you want to try it (anim.) on?
	kiwî-kociškawâw nâ nêsta palacîs?	Do you want to try on the pants too?
	âtiht	some, several
	âtiht ililiwak otinamwak kêkwâna, môla mâka nahiškamwak.	Some people buy (take) things but they don't fit them.
Twâmas:	nimikwaškâtêlihtên	I worry about it
	môla nimikwaškâtêlihtên nêsta niwîkimâkan.	I don't worry about it, nor does my wife.
	pohciškam	he puts it on
	pêyak awâšiš	one of the children
	pêyak awâšiš môšak ta-kî-pohciškam.	One of the children can always put them on.
Okimâšiš:	milonâkwan	it looks good
	êhê, šâkoc mâka môla nâspic milonâkwan.	Yes, but it certainly doesn't look very smart.
Twâmas:	mâmaw	altogether, together
	tânîlikohk mâka êspalik mâmaw?	How much does that come to altogether?

[3] nanâtawâpam- also occurs in contracted form as both 'nâtawâpam- and nân'tawâpam-, reduplicated form of natawâpam-, natawâpaht-, *q.v.*

Okimâšiš:	nistošâpw-ahtay	thirteen dollars
	niyâlomitana šânk	fifty-nine
	nistošâpw-ahtay mîna niyâlomitana šânk sêns.	Thirteen dollars and fifty-nine cents.
	n'ka-mâkwahpitên	I'll tie it
	n'ka-walahpitên	I'll wrap it up
	n'ka-walahpitên, n'ka-mâkwahpitên mâka.	I'll wrap it up and tie it.
Twâmas:	mîkwêc.	Thank you.

B. DISCUSSION OF GRAMMAR

1. Verbs

1.1 Transitive Stem Finals

The minimum number of components needed to build a basic, transitive verb stem, is a *root* and a *final* element. The *root* may be thought of as embodying the core meaning of the verb, the *final* as showing how the action is carried out: *e.g.,*

√ pîkw... break, + ...ɩn- by hand: pîkonam he breaks it by hand,
√ koc... try, + ...ɩšk(aw)- by body movement: kociškam he tries it on,
√ pâsk... burst, + ...ɩs(w)- by heat: pâskiswêw he shoots him.

These transitive stem finals, or *instrumentals,* go in pairs and, given either the VTA or VTI form, one can ordinarily predict what the other will be. (The very small number of irregularities can be learned as they occur.) The following list will illustrate certain stem finals with inflectional endings.

	pohc...ɩ**škaw**-êw pohc...ɩ**šk**-am	aki...**m**-êw aki...**ht**-am	ot...ɩ**n**-êw ot...ɩ**n**-am	otâm...**ahw**-êw otâm...**ah**-am
	koc...ɩ**škaw**-êw koc...ɩ**šk**-am	kîhkâ...**m**-êw kîhkâ...**ht**-am	tahk...ɩ**n**-êw tahk...ɩ**n**-am	pist...**ahw**-êw pist...**ah**-am
	nah...ɩ**škaw**-êw nah...ɩ**šk**-am	milâ...**m**-êw milâ...**ht**-am	wêp...ɩ**n**-êw wêp...ɩ**n**-am	cîk...**ahw**-êw cîk...**ah**-am
VTA VTI	...ɩ**škaw**- ...ɩ**šk**-	...**m**- ...**ht**-	...ɩ**n**- ...ɩ**n**-	...**ahw** ...**ah**-
	"by foot or body movement"	"by speech or perception"	"by hand"	"by instrument"

pâsk...ɩ**sw**-êw pâsk...ɩ**s**-am	têpwâ...**t**-êw têpwâ...**t**-am	wani...**h**-êw wani...**htâ**-w (VAI-T)

	kîs...ιsw-êw kîs...ιs-am	naka...t-êw naka...t-am	oši...h-êw oši...htâ-w
	iskwâ...ιsw-êw [scorch] iskwâ...ιs-am (> iskwâsw-, iskwâs-)	kitot...t-êw kitot...t-am	itohta...h-êw itohta...htâ-w
VTA VTI	...ιsw- ...ιs- "by heat"	...t- ...t- abstract final: hard to specify concrete meaning	...h- ...htâ- abstract finals often associated with causative meaning

Other finals will be met as we proceed, sometimes in a slightly different form: *e.g.*,...**am-**, ...**aht-**, as in wâp...am- see s.o., wâp...aht-, see s.t.

These stem elements, called *instrumentals*, often convey certain concrete meanings as we have shown. ...ιšk- (with a plus of ...aw in the VTA: *i.e.*, ...ιškaw-), often points to an action involving large body movement or movement of the legs: *e.g.*, pohcιškam he puts it on; pîkoškam (< pîkw...ιšk-am) he breaks it (as by sitting on it). ...m-, ...ht- have to do with activity from the area of the face: *e.g.*, akimêw he counts them, milâhtam he smells it and, in lengthened form, ...am-, ...aht-: wâpamêw she sees them, wâpahtam he sees it. Action by hand is often signalled by the stem final ...ιn- : *e.g.*, itinam he holds it so, pîkonam he breaks it (by hand). Final ...ahw- and ...ah- normally indicate the use of an instrument: otâmahwêw she hits him, kawaham he knocks it down. The stem final, ...ιsw-, ιs-, typifies action by heat: *e.g.*, pâskiswêw he shoots them (√ pâsk... burst, explode + ...ιsw- by heat), kîsisam he cooks it. Verbs are frequently met in which two or more of these stem forming elements occur. Consequently, when you meet nearly identical words with minor variations on a basic meaning, check the stems throughout: *e.g.*,

pîko**h**am	he breaks it by instrument (√ pîkw... + ...ah-)
pîko**n**am	he breaks it by hand
pîko**šk**am	he breaks it by some kind of bodily action.

Study the following sentences.

1. ta-kocihêw apwoya. — He will try the paddle.
2. môla ohci-kociškawêw ašikana. — She hasn't tried (on) the socks.
3. cwân kî-pîkonam omasinahikanâhtik. — John has broken his pencil.

4. otâmaha, mistik ê-âpacihtâyan, ka-pîkohên mâka. — Hit it with (using) a stick and you'll break it.
5. cîmânihk n'kî-iši-apin, n'kî-pîkoškên mâka. — I sat on the canoe and I broke it.
6. tahkonêw apwoya, tahkwatêhtam nêsta pîšâkanâpîliw. — He's holding the paddle (by hand) and the line (in his mouth).
7. pâhkân n'ka-kociškên. — I"ll try it (on) presently.
8. ka-kawinênânaw mâhkiy. — We'll take down the tent.
9. kîla mâka, ka-kî-kawipitên. — But you can pull it down.
10. ka-kawiškênânaw nêstapiko ka-kawahênânaw. — We'll push it down (by leaning on it) or we'll cut it down.

1.2 Stem Formatives

We have seen that the minimal requirement for a full verb stem is a *root* and a *final*. Without the one or the other, there is no stem; and there must be a stem before any inflectional material can be added. Examples have occurred beginning with roots such as nataw..., kanaw..., etc. (Unit 8.B.2.3), coupled with other elements; and in the present unit there occurs a reduplicated form related to nataw...: *i.e.*, nân'taw... or nanâtaw....

One common stem building element is ...êli..., by thought, commonly occurring as a so-called *pre-final* in transitive verb stems as ...**êlim**..., ...**êliht**... : *e.g.*,

it...	so, thus	it...**êlim**-êw it...**êliht**-am	he thinks him so he thinks it so
milo...	good, fine	milw...**êliht**-am	he likes it
nataw...	seek, go after	nataw...**êliht**-am	he wants it
kanaw...	focus on, retain	kanaw...**êliht**-am kanaw...**âpam**-êw	he keeps it he looks at him
wîyat...	funny, amuse	wîyat...**êli**...htâkwan *lit.,* funny...to-the-mind...it sounds	it sounds funny

Study the following sentences.

11. kititêlimâw nâ âniy ê-iskôliwit? — Do you think Annie goes to school?
12. môla nâspic milwêlihtam ôta. — She doesn't like it very much here.
13. ninatawêlihtên oški-maskisina nêsta pakwayân. — I need new shoes and a shirt.

14.	môšak mâka kimikwaškâtêlihtênâwâw ôho kêkwâna.	You're forever worrying about these things.
15.	nikî-kanawêlimikonân nimis.	My older sister took care of us.
16.	wîyatêlihtâkosiw ana ililiw.	That person is amusing.

...**pit**- by pulling action

17.	nîla n'ka-kâhtinên; kîla mâka ocipita.	I'll push; you pull.
18.	kî-tahkopitêwak atimwa otâkošîhk.	They tied the dog up yesterday.
19.	pîkopitam pakwayâniliw.	She's tearing up a shirt.
20.	kîla ka-kî-walahpitên. n'ka-mâkwahpitên mâka nîla.	You can wrap it up and I'll tie it.

———DRILLS 1 AND 2———

1.3 ...**kê**-: Verb Final Marking Generalized Goal

The verb final ...**kê**- is often added to VTI stems with the concrete meaning of "doing things generally": *i.e.*, directing the verb function to a generalized goal. From pâskis..., shoot it, + connective /i/ + ...kê- is built the VAI stem, pâskisikê-, shoot things generally. The parallels between VTI and VAI stems and related nouns with ...**kan**- as a noun stem final may readily be seen:

pâskis...am	pâskisikêw nipâskisikân	pâskisikan	a gun
cîkah...am	nicîkahikân	cîkahikan	an axe
masinah...am	nimasinahikân	masinahikan	a book
kwâškwêpit...am	nikwâškwêpicikân	kwâškwêpicikan	a fish hook

There are, of course, possible formations of this sort not exploited by Cree: *e.g.*, mitonêlihcikan mind, occurs; but the analogous mitonêlihcikê- VAI is met rarely if at all. Ordinary Cree usage requires a VTI (*e.g.*, mâmitonêliht-) for the meaning, ponder s.t., reflect on s.t., cogitate about s.t..

———DRILL 3———

2. Nouns: Expressions of Measure

Expressions of quantity or measurement in Cree do not involve the plural form of the unit of measurement when it is coupled with a numeral denoting the quantity: *e.g.*,

pêyakw-ahtay	(amount of) one dollar
nîšw-ahtay	(amount of) two dollars
nisto-šânkwêš	three quarters (of a dollar)

When the numeral is combined with the unit of measurement the two form one compound word (which we have occasionally written without a hyphen simply because of frequency of occurrence). Forms such as pêyako-tipahikan "per gallon (unit)", instead of pêyak tipahikan, which might have been expected, have already been encountered.

———DRILL 4———

3. Pronouns

The singular and plural (proximate) of the demonstratives are as follows:

	Animate				Inanimate			
Sg.	**awa**	this	**ana**	that	**ôma**	this	**anima**	that
Pl.	**ôko**	these	**aniki**	those	**ôho**	these	**anihi**	those

Alternate forms used in the Moose area are **ôki** *these* (anim. pl.) and **ôhi** *these* (inan. pl.). Demonstratives, like nouns, show no formal distinction in number for the animate pronoun in the obviative. For the inanimate, however, distinction in form is shown between singular and plural. The full paradigm is as follows:

	Animate				Inanimate			
Sg.	**ôho**	this	**anihi**	that	**ômêliw**	this	**animêliw**	that
Pl.		these		those	**ôho**	these	**anihi**	those

For anihi, both animate and inanimate plural, the alternative **anihêliwa** is reported in the Moose Dialect, although anihi seems to be current usage. The corresponding forms for **kotak** (Unit 5.B.3) are—

		Animate	Inanimate
Prox.	Sg.	**kotak**	**kotak**
	Pl.	**kotakiyak**	**kotakiya**
Obv.	Sg.	**kotakiya**	**kotakîliw**
	Pl.		**kotakiya**

———DRILL 5———

4. A Note on Grammar—"All Grammars Leak"

In all languages there are so-called "rules of grammar". These rules should not be regarded as arbitrary laws which the language MUST obey, but rather as a set of systematized observations on the way the signal code appears to function. In this sense, grammatical rules are like the 'laws' of nature: they reflect our understanding of the system as far as we have been able to discern it.

When a verb takes an object, the use of a transitive verb form is ordinarily indicated. Yet in Cree one says, n'kî-otinikân (*or* n'kî-šwâpihkân) kêkwân, I bought something. Both verbs bear all the earmarks of the VAI type. This, however, is not a violation of any rule. Actually, the kêkwân represents the goal towards which the action of the verb is directed: I shopped (*in relation to*) something.

One hears matakwan šôliyân, There is no money. matakwan is a VII, even though šôliyân is classed as an animate noun. Simply take note of such usage when you observe it, and follow it. A comment by Edward Sapir is worth remembering:

> "—all languages have an inherent tendency to economy of expression. ...The fact of grammar, a universal trait of language, is simply a generalized expression of the feeling that analogous concepts and relations are most conveniently symbolized in analogous forms. Were a language ever completely 'grammatical' it would be a perfect engine of conceptual expression. Unfortunately, or luckily, no language is tyrannically consistent. All grammars leak."[1]

When you hear an expression which you have difficulty fitting into any grammatical pattern known to you, learn how and where to use it. This is of first importance. Worry later about the logic involved, if any.

[1] Edward Sapir, *Language,* Harcourt Brace and Company, 1921; p. 39. Quoted by permission.

C. DRILLS

1. Transitive Stem Finals. Circle the word containing the instrumental that corresponds to the action in the picture.

(Check column)

1. pîkoham

   pîkonam

   pîkoškam

1. pîkonam

2. pîkoham

   pîkoškam

   pîkonam

2. pîkoham

3. pîkonam

   pîkoškam

   pîkoham

3. pîkoškam

4. tahkonam

   tahkwatêhtam

   tahkwaham

4. tahkonam

(Check column)

5. tahkwatêhtam

tahkoškam

tahkonam

5. tahkwatêhtam

6. tahkoškam

tahkonam

tahkwaham

6. tahkoškam

7. kawinam

kawaham

kawiškam

7. kawinam

8. kawiškam

kawaham

kawinam

8. kawaham

9. ohpinam

ohpaham

9. ohpinam

(Check column)

10. ohpaham

ohpinam

ohpipitam

10. ohpaham

2. Fill in the gaps in the following conversation with an appropriate word from the list supplied. Each word should be used once only.

kitayâwâw, ka-kî-mîšahên, n'ka-kociškên, nahiškamwak, n'kî-pîkoškên, n'ka-kisiwâsîstâk, ta-kî-pohciškawêw, kin'tawêl'tên, ka-natawi-kanawâpahtênânaw, ka-kî-tahkonâw, n'ka-masinahikân, niwî-itohtân, ninatawêlimâw, niwî-nanâtawâpamâwak, ka-kî-nôcihtânânaw.

Cîmis: anohcîhkê cîmânihk n'kî-iši-apin, ________________ mâka.
 mâškôc ________________ nistês.

Twâmas: ______________ nâ, kititêl'tên? n'tawâc mwêhci ________
 __________________.

Cîmis: môl' âpatan, šwâpihk ______________ pitamâ.

Twâmas: ______________ nâ kêkwân? mâškôc oški-wîlâhcikana.

Cîmis: êhê. palacîs ________________ nêsta ašikanak. mâškôc
 ______________ nêsta maskisina. âtiht ililiwak otinamwak,
 môla mâka ______________.

Twâmas: môla mâškôc ________________ 'wênihkân ašikana.
 ___________ nâ šôliyân?

Cîmis: môla, ________________ piko. kwayask n'kiskêlimik okimâw.

Twâmas: ________________ nâ awa apwoy? ______________________
 kâ-pîsisicik šôliyânak. nâkê mâškôc cîmân __________________.

3. VTI Stems + …kê- Verb Final

Given the corresponding nouns, try your hand at producing the related verb forms on the pattern:

Recording: cîkahikan ê-âpacihtâyân, ______________.
Reply: cîkahikan ê-âpacihtâyân, n'ka-cîkahikân.
 Using an axe, I'll chop.

1. cîkahikan ê-âpacihtâyân, ______________.
2. masinahikan ê-âpacihtâyân, ______________.
3. kînipocikan [file] ê-âpacihtâyân, ______________.
4. pâskisikan ê-âpacihtâyân, ______________.
5. kwâškwêpicikan ê-âpacihtâyân, ______________.
6. kîškipocikan [cross cut saw] ê-âpacihtâyân, ______________.
7. pôtâcikan [bugle, trumpet] ê-âpacihtâyân, ______________.
8. kitohcikan [musical instrument] ê-âpacihtâyân, ______________.

4. Sizes and Prices

4.1 To the question, tân' êspihcâk anima astotin?
Reply on the pattern, nîswâs ispihcâw (It's size 7.) *or*
nîswâs mîna âpihtaw ispihcâw (Size 7 ½).

—And so on throughout the exercise, varying your reply with each size. The recording gives sizes and prices in English throughout this section. There is time for mimicry at each step.

		(Check column)	
4.1.1 tân' êspihcâk anima astotin?	6	n'kotwâs	ispihcâw.
tân' êspihcâk anima kotak astotin?	6 ½	n'kotwâs mîna âpihtaw	ispihcâw.
tân' êspihcâk anima astotin?	7	nîswâs	ispihcâw.
tân' êspihcâk anima kotak astotin?	7 ½	nîswâs mîna âpihtaw	ispihcâw.
tân' êspihcâk anima astotin?	8	niyânânêw	ispihcâw.
4.1.2 tân' êspihcâk anima pakwayân?	12	nîšošâp	ispihcâw.
	12 ½	nîšošâp mîna âpihtaw	ispihcâw.
	13	nistošâp	ispihcâw.
	13 ½	nistošâp mîna âpihtaw	ispihcâw.
	14	nêw'šâp[1]	ispihcâw.
	14 ½	nêw'šâp mîna âpihtaw	ispihcâw.
	20	nîšitana	ispihcâw.
4.1.3 tân' êtikitit[2] ana palacîs?	30	nistomitana	itikitiw.
	30 ½	nistomitana mîna âpihtaw	itikitiw.
	36	nistomitana n'kotwâs	itikitiw.
	37	nistomitana nîswâs	itikitiw.
	38	nistomitana niyânânêw	itikitiw.
	39	nistomitana šânk	itikitiw.
	40	nêmitana	itikitiw.
	41	nêmitana pêyak	itikitiw.
	42	nêmitana nîšo	itikitiw.
	43	nêmitana nisto	itikitiw.

1 < nêwišâp: [nêyošâp] by /w + i / > /o/. Insertion of /y/ required since Cree does not permit two vowels to occur adjacent to each other.
2 Alternative form: tân' êspîhcikitit? ... ispîhcikiti-.

4.1.4 tân' êspihcâki anihi maskisina?	7(½)	nîswâs (mîna âpihtaw)	ispihcâwa.
	8	niyânânêw	ispihcâwa.
	9	šânk (*or* šâkitât)	ispihcâwa.
	10	mitâht	ispihcâwa.
	11	pêyakošâp	ispihcâwa.
	12	nîšošâp	ispihcâwa.

4.1.5 tân' êspicâk anima wâpwayân?	56	niyâlomitana n'kotwâs	ispihcâw.
	58	niyâlomitana niyânânĕw	ispihcâw.
	59	niyâlomitana šânk	ispihcâw.
	60	n'kotwâsomitana	ispihcâw.
	70	nîswâsomitana	ispihcâw.
	80	niyânânêyamitana	ispihcâw.

4.1.6 tân' êspîhcikitit ana ašikan?	7(½)	nîswâs (mîna âpihtaw)	ispîhcikitiw.
	8	niyânânêw	ispîhcikitiw.
	9	šânk (*or* šâkitât)	ispîhcikitiw.
tân' êtikiticik aniki ašikanak?	10	mitâht	itikitiwak.
	11	pêyakošâp	itikitiwak.
	12	nîšošâp	itikitiwak.

4.2 The customary form for asking and indicating price is—

Question: tânîlikohk mâka êspalik?
How much does it come to?
Answer: pêyakw-ahtay mîna pêyakošâp sêns ispaliw.
It comes to one dollar and eleven cents.

First drill the above formula, then in the following sections drill the amounts alone. Mimic the recording.

4.2.1	$1.00	pêyakw-ahtay
	$1.50	pêyakw-ahtay mîna âpihtaw
	$2.00	nîšw-ahtay
	$2.50	nîšw-ahtay mîna âpihtaw
	$3.00	nistw-ahtay
	$3.50	nistw-ahtay mîna âpihtaw
	$4.00	nêw-ahtay
	$4.50	nêw-ahtay mîna âpihtaw
	$5.00	niyâlw-ahtay
	$5.50	niyâlw-ahtay mîna âpihtaw

$6.00	n'kotwâsw-ahtay
$6.50	n'kotwâsw-ahtay mîna âpihtaw
$10.00	mitâhtw-ahtay
$10.50	mitâhtw-ahtay mîna âpihtaw
$11.00	pêyakošâpw-ahtay
$11.50	pêyakošâpw-ahtay mîna âpihtaw
$12.00	nîšošâpw-ahtay
$12.50	nîšošâpw-ahtay mîna âpihtaw (*Cf.* B.2 above.)

4.2.2 šânkwêš means a quarter (of a dollar) or 25¢. (*Cf.* Ojibwa šânkwêšši-, mink.)

$1.25	pêyakw-ahtay mîna šânkwêš
$1.75	pêyakw-ahtay mîna nisto-šânkwêš
$2.25	nîšo mîna šânkwêš
$2.75	nîšo mîna nisto-šânkwêš
$3.25	nisto mîna šânkwêš
$3.75	nisto mîna nisto-šânkwêš
$10.25	mitâht mîna šânkwêš
$10.75	mitâht mîna nisto-šânkwêš
$11.25	pêyakošâp mîna šânkwêš
$11.75	pêyakošâp mîna nisto-šânkwêš
$12.25	nîšošâp mîna šânkwêš
$12.75	nîšošâp mîna nisto-šânkwêš

(Note that šânkwêš, like ahtay, when coupled with a numeral to indicate an amount, forms a compound and occurs always in singular form. *Cf.* B.2 above.)

4.2.3 Drill the following sequence several times until you can look at the Arabic numerals and give the amount in Cree without hesaitation.

$9.95	šânkw-ahtay mîna šânkomitana niyâlan sêns
$10.01	mitâhtw-ahtay mîna pêyak sêns
$11.21	pêyakošâpw-ahtay mîna nîšitana pêyak sêns
$12.22	nîšošâpw-ahtay mîna nîšitana nîšo sêns
$13.33	nistošâpw-ahtay mîna nistomitana nisto sêns
$14.44	nêw'šâpw-ahtay mîna nêmitana nêw sêns
$15.55	niyâlošâpw-ahtay mîna niyâlomitana niyâlan sêns
$16.66	n'kotwâsošâpw-ahtay mîna n'kotwâsomitana n'kotwâs sêns
$17.77	nîswâsošâpw-ahtay mîna nîswâsomitana nîswâs sêns
$18.88	niyânânêw'šâpw-ahtay mîna niyânânêyamitana niyânânêw sêns
$19.99	šânkošâpw-ahtay mîna šânkomitana šânk sêns

4.2.4 The numeral will be repeated once, the amount in dollars three times. Mimic the recording carefully, and THINK THE MEANING IN CREE as you repeat.

20	nîšitana
$20.00	nîšitanawêhtay *or* nîšitana tahtw-ahtay
21	nîšitana pêyak
$21.00	nîšitana pêyak tahtw-ahtay
22	nîšitana nîšo
$22.00	nîšitana nîšo tahtw-ahtay
30	nistomitana
$30.00	nistomitanawêhtay *or* nistomitana tahtw-ahtay
33	nistomitana nisto
$33.00	nistomitana nisto tahtw-ahtay
34	nistomitana nêw
$34.00	nistomitana nêw tahtw-ahtay
40	nêmitana
$40.00	nêmitanawêhtay *or* nêmitana tahtw-ahtay
45	nêmitana niyâlan
$45.00	nêmitana niyâlan tahtw-ahtay
46	nêmitana n'kotwâs
$46.00	nêmitana n'kotwâs tahtw-ahtay
50	niyâlomitana
$50.00	niyâlomitanawêhtay *or* niyâlomitana tahtw-ahtay
57	niyâlomitana nîswâs
$57.00	niyâlomitana nîswâs tahtw-ahtay
58	niyâlomitana niyânânêw
$58.00	niyâlomitana niyânânêw tahtw-ahtay
59	niyâlomitana šânk
$59.00	niyâlomitana šânk tahtw-ahtay
60	n'kotwâsomitana
$60.00	n'kotwâsomitanawêhtay *or* n'kotwâsomitana tahtw-ahtay
70	nîswâsomitana
$70.00	nîswâsomitanawêhtay *or* nîswâsomitana tahtw-ahtay
80	niyânânêyamitana
$80.00	niyânânêyamitanawêhtay *or* niyânânêyamitana tahtw-ahtay
90	šânkomitana
$90.00	šânkomitanawêhtay *or* šânkomitana tahtw-ahtay

100	mitâhtomitana
$100.00	mitâhtomitanawêhtay *or* mitâhtomitana tahtw-ahtay
twice	nîšwâ
200	nîšwâ mitâhtomitana
$200.00	nîšwâ mitâhtomitanawêhtay *or* nîšwâ mitâhtomitana tahtw-ahtay
thrice	nistwâ
300	nistwâ mitâhtomitana
$300.00	nistwâ mitâhtomitanawêhtay *or* nistwâ mitâhtomitana tahtw-ahtay
1,000	kišê-mitâhtomitana
$1,000	kišê-mitâhtomitanawêhtay *or* kišê-mitâhtomitana tahtw-ahtay

5. Demonstrative Pronouns

Listen to the recording twice, then mimic the recorded utterance, completing it with the correct form from the brackets.

		(Check column)
1.	kî-pêhtawâw nâ ana _______ (atim ~ cîmân)?	atim
2.	môla n'tôhci-miskênân anihi _______ (ašikanak ~ mâhkiya).	mâhkiya
3.	tântê anima _______ (awâšiš ~ mêskanaw)?	mêskanaw
4.	wîpac mâškôc ka-kociškawânawak ôko ________ (palacîsak ~ astotina).	palacîsak
5.	kin'tawêlimâw nâ awa ________ (askihk ~ pâskisikan)?	askihk
6.	môla ka-kî-ayânâwâw ôma ________ (cîmân ~ acimošiš).	cîmân
7.	tâpwê nâspic milwâšinwa ôho _______ (namêsak ~ maskisina).	maskisina
8.	n'ka-kî-pâskiswânân nâ ana ________ (šîšîp ~ pâskisikan)?	šîšîp
9.	wêsâ mâškôc mišikitiwak aniki _______ (atimwak ~ pakwayâna).	atimwak
10.	tân' êspîhcikitit awa _________ (ašikan ~ pîskâkan)?	ašikan
11.	n'ka-nahiškên nâ ôma _________ (palacîs ~ astotin)?	astotin
12.	tânîlikohk mâka êspalik anima ______ (apwoy ~ wâpwayân)?	wâpwayân
13.	âšay wîpac ka-wâpahtênânaw ôho ________ (ililiwak ~ sîpiya).	sîpiya
14.	kî-wî-pohciškênâwâw nâ anihi ________ (pîskâkana ~ palacîs)?	pîskâkana
15.	kišâstaw wîstâsihtâkosiwak ôko ____ (pilêsiwak ~ pâskisikana)!	pilêsiwak

Drill 5, Unit 5.C may be used as a review of the obviative of pronouns.

D. CONVERSATION PRACTICE

1. Review the Basic Conversation. Cover the Cree column and, working from the English, produce the Cree equivalents. Uncover the Cree text line by line to check yourself. Go through the whole conversation, checking the items which you cannot produce without hesitation. When you have finished, learn these thoroughly; then repeat the entire conversation.

Check the drills to make sure you can repeat them correctly and unhesitatingly. Do not proceed to the next unit until you feel you have achieved mastery of the material in the present one.

2. Imagine yourself to be looking at various articles of clothing in the store. Explain what you want, what size, how many, etc. Finally, haggle over the price.

Useful expressions: tân' êtakihtêk? How much does it (inan.) cost?
tân' êtakisot? How much does it (anim.) cost ?

itakisow	VAI	it (anim.) costs ......
itakihtêw	VII	it (inan.) costs ......
âlimakisow	VAI	it (anim.) is expensive
âlimakihtêw	VII	it (inan.) is expensive
wêhtakisow	VAI	it (anim.) is cheap
wêhtakihtêw	VII	it (inan.) is cheap

A frequently heard expression is, wêsâ âliman it's too expensive: *i.e.,* too difficult.

3. Ask whether you may try on various types of clothing. Say whether they fit or not, are too large, too small, etc. You don't have any cash. Ask whether you may sign for them or use a credit card.

n'ka-kî-âpacihâw nâ plâstiko-têhamân?
May I use a credit card?

êhê. masinaha kitišinihkâsowin ôta.
Yes. Sign your name here.

or êhê. masinahotiso ôta. *(a reciprocal imperative)*
Yes. Sign here: *lit.,* Sign yourself here.

4. You have been working at the store, have a good deal of money and want to buy a new gun. Your old one is broken. Perhaps you even need a new canoe. Tell a friend about this and discuss the prices of guns, canoes, etc. You enjoy eating ducks, geese, and your wife is a good cook (milotêpo-VAI). Then conclude the conversation, saying you are going upriver. Your friends are staying there and they want to break camp.

E. LISTENING IN

Cîmis:	nawac milwêl'tâkwan ôta ê-takwâkihk, manâ?
Saylas:	êhê. šâkoc mâka ta-ati-tahkâyâw nâkê nawac.
Cîmis:	kî-wâpamâwak nâ âšay pilêsiwak?
Saylas:	môla. môl' êškwâ pâpihlâwak pilêsiwak. wîpac mâškôc âšay ta-ati-pâpihlâwak mâka. nâsic[1] mâškôc ta-lipâci-kîšikâw kê-wâpahk, n'titêl'tên.
Cîmis:	kitayâwâwak nâ kâ-pîsisicik šôliyânak? niwî-otinikân[2] sikalêtak.[3]
Saylas:	n'tayâwâwak nêw-ahtay mîna niyâlomitana šânk nipwâkitimihk.[4] kayâm[5] ka-kî-ayâwâw niyâlomitana šânk.
Cîmis:	mîkwêc. nin'tawêlimâw nistomitana niyâlan sêns piko. kâ-atâwêt ayâw oški-kêkwâna. n'kî-kociškên nimaskisina têpiskâk. âšay mêscipaliwa.
Saylas:	mêscipaliw nipalacîs, nêsta mâka nin'tawêlimâwak oški-ašikanak; môla mâka n'tayâwâw šôliyân. môla mâka n'ka-kî-tipahên anohc wîla.
Cîmis:	šâkoc mâka kitayâwâw nêw-ahtay. ka-kî-ayâwâwak mâka ašikanak anohc. nêw-ahtay ê-ayâwacik[6] ka-kî-šwâpihkân ašikanak nêsta mâka pakwayân.
Saylas:	ka-kî-tahkonên nâ ôma walahpicikan? nimikwaškâtêl'tên nipalacîs ohci. pîkopaliw,—niwî-mâkwahpitâw mâka.
Cîmis:	tân' êtikitit?
Saylas:	nistomitana pêyak mîna âpihtaw itikitiw mwêhci kwayask. tânîlikohk êtakisocik oški-ayahâwak?
Cîmis:	môla mwêhci kwayask n'kiskêl'tên. mâškôc niyâlan mîna âpihtaw n'titêl'tên. môla mâškôc ka-kî-masinahikân.
Saylas:	môla mâškôc. nakiskaw mâškôc kêyâpac ta-ispaliw.[7]
Cîmis:	kikiskêl'tên nâ kêkwân? n'kî-miskawâwak nîšo apwoyak mâmihk sîpîhk otâkošîhk.
Saylas:	awênihkân?

[1] nâsic: *variant for* nâspic
[2] niwî-otinikân I want to buy
[3] sikalêt- NA cigarette
[4] nipwâkitimihk in my pocket
[5] kayâm all right
[6] ê-ayâwacik in your having them (*anim.*)
[7] nakiskaw ta-ispaliw it will last a little while

Cîmis: kî-kihtohtêw êntiniy,[8]—nêstapiko wîla otayâna.
Saylas: nêsta nîla n'kihtohtân nakiskaw piko,—nakiskaw piko nâspic.
Cîmas: n'tohta! Kêkwân anima? awâšiš mâškôc?
Saylas: môla mâškôc. ôlow n'cêmišiš piko. lâlatin n'kî-iši-miskawâw namês; wîla mâka acimošiš n'tawêlimêw namêsa.
Cîmis: êko wâs' âni. wâciyê.
Saylas: wâciyê.

8 êntiniy NA Henry

F. REFERENCE LIST

ahtay-	NA	a fur; a dollar
anihi	PR dem. inan. pl.	those (ones)
aniki	PR dem. anim. pl.	those (ones)
askihkw-	NA	kettle, pail
ašikan-	NA	sock, stocking
atâwêwikamikw-	NI	trading post, store
âlimakihtê-	VII	be expensive
âlimakiso-	VAI	be expensive
âpihtaw	IPC	half
ispali-	VA / VII	it so goes, it lasts
ispihcâ-	VII	be so large, be of such a size *v.* ispîhcâ-.
ispîhcâ-	VII	be so large, be of such a size: tân' êspîhcâk? How large is it? *v.* ispihcâ-.
ispîhcikiti-	VAI	be so large, be of such a size: tân' êspîhcikitit? How large is he (*or* it [anim.])?
išicišahikan-	NI	parcel to be sent *v.* walahpicikan-.
itakihtê-	VII	cost so much
itakiso-	VAI	cost so much
itikiti-	VAI	be so big: tân' êtikitit? How big is it (anim.)?
kawah-	VTI	take s.t. down *or* knock s.t. down with an instrument
kawahw-	VTA	take s.o. down *or* knock s.o. down with an instrument
kawipit-	VTA / VTI	pull s.o./ s.t. down
kawišk-	VTI	bring *or* knock s.t. down by body action
kawiškaw-	VTA	bring *or* knock s.o. down by body action
kayâm	IPC	all right!
kâ-pîsisicik šôliyânak	Nom. A pl.	small change
kîhkêhtakâhk	IPC	in the corner
kocišk-	VTI	try s.t. on (clothing)
kociškaw-	VTA	try s.o. on (clothing)
masinahikê-	VAI	write, get "debt" (*i.e.,* credit) at the store
maskisin-	NI	shoe, boot, moccasin
mâkwahpit-	VTA / VTI	tie s.o./ s.t. up

mâmaw	IPC	together, altogether
mikwaškâtêliht-	VTI	worry about s.t.
mikwaškâtêlim-	VTA	worry about s.o.
milonâkosi-	VAI	look nice
milonâkwan-	VII	look nice
milotêpo-	VAI	be a good cook, be good at cooking
nahišk-	VTI	fit s.t. (in Cree the person fits the garment)
nahiškaw-	VTA	fit s.o. (*i.e.,* a garment represented by an NA)
nanâtawâpaht-	VTI	look for s.t., search for s.t.
nanâtawâpam-	VTA	look for s.o., search for s.o.
nânatawâpaht-	VTI	*variant of* nanâtawâpaht-, *q.v.*
nânatawâpam-	VTA	*variant of* nanâtawâpam-, *q.v.*
nâsic	IPC	very, very much *synon. for* nâspic
nêmitana	IPC	forty
nêmitanawêhtay-	NA	forty dollars
nêw-ahtay-	NA	four dollars
nêw'šâpw	IPC	fourteen
nikotwâsomitana	IPC	sixty
nikotwâsošâpw	IPC	sixteen
nistomitana	IPC	thirty
nistošâpw	IPC	thirteen
nistwâ	IPC	three times
niyâlomitana	IPC	fifty
niyâlošâpw	IPC	fifteen
niyânânêw'šâpw	IPC	eighteen
niyânânêyamitana	IPC	eighty
nîswâsomitana	IPC	seventy
nîswâsošâpw	IPC	seventeen
nîšošâpw	IPC	twelve
nîšitana	IPC	twenty
nîšwâ	IPC	twice
ôhi	PR dem. anim. obv. and inan. pl.	*MC variant of* ôho, *q.v.*
ôho	PR dem. anim. obv.; inan. prox. & obv. pl.	this (one), these (ones) these (ones)
ôki	PR dem. anim. prox. pl.	*MC variant of* ôko, *q.v*
ôko	PR dem. anim. prox. pl.	these (ones)
pakwayân-	NI	shirt
pâhkân	IPC	presently, shortly

pêyakošâpw	IPC	eleven
pîkoh-	VTI	break s.t. by instrument
pîkohw-	VTA	break s.o. by instrument
pîkošk-	VTI	break s.t. by body action
pîkoškaw-	VTA	break s.o. by body action
pîsisi-	VAI	be in bits, be in pieces
pîsiskâkan-	NI	coat, jacket
plâstiko-têhamân-	NA	credit card
pohcišk-	VTI	put s.t. on
pohciškaw-	VTA	put s.o. on
pôtâcikan-	NI	bugle, trumpet, blowing instrument (of music)
pwâkit-	NI	pocket
sêns-	NA	cent
sikalêt-	NA	cigarette
šânkomitana	IPC	ninety
šânkošâpw	IPC	nineteen
šânkw-ahtay-	NA	nine dollars
šânkwêš-	NA	quarter; twenty-five cents
šwâpihkê-	VAI	buy, shop
tahkon-	VTA / VTI	hold s.o./ s.t. by hand
tahkošk-	VTI	hold s.t. by leg *or* body action
tahkoškaw-	VTA	hold s.o. by leg *or* body action
tahkwah-	VTI	hold s.t. by instrument; steer s.t.
tahkwatêht-	VTI	hold s.t. in the mouth (with the teeth)
tahkwatêm-	VTA	hold s.o. in the mouth (with the teeth)
tahtw-ahtay-	NA	so many dollars *v.* tân'tahto- how many?
tânîlikohk	IPC	(up to) how much, to what extent
têhamân-	NA	card
tipah-	VTI	pay for s.t., measure s.t.
tipahw-	VTA	pay for s.o., measure s.o.
walahpicikan-	NI	(wrapped) parcel. *Cf.* parcel to be sent: išicišahikan-.
walahpit-	VTA / VTI	wrap s.o./ s.t. up
wêhtakiht-	VII	be inexpensive, be cheap
wêhtakiso-	VAI	be inexpensive, be cheap

G. REVIEW

10.A Kakwêcihkêmôwina—Questions

Answer each question with a full sentence and elaborate your reply if you can: *e.g.,* to #1 you might add, They're nice too, but I don't think they'll fit.

1. tân' êtakisot awa palacîs?
2. tân' êspihcâk anima pakwayân?
3. tântê okimâw? atâwêwikamikohk nâ?
4. mêscipaliwak nâ kitašikanak?
5. awênihkânak aniki wîlawâw?
6. kin'tawêlimâw nâ palacîs nêstapiko astotin?
7. môla nâ kin'tawêlimâwak ôko ašikanak?
8. ta-kî-kanawêl'tam nâ opâskisikan omâhkîmihk?
9. kiwî-masinahikân nâ?
10. n'tawêl'tam nâ nêsta pakwayâniliw?
11. tân' êspihcâk mâka anima astotin?
12. tântê omaskisina? kîhkêhtakâhk nâ?
13. kotak nâ kêkwân kin'tawêl'tên?
14. tânîlikohk aniki askihkwak?
15. ka-kî-tipahênâwâw nâ mâka kê-wâpahk ôho?
16. n'ka-otinên nâ ôma walahpicikan?
17. ta-otinamwak nâ ililiwak ôho kêkwâna?
18. milonâkwan nâ kititêl'tên ôma pîskâkan?
19. kiwî-kociškênâwâw nâ ôho maskisina?
20. âšay nâ kî-pohciškam owîlâhcikana?
21. ninahiškawânânak nâ ôko ašikanak?
22. kitayân nâ pakwayâna anohc kâ-kîšikâk?
23. awênihkân omaskisina kîhkêhtakâhk anta?

10.B Naskwêwasihtwâwina—Answers

Formulate questions to which the following might be appropriate answers.

1. šâkoc otinamwak.
2. êhê, n'ka-walahpitên ôho.
3. nêmitanawêhtay mîna n'kotwâsomitana nîswâs sêns.
4. pêyakošâp mîna âpihtaw itikitiwak.
5. šwâpihk mâškôc ihtâw.
6. môla mwêhci n'kiskêl'tên.
7. tâpwê. nâspic milwâšišiwak.
8. ayahâw, —mâškôc n'ka-otinên nêsta maskisina.
9. môla. ka-nahiškên mâškôc.
10. nîšitana pêyak nêstapiko nîsitana nîšo itikitiw.
11. êhê, nin'tawêlimâwak nîšo askihkwak.
12. môla môšak nahiškamwak owîlâhcikaniwâwa.
13. êhê. šâkoc mâka ta-ati-tahkâyâw nâkê nawac.
14. môl' êškwâ pâpihlâwak pilêsiwak.
15. šwâpihk. niwî-otinikân sikalêtak.
16. nin'tawêlimâw nistomitana niyâlan sêns piko.
17. môla niwî-pohciškawâwak ôko ašikanak. kêkât mêscipaliwak.
18. môšak mâškôc ta-kî-masinahikêw.
19. awâšiš mâškôc.
20. mâškôc. ôlow nicêmišiš piko.
21. môla. apišîš piko pîkopaliw. nakiskaw mâškôc kêyâpac ta-ispaliw.
22. matêw. âšay kî-kihtohtêw.
23. mâškôc êntiniy otayâna.

UNIT ELEVEN

A. BASIC CONVERSATION

1. Fall Fishing

Kiyâsk (Seagull) meets a friend, Šinkipiš[1] (Diver Duck), who has returned from the fishing grounds.

Kiyâsk:	kî-wâpamitin kêkišêp.	I saw you this morning.
Šinkipiš:	wîpac nawac n'kî-mišakânân.	We came to shore pretty early.
Kiyâsk:	êhê, kî-pêhtâtinâwâw.	Yes, I heard you.
Šinkipiš:	kâ-iši-nôtamêsêyâhk	where we (1p) fish
	n'kî-pêci-kîwânân	we (1p) came back
	n'kî-pêci-kîwânân kâ-iši-nôtamêsêyâhk ohci.	We came back from the fishing grounds.
	alapiy-	fish net
	kitawihin	you (2) lend me
	ka-kî-awihin nâ alapiy?	Can you lend me a fish net?
Kiyâsk:	otânâhk kâ-tawâstêk	last week
	anohcîhkê	just now, recently
	kî-kakwêcimin nâ	did you (2) ask me (about s.t.)?
	êhê. kî-kakwêcimin[2] nâ anohcîhkê,—nêstapiko otânâhk kâ-tawâstêk? kikiskisin nâ?	Yes. Did you ask me (about it) just now,—or was it last week? Do you remember?
Šinkipiš:	kî-kakwêcimitin[2]	I asked you (2)
	otâkošîhk kî-natotamâtin.	I asked you (for it) yesterday.
Kiyâsk:	pêyakwâ ê-kîšikâk	some day
	ka-mîlitin	I'll give (it to) you (2)

[1] See B.6 below: šinkipiš.

[2] kakwêcim- VTA ask s.o. a question (*about* s.t.), make a request of s.o. Ask, request, entreat, beseech, beg s.o. *for* s.t. is expressed by natotamaw- VTA.

	mâškôc ka-mîlitin pêyakwâ ê-kîšikâk.	Perhaps I'll give it to you some day.
	ka-âpacihâw	you will use him
	kîla ka-âpacihâw awasitê ispîš nîla.	*You'll* use it (anim.) more than I do.
	ê-pakitahwâniwahk	in (one's) setting nets
	milopaliw nâ ê-pakitahwâniwahk?	Is the (net-) fishing good?
Šinkipiš:	oški-kîšikâw	it is Monday
	n'kî-natawi-kapêšinân	we (1p) went to pitch camp
	n'kî-n'tawi-kapêšinân ê-oški-kîšikâk.	We went to pitch camp on Monday.
	ê-kî-iškwâ-âpihtâ-kîšikâk	in the afternoon
	pakitahwâw	he sets nets
	n'kî-pakitahwânân ê-kî-iškwâ-âpihtâ-kîšikâk.	We put out the nets in the after noon.
	kâ-iškwâ-nisto-kîšikâk	after the third day (*i.e.,* when-it-had-finished-three-daying)
	n'kî-pâswânânak	we (1p) dried them
	kâ-iškwâ-nisto-kîšikâk n'kî-otinânânak alapiyak. n'kî-pâswânânak mâka.	Three days later we took the nets (up) and dried them out.
Kiyâsk:	mihkwacakâš	sucker (red)
	kî-nipahâwâwak	you (2) killed them (anim.)
	atihkamêk	whitefish
	mâškôc awasitê atihkamêkwak kî-nipahâwâwak nêsta mihkwacakâšak.	I guess you got mostly whitefish and suckers.
Šinkipiš:	ka-kî-ohci-kâhcitinâw	you'll be able to catch him from-
	misiwê piko tôwi-namês	every kind of fish
	misiwê piko tôwi-namês ka-kî-ohci- kâhcitinâw alapîhk.	You can get every kind of fish from a net.
Kiyâsk:	wîskâc nâ kikwâškwêpicikân?	Do you ever fish with a hook?
Šinkipiš:	mâsamêkos	speckled trout
	kinošêw	pike, jackfish

	môla, môl' âpatan. n'kî-ayâwânânak kinošêwak nêsta mâsamêkosak.	No, it's not worth it. We (1p) got some jackfish and speckled trout too.
	kêposkâhk	at Kapiskau
	pêšoc	near to, close to (+ loc.)
	âhkwatin	it is freezing
	âšay wîpac kî-ati-âhkwatin mâka pêšoc kêposkâhk.	It soon began to freeze though near Kapiskau.

2. Camp Activities

Kiyâsk:	kî-takošininâwâw	you (2p) arrived
	misiwê nâ mâka kî-takošininâwâw?	Did you all arrive (together)?
Šinkipiš:	ništam	first (in order)
	môla. nîla ništam n'kî-takošinin.	No. I arrived first.
	kêšîciwan	Kashechewan (near mouth of Albany River)
	kê-otâkošinilik (*obviative*)	this afternoon, early evening
	ta-takošin nikosis kêšîciwanohk kê-otâkošinilik.	My son will come to Kashechewan (late) this afternoon.
Kiyâsk:	ka-âhkwatimâwâwak	you (2p) will freeze them (anim.)
	ka-šîwahwâwâwak	you (2p) will salt them (anim.)
	ka-šîwahwâwâwak nâ mâka namêsak nêstapiko ka-âhkwatimâwâwak?	Will you salt the fish down or freeze them?
Šinkipiš:	mâškôc n'ka-akwâpaswânânak.	Perhaps we'll smoke them.
Kiyâsk:	ka-kî-pêcicišahamawinân nâ?	Will you be able to send us some?
Šinkipiš:	mwêhci anohc ka-išicišahamâtinâwâw.	I'll send you some right over.
Kiyâsk:	milwâšin! ka-tipahamâtin.	Good! I'll pay you.
	iskali-kîšik	all day
	tân' êhtôtaman iskali-kîšik nêtê?	What do you do all day down there?

Šinkipiš:	nicîkahênân	we (1p) chop it
	nipîsikahênân	we (1p) split it
	n'tôtâpânân	we (1p) haul
	n'tôtâpânân nêsta nipîsikahênân,— nêstapiko nin'tawi-cîkahênân nôhcimihk.	Oh, we haul (wood) and split it,— or we go out to chop it in the bush.
Kiyâsk:	êti-otâkošihki (*changed conj. subj.*)	whenever evening comes on
	kôskawâtêlihtâkwan	it is quiet, it is tranquil
	šâkoc kôskawâtêlihtâkwan êti-otâkošihki.	I'll bet it's quiet in the evenings.
Šinkipiš:	wâšakâm	around
	nipimâskošininân	we lie lengthwise (on a solid surface)
	êhê. nipimâskošininân wâšakâm iškotêhk walawîtimihk.	Yes. We lie around the fire outside.
	n'tapwânân	we barbecue, we roast over a fire
	ayawiši-namês milwâšišiw. n'tapwânân iškotêhk.	Fresh fish is good. We barbecue (it) over the fire.
	itinêw	he holds him so
	itin (*VTA imperative*)	hold him so
	otônihk	in his mouth
	tâpišahwêw	he strings him, he threads him
	tâpišaw (*VTA imperative*)	string him, thread him
	tâpišaw otônihk mistikoliw, iškotêhk mâka itin.	Insert a stick in his mouth, and hold him over the fire.

B. DISCUSSION OF GRAMMAR

1. Verbs

1.1 Transitive Animate Local Inflection: 2 -1 :: 1 - 2

Up to this point we have studied two sets of VTA forms, the Direct (1 → 3, etc.) and the Inverse (1 ← 3, etc.). It is now time to learn two further short sets where first and second persons interact: the Local inflection. In the following paradigm 1p stands for "we-*exclusive*".

2 → 1	ki...wâpam...in	1 → 2	ki...wâpam...ιtin
2 → 1p	ki...wâpam...inân	1p → 2	ki...wâpam...ιtinân
2p → 1/1p	ki...wâpam...inâwâw	1/1p → 2p	ki...wâpam...ιtinâwâw

NOTE. i. The personal prefix is always ki....
ii. Wherever 2nd person, as either actor or goal, is plural the verb gives no formal indication of number for 1st person.

Use of aspect markers and preverbs follows the regular order: *e.g.,*

kiwî-pêci-wâpamin nâ?	Do you want to come and see me?
môla kitôhci-wâpaminân.	You didn't see us.

1.2 Contraction: /aw- + ...ιtin/ > /âtin/

In this unit you meet a number of verb stems ending in /aw/: *e.g.,* pêhtaw-, miskaw-, tipahamaw-. In the Local inflection contraction takes place, but on the 1 - 2 side only. /aw- + ...ιtin/ becomes /âtin/: *e.g.,*

	You would expect	but you get
1 → 2	kipêht**aw**ιtin	kipêhtâtin
1p → 2	kipêht**aw**ιtinân	kipêhtâtinân
1/1p → 2p	kipêht**aw**ιtinâwâw	kipêhtâtinâwâw (*v.* Unit 7.B.3.)

There is no contraction for 2 - 1 (you - me / us) forms:

2 - 1	kipêhtawin
2 - 1p	kipêhtawinân
2p - 1/1p	kipêhtawinâwâw

HISTORICAL NOTE: The endings for 1 → 2 are based on a Cree suffix, ...ιtin, etc., which is reconstructed for Proto-Algonquian, the parent language, as *...eθene. Note the short vowel, *e, which no longer occurs in Cree. Over time *e and *i merged, appearing as the single vowel, /i/, in Modern Cree, but not before the contraction, *aw + *e > *â, had taken place. This contraction remains in present day Cree wherever /i/ occurs in the place of former *e. Such occurrences, when they are at the beginning of a suffix form, have been written ι: *e.g.,* ...ιhk, ...ιtin. (Unit 1.B.2.3, fn. 3, p. 7.) The endings for the 2 → 1 inflection began with the historic vowel *i, not *e: *e.g.,* *...in, *...inân, *...inâwâw, which has remained as modern /i/ and did not contract with *aw. Hence we have uncontracted forms of the type, kipêht**awin**, kimisk**awin**ân, kitipaham**awin**âwâw. (* is used to mark a reconstructed form or segment, / / the distinctive sounds of present day Cree.)

———DRILL 1———

1.3 The Double Object

Certain verbs, such as give, lend, show, often take two objects: *e.g.,*

He gives *you* the *ball.*

Conventional English grammars classify *ball* as the direct object of the verb and *you* as the indirect object. In Cree the *you* is the immediate object of the verb, just as much as in a statement such as

I see *you* - kiwâpamitin.

Note the parallel: I give *you* - kimîlitin. Any further object is simply one place further removed, or next-in-line, as in

I give *you* the *canoe* - kimîlitin cîmân.

Where the immediate object is already in 3rd person position: *e.g.,* I give *John* the *canoe* or I give *him* the *canoe,* the further object slides over into the next slot, the obviative position:

kimîlâw nâ cîmâniliw?	Are you giving *him* the *canoe*?
n'ka-wâpahtilâw awâšiša.	I'll show *her* the *child.*

In short, there is no such thing in Cree as an *indirect* object. The *person* to whom a thing is given, lent, shown, told, sent, etc., is the immediate object of the verb. The *thing* given, lent, shown, etc., is the second object, and so is one position further removed.

Study the following sentences.

1.	môla kikiskêlimitin.	I don't know you.
2.	nôhcimihk kî-iši-wanihitinân.	We lost you (2) in the bush.
3.	kiwî-ayamihitinâwâw.	I (*or* we) want to talk to you (2p).
4.	lâlatin kî-iši-wâpamin.	You (2) saw me at the waterside.
5.	anohc mâka ka-kî-kakwêciminân.	You (2) can ask us right now.
6.	kiwî-âpacihinâwâw nâ?	D you (2p) want to work for me (*or* us)?
7.	môla mwêhci kinisitohtâtin.	I don't quite understand you (2).
8.	âšay kipêhtâtinâwâw.	Now I hear you (2p).
9.	kiwî-tipahamâtinâwâw mwêhci anohc.	I (*or* we) want to pay you (2p) right now.
10.	kî-pêci-mîlitin šôliyân.	I came to give you (2) (some) money.
11.	ka-kî-awihinân nâ apwoy?	Can you (2) lend us a paddle?
12.	kiwî-wîhtamawinâwâw nâ kêkwân?	Do you (2p) want to tell me (*or* us) something?

———DRILLS 2 AND 3———

1.4 More on Compound Stems

The practice of stem composition, especially with verbs, is already familiar to you (Unit 7.B.2), although the length to which this can be carried in Cree may at first be unexpected. A number of such compound stems have been introduced in the present unit. Sometimes the English gloss may obscure as much of the meaning as it reveals. "Cree Grammar" (p. xxxiv) illustrated typical constructions of this kind. The following segment by segment paraphrase will clarify some of the structural and perceptual differences involved. Remember, the English is not an exact translation of the corresponding Cree segment. It is merely intended to convey something of the idea embodied in the Cree. All of the forms immediately following are in the conjunct order of the verb (*v.* Unit 5.B.4).

kê-otâkošihk	this (late) afternoon *or* this (early) evening: *lit.,* when (it)-will-be-evening

ê-oški-kîšikâk	on Monday: *lit.*, in (its)-new-daying
kâ-iškwâ-nisto-kîšikâk	three days later: *lit.*, when (it) had-ended-three-daying
kâ-iškwâ-âpihta-kîšikâk	in the afternoon: *lit.*, when (it) had-ended-half-daying

All four expressions above are single words in Cree. Insertion of hyphens in the English literal rendering is merely intended to help recognition of the Cree components.

Two other forms which have occurred might be noted:

i. ka-kî-ohci-kâhcitinâw. From the English translation in the Basic Conversation an English speaker might expect to find ohci linked immediately to alapiy rather than forming part of the verb stem. In Cree, however, it is common for ohci to form part of the verb stem: ohci-kâhcitinam - he "from-catches" it, and the source from which he catches it goes into the locative case. In the same way one can "from-fall" a rock, or "from-travel" a place. Pay particular attention to the construction at this point and it will not seem so strange when it occurs later in conversations and drills. (*v.* Unit 17.C.4.)

ii. ništam n'kî-takošinin (*v.* A.2, above). The statement consists of two words. An alternative way of saying this is in one compound word: n'kî-ništami-takošinin, where ništami is now a preverb (*v.* Unit 9.B.3). This latter usage is commonly heard around Norway House and in the area about Lake Winnipeg.

1.5 ıši: Position in Compound Stems

Whenever a locating expression, either a particle or noun in the locative, precedes the verb with which it is constructed, the verb stem is preceded by ıši (Unit 3.B.1.5, p. 53): *e.g.*,

nêtê iši-âpatisiw	he is working over there
šwâpihk n'kî-iši-wâpamâwak	I saw them at the store

It often happens that a stem such as wâpam-, âpatisi-, etc., may have one or more preverbs attached: *e.g.*,

	kakwê-ohpinam	she's trying to lift it
	ati-tipiskâw	it's beginning to get dark.

Some of these preverbs display a limited freedom of position in relation to others, depending on the meaning (Unit 7.B.1.2, p. 166): *e.g.,*

	kitati-kakwê-âpatisin	you are beginning to try to work
or	kikakwê-ati-âpatisin	you are trying to begin to work.

ιši, when required as part of such a compound stem, occurs after any aspect markers, including wî, and before any other preverbs: *e.g.,*

	kika-wî-kakwê-ati-âpatisin	you will want to try to begin to work
but	šwâpihk kika-wî-ιši-kakwê-ati-âpatisin	you will want to try to begin to work at the store.

——DRILL 4——

1.6 n-Stems

The Basic Conversation has introduced two new VAI n-stems: takošin arrive, and pimâskošin lie on a solid surface. Take special note of the forms in which these verbs appear. VAI n-stems will be studied fully in Unit 12.

2. **Nouns**

2.1 tôwi

misiwê piko tôwi- is glossed in the Basic Conversation as "every kind of - ". You have already met the form in an earlier drill: kêko tôwi-masinahikan? What kind of book? (Unit 5.C.1, #19). tôwi in this position is a prenoun, conditioning the meaning of the stem that follows: *e.g.,*

misiwê piko tôwi-namês	every kind of fish
misiwê piko tôwi-cîmân	every kind of canoe

2.2 Dialect Variation

One of the two speakers in the Basic Conversation is called Šinkipiš. The word in this form appears to be a borrowing from Ojibwa, and is used at Kashechewan as the name for a diver duck, probably the small or hooded merganser. The term is reported from other areas as applied to the coot; and in still other Cree speaking areas it is not known at all. The form, šihkipiš is attested north of Kashechewan; but the species of duck is more common in Ojibwa speaking country and this may account for the Ojibwa sounding shape of the name. Šinkipiš is also a well known figure of Cree legend.

mâsamêkos is the generic term for trout in the area of Kashechewan. It refers to the speckled or river trout, the kind usually caught in that region. The term, namêkos, lake trout, is heard elsewhere.

mihkwacakâš is used at Kashechewan for the sucker. It denotes the red-horse sucker. The large inland sucker is known as namêpil; and elsewhere than at Kashechewan this may be the generic term.

kinošêw is glossed as pike, jackfish. Further west kinošêw (Plains Cree kinosêw) is the generic word for fish of any kind. In the Kashechewan region the generic word is namês, containing a root obviously shared by namêw, sturgeon and namêkos, lake trout.

2.3 Personal Names

In many parts of the country speakers of an Indian language use names of European origin in their daily contacts with fellow Canadians. Within Cree speaking communities, however, the use of Indian names, sometimes nick-names, is very common. Nicknames may describe a characteristic or event in the life of a person, or they may be functional titles. The two names, Kiyâsk and Šinkipiš were actually used by two people officially called something quite different. Until you know a person well and are an accepted member of the community, it is wiser to use a person's official name. A man might not object to being called Thin Ears, Dirty Neck or Old Fox by close friends. (Indeed,the names might have a different connotation than the outsider would at first suspect.) It might, however, be wise to check whether liberties in this direction are acceptable, coming from a stranger.

C. DRILLS

1. Pronunciation Drill. Listen to the following words and pronounce them carefully after the recording or your teacher's voice. (Some of this is a review of material covered in Unit One. *v.* U1, Pronunciation Drills, c.i and ii.)

pâskiswêw	nipâskiswânân
cîkahwêw	nicîkahwânân
pâswêw	nipâswânân
mîšahwêw	nimîšahwânân
akwâpaswêw	n'takwâpaswânân
pîhtokwêw	nipîhtokwânân
âhtakwêw	n'tâhtakwânân
kî-itwêw	n'kî-itwânân
apwêw	n'tapwânân

2. In the following question-answer sequences repeat the question after the recording, then answer immediately in the affirmative. The recording will then provide the correct reply.

2.1 $2 \rightarrow 1 :: 1 \rightarrow 2$

	(Check column)
kiwâpamin nâ?	êhê, kiwâpamitin.
kimilwêlimin nâ?	êhê, kimilwêlimitin.
kî-kiskêlimin nâ?	êhê, kî-kiskêlimitin.
ka-išiwilin nâ?	êhê, ka-išiwilitin.
kî-wî-kakwêcimin nâ?	êhê, kî-wî-kakwêcimitin.
kipêhtawin nâ?	êhê, kipêhtâtin.
kinisitohtawin nâ?	êhê, kinisitohtâtin.
kinatohtawin nâ?	êhê, kinatohtâtin.
kî-tipahamawin nâ?	êhê, kî-tipahamâtin.
ka-kî-miskawin nâ?	êhê, ka-kî-miskâtin.

2.2 2 → 1p :: 1p → 2

	(Check column)
kiwâpaminân nâ?	êhê, kiwâpamitinâwâw.
kimilwêliminân nâ?	êhê, kimilwêlimitinâwâw.
kikiskêliminân nâ?	êhê, kikiskêlimitinâwâw.
ka-išiwilinân nâ?	êhê, ka-išiwilitinâwâw.
kî-wî-kakwêciminân nâ?	êhê, kî-wî-kakwêcimitinâwâw.
kipêhtawinân nâ?	êhê, kipêhtâtinâwâw.
kinisitohtawinân nâ?	êhê, kinisitohtâtinâwâw.
kinatohtawinân nâ?	êhê, kinatohtâtinâwâw.
kî-tipahamawinân nâ?	êhê, kî-tipahamâtinâwâw.
ka-kî-miskawinân nâ?	êhê, ka-kî-miskâtinâwâw.

2.3 2p → 1(p) :: 1(p) → 2p

kiwâpaminâwâw nâ?	êhê, kiwâpamitinân.
kimilwêliminâwâw nâ?	êhê, kimilwêlimitinân.
kî-kiskêliminâwâw nâ?	êhê, kî-kiskêlimitinân.
ka-išiwilinâwâw nâ?	êhê, ka-išiwilitinân.
kî-wî-kakwêciminâwâw nâ?	êhê, kî-wî-kakwêcimitinân.
kipêhtawinâwâw nâ?	êhê, kipêhtâtinân.
kinisitohtawinâwâw nâ?	êhê, kinisitohtâtinân.
kinatohtawinâwâw nâ?	êhê, kinatohtâtinân.
kitipahamawinâwâw nâ?	êhê, kitipahamâtinân.
ka-kî-miskawinâwâw nâ?	êhê, ka-kî-miskâtinân.

2.4 Mixed

kimilwêlimin nâ?	êhê, kimilwêlimitin.
kî-wî-kakwêciminâwâw nâ?	êhê, kî-wî-kakwêcimitinân.
kiwâpaminân nâ?	êhê, kiwâpamitinâwâw.
kî-kiskêliminâwâw nâ?	êhê, kî-kiskêlimitinân.
kipêhtawin nâ?	êhê, kipêhtâtinân.
kinatohtawin nâ?	êhê, kinatohtâtin.
ka-kî-miskawinân nâ?	êhê, ka-kî-miskâtinâwâw.
kî-tipahamawinân nâ?	êhê, kî-tipahamâtinâwâw.
ka-išiwilinâwâw nâ?	êhê, ka-išiwilitinân.
kinisitohtawinâwâw nâ?	êhê, kinisitohtâtinân.

3. The Double Object

In the sentences,

> Give *him* the book, or Give the book *to him,*
> Show *me* the canoe, or Show the canoe *to me,*

the italicised part is called in conventional English grammar the *indirect* object. In all cases Cree treats the *him, me,* or any personal recipient, as the immediate object of the verb. (*v.* B.1.3 above.) Whatever is given or shown, as in the above examples, then becomes a further, or second, object. Verbs of this type are said to take a *double object.*

3.1 In the following exchanges respond on the model:

Question:	kiwî-awihin nâ cîmân?
Reply:	tâpwê, kiwî-awihitin cîmân.

	(Check column)
kiwî-awihin nâ cîmân?	tâpwê, kiwî-awihitin cîmân.
kiwî-wâpahtilin nâ cîmân?	tâpwê, kiwî-wâpahtilitin cîmân.
kiwî-pêcicišahamawin[1] nâ cîmân?	tâpwê, kiwî-išicišahamâtin[2] cîmân.
(Replace tâpwê with êhê.)	
ka-kî-mîlinân nâ askihkwak?	êhê, ka-kî-mîlitinâwâw askihkwak.
ka-kî-tipahamawinân nâ askihkwak?	êhê, ka-kî-tipahamâtinâwâw askihkwak.
ka-kî-pêcicišahamawinân[1] nâ...?	êhê, ka-kî-išicišahamâtinâwâw[2]...
(Now reply in the negative: môla. môla ka-kî-......)	
ka-kî-awihinâwâw nâ apwoy?	môla. môla ka-kî-awihitinâwâw apwoy.
ka-kî-mîlinâwâw nâ apwoy?	môla. môla ka-kî-mîlitinâwâw apwoy.

3.2 The Double Object and the Obviative

Where the first object of a double object verb is a 3rd person, or proximate, the further object must be one position further removed: *i.e.,* must be obviative. Respond to the following questions on the model given. The recording will check you but allow no time for mimicry.

Question:	âšay nâ ka-kî-mîlin maskisin?
Response:	êhê, nêsta cwân, n'ka-mîlâw maskisiniliw.

[1] pêci... send towards speaker
[2] iši... send away from speaker

âšay nâ ka-kî-mîlin maskisin?	êhê, nêsta cwân n'ka-mîlâw maskisiniliw.
âšay nâ ka-kî-awihin alapiy?	êhê, nêsta cwân, n'ka-awihâw alapiya.
âšay nâ ka-kî-tipahamawin askihk?	êhê, nêsta cwân n'ka-tipahamawâw askihkwa.
âšay nâ ka-kî-pêcicišahamawin namês?	êhê, nêsta cwân n'ka-pêcicišahamawâw namêsa.
âšay nâ ka-kî-pêci-mîlin pîskâkan?	êhê, nêsta cwân, n'ka-pêci-mîlâw pîskâkaniliw.
âšay nâ ki-wî-kakwêcimin kêkwân?	êhê, nêsta cwân, niwî-kakwêcimâw kêkwâliw.
âšay nâ ki-wî-wîhtamawin kêkwân?	êhê, nêsta cwân, niwî-wîhtamawâw kêkwâliw.
âšay nâ kiwî-wâpahtilin apwoy?	êhê, nêsta cwân, niwî-wâpahtilâw apwoya.

4. Compound Stems

In Unit 2.C.8.1 and 2 you practised putting certain independent particles in the right order in a sentence. Building words involves another level of ordering, as components fit into their appropriate places *within the word*. The following drill will help you to see the systematic pattern in certain compound stems. Remember, the members of a compound stem together form one word.

4.1 Add each of the following particle prefixes to form an increasingly long, compound stem.

Recording: nimawâpin.
Add pêci to produce nipêci-mawâpin, and keep adding as each new particle prefix comes up.

nimawâpin
pêci
kakwê
ati
kî
ka
____
mâškŏc

4.2 Repeat as above, adding the following particle prefixes to the base, pakitahwâw.

pakitahwâw
natawi
kakwê
ati
wî
kî (*completed action*)

---

môla (Note that môla requires change of kî to ohci.)

4.3 Add the following elements in the proper order to the given base.

kitâpatisin
ati
kakwê
wî
ka

šwâpihk (Note the addition of iši, after the aspect markers and before other preverbs, with šwâpihk marking location. Also note possible, variable order of ati, kakwê)

4.4 Repeat as in 4.3.

kîšikâw
milo
âpihtâ
iškwâ
ta

---

wîpac

4.5 In this drill the order is scrambled. Insert the components in the correct place as you build the compound word from the base, nikapatênâsonân 'we are unloading'.

	nikapatênâsonân
	(Check column)
ka	nika
mâci	ka-mâci
kî	ka-kî-mâci-
pêci	ka-kî-pêci-mâci
kakwê	ka-kî-kakwê-pêci-mâci
âšokanihk	nika-kî-iši-kakwê-pêci-mâci-kapatênâsonân

5. Complete each of the following sentences with the appropriate word.

You have just come ashore and your friend, Kiyâsk, remarks that he saw you this morning: K: ______________ kêkišêp!

You respond that you came ashore pretty early: wîpac ________ ________________.

He rejoins: êhê, _____________.

You explain that you are just back from the fishing grounds: n'kî-pêci-kîwânân ___________________________ ohci.

Then you ask whether he can lend you a fish net: ______________ __ alapiy?

He agrees, but can't quite remember whether you've asked him recently, or last week: êhê, ________________ ___ anohcîhkê, - nêstapiko _________ __________?

It was yesterday that you asked him, and you tell him so: ___________ ___________.

On reflection, he says that he may give it to you some day: mâškôc __________________ pêyakwâ ________________.
You change the subject slightly and note that you (pl.) went to pitch camp on Monday: n'kî- ___________________ __________________ ; and that you set out your nets in the afternoon: _______________ ________________________.

Three days later, you tell him, you took up the nets and dried them out: ____________________________ n'kî-otinânânak alapiyak, _________________ mâka.

He hazards a guess as to the kinds of fish you caught: mâškôc awasitê ________________ ______________ nêsta ________________ ; then he asks whether you ever fish with a hook: wîskâc nâ _______________________?

You reply that it's not worth it, but you tell him what other fish you caught: môl' __________. n'kî-ayâwânânak _____________ nêsta ________________.

D. CONVERSATION PRACTICE

1. Cover the Cree column of the Basic Conversation and, working from the English, repeat the conversation in Cree. Where you cannot produce the Cree equivalent without undue hesitation, mark the section and keep going. Then learn carefully the sections you have marked. Finally, working from the English, repeat the conversation as a whole.

2. Check the drills to make sure you control the material with ease.

3. Ask whether your friend, Sinkipiš, is still camped in the bush or has gone downriver to set nets. Discuss the price of nets.

âlimisi-	VAI	be expensive (*v.* âliman, in last unit.)
wêhtisi-	VAI	be inexpensive, be cheap (*i.e.*, be easy)
wêhtan-	VII	be inexpensive, be cheap

You don't want to buy a new net yet. Your old one is worn out, but you would rather mend it.

4. Discuss the kind of fish you get in a net. You net fished all night and got back early this morning.

akwâpicikê-	VAI	fish with a seine net
iskali-tipisk	IPC	all night

Down at the shore your wife cooked some fresh trout for you and you rather liked it. She also barbecued some whitefish. You will freeze the suckers and give them to the dogs.

5. Make up further conversations. Keep them simple but use the several hundred words you already know in Cree. Practise at every opportunity outside the classroom. "The man who never made a grammatical mistake, never learned to talk *any* language." (E.A. Nida)

E. LISTENING IN

Mâtyiw: môla nâspic milopaliw ê-pakitahwâniwahk.
Alik: êhê, môla nâspic milopaliw.
Mâtyiw: n'kî-pakitahwânân ê-oški-kîšikâk. kâ-iškwâ mâka nisto-kîšikâk kêkât[1] môla kêkwân n'tôhci-kâhcitinênân.
Alik: šâ! môla nâspic milwâšin anohc kâ-nîpihk.[2]
Mâtyiw: tâpwê! awasitê mihkwacakâšak n'kî-nipahânânak. milwâšišiwak atim omîcim ohci piko.
Alik: kiwî-kakwêcimitin kêkwân.
Mâtyiw: êko,—kakwêcimin.
Alik: kitayân nâ apahkwâson?[3] apišîš piko nin'tawêl'tên. niwî-cimatân nimâhkîm.
Mâtyiw: môla wîla kêkwân n'tayân. ayâw wîla n'kosis mâka. âšay mâka mâškôc kî-pôsiw.
Alik: wâ! n'kî-'nâtawâpahtên kêkišêp. matakwan apahkwâson šwâpihk.
Mâtyiw: ayahâw,—mâškôc ta-ayâw sayman kôsîs. âskaw kanawêl'tam wîla aliwâk[4] ilikohk kâ-n'tawêl'tahk.
Alik: tâpwê nâ? n'ka-'nâtawâpamâw.
Mâtyiw: êškwâ pitamâ. ka-kî-awihin nâ kêkwân?
Alik: n'cîmân nâ?
Mâtyiw: môla. kitêncinim.
Alik: êhê,—matakwan mâka pimiy.[5]
Mâtyiw: ê'kwâni. n'ka-šwâpihkân nîla. mâškôc n'ka-pôsinân kê-wâpahk.
Alik: ka-kî-nakatên lâlatin kê-otâkošihk.
Mâtyiw: anohc nâ mîna ka-ati-kapêšin sîpîhk n'timihk?
Alik: môla nâspic nisâpêl'tên. šâkoc pâhkwatinâw; môla mâka n'tôhci wâpamâwak namêsak anta.
Mâtyiw: okimâw kî-kwâškwêpicikêw âšokanihk ohci otâkošîhk.
Alik: môl' âpatan. môla kêkwâliw ta-kî-kâhcitinam anta.
Mâtyiw: âšay wîpac mîna ta-ati-takwâkin. mâškôc kêposkâhk ta-âhkwatin ništam, êko mîna kêšîciwanohk.

1 kêkât	IPC	almost, nearly
2 anohc kâ-nîpihk		this summer *v.* anohc kâ-kîšikâk.
3 apahkwâson-	NI	canvas
4 aliwâk	IPC	in excess, over and above: aliwâk ilikohk kâ-n'tawêl'tahk more than he needs
5 pimiy-	NI	oil, grease: *i.e.,* fuel

Alik: mihcêt nâ ka-otâpân mihta?

Mâtyiw: môla mâškôc n'titêl'tên. niwî-šîwahwâwak namêsak nêsta niskak. n'kosis ta-kî-otâpêw mihta. âtiht piko nîla n'ka-pîsikahên.

Alik: kôskawâtêl'tâkwan wîla kêposkâhk.

Mâtyiw: tâpwê, n'kiskisin. misiwê 'wênihkân pimâškošin wâsakâm iškotêhk ê-tipiskâlik.[6] nimilwêl'tên mâka šâkoc ôta.

[6] ê-tipiskâlik — at night, in the late evening. Note the obviative in a dependent clause, 'when it is night', where the subject of the main clause is a 3rd person, animate.

F. REFERENCE LIST

akwâpasw-	VTA	smoke dry s.o.
akwâpicikê-	VAI	fish with a seine net
alapiy-	NA	fish net
aliwâk	IPC	in excess, over and above
anohcîhkê	IPC	just now, a few minutes ago, recently
apahkwâson-	NI	canvas
apwê-	VAI	barbecue, roast over an open fire
atihkamêkw-	NA	whitefish: *lit.,* caribou fish
awih-	VTA	lend (to) s.o.
âhkwatim-	VTA	freeze s.o.
âhkwatin-	VII	be freezing
âlikw-	NA [personal name]	Alec, Alex
âliman-	VII	be difficult, be expensive
âlimisi-	VAI	be difficult, be expensive
âpacih-	VTA	use s.o.
âpacihtâ-	VAI-T	use s.t.
cîkah-	VTI	chop s.t.
cîkahw-	VTA	chop s.o.
ê-kî-iškwâ-âpihtâ-kîšikâk	VII conj. indic.	in the afternoon
êti-otâkošihki	VII changed conj. subj.	of an evening, whenever it is evening
iskali	IPN	whole, entire, all *v.* iskali-kîšik.
iskali-kîšik	IPC	all day
iskali-tipisk	IPC (Sect. D)	all night
išicišahamaw-	VTA	send to s.o.
iškwâ	IPV	finish, complete *v.* ê-kî-iškwâ-âpihtâ-kîšikâk.
itin-	VTA / VTI	hold s.o./ s.t. so
kakwêcim-	VTA	ask s.o. (about s.t.) request s.o. *v.* natotamaw-.
kapêši-	VAI	camp
kêkât	IPC	almost, nearly

kê-otâkošihk	VII conj. indic.	late this afternoon, early this evening
kêposkâw-	NI	Kapiskau (place name): *lit.,* reeds are abundant
kêšîciwanw-	NI	Kashechewan, formerly Albany Post, Ontario: *lit.,* Swift Flow, Swift Current
kicistâpâwahtâ-	VAI-T	wash s.t.
kicistâpâwal-	VTA	wash s.o.
kinošêw-	NA	pike, jackfish *v.* B.2.2 above, Dialect Variation.
kiyâskw-	NA	seagull
kôskawâtêlihtâkwan-	VII	be quiet, be tranquil
kwâškwêpicikê-	VAI	fish with a hook, angle
mâsamêkos-	NA	(speckled) trout *v.* B.2.2 above, Dialect Variation
mihkwacakâš-	NA	(red horse) sucker *v.* B.2.2 above, Dialect Variation
mistikw-	NI	stick
mišakâ-	VAI	land, come to shore
natawi-kapêši-	VAI	go to pitch camp
natotamaw-	VTA	ask s.o. for s.t., request s.t. of s.o. *v.* kakwêcim-.
ništam	IPC	first
nîpin-	VII	be Summer *v.* anohc kâ-nîpihk this Summer
nôtamêsê-	VAI	fish
ohci-kâhcitin-	VTA / VTI	catch s.o./ s.t. from...
oški-kîšikâ-	VII	be Monday
otânâhk	IPC	behind, latterly
otânâhk kâ-tawâstêk		last week *v.* tawâstê-.
otâpê-	VAI	haul (wood)
otôn-	NDI	his / her mouth: nitôn-, kitôn-, etc.
pakitahwâ-	VAI	set out nets
pâs-	VTI	dry s.t. out
pâsw-	VTA	dry s.o. out
pêcicišahamaw-	VTA	send s.t. (to) s.o. (pêci in direction of speaker)
pêci-kîwê-	VAI	come back home, return
pêšoc	IPC	near to (*w. loc.*), nearby
pêyakwâ	IPC	once
pimâskošin-	VAI	lie lengthwise (on a solid surface)
pimiy-	NI	oil, grease: *i.e.,* fuel
pîsikah-	VTI	split s.t.
pîsikahw-	VTA	split s.o.

šinkipiš-	VTA	diver duck, probably the small or hooded merganser *v.* B.2.2. above.
šîwah-	VTI	salt s.t. down
šîwahw-	VTA	salt s.o. down
takošin-	VAI	arrive
tawâstê-	VII	be a week
tawâstêw-	NI	week
tâpišah-	VTI	string s.t., thread s.t.
tâpišahw-	VTA	string s.o., thread s.o.
tipahamaw-	VTA	pay s.o. (for s.t.)
tôwi	IPN	kind of: êwakwâna tôwi-awênihkân that's the kind of person she is; êwakwânima tôwi-kêkwân that's the kind of thing it is
wâšakâm	IPC (w. loc.)	around: nipimâškošininân wâšakâm iškotêhk we lie (along the ground) around the fire
wêhtan-	VII	be cheap, be inexpensive (*i.e.* be easy)
wêhtisi-	VAI	be cheap, be inexpensive (*i.e.,*be easy)

G. REVIEW

11.A Kakwêcihkêmôwina—Questions

Answer each question with a full sentence, expanding your reply if you are able. Use materials from the conversations, drills, etc., but also use your imagination.

1. otâkošîhk nâ kî-kakwêcimin ana alapiy?
2. awasitê nâ kimilwêl'tên kêšîciwanohk ispîš wîla môsonîhk?
3. môšak nâ kitâpacihâw alapiy?
4. kitâpacihâw nâ apwoy nêstapiko êncin?
5. kî-ihtâw nâ Šinkipiš ôta kêkišêp?
6. wîskâc nâ kwâškwêpicikêwak?
7. âšay nâ kî-ati-âhkwatin kêposkâhk?
8. milopaliw nâ ê-pakitahwâniwahk?
9. kî-kâhcitinâwak nâ namêsak mâmihk sîpîhk?
10. ka-âhkwatimâwâwak nâ namêsak?
11. tân' êhtôtaman iskali-kîšik nêtê?
12. ka-kî-pêcicišahamawinân nâ?
13. kôskawâtêl'tâkwan nâ êti-otâkošihki?
14. kitapwânâwâw nâ ayawiši-namês?
15. âšay nâ ka-tipahamâtinâwâw nêstapiko nâkê?
16. kî-natotamawêw nâ Šinkipiš otôtêma otalapîlîw?
17. otâkošîhk nâ kî-kakwêcimitin, nêstapiko otânâhk kâ-tawâstêk?
18. nâspic awasitê kitâpacihtân ôma cîmân ispîš nîla, manâ?
19. kî-pêhtawin nâ ê-mišakâyân (coming ashore)?
20. misiwê nâ mâka kî-takošininâwâw?
22. âšay nâ kî-pâswâwâwak kitalapiyak?
23. milopaliw nâ ê-kapêšinâniwahk natimihk sîpîhk?
24. kîla nâ ništam kî-takošinin?

11.B Naskwêwasihtwâwina—Answers

Make up questions which may be answered by the following statements.

1. kwâškwêpicikêw âšokanihk.
2. môla. niwîkimâkan nêsta nîla ništam n'kî-takošininân.
3. šâkoc ka-awihitin n'tastotin.
4. môla nâspic awasitê otakikomiw ispîš nîla.
5. âskaw n'tapwânân namês iškotêhk.
6. êhê, ka-awihitinân pâskisikan.
7. mâškôc n'ka-awihâw apwoya ispîš wîla cîmâniliw
8. tâpwê. mâškôc ayâw aliwâk ilikohk kâ-n'tawêl'tahk.
9. mîna mâškôc n'ka-pêci-takošininân.
10. âšay kî-takošin.
11. wîpac mâškôc ka-kihtohtânânaw.
12. šâkoc wêsâ âliman!
13. nêtê cîmânihk.
14. êhê, kiwî-kakwêcimitin kêkwân.
15. môla. pitamâ ta-mîšahwêw otalapiya.
16. nâspic milwêlimêw ayawiši-namêsa.
17. wîpac nawac n'ka-mišakânân.
18. môla kitôhci-pêhtâtin.
19. kê-wâpahk n'ka-n'tawêlimâw alapiy.
20. awasitê mâškôc atihkamêkwak ka-kâhcitinânawak.
21. kêkât môšak alapiy n'tâpacihânân.
22. otânâhk kâ-tawâstêk n'titêl'tên.
23. môla n'tôhci-kapêšinân ê-oški-kîšikâk.
24. êhê, wîla ništam kî-takošin nikosis.

Supplementary Conversation I

If you have been studying under formal, classroom conditions, particularly in an urban setting, the life of a Cree village may seem somewhat remote. You might like a few Cree terms to talk about your own day-to-day activities in town or on campus. The following conversation will provide some useful expressions.

kî-iškwâ-kiskinohamâsonâniwahkê	**After Class**
kišâstaw! môla nisâpêl'tên ôma ê-kîšikâk.	Gosh! I don't like this weather much.
tânt' êt'-îtohtêyin anohc?	Where are you off to now?
môla n'kiskêl'tên. mâškôc mîcisôwikamikohk n'ka-itohtân.	I don't know. Maybe to the restaurant.
n'tawê-mîcisôwipalihotâ(k).	Let's go for a quick snack.
tântê kê-itohtêyin kî-iškwâ-kiskinohamâsoyinê?	Where are you going after class?
nîkihk mâškôc.	Home I guess.
mâškôc n'ka-natawê-šwâpihkân.	Maybe I'll go shopping.
" n'ka-natawê-âpatisin.	" I'll go to work.
" n'ka-kiskinohamâson.	" I'll study.
ka-otamîn nâ kê-otâkošihk?	Will you be busy this evening?
n'ka-minawân kê-otâkošihk.	I'll / I have to get supper this evening.
tân' êspalik mâna kîla ê-iši-mîcisoyan?	What time do you usually eat?
n'kotwâs ê-ispalik,—nîswâs ê-ispalik.	Six o'clock,—seven o'clock.
tântê kê-itohtêyin kê-otâkošihk?	Where will you be going this evening?
" " anohc kê-mâtinawê-kîšikâk?	" this Saturday?
" " anohc kê-ati-kîšipalik ê-tawâstêk?	" this weekend?
mâškôc n'ka-itohtân kâ-iši-nîminâniwahk.	I'll probably go to a dance.
" " kâ-iši-mêtawâniwahk.	" " a party.

ta-ihtâwak kê-kitohcikêcik.	There's a good band (musicians) coming.
" kê-nikamocik.	" (singers) coming.
" kê-matwêhiskohkwêcik.	" (drummers) coming.
âh! âstatâpwê! âšay takopaliw "pas".	Whoops! Aw-w-h! There's the bus.
n'ka-šwâpihkân tikita.	I have to buy tickets.
tânîlikohk *or* tân' êtakihtêki anihi tikita?	How much are those tickets ?
nîswâs-ahtay mîna niyânânêyamitana sêns nîšošâp ohci.	$7.80 for twelve.
kî-ayamihitin têpiskâk, môla mâka kititâhtay.	I phoned you last night, but you weren't there.
kinaškwêwašihtwâwiniyâpiy mâka itwêmakanôpan: "wâciyê. êkoši pakitina kitišinihkâsowin nêsta kitakihtâsowin: wîpac mâka mîna ka-pêci-ayamihitin. mînkwêc."	Your answering machine said: "Hello. Please leave your name and number; and I"ll get back to you soon. Thank you."
pêci-ayamihîhkan ci kê-otâkošihk.	Give me a phone-call this evening if you don't mind.
tân' êtasinâsoyin kîkihk?	What's your phone number?
nêw, niyânânêw, nîswâs, "zero", nisto, nîšo, nîšo.	487-0322
ka-kî-pakitinên naškwêwašihikaniyâpîhk.	You can leave a message on the answering machine.
mâškôc pâmâšakwêtâ(k).	Let's go for a stroll perhaps.
êhê, êkwâni pitamâ. nakiškawin nêtê pânkihk êko mâka lwâriyê.	Right. See you later. Meet me at Bank and Laurier (streets).
wâciyê.	Good-bye.

kî-iškwâ-kiskinohamâsonâniwahkê		conjunct subjunctive = "when, if", pointing to the future: *lit.*, when one will have finished learning
ôma ê-'ši-kîšikâk		this kind of day: *lit.*, this one in-its-so-being-day
mîcisôwikamikw-	NI	restaurant, *lit.*, eating building
natawê	IPV	go (to do s.t.): *variant of* natawi
mîcisôwipaliho-	VAI	have a quick snack
tântê kê-itohtêyin		**kê** + conj. indic. *looks to future*: where will you be going? *v.* **kê**-otâkošihk, *etc.*
kî-iškwâ-kiskinohamâsoyinê		when you will have finished learning: *cf.* title.
otamî-	VAI	be busy
minawê-	VAI	cook
tân' êspalik (pîsimohkânihk *understood*)		*lit.*, How does it so-go (on the clock)?
mâna	IPC	repeatedly, usually
nîmi-: kâ-iši-nîminâniwahk	VAI	dance: where one dances
mêtawê-: kâ-iši-mêtawâniwahk	VAI	play: where one plays
kitohcikê-: kê-kitohcikêcik	VAI	make music: who WILL make music
nikamo-: kê-nikamocik	VAI	sing: who WILL sing
matwêhiskohkwê-: kê-matwêhiskohkwêcik	VAI	drum: who WILL drum
naškwêwašihtwâwiniyâpiy-	NI	telephone answering machine
âstatâpwê!	IPC	Alas!
ayamihîhkan	VTA	2 - 1 future imperative
ci	IPC	"if you wouldn't mind" (not quite English "please")
itasinâso- : tân' êtasinâsoyin?	VAI	be marked, be listed: How are you listed?
naškwêwašihikaniyâpiy-	NI	telephone answering machine (*alternate term*)
pâmâšakwê-	VAI	go for a stroll around

UNIT TWELVE

A. BASIC CONVERSATION

Canoe Loading

Okimâw:	kimâmitonêlihtên	you are pondering it
	kimâmitonêlihtên nâ kêkwân?	Got something on your mind?
Alik:	pikiwaskisina	rubber boots
	ka-awihâsomitin	I'll borrow (from) you
	mâškôc ka-awihâsomitin kipikiwaskisina.	Maybe I can borrow your rubber boots.
Okimâw:	ka-pišošimikon[1]	it will trip you
	wêsâ mišâwa	they (inan.) are too big
	kayâm. wêsâ mâka piko mišâwa. mâškôc ka-pišošimikon.	All right. They're too big, though. You may trip.
Alik:	kiwî-wâpahtilitin	I want to show you
	nipôsihtâsonân	we are loading (freight)
	nipôsihtâsonân. kiwî-wâpahtilitin kêkwân.	We're loading freight. I want to show you something.
	pišišikwâw	it's empty
	pišišik	continuously, throughout
	kîšponêw	it is full
	tân' êšinâkwahk?	how does it look?
	tân' êšinâkwahk anima? pêyak cîmân kîšponêw pišišik mîcim,—kotakiy mâka cîmân pišišikwâw.	How does that look? One canoe is full of food,—and the other is empty.
Okimâw:	ta-kosâpêw	it will sink
	wêsâ kîšponêw. ta-kosâpêw.	It's too full. It will sink.

[1] *v.* Unit 9.B.1.3: niwanâhikon.

Alik:	tawâw	there's room
	astêw	it is set, it is placed
	kê-iši-astêki[2] kêkwâna	where things will be placed
	kêyâpac tawâw kê-iši-astêki kêkwâna.	There's still room for more stuff.
Okimâw:	nistwâ kišê-mitâhtomitana	three thousand
	tipâpêskocikan	pound
	âšay mâka nistwâ kišê-mitâhtomitana tipâpêskocikan kitayân.	But by now you've got three thousand pounds (in there).
Alik:	'kâwila mikwaškâtêl'ta	Don't worry (2 sg.)
	nipakitinênân mîcim	we are putting the food
	pahkân	separately
	misiwê pahkân nipakitinênân mîcim, nêsta pahkân atimwak.	We're putting all the food in one, and the dogs in the other.
Okimâw:	êncini-pimiy	gasoline
	sîhcâw	it's crowded, it's tight fitting
	nawac sîhcâw. tântê apahkwâsona nêsta êncini-pimiy?	It's pretty well crammed. Where are the canvases and gas?
Alik:	anohcîhkê n'kî-îkatênên.	I moved them aside just a while ago.
	iškotêhkân	a stove
	mâhkîw'-iškotêhkân	camp stove
	n'kî-astân	I set it, I placed it
	âšokanihk n'kî-iši-astân, pêšoc mâhkîw'-iškotêhkânihk.	I set them on the wharf, near the camp stove.
	nitalâw	I set him, I place him
	âšokanihk n'kî-iši-alâwak nêsta askihkwak.	I set the kettles on the wharf too.
Okimâw:	kê-tipiskâk	tonight (*looking forward*)
	ka-kî-pêci-n'tawâpaminâwâw nâ kê-tipiskâk?[2]	Will you folks be seeing us tonight?

[2] *v.* Unit 8.A.2, kê-wâpahk and Unit 11.B.1.4 kê-otâkošihk, where kê points to the future: kê-iši-astêki where they (inan. pl.) WILL be placed. Cf. also Supplementary Converstion 1: kê-kitohcikêcik, etc.

Alik:	pwâmoši [+ conj. indic.]	before
	pwâmoši pôsiyâhk	before we leave (by conveyance)
	'kišêpâyâkê	when it will be morning
	ka-wâpamitinâwâw 'kišêpâyâkê mâškôc, pwâmoši pôsiyâhk.	We'll see you (pl.) in the morning, I guess, before we leave.
Okimâw:	ka-kotikošinin	you'll sprain yourself (sg.)
	yâkwâ!	look out!
	kikilišinin	you're slipping (sg.)
	yâkwâ! kikilišinin. ka-kotikošinin.	Look out! You're slipping. You'll sprain yourself.
Alik:	môla wayêš n'ka-ihtin	I'll be all right
	môla wayêš n'ka-ihtin. nakiskaw mâškôc n'ka-ispêlohkân.	Oh, I'll be all right. Maybe I'll take a break for a bit.
Okimâw:	alwêpiw	he takes a rest, he takes a holiday
	âšay alwêpiw wîla cîmis.	James there is taking a rest already.
	môla ta-pahkišin	he won't fall
	ê-pimišihk	in-his-lying-down
	ê-tôtahk	in-his-doing-it
	ê'ko n'âni ê-tôtahk	is that it?
	ê'ko n'âni ê-tôtahk? ê-pimišihk môla ta-pahkišin.	Is that what he's doing? When he's lying down, he won't fall.
Alik:	anohc kâ-nîpihk	this Summer
	âpatisîwin	work
	misawâc	at any rate, anyway
	ê'kwâni kwayask. wêsâ misawâc kišitêw âpatisîwin ohci anohc kâ-nîpihk.	That's right. Anyway, it's too hot for work this Summer.

B. DISCUSSION OF GRAMMAR

1. Verbs

1.1 VAI n-Stems

A number of animate intransitive verbs (VAI) show a stem ending in /n/ rather than a vowel. Among these are many with a high frequency of occurrence: *e.g.,*

pimišin	he lies down
pahkišin	he falls
kilišin	he slips
takošin	he arrives (by land)

For all but 3rd person subjects the n-stem shows an added /i/: *i.e.,* pimišini-, followed by the same inflectional endings as for vowel stems. 3rd person subjects take the simple n-stem:

3	takošin......w
3p	takošin......wak
3′	takošin.....ɩliwa[1]
1	nitakošini...n
2	kitakošini...n
11	nitakošini...nân
21	kitakošini...nânaw
2p	kitakošini...nâwâw

In the form for 3 subject, takošinw becomes takošin by the regular sound rule that /w/ in final position after a consonant is dropped (Unit 3.B.2.1.2).

1.2 VAI-VII n-Stem Pairs

Most n-stem verbs show an inanimate intransitive stem on the pattern:

pimišin	~	pimi**ht**in
pahkišin	~	pahki**ht**in
kilišin	~	kili**ht**in

[1] V. Unit 3.B.1.1 and 1.2.

takošin is a noteworthy exception with VII takošinômakan, the pattern followed by VAI vowel-stems, where no parallel VII form exists: *e.g.,* apîmakan mohcihtak it sits on the floor.

Study the following sentences.

1. môla ta-pahkišin /...wak.	He /...they won't fall.
2. nîla ništam n'kî-takošinin.	I arrived first.
3. ašiškîhk ka-iši-kilišininânaw.	We (21) will slip on the mud.
4. 'yâkwâ! mâškôc ka-kotikošinin.	Look out! You'll sprain yourself.
5. nipimâskošininân wâšakâm iškotêhk.	We (11) lie around the fire.
6. misiwê kipišošinâwâw ê-tipiskâk.	You are all stumbling in the dark.

———DRILLS 2.1 THROUGH 2.4———

1.3 Transitive Stems: VTA in final /l/; VAI-T in final /tâ/ *or* /stâ/

Certain transitive verbs display stems ending in /l/, with the parallel VAI-T forms showing a stem in final /tâ/ or /stâ/. You have already met several of these verbs and below are a few more:

VTA		VAI-T	
	akol...êw		akotâ...w
	išiwil...êw		išiwitâ...w
	kicistâpâwal...êw		kicistâpâwatâ...w
	al...êw		astâ...w
	mîl...êw		————

In Moose Cree stem final /l/ is regularly heard as such. In Swampy Cree (N-Dialect) the VTA stem in /l/ sounds exactly like the stem finals in /n/: *e.g.,* akônêw; so when learning a new word of this class, make sure to learn the VAI-T form as well. In a language which shows as heavy a dependence on inflection as Cree, misanalogizing from VTA to VTI on the basis of an ...n- VTA stem final might easily render your meaning quite unintelligible.

Study the following sentences.

7. kî-akolêw asâma, kî-akotâw nêsta maskisina.	He hung up the snow-shoes and he hung up the moccasins too.
8. apwoyak kîla âšokanihk ka-kî-išiwilâwak, wîla pimiy n'ka-išiwitân.	You can take the paddles to the wharf, I'll take the oil.
9. kî-kicistâpâwalêw ašikana, kî-kicistâpâwatâw nêsta wâpwayân.	She washed some socks, she also washed a blanket.

10. olâkana mîcisonâhtikohk n'kî-iši-astânân; askihkwak mâka ka-kî alâwâwak iškotêhkânihk. — We set the dishes on the table, but the kettles you may set on the stove.

11. mîcimiliw n'kî-mîlik otâkošîhk, âšay mâka kêkwân kiwî-mîlitin. — He gave me some food yesterday and now I want to give you something.

——— DRILLS 3.1 AND 3.2———

2. Syntax

2.1 Conjunct Order and the Obviative in Dependent Clauses

From time to time forms of the verb listed as "conjunct" have been introduced into the Basic Conversation; and Unit Five presents content questions in which the verb is in the conjunct order.

The conjunct order of the verb occurs regularly in dependent clauses: *i.e.,* clauses linked to a preceding main or principal clause. For example: We left (*principal clause*), while he was speaking (*dependent clause*), in Cree, n'kî-kihtohtânân (*principal clause*), mêkwâc ê-ayamit (*dependent clause*). ê-pimišihk when he lies down, ê-kî-iškwâ-âpihtâ-kîšikâk in-its-having-ended-being-half-day, *i.e.,* in the afternoon, are dependent clauses in Cree. In the case of content questions, the question words, "how, when, where", etc., are used predicatively: tânt' êtohtêyan? Where [is it] (*principal clause*) that-you-are-going (*dependent clause*)?

Nouns appear in the obviative if possessed by a third person, animate possessor, or when used as the object of a verb with third person, animate subject. In the case of verbs, the presence of a dependent clause implies the existence of a principal or main clause somewhere. Where the subject of the verb in a main clause is a *third person animate*, any verb with a further third person subject (animate or inanimate), dependent on the verb in the main clause, moves from the proximate into the obviative position: *e.g.,*

> ta-pêci-pîhtokwêw mêkwâc ê-mîcisolici atimwa.
> He will come inside while the dogs are eating.
>
> ta-takošin nikosis kêšîciwanohk kê-otâkošinilik.
> My son will arrive at Kashechewan this evening.

A number of conjunct endings, especially VAI and VII, have appeared in addition to those listed in the table in 5.B.4. Note VII ending,...k (ê-kîšikâk) and both VAI and VII ...hk (ê-otâkošihk, ê-pimišihk), where ...n stem-final changes from /n/ to /h/ before conjunct ending ...k, for 3 and 0 subjects.

You have also met VAI ...yâhk (pôsiyâhk) and, in the two examples immediately above, VAI 3′ ...ɩlici (ê-mîcisolici) and VII 0′ ...ɩlik (kê-otâkošinilik).

———DRILL 4———

As these forms appear from time to time you might like to begin organizing your own table of conjunct endings by expanding the list in Unit 5.B.4 as the course proceeds. The following summary of expressions in which the conjunct order is used, up to and including Unit 12, will help you to get started.

2.2 Expressions in Which the Conjunct Indicative Is Used: Units 1–12

U1.E & U2.A.1	tân′ êšihihkâsoyin?	What is your name?
U2.A.1	tânt′ êtohtêyin mâka anohc?	But where are you going now?
B.2	tân′ êhtiyin anohc kâ-kîšikâk?	How are you (faring) today?
U3.A.1	tân′ êtamahcihoyin kîla?	How are *you* feeling?
U4.A.2	tân′ êšinihkâtêk anima (kêkwân) ê-ililîmonâniwahk?	What is that (thing) called in (your) speaking Cree?
U5.A.2	tân′ êhtiyin?	How are you faring? How are you doing?
	tân′ êhtit mâka awâšiš?	And what's wrong with the child?
	tânt′ êtohtêt?	Where is he going?
	kêkwân wiyâpahtaman?	What (is it) that you see? What do you see?
	awênihkân wiyâpamat anta?	Who (is it) that you see there?
	môla n′kiskêlimâw ... tân′ êšinihkâsot.	I don't know ... what his name is.
	kêkwâliw nêtawêlihtahk?	What (is it) that he / she wants?
	tân′ êhtôtaman anta?	What (is it) that you are doing there?
	tân′ êhtôtahk?	What is it that he / she is doing?
U6.A.1	ê-ililîmoyan	in your speaking Cree
	′ci-kiskêlihtaman	that you know it
A.2	tân′tahto-wiyâpahtaman?	How many (NI) do you see?

U7.A.2	kici-ispaliyahk kê-pônihkêyahk	that we (21) so go that we will make a fire
	ê-wêmistikôšîmonâniwahk	in (one's) speaking English
A.3	mâhcic kâ-kî-ayamihê'-kîšikâk	last Sunday
D	ê-ililîmocik	in their speaking Cree
U8.A.1	tân' êtakisot?	How much does it (*anim.*) cost?
	kâ-atâwêt	(the one) who trades: *i.e.,* the trader
A.2	tân' êhkihk?	What's happening?
U9.A.1, 3	kâ-kiskinohamâkêt	(the one) who teaches: *i.e.,* the teacher
	'ci-iskôliwiyân	that I go to school
	(ka-tôtâk) 'ci-kîwêyin	(she will do to you) that you go home
A.2	tân' êhtiyêk? going on with you?	How are you (pl.) faring? What's
	ê-mâtot	in his / her crying
	ê-ayamihtâyan	in your reading it
A.3	kici-mîcisonâniwahk	that one eat
U10.A	anohc kâ-kîšikâk	today
	tân' êspîhcâk?	What size is it (*inan.*)?
	tân' êspîhcikitit?	What size is it (*anim.*)?
	kâ-pîsisicik šôliyânak	small change: *lit.,*monies which are in bits
U11.A.1	kâ-iši-nôtamêsêyâhk	where we fish
	otânâhk kâ-tawâstêk	last week
	pêyakwâ ê-kîšikâk	some day, one day
	ê-pakitahwâniwahk	in one's net fishing
	ê-oški-kîšikâk	on Monday
	ê-kî-iškwâ-âpihtâ-kîšikâk	in the afternoon
	kâ-iškwâ-nisto-kîšikâk	three days later
A.2	kê-otâkošinilik	(late) this afternoon, this evening
	tân' êhtôtaman?	What do you do? What are you doing?

Supplementary Conversation 1. *v.* pp. 297–99.

U12.A	tân' êšinâkwahk anima?	How does that look?
	kê-iši-astêki kêkwâna	Where things will be placed
	kê-tipiskâk	tonight, this coming night
	pwâmoši pôsiyâhk	before we leave
	ê'ko n'âni ê-tôtahk?	Is that what he's doing?
	ê-pimišihk	as he lies down
	anohc kâ-nîpihk	this Summer
B.2	ê-mîcisolici atimwa	as / while the dogs are eating

C. DRILLS

1. Pronunciation Drill: Pre-aspirated Stops

Listen carefully to the following eight pairs of words. In the first five the only thing which keeps two otherwise identical utterances apart is the presence of an /h/ before a stop consonant in one and its absence in the corresponding position in the other. (*v.* "Cree Sound System", p. xxvii). Such pairs are called "minimal pairs". The last three pairs contain members kept apart by more than one feature: in #6 the aspirate occurs in a different position with the further /l ~ n/ distinction in the L but not in the N Dialect; in #7 and #8 the members of each pair in the left column show no pre-aspirated stop. The right hand members show two; and these mark the distinction between the two terms.

Mimic the recording carefully for each pair.

1.	pêtâw	he brings it	pêhtâw	he waits for it
2.	akocin	he hangs	akohcin	he floats
3.	otinam	he takes it	ohtinam	he takes it from
4.	pakân	nut	pahkân	separately
5.	pimotêw	he throws it at him	pimohtêw	he walks about
6.	nipâpihlân	I'm flying in for a landing	nipâhpinân	we are laughing
7.	(ê-) apit	as he sits	ahpiht	flint
8.	pakitin	put him, let him	pahkihtin	it falls

2. n-Stem Verbs

2.1 Drill the following question-answer exchanges, repeating the question and answering immediately on the pattern:

Question: âšay nâ kî-takošinin?
Answer: êhê, anohcîhkê piko n'kî-takošinin.

The recording will check you; but in these and the following sequences there will be no time for mimicry of the correct reply.

	(Check column)
âšay nâ kî-takošinin?	êhê, anohcîhkê piko n'kî-takošinin.
âšay nâ kî-pimišinin?	êhê, anohcîhkê piko n'kî-pimišinin.
âšay nâ kî-pahkišinin?	êhê, anohcîhkê piko n'kî-pahkišinin.
âšay nâ kî-kilišinin?	êhê, anohcîhkê piko n'kî-kilišinin.
âšay nâ kî-kotikošinin?	êhê, anohcîhkê piko n'kî-kotikošinin.

2.2 Continue on the same pattern,

Question: âšay nâ kî-takošininâwâw?
Answer: êhê, anohcîhkê piko n'kî-takošininân.

âšay nâ kî-takošininâwâw?	êhê, anohcîhkê piko n'kî-takošininân.
âšay nâ kî-pahkišininâwâw?	êhê, anohcîhkê piko n'kî-pahkišininân.
âšay nâ kî-kilišininâwâw?	êhê, anohcîhkê piko n'kî-kilišininân.
âšay nâ kî-pimišininâwâw?	êhê, anohcîhkê piko n'kî-pimišininân.
âšay nâ kî-kotikošininâwâw?	êhê, anohcîhkê piko n'kî-kotikošininân.
âšay nâ kî-pimâskošininâwâw?	êhê, anohcîhkê piko n'kî-pimâskošininân.

2.3 Continue on the pattern,

Question: wîpac nâ ka-takošininânaw?
Answer: wîpac mâškôc ka-takošininânaw.

wîpac nâ ka-takošininânaw?	wîpac mâškôc ka-takošininânaw.
wîpac nâ ka-pimišininânaw?	wîpac mâškôc ka-pimišininânaw.
wîpac nâ ka-kilišininânaw?	wîpac mâškôc ka-kilišininânaw.
wîpac nâ ka-pahkišininânaw?	wîpac mâškôc ka-pahkišininânaw
wîpac nâ ka-pimâskošininânaw?	wîpac mâškôc ka-pimâskošininânaw.

2.4 Follow the pattern,

Question: wîpac nâ ta-takošin?
Answer: wîpac ta-takošinwak misiwê.

wîpac nâ ta-takošin?	wîpac ta-takošinwak misiwê.
wîpac nâ ta-pimišin?	wîpac ta-pimišinwak misiwê.
wîpac nâ ta-kotikošin?	wîpac ta-kotikošinwak misiwê.
wîpac nâ ta-pahkišin?	wîpac ta-pahkišinwak misiwê.
wîpac nâ ta-kilišin?	wîpac ta-kilišinwak misiwê.

3. Transitive Stems: VTA stems in final /l/; VAI-T in /tâ/ *or* /stâ/.

3.1 Select the appropriate noun to stand as object to the verb. The recording will provide two nouns followed by a sentence fragment. Complete the fragment with the right noun. The recording will then give the correct form.

1. nêtê iškwâtêmihk kî-iši-akolêw ..... (omaskisina ~ otašikana).
2. môla mâškôc n'ka-išiwitân ..... (iškotêhkân ~ askihk) kê-wâpahk.
3. âšay nâ kicistâpâwatâliwa okâwiya ..... (wâpwayâniliw ~ awâšiša)?
4. âšokanihk n'kî-iši-astân ..... (pimîwi-kân ~ pahkwêšikan).
5. môšak nimîlânânak ..... (masinahikanâhtik ~ šôliyâna).
6. iškotêhkânihk ta-iši-alêwak ..... (namêsa ~ mîcimiliw).
7. anohc mâka môla ka-kî-kicistâpâwalâwâwak ..... (olâkana ~ astisak).
8. wîskâc nâ kitišiwilâw ..... (awâšiš ~ cîmân) sîpîhk?
9. wâskâhikanihk n'kî-iši-akotânân ..... (alapiy ~ wâpwayân).
10. n'kotwâsošâp ayâwêliwa ..... (šîšîpa ~ cîkahikana) ostêsa.

1. otašikana
2. iškotêhkân
3. wâpwayâniliw
4. pimîwi-kân
5. šôliyâna
6. namêsa
7. astisak
8. awâšiš
9. wâpwayân
10. šîšîpa

3.2 Select the verb form required by the object.

1. askihkwak nêtê ..... (n'ka-iši-astân ~ n'ka-iši-alâwak).
2. môla tawâw kê-iši-astêki kêkwâna. walawîtimihk ..... (ka-kî-išiwilâwak ~ ka-kî-išiwitân).
3. môla wîskâc alapiy ..... (nitakotânân ~ nitakolânân).
4. âšokanihk apahkwâsoniliw .....(kî-iši-alêw ~ kî-iši-astâw).
5. âšay nâ namêsak ..... (ka-kicistâpâwalânawak ~ ka-kicistâpâwatânânaw)?
6. pakwayân pîhtokwamihk ..... (n'ka-iši-akolâw ~ n'ka-iši-akotân).
7. wîpac mâka walahpicikan ..... (ka-kî-išiwitân ~ ka-kî-išiwilâw).
8. âšay pišišikwâw cîmân ..... . (ka-kî-kicistâpâwalâwâw ~ ka-kî-kicistâpâwatânâwâw).

1. n'ka-iši-alâwak
2. ka-kî-iširwitân
3. nitakolânân
4. kî-iši-astâw
5. ka-kicistâpâwalânawak
6. n'ka-iši-akotân
7. ka-kî-iširwitân
8. ka-kî-kicistâpâwatânâwâw

4. Obviative of VII Forms in the Conjunct.

Drill each sequence on the pattern:

Recording: mâškôc n'ka-pôsin kê-wâpahk.
Response: nêsta wîla, mâškôc ta-pôsiw kê-wâpanilik.

		(Check column)
1.	mâškôc n'ka-pôsin kê-wâpahk.	kê-wâpanilik
2.	mâškôc n'ka-âpatisin kê-otâkošihk.	kê-otâkošinilik
3.	šâkoc n'ka-nipân kê-tipiskâk.	kê-tipiskâlik
4.	âskaw n'takwâpicikân ê-takwâkihk.	ê-takwâkinilik
5.	môšak n'talwêpinân ê-nîpihk.	ê-nîpinilik.
6.	môla nimilwêl'tênân ê-kimiwahk.	ê-kimiwanilik
7.	âskaw n'tôtakikomin ê-tahkâyâk.	ê-tahkâyâlik
8.	niwî-ispêlohkân ê-kišitêk.	ê-kišitêlik
9.	n'kî-n'tawi-kapêšin ê-oški-kîšikâk.	ê-oški-kîšikâlik
10.	n'kî-pakitahwânân ê-kî-iškwâ-âpihtâ-kîšikâk.	ê-kî-iškwâ-âpihtâ-kîšikâlik
11.	kâ-iškwâ-nisto-kîšikâk n'kî-otinânânak alapiyak.	kâ-iškwâ-nisto-kîšikâlik
12.	mîna n'kî-pêci-kîwân otânâhk kâ-tawâstêk.	otânâhk kâ-tawâstêlik

5. Days of the Week

Repeat these after the recording or your teacher.

(it is) Sunday	ayamihê'-kîšikâw
(it is) Monday	oški-kîšikâw
(it is) Tuesday	nîšo-kîšikâw
(it is) Wednesday	âpihtawan
(it is) Thursday	nêw'-kîšikâw
(it is) Friday	mâtinawê-kîšikâšin
(it is) Saturday	mâtinawê-kîšikâw

Except for the terms applied to Friday and Saturday, all these words or their constituent parts have occurred in the lessons. Saturday was the usual day for giving out rations at the Hudson's Bay Company posts, and from this comes the name *Serving-out Day* or *Distribution Day*: mâtinamâkê- VAI or mâtinawê-, distribute, apportion, allot; hence, mâtinawê-kîšikâw. Friday, *Little Distribution Day,* is also known as niyâlano-kîšikâw, *Fifth Day*; and in predominantly Roman Catholic areas it is known as cîpayâhtiko-kîšikâw, *Cross Day.*

6. Complete each sentence with the appropriate form from one of the verb stems listed at the left.

mâmitonêliht-	Okimâw:	____________ nâ kêkwân?
išinâkwan-	Alik:	mâškôc ka-____________ kipikiwaskisina.
kîšponê-		âšay nipôsihtâsonân. kiwî-____________
wâpahtil-		kêkwân. tân' ____________ anima? pêyak
awihâsom-		cîmân ____________ pišišik mîcim; kotakiy
pišišikwâ-		mâka cîmân ____________.
kosâpê- [sink]	Okimâw:	wêsâ kîšponêw. mâškôc ta-____________.
kilišin-		ka-kî-______-____________ nâ kê-tipiskâk?
mikwaškâtêliht-	Alik:	môla mâškôc. ka-____________ mâka
wâpam-		kišêpâyâkê pwâmoši pôsiyâhk.
ihti-	Okimâw:	yâkwâ! ____________!
ispêlohkê-	Alik:	'kâwila ____________. môla wayêš
pimišin-		n'ka-____________. nakiskaw mâškôc n'ka-____________.
alwêpi-		âšay ____________ cîmis. šîpâyâhtikohk [under
pêci-natawâpam-		the tree] iši-____________.

D. CONVERSATION PRACTICE

1. As in former units, cover the Cree column in the Basic Conversation and test yourself, working from the English equivalents. Mark points of hesitation or other difficulties, but *keep on going*. Return to the points of difficulty and learn the material thoroughly. Then repeat the whole conversation from the beginning.

NOTE: The present unit has a relatively short drill section. Under the circumstances it is of vital importance to control the conversation with particular competence. Do not proceed to the next unit until you are satisfied that you know the material in the present one.

2. You are loading your canoe to go and camp upstream this evening, and somewhere else (pîtoš wayêš) tomorrow. A friend meets you and you discuss the price of supplies, how much a canoe can hold, how yours turned over (kwatapipali- VA/II) last week and you lost everything, including your rubber boots.

3. Discuss how James and Alec don't like working in the heat, and always take a break in the afternoon. James always grumbles when it rains, and was repairing his tent last Monday when he slipped on the mud, down the bank, and sprained himself.

4. You are unloading a boat (kikapatênâson cîmân). It is very hot this Summer, far too hot for work and you have just lain down under a tree to rest. The Store Manager approaches and asks whether you are tired (ayêskosi- VAI) or just lazy (kihtimi- VAI). You point out that you are not really either, but that you are just taking a rest. Anyway, the ground is dry and the wharf is wet. Yesterday you fell in the river and don't want to slip again right now. You'll unload another boat later on — mâškôc kotak cîmân ka-kapatênâson nâkê.

5. Work out the above conversations or any others, either with someone else or by yourself. Use your imagination to the full. If you find yourself looking for an expression which you do not have or cannot remember, try to say the same thing in words which you do have. Remember, a good control of a language involves not only the use of a great many words and expressions, but also the ability to get the greatest mileage out of the expressions and words which you already know.

E. LISTENING IN

Alik: tânilikohk pêyako-tipahikan pimiy?

Okimâw: niyânânêyamitana-niyâlan sêns pêyak tipahikan. nâspic âliman. nipôsihtâsonân pîliš[1] kêšîciwanohk.

Alik: niwî-šwâpihkân misawâc.

Okimâw: kî-mišakân nâ kêkišêp?

Alik: êhê, n'kî-mišakânân n'timihk ohci, kâ-iši-nôtamêsêyâhk ohci.

Okimâw: wîpac n'ka-itohtân šwâpihk.

Alik: kin'tawêlimâw nâ ayawiši-namês? n'tayâwâwak âtiht mâsamêkosak.

Okimâw: kihci[2]-mîkwêc! milopaliw nâ ê-pakitahwâniwahk?

Alik: môla wîla oskac. n'kî-kapêšinân otânâhk kâ-kî-tawâstêk; kâ-nîšo-kîšikâk[3] mâka n'kî-pakitahwân. kâ-iškwâ-nîšo-kîšikâk mâka mitoni[4] kî-kîšponêw alapiy.

Okimâw: tâpwê nâ? mâškôc atihkamêkwak mâwac kî-ayâwâwak.

Alik: —mihkwacakâšak ašic. niwîkimâkan kêyâpac akwâpaswêw atihkamêkwa.

Okimâw: ka-pêci-mawâpîstâtinâwâw[5] nêtê. niwî-kwâškwêpicikân.

Alik: n'kosis nêsta nîla n'ka-kîwânân kê-wâpahk.

Okimâw: môla mâškôc n'ka-kî-kihtohtân kê-wâpahk. niwîkimâkan kî-pahkišin mâhcic kâ-kî-tawâstêk. kî-kotikošin. môla nâspic milomâtisiw.

Alik: ta-kî-alwêpiw antê,—mâškôc ta-kî-mîšahwêw alapiya.

Okimâw: ka-wîhtamâtin êškwâ,[6]—n'ka-kakwêcimâw niwîkimâkan. mâškôc n'ka-kî-pêc'-îtohtân.

Alik: mâškôc ka-otihtahênânaw[7] nimâhkîmihk kê-wâpahk.

Okimâw: milwâšin. kî-kakwêcimin[8] mâhkîw'-iškotêhkân. n'tayân pêyak šwâpihk. kêyâpac nâ tawâw kê-iši-astêki kêkwâna kicîmânihk?

Alik: apišîš piko. kêkât kîšponêwa nîšo cîmâna. misiwê pahkân n'kî-pakitinên mîcim, nêsta pahkân atimwak. môšak wî-mîcisowak.

1	pîliš	IPC	up to, as far as, until
2	kihci	IPN / V	great, big
3	kâ-nîšo-kîšikâk		on Tuesday (past)
4	mitoni	IPC	entirely, utterly
5	kâ-pêci-mawâpîstâtinâwâw		I'll come visit you
6	ka-wîhtamâtin êškwâ		I'll tell you later
7	otihtah-	VTI	come to s.t., reach s.t.
8	kakwêcim-	VTA	ask s.o. *about* s.t., *vs.* natotamaw- ask s.o. *for* s.t.

Okimâw:	šâkoc wêsâ âliman pimiy atim ohci.
Alik:	tâpwê. mâškôc ka-pêci-n'tawâpamitin pwâmoši pôsiyâhk.
Okimâw:	nâspic kimiwan ôho kîšikâwa manâ?
Alik:	tâpwê. môla wâwâc nâspic milo-kîšikâw anohc kâ-nîpihk. ta-milwâšin mâka cîmâna ohci. awasitê ta-kî-opahipêwa.[9]
Okimâw:	tântê kistês? môla n'tôhci-wâpamâw anohc kâ-kišêpâyâk.
Alik:	êhê. anohcîhkê kî-pêci-kîwêw mâmihk ohci. âšay otâpêw nôhcimihk. wîpac mâškôc ta-ihtâw ôta. ayahâw mâka, —mâhkîw'-iškotêhkân: apišîš piko tawâw cîmânihk. mâškôc n'ka-otinên. atâmihk[10] n'ka-pakitinên apahkwâsonihk.
Okimâw:	yâkwâ! pêyak 'wênihkân kî-astâw pimîwi-kâniliw[11] âšokanihk,— kî-ohcikawiniliw mâka. mâškôc ka-kilišinin.
Alik:	'kâwila mikwaškâtêl'ta. n'ka-nâkacihtân. ka-wâpamitinân nâ kišêpâyâkê?
Okimâw:	êhê. n'ka-ayamihâw niwîkimâkan; ka-wîhtamâtin mâka kê-wâpahk.

Play the above Listening In several times over, checking the additional words in the appended list. Do this until you can close your text and follow the recording with understanding.

9	opahipê-	VII	float
10	atâmihk	IPC	underneath
11	pimîwi-kân-	NI	oil can

F. REFERENCE LIST

al-	VTA	set s.o., place s.o. *v.*. astâ-.
alwêpi-	VAI	take a rest, take a holiday
anohc kâ-nîpihk		this Summer
astâ-	VAI-T	set s.t., place s.t. *v.* al-.
astê-	VII	be set, be placed
atâmihk	IPC	underneath, below
awihâsom-	VTA	borrow (from) s.o.
ayamihê'-kîšikâ-	VII	be Sunday
ayêskosi-	VAI	be tired
âpatisîwin-	NI	work
âpihtawan-	VII	be Wednesday
cîpayâhtiko-kîšikâ-	VII	be Friday: *v.* mâtinawê-kîšikâšin-, niyâlano-kîšikâ-.
êmwayêš	IPC [+ conj. indic.]	before (Lake Winnipeg area) *v.* pwâmoši.
êncini-pimiy-	NI	gasoline
ispêlohkê-	VAI	take a short rest from work
(išinâkosi-	VAI	appear so)
išinâkwan-	VII	appear so
iškotêhkân-	NI	stove
îkatên-	VTA / VTI	put s.o./ s.t. aside, store s.o. /s.t. away (for a short time)
kapatênâso-	VAI	unload (a boat), put (things) ashore
kayâm	IPC	quietly, tranquilly; "All right!"
kê-tipiskâk	VII conj. indic.	tonight (looking forward)
kihtimi-	VAI	be lazy
kilihtin-	VII	slip
kilišin-	VAI	slip
kišêpâyâkê	VII conj. subj.	in the morning (looking forward) *or* kêkišêpâyâkê
kîšponê-	VII	be full
kosâpê-	VAI / VII	sink
kosikwan-	VII	be heavy
(kosikwati-	VAI	be heavy)

kotikošin-	VAI	sprain oneself
kwatapipali-	VA/II	capsize
mawâpîstaw-	VTA	visit s.o.
mâhkîw'-iškotêhkân-	NI	camp stove: *lit.*, tent stove
mâmitonêliht-	VTI	think about s.t., ponder s.t.
mâtinamâkê-	VAI	distribute, apportion, allot
mâtinawê-	VAI	distribute, apportion, allot
mâtinawê-kîšikâ-	VII	be Saturday
mâtinawê-kîšikâšin-	VII	be Friday: *v.* cîpayâhtiko-kîšikâ-, niyâlano-kîšikâ-.
milomâtisi-	VAI	be well
mišâ-	VII	be big
(mišikiti-	VAI	be big)
nêw'-kîšikâ-	VII	be Thursday
niyâlano-kîšikâ-	VII	be Friday *v.* cîpayâhtiko-kîšikâ-, mâtinawê-kîšikâšin-.
nîšo-kîšikâ-	VII	be Tuesday
opahipê-	VII	float
otihtah-	VTI	come up to s.t., reach s.t.
pahkân	IPC	separately
pahkihtin-	VII	fall
pahkišin-	VAI	fall
pahkwêšikan-	NA	flour
pakitin-	VTA / VTI	put s.o./ s.t., let s.o./ s.t.
pikiwaskisin-	NI	rubber boot, gum boot
pimihtin-	VII	lie
pimišin-	VAI	lie
pimîwi-kân-	NI	oil can
pišišik	IPC	consistently, throughout
pišišikosi-	VAI	be empty
pišišikwâ-	VII	be empty
pišošim-	VTA	trip s.o., cause s.o. to stumble
pišošin-	VAI	stumble
pîliš	IPC	up to, until
pîtoš	IPC	differently, different
pîtoš wayêš	IPC	somewhere else, elsewhere
pôsihtâso-	VAI	load (freight on a canoe)
pwâmoši	IPC + conj. indic.	before: *v.* êmwayêš.

sîhcâ-	VII	be tight-packed, be tight-fitting; be crowded
(sîhcisi-	VAI	be tight-packed, be tight-fitting)
šîpâ	IPC	under
šîpâyâhtikohk	IPC	under a / the tree(s)
takošinômakan-	VII	arrive
tawâ-	VII	be room (for s.t.)
tipâpêskocikan-	NI	pound
wâpahtil-	VTA	show (to) s.o.
wâwâc	IPC	especially, even, equally so
'yâkwâ	IPC [interjection]	Look out!

G. REVIEW

12.A Kakwêcihkêmôwina—Questions

Answer each question with a full sentence, expanding your reply if you are able.

Use materials from any section of past units and in this way keep up your review.

1. tân' êhtiyan? kî-kotikošinin nâ mêkwâc ê-mêtawêyin?
2. kî-wî-alwêpiw nâ âlik?
3. kî-wâpaminân nâ kêkišêp?
4. ka-kî-pêci-natawâpaminân nâ kê-tipiskâk?
5. awasitê nâ âliman êncini-pimiy ispîš wîla pahkwêšikan?
6. ta-opahipêw nâ anima cîmân? nâspic kîšponêw.
7. tântê kê-iši-astêki ôho kêkwâna?
8. ka-awihâsomitin nâ kipikiwaskisina?
9. wêsâ nâ mišâwa anihi maskisina?
10. tân' êšinâkwahk anima cîmân?
11. ta-kosâpêw nâ kititêl'tên?
12. misiwê nâ kî-pakitinênâwâw pahkân mîcim?
13. pišišikwâw nâ kotakiy cîmân?
14. kiwî-mîlin nâ kêkwân?
15. kêyâpac nâ tawâw kimâhkîmihk?
16. kî-mâmitonêl'tam nâ âlik kêkwâliw?
17. tântê apahkwâsona nêsta êncini-pimiy?
18. atâmihk nâ kî-iši-pakitinâwak askihkwak?
19. tânt' êši-pimišihk cîmis?
20. tân' êhtôtahk okimâw?
21. šîpâyâhtikohk nâ iši-nipâw?
22. nakiskaw nâ kiwî-ispêlohkân kî-iškwâ-kiskinohamâsonâniwahkê?
23. ayêskosiwak nâ ililiwak mêkwâc ê-kišitêlik?
24. kiwî-kwâškwêpicikân nâ âšokanihk ohci?
25. âšay nâ mîna pôsihtâsow?

12.B Naškwêwašihtwâwina—Answers

Make up questions which nay be answered by the following replies.

1. nakiskaw wî-alwêpiw šîpâyâhtikohk.
2. ê'konâni ê-tôtahk! môla n'tôhci-wâpamâw.
3. apišîš kihtimiw piko, n'titêl'tên.
4. êhê, n'kî-kotikošinin otâkošîhk.
5. nêtê âšokanihk iši-kwâškwêpicikêw šîpâyâhtikohk.
6. êhê, kiwî-awihâsomitinân pâskisikan.
7. wêsâ kîšponêw. ta-kosâpêw.
8. mâškôc. âšay mâka nîšwâ kišê-mitâhtomitana tipâpêskocikan n'tayân.
9. tâpwê, wêsâ kosikwan.
10. kêyâpac mâškôc ta-opahipêw.
11. nipôsihtâson piko.
12. âšokanihk n'kî-iši-nakatên. mitoni pišišikwâw.
13. êhê, wîlawâw ništam kî-takošinwak nikosisak.
14. tâpwê ihtâwak kotakiyak: mihkwacakâšak nêsta kinošêwak.
15. kayâm. wêsâ mâka piko apišâšin.
16. êhê. âstam pitamâ! kiwî-wâpahtilitin kêkwân.
17. apišîš piko kêyâpac tawâw kê-iši-astêki kêkwâna.
18. tâpwê. pišišik kîšponêw.
19. mâškôc n'ka-pišošimikon.
20. âšokanihk n'kî-iši-astân,—nêtê piko, šîpâyâhtikohk.
21. anta, pêšoc mâhkîw'-iškotêhkânihk.
22. êhê, âlimisiw nêsta pahkwêšikan.
23. âšay ninisitohtên. awasitê milwêl'tam ê-pakitahwâniwanilik.
24. cikêmânima! wêsâ misawâc kišitêw âpatisîwin ohci.
25. ê'kwâni kwayask. môla n'ka-âpatisinân anohc kâ-nîpihk.

UNIT THIRTEEN

A. BASIC CONVERSATION

The Old Folks

Sayman:	kimošôm	your grandfather
	n'kî-mayâwahwâw	I passed him (on water)
	n'kî-mayâwahomâwa otalapiya	I passed by his nets
	n'kî-mayâwahomâwa kimošôm otalapiya n'timihk sîpîhk.	I passed by your grandfather's nets upstream.
Côwil:	nôhkoma (*obviative*)	my grandmother
	wîcêwêpan	he was accompanying her
	wîcêwêpan nâ nôhkoma?	Was he with my grandmother?
	kî-nâtahomâwâwa otâšokana	you (2p) approached his wharf
	môla mâškôc kitôhci-nâtahomâwâwa pêšoc otâšokana.	You probably didn't go near his wharf.
Sayman:	n'kî-pisiskâpam...im...ânânih	we (1p) noticed her (*obv.*)
	môla n'tôhci-pisiskâpamimânânih wîwa.	We didn't notice his wife.
	nipîwâpiskominân	our (1p) motor
	môla mâškôc ohci-pêhtam m'pîwâpiskominân.	He probably didn't hear our motor.
Côwil:	môla osihtêw	he's hard of hearing
	kišê-'liliw	the old man
	tâpwê! kišê-'liliw apišîš môla osihtêw.	Quite likely! The old man's a little hard of hearing.
	kicîmâniliw (*obviative*)	your canoe
	wâwâc	even
	môla mâškôc nêsta wâwâc ohci-wâpahtam kicîmâniliw.	He probably didn't even see your canoe.
Sayman:	kišê-'lilîwiw	he is an old person
	nâspic kišê-'lilîwiw, manâ?	He's very old, isn't he?
	tâpwê môla n'tôhci-wâpamikonân.	He certainly didn't see us.

	ôsisima	his grandchild(ren)
	mihcêt nâ ayâwêw ôsisima?	Has he many grandchildren?
Côwil:	onahâhkaniskwêma	his daughter-in-law
	cakawâšišiliwa	they (*obviative*) are few
	cakawâšišiliwa piko. pêyak ayâwêw onahâhkaniskwêma.	Only a few. He has one daughter-in-law.
	wîkitoliwa	they (*obviative*) are married
	onahâhkišîma	his sons-in-law
	nîšiliwa	they (*obviative*) are two
	nîšiliwa onahâhkišîma. misiwê wîkitoliwa ocawâšimiša.	He has two sons-in-law. All his children are married.
	n'kî-wîci-tašîhkê...m...ikonânih[1]	they (3') stayed with us
	n'kî-wîci-tašîhkêmikonânih onahâhkišîma piponohk.	His sons-in-law stayed with us last Winter.
Sayman:	pêyakwâ ê-kîšikâlik (*obv.*)	one day
	kî-wîci-nâtawahomânawa[2]	we (21) hunted with them (*obv.*)
	êhê, n'kiskêl'tên. kî-wîci-natawah... omânawa pêyakwâ ê-kîšikâlik. kikiskisin nâ?	Yes, I know. We hunted with them one day. Remember?
	ocawâšimišilîw	her (3') children (3")
	milo-wâhkom...im...êw	he (3) gets on well with them (3")
	kišê-ililiw nâ milo-wâhkomimêw otânisa ocawâšimišilîw?	Does the old chap get along well with his daughter's children?
Côwil:	nahêlim...êliwa	she (3') is pleased with them (3")
	nahêlim...im...êw	he (3) is satisfied with them (3")
	êhê, nâsic nahêlimimêw. nêsta owîkimâkana nahêlimêliwa.	Oh yes, he's very pleased with them. His wife is pleased with them too.
	mihcêtwâ	many times
	wît...api...m...im...êwak	they (3p) sit with them (3")
	tâpwêwin ohci	as a matter of fact, to tell the truth
	tâpwêwin ohci, kišê-'liliwak wîtapimimêwak otânisiwâwa ocawâšimišilîw mihcêtwâ nawac.	As a matter of fact, the old people sit with their daughter's children quite often.

[1] Speaker slipped into 1p ← 3p, instead of the expected 1p ← 3'.

[2] < nâtawahw...ɩm...ânawa.

	iko	only
	pêyako-tipisk	one night ('s length)
	mîskaw	for a change
	onîkihikowâwa	their parents
	mîskaw awâšišak onîkihikowâwa pêyako-tipisk iko itâpicîliwa.	For a change, the children's parents are away overnight.
Sayman:	n'kî-mayâškawimâwa otêma	I passed by her dogs (walking)
	tâpwê nâ? n'kî-mayâškawimâwa kimis otêma otâkošîhk.	Really? I walked past your sister's dogs yesterday.
	wîci-mêtawê...m...êpan	he was playing together with him
	pêyak awâšiš wîci-mêtawêmêpan acimošiša.	One of the children was playing with a puppy.
Côwil:	kî-wî-ayamihikoliwa	he (3') wanted to speak to you
	nimis onâpêma kî-wî-ayamihikoliwa. wîci-tašîhkêmikowak nîšo okosisa. wî-kiskêl'tamiliwa: ka-kî-wîcêwitinâwâw nâ ê-n'taminahoyêk?[3]	My sister's husband wanted to speak to you. His two sons are living with them. He wants to know if they can go off hunting with you folks.
Sayman:	cikêmânima, ka-kî-wîcêwinâwâw!	Of course they may come with us.

[3] Note use of direct discourse.

B. DISCUSSION OF GRAMMAR

1. Verbs

1.1 VTA with 3′ or 3″ Object: Independent Order, Direct

You will recall from 3.B.1.4.2 that you were cautioned against trying to say things such as 'I see his canoe' or 'You lost his paddle', etc., that is, not to combine a ni... or ki... subject with an object possessed by a third person. In this unit you are going to learn how to do just that, beginning with the transitive animate verb.

When the subject of a verb is ni... or ki..., the next position further out, so to speak, is 3, followed by 3′, still further out. In the sentences above, canoe and paddle are nouns possessed by a third person possessor, which pushes them out to *further* third person, or obviative, position. In moving from a first or second person subject to a *further* third person object, it is as though the third person proximate position were being skipped. The case is the same when moving from 3 subject to 3″ object. To show this skipping of one position an additional element, ...**ιm**, is inserted after the VTA stem. If the subject is ni... or ki... the obviative indicator, ...**a** is then added to the verb endings for proximate object. There is no marker to show whether the 3′ object is singular or plural.

Where the subject is 3 or 3p, the use of ...**ιm** shows that the object is 3″ ; and in this case the obviative indicator, ...**a**, does not appear. Study the following paradigm noting where a position is skipped between subject and object.

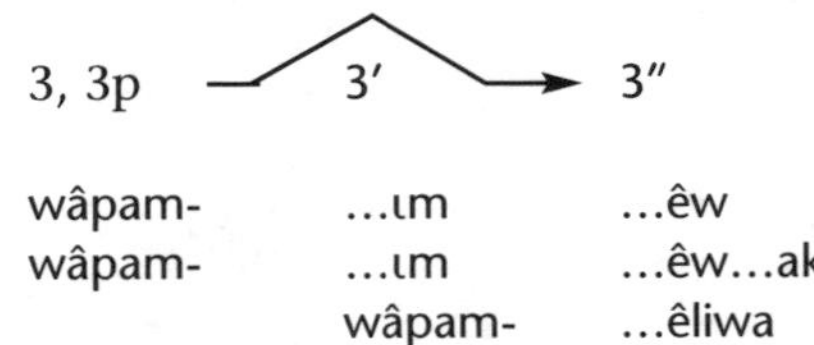

1}
2} ———————— 3, 3p ————→ 3′

1-	ni...	wâpam-	...ιm	...âw...a
1p-	"	"	...ιm	...ânân...a, ...ih
2-	ki...	"	...ιm	...âw...a
21-	"	"	...ιm	...ânaw...a
2p-	"	"	...ιm	...âwâw...a

Note, where the subject is 1p, the obviative indicator, ...a, displays a dialect variant, ...ih: *e.g.,* niwâpamimânânih otalapiya, we see his nets.

Study the following sentences.

1. n'kî-ayamihimânâna ôsisima otâkošîhk. We spoke to his grandchild yesterday.
2. nâsic nahêlimimêw otânisa ocawâšimišilîw. She's very pleased with her daughter's children.
3. kî-nâtahomâwâwa nâ âlik otâšokana? Did you go near Alec's wharf?
4. kî-mayâwahomânawa nimošôm otalapiya. We (21) passed by my grandfather's nets.
5. môla n'tôhci-pisiskâpamimâwa wîwa. I didn't notice his wife.
6. mâškôc ka-kî-wîci-natawahomâwa ostêsa. Maybe you can hunt with his older brother.
7. kî-miskâmêwak okosisiwâwa ocêmišišilîw. They found their son's pups.

———DRILLS 1 THROUGH 3———

1.2 VTA with 3′ or 3″ Actor: Independent Order, Inverse

To our repertoire of inverse suffixes we can now add those for 3′ actor with ni... and ki... goals. The suffixes introduced in this unit are the ones shown in square brackets in Unit 9.B.1.1. Study their relation in shape to the other forms charted in the diagram following.

		3-	3p-	3′-	3″-
-3				...ιkow	
-3p				...ιkowak	
-3′					...ιkoliwa
-1	ni(t)	...ιk	...ιkwak	...ιkoliwa	
-2	ki(t)	...ιk	...ιkwak	...ιkoliwa	
-1p	ni(t)	...ιkonân	...ιkonânak	...ιkonâna	
-21	ki(t)	...ιkonaw	...ιkonawak	...ιkonawa	
-2p	ki(t)	...ιkowâw	...ιkowâwak	...ιkowâwa	

Note in particular: the terms, *actor* and *goal* rather than subject and object were used above. In word-building, each component has its appropriate slot: *ni...wâpam...â...ιnân...ak, where ni... represents the grammatical subject and ...ak the plural object in the direct form. In the inverse the only change is in the direction signal: ...a... is replaced by ...ιkw...: *i.e.,* the grammatical subject and object remain the same. (Think of the English passive: *we are seen,* where *we* remains the grammatical subject but is now the recipient or *goal* of the action.) In the inverse, grammatical subject and object remain the same; the subject, however, is now the recipient or *goal* of the 1p ← 3p action in the example above. ...ak now signals the 3p *actor,* no longer the goal.

Study the following sentences carefully.

8.	n'kî-ayamihikonâna ôsisima otâkošîhk.	His grandchild(ren) spoke to us yesterday.
9.	nâsic nahêlimikoliwa otânisa ocawâšimišilîw.	Her daughter's children are very fond of her.
10.	kî-wâpamikoliwa nâ âlik ostêsa?	Did Alec's young brother see you?
11.	nimis okosisa kî-miskâkonawa natimihk.	My sister's son found us upriver.
12.	môla n'tôhci-wâpamikonâna wîwa.	His wife didn't see us.
13.	ka-kî-pêci-wîci-natawahokoliwa ošîma.	His young brother will be able to come and hunt with you.
14.	kî-wîhtamâkowak onahâhkaniskwêma.	Their daughter-in-law told them.
15.	wîwa ošîmilîw kî-wîtapimikoliwa pêyako-tipisk.	His wife's young sister stayed with her for one night.

———DRILLS 4 AND 5———

1.3 wîci + VAI Stems

The verbal prefix, wîci, when used with animate intransitive verbs, signals that the actor does whatever the verb indicates, *together with* someone else. The VAI stem follows the prefix and is in turn followed by the VTA stem final, ...m-, and the regular VTA inflectional suffixes. The partner to the activity is then grammatically the object of the verb: *e.g.,*

ki... mîciso ...n.	You are eating.
ki...wîci-mîciso...m...âw.	You are eating with him.
nîmi ...w.	She is dancing.
wîci-nîmi...m...êw.	She is dancing with him.

wîci, the preverb particle, is formed from the root, wît..., as in wîtapimikoliwa (#15 above). You have already met a parallel in the preverb particle, pêci, and pêt..., the root in pêtâpan-, "dawn is coming". Roots, unlike preverb particles, are not followed by a hyphen since they are part of the primary stem itself. Learn verbs such as pêtâpan- and wîtapim- as you go along. They will be useful points of reference when we come to study such formations in full.

2. Nouns

2.1 Obviative of Possessed Nouns, *continued*

We have already met the obviative of possessed nouns (Unit 4.B.6.2; Unit 5.B.2.1). *Animate* nouns, whether possessed by singular or plural possessor, mark obviation by the addition of...a, or when 3′ is possessor, by the addition of ...ilîw: *e.g.,*

kî-wîtapimêw nicawâšimiša. — She sat with my child.
kî-pâskisomêw kitêmiwâwa. — He shot your (2p) dog.
twâmas kî-miskâmêw cwâna otapwôlîw. — Thomas found John's paddle.

BUT, *inanimate* nouns possessed by ni... or ki... *plural* take no formal marker to show the obviative: *e.g.,*

kî-miskam kitastotiniliw. — He found your (2) hat.
but kî-miskam kitastotiniwâw. — He found your (2p) hat.

3. Sound System

3.1 Contraction of /w/ + /i/ to /o/ across morpheme boundary

Where a stem or other component ends in a Consonant + /w/, symbolized by Cw, and is followed by a further element beginning with /i/, the combination of /w/ + /i/ across the boundary regularly results in the vowel /o/. This is reflected in conventional spelling where

*otâmah**w**...ιm...êw > otâmah**o**mêw
and *pâskis**w**...ιm...êw > pâskis**o**mêw.

This is, of course, the same change as that which operates in the forms,

mistikohk < mistikw...ιhk (Unit 3.B.2.1.2)

and the change affects the modern vowel /i/, regardless of its historic origin (*v.* Unit 11.B.1.2, HISTORICAL NOTE.):

kî-otâmahon you struck me < kî-otâmahw...in.

The change may be neatly symbolized by the formula: /Cw/ + /i/ > /Co/.

3.2 Contraction of /aw/ + /i/(< ι̲), *continued*

VTA stems in /aw/ final were described (Unit 11.B.1.2) as always showing a regular type of contraction in the 1 → 2 inflectional set. The contraction is, in fact, a regular sound change occurring in forms such as nisitohtâtowak < *nisitohtaw...ιtowak and miskâmêw < *miskaw...ιmêw in the present unit. Forms such as kawinêw (Unit 6.A.3) show no contraction, possibly because a shortened form, *kânêw, might obscure the identity of the root. Whatever the reason, the occurrence of forms like pêhtawimêw (C.1.8.c below) rather than pêhtâmêw and n'kî-mayâškawimâwa instead of n'kî-mayâškâmâwa serves to recall the admonition of Edward Sapir (Unit 10.B.4).

3.3 Palatalization of /t/ by assimilation

You may have wondered why awâšiš, when possessed, takes the form ocawâšimiša, instead of otawâšimiša. In rapid English speech adjoining sounds are often run together so that at least one of them is changed: *e.g.,* Didja? for Did you? This change, by which one speech sound is influenced by another to become more like it is known as *assimilation.* It usually happens when two sounds are adjacent or, at least, close together. Sometimes, however, sounds may be somewhat further apart and still influence each other.

In awâšimiša there are two occurrences of /š/. This sound is made by holding the *blade* of the tongue close to the alveolar ridge, a little back towards the palate (*v.* diagram, "Cree Sound System", p. xxvii). As the tongue gets ready to go into position for /š/, it moves, slightly altered, backwards in the mouth and this has the effect of changing preceding /t/ to a /c/. As a result, instead of atimošiš one hears acimošiš, and instead of otawâšimiša the form is ocawâšimiša. This "long distance" assimilation is technically described as *non-contiguous* assimilation. (As a matter of interest, failure to carry out this kind of assimilation in the prescribed place often conveys the impression of baby-talk to a native speaker. The same thing seems to hold true with failure to observe the important distinction between preaspirated and non-preaspirated stops. [*v.* Unit 12.C.1.])

4. Syntax

Attention is drawn to the Cree preference for directly reported speech, as in the final exchange in the Basic Conversation above where the direct words of the speaker are cited:

> wî-kiskêl'tamiliwa: ka-kî-wîcêwitinâwâw nâ ê-n'taminahoyêk?
> He wants to know whether they can go hunting with you folks.

This is common in Cree and from time to time you will note other instances in the text.

C. DRILLS

The drills below contain two or three unfamiliar verbs. Treat them as you would familiar words belonging to the same stem class and do not worry about their dictionary meaning yet.

1. Transitive Animate Verbs, Direct, with obviative object

Repeat the fragment given by the recording and expand it with the verb form proper to a 3′ object or, where the subject is already 3, proper to a 3″ object. The model is

Recording: n'kî-otinâw nitêm. (twice)
Response: n'kî-otinâw nitêm, n'kî-otinimâwa nêsta cwân otêma.

1.a n'kî-otinâw kitêm, __________ nêsta cwân otêma.
1.b n'kî-pâskiswâw kitêm, __________ nêsta cwân otêma.
1.c n'kî-miskawâw kitêm, __________ nêsta cwân otêma.

2.a kî-wâpamêw okosisa, __________ nêsta cwâna okosisilîw.
2.b kî-otâmahwêw okosisa, __________ nêsta cwâna okosisilîw.
2.c kî-wîhtamawêw okosisa, __________ nêsta cwâna okosisilîw.

3.a ka-wanihânawak kitapwoyak, __________ nêsta cwân otapwoya.
3.b ka-pîkohwânawak kitapwoyak, __________ nêsta cwân otapwoya.
3.c ka-miskawânawak kitapwoyak, __________ nêsta cwân otapwoya.

4.a ta-âhkohêwak kikosisa, __________ nêsta cwâna okosisilîw.
4.b ta-cîstahwêwak kikosisa, __________ nêsta cwâna okosisilîw.
4.c ta-tipahamawêwak kikosisa, __________ nêsta cwâna okosisilîw.

5.a kikanawâpamâwâw nipalacîs, __________ nêsta cwân opalacîsa.
5.b kimâcišwâwâw nipalacîs, __________ nêsta cwân opalacîsa.
5.c kikociškawâwâw nipalacîs, __________ nêsta cwân opalacîsa.

6.a âskaw niwâpamânân kimošôm, âskaw nêsta __________ cwân omošôma.
6.b âskaw nimayâwahwânân kimošôm, âskaw nêsta __________ cwân omošôma.
6.c âskaw nimawâpîstawânân kimošôm, âskaw nêsta __________ cwân omošôma.

7.a môla wîskâc kitôhci-âpacihâw n'talapiy, môla nêsta wîskâc __________ cwân otalapiya.
7.b môla wîskâc kitôhci-mayâwahwâw n'talapiy, môla nêsta wîskâc __________ cwân otalapiya.
7.c môla wîskâc kitôhci-mayâškawâw n'talapiy, môla nêsta wîskâc __________ cwân otalapiya.

8.a natomimêw cwân okosisa otêmilîw, nêsta okosisa __________ otêmilîw.
8.b otâmahomêw cwân okosisa otêmilîw, nêsta okosisa __________ otêmilîw.
8.c pêhtawimêw cwân okosisa otêmilîw, nêsta okosisa __________ otêmilîw.

(Checklist)

1.a n'kî-otinimâwa
1.b n'kî-pâskisomâwa
1.c n'kî-miskâmâwa
2.a kî-wâpamimêw
2.b kî-otâmahomêw
2.c kî-wîhtamâmêw
3.a ka-wanihimânawa
3.b ka-pîkohomânawa
3.c ka-miskâmânawa
4.a ta-âhkohimêwak
4.b ta-cîstahomêwak
4.c ta-tipahamâmêwak
5.a kikanawâpamimâwâwa
5.b kimâcišomâwâwa
5.c kikociškâmâwâwa
6.a niwâpamimânâna
6.b nimayâwahomânâna
6.c nimawâpîstâmânâna
7.a kitôhci-âpacihimâwa
7.b kitôhci-mayâwahomâwa
7.c kitôhci-mayâškâmâwa
8.a natomêliwa
8.b otâmahwêliwa
8.c pêhtawêliwa

2. Transitive Animate Verbs: Independent Direct ni..., ki... → 3'; 3, 3p → 3"

2.1 Mimic the recording across each row, noting the contrast in form.

wîcêwêw okimâwa	wîcêwimêw okimâwa okosisilîw
pisiskâpamêw ililiwa	pisiskâpamimêw ililiwa wîwilîw
mayâ'hwêw kimošôma	mayâ'homêw kimošôma otalapîlîw
nâtahwêw kišê-'liliwa	nâtahomêw kišê-'liliwa otâšokanilîw
pâskiswêwak kotakiya	pâskisomêwak kotakiya otêmilîw
wîhtamawêwak omisa	wîhtamâmêwak omisa ocawâšimišilîw
miskawêwak kôhtâwiya	miskâmêwak kôhtâwiya otapwôlîw
ayâwêwak kôhkoma anta	ayâwimêwak kôhkoma otaskhikolîw

ôhtâwiya ayamihêliwa wîwilîw
ôsisima kî-otinêliwa otapwôlîw
wîwa ta-kîsiswêliwa otâlahkonâmilîw
otânisa kî-miskawêliwa otalapîlîw

2.2 Continue to repeat after the recording, as above.

nikawinâw âšokan ka-ohpahâwak nâ alapiyak?	nikawinimâwa cwân otâšokana ka-ohpahimâwa nâ cwân otalapiya?
niwâpamânân iskwêw nitakimânânak šôliyânak	niwâpamimânânih cwân otiskwêma nitakimimânânih cwân ošôliyânima
kikociškawânaw palacîs kitayâwânawak šîšîpak	kikociškâmânawa cwân opalacîsa kitayâwimânawa cwân ošîšîpima
kî-šîwahwâwâw namês kî-pâskiswâwâwak atimwak	kî-šîwahomâwâwa cwân onamêsima kî-pâskisomâwâwa cwân otêma

3. Further drill on the obviative of possessed nouns

3.1 The voice on the recording will give the object of the verb, then two verb phrases twice. After the second time, you select the verb form required to complete the sentence correctly; then repeat the sentence as a whole: *e.g.*,

Cue:	kicîmâniliw: then, mâškôc n'tawêl'tam ~ mâškôc n'ka-n'tawêl'tên (twice)
Reply:	mâškôc n'tawêl'tam kicîmâniliw.

The recording will then provide a correct version of the sentence. (In this and in Drill 3.2, use only as much of the material as you need; but be sure you control the forms.)

1. (mâškôc n'tawêl'tam ~ mâškôc n'ka-n'tawêl'tên) kicîmâniliw.
2. (kî-awihâsomâw nâ ~ kî-awihâsomêw nâ) opâskisikan?
3. ka-wawêšihtân nâ ~ ta-wawêšihtâw nâ) niwâskâhikanimiliw?
4. (kî-otinamwak ~ kî-otinênâwâw) nipîskâkaniliw.
5. ka-mîlitinâwâw nâ ~ ka-mîlânaw nâ) cwân kitapwoya?
6. (n'ka-mîlânân nâ ~ ta-mîlêw nâ) cwâna otapwôlîw?
7. (kî-ayamihâw nâ ~ kî-ayamihêw nâ) kitânisa?
8. (mihcêtwâ wîtapimêwak ~ mihcêtwâ wîtapimimêwak) osisimiwâwa.
9. (wîskâc nâ ohci-wâpamêwak ~ wîskâc nâ kitôhci-wâpamâw) nôhtâwiya?

10. (tâpwê kî-wîcêwâw ~ tâpwê kî-wîcêwêpan) kôhkoma.
11. (kî-milwêl'tam nâ kikosis ~ kî-milwêl'tên nâ) kipîwâpiskomiliw?
12. ta-âpacihêw nâ ~ ta-âpacihimêw nâ) kikosisa otâšokwanilîw?
13. (okâwiya nâ kî-âpacihêliwa ~ okâwiya nâ kî-âpacihêw) otaskihkolîw?
14. kî-kanawâpahtam nâ ~ kî-kanawâpahtên nâ) niwâskâhikanim?
15. (n'ka-mayâwahwâwak nâ ~ n'ka-mayâ'homâwa nâ) kinahâhkišîm otalapiya?
16. (môla mâškôc n'ka-milo-wâhkomânânak ~ môla mâškôc n'ka-milo-wâhkomimânânih) kišê-'liliwak onahâhkaniskwêmiwâwa.

(Remainder of drill not recorded)

17. (cwân nâ kî-miskawêliwa ~ cwân nâ kî-miskâmêw) okosisa otêmilîw?
18. (ka-nahêlimimâwâwa ~ ka-nahêlimâwâwak) kišê-iskwêw ocawâšimišiwâwa.
19. (môla ohci-têpwâtêw ~ môla ohci-têpwâtimêw) nitânisa.
20. (môla n'tôhci-pipiskâpamimânânih ~ môla n'tôhci-pipiskâpamâw[1]) wîwa.
21. (kî-nâtahwâwâw nâ ~ kî-nâtahomâwâwa nâ) pêšoc otâšokwana?
22. (awâšišak kî-wîci-mêtawêmêwak ~ awâšišak kî-wîci-mêtawêmêliwa) acimošiša.

1. n'tawêl'tam
2. kî-awihâsomâw
3. ta-wawêšihtâw
4. kî-otinamwak
5. ka-mîlânaw
6. ta-mîlêw
7. kî-ayamihêw
8. wîtapimêwak
9. ohci-wâpamêwak
10. kî-wîcêwêpan
11. kî-milwêl'tam
12. ta-âpacihimêw
13. kî-âpacihêliwa
14. kî-kanawâpahtên
15. n'ka-mayâ'homâwa
16. n'ka-milo-wâhkomimânânih
17. kî-miskâmêw
18. ka-nahêlimimâwâwa
19. ohci-têpwâtêw
20. n'tôhci-pipiskâpamimânânih
21. kî-nâtahomâwâwa
22. kî-wîci-mêtawêmêwak

3.2 In the following drill choose the form of the possessed noun required to produce a grammatically correct sentence.

1. nâspic milwêlimêw (otapwoya ~ otapwôlîw).
2. ta-pâskiswêw nâ (nitêm ~ nitêma)?
3. kî-pâskisomêw (ošîma otêmilîw ~ otêma).
4. môla mâškôc ta-wî'-tašîhkêmêw[2] (kitôtêmiwâwak ~ kitôtêmiwâwa).
5. nahiškawêw nâ âlik (kipalacîs ~ kipalacîsa)?
6. môla nâspic ninahêlimimâwa (cîmis ~ cîmis ošîma).

[1] pipisk..., alternative heard for pisisk....
[2] wî': here a contracted form for wîci.

7. kin'tawêlimâw nâ (n'tapwoy ~ n'tapwoya)?
8. n'ka-wîtapimimânânih nâ (awîšišak ~ ocawâšimišiwâwa)?
9. mâškôc ta-kî-wawêšihêwak (kitâšokwana ~ kitâšokwan).
10. âšay nâ kî-wâpamimêwak (otalapiya ~ okosisa otalapîlîw)?
11. ta-n'tawêl'tam nâ (nicîmân ~ nicîmâniliw) kititêlihtên?
12. tâpwê! kî-miskamwak (nipâskisikaninân ~ nipâskisikaninân).

(Right! An inanimate noun possessed by 1p, 21 or 2p does not show ...iliw to mark the obviative.)

13. kî-wâpahtam (kicîmâniwâw ~ kicîmâniwâw).
14. kî-wâpahtam (kicîmân ~ kicîmâniliw).
15. wîpac mâškôc ta-wawêšihimêw omošôma (otapwoya ~ otapwôlîw).
16. kiwî-sakahpitimâwâwa nâ (nitêminân ~ otêmiwâwa).
17. wîskâc nâ ka-kî-ohci-wâpamânawak (kinîkihikonawak ~ onîkihikowâwa)?
18. ka-kociškâmâwa nâ (kitastisak ~ otastisa)?
19. môla mâškôc ta-mayâwahwêw (n'tâšokwana ~ otâšokwan).
20. môla ohci-nâtahwêwak pêšoc (nitalapînân ~ nitalapînâna).
21. tâpwê nâ kî-milo-wâhkomêw (kitôkimâminawa ~ kitôkimâminaw)?
22. mâškôc ka-wîcêwimânawa (ôhtâwiya ~ kôhtâwiy).
23. wîcêwêpan nâ (nôhkom ~ nôhkoma)?
24. kî-mawâpîstawêw (ninîkihikonânak ~ ninîkihikonânih).
25. ayâwimêw nâ (cwâna opalacîsilîw ~ opalacîsa)?

1. otapwoya
2. nitêma
3. ošîma otêmilîw
4. kitôtêmiwâwa
5. kipalacîsa
6. cîmis ošîma
7. n'tapwoy
8. ocawâšimišiwâwa
9. kitâšokwana
10. okosisa otalapîlîw
11. nicîmâniliw
12. nipâskisikaninân
13. kicîmâniwâw
14. kicîmâniliw
15. otapwôlîw
16. otêmiwâwa
17. kinîkihikonawak
18. otastisa
19. n'tâšokwana
20. nitalapînâna
21. kitôkimâminawa
22. ôhtâwiya
23. nôhkoma
24. ninîkihikonânih
25. cwâna opalacîsilîw

4. Transitive Animate Verbs, Inverse, with obviative actor

Repeat the fragment given by the recording and expand it with the verb form proper to the obviative actor, on the model,

Recording: n'kî-ayamihik nitôtêm.
Response: n'kî-ayamihikoliwa nêsta cwân otôtêma.

1.a n'kî-ayamihik n'tôtêm,... nêsta cwân otôtêma,
1.b n'kî-pâskisok n'tôtêm,... nêsta cwân otôtêma,
1.c n'kî-wîhtamâk n'tôtêm,... nêsta cwân otôtêma,

2.a kî-kanawâpamikow omisa,... nêsta cwâna omisilîw,
2.b awâšiš kî-pâsokow omisa,... nêsta cwâna omisilîw,
2.c kî-mayâškâkow omisa,... nêsta cwâna omisilîw,

3.a ka-mîlik kišê-'liliw,... nêsta wîwa,
3.b ka-otâmahok kišê-'liliw,... nêsta wîwa,
3.c ka-tipahamâk kišê-'liliw,... nêsta wîwa,

4.a n'ka-wîtapimikonân nikâwînân,... nêsta nikâwînân omisa,
4.b n'ka-mayâwahokonân nikâwînân,... nêsta nikâwînân omisa,
4.c n'ka-miskâkonân nikâwînân,... nêsta nikâwînân omisa,

5.a kikanawêlimikonawak kotakiyak,... nêsta owâhkomâkaniwâwa,
5.b kipâskisokonawak kotakiyak,... nêsta owâhkomâkaniwâwa,
5.c kiwîhtamâkonawak kotakiyak,... nêsta owâhkomâkaniwâwa,

6.a ka-nakatikowâw âšokanihk,... nêsta ôhtâwiya,
6.b ka-mayâwahokowâw âšokanihk,... nêsta ôhtâwiya,
6.c ka-tipahamâkowâw âšokanihk,... nêsta ôhtâwiya,

7.a kî-môhikowak mêrîwa,... nêsta mêrîwa ošîmilîw,
7.b kî-pâsokowak mêrîwa,... nêsta mêrîwa ošîmilîw,
7.c kî-kisiwâsîstâkowak mêrîwa,... nêsta mêrîwa ošîmilîw,

1.a n'kî-ayamihikoliwa
1.b n'kî-pâskisokoliwa
1.c n'kî-wîhtamâkoliwa

2.a kî-kanawâpamikoliwa
2.b kî-pâsokoliwa
2.c kî-mayâškâkoliwa

3.a ka-mîlikoliwa
3.b ka-otâmahokoliwa
3.c ka-tipahamâkoliwa

4.a n'ka-wîtapimikonâna
4.b n'ka-mayâwahokonâna
4.c n'ka-miskâkonâna

5.a kikanawêlimikonawa
5.b kipâskisokonawa
5.c kiwîhtamâkonawa

6.a ka-nakatikowâwa
6.b ka-mayâwahokowâwa
6.c ka-tipahamâkowâwa

7.a kî-môhikoliwa
7.b kî-pâsokoliwa
7.c kî-kisiwâsîstâkoliwa

5. Transitive Animate Verbs: Independent Inverse with obviative actor.

5.1 Select the form in brackets required by the verb.

Recording: n'kî-kîwêhtahikonâna (êntiriy ~ êntiriy ostêsa).
Response: n'kî-kîwêhtahikonâna êntiriy ostêsa.

1. n'kî-kîwêhtahikonâna (êntiriy ~ êntiriy[3] ostêsa).
2. nâsic nahêlimikoliwa (otânisa onâpêmilîw ~ otânisa).
3. ka-miskâkonawak (kitôtêmak okâwîwâwa ~ kitôtêmak).
4. n'kî-kitotikoliwa (nitôtêm ~ otôtêma).
5. kî-otâmahok nâ (kistês ~ kistêsa) ?
6. kî-otâmahokowak nâ (kistês ~ kistêsa)?
7. tâpask ka-kitotikowâw (ana iskwêw ~ anihi iskwêwa).
8. môšak kimôhikowâwa (âlik ~ âlik ostêsa).
9. kî-pêhtâkonawa nâ (kitêminaw ~ otêmiwâwa)?
10. mâškôc ka-tôtâkoliwa 'ci-iskôliwiyan (kôhkom ~ ôhkoma).

1. êntiriy ostêsa
2. otânisa onâpêmilîw
3. kitôtêmak
4. otôtêma
5. kistês
6. kistêsa
7. ana iskwêw
8. âlik ostêsa
9. otêmiwâwa
10. ôhkoma

5.2 Select the verb form required.

Recording: ostêsa âšay (nipâhpihikonân ~ nipâhpihikonâna).
Response: ostêsa âšay nipâhpihikonâna.

1. ostêsa âšay (nipâhpihikonân ~ nipâhpihikonâna).
2. tâpask ocawâšimiša (ka-wanâhikonawa ~ ka-wanâhikonawak).
3. mihcêtwâw wîwa (kitayamihikoliwa ~ kitayamihik).
4. ana iskwêšiš nâpêšiša (kî-otâmahokoliwa ~ kî-otâmahokow).
5. šâ! mâškôc otêma (n'ka-pêhtâkoliwa ~ n'ka-pêhtâk).
6. otôtêma misiwê (kî-papâmohtahikowâwak ~ kî-papâmohtahikowâwa).
7. ocawâšimišiwâwa nâ (kî-pâhpihikwak ~ kî-pâhpihikowak)?
8. otôkimâma okosisilîw (kî-wîcihikow ~ kî-wîcihikoliwa).
9. nipîhk kî-iši-pahkišinin. mêriy okâwiya (ka-pâsok ~ ka-pâsokoliwa).
10. ôsisima otâkošîhk (kî-pêci-mawâpîstâkonawa ~ kî-pêci-mawâpîstâkwak).

[3] Also heard as êntiniy.

1. nipâhpihikonâna
2. ka-wanâhikonawa
3. kitayamihihikoliwa
4. kî-otâmahokow
5. n'ka-pêhtâkoliwa
6. kî-papâmohtahikowâwa
7. kî-pâhpihikowak
8. kî-wîcihikoliwa
9. ka-pâsokoliwa
10. kî-pêci-mawâpîstâkonawa

6. Complete each sentence with the appropriate form from the stems listed on the left.

	Simon and Joel are chatting about the old folks in the village. Simon remarks: "I passed by your grandfather's nets upriver."
mayâwahw-	____________________ kimošôm ____________
alapiy-	n'timihk sîpîhk.
	Joel wonders whether his grandfather was accompanied by
wîcêw-	his grandmother: ________________ nâ nôhkoma?
	Simon replies that they didn't notice the grandfather's wife and the old gentleman probably didn't even hear their motor:
pisiskâpam-	môla ________________ wîwa. môla mâškôc ohci-
pêht-	__________ m'pîwâpiskominân.
	He adds, "He certainly didn't see us:" tâpwê môla
wâpam-	______________________. nâspic kišê-ililîwiw,
ayâw-	manâ? Then he asks: mihcêt nâ __________ ôsisima?
wîkito-	To which Joel replies: misiwê ocawâšimiša __________.
wîci-tašîhkêm-	In fact, ________________________ onahâhkišîma. piponohk.
wîci-nâtawahw-	"I know," rejoins Simon: ________________ pêyakwâ ê-kîšikâlik.
milo-wâhkom-	Then he inquires: kišê-ililiw nâ __________________ otânisa ocawâšimišilîw?
nahêlim-	"Yes," replies Joel: nâsic ______________ ; and so does his wife: nêsta owîkimâkana ________________.
wîtapim-	As a matter of fact, kišê-ililiwak __________________ otânisiwâwa ocawâšimišilîw mihcêtwâ nawac.
	Changing the subject, Simon observes that he walked past
mayâškaw-	your sister's dogs yesterday: ______________ kimis otêma otâkošîhk. One of the youngsters was playing with a puppy:
wîci-mêtawêm-	pêyak awâšiš ____________________ acimošiša.
	Her two sons are still living with them:
wîci-tašîhkêm-	kêyâpac __________________ nîšo okosisa.

D. CONVERSATION PRACTICE

1. Cover the Cree column in the Basic Conversation and proceed as in earlier units. Remember, even if you get stuck, KEEP GOING. Mark difficult points and return to learn them. Then drill the whole conversation again from the beginning.

2. Check the drills for difficulties. To counteract the likelihood of memorizing the order in which responses occur, work with another member of the class, selecting sentences at random. You might then practise the forms on a question-answer basis:

Do you ______?	Yes, I ______.
Do I ______ ?	Yes, you ______.
Do we ______?	Yes, you (pl.) ______.

3. You have been to visit Alec in his house or tent. You spoke to his wife and saw his grand-children; but you couldn't find his son. Later on you passed Alec on the river and noticed his son lying under a tree. He was just resting, he said; then he was going to set out nets. Alec's son's wife often bakes bread and it's delicious. She was baking some before they went away, she said. She remarked that they intended to pitch camp upriver at the fishing grounds.

4. Discuss someone's relatives, in-laws (nîstâw- NDA my brother-in-law, nîtimw- NDA my sister-in-law), how you visited them, spoke to them, hunted with them, etc. Supplementary Conversation 2, which follows this unit, will provide a number of further useful expressions to discuss family matters.

E. LISTENING IN

Listen to the following conversation several times with your text closed. When you have recognized all or most of the material already learned, there will still be unfamiliar items. Try to guess at the meaning, first on the basis of the part of speech to which the new word seems to belong, on the basis of its form (*e.g.*, locative, obviative, inverse), or from any clue given by its position in the sentence. Now check your attempts at "educated guesswork" by following the text and looking at the glosses below. Remember, one of the ways in which you learned the meaning of words in your own language was by noting their recurrence in a given context.

Côw:	mwêhci anohcîhkê n'kî-nâtawâpamimânânih nimošôm otalapiya.
Tânyil:	kitayâwimâwa nâ anta âtiht onamêsima?
Côw:	môla. n'kî-nakatimâwa âšokanihk. nimilwêlimimâwa otâšokana awasitê ispîš nîlanân. têhtêpahipêliwa.[1]
Tânyil:	wâhtâkana[2] nâ šîpâ kî-pakitinam?
Côw:	nêw wâhtâkana. nâsic mâmišâwa.[3]
Tânyil:	ka-kî-âpacihimânawa nâ kititêl'tên otapwoya? nêsta nîla niwî-natawâpamimâwa nôhtâwiy otalapiya.
Côw:	mihcêtwâ n'tôtinimâwa otapwoya. môla wayêš itêl'tam. môla mistahi[4] âpacihêw anohc.
Tânyil:	ka-kî-kihciwilimânawa[5] nêsta nôhkom otaskihkwa; ka-kî-tîwâpohkânânaw[6] nêsta ministikohk.[7]
Côw:	ê'kwâni milwâšin.
Tânyil:	n'ka-natawâpamimâwa mwêhci anohc. mâmîšahomêw onâpêma otalapîlîw.
Côw:	ka-nakiškâtin[8] lâsipêtimihk.[9] ka-kî-âpacihimânawa kôhtâwiy otâšokana. wîpac anta n'ka-ihtân.
Tânyil:	milwâšin. ka-kî-pêtân cîkahikan. ka-cimatânânaw mâhkiy.

1 tehtêpahipê	VAI/VII	float (on the surface)
2 wâhtâkana	NI pl.	barrels: *contraction* of wiyâhtâkana
3 mâmiša	VII rdpl.	be large (Collectively) v. mâmîšahomêw
4 mistahi	IPC	much
5 kihciwil-	VTA	carry s.o. off, carry s.o. away
6 tîwâpohkê-	VTA	make tea
7 ministik...ohk	NI loc.	on an island, on the island
8 nakiškâtin	VTA	meet s.o.
9 lâsipêtimihk	IPC	down the bank

F. REFERENCE LIST

âhkoh-	VTA	hurt s.o.
cakawâšiši-	VAI	be few
iko	IPC	only
kihciwil-	VTA	carry s.o. off, carry s.o. away
(kihciwitâ-	VAI-T	carry s.t. off, carry s.t. away)
kimošôm-	NDA	your (2) grandfather *v.* nimošôm-, omošôma.
kinahâhkaniskwêm-	NDA	your (2) daughter-in-law *v.* ninahâhkaniskwêm-, onahâhkaniskwêma.
kinahâhkišîm-	NDA	your (2) son-in-law *v.* ninahâhkišîm-, onahâhkišîma.
kinîkihikwak	NDA	your (2) parents *v.* ninîkihikwak, onîkihikwa.
kišê-ililiw-	NA	old person (*contracted to* kišê-'liliw)
kišê-ililîwi-	VAI	be an old person
kîstâw-	NDA	your (2) brother-in-law *v.* nîstâw-, wîstâwa.
kîtimw-	NDA	your (2) sister-in-law *v.* nîtimw-, wîtimwa.
kôsisim-	NDA	your (2) grandchild *v.* nôsisim-, ôsisima.
lâsipêtimihk	IPC	down the bank
mayâškaw-	VTA	pass s.o. (walking)
mayâwahw-	VTA	pass s.o. (by water)
(mâciš-	VTI	cut s.t.)
mâcišw-	VTA	cut s.o., operate (surgically) on s.o.
mâmišâ-	VII rdpl.	be large (collectively), be large all over *v.* mišâ.
mâmîšahw-	VTA rdpl.	mend all over, mend here and there *v.* mîšahw-.
mêtawê-	VAI	play
mihcêtwâ	IPC	many times
milo-wâhkom-	VTA	get on well with s.o.
ministikw-	NI	island
mistahi	IPC	much
mîskaw	IPC	by way of a change, for a change

nahêlim-	VTA	be fond of s.o.
nakiškaw-	VTA	meet s.o.
natawaho-	VAI	hunt
nâtahw-	VTA	approach s.o. (by water)
nimošôm-	NDA	my grandfather *v.* kimošôm-, omošôma.
ninahâhkaniskwêm-	NDA	my daughter-in-law *v.* kinahâhkaniskwêm-, onahâhkaniskwêma.
ninahâhkišîm-	NDA	my son-in-law *v.* kinahâhkišîm-, onahâhkišîma.
ninîkihikwak	NDA	my parents *v.* kinîkihikwak, onîkihikwa.
nîmin-	VTA / VTI	hold s.o./s.t. up (by hand)
nîstâw-	NDA	my brother-in-law *v.* kîstâw-, wîstâwa.
nîši-	VAI	be two
nîtimw-	NDA	my sister-in-law *v.* kîtimw-, wîtimwa.
nôsisim-	NDA	my grandchild *v.* kôsisim-, ôsisima.
omošôma	NDA	his / her grandfather *v.* kimošôm-, nimošôm-.
onahâhkaniskwêma	NDA	his / her daughter-in-law *v.* kinahâhkaniskwêm-, ninahâhkaniskwêm-.
onahâhkišîma	NDA	his / her son-in-law *v.* kinahâhkišîm-, ninahâhkišîm-.
onîkihikwa	NDA	his / her parents *v.* ninîkihikwak, kinîkihikwak.
osihtê-	VAI	hear: *used with negative,* be hard of hearing, be deaf
ôhkoma	NDA	his / her grandmother *v.* kôhkom-, nôhkom-.
ôsisima	NDA	his / her grandchild *v.* kôsisim-, nôsisim-.
pêyako-tipisk	IPC	period of one night, overnight
piponohk	NI loc. / IPC	last Winter
pîwâpiskw-	NI	metal; motor
tâpwêwin-	NI	truth
têhtêpahipê-	VA/II	float (upon the surface)
tîwâpohkê-	VAI	make tea
wâhtâkan-	NI	barrel: *contraction of* wiyâhtâkan-.
wâwâc	IPC	even
wîcêw-	VTA	accompany s.o., be with s.o.
wîci	IPV	together with, co-
wîci-mêtawêm-	VTA	play together with s.o. *v.* mêtawê-.
wîci-natawahom-	VTA	hunt with s.o. *v.* natawaho-. (*In the text one would expect* kî-wîci-natawahomımânawa *for 3′ object.*) *Probable haplology.*
wîci-tašîhkêm-	VTA	dwell together with s.o.
wîkito-	VAI reciprocal	marry, marry each other
wîstâwa	NDA	his brother-in-law *v.* kîstâw-, nîstăw-.
wîtapim-	VTA	sit with s.o.
wîtimwa	NDA	his sister-in-law *v.* kîtimw-, nîtimw-.

G. REVIEW

13.A Kakwêcihkêmôwina—Questions

Answer each question with a full sentence, expanding your reply if you are able.

Use materials from the conversations, drills, etc., and some imagination.

1. ka-mayâwahomâwa nâ nimošôm otâšokana?
2. môla mâškôc ka-nâtimâwâwa pêšoc otalapiya, manâ?
3. ta-kî-mîšaham nâ nistês kicîmâniliw?
4. ka-nakiškâmânawa nâ cîmis ôsisima anta âšokanihk?
5. milo-wâhkomimêw nâ cwân wîwa okâwîlîw?
6. kî-nakiškawêw nâ ana kišê-ililiw kikosisa mêskanâhk?
7. kinahêlimimâwa nâ kistês ocawâšimiša?
8. ka-nakatimânawa nâ kišê-ililiw onamêsima askihkohk?
9. ta-âpacihêw nâ kinahâhkišîm kitapwoya?
10. kî-wîcêwêw nâ cwân ôhkoma otâkošîhk
11. kî-mâmîšahwêw nâ âniy n'talapînânih otâkošîhk?
12. kimošôm nâ ta-kî-miskâmêw owîkimâkana otaskihkolîw?
13. owîkimâkana nâ kî-wâpamêliwa onahâhkaniskwêmilîw?
14. awâšišak nâ kî-wîci-mêtawêmêwak acimošiša?
15. kî-kanawâpamimâwa nâ kôhtâwînaw otalapiya?
16. âšay nâ kî-sakahpitimâwa kistês otêma?
17. ka-mîlimânawa nâ kišê-ililiw owîkimâkana âtiht niska?
18. ka-kî-akimimâwa nâ oniskima?
19. kinatawêlimimânawa nâ kôhtâwiy otapwoya cîmânihk?
20. n'ka-šîwahomânânih nâ onamêsima mwêhci anohc?
21. kî-pisiskâpamimêw nâ sayman kišê-ililiwa owîkimâkanilîw?

13.B Naškwêwašihtwâwina—Answers

Formulate questions which may be answered by the following statements.

1. cikêma, n'ka-wîcêwimâwa âniy onâpêma.
2. êhê, kišê-ililiwak tašinê witapimimêwak otânisiwâwa ocawâšimišilîw.
3. môla. môla mâškôc pêšoc ka-nâtahomânawa otalapîlîw.
4. mîskaw onîkihikowâwa pêyako-tipisk itâpicîliwa.
5. tâpwêwin ohci môla wâwâc n'tôhci-pisiskâpamimânânih otastisa.
6. môla. môla n'tôhci-wâpamimâwa otapwoya cîmânihk.
7. môla mâškôc wâwâc ohci-wâpahtamwak n'cîmâninân.
8. êhê, nâspic kišê-ililîwiw.
9. n'kotwâsošâp ayâwêw ôsisima.
10. nisto ayâwêw onahâhkišîma.
11. cikêma, wîwa nêsta nahêlimêliwa ôsisímilîw.
12. tâpwêwin ohci, wîci-natawahomêw wîwa ošîmilîw.
13. môla, môla ka-kî-âpacihimânawa âlik otâšokana.
14. pêyak awâšiš wîci-mêtawêmêpan kicêmošiša.
15. ka-âpacihimâwa nôhkom otaskihkwa kitîminaw (*our tea*) ohci.
16. êhê, mâwac nimilwêlimimâwa ostêsa ispîš ililiwa ôta.
17. môšak âpacihimêw omisa otaskihkolîw.
18. mâškôc n'ka-pâskisomâwa âtiht otêma.
19. êhê, âšay wîci-mêtawêmimêwak sopâyawa ocêmišišilîw.
20. n'kî-wâpamimâwa onahâhkaniskwêma otâkošîhk.

Supplementary Conversation II

You may wish to talk about home and family with new Cree speaking friends. Here are a few more helps to conversation.

ê-âlimômihcik kîcišânak	**Talking about your Family**
kipêyakon nâ kîkihk, nêstapiko kiwîci-tašîhkêmâwak nâ kîcišânak?	Do you live alone, or do you have a family?
iskonikanihk ihtâwak nîcišânak.	My family lives on the reservation.
pêyak ê-piskihcâk wâskâhikanihk n'tiši-wîkin ôta.	I have a room in a house here.
tân' êtašiyêk kîlawâw pêyak ôtênaw?	How large is your family?
nitôhtâwin, nitôšîmin, nitôstêsin ...	I have a father, a younger sibling, (an) older brother(s) ...
tân' êtašicik kimisak?	How many older sisters do you have?
pêyakow nimis, nîšiwak mâka nistêsak.	I have one older sister, but two older brothers.
nitôsis n'kî-ohpikihikonân.	My aunt / stepmother brought us up.
kitôcawâšimišin nâ mâka kîla?	Do YOU have any children?
êhê, nîšiwak nikosisak, pêyakow mâka nitânis.	Yes, I have two sons and one daughter.

âlimôm-	VTA	talk about s.o.
âlimôt-	VTA	talk about s.t.
pêyako-	VAI	be one, be alone
mihcêti-	VAI	be many
kîcišân-	NDA	member of your kin group
iskonikan-	NI	reservation: *lit.,* left-over.
piskihcâ-	VII	be separate, be distinct: kâ-piskihcâk what is separate, *i.e.,* a room.
wîki-	VAI	dwell (in), live (in)
itašiwak	VAI 3p	they are so many
tân' êtašiyêk?		How many are you?
tân' êtašicik?		How many are they?
pêyak ôtênaw		as one family
ôhtâwi-	VAI	have a father
ošîmi-	VAI	have a younger sibling
ostêsi-	VAI	have an older brother
ôtênaw	NI	dwelling group, town; *here as* family: tân'taht'-ôtênaw in how many families? pêyak ôtênaw as one family
nitôsis-	NDA	my aunt / stepmother
nôhkomis-	NDA	my uncle / stepfather
ohpiki-	VAI	grow up
ohpikih-	VTA	bring up, raise
ocawâšimiši-	VAI	have child(ren)

SOME RELATIVES AND IN-LAWS

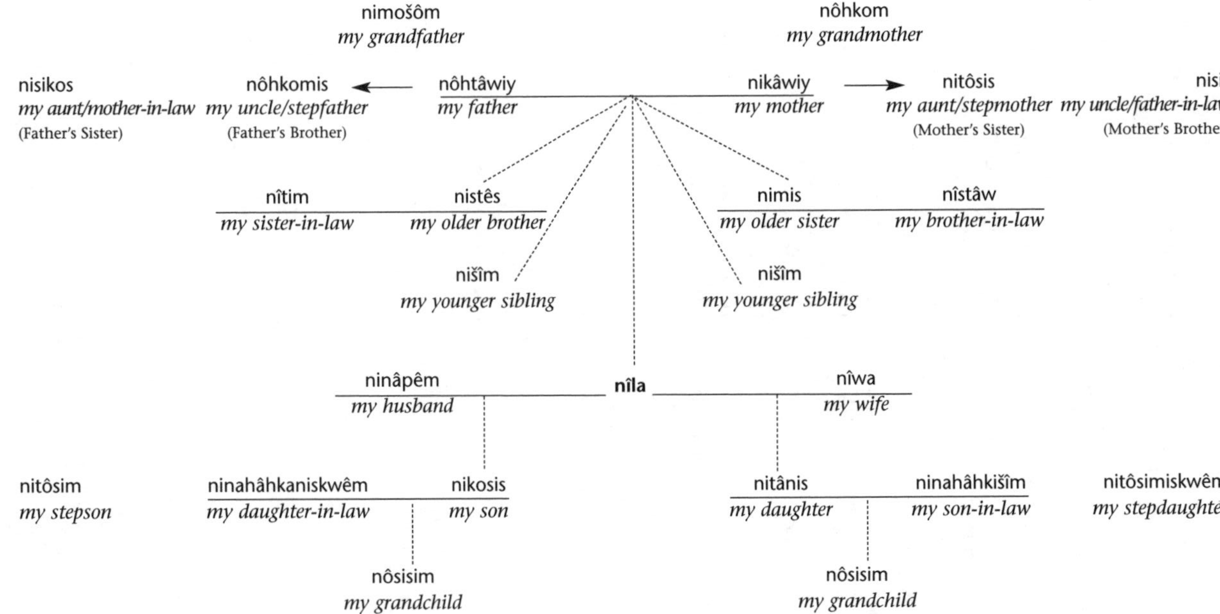

UNIT FOURTEEN

A. BASIC CONVERSATION

1. Send for the Nurse

Wâlta:	n'kî-mayâškên mâhkiy	I passed the tent (on foot)
	n'kî-mayâšk...amw...ân omâhkîm	I passed by his tent
	n'kî-pêci-mayâškamwân sayman omâhkîm kêkišêp.	I came past Simon's tent this morning.
	matê	at a distance
	âtiht 'wênihkânak kî-matê-ayamihitowak.	Some people were chatting in the distance (*or* could be heard chatting)
Sâpiyê:	kotakiya 'wênihkâna anohc mwêhci kî-matê-pîhtokwêliwa omâhkîmihk.	Someone else went into his tent just now.
	kêkwân kênawâpahtaman?	What are you staring at?
Wâlta:	kâ-tôtahk	which he is doing
	animêliw	that one (0')
	nicîhkêlihtên[1]	I am interested in it
	nicîhkêliht...am...wân	I am interested in it (in relation to someone else)
	nawac nicîhkêlihtamwân animêliw kâ-tôtahk ana ililiw.	I am rather interested in what that fellow is doing.
	âpacihtâ...w...êw	he uses his (someone else's) canoe
	na! âpacihtâwêw saymana ocîmânilîw.	Look! He's using Simon's canoe.
	kî-âpaham	he loosened it
	kî-âpah...amw...êw	he loosened it (in rel. to s.o. else)
	anohc kî-âpahamwêw.	He loosened it just now.

[1] Kêšîciwan usage. At Moose, nikistêlihtên; N.W coast of James Bay and Hudson's Bay, nikišišawêlihtên.

Sâpiyê:	mâškôc âhkosiw Sôsan.	Perhaps Susan is ill.
	kî-ihtâ...w...êw	she stayed (in rel. to s.o. else)
	kî-ihtâwêw okâwiya wîkilîhk otâkošîhk	She stayed at her mother's yesterday.
Wâlta:	nâcipahêwak	they are fetching her
	mâškôc nâcipahêwak n'tohkolon-iskwêwa.	Perhaps they are fetching the nurse.
	maškawîmakan	it is more powerful
	nipîwâpiskom awasitê maškawîmakan.	My motor is more powerful.
	ka-kî-pakitin...amw...ânânaw	we (21) can put it (in rel. to s.o.)
	ka-kî-pakitinamwânânaw ocîmânihk.	We can put it on his canoe.

2. Have You Known Them Long?

Sâpiyê:	wîskâc nâ kinwêš kitôhci-ihtâ...w...ânâwâw omâhkîmiwâhk?	Have you ever been in their tent for long?
Wâlta:	nimawâpi...w...ân	I visit (in rel. to s.o.)
	tašinê	constantly, all the time, incessantly
	môla. môla tašinê nimawâpiwân omâhkîmiwâhk.	No. I don't visit in their tent all the time.
Sâpiyê:	kitimâkisiwak	they are poor, they are piteous
	nâspic kitimâkisiwak, ohcikawinilw mâka omâhkîmiwâw.	They are very poor and their tent leaks.
	kî-šâpopaliw	it came through
	ê-kimiwahk	as it rained
	ê-kimiwahk kî-šâpopaliw apahkwâsonihk.	The rain came through the canvas.
	pêšoc otiškotêhkânihk	near his stove
	n'kî-mîciso...w...ânân	we ate (in rel. to s.o.)
	côsip nêsta nîla pêšoc n'kî-mîcisowânân otiškotêhkânihk.	Joseph and I ate beside his stove.

	okihciniskîlîhk	on his (3′) right
	kî-api…w…êw	he sat (in rel. to s.o.)
	êhê, n'kiskisin. côw kî-apiwêw saymana okihciniskîlîhk.	Yes, I remember. Joe sat on Simon's right.
	onamatiniskîhk	on his left
	kî-nîpawi…w…ân	you stood (in rel. to s.o.)
	kîla mâka kî-nîpawiwân onamatiniskîhk.	But *you* stood on his left.
Wâlta:	tâpiskôc	alike, together
	tâpiskôc kî-nipîwinânaw.	We both got wet.
	mîšakisîwak	they are rich
	môla nâspic mîšakisîwak.	They're not very well off.
Sâpiyê:	kî-mâmîšah…amw…ânâwâw	you (pl.) mended it here and there (rel.)
	kî-mâmîšahamwânâwâw otapahkwâsoniwâw, manâ?	You mended their canvas, didn't you?
Wâlta:	wêskac ohci…	as of a long time ago
	êhê, wêskac n'tôhci-kiskêlimâwak.	Yes, I've known them for a long time.
	owîkitôwiniwâw	their wedding
	owîkitôwiniwâhk	at their wedding
	n'kî-kitohcikê…w…ân	I played music (in rel. to s.o.)
	n'kî-kitohcikêwân owîkitôwiniwâhk.	I played the fiddle at their wedding.
Sâpiyê:	ê-âhkosit	as she is ill, in her-being-ill
	nimihcilawêsin ê-âhkosit sôsan.	I'm sorry Susan is ill.
	nôkosiw	she appears
	âšay mâka pêci-nôkosiw n'tohkolon-iskwêw.	Here comes the nurse now, though.

B. DISCUSSION OF GRAMMAR

1. VAI and VTI Relational Inflection

In Unit Thirteen we saw that when the object of a transitive animate verb (VTA) is two positions removed from the subject, the skipping of one position is marked in the direct by the addition of ...ım... between the verb stem and the inflectional suffixes.

In the case of VAI and VTI, where the action is carried out *in relation to* another person one position removed from the subject, VAI stems add ...w..., VTI stems, ...amw... to the stem to form the new relational inflection. For this purpose ni... and ki... are treated as sharing one position relative to 3 (or 3p) and 3'. (*v.* Unit 13.B.11.) To this relational base is added the stem vowel, /ê/ for third person subjects, changing to /â/ for ni... and ki... subjects, followed by the regular VAI inflectional suffixes (Unit 1.B.1.1; Unit 5.B.1; Unit 6.B.1.1): *e.g.,*

	Non-Relational	Relational
VAI	nipâ...w	nipâ...w...ê...w
	ninipâ...n	ninipâ...w...â...n
VTI	âpah...am	âpah...amw...ê...w
	nitâpah...ên	nitâpah...amw...â...n

The Basic Conversation has provided examples of the use of the Relational Inflection: *e.g.,*

apiwêw okihciniskîlîhk he (3) sits on his (3') right hand.

An interesting instance occurs in the Cree version of Pilgrim's Progress where Christian says to the gatekeeper: "Evangelist bid me come hither ...". The Cree version (translated by a native speaker, highly literate in both Cree and English) reads:

kici-pêci-itohtê...**w**...ak that I come hither (in relation to him), where the relational ...w... occurs immediately after the VAI stem vowel and before the (conjunct) personal suffix.

The paradigm for the relational inflection, independent order, neutral (*or* present) tense for VAI and VTI is as follows:

	VAI	VTI	
3	...w	...amw	...ê...w
3p	...w	...amw	...ê...wak
3′			...ɩliwa (VAI), ...amiliwa (VTI)
1	...w	...amw	...â... n
2	...w	...amw	...â... n
1p	...w	...amw	...â...nân
21	...w	...amw	...â...nânaw
2p	...w	...amw	...â...nâwâw

All VAI-T form the relational inflection like VAI â-stems.

Study the following sentences.

1.	n'ka-pîhtokwêwân omâhkîmihk.	I'll go into his tent.
2.	wâlta kî-pôsiwêw ošîma ocîmâniliîhk.	Walter embarked in his young brother's canoe.
3.	apiwêwak âniwa onamatiniskîlîhk.	They're sitting on Annie's left.
4.	kê-wâpahk ka-ihtâwânâwâw wîkiwâhk.	Tomorrow you will stay at their place.
5.	kî-mîšahamwêw opîskâkanilîw.	She mended his jacket.
6.	kiwâpahtamwân nâ kimošôm opâskisikan?	Do you see your grandpa's gun?
7.	n'kî-kilišiniwân šîpâ otâšokanihk.	I slipped underneath his dock.
8.	ka-pîhtokwêwânânaw nâ wîkiwâmiwâhk?	Shall we (21) go into their tent?

———DRILLS 1 THROUGH 4———

NOTE. The use of the relational inflection, particularly with transitive inanimate verbs, clearly shows broad, syntactic parallels with that of the VTA inflection for (1, 2) → 3′ and 3 → 3″ and identical personal suffixes in the conjunct order. This led some earlier grammarians to discuss both relational and VTA forms for obviative objects under the same heading. Cf. further, Unit 24.B.1, fn.2 in *Spoken Cree, Level II.*

2. ohci in Compound Stems: "Present Perfective" Use

Unit 11.A and B.3, illustrate the use of ohci in forming a compound stem, where the verb is associated with a noun in the locative:

ka-kî-ohci-kâhcitinâw alapîhk	You can catch him from a net: *lit.,* You can "from-catch" him a net.

A corresponding use occurs with many particles denoting time:

kinwêš nâ kitôhci-ililîmon?	Have you been speaking Cree long? *lit.,* as-of a long time
wîskâc nâ kinwêš kitôhci-ihtâwânâwâw omâhkîmiwâhk?	Have you (2p) ever stayed in their tent for a long time?
êhê, wêskac n'tôhci-kiskêlimâwak.	Yes, I've known them for a long time: *lit.,* from long ago

Note in each case the use of "have" plus the past participle, *i.e.,* the "present-perfective", in English to convey the sense of ohci in the Cree verb. Both the second and fourth examples picture a situation beginning in the past and continuing into the time of speaking. In the third example the action is pictured as beginning in the past and continuing up to a later point in time. This parallels the English,

Have you *been* here long?	kinwêš nâ kitôhci-ihtân ôta?

as contrasted with the simple past:

Were you here?	kî-ihtân nâ ôta?

3. kî Potential + ohci

In Drill 1 below, #3 and #6, one might expect the order to be

* môla n'tôhci-kî-nîmiwân ...
and * môla nâ kitôhci-kî-wâpiwân ..., respectively,

on the basis of the relative order of kî, the potential particle (Unit 3.B.1.3) and the aspect markers. When the particles, kî-potential and ohci are in sequence, however, kî precedes.

C. DRILLS

1. VAI Relational Inflection: Independent Order

Where you do not know the dictionary meaning of a word, the grammatical form alone should provide a sufficient clue for doing the drill.

1.1 Show that you recognize whether the verb is in the relational inflection or not by completing each fragment with omâhkîmihk where the verb is relational, or with kimâhkîminâhk where the verb is non-relational.

		(Check column)
1.	ka-nipân nâ ________?	kimâhkîminâhk
2.	anohcîhkê n'kî-pîhtokwêwân ________.	omâhkîmihk
3.	môla n'kî-ohci-nîmiwân ________ ê-pâhpiyân ohci.	omâhkîmihk
4.	wîpac n'ka-ispêlohkân ________.	kimâhkîminâhk
5.	n'kî-wîyatwêwânân ________ têpiskâlik.	omâhkîmihk
6.	môla nâ kikî-ohci-wâpiwân ________?	omâhkîmihk
7.	môla mâskôc ta-ihtâw ________.	kimâhkîminâhk
8.	môšak wî-mawâpiw ________.	kimâhkîminâhk
9.	kî-ati-otakikomiw ________ ê-ihtât.	kimâhkîminâhk
10.	šâ! âpihkow atim ________.	kimâhkîminâhk
11.	wîpac mâškôc n'ka-tîwâpohkêwânân ________.	omâhkîmihk
12.	ka-mîcisowân nâ ________?	omâhkîmihk
13.	n'ka-kwâškwêpicikân pêšoc ________.	kimâhkîminâhk
14.	ka-kî-tašîhkêwânânaw ________.	omâhkîmihk
15.	kî-apiw ________.	kimâhkîminâhk
16.	nâspic ka-apwêsiwânâwâw [perspire] ________.	omâhkîmihk
17.	misiwê 'wênihkânak 'êmistikôšîmowak ________.	kimâhkîminâhk
18.	n'ka-apiwân astamitê itêhkê ________.	omâhkîmihk

1.2 In each sentence pick the verb form required by the succeeding noun. If using a recording, listen to the fragment twice, then repeat the form of the verb required by the noun. The recording will be your check.

		(Check column)
1. kî-wawêšihtâwân nâ kî-wawêšihtân nâ	omaskisina?	kî-wawêšihtâwân
2. n'kî-kwâškwêpicikêwân n'kî-kwâškwêpicikân	otâšokanihk ohci?	n'kî-kwâškwêpicikêwân
3. n'ka-apiwân n'ka-apin	okihciniskîhk.	n'ka-apiwân
4. cwân mâka kî-apiw cwân mâka kî-apiwêw	onamatiniskîlîhk.	kî-apiwêw
5. n'ka-pêc'-îtohtêwân n'ka-pêc'-îtohtân	kimâhkîmihk kê-wâpahk.	n'ka-pêc'-îtohtân.
6. nîpawiwêw nîpawiw	cîkic [beside] niwâskâhikanimihk.	nîpawiw
7. nâspic kî-sîhkaciwêw nâspic kî-sîhkaciw [be cold]	kâ-pêci-pîhtokwêt nîkinâhk.	kî-sîhkaciw
8. niwî-ispêlohkêwânân niwî-ispêlohkânân	wîkiwâhk nakiskaw.	niwî-ispêlohkêwânân
9. ka-nipâwânâwâw nâ ka-nipânâwâw nâ	kistêsiwâw omâhkîmihk?	ka-nipâwânâwâw
10. âkinis kî-pêci-walawîw âkinis kî-pêci-walawîwêw	âlikwa ošwâpimilîhk ohci.	kî-pêci-walawîwêw
11. mâškôc ta-masinahikêwêw mâškôc ta-masinahikêw	šwâpihk.	ta-masinahikêw
12. mâškôc ta-masinahikêwêw mâškôc ta-masinahikêw	têpita ošwâpimilîhk.	ta-masinahikêwêw

2. Replace the non-relational form of the verb with a relational form on the model:

2.1 Cue: ka-ihtân nâ nîkinâhk?
Response: môla, n'ka-ihtâwân mâka câlis wîkihk.

Correct responses are on the recording and in the check column.

		(Check column)
1.	ka-mawâpin nâ nîkinâhk?	môla, n'ka-mawâpiwân mâka câlis wîkihk.
2.	ka-nipân nâ nîkinâhk?	n'ka-nipâwân
3.	ka-mîcison nâ nîkinâhk?	n'ka-mîcisowân
4.	ka-tašîhkân nâ nîkinâhk?	n'ka-tašîhkêwân
5.	ka-tîwâpohkân nâ nîkinâhk?	n'ka-tîwâpohkêwân
6.	ka-pêhon nâ nîkinâhk?	n'ka-pêhowân
7.	ka-alwêpin nâ nîkinâhk?	n'ka-alwêpiwân

2.2 Cue: ihtâw nâ kîkihk?
Response: môla, ihtâwêw cwâna omâhkîmilîhk.

1.	ihtâw nâ kîkihk?	môla, ihtâwêw cwâna omâhkîmilîhk.
2.	âpatisiw nâ kîkihk?	âpatisiwêw
3.	nîmiw nâ kîkihk?	nîmiwêw
4.	apiw nâ kîkihk?	apiwêw
5.	ispêlohkêw nâ kîkihk?	ispêlohkêwêw
6.	pêhow nâ kîkihk?	pêhowêw
7.	pimišin nâ kîkihk?	pimišiniwêw

2.3 Cue: ka-pîhtokwânâwâw nâ nimîkiwâmihk [my wigwam]?[1]
Response: âšay nipîhtokwêwânân cîmis omîkiwâmihk.

1.	ka-pîhtokwânâwâw nâ nimîkiwâmihk?	nipîhtokwêwânân
2.	ka-apinâwâw nâ nimîkiwâmihk?	nitapiwânân
3.	ka-ihtânâwâw nâ nimîkiwâmihk?	nitihtâwânân
4.	ka-tašîhkânâwâw nâ nimîkiwâmihk?	nitašîhkêwânân
5.	ka-pimišininâwâw nâ nimîkiwâmihk?	nipimišiniwânân
6.	ka-nîminâwâw nâ nimîkiwâmihk?	ninîmiwânân
7.	ka-mêtawânâwâw nâ nimîkiwâmihk?	nimêtawêwânân

[1] mîkiwâm—treated here as NI. See mîkiwâm and note in §F. Reference List, below.

3. VTI and VAI-T Relational Inflection: Independent Order

3.1 Show that you recognize which of the transitive inanimate verb forms are in the relational inflection by completing the fragment with the correct form from the bracketed choices.

1. kitâpacihtâwân nâ (kicîmân ~ ocîmân)?
2. môla mâškôc ohci-otinamwêw (âlik otôtâmahikan ~ âlikwa otôtâmahikanilîw).
3. tašinê n'kî-âlimôtên (nipîwâpiskom ~ opîwâpiskom).
4. mâškôc wî-kocihtâwêwak (ocîkahikaniwâw ~ ocîkahikanilîw).
5. ka-kî-otinamwânâwâw (omaskisina ~ kimaskisiniwâwa).
6. ka-kî-otinênâwâw (opîwâpiskomiwâw ~ nipîwâpiskominân).
7. kî-nakatamwêwak (otôtâmahikaniwâw ~ otôtâmahikanilîw).
8. anta n'kî-iši-nakatamwânân (ocîmâniwâw ~ nicîmâninân)
9. âšay nâ kitayân (kitastotin ~ otastotin)?
10. âšay nâ kitayâwân (kicîmân ~ ocîmân)?
11. môla mâškôc ka-n'tamwêl'tamwânânaw (omâhkîmiwâw ~ kimâhkîminaw).
12. n'kî-pîkopitên (cîkahikan ~ ocîkahikan).
13. kî-mîšahamwân nâ (kitapahkwâson ~ otapahkwâson)?
14. kî-kiciskinênânaw (kipîskâkaniwâwa ~ opîskâkaniwâwa).
15. kî-pêhtên nâ (nicîkahikan ~ ocîkahikan) ê-pahkitihk?
16. cwân kî-wanihtâwêw (otôtâmahikan ~ otôtâmahikanilîw).

1. ocîmân
2. âlikwa otôtâmahikanilîw
3. nipîwâpiskom
4. ocîkahikanilîw
5. omaskisina
6. nipîwâpiskominân
7. otôtâmahikanilîw
8. ocîmâniwâw
9. kitastotin
10. ocîmân
11. omâhkîmiwâw
12. cîkahikan
13. otapahkwâson
14. kipîskâkaniwâwa
15. nicîkahikan
16. otôtâmahikanilîw

3.2 In each sentence pick the verb form required by the succeeding noun. If using a recording, listen to the fragment twice, then repeat the form of the verb required by the noun. The recording will be your check.

			(Check column)
1.	êntiniy kî-nakatam êntiniy kî-nakatamwêw	cwâna ocîmânilîw âšokanihk	kî-nakatamwêw
2.	n'kî-ayamihtân n'kî-ayamihtâwân	omasinahikan.	n'kî-ayamihtâwân.
3.	kî-tahkopitên nâ kî-tahkopitamwân nâ	nicîmân?	kî-tahkopitên nâ
4.	pêyakwâ ê-kîšikâlik ta-n'tawêl'tam ta-n'tamwêl'tamwêw	nipîskâkaniliw.	ta-n'tawêl'tam
5.	ka-miskênâwâw ka-miskamwânâwâw	otastotin mâhkîhk.	ka-miskamwânâwâw
6.	mitoni kwayask kî-sêskipitênânaw kî-sêskipitamwânânaw	kicîmâninaw.	kî-sêskipitênânaw
7.	âskaw nimâmîšahên âskaw nimâmîšahamwân	têpit ošîpâstêwayân.	nimâmîšahamwân.
8.	ka-kî-tahkonên ka-kî-tahkonamwân	nipîskâkaninânih.	ka-kî-tahkonên
9.	šâpopêkan ôta. n'ka-pîhtahên n'ka-pîhtahamwân	otayâna wâhtâkanihk.	n'ka-pîhtahamwân
10.	nâspic nahêl'tamwak nâspic nahêl'tamwêwak	otôški-wâskâhikanimiwâw.	nahêl'tamwak
11.	n'kî-pâsênân n'kî-pâsamwânân	owâpwayân.	n'kî-pâsamwânân
12.	kî-wanihtân kî-wanihtâwân	osakahikana (screws).	kî-wanihtâwân
13.	išiwitâwak nâ išiwitâwêwak nâ	kicîkahikaniliw.	išiwitâwak
14.	wîskâc nâ kitôhci-wâpahtên kitôhci-wâpahtamwân	kâ-tôtahk?	kitôhci-wâpahtamwân

4. Complete the sentence fragment in the cue by filling in the blank with the appropriate relational form of the verb and repeating the second part, on the model:

4.1 Cue: kî-pîkoham ocîmân, _________ nêsta saymana ocîmânilîw.
Response: kî-pîkohamwêw nêsta saymana ocîmânilîw.

1. kî-pîkoham ocîmân, _________ nêsta saymana ocîmânilîw.
2. kî-wawêšihtâw opîwâpiskom, _________ nêsta cwâna opîwâpiskomilîw.
3. kî-kiškam otastotin, _________ nêsta coca otastotinilîw.
4. ta-kî-otinam wîwat, _________ nêsta ošîma wîwatilîw.
5. môla nahiškam opîskâkan, môla nêsta _________ ôhtâwiya opîskâkanilîw.
6. milwêl'tam okitohcikan, _________ nêsta saylasa okitohcikanilîw.

1. kî-pîkohamwêw
2. kî-wawêšihtâwêw
3. kî-kiškamwêw
4. ta-kî-otinamwêw
5. nahiškamwêw
6. milwêl'tamwêw

4.2 Cue: kî-miskên nâ kicîmân? _________ nêsta sayman ocîmân.
Response: êhê, n'kî-miskamwân nêsta sayman ocîmân.

1. kî-miskên nâ kicîmân? _________ nêsta sayman ocîmân.
2. kî-kociškên nâ kimaskisina? _________ nêsta sayman omaskisina.
3. kî-wanihtân nâ kipâskisikan? _________ nêsta côw opâskisikan.
4. kiwâpahtên nâ kîki? _________ nêsta cwân wîki.
5. kitayân nâ kicîkahikan? _________ nêsta cwân ocîkahikan.
6. ka-kocihtân nâ nikitohcikan? _________ nêsta âlik okitohcikan.

1. n'kî-miskamwân
2. n'kî-kociškamwân
3. n'kî-wanihtâwân
4. niwâpahtamwân
5. nitayâwân
6. n'ka-kocihtâwân

4.3 Cue: n'ka-mîšahênân niwîlâhcikaninâna, _________ nêsta âniy owîlâhcikana.
Response: n'ka-mîšahamwânân nêsta âniy owîlâhcikana.

1. n'ka-mîšahênân niwîlâhcikaninâna, _________ nêsta âniy owîlâhcikana.
2. n'ka-otinênân nîwatinân, _________ nêsta côsip wîwat.
3. n'ka-âpacihtânân niwâpwayâninân, _________ nêsta sopâya owâpwayân.

4. nipimiwitânân nipâskisikaninâna, _________ nêsta okimâw opâskisikana.
5. nimilwêl'tênân nîkinân, _________ nêsta êntiniy wîki.
6. niwî-kocihtânân ôma kitohcikan, _________ nêsta saylas okitohcikan.

1. n'ka-mîšahamwânân
2. n'ka-otinamwânân
3. n'ka-âpacihtâwânân
4. nipimiwitâwânân
5. nimilwêl'tamwânân
6. niwî-kocihtâwânân

4.4 Cue: môla kitôhci-kawinênâwâw mâhkiy, _________ cwân omâhkîm.
Response: môla kitôhci-kawinamwânâwâw cwân omâhkîm.

1. môla kitôhci-kawinênâwâw mâhkiy, _________ cwân omâhkîm.
2. môla kitôhci-pêtânâwâw otâmahikan, _________ cwân otôtâmahikan.
3. môla kitôhci-tahkonênâwâw wîlâhcikan, _________ mêriy owîlâhcikan.
4. ka-pîsikahênâwâw mihta, _________ ayamihêwikimâw omihtima.
5. kî-wanihtânâwâw n'tôtâmahikan, _________ êtiy otôtâmahikan.
6. kî-ayamihtânâwâw nâ ôma masinahikan? _________ wâlta omasinahikan.

1. kitôhci-kawinamwânâwâw
2. kitôhci-pêtâwânâwâw
3. kitôhci-tahkonamwânâwâw
4. ka-pîsikahamwânâwâw
5. kî-wanihtâwânâwâw
6. kî-ayamihtâwânâwâw

4.5 Cue: ka-nakatênânaw nâ astotin ôta? _________ têpit otastotin?
Response: ka-nakatamwânânaw nâ têpit otastotin ôta?

1. ka-nakatênânaw nâ astotin ôta? _________ têpit otastotin?
2. ka-kîsisênânaw nâ mîcim ôta? _________ têpit omîcim?
3. ka-pâsênânaw nâ šîpâstêwayân ôta? _________ têpit ošîpâstêwayân?
4. ka-sêskipitênânaw nâ cîmân ôta? _________ cîmis ocîmân?
5. nôhcimihk kî-iši-cimatânânaw wâskâhikan. _________ owâskâhikanim.
6. ka-kî-išiwitânânaw cîkahikan nêtê. _________ ocîkahikan.

1. ka-nakatamwânânaw
2. ka-kîsisamwânânaw
3. ka-pâsamwânânaw
4. ka-sêskipitamwânânaw
5. kî-iši-cimatâwânânaw
6. ka-kî-išiwitâwânânaw

5. Complete each sentence with an appropriate form from the stems listed on the left.

Walter meets Xavier and remarks that something seemed to be happening at Simon's tent when he came past it this morning. He says:

mayâšk- _______________ sayman omâhkîm kêkišêp.

Some people could be made out in the distance talking to each other:

matê-ayamihito- âtiht 'wênihkânak _______________.

Xavier interjects: "Someone else went into his (Simon's) tent just now."

pîhtokwê- kotakiya 'wênihkâna anohc mwêhci _______________ omâhkîmihk. Walter's attention seems to be wandering, and Xavier asks: "What are you looking at?"

kanawâpaht- kêkwân _______________? (Note change on first vowel of verb.)

—to which Walter replies that he's interested in what some one whom he sees is doing:

cîhkêliht- nawac _______________ animêliw kâ-tôtahk ana ililiw.

"Look!", he says. "He's using Simon"s canoe."

âpacihtâ- na! _______________ saymana ocîmânilîw.

"He loosened it just now, I think," says Xavier:

âpah- anohc _______________, n'titêl'tên,—he exclaims, adding "Perhaps Susan is ill. She stayed at her mother's place yesterday":

ihtâ- mâškôc âhkosiw sôsan. _______________ okâwiya wîkilîhk otâkošîhk.

"If they want," suggests Walter, "we (21) can put my motor on Simon's canoe."

pakitin- n'tawêl'tahkwâwê,[1] _______________ nipîwâpiskom sayman ocîmânihk. "What with the poor fur market and general recession," he adds, "Susan and Simon are having a rough time."

âlimisi- _______________. "In fact, they're very poor," agrees Xavier.

kitimâkisi- tâpwê mâka nâspic _______________. "Have you ever been in their tent for an extended period of time?" he asks.

ihtâ- wîskâc nâ kinwêš _______________ omâhkîmiwâhk?

"One rainy day," answers Walter, "Joseph and I ate near his stove."

[1] Conjunct subjunctive, "if they want it".

mîciso-	côsip nêsta nîla pêšoc ________________ otiškotêhkânihk.
api-	"Joe sat on Simon's right:" côw ________________ saymana okihciniskîlîhk. "I stood to his left,"
nîpawi-	nîla mâka, n'kî-________________ onamatiniskîhk,
nipîwi-	"and we both got wet, tâpiskôc n'kî-______________, because[2] their tent leaked so much."
ohcikawin-	ê-ispîhci-______________...ilik omâhkîmiwâw. "Tch. tch! What a pity!" murmurs Xavier." šâ! __________________! "Joe mended their canvas, though, didn't he?"
mâmîšah-	côw mâka, ________________ otapahkwâsoniliw, manâ?
kiskêlim-	"I've known them for a long time." wêskac n'tôhci-________________.
kitohcikê-	"I played the fiddle at their wedding." _____________________ owîkitôwiniwâhk. (*v.* wîkitoliwa, p. 328.)

[2] Note how "because" is expressed by ê + conjunct: *i.e.,* in-that-it-leaked so much

D. CONVERSATION PRACTICE

1. Review the Basic Conversation as in previous units, making sure that you have learned each section so that there is no hesitation in the responses when you cover the Cree column.

2. Check the drills to be certain that you have mastered both the form and use of the relational inflection as far as it is presented in this unit.

3.1 Go back over earlier units and make a list of verbs: VTA, VTI and both VAI and VAI-T. Using your list, drill the use of ...ιm... with verbs of the VTA group where subject → object relationship is (ni..., ki...,) → 3′, or 3 → 3″. Then practise the VTA with the corresponding inverse forms.

3.2 Practise the use of the relational inflection for verbs of the VTI, VAI and VAI-T group. Use drills in this and preceding units as examples, and make up your own questions and answers. Do this kind of review with a partner if you can.

4. Practise free conversation, using any of the topics suggested in earlier units (or others which you have thought up). It helps to prepare a set of topics and conversational exchanges ahead of time so that you can focus on the new usage and not have to think of what to say next.

E. LISTENING IN

Wâlta: âsay nâ kî-wâpahtamwân cwân otôški-pîwâpiskom?

Sîmyan: êhê, anohc n'kî-wâpahtamwân. nâspic kî-milwêl'tamwêw cim[1] opîwâpiskomilîw. otânâhk kâ-kî-tawâstêlik kî-ayâw animêliw mwêhci tôwihkâniliw.

Wâlta: niwîkimâkan kî-mayâškamwêw wîkilîw kêkišêp.

Sîmyan: kî-pîhtokwêwêw pâtnîwa[2] omâhkîmilîhk, manâ?

Wâlta: êhê, nîla mâka n'kî-nîpawiwân piko lâlih[3] omâhkîmihk. okosisa wawêšihtâliwa n'cîmâniliw. n'kî-wî-wâpahtamwân piko tân' êtôtahk. niwîkimâkan nêsta kî-wî-kiskêl'tamwêw tân' êhtôtamilici.[4]

Sîmyan: kimilwêl'tamwânâwâw nâ owâskâhikanimiwâw anta ministikohk?

Wâlta: êhê, n'kî-wâpahtamwân, môla mâka wîskâc n'tôhci-pîhtokwêwân.

Sîmyan: nâspic n'kî-cîhkêl'tamwânân animêliw kâ-cimatâcik.[5] cwân âsay kî-iškwâ-pakitinamwêw otôsk'-îškotêhkânilîw kicinihk.[6]

Wâlta: êhê, n'kiskêl'tên. n'kî-otinikêwân okayâši-iškotêhkâniwâw. pêyakwâ n'kî-nipâwâhtân[7] cwân omâhkîmihk; môla mâka wîskâc šâkoc n'tôhci-wâpahtamwân owâskâhikanimiwâw ministikohk.

[1] cim	NA	Jim
[2] pâtniy	NA	Evadney: a fairly common name in this area.
[3] lâlih	IPC + loc.	beside
[4] tân' êhtôtamilici	VTI conj. indic. 3' subject.	
[5] kâ-cimatâcik	VAI-T conj. indic. 3' subject:	which they are setting up, which they are building *v.* cimatâ-.
[6] kicinihk	NI loc.	in the kitchen
[7] n'kî-nipâwâhtân	VAI kî + preterit (distant past) 1p subject	**had** slept

F. REFERENCE LIST

apwêsi-	VAI	perspire
câlis-	NA [personal name]	Charles
cim-	NA [personal name]	Jim
cimatâ-	VAI-T	set s.t. up (*e.g.,*a tent), build s.t. (*e.g.,* a house), erect s.t.
cîhkêliht-	VTI	be interested in s.t. *v.* kišišawêliht, kistêliht-.
cîhkêlim-	VTA	be interested in s.o., *v.* kišišawêlim-, kistêlim-.
cîkic	IPC + loc.	beside
coc-	NA [personal name]	George
côw-	NA [personal name]	Joe
ê-kimiwahk	VII conj. indic.	in that it rains, as it rains
kawin-	VTA / VTI	knock s.o./ s.t. down (*e.g.,* a tent)
kicin-	NI [loanword]	kitchen
kihciniskîhk	IPC	on the right
-kimiwahk		*v.* ê-kimiwahk.
kinwêš	IPC	a long time, extended period of time *v.* wêskac.
kistêliht-	VTI	be interested in s.t., respect s.t.; esteem s.t. *v.* cîhkêliht-, kišišawêliht-.
kistêlim-	VTA	be interested in s.o., respect s.o., esteem s.o. *v.* cîhkêlim-, kišišawêlim-.
kišišawêliht-	VTI	be interested in s.t. *v.* cîhkêliht-, kistêliht-. (N.W. James Bay)
kišišawêlim-	VTA	be interested in s.o. *v.* cîhkêlim-, kistêlim-. (N.W. James Bay)
kišk-	VTI	wear s.t.
kiškaw-	VTA	wear s.o.
kitimâkisi-	VAI	be poor, be pitiable
kitohcikan-	NI	musical instrument, fiddle
kitohcikê-	VAI	play music
kîwat-	NDI	your (2) (hunting) bag *v.* mîwat-, nîwat-, wîwat-.

lâlih	IPC + loc.	beside
maškawîmakan-	VII	be powerful
mat(w)ê	IPV	at a distance, just discernible (either by hearing or sight)
mayâšk-	VTI	pass s.t. walking
mayâškaw-	VTA	pass s.o. walking
mêliy-	NA [personal name]	Mary *MC*
mêniy-	NA [personal name]	Mary *SC*
mêriy-	NA [personal name]	Mary *adoption of* /ɪ/ *from English*
mîkiwâm-	NI and NDI	wigwam-type tent, tipi

(There is some vacillation among MC speakers in treating mîkiwâm as NI or NDI. Both omîkiwâm and owîkiwâm may be heard, the o... probably borrowed from NI possessed forms, rather than wîkiwâm-, NDI attested elsewhere.)

mîšakisî-	VAI	be rich, be well off
mîwat-	NDI	(hunting) bag *v.* kîwat-, nîwat-, wîwat-.
namatiniskîhk	IPC	on the left
nâcipah-	VTA	fetch s.o.
(nâcipahtâ-, nâcipahtwâ-,	VAI-T	fetch s.t.)
nîpawi-	VAI	stand
nîwat-	NDI	my (hunting) bag *v.* kîwat-, mîwat-, wîwat-.
nôkosi-	VAI	appear
pâtniy-	NA [personal name]	Evadney
pimiwil-	VTA	carry s.o. (general word for carrying in the arms); *v.* išiwil-.
pimiwitâ-	VAI-T	carry s.t. (general word for carrying in the arms)" *v.* išiwitâ-.
sakahikan-	NI	screw (Do not confuse with sâkahikan, lake.)
sayman-	NA [personal name]	Simon
sâpiyê-	NA	Xavier
sîhkaci-	VAI	be cold (of a person)
sopâya-	NA [personal name]	Sophia
šâpopali-	VA / VII	go through
šîpâ	IPC + loc.	under, underneath
šîpâstêwayân-	NI	sweater

tašinê	IPC	all the time, continually, incessantly
wâlta-	NA [personal name]	Walter
wêskac	IPC	long ago *v.* kinwêš.
wîkitôwin-	NI	wedding
wîwat-	NDI	his (hunting) bag *v.* kîwat-, mîwat-, nîwat-.

G. REVIEW

14.A Kakwêcihkêmôwina—Questions

Answer each question with a full sentence, adding comment where you can.

1. âšay nâ kî-pêci-nôkosiw n'tohkolon-iskwêw?
2. tâpwê nâ kî-kitohcikêwân sayman nêsta âniy owîkitôwiniwâhk?
3. âšay nâ kî-mâmîšahamwân ocîmâniwâw?
4. âšay nâ kî-mâmîšahamwak kicîmâniliw?
5. kinwêš nâ kitôhci-kiskêlimâwak cwân nêsta mêliy?
6. mîšakisîwak nâ?
7. wîskâc nâ kitôhci-tašîhkêwânâwâw kimisiwâw omâhkîmihk?
8. côw nâ wî-apiwêw mêlîwa okihciniskîlîhk?
9. ka-mawâpiwânânaw nâ omâhkîmiwâhk?
10. ka-pakitinamwânânaw nâ pîwâpisk côw ocîmânihk?
11. kî-ihtâwêw nâ sôsan okâwiya wîkilîhk kâ-kî-tipiskâlik?
12. kiwî-kanawâpahtamwân nâ cim opâskisikan? mâškôc pîkopaliliw.
13. awâšišak nâ cîhkêl'tamwêwak kâ-tôtamilici saymana?
14. awênihkân nâ kî-pîhtokwêwêw saymana wîkilîhk?
15. cwân nâ ta-kî-wawêšihtâw nimâhkîmiliw, kititêl'tên?
16. cim nâ kî-otinam n'tastotiniliw, nestapiko n'kî-otinamwân wîla otastotin?
17. awâšišak nâ n'tawêl'tamwak kipîskâkaniliw?
18. âšay nâ kî-pêhtamwânâwâw cim opîwâpiskom?
19. n'ka-kawinamwânân nâ kisê-ililiwak ôta omâhkîmiwâw?
20. awâšišak nâ kî-otinamwêwak omošômiwâwa opâskisikanilîw?
21. kî-mâkwahpitamwân nâ nimošôm ocîmân?
22. cîmis nâ kî-kihciwitâw kimîcimiwâw?

14.B Naškwêwašihtwâwina—Answers

Formulate questions to which the following statements could be answers.

1. êhê, nitahkonamwân cîmis owalahpicikan.
2. môla, kociškam kitastotiniliw.
3. êhê, n'kî-mâkwahpitamwân kimošôm ocîmân âšokanihk.
4. niwî-kanawâpahtamwânân pîskâkana kâ-ayât kâ-atâwêt.
5. môla nâspic kinwêš n'kî-ihtâwânân omâhkîmihk.
6. môla. môla ohci-kocihtâw nipâskisikaniliw; nîla mâka šâkoc n'kî-kocihtâwân wîla opâskisikan.
7. êhê, n'kî-otinamwân omaskisina, n'kî-wîyatwêwân mâka piko.
8. ka-kî-wîcêwâwâw. ka-kî-cîkahamwânâwâw omihtima.
9. n'ka-tipahên nîla nipimîm; môla mâka šâkoc n'ka-kî-tipahamwân wîla.
10. êhê, n'kî-mayâškamwân sayman omâhkîm kêkišêp.
11. môla 'wênihkân ohci-ihtâw omâhkîmihk.
12. cikêmânima! nâspic n'cîhkêl'tamwân animêliw kâ-tôtahk.
13. kišê-ililiwak tašinê âpacihtâwêwak onahâhkišîmiwâwa ocîmânilîw.
14. n'tawâc ka-nakatamwânânaw kôhtâwiy opâskisikan ôta.
15. môla, ka-kî-pakitinamwân kipîwâpiskom ocîmânihk.
16. ninipîwin ê-kimiwahk ohci; šâkoc mâka ka-kî-pîhtokwêwânânaw mêliy omâhkîmihk. ka-kî-pâsênânaw mâka kipîskâkanínawa anta.
17. môla, n'kî-apiwânân lâlih wîkihk.
18. ka-kî-mîšahamwânâwâw cwân ocîmân kê-wâpahk.
19. nawac kinwêš. n'kî-kitohcikêwân owîkitôwiniwâhk.
20. mwêhci anohc kî-âpahamwêwak n'tohkolon-iskwêwa ocîmânilîw.
21. âšay wîpac ta-kîwêliwa.

UNIT FIFTEEN

A. BASIC CONVERSATION

1. Let's Go for a Ride

Âniy:	'pâmpali...tâk[1]	let us ride (around)
	âpah...a	open it (2 sg.)
	âpaha cîmân. âstam 'pâm'palitâk.	Untie the canoe. Let's go for a ride.
Mâkrit:	tânt' êhtakwahk?	Where is it?
Âniy:	mêkwayêš (+ loc.)	among
	itâpi	look (there)
	tântê piko	Goodness knows where!
	tântê piko. itâpi mêkwayêš mistikohk.	Goodness knows where! Look over there among the trees.
	n'ka-ocipitên	I'll pull it
	kâhtin...a	push it (2 sg.)
	nêma	yonder one
	mâtika	behold
	mâtika nêma! kâhtina, nîla mâka n'ka-ocipitên.	There it is! You push it and I'll pull it.
Mâkrit:	âšowah...êtâk	let's cross it
	âšow'hêtâk sâkahikan.	Let's cross the lake.
	nâtakah...êtâk	let's bring it to shore (paddling)
	kwêskah...a cîmân	turn (2 sg.) the canoe
	kwêskaha cîmân ôta. nâtakahêtâk mâka.	Turn the canoe here. Let's bring it to shore.
Âniy:	mâkwahpit...a	tie (2 sg.) it up
	mâkwahpita cîmân.	Tie up the canoe.

[1] Where final /k/ is pronounced, the preceding vowel is shortened.

2. A Drop-in Visit

Âniy:	pîhtokwê...wâtâk	let us enter (*relational*)
	âstam, pîhtokwêwâtâk sopiy owâskâhikanimihk.	Come on, let's go into Sophie's house.
Mâkrit:	ihtâ...wâtâk	let's stay (*relational*)
	ihtâwâtâk wîkihk nakiskaw piko.	Let's just stay a little while at her place.
	iškwâhtêmihk	on the door
	pâpawahikê	knock, rap (2 sg.)
	pâpawahikê iškwâhtêmihk.	Knock on the door.
Sopiy:	awêna?	Who (is it)?
Âniy:	nîla ô	it's me
	nîla ô! âpaha iškwâhtêm.	It's me! Open the door.
Sopiy:	api	sit (2 sg.)
	pîhtokwê	enter (2 sg.)
	pîhtokwê! api mâka.	Come in! Sit down.
	onipêwinihk	on his bed
	api...w	sit (2 sg., *relational*)
	apiw âlik onipêwinihk.	Sit on Alec's bed.
Âniy:	ê'kwâwa n'tôtêm, mâkrit.	This is my friend, Margaret.
	mêšakwani-pipon	every year
	môšak pêci-mawâpiw ôta mêšakwani-pipon.	She always comes visiting here every year.
Sopiy:	api...k	sit (2p)
	pîhtokwê...k	enter (2p)
	pîhtokwêk, apik mâka.	Come in and sit down.
Âniy:	lâlihtak	along by the wall
	api...tâk	let's sit
	êkoši	so then
	kipah...amok	close it (2p)
	kipahamok iškwâhtêm. êkoši apitâk lâlihtak.	Close the door. Let's sit by the wall, then.

Sopiy:	tiy	tea
	minihkwê-tâk	let's drink
	minihkwêtâk tiy.	Let's drink some tea.

3. At Sophie's House

Âniy:	ê-âpatisiyan	in (your) working
	êkâwila kipihcî	don't stop (2 sg.)
	'kâwila kipihcî ê-âpatisiyan.	Don't stop working
	nakiskaw ô	just for a little while, see!
	nakiskaw ô piko n'kî-pîhtokwânân.	We just dropped in for a few minutes.
Sopiy:	kicistâpâwacikêw	she is washing
	nikicistâpâwacikân piko.	I'm just doing the washing.
	akotâ...w	hang it (2 sg., *relational*)
	otin...am	take it (2 sg., *relational*)
		(speaking to someone in the house:)
	otinam âniy wîwat, akotâw mâka.	Take Annie's bag and hang it up.
Mâkrit:	wîhcêki...nâkwan	it looks dirty (*lit.,* foul...it looks)
	sîpîwâpoy	river water
	sîpîwâpoy nâspic wîhcêkinâkwan.	The river water looks very dirty.
Sopiy:	wâšêy...âkamin	it is clear (of liquids)
	kimiwanâpoy	rain water
	kimiwanâpoy âpacihtâ. awasitê wâšêyâkamin.	Use rain water. It's clearer.
	kwâpahipân	dipper. jug
	pêtâ	bring it (2 sg.)
	pêtâ anima kwâpahipân.	Bring that jug (*or* dipper).
	olâkanihk	in the basin, in the dish
	alisipiy	plain water
	sîkin...a	pour it (2 sg.)
	otin...a	take it (2 sg.)
	otina, sîkina mâka alisipiy ôta olâkanihk.	Take it and pour some plain water here in the basin.

	kanawâpaht...amok	look at it (2p)
	kanawâpahtamok. tâpwê wâšêyâkamin.	Look at it. It's certainly clear.
Mâkrit:	pimihtakâhk[2]	on the wall
	kâ-akôtêki	which hang (*pl.*)
	kêkwân anihi kâ-akôtêki pimihtakâhk?	What are those (things) hanging on the wall ?
Sopiy:	nîhtin...amwâhk	take it / them down (2p *rel.*)
		(*—to the children:*)
	nîhtinamwâhk kôhtâwîwâw omaskisina pimihtakâhk ohci.	Take your father's moccasins down from the wall.
	wâpahtil...ihk	show (2p) her
	wâpahtil...ihkok	show (2p) them
	wâpahtilihkok iskwêwak.	Show the ladies.
	kîwê (*prefix form*)	back again, return
	kîwê-pakitin...amwâtâk	let's put it / them back (*rel.*)
	êkoši kîwê-pakitinamwâtâk pâpâ omaskisina.	Now let's put Daddy's moccasins back.
Âniy:	êko wâs' âni,—âšay mâškôc ka-kihtohtânânaw.	Well, that's that,—I guess we'll run along now.

2 Moose Cree variant: pimicihtakâhk.

B. DISCUSSION OF GRAMMAR

1. VAI and VTI Present Imperative: Relational and Non-relational Inflections

In the present unit the imperative order of suffixes is introduced for animate intransitive verbs (VAI) and transitive inanimate (VTI). There are actually two sets of imperative forms in Cree: one refers to the immediate situation, the so-called *immediate* or *present* imperative, to which the forms in the present unit belong. The other, the so-called *delayed* or *future* imperative, refers to an action to be carried out at some future time: *e.g.,* "When you come back, put the canoe away". This will be introduced later on.

VAI and VTI show forms for both relational and non-relational inflections:

	Non-relational		Relational	
VAI	2	... Ø	2	... w
	21	...tâ (k)	21	...wâtâ (k)
	2p	... k	2p	...wâhk
VTI	2	... a	2	... am
	21	...êtâ (k)	21	...amwâtâ (k)
	2p	...amok	2p	...amwâhk

Final /k/ in the forms for 21 subject often seems to be present but unreleased in the area of Kashechewan and the preceding vowel is phonetically somewhere between long and short. Some speakers drop the /k/ entirely, in which case the vowel is long. Study the following sentences.

	Non-relational	Relational
1.	api cîmânihk. Sit in the canoe.	apiw cwân ocîmânihk. Sit in John's canoe.
2.	ihtâtâk kîkinâhk. Let's stay at our place.	ihtâwâtâk âniy wîkihk. Let's stay at Annie's place.
3.	pêci-pîhtokwêk wâskâhikanihk. Come into the house.	pêci-pîhtokwêwâhk owâskâhikanimiwâhk. Come into their house.

4.	âpaha cîmân. Untie the canoe.	âpaham ocîmân. Untie his canoe.
5.	kipahêtâk iškwâhtêm. Let's close the door.	kipahamwâtâk otiškwâhtêmiwâw. Let's close their door.
6.	otinamok anihi mîwata, akotâk mâka. Take those bags and hang them up.	otinamwâhk âlik wîwata, akotâwâhk mâka. Take Alec's bags and hang them up.

NOTE. VAI relational imperatives for 2 and 2p are widely replaced by non-relational forms such as api, pêci-pîhtokwêk, even in a clearly relational context. Follow local usage in this matter. Use of VTI relational imperatives seems to be maintained: *e.g.,* âpaha has not replaced âpaham.

2. âstam, âstamik

âstam, "in facing direction", is often used as a command, "Come, come here". See Unit 4.A.2, êtiy, âstam pitamâ, "Eddie, come here a minute", and the recurrent âstamitê, "to this side".

Although âstam is not a verb, a 2p imperative is formed by the addition of ...ik: *i.e.,* âstamik. An older 2p imperative, âstamitok, is regularly encountered in the literature and may still be in colloquial use in some areas.

3. A Note on Pronunciation: /r/

Attention is drawn to the introduction in this unit of the /r/ phoneme, as in Mâkrit. In Cree, as spoken at Moosonee, Moose Factory and on the west coast of James Bay, this is clearly a borrowing from English, although it is reported as part of the native phonemic inventory at Isle à la Crosse, where nîla or nîna would be nîra (J. Horden, *A Grammar of the Cree Language,* S.P.C.K., 1881; p. 3). The sound is now widely heard in borrowed words, especially proper names, and various dialect provisions have been made for it in Cree syllabic writing (*v.* Unit 18.B.2.3).

C. DRILLS

In the following drills you will meet the occasional unfamiliar word. Even though you may not know its meaning, it will display a familiar grammatical form. Concentrate on the *form* of the word and this will provide your clue to a correct response.

1. Show that you recognize which forms of the imperative are relational and which non-relational by completing the sentence with the correct item from the bracketed alternatives.

		(Check column)
1.	nâtakahêtâk (kicîmân ~ ocîmân)	kicîmân
2.	'kâwila nôcihtâk (opâskisikan ~ kipâskisikaniwâw).	kipâskisikaniwâw
3.	'kâwila apiw (wîwatihk ~ nîwatihk).	wîwatihk
4.	mâkwahpita (kicîmâninaw ~ ocîmâniwâw).	kicîmâninaw
5.	kipahamok (iškwâhtêm ~ otiškwâhtêm).	iškwâhtêm
6.	otinam (kwâpahipân ~ okwâpahipân).	okwâpahipân
7.	akotâwâhk (cwân opîskâkan ~ nipîskâkan).	cwân opîskâkan
8.	pîhtokwêwâtâk (niwâskâhikanimihk ~ âniy owâskâhikanimihk).	âniy owâskâhikanimihk
9.	mâkwahpitêtâk (kicîmâninaw ~ ocîmâniwâw).	kicîmâninaw
10.	mâkwahpitamwâtâk (ocîmâniwâw ~ kicîmâninaw)	ocîmâniwâw
11.	'kâwila nipâ (onipêwinihk ~ nipêwinihk).	nipêwinihk
12.	papâm'palitâk (kicîmâninâhk ~ ocîmâniwâhk).	kicîmâninâhk
13.	mîcisowâhk (cîmis wîkihk ~ nîkihk).	cîmis wîkihk
14.	pakitinamok (wîwatihk ~ mîwatihk).	mîwatihk
15.	tîwâpohkêw (otaskihkohk ~ n'taskihkohk).	otaskihkohk
16.	âpatisiwâhk (nišwâpimihk ~ cwân ošwâpimihk).	cwân ošwâpimihk
17.	nipâk (owâskâhikanimihk ~ niwâskâhikanimihk).	niwâskâhikanimihk
18.	'kâwila pahkišiniwâtâk (otâšokanihk ohci ~ kitâšokanihk ohci).	otâšokanihk ohci

2. Answer each question, using the same verb but in the imperative order as in the model sentence. If you are using a recording, listen to the question repeated twice.

2.1 Question: n'ka-apin nâ ôta?
Reply: môla, nêtê iši-api mêkwayâhtik.

		(Check column)
1.	n'ka-apin nâ ôta?	iši-api
2.	n'ka-nipân nâ ôta?	iši-nipâ
3.	n'ka-mîcison nâ ôta?	iši-mîciso
4.	n'ka-âpatisin nâ ôta?	iši-âpatisi
5.	n'ka-ihtân nâ ôta?	ihtâ
6.	n'ka-pimišinin nâ ôta?	iši-pimišini
7.	n'ka-kapêšin [camp] nâ ôta?	iši-kapêši
8.	n'ka-kotawân nâ ôta?	iši-kotawê
9.	n'ka-alwêpin nâ ôta?	iši-alwêpi
10.	n'ka-cîkahikân nâ ôta?	iši-cîkahikê

2.2 Question: kiwî-apinâwâw nâ ôta?
Reply: môla nîlanân, kîlawâw mâka apik.

1.	kiwî-apinâwâw nâ ôta?	apik
2.	kiwî-nipânâwâw nâ ôta?	nipâk
3.	kiwî-ihtânâwâw nâ ôta?	ihtâk
4.	kiwî-âpatisinâwâw nâ ôta?	âpatisik
5.	kiwî-mîcisonâwâw nâ ôta?	mîcisok
6.	kiwî-kapêšinâwâw nâ ôta?	kapêšik
7.	kiwî-pimišininâwâw nâ ôta?	pimišinik
8.	kiwî-kotawânâwâw nâ ôta?	kotawêk
9.	kiwî-tîwâpohkânâwâw nâ ôta?	tîwâpohkêk
10.	kiwî-alwêpinâwâw nâ ôta?	alwêpik
11.	kiwî-cîkahikânâwâw nâ ôta?	cîkahikêk
12.	kiwî-mêtawânâwâw nâ ôta?	mêtawêk

2.3 Question: ka-apinânaw nâ ôta?
Reply: êhê, apitâ nakiskaw.

NOTE. When final /k/ is dropped from apitâk, final /â/ sounds longer. When /k/ is retained, the /â/ is phonetically shorter. Familiarize yourself with both forms and follow local usage.

		(Check column)
1.	ka-apinânaw nâ ôta?	apitâ(k)
2.	ka-nipânânaw nâ ôta?	nipâtâ(k)
3.	ka-ihtânânaw nâ ôta?	ihtâtâ(k)
4.	ka-âpatisinânaw nâ ôta?	âpatisitâ(k)
5.	ka-mîcisonânaw nâ ôta?	mîcisotâ(k)
6.	ka-kapêšinânaw nâ ôta?	kapêšitâ(k)
7.	ka-pimišininânaw nâ ôta?	pimišinitâ(k)
8.	ka-kotawânânaw nâ ôta?	kotawêtâ(k)
9.	ka-tîwâpohkânânaw nâ ôta?	tîwâpohkêtâ(k)
10.	ka-alwêpinânaw nâ ôta?	alwêpitâ(k)
11.	ka-cîkahikânânaw nâ ôta?	cîkahikêtâ(k)
12.	ka-mêtawânânaw nâ ôta?	mêtawêtâ(k)

3. Answer each question using the relational form of the imperative wherever the verb in the question is relational, the non-relational form where it is non-relational. On the recording the question is repeated twice and the correct reply is given.

3.1 Question: n'ka-apiwân nâ omâhkîmihk?
Reply: êhê, apiw âlik omâhkîmihk.

1.	n'ka-apiwân nâ omâhkîmihk?	apiw
2.	n'ka-nipâwân nâ omâhkîmihk?	nipâw
3.	n'ka-mîcisowân nâ omâhkîmihk?	mîcisow
4.	n'ka-minihkwân nâ mâhkîhk?	minihkwê
5.	n'ka-âpatisiwân nâ omâhkîmihk?	âpatisiw
6.	n'ka-minihkwêwân nâ omâhkîmihk?	minihkwêw
7.	n'ka-ihtâwân nâ omâhkîmihk?	ihtâw
8.	n'ka-tašîhkêwân nâ omâhkîmihk?	tašîhkêw
9.	n'ka-alwêpiwân nâ omâhkîmihk?	alwêpiw
10.	n'ka-pîhtokwân nâ mâhkîhk?	pîhtokwê
11.	n'ka-mêtawân nâ mâhkîhk?	mêtawê
12.	n'ka-mêtawêwân nâ omâhkîmihk?	mêtawêw

3.2 Each question below shows the verb in the non-relational inflection. You reply in each case with the 21 relational imperative: Let's ......

Question: kiwî-apin nâ anta?
Reply: apiwâtâ(k) cîmis wîkihk.

	(Check column)
1. kiwî-apin nâ anta?	apiwâtâ(k)
2. kiwî-mîcison nâ anta?	mîcisowâtâ(k)
3. kiwî-âpatisin nâ anta?	âpatisiwâtâ(k)
4. kiwî-tašîhkân nâ anta?	tašîhkêwâtâ(k)
5. kiwî-pimišinin nâ anta?	pimišiniwâtâ(k)
6. kiwî-nipân nâ anta?	nipâwâtâ(k)
7. kiwî-kotawân nâ anta?	kotawêwâtâ(k)
8. kiwî-tîwâpohkân nâ anta?	tîwâpohkêwâtâ(k)
9. kiwî-alwêpin nâ anta?	alwêpiwâtâ(k)
10. kiwî-mêtawân nâ anta?	mêtawêwâtâ(k)

3.3 To the question, "Shall we ...?" reply with the relational imperative, "You (2p)": *e.g.*,

Question: âšay nâ n'ka-apinân?
Reply: apiwâhk cîmis wîkihk, kišâspin sâpêl'tamêkwê.
(- if you (2p) like)

1. âšay nâ n'ka-apinân?	apiwâhk
2. âsay nâ n'ka-mîcisonân?	mîcisowâhk
3. âšay nâ n'ka-âpatisinân?	âpatisiwâhk
4. âšay nâ n'ka-pimišininân?	pimišiniwâhk
5. âšay nâ n'ka-nipânân?	nipâwâhk
6. âšay nâ n'ka-tîwâpohkânân?	tîwâpohkêwâhk
7. âšay nâ n'ka-mêtawânân?	mêtawêwâhk
8. âšay nâ n'ka-nîminân?	nîmiwâhk
9. âšay nâ n'ka-akotânân?	akotâwâhk
10. âšay nâ n'ka-pîhtokwânân?	pîhtokwêwâhk

4. In the following drill, where the verb is in the relational inflection, answer with the relational imperative, where it is non-relational answer with the non-relational imperative.

4.1 Question: n'ka-nakatên nâ mihta?
Reply: cikêma, nakata ôta mihta.
but to
Question: n'ka-nakatamwân nâ omihtima?
Reply: cikêma, nakatam ôta omihtima.

	(Check column)
1. n'ka-nakatên nâ mihta?	nakata
2. n'ka-tipahamwân nâ omihtima?	tipaham

3. n'ka-nôcihtân nâ mihta? — nôcihtâ
4. n'ka-otinên nâ mihta? — otina
5. n'ka-akihtamwân nâ omihtima? — akihtam
6. n'ka-tahkoskâtên [step on] nâ mihta? — tahkoskâta
7. n'ka-tipahên nâ mihta? — tipaha
8. n'ka-wêpinamwân nâ omihtima? — wêpinam
9. n'ka-walastân nâ mihta? — walastâ
10. n'ka-ohpinên nâ mihta? — ohpina
11. n'ka-otinamwân nâ omihtima? — otinam
12. n'ka-cîkahên nâ mihta? — cîkaha

4.2 To the questions below, reply as above but with 21 subject:

Question: kiwî-nakatamwân nâ ôta omihtima?
Reply: êhê, nakatamwâtâ(k) ôta omihtima.

1. kiwî-nakatamwân nâ ôta omihtima? — nakatamwâtâ(k)
2. kiwî-cîkahên nâ ôta mihta? — cîkahêtâ(k)
3. kiwî-pakici-wêpinên [throw down] nâ ôta mihta? — pakici-wêpinêtâ(k)
4. kiwî-akihtên nâ ôta mihta? — akihtêtâ(k)
5. kiwî-akihtamwân nâ ôta omihtima? — akihtamwâtâ(k)
6. kiwî-walastâwân nâ ôta omihtima? — walastâwâtâ(k)
7. kiwî-iskwâsên nâ ôta mihta? — iskwâsêtâ(k)
8. kiwî-otinamwân nâ ôta omihtima? — otinamwâtâ(k)
9. kiwî-tipahamwân nâ ôta omihtima? — tipahamwâtâ(k)
10. kiwî-nôcihtân nâ ôta mihta? — nôcihtâtâ(k)

4.3 To the following statements respond with a 2p *negative* imperative on the model:

Statement: n'ka-mâkwahpitênân ôta.
Response: 'kâwila mâkwahpitamok ôta.

But to relational: n'ka-pâsamwânân otâšokanihk,
respond 'kâwila pâsamwâhk otâšokanihk.

1. n'ka-otinênân ôta. — 'kâwila otinamok
2. n'ka-âpacihtânân ôta. — 'kâwila âpacihtâ(k)
3. n'ka-otinamwânân otâšokanihk. — 'kâwila otinamwâhk
4. n'ka-pâsênân ôta. — 'kâwila pâsamok
5. n'ka-cîkahênân ôta. — 'kâwila cîkahamok
6. n'ka-cîkahamwânân otâšokanihk. — 'kâwila cîkahamwâhk

7.	n'ka-natawi-kanawâpahtamwânân otâšokanihk.	'kâwila natawi-kanawâpaht... amwâhk
8.	n'ka-nôcihtânân ôta.	'kâwila nôcihtâk
9.	n'ka-walastânân ôta.	'kâwila walastâk
10.	n'ka-âpacihtâwânân otâšokanihk.	'kâwila âpacihtâwâhk
11.	n'ka-mâkwahpitênân ôta.	'kâwila mâkwahpitamok
12.	n'ka-tipahamwânân otâšokanihk.	'kâwila tipahamwâhk

5. Complete each sentence with an appropriate form from the stems listed on the left.

5.1	Imagine that you and a friend have some free time and decide to go for a canoe ride. You say to your friend: Untie the canoe. C'mon, let's go for a ride.
âpah-	__________ cîmân. âstam ________________.
'pâmipali-	
	The friend doesn't know where you've moored the canoe, and asks:
ihtakwan-	tânt' ____________? Apparently it's drifted away and you reply: Goodness knows where. Look around among the trees.
itâpi-	________ ______. ___________ mêkwayêš mistikohk. It's stuck and needs prying loose; so you say
ocipit-	There it is! Pull it and I'll push it.
kâhtin-	mâtika nêma! ____________, nîla mâka _____________.
âšowah-	Once afloat, you suggest: Let's cross the lake and beach the canoe.
nâtakah-	______________ sâkahikan; _______________ mâka cîmân.
kwêskah-	Turn it here, you say; but be careful. _____________ ôta;
ayâkwâmisî-	__________________ mâka.
mâkwahpit-	That's it. Tie it up; but look out for that dog.
'yâkwâ	ê'kwâni. ______________ ; __________ ana atim!
5.2	Once landed, you say: C'mon, let's go into Susan's house and stay a while.
pîhtokwê-	âstam, _________________ sôsan owâskâhikanimihk;
ihtâ-	__________________ nakiskaw piko.
	Unrequired though it may be in local practice, you nonetheless say:
pâpawahikê-	Rap on the door. _________________ iškwâhtêmihk. A voice calls out: Who is it?___________? To which you reply:
âpah-	It's me. Open the door. nîla ô! ____________ iškwâhtêm. From inside Susan responds sociably:
pîhtokwê-, api-	Come in. Sit down. Did you come alone?

pêci-pêyako-	____________. ______ mâka. kî- __________________ nâ?
	At this point Susan notices your friend and, addressing **you both**, says:
pîhtokwê-, api-	Come in and sit down; but close the door. There are too many insects.
kipah-,	___________, _______ mâka; ___________ iškwâhtêm. wêsâ
mihcêti-	______________ man'côšak.
pêtâ-,	Bring that dipper, she calls to one of the children. I'll make tea.
tîwâpohkê-	_______ anima kwâpahipân. n'ka-__________________.
5.3	Realising that Susan was busy at something, you hasten to say:
kipihcî-	Don't stop working. We just dropped in for a few minutes.
pîhtokwê-	êkâwila _____________ ê-âpatisiyan. nakiskaw piko ____________.
	Susan notices that you're carrying a bag and says to one of the children:
otin-	Take that bag. __________ anima mîwat.
	The youngster doesn't know which bag; so Susan explains: Take
otin-, akotâ-	Annie's bag and hang it up. ________ âniy wîwat; _________ mâka.
	By this time the child has brought the dipper, and Susan tells her: Take it and pour some plain water here in the basin.
otin-, sîkin-	__________, ____________ mâka alisipiy ôta _______________.
	She's pleased that it's not too muddy after the rain, and remarks:
kanawâpaht-	(2p) Look at it! It's certainly clear (liquid). _______________!
wâšêyâkamin-	tâpwê _________________.
	Indicating some brand new moccasins hanging on the wall, she says to two of the children: Take down your father's moccasins and show the ladies.
nîhtin-, wâpahtil-	____________ kôhtâwîwâw omaskisina; _____________ iskwêwak.
	Now, she adds after a moment, let's put Daddy's moccasins back.
kîwê-pakitin-	êkoši, kîwê-____________________ pâpa omaskisina.
	Well, I guess we'll probably be on our way, you say to your friend.
kihtohtê-	êko wâs' âni, âšay mâškôc ___________________, and the visit is over.

D. CONVERSATION PRACTICE

1. Review the Basic Conversation as in preceding units and REMEMBER, *do not stop* when you get stuck. Keep going but mark the difficult points. Then return and learn the items which you have marked. Repeat the review of the whole conversation.

2. Check the drills for difficulties. Practise by yourself, with another member of the class or with a recording; but whichever way you choose, be sure you can give the responses without undue hesitation.

3.1 Imagine a situation in which you arrange with someone to chop wood for you. Direct him to chop it, where to throw it down or pile it in relation to someone's house or tent.

mihti	NI sg.	log of wood; mihta NI pl.
mihtikân-	NI	woodpile
pakici-wêpin-	VTA / VTI	throw s.t. down
piskwastâ-	VAI-T	pile s.t. in a heap
mâwisikostâ-	VAI-T	pile s.t. together, stack s.t. together
otânâhk wâskâhikanihk		behind the house; opiskoni w. at the back of ...

3.2 Pretend you have just arrived to visit your aunt. Her dog begins to bark and you warn your friend: "Look out for that dog!" Your aunt happens to be busy doing the washing and tells you to sit down on someone's bed while she works. (mêkwâc ê-âpatisiyân while I work; mêkwâc ê-âpatisit while she works) You urge her not to stop working,—you have just come for a short while. You didn't come alone (môla n'tôhci-pêci-pêyakon); and when you introduce your companion, she insists that you stay and have tea. You chat about other friends who have just recently come back from upriver and then remark that you will be going. You want to get home before dark (pwâmoši ati-tipiskâk).

3.3 Engage in any other conversation which enables you to make use of imperative forms, both non-relational and relational. Suggest to your friend that you put the canoe in to shore and build a fire (kotawê- VAI) since it is cold (ê-tahkâyâk). Your friend warns: "Don't make a fire among the trees!"

You suggest making tea. Your friend agrees and suggests that you camp on the spot.

It always saves time and makes for more rewarding conversation to rough out the subject matter ahead of time, noting words and expressions which you would like to use. You can then concentrate on the language instead of trying to think of what to say next.

E. LISTENING IN

Mâkrit:	wî-kakwê-tahkona[1] ôma wâhtâkan,—'yâkwâmisî mâka. nâspic kosikwan.[2]
Sêra:	kayâm! mâtih,[3] kwêskahêtâk cîmân ôta. awênihkân owâskâhikanim animêliw? âlik nâ?
Mâkrit:	êhê, mâškôc n'titêl'tên. nôhcimihk kî-ohcipiciw[4] otânâhk kâ-kî-tawâstêlik.
Sêra:	pêtâ cîmân ôtê, âšokanihk mâka pakitina êncin. 'yâkwâmisî, mâškôc ka-pahkišinin.
Mâkrit:	mâcika nâha sopiy! têpwêw. tân' êtwêt?
Sêra:	"pêci-pîhtokwêk", itwêw. "mâkwahpitamok kicîmâniwâw mêkwayêš mistikohk."
Mâkrit:	ê'kotôta mâkwahpitêtâk. kîla ocipita, n'ka-kâhtinên nîla. ââ, milwâšin.
Sêra:	mâca kîla nîkânî.[5] ihtâwâtâk otiškotêhkânihk. apišîš tahkâyâw ôta.
Mâkrit:	nipîwanwa kimaskisina. âpacihtâ anihi kotakiya nimaskisina. nîwatihk anta pîhcihtinwa.[6] êliwêk ašiškîwan! kêkât môla ka-kî-pimohtân.
Sêra:	êhê, n'kiskêl'tên. sîkina apišîš nipiy ôta n'cihcîhk.[7] pêtâ ašic kîwat. mâškôc ta-kimiwan.
Mâkrit:	kapêšitâk ôta anohc kâ-tipiskâk. akotâ kimaskisina opiskoni[8] sopiy otiškotêhkânihk. wîpac ta-pâstêwa.[9]
Sêra:	kicistâpâwacikêliwa âlik wîwa. niwâpamimâwa lâlih wâskâhikanihk.

1 kakwê	IPV	try to
2 kosikwan-	VII	be heavy
3 mâtih	IPC	see then! look then!
4 ohcipici-	VAI	move (with one's family and belongings)
5 nîkânî-	VAI	go ahead, go in advance
6 pîhcitinwa	VII 0 pl.	they are inside
7 nicihciy-	NDI	my hand: n'cihcîhk in my hand
8 opiskoni	IPC + loc.	back of
9 pâstê-	VII	dry, dry out: ta-pâstêwa they will dry

Mâkrit: sîpîwâpoy nâspic wîhcêkinâkwan.

Sêra: mâškôc kimiwanâpoliw âpacihtâtokwê.[10] awasitê wâšêyâkamin. ihtâwâtâk owâskâhikanimiwâhk kê-tipiskâlik. mâca, ati-pîhtokwê. nâkê n'ka-pêci-pîhtokwân.

10 âpacihtâtokwêVAI dubitative mode she must be using

F. REFERENCE LIST

(akôl-	VTA	hang s.o. up *v.* akôtâ-.)
akotâ-	VAI-T	hang s.t. up *v.* akôl-.
akotê-	VII	hang: kâ-akôtêki things which hang
alisipiy-	NI	plain water
awêna	PR interrogative	who? *used predicatively*: Who is it?
ayâkwâmisî-	VAI	be careful, be cautious
âpacihtâtokwê	VAI-T indep. dubit.	he must be using it
âšawah-	VTI	cross s.t. (*e.g.*, a river)
êkoši	IPC	so then (*used as a polite introduction to a directive*)
iškwâhtêm-	NI	door
itâpi-	VAI	look there, look about
kakwê	IPV	try (to)
kâhtin-	VTA / VTI	push s.o./ s.t.
kicihciy-	NDI	your (2) hand *v.* micihciy-, nicihciy-, ocihciy-.
kicistâpâwacikê-	VAI	wash, do the washing
kimiwanâpoy-	NI	rain water
kipah-	VTI	close s.t., shut (off) s.t., *v.* okipahowêsiw-, Unit 7.A.2.
(kipahw-	VTA	close s.o., shut (off) s.o.)
kipihcî-	VAI	stop, come to a standstill
kîšowa-	VII	be warm
kîwat-	NDI	your (2) bag *v.* mîwat-, nîwat-, wîwat-.
kotawê-	VAI	build an open fire
kwâpahipân-	NI	dipper, jug
kwêskah-	VTA / VTI	turn s.o./ s.t. (*e.g.*, a canoe) using a paddle
lâlihtak	IPC	along by the wall
mâtih	IPC	see then! look then!
mâtika	IPC	behold! look!
mâwisikostâ-	VAI-T	pile s.t. together, stack s.t. *v.* piskwastâ-.
mêkwayâhtikw	IPC	among the trees (on land)

mêkwayêš	IPC + loc.	among: mêkwayêš mistikohk among the trees (as a clump in the water)
mêšakwani-piponw	IPC	every year, *lit.,* every Winter
micihciy-	NDI	a / the hand *v.* kicihciy-, nicihciy-, ocihciy-.
mihcêti-	VAI	be many
minihkwâkan-	NI	drinking vessel, cup, glass
mîwat-	NDI	a / the bag *v.* kîwat-, nîwat-, wîwat-.
nâha	PR dem. anim prox. sg.	yonder one *v.* nêma.
nâtakah-	VTI	bring s.t. (by instrument, *i.e.,* a paddle) to shore (Verb implying use of a motor is sêskipalihtwâ-.)
nêma	PR dem. inan. prox. sg.	yonder one *v.* nâha.
nicihciy-	NDI	my hand *v.* kicihciy-, micihciy-, ocihciy-.
nipêwin-	NI	bed, bunk
nîhtin-	VTA / VTI	hand s.o./ s.t. down
nîkânî-	VAI	go ahead, go in lead position
nîwat-	NDI	my bag *v.* kîwat-, mîwat-, wîwat-.
ocihciy-	NDI	his hand *v.* kicihciy-, micihciy-, nicihciy-.
ocipit-	VTA / VTI	pull s.o./ s.t.
ohcipici-	VAI	move (with family and belongings) from
olâkan-	NI	dish, basin
opiskoni	IPC + loc.	(at the) back of
otânâhk	IPC + loc.	behind
ô	IPC	reference to immediate vicinity: *e.g.,* nîla ô it's me, *lit.,*me here; tânta ô? where (right around here)?
pakici-wêpin-	VTA / VTI	throw s.o./ s.t. down
papâmipali-	VA / VII	travel about, move about: *contracted to* 'pâm'pali-.
pâpawahikê-	VAI	knock, rap
pâstê-	VII	dry
pêci-pêyako-	VAI	come alone
(pêšiw-	VTA	bring s.o. Unit 8.C.3.3)
pêtâ-	VAI-T	bring s.t.
pêyako-	VAI	be alone
pimicihtakâhk	IPC	on the wall (*MC*)
pimihtakâhk	IPC	on the wall
piskwastâ-	VAI-T	pile in a heap *v.* mâwisikostâ-.
pîhcihtin-	VII	be inside, be contained inside
(pîhcišin-	VAI	lie inside, be inside)

sîkin-	VTA / VTI	pour s.o./ s.t.
sîpîwâpoy-	NI	river water
wâšêyâkamin-	VII	be clear (liquid)
wîhcêkinâkosi-	VAI	appear dirty
wîhcêkinâkwan-	VII	appear dirty
wîwat-	NDI	his bag *v.* kîwat-, mîwat-, nîwat-.

G. REVIEW

15.A Kakwêcihkêmôwina—Questions

Answer the following questions using material from the conversations and drills.

Wherever you have a choice, try to use an imperative form in your reply.

1. n'ka-kwêskahên nâ cîmân ôta?
2. ka-mîcisowânânaw nâ cîmis omâhkîmihk?
3. n'ka-kotawânân nâ ôta?
4. n'ka-pâpawahikân nâ?
5. n'ka-sêskipitamwân nâ saylas ocîmân mwêhci ôta?
6. ka-kî-tašîhkêwânânaw nâ âlik omâhkîmihk?
7. n'ka-âpahênân nâ iškwâhtêm?
8. kî-itwêw nâ âlik kêkwâliw?
9. n'ka-apiwân nâ cîkic otiškotêhkânihk?
10. kinwêš nâ ka-ihtâwânânaw sopiy omâhkîmihk?
11. kišâstaw! tâpwê tahkâyâw, manâ?
12. n'ka-sîkinên nâ kwâpiy kiminihkwâkanihk [in your cup]?
13. mâškôc n'ka-kotawân mêkwayêš mistikohk, manâ?
14. n'ka-nîhtinamwânân nâ âlik omaskisina pimihtakâhk ohci?
15. kin'tawêl'tên nâ alisipiy olâkanihk?
16. n'ka-kî-wâpahtênân nâ kitôški-pâskisikan?
17. n'ka-âpacihtâwân nâ nôhkom okwâpahipân?
18. ka-tîwâpohkêwânânaw nâ sopiy wîkihk?
19. n'ka-kî-apin nâ pîhci cîmânihk?
20. âšay nâ kikicistâpâwacikân, nêstapiko n'ka-kî-pîhtokwânân nâ?

15.B Naškwêwašihtwâwina—Answers

Formulate questions which may be answered by the following statements.

1. êhê. mâkwahpita ôta âšokanihk.
2. môla. 'kâwila tahkopita nîla n'cîmân; wîla mâka ocîmân tahkopitam.
3. êhê, kipaha iškwâhtêm; awasitê mâka ta-kîšowâw (be warm) pîhtokwamihk.
4. kayâm. tîwâpohkêk.
5. âniy kî-itwêw: " 'pam'palitâ".
6. êhê, 'kâwila mâka kotawê mêkwayêš mistikohk.
7. môla. 'kâwila mâka pâpawahikê. n'kiskêlimâwak kwayask.
8. pêci-pîhtokêk, apiwâhk mâka âlik onipêwinihk.
9. kimiwanâpoy âpacihtâ. mistahi awasitê wâšêyâkamin.
10. 'kâwila kipihcî ê-kicistâpâwacikêyan. wîpac n'ka-kihtohtânân.
11. 'kâwila nakata anta. pimihtakâhk iši-akotâ.
12. êhê, kîwê-pakitinamwâtâk mâka pâpâ omaskisina.
13. êhê, alisipiy sîkina kwâpahipânihk.
14. itohtahtâ maskisina wâskâhikanihk, nakata mâka mîwat ôta.
15. cikêmânima, mâkwahpita.
16. kayâm, êkoši âšow'hêtâk sâkahikan mwêhci anohc.
17. êhê, ocipita; êkâwila mâka kâhtina.
18. tâpwê kišitêw ôta. âpaha iškwâhtêm.
19. pêci-pêyako. môla ka-wanišinin.
20. sêskipitamok cîmân; êko mâka pêci-pîhtokêk mâhkîhk.

UNIT SIXTEEN

A. BASIC CONVERSATION

1. The Public Health Nurse

Atôskêlâkan (Assistant):		
	tahkoskât...êw	he steps on him
	tahkoskâš	(2) step on him
	tahkoskâš âšokan.	Step on the wharf.
P.H.N. (Public Health Nurse):		
	pimót...êw	he throws at him
	pimoš	(2) throw at him
	pimoš kêkwâliw ana atim.	Throw something at that dog.
Atôskêlâkan:	natom...êw	he calls to him, beckons to him
	natom	(2) call to him, invite him
	cêniy, natom kitêm.	Janie, call your dog.
P.H.N.	pakitin...ik	(2) put them (*anim.*)
	natom...ik	(2) call them, invite them
	pakitinik apwoyak cîmânihk, —n'tomik mâka aniki iskwêwak wâskâhikanihk.	Put the paddles in the canoe, —and call those women into the house.
(—to a bystander)		
	kisisow	he is warm
	kisisow awa awâšiš.	This child has a fever.
	mâtow	he is crying
	môšak nâ mâtow?	Does he always cry?
	têhtal...êw	he sets him (on top of...)
	têhtal	(2) set him
	têhtal anta têhtapiwinihk.	Set him there on the chair.
	mohcihtak	on the floor
	pakitin...im	(2) put him (3')
	pakitinim otašíkana mohcihtak.	Put his socks on the floor.

	n'ka-nanâtawimâw	I'll examine him
	tahkon	(2) you hold him
	tahkon, n'ka-nanâtawimâw mâka.	Hold him and I'll examine him.
Atôskêlâkan:	kanawâpam	(2) you look at him
	kanawâpam...im	(2) look at him (3')
	kanawâpamim nêsta ostêsa.	Look at his older brother too.
P.H.N.	kanawâpam...âtâk	let's look at him
	êkoši kanawâpamâtâk pitamâ.	Let's look at him first.
	olihkwa	his tonsils
	kanawâpam...im...âtânih	let's look at him (3')
	kanawâpamimâtânih olihkwa.	Let's look at his tonsils.
	mistikwân	head
	mistikwâni-	*compounding form of* head
	mistikwâni-n'tohkoliy	aspirin
	mîl	(2) give him
	mîl mistikwâni-n'tohkolîliw.	Give him an aspirin.
	kîšôh-...êw	he keeps him warm
	kîšôy	(2) keep him warm
	kîwêhtah...êw	he takes him home
	kîwêhtay	(2) take him home
	kîwêhtay anohc, kîšôy mâka.	Take him home now and keep him warm.
	kîwêhtah...im	(2) take him (3') home
	kîwêhtahim nêsta ostêsa.	Take his (older) brother home too.
	pâtimâ	later on, bye-and-bye
	'nâtawim...âtânik	let's examine them
	êškwâ 'nâtawimâtânik misiwê kotakiyak pâtimâ.	Let's examine all the others later.

2. At the Clinic

Doctor:	têpwâš	(2) call him
	têpwâš kotak 'wênihkân.	Call someone else.
Nurse:	nanâtawim	(2) you examine him
	nanâtawim awa ililiw ništam,	Examine this man first,

	'nâtawicikan	thermometre
	mîlin	(2) give me
	—mîlin mâka ani 'nâtawicikan.	—and give me that thermometre.
Doctor:	opîwâpiskom	his "temperature", *lit.,* metal
	pêci-pîhtokah...êw	he brings him in
	pêci-pîhtokay	(2) bring him in
	pêci-pîhtokay, otinam mâka opîwâpiskom.	Bring him in and take his temperature.
Nurse:	apišîš kikisison.	You have a bit of a temperature.
Doctor:	ospitonihk	in his arm
	otêhi	his heart
	otêhiyâpiy-	his artery, *lit.,* heart-line
	kotinam	(2) test it by hand (*relational*)
	kotinam otêhiyâpiy ospitonihk.	Check his pulse.
(*—to patient*)		
	'ci-kîsôsiyan	that you may be warm
	pimišini	(2) lie
	pimišini kinipêwinihk 'ci-kîsôsiyan.	Get in bed and keep warm.

3. Treatment

Nurse:	manicôš	an insect, a "boil"
	omanicôš...im...iw[1]	he has a boil
	oman'côšimiw awa awâšiš.	This child has a boil.
Doctor:	âpacih...êw	he uses him
	âpaciy	(2) use him
	alôminask	linseed meal
	alôminask âpaciy.	Use linseed meal.
	pakitin	(2) put him
	ohtêw	it boils
	ê-ohtêk	in its boiling
	ê-ohtêk nipiy pakitin.	Put it (*anim.*) in boiling water.
	kâ + iši	where
	kâ-iši-omanicôšimit	where he has a boil
	êko mâka	and then

[1] Alternative further west, o...sîkihp...im...iw.

	'ci-tahkisit	that it (*anim.*) cool
	pêh...êw	he waits for him
	pêy	(2) wait for him
	pêy 'ci-tahkisit; êko mâka pakitin kâ-iši-oman'côšimit.	Wait for it (alôminask) to cool; then put it on the boil.
Nurse:	cîstahw...êw	he pricks him, he injects him
	n'ka-cîstahwâw nâ?	Shall I give him an injection?
Doctor:	êhê, cîstaw.	Yes, give him an injection.

(*—to child's mother*)

sôp	soap
âpacih...ihk	(2p) use it (*anim.*)
tâpiskôc âpacihihk awa sôp.	Both of you use this soap.
kîlawâw ôko kitastisiwâwak.	These mitts are yours (2p).
otin...ihkok.	(2p) take them.
tân' êspalit	how he gets on
kiskêl'tamohinân	(2p) let us know
kiskêl'tamohinân tân' êspalit.	Let us know how he gets on.

4. "Third Man" Theme

sikalêtak[2]	cigarettes
cahkišim...êw	he stubs him (a cigarette)
kata	*future marker, full form with other than* ni... *or* ki... prefix
êkâwila ililiwak kata-cahkišimêwak sikalêta mohcihtak.	People will kindly not stub cigarettes on the floor.
êkoši misiw' 'wênihkân ta-akotâw opîskâkan.	Will everyone please hang up his coat.
êkâwila kata-mâkwahpitamwak ililiwak cîmâna ôta âšokanihk.	People will kindly not tie boats to this wharf.

(In Cree one does not say awa âšokanihk: v. Unit 5.B.3.2.)

êkoši kata-kipahamwak ililiwak iškwâhtêmiliw.	Will people please close the door.

[2] Often heard as sikarêtak.

B. DISCUSSION OF GRAMMAR

1. Verbs

1.1 Present Imperative and Jussive

To form the present (*or* "immediate") imperative of the transitive animate verb the following inflectional endings are added to the stem:

Present (Immediate) Imperative

(š)	2 - 1	...in	(š)[1]	-3	...y > Ø	(š)	-3′	...ım
(š)	2 - 1p	...inân	(š)	-3p	...ik			
	21		(t)	-3	...âtâk	(t)	-3′	...ımâtânih
			(t)	-3p	...âtânik			*or* ...ımâtâna
				or	...âtânak			
(š)	2p - 1	...ik	(t)	-3	...ıhkw	(t)	-3′	...ımâhk
(š)	2p - 1p	...inân	(t)	-3p	...ıhkok			

Jussive (3rd person imperative)

3 - 3′	êkoši êkâwila	kata	+ VTA Stem	+ ...êw
3p - 3′	êkoši êkâwila	kata	+ VTA Stem	+ ...êwak

1.2 Sound Change

1.2.1 (š) in the paradigm[1] above indicates change of stem-final /t/ to /š/: *e.g.,*

têpwât...êw	he calls him
têpwâš	call him (2 imperative)

[1] Stem final /t/ > /š/ before /y/. /y/ final like /w/ final after a consonant disappears leaving têpwâš alone as the 2→3 imperative form. See HISTORICAL NOTE, p. 408.

This normally takes place throughout all present imperative forms for 2 actor and in the 2p - 1/1p set, although both têpwâtim and têpwâšim may be heard for 2–3′, the latter on the analogy of other forms in the 2 subject set. (Recall the sound change noted in Unit 1.B, fn. 3, p. 7 and the HISTORICAL NOTE, Unit 11.B.1.2, p. 278.)

HISTORICAL NOTE. The final /t/ of têpwât- and other t-stem verbs comes from a sound in the parent language (Proto-Algonquian) which we write as <θ>, a kind of "t" sound, although its exact phonetic features are not known. This sound, whenever it preceded * e in PA, became /t/ in modern Cree: hence têpwâtisk from earlier ...*θesk, and modern atim from earlier *aθemw-. By contrast, *θ before historic *i and *y became /š/, to yield forms such as têpwâšit from earlier ...*θit, or the particle prefix, ιši, from the old root, *eθ..., when followed by *i, and the 2 - 3 imperative, têpwâš, from *têpwâθ...y. /y/, like /w/, disappears in final CY position leaving the verb stem alone as indicated by Ø in the paradigm. When PA *e and *i had merged into one vowel in Modern Cree, the effect of the old sound changes, *θ into /t/ or /š/, remained. The symbol <ι> in this text represents modern /i/ where it is descended from *e in the parent language.

1.2.2 /h/ as stem-final

Where /h/ occurs in stem-final position one would expect the 2 - 3 imperative to take forms such as pêh, sâkih, kîšoh, pîhtokwah, etc. As the transcription in the Basic Conversation indicates, a stem-final /h/ is normally realised in this dialect as [y]. This does not hold for all dialect areas. In some localities pêy, sâkiy, etc., may be heard as pêhi(h) or sâkih. Forms of the type, sâkihik and sâkihihkok, however, occur regularly, even where the 2 - 3 norm is pêy, sâkiy, kîšôy, pîhtokay, etc.

1.2.3 /w/ stem-final with ...ahw-, ...ιsw-, ...ιšw-

Where /hw/ occurs in stem-final position, the 2 - 3 imperative drops the /h/ before final /w/: *e.g.,*

cîstahw...êw	he punctures him, he gives him an injection
cîstaw	puncture him, give him an injection (2 - 3)

Where /sw/ or /šw/ occurs in stem-final position, final /w/ is dropped: *e.g.,*

pâskisw...êw	he shoots him
pâskis	shoot him (2 - 3) *v.* Unit 3.B.2.1.2.

1.3 êkoši and êkâwila with Jussive

The jussive form is obtained with the use of êkoši, for affirmative statements, or êkâwila, for negative statements, with kata + independent indicative to yield a 3(p) - 3′ imperative or "jussive" as expressed in English by, "Let him / them do so-and-so", in the sense, "See that he does so-and-so": *e.g.,*

> êkoši kata-mâkwahpitam cîmâniliw.
> Let her tie up the canoe.
>
> êkâwila kata-ayamihêw omošôma.
> Let him not speak to his grandfather.

A corresponding usage with ka + independent indicative exists for 1st and 2nd person actors but is not as frequently encountered.

———DRILLS 1 THROUGH 6———

2. Stem Composition

2.1 Connective /i/ and /wi/

An increasing number of forms will be met showing the composition of two noun stems: *e.g.,* mistikwâni-natohkoliy, aspirin, *lit.,* "head medicine". Stem composition will be studied in greater detail as we proceed; meanwhile it should be noted that in compound stems where both members are nouns, the prior member is linked to the second by means of the so-called "*connective* /i/": *e.g.,*

mistikwân...i-natohkoliy	>	mistikwâni-natohkoliy
êncin...i-pimiy	>	êncini-pimiy

In each case the resultant compound is **one word.** The addition of /i/ does not turn a noun into an "adjective", but into the initial member of a compound stem.

Correspondingly, VAI stems, with the addition of /wi/, also occur as prior members in composition with nouns: *e.g.,*

nikamo...w		he sings
masinahikan		book
nikamo...wi-masinahikan	>	nikamowi-masinahikan
		song book, hymn book

Study the following sentences.

1.	kanawâpam awâšiš.	(2)	Look at the child.
2.	kanawêlimik awâšišak.	"	Take care of the children.
3.	ayamihim ošîma.	"	Speak to his young brother.
4.	mîl sikalêta.	"	Give him a cigarette.
5.	mîlin sikalêt.	"	Give me a cigarette.
6.	mîlinân cîstêmâw.	"	Give us some tobacco.
7.	pâskisok pilêsiwak.	"	Shoot the birds.
8.	êkâwila otâmahonân. otâmaw mâka wîla; otâmahom nêsta ostêsa.	"	Don't hit us. Hit him though, and hit his big brother too.
9.	nakaš ana apwoy, nakašik nêsta kotakiyak.	"	Leave that paddle and leave the others too.
10.	nakatihk ana apwoy, nakatihkok nêsta kotakiyak.	(2p)	Leave that paddle and leave the other others too.
11.	natawâpamihk awâšiš.	"	Go fetch the child.
12.	šawêlimihkok awâšišak.	"	Have compassion on the children.
13.	pêhimâhk ôhtâwiya.	"	Wait for his father.
14.	mîlik namêsa.	(2)	Give them the fish.
15.	mîlik namêsak.	(2p)	Give me the fish.
16.	wîcihinân. išiwilinân mwêhci anohc.	(2 *or* 2p)	Help us. Take us right now.
17.	têhtalâtâk mohcihtak.	(21)	Let's set him on the floor.
18.	akimâtânak (*or* akimâtânik) šîšîpak.	"	Let's count the ducks.
19.	natomimâtâna (*or* natominâtânih) onîkihikwa.	"	Let's invite her parents.

C. DRILLS

The purpose of the drills is to promote "overlearning": *i.e.,* to lead you to make automatic—and correct—responses without having to stop and think. The unusually extensive exchanges below have been supplied to facilitate mastery of the rich, inflectional character of the VTA imperative. If, part way through a sequence, you find yourself in full control of the material, avoid tedium by moving ahead directly to the next set of exchanges.

1. Answer the questions in each exchange with the required form of the imperative. Each question is recorded twice with a check repetition of the answer.

1.1 Answer with 2 - 3 imperative on the model:

Question: n'ka-natomâw nâ?
Shall I invite him / her?
Reply: êhê, natom anohc.
Yes, invite him / her now.

		(Check column)
1.	n'ka-natomâw nâ?	natom
2.	n'ka-išiwilâw nâ?	išiwil
3.	n'ka-kîšônâw nâ?	kîšôn
4.	n'ka-kîwêhtahâw nâ?	kîwêhtay
5.	n'ka-natohtawâw nâ?	natohtaw
6.	n'ka-pâskiswâw nâ?	pâskis
7.	n'ka-cîkahwâw nâ?	cîkaw
8.	n'ka-nakatâw nâ?	nakaš
9.	n'ka-ocipitâw nâ?	ocipiš
10.	n'ka-tahkoskâtâw nâ?	tahkoskâš

1.2 Answer, as above, but with 2 - 3p imperative, on the model:

Question:	n'ka-kî-natomâwak nâ? May I invite them?
Reply:	cikêmânima, natomik misiwê. Of course, invite them all.

		(Check column)
1.	n'ka-kî-kanawâpamâwak nâ?	kanawâpamik
2.	n'ka-kî-têhtalâwak nâ?	têhtalik
3.	n'ka-otinâwak nâ?	otinik
4.	n'ka-kî-pîhtokwahâwak nâ?	pîhtokwahik
5.	n'ka-kî-wîcêwâwak nâ?	wîcêwik
6.	n'ka-kî-kîsiswâwak nâ?	kîsisok
7.	n'ka-kî-otâmahwâwak nâ?	otâmahok
8.	n'ka-kî-têpwâtâwak nâ?	têpwâšik
9.	n'ka-wîskwêpitâwak nâ?	wîskwêpišik
10.	n'ka-kî-tahkoskâtâwak nâ?	tahkoskâšik

1.3 Respond to the cue with 2 - 3' imperative on the model:

Cue:	mâškôc n'ka-natomimâwa ostêsa. Perhaps I'll invite his brother.
Response:	milwâšin, n'tomim ostêsa anohc. Good, invite his brother now.

1.	mâškôc n'ka-natomimâwa ostêsa.	n'tomim
2.	n'ka-têhtalimâwa otapwoya.	têhtalim
3.	n'ka-tahkonimâwa ostêsa.	tahkonim
4.	n'ka-ayamihimâwa ostêsa.	ayamihim
5.	n'ka-pêšiwimâwa ostêsa.	pêšiwim
6.	n'ka-pêhtawimâwa ostêsa.	pêhtawim
7.	n'ka-mâcišomâwa opalacîsa.	mâcišom
8.	n'ka-cîstahomâwa okosisa.	cîstahom
9.	n'ka-têpwâtimâwa ostêsa.	têpwâšim
10.	n'ka-nakatimâwa ostêsa.	nakašim

Note nos. 5 and 6, where no contraction takes place, and nos. 9 and 10, where /t/ > /š/ before ...im. *v.* B.2.1, above, paradigm for 2 - 3'.

2. Reply to the questions in each exchange as indicated.

2.1 Answer with 21 - 3 *or* 3′ imperative on the model:

Question: ka-kanawêlimânaw nâ?
Shall we (21) keep him?
Reply: môla wayêš ihkin, kanawêlimâtâk piko.
It doesn't matter, let's keep him.

		(Check column)
1.	ka-kamawêlimânaw nâ?	kanawêlimâtâk
2.	ka-ašamânaw nâ?	ašamâtâk
3.	ka-wîtapimânaw nâ?	wîtapimâtâk
4.	ka-kanawêlimânawak nâ?	kanawêlimâtânak
5.	ka-natomânawak nâ?	natomâtânak
6.	ka-kakwêcimânawak nâ?	kakwêcimâtânak
7.	ka-ašamimânawa nâ ostêsa?	ašamimâtâna
8.	ka-wîtapimimânawa nâ ostêsa?	wîtapimimâtâna
9.	ka-natomimânawa nâ ostêsa?	natomimâtâna

2.2 In the following drill 3, 3p and 3′ objects have been scrambled. Answer with the 21 imperative for the appropriate object on the pattern:

Question: ka-kihciwilânawak nâ astisak?
Shall we carry his mitts away?
Reply: Twoyêhk (immediately) kihciwilâtânak.
Let's carry them away immediately.

Note 21 - 3 replies below where final /k/ is dropped and *v.* NOTE following E. Listening In.

1.	ka-kihciwilânawak nâ astisak?	kihciwilâtânak
2.	ka-išiwilânaw nâ astis?	išiwilâtâ
3.	ka-têhtalânaw nâ astis?	têhtalâtâ
4.	ka-akolânawak nâ astisak?	akolâtânak
5.	ka-otinimânawa nâ otastisa?	otinimâtâna
6.	ka-tahkonimânawa nâ otastisa?	tahkonimâtâna
7.	ka-tahkonânawak nâ astisak?	tahkonâtânak
8.	ka-otinânaw nâ astis?	otinâtâ
9.	ka-akolânaw nâ astis?	akolâtâ
10.	ka-kîšônânawak nâ astisak?	kîšônâtânak

11.	ka-kicistâpâwalânaw nâ astis?	kicistâpâwalâtâ
12.	ka-têhtalimânawa nâ otastisa?	têhtalimâtâna
13.	ka-sâminânawak nâ astisak?	sâminâtânak
14.	ka-kicistâpâwalimânawa nâ otastisa?	kicistâpâwalimâtâna
15.	ka-sâminânaw nâ astis?	sâminâtâ

2.3 Answer as in 2.2 above but on the pattern:

Question: ka-kîwêhtahâw nâ?
Will you (2) take him home?
Reply: êhê, kîwêhtahâtâk tâpiskôc.
Yes, let's both take him home.

1.	ka-kîwêhtahâw nâ?	kîwêhtahâtâk
2.	ka-kîwêhtahâwak nâ?	kîwêhtahâtânak
3.	ka-kîwêhtahimâwa nâ ošîma?	kîwêhtahimâtâna
4.	ka-natohtawânaw nâ?	natohtawâtâk
5.	ka-natohtawânawak nâ?	natohtawâtânak
6.	ka-natohtawimânawa nâ otôtêma?	natohtawimâtânih
7.	ka-pêhtawânaw nâ?	pêhtawâtâk
8.	ka-wîcihâwak nâ?	wîcihâtânak
9.	ka-pêhtawimânawa nâ otôtêma?	pêhtawimâtânih
10.	ka-wîcêwimânawa nâ otôtêma?	wîcêwimâtânih
11.	ka-miskawânawak nâ?	miskawâtânak
12.	ka-wîcêwânaw nâ?	wîcêwâtâk
13.	ka-wîcihimâwa nâ ošîma?	wîcihimâtânih
14.	ka-pîhtokwahâw nâ?	pîhtokwahâtâk
15.	ka-wîcihâw nâ?	wîcihâtâk

2.4 Answer as in 2.2, but using the pattern,

Question: âšay nâ ka-pâskiswânaw?
Shall we (21) shoot him now?
Reply: cikêma, pâskiswâtâk anohc.
Certainly, let's shoot him (right) now.

1.	âsay nâ ka-pâskiswânaw?	pâskiswâtâk
2.	âšay nâ ka-pâskiswânawak?	pâskiswâtânak
3.	âšay nâ ka-pâskisomânawa oniskima?	pâskisomâtânih
4.	âšay nâ ka-mâcišomânawa oniskima?	mâcišomâtânih
5.	âšay nâ ka-mâcišwânawak?	mâcišwâtânak
6.	âšay nâ ka-cîstahomânawa ošîma?	cîstahomâtânih
7.	âšay nâ ka-mâcišwânaw?	mâcišwâtâk

8.	âšay nâ ka-šîwahwânaw?	šîwahwâtâk
9.	âšay nâ ka-šîwahwânawak?	šîwahwâtânak
10.	âšay nâ ka-cîstahwânawak?	cîstahwâtânak
11.	âšay nâ ka-cîstahwânaw?	cîstahwâtâk
12.	âšay nâ ka-šîwahomânawa oniskima?	šîwahomâtânih

2.5 Answer as in 2.4, above, but on the pattern,

Question: ka-têpwâtânaw nâ?
Reply: môla, 'kâwila têpwâtâtâk.

1.	ka-têpwâtânaw nâ?	têpwâtâtâk
2.	ka-têpwâtânawak nâ?	têpwâtâtânak
3.	ka-têpwâtimânawa nâ ostêsa?	têpwâtimâtânih
4.	ka-nakatimânawa nâ ostêsa?	nakatimâtânih
5.	ka-nakatânawak nâ?	nakatâtânak
6.	ka-tahkoskâtânaw nâ?	tahkoskâtâtâk
7.	ka-tahkoskâtimânawa nâ?	tahkoskâtimâtânih
8.	ka-nakatânaw nâ?	nakatâtâk
9.	ka-ocipitânaw nâ?	ocipitâtâk
10.	ka-tahkoskâtânawak nâ?	tahkoskâtânik
11.	ka-ocipitimânawa nâ ostêsa?	ocipitimâtânih
12.	ka-ocipitânawak nâ?	ocipitâtânak

3. Reply to the questions in each exchange as indicated.

3.1 Answer with 2p - 3, 3p or 3' imperative on the model:

Question: kiwî-têhtalâw nâ askihk?
Do you want to set the kettle (on something)?
Reply: môla, têhtalihk kîlawâw.
No, you (2p) set it.

1.	kiwî-têhtalâw nâ askihk?	têhtalihk
2.	kiwî-akolâw nâ askihk?	akolihk
3.	kiwî-išiwilâw nâ askihk?	išiwilihk
4.	kiwî-kihciwilâw nâ askihk?	kihciwilihk
5.	kiwî-têhtalâwak nâ askihkwak?	têhtalihkok
6.	kiwî-akolâwak nâ askihkwak?	akolihkok
7.	kiwî-išiwilâwak nâ askihkwak?	išiwilihkok
8.	kiwî-kihciwilâwak nâ askihkwak?	kihciwilihkok
9.	kiwî-têhtalimâwa nâ cwân otaskihkwa?	têhtalimâhk
10.	kiwî-akolimâwa nâ cwân otaskihkwa?	akolimâhk

11. kiwî-išiwilimâwa nâ cwân otaskihkwa? — išiwilimâhk
12. kiwî-kihciwilimâwa nâ cwân otaskihkwa? — kihciwilimâhk

3.2 In the following, 3, 3p and 3′ objects have been scrambled. Answer with the 2p imperative for the appropriate object.

Reply: cikêmânima, _______________.

1. n'ka-kotinânânak nâ atimwak? — kotinihkok
2. n'ka-wîtapimânân nâ atim? — wîtapimihk
3. n'ka-âlimômânân nâ atim? — âlimômihk
4. n'ka-natomimânâna nâ otêma? — natomimâhk
5. n'ka-tahkonânânak nâ atimwak? — tahkonihkok
6. n'ka-ašamimânâna nâ otêma? — ašamimâhk
7. n'ka-otinimânâna nâ otêma? — otinimâhk
8. n'ka-kanawêlimânânak nâ atimwak? — kanawêlimihkok
9. n'ka-kanawêlimânân nâ atim? — kanawêlimihk
10. n'ka-kîšônânân nâ atim? — kîšônihk
11. n'ka-otinânânak nâ atimwak? — otinihkok
12 n'ka-kotinânân nâ atim? — kotinihk
13. n'ka-sâminimânâna nâ otêma? — sâminimâhk
14. n'ka-âlimômânânak nâ atimwak? — âlimômihkok
15. n'ka-kanawêlimimânâna nâ otêma? — kanawêlimimâhk

3.3 Answer on the model:

Question: n'ka-kî-kîwêhtahânân nâ?
Will we be able to take him back?
Reply: 'kâwil' êškwâ kîwêhtahihk.
Don't (2p) take him back yet.

1. n'ka-kî-kîwêhtahânân nâ? — kîwêhtahihk
2. n'ka-kî-kîwêhtahânânak nâ? — kîwêhtahihkok
3. n'ka-kî-mowimânâna nâ oniskima? — mowimâhk
4. n'ka-kî-têpwâtânânak nâ? — têpwâtihkok
5 n'ka-kî-wîcêwânân nâ? — wîcêwihk
6. n'ka-kî-wîcêwimânâna nâ omošôma? — wîcêwimâhk
7. n'ka-kî nakatânân nâ? — nakatihk
8. n'ka-kî-mawâpîstawânân nâ? — mawâpîstawihk
9. n'ka-kî-ocipitânânak nâ? — ocipitihkok
10. n'ka-kî-wîcihimânâna nâ otôtêma? — wîcihimâhk

3.4 Answer on the model:

Question:	n'ka-kî-pâskiswânânak nâ? Will we be able to shoot them?
Reply:	Tâpwê, pâskisohkok. Certainly, (2p) shoot them.

		(Check column)
1.	n'ka-kî-pâskiswânânak nâ?	pâskisohkok
2.	n'ka-kî-pâskiswânân nâ?	pâskisohk
3.	n'ka-kî-pâskisomânâna nâ otêma?	pâskisomâhk
4.	n'ka-kî-otâmahwânân nâ?	otâmahohk
5.	n'ka-kî-cîkahwânânak nâ?	cîkahohkok
6.	n'ka-kî-kîsisomânâna nâ onamêsima?	kîsisomâhk
7.	n'ka-kî-otâmahomânâna nâ otôtêma?	otâmahomâhk
8.	n'ka-kî-mâcišwânân nâ?	mâcišohk
9.	n'ka-kî-kîsiswânânak nâ?	kîsisohkok
10.	n'ka-kî-cîkahomânâna nâ omistikoma?	cîkahomâhk

4. Answer each set of exchanges on the pattern indicated.

4.1 Answer with the 2 - 1 imperative on the model:

Question:	ka-kî-wâpamitin nâ? May I see you?
Reply:	môla, 'kâwil' êškwâ wâpamin. No, don't see me yet.

1.	ka-kî-wâpamitin nâ?	wâpamin
2.	ka-kî-wanâhitin nâ?	wanâhin
3.	ka-kî-mîlitin nâ?	mîlin
4.	ka-kî-išiwilitin nâ?	išiwilin
5.	ka-kî-sâminitin nâ?	sâminin
6.	ka-kî-kîwêhtahitin nâ?	kîwêhtahin
7.	ka-kî-wîcihitin nâ?	wîcihin
8.	ka-kî-wîcêwitin nâ?	wîcêwin
9.	ka-kî-pêšîtin (*or* pêšiwitin) nâ?	pêšiwin
10.	ka-kî-wîhtamâtin nâ?	wîhtamawin
11.	ka-kî-cîstahotin nâ?	cîstahon
12.	ka-kî-nakatitin nâ?	nakašin

4.2 To the following 1p - 2 questions reply with the 2p - 1 imperative form:

Question: ka-mâkwahpititinân nâ?
Shall we tie you (2) up?
Reply: 'kâwil' êškwâ mâkwahpišik.
Don't (2p) tie me up yet.

		(Check column)
1.	ka-mâkwahpititinân nâ?	mâkwahpišik
2.	ka-nakatitinân nâ?	nakašik
3.	ka-mâcišotinân nâ?	mâcišok
4.	kî-pâsotinân nâ?	pâsok
5.	ka-otâmahotinân nâ?	otâmahok
6.	ka-natohtâtinân nâ?	natohtawik
7.	ka-miskâtinân nâ?	miskawik
8.	ka-mawâpîstâtinân nâ?	mawâpîstawik
9.	ka-wîcêwitinân nâ?	wîcêwik
10.	ka-pîhtokwahitinân nâ?	pîhtokwahik
11.	ka-wîcihitinân nâ?	wîcihik
12.	ka-ayamihitinân nâ?	ayamihik

4.3 To the following 1 *or* 1p - 2p questions reply with the 2 - 1p imperative on the model:

Question: ka-kî-'nâtawimitinâwâw nâ?
Can I (*or* we) examine you (pl.)?
Reply: cikêmânima, 'nâtawiminân.
Of course, examine us.

1.	ka-kî-'nâtawimitinâwâw nâ?	'nâtawiminân
2.	ka-kî-ašitakimitinâwâw nâ?	ašitakiminân
3.	ka-kî-têhtalitinâwâw nâ?	têhtalinân
4.	ka-kî-wanâhitinâwâw nâ?	wanâhinân
5.	ka-kî-sâminitinâwâw nâ?	sâmininân
6.	ka-kî-ayamihitinâwâw nâ?	ayamihinân
7.	ka-kî-payêhkihitinâwâw [clean you up] nâ?	payêhkihinân
8.	ka-kî-pîhtokwahitinâwâw nâ?	pîhtokwahinân
9.	ka-kî-wîcêwitinâwâw nâ?	wîcêwinân
10.	ka-kî-pêhtâtinâwâw nâ?	pêhtawinân
11.	ka-kî-otâmahotinâwâw nâ?	otâmahonân
12.	ka-kî-têpwâtitinâwâw nâ?	têpwâšinân

5. Recognition Drills

5.1 Show your recognition of the imperative forms by expanding the full sentence with the correct one of the two nouns in brackets. (On the recording there will be two repetitions of the partial sentence, a pause for you to repeat the full sentence expanded with the bracketed form, and a check repetition.)

		(Check column)
1.	mîl (nâpêšiš ~ nâpêšiša) ômêliw cîmâniliw.	nâpêšiš
2.	kîšôhâtâk (awâšiš ~ awâšišak).	awâšiš
3.	išiwilihkok (ililiwak ~ ililiw) âhkosîwikamikohk.	ililiwak
4.	têpwâšim (otânisa ~ kitânis) mwêhci anohc.	otânisa
5.	êkoši natomimâtânih (atim ~ otêma).	otêma
6.	kîwêhtahimâhk (ocawâšimiša ~ awâšišak).	ocawâšimiša
7.	awihâsomik (nâpêwa ~ nâpêwak) nipâskisikaniliw.	nâpêwak
8.	êkâwila otâmahwâtânik (awâšiš ~ awâšišak).	awâšišak
9.	wîcêwim (otôtêma ~ kitôtêm).	otôtêma
10.	wîcêwihkok (ililiwa ~ ililiwak).	ililiwak
11.	ayamiy (nâpêšiš ~ nâpêšišak).	nâpêšiš
12.	nâtawi-miskâm (nitêm ~ otêma).	otêma
13.	natohtawihkok (nâpêšiš ~ nâpêšišak).	nâpêšišak
14.	tahkonik (ašikanak ~ ašikana).	ašikanak
15.	kîwêhtahik (awâšiša ~ awâšišak).	awâšišak
16.	wanâhâtânak (ililiwak ~ ililiwa).	ililiwak
17.	kanawâpam (atim ~ atimwak).	atim
18.	'nâtawimim (nimis ~ omisa).	omisa
19.	natomihk (kitêmiwâw ~ kitêmiwâwak).	kitêmiwâw
20.	akimihkok (apwoyak ~ apwoya).	apwoyak
21.	êkoši natohtawâtâk (awâšiš ~ awâšišak).	awâšiš
22.	têpwâš (okosisa ~ kikosis).	kikosis
23.	mîlimâhk (kôhtâwîwâw ~ ôhtâwîwâwa).	ôhtâwîwâwa
24.	ayamihimâtânih (ošîma ~ nišîm).	ošîma

5.2 Turn the following imperative forms into statements, in each case using the independent order with the same subject and object: *e.g.,*

Cue: wîhtamawihk
(2p) Tell him.
Reply: kiwîhtamawâwâw
You (2p) are telling him.

1.	wîhtamawihk.	kiwîhtamawâwâw
2.	mîlin kotak apwoy.	kimîlin
3.	'nâtawiminân.	ki'nâtawiminân
4.	kakwêcimin.	kikakwêcimin

5.	kîwêhtahihk.	kikîwêhtahâwâw
6.	'kâwila pâskison.	môla kipâskison
7.	cîstahonân.	kicîstahonân
8.	êkâwila otâmahon.	môla kitotâmahon
9.	kanawâpaminân.	kikanawâpaminân
10.	êkâwila nakašin.	môla kinakašin
11.	akimâtânik šîšîpak.	kitakimânawak
12.	pêhin.	kipêhin.
13.	išiwilihk âhkosîwikamikohk.	kitišiwilâwâw
14.	wîcêwik.	kiwîcêwâwak *or* kiwîcêwinâwâw
15.	êkâwila nakaš.	môla kinakatâw
16.	natohtawihkok.	kinatohtawâwâwak
17.	êkâwila pêhimâhk.	môla kipêhimâwâwa.
18.	mawâpîstawâtânik.	kimawâpîstawânawak
19.	natomâtâk atim.	kinatomânaw
20.	cîstahom nêsta ostêsa.	kicîstahomâwa
21.	têpwâtimâtânih ocawâsimiša.	kitêpwâtimânawa
22.	pâskisomâhk otêma.	kipâskisomâwâwa

6. Complete each sentence with an appropriate verb form from the stems listed on the left. (Before you tackle this re-read B.1.1 through 1.3 **carefully**, and don't forget Unit 15.B.1.)

As the Public Health Nurse (PHN) ties her canoe to a wharf, one of the village dogs approaches menacingly. Turning to her assistant (atôskêlâkan), she says:

tahkoskât-, pimot- ______________ âšokan. __________ kêkwâliw ana atim.
pakitin-, natom- ______________ apwoyak cîmânihk. __________ mâka aniki iskwêwak wâskâhikanihk.

On entering the house that serves as a clinic, the PHN observes a mother with a fretful child.

kisiso- ______________ awa awâšiš, she remarks.
kanawâpam- Let's look at her first: ______________ pitamâ. Hm-m!
kanawâpam- Nasty throat! ________________ olihkwa.
nanâtawim- êškwâ __________________ misiwê kotakiyak pâtimâ.

At this point the local doctor arrives and indicates that he's ready to see a patient. Call someone else, he says
têpwât to the assistant: ____________ kotak 'wênihkân.
pêci-pîhtokah- Bring him in and take his temperature: ____________;
otin- ___________ mâka opîwâpiskom; then hand me a
mîl- thermometer; and check his pulse: _________ mâka ani

kotin-	'nâtawicikan; __________ nêsta otêhiyâpiy ospitonihk. n'ka-
cîstahw-	cîstahwâw nâ? inquires the nurse. êhê, __________, replies
	the doctor. Turning to two patients with a skin complaint,
âpacih-	he prescribes: tâpiskôc __________ awa sôp. As they leave,
	he points to their mitts on a chair and says:
otin-	____________ kitastisiwâwak.
	Turning to the mother whose child had a fever he says to
	her, Let us know how he gets on:
kiskêlihtamoh-	____________________ tân' êspalit.
	Someone, on the way out, stubs a cigarette on the floor.
	The assistant points to a sign which reads: êkâwila ililiwak
cahkišim-	______-_______________ sikalêta mohcihtak.
	A further sign just before the exit carries the request:
kipah-	êkoši ______-_______________ ililiwak iškwâhtêmiliw.

D. CONVERSATION PRACTICE

1. Review the Basic Conversation carefully as for former units, making sure that you can give the Cree equivalents for items in the English column.

2. Check the drills. You should be able to select or provide the correct form of the imperative as required, or recognize what form is being used, before you proceed to Unit 17. There should be no marked hesitation in your responses.

3. Look over the subject matter of the Basic Conversations and make a list of topics covered. This not only refreshes older material in your mind but helps broaden the area in which you can communicate. Then undertake a conversation with a friend, ranging over a variety of such topics. Make as full use as you can of imperative forms but try to keep the conversation from degenerating into a sequence of mere "Shall I...?" "Yes, do so-an-so", exchanges.

4. Imagine yourself to be operating a dispensary. Let someone else take the part of the patient. The following are some additional terms, useful in the clinic:

mitôn- (nitôn-, etc.)	NDI	mouth
mispiton- (nispiton-, etc.)	NDI	arm
miskât- (niskât-, etc.)	NDI	leg
misit- (nisit-, etc.)	NDI	foot
wîsakêliht-	VTI	have a pain
tânt' êši-wîsakêl'taman?		Where do you have a pain?
pihcišitiso-	VAI	cut oneself accidentally.
pâkisê-	VII	be swollen
sîtwahpit-	VTA / VTI	bandage s.o./ s.t, bind s.o./ s.t as for a splint
n'ka-sîtwahpitâw		I shall bandage him
sîtwahpicikan-	NI	bandage, binding
pahkišin-	VAI	fall; have a rupture
têwistikwânê-	VAI	have a headache
matay- (natay-, etc.)	NDI	belly, stomach
pâsitêniko-	VAI	have heartburn, stomach distress
mošihtâ-	VAI-T	feel s.t., experience a sensation of s.t.

apišîš n'têhi nimošihtân		I feel my heart a little (Probably indigestion is what often gives rise to this expression.)
lîsamawi-n'tohkolon-	NI	bicarbonate of soda *Cf. MC* -natohkoliy-.
otwâwê-	VAI	have hiccoughs
pêkatê-	VAI	belch
mîsî-	VAI	defecate
tâpitâw nâ mîsîw?		Does he have regular bowel movements?
mîsîwi-n'tohkolon-	NI	castor oil *Cf. MC* -natohkoliy-.
walawîwi-n'tohkolon-	NI	milk of magnesia *Cf. MC* -natohkoliy-.
maškawisî-	VAI	be healthy
wîsakikohtaskwê-	VAI	have a sore throat

E. LISTENING IN

Alik: akimik šîšîpak anta ašiškîhk.

Mâtyiw: n'ka-pâskiswâwak nâ?

Alik: môla. 'kâwil' êškwâ pâskisok. ka-wîhtamâtin ispî.[1] wîhtamaw cwân 'ci-kôskawâtapit.[2] wêsâ mistahi[3] têpwêw. misiwê ta ohpahowak.[4]

Mâtyiw: wîhtamawimâtânih wîwa; wîla mâka ta-wîhtamawêw cwâna.

Alik: kîwêtâk êko, mîna mâka ka-pêci-itohtânânaw nâkê. n'ka-išiwilâw nišîm n'tohkolon-iskwêwa.

Mâtyiw: âhkosiw nâ?

Alik: âhkosiw olihkwa. "nîšo mistikwâni-n'tohkoliya mîl, kîšôy mâka," kî-itwêliwa n'tohkolon-iskwêwa otâkošîhk.

Mâtyiw: êkoši, kata-cîstahwêw.

Alik: 'kâwila nîla wîhtamawin. wîla wîhtamaw,—'yâkwâ! tânt' êtohtêyan? pakitinik kitapwoyak anta âšokanihk.

Mâtyiw: môla wayêš n'ka-ihtin. mâškôc nêsta anta n'tohkolon ta-ihtâw. kakwêcimik tâpiskôc. kîla nêsta kišîm kakwêcimihkok tâpiskôc.

Alik: êko itohtêtâk, išiwilâtâk n'tohkolonikamikohk anohc. têpwâšim okâwiya. išiwilâtânik aniki tâpiskôc.

Mâtyiw: êko âpacihâtânik aniki apwoyak. môla wayêš ilâpatan[5] anta ê-apicik âšokanihk. pêyak pakitin cîmânihk, otin mâka ana kotak. n'ka-âpahên anohc mwêhci cîmân.

NOTE the forms, kîwêtâk, itohtêtâk and išiwilâtâk above. The speaker whose voice you hear on the recording comes from Moose Factory where the final /k/ in the forms noted is usually dropped. You will hear them quite clearly recorded as kîwêtâ, itohtêtâ and išiwilâtâ.

In liturgical texts in Moose Cree a further variant on the 21 imperative suffix occurs. Final /k/ is replaced by /w/, yielding, *e.g.,* ayamihâtâ**w** - Let us pray. In Plains Cree the corresponding form is ayamihâtâ**n**.

[1] ispî — IPC — when
[2] kôskawâtapi- — VAI — sit still 'ci-kôskawâtapit to sit still
[3] wêsâ mistahi — too much
[4] ohpaho- — VAI — fly up
[5] ilâpatan- — VII — be good for

F. REFERENCE LIST

alôminaskw-	NA	linseed meal
astis-	NA	mitt
atôskêlâkan-	NA	servant
cahkišim-	VTA	stub s.o. (a cigarette): not used for "stubbing" a toe. *v.* pišošimiko-.
cîstah-	VTI	puncture s.t., prick s.t.
cîstahw-	VTA	puncture s.o., prick s.o., give an injection to s.o.
cîstêmâw-	NA	tobacco
ilâpatan-	VII	be good for
ispî	IPC	when
kisiso-	VAI	be warm (over -warm), have a fever
kiskêlihtamoh-	VTA	inform s.o., *lit.*, make s.o. to know
kîsôsi-	VAI	be (snug) warm
kîšowâ-	VII	be warm
kîšôh-	VTA	keep s.o. warm (as with a blanket)
kîšôn-	VTA	keep s.o. warm (by holding him)
kotin-	VTA / VTI	test s.o./ s.t. by hand
kôskawâtapi-	VAI	sit still, sit quietly
lîsamawi-natohkoliy-	NI	bicarbonate of soda
maškawisî-	VAI	be healthy
matay-	NDI	belly, stomach: katay-, natay-, watay-, etc.
mâciš-	VTI	cut s.t.
mâcišw-	VTA	cut s.o., operate (surgically) on s.o.
milihkw-	NDA	tonsil: kilihkwak, nilihkwak, olihkwa, etc.
misit-	NDI	foot: kisit-, nisit-, osit-, etc.
miskât-	NDI	leg: kiskât-, niskât-, oskât-, etc.
mispiton-	NDI	arm: kispiton-, nispiton-, ospiton-, etc.
mistahi	IPC	much
mistikwân-	NDI	head: kistikwân-, nistikwân-, ostikwân, etc.
mistikwâni-natohkoliy-	NI	aspirin: *lit.*, head-medicine; 3 poss. omistikwâni-natohkolîm.

mitêhi-	NDI	heart: kitêhi-, nitêhi-, otêhi-, etc.
mitêhiyâpiy-	NDI	artery: *lit.*, heart line *v.* nitêhiyâpiy-, otêhiyâpiy-.
mitôn-	NDI	mouth: kitôn-, nitôn-, otôn-, etc.
mîsî-	VAI	defecate *v.* šiki-.
mîsîwi-natohkoliy-	NI	castor oil *v.* walawîwi-natohkoliy-.
mohcihtak	IPC	on the floor
mošihtâ-	VAI-T	feel s.t., experience sense of s.t.
nanâtawim-	VTA rdpl.	examine s.o.
natoht-	VTI	listen to s.t.
natohtaw-	VTA	listen to s.o.
natom-	VTA	call s.o., invite s.o., "beckon to" s.o.
'nâtawicikan-	NI	thermometre
'nâtawim-	VTA	*contraction of* nanâtawim- *q.v.*
nitêhiyâpiy-	NDI	my artery *v.* mitêhiyâpiy-, otêhiyâpiy-.
ohpaho-	VAI	fly up
ohtê-	VII	boil *v.* oso-.
olihkwa	NDA	his tonsils *v.* milihkw-.
o...manicôš...im...i-	VAI	have a boil, *lit.*,an "insect". While use of manicôš- NA for "boil" is common, the term in much Swampy Cree country is kâsîp- NA: nit...ô...kâsîp...im...in I have a boil. A further term is o...sîkihp...im...iw *v.* sîkihp-.
oso-	VAI	boil *v.* ohtê-.
ospiton-	NDI	his arm *v.* mispiton-.
otêhi-	NDI	his heart *v.* mitêhi-.
otêhiyâpiy-	NDI	his artery *v.* mitêhiyâpiy-, nitêhiyâpiy-.
otwâwê-	VAI	have hiccoughs
pahkišin-	VAI	fall; have a rupture
pâhpih-	VTA	laugh at s.o.
pâhpitâ-	VAI-T	laugh at s.t.
pâkisê-	VII	be swollen
pâsitêniko-	VAI	have heartburn, have stomach distress
pêh-	VTA	wait for s.o.
pêhtâ-	VAI-T	wait for s.t. (Not to be confused with pêtâ- VAI-T bring s.t.)
pêkatê-	VAI	belch
pihcišitiso-	VAI	cut oneself accidentally
pimot-	VTA	throw (s.t.) at s.o.
pîhtokah-	VTA	bring s.o. in
pîhtokwah-	VTA	bring s.o. in

sâmin-	VTA / VTI	touch s.o./ s.t.
sikalêt-	NA	cigarette
sîkihp-	NA	boil (swelling on skin)
sîtwahpicikan-	NI	bandage, binding
sîtwahpit-	VTA / VTI	bandage s.o., bind up s.t.
sôp-	NA	soap
šiki-	VAI	urinate *v.* mîsî-.
tahkisi-	VAI	grow cool, cool off
tahkoskât-	VTA / VTI	step on s.o./ s.t.
tâpitâw	IPC	regularly
têhtal-	VTA	set s.o. upon, place s.o. upon
têhtapiwin-	NI	seat, chair
têhtastâ-	VAI-T	set s.t. upon, place s.t. upon
têwistikwânê-	VAI	have a headache
twoyêhk	IPC	immediately, directly
walawîwi-n'tohkoliy-	NI	milk of magnesia *v.* mîsîwi-natohkoliy-.
wêsâ	IPC	too, too much so
wîcih-	VTA	help s.o.
wîsakêliht-	VTI	have a pain
wîsakikohtaskwê-	VAI	have a sore throat

G. REVIEW

16.A Kakwêcihkêmôwina—Questions

Answer each question with a full sentence, expanding your reply if you are able. Draw on any of past conversations, drills, and your own imagination for materials.

1. n'ka-pimotimâwa nâ kêkwâliw otêma?
2. mâškôc n'ka-kî-'nâtawimânânik kotakiyak pâtimâ, manâ?
3. n'ka-têpwâtânânik nâ aniki iskwêwak?
4. n'ka-têhtalâw nâ awâšiš têhtapiwinihk?
5. kiwî-nanâtawimâw nâ nikosis?
6. ka-nakatânawak nâ apwoyak cîmânihk?
7. ka-nakatimânawa nâ cim otapwoya cîmânihk?
8. kata-kî-âpacihimêw nâ cêniy kikâwiya otaskihkolîw?
9. ta-kî-kihciwilêw nâ cwân otapwoya?
10. ka-tahkonâw nâ awâšiš, nêstapiko n'ka-tahkonâw nâ nîla?
11. natawêlihtamwak nâ mistikwâni-natohkolîliw?
12. n'ka-išicišahamawânânik nâ natohkolîliw?
13. kiwî-wâpahtênâwâw nâ n'tôški-pâskisikan?
14. ka-wîhtamâtin nâ tân' êspalit?
15. n'ka-kî-kanawâpamâwak nâ kilihkwak?
16. n'ka-kî-kanawâpamimâwa nâ kicawâšimiš olihkwa?
17. ka-cîstahwânaw nâ awa ililiw?
18. ka-mîlitinân nâ sôp?
19. n'ka-pêhâw nâ?
20. n'ka-pêhâwak nâ awâšišak?
21. ka-pêhitinân nâ?
22. n'ka-nanâtawimânânik nâ?
23. tâni kâ-itwêt sikarêta ohci?

16.B Naškwêwašihtwâwina—Answers

Formulate questions to which the following statements might be reasonable answers.

1. êkoši pitamâ kata-nanâtawimêw n'tohkolon-iskwêw.
2. êhê, pakitinam omaskisina mohcihtak.
3. natomihk kitêmiwâw.
4. sakahpitihkok kitêmiwâwak.
5. êhê, išicišahamâhkok ostostocikanâpôliw.
6. mîl awâšiš nîšo mistikwâni-natohkoliya.
7. awihin kitastotin. kimiwan.
8. kiskêlihtamohinân tân' êspalit.
9. êkoši, cîstahwâtânik misiwê awâšišak.
10. êkoši, cîstahwâtâ(k) awa awâšiš.
11. cîstahomâtânih cwân ocawâšimiša.
12. išicišahamawinân namêsak, ka-tipahamâtinân mâka.
13. môla, êkâwila âpacihik aniki apwoyak.
14. êhê, kociškawik ôko ašikanak.
15. êkâwila âpacihihk ana askihk. kotakiyak âpacihihkok.
16. tâpwê, kakwêcimin.
17. išiwilik astisak.
18. êkâwila âpaciy alôminask mwêhci anohc. pêy 'ci-tahkisit.
19. cikêmânima, pêci-pîhtokahik. tahkâyâw walawîtimihk.
20. tâpwê, wâpahtilinân kitôški-pâskisikan.
21. namawila awêna kata-nakatêw apwoya âšokwanihk.
    [awêna here = awênihkân]
22. natom kotak awêna. n'ka-nanâtawimâw mwêhci anohc.
23. kî-itwêw, "êkâwila ililiwak kata-tahkoskâtêwak sikarêta mohcihtak".
24. môla. mîl nîla n'cîmâniliw.

UNIT SEVENTEEN

A. BASIC CONVERSATION

Guess Again

Old Clara appears struggling up the river bank with a large, oblong pack over her shoulder. Two onlookers try to guess what's in the pack.

Cêniy:	wîwašiw	she is carrying (on her back)
	kišâstaw, mistahi wîwašiw.	Gosh, she's carrying a load!
	ohpinam	she lifts it
	kakwê-ohpinam	she tries to lift it
	mâšihtâw	she fights (with) it
	mâšihtâw nâ, nêstapiko kakwê-ohpinam?	Is she fighting with it or trying to lift it?
Sôsan:	wakîtatin	on top of the bank
	kospihtatâw	she's carrying it up the bank
	mâškôc wî-kospihtatâw. wakîtatin wî-iši-astâw.	I think she wants to carry it up and set it on top of the bank.
Cêniy:	'ci-lâsipêhtatât	that she carry it down
	ta-wêhtanôpan	it would be easy
	awasitê ta-wêhtanôpan 'ci-lâsipêhtatât.	It would be easier (for her) to carry it down.
	kêkwânihkân?	what sort of thing (is it)?
	apwêsiw	she is perspiring
	šâkoc apwêsiw! kêkwânihkân?	She sure is perspiring! What sort of thing is it?
Sôsan:	ê-kosikwahk	in its being heavy
	kinanâtoštahikân	you (2) are guessing
	ka-kî-nanâtoštahikân[1] nâ? išinâkwan ê-kosikwahk.	Can you guess? It looks heavy.

[1] Common local use: ka-kî-wihtên nâ? Can you tell (it)?

Cêniy:	kosikwan	it is heavy
	kây, klêra,—kosikwan nâ?	Hey, Clara,—is it heavy?
Klêra:	'ci-pimiwitâyân	that I can carry it about (in my arms)
	nîšwâ	twice
	lâhkašin	it is light (in weight)
	môla, lâhkašin. n'kaškihtân nîšwâ awasitê 'ci-pimiwitâyân	No, it's light. I can carry twice as much.
Sôsan:	atâmihk itêhkê	at the bottom
	apišâšin	it is small
	kahkahkîhkêyâw	it is square
	kahkahkîhkêyâw išpimihk, apišâšin mâka atâmihk itêhkê.	It's square at the top and small at the bottom.
Cêniy:	wâwiyêyâw	it is round (disk-like)
	wâwiyênâkwan	it looks round (disk-like)
	wâwiyênâkwan isa wîla ôta ohci.	It looks round from here.
Sôsan:	namês...iwan	it is a fish
	mâškôc namêsiwan.	Maybe it's a fish.
	wakîc	on top (of), at the top
	nôtimisiw	he is round (spherical *or* cylindrical)
	apišîšišiw	he is small
	namês ta-kî-nôtimisiw wakîc nêsta ta-apišîšišiw atâmihk.	A fish can be round at the top and small at the bottom.
Cêniy:	ê-kišipâk	in its ending
	cîpwâw	it is pointed
	pimic itêhkê	on the side (of an object)
	napakâw	it is flat
	napakâw nêsta pimic itêhkê, cîpwâw mâka ê-kišipâk.	It's flat on the side too, and pointed on the end.
Sôsan:	ê-kišipisicik	in their (*anim.*) ending
	cîposiwak	they are pointed
	napakisiwak	they are flat
	âtiht namêsak napakisiwak pimicitêhkê, cîposiwak mâka ê-kišipisicik.	Some fish are flat on the side and pointed on the end.

Cêniy:	mipwâm	thigh, back leg
	môs opwâm	a moose's leg
	mayêw[2] tâpiskôc môs opwâm.	It's not like a leg of moose.
Klêra:	kâšisiw	he is sharp
	lôskisiw	he is soft
	ê'kwâni tâpwê	that's so, that's right
	ê'kwâni tâpwê. tâpwê lôskisiw môs môla mâka nâspic kâšisiw.	That's so. A moose is soft all right, and not very sharp.
	tahkwâw	it is short
	tahkonikan	a handle
	kiwâpahtên nâ tahkonikan? nawac tahkwâw.	Do you see a handle? It's quite short.
Sôsan:	kihcipalihcikan	outboard motor, "kicker"
	kihcipalihcikan...iwan	it is a kicker
	êhê,—tâpwê kihcipalihcikaniwan.	Yes,—it's actually a kicker.
Klêra:	kiwî-lâsipânâwâw nâ?	are you (2p) coming down the bank?
	mayêw[2] wîla cîmân	it is not a canoe
	ê'kwâni tâpwê! tâpwê mayêw wîla cîmân.	That's right! It's certainly not a canoe.
	kiwî-lâsipânâwâw nâ?	Are you coming down the bank?
Cêniy:	'ci-wîcihikawiyin	that you (2) be helped
	kêkwân ohci? kin'tawêl'tên nâ 'ci-wîcihikawiyin?	Why? Do you need help?
Klêra:	n'ka-kospin	I'll come up the bank
	îkatêsik	get out of the way (2p)
	môla, îkatêsik nawac; n'ka-pêci-kospin mâka.	No, just stay out of the way and I'll come up.

2 *v.* Unit 3.A.2: mayêw tôwihkân.

B. DISCUSSION OF GRAMMAR

1. Describing Words

In "Cree Grammar" under the section Preference for Verbal Constructions (p. xxxii), it was noted that describing words in Cree are not adjectives. Some describing terms are verb or noun prefixes, like milo, oški, mistikwâni, etc.; but perhaps the great bulk of describing words which correspond to many of the most common English adjectives are intransitive verbs. Since nouns belong to one of two gender classes, *animate* or *inanimate*, describing verbs must show forms to go with both. Hence, one meets

VAI	mišikitiw	he is big	wîyatêlihtâkosiw	he is funny
VII	mišâw	it is big	wîyatêlihtâkwan	it is funny
VAI	pâhkosiw	he is dry	milwâšišiw	he is nice
VII	pâhkwâw	it is dry	milwâšin	it is nice

These describing verbs display all the features common to intransitive verbs, both *animate* and *inanimate*, and are conjugated regularly throughout (*v.* paradigm, Unit 3.B.l.2). Note also that, unlike VAI, VII *do* show a formal difference for singular versus plural subject in the obviative. (*v.* Drill 1.2, below.)

———DRILLS 1 AND 2———

2. Verbs of Being

Cree, unlike English, distinguishes between "be"

1. in the sense of "be located in a given place": *e.g.,* âšokwanihk ihtâw - he **is** at the wharf,
2. be in the sense of "equals, is to be identified as": *e.g.,* this **is** a canoe, and
3. be, in the sense of "exist": To **be** or not to **be** -, etc.

You are by now familiar with the first two types of be; but at this point we pause to consider type 2 at greater length. Sentences such as atim awa, This is a dog, and cîmân ôma, This is a canoe,.... so-called *equational sentences,* commonly require no verb (Unit 2.B.4.3). Others which use a particle or pronoun predicatively but fall rather into type 1: *e.g.,* tântê nôhtâwiy, Where is my father?—also require no verb. Drill 3 of this unit, however, demonstrates a regular pattern for expressing the predication, "he / it **is** (a) something", or in a fairly wide sense, "displays (the) characteristics of something". To the noun stem (represented by "something") is added the verbalizing affix, ...iw..., VAI stem vowel, ...i..., and the appropriate inflectional suffix: *e.g.,* ...iwiw. This is subject to the usual phonological conditioning.

acimošiš + ...iwiw > acimošišiwiw he is a puppy

atim (< atimw-) + ...iwiw > *atimwiwiw, which by /w + i > o / becomes the surface form, atimowiw he is a dog

okimâw
nâpêw + ...iwiw > *okimâwiwiw, *nâpêwiwiw, and by contraction,

okimâwiw he is the manager
nâpêwiw he is a man

ililiw
apwoy and other stems with a short vowel before final /w/ or /y/ also show contraction. The short vowel is lengthened, /y/ replaced by /w/, and the form then parallels okimâwiw: *e.g.,*

ililiw
apwoy + ...iwiw > *ililiwiwiw > ililîwiw he is an Indian
*apwoyiwiw > apwôwiw it is a paddle

Corresponding VII forms appear:

cîmân + ...iwan > cîmâniwan it is a boat, it is boat-like

mistik (< mistikw-) + ...iwan > *mistikwiwan, which by /w + i > o/ becomes mistikowan it is of wood, it is wooden

iškotêw + ...iwan > *iškotêwiwan, and by contraction becomes iškotêwan it is fiery

mêskanaw + ...iwan > *mêskanawiwan > mêskanâwan it is a path, it features a path

sîpiy *sîpiyiwan > sîpîwan it is supplied / with (a) river(s)

The affix, ...iw..., is a so-called *derivational* affix and changes the part of speech classification of the word from noun to verb.

As demonstrated in Drill 3 below, there is no single construction in English which matches exactly the area of meaning covered by the ...iw... affix. It is worth remembering that there are probably very few, if any, words and / or expressions in any language which bear a one to one semantic relationship to words and / or expressions in any other language. Even commonly occurring nouns: door, chair, and verbs: carry, walk, etc., often do not match their nearest equivalents in other languages exactly. Abstract words are particularly notorious in this respect. Similarly, the area of meaning covered by the predicative, verbalizing affix which we shall represent as {...IW...} may be shown to overlap several related areas in English. The solid circle below represents the area of meaning for a Cree speaker, the dot separated areas, those of an English speaker.

———DRILL 3———

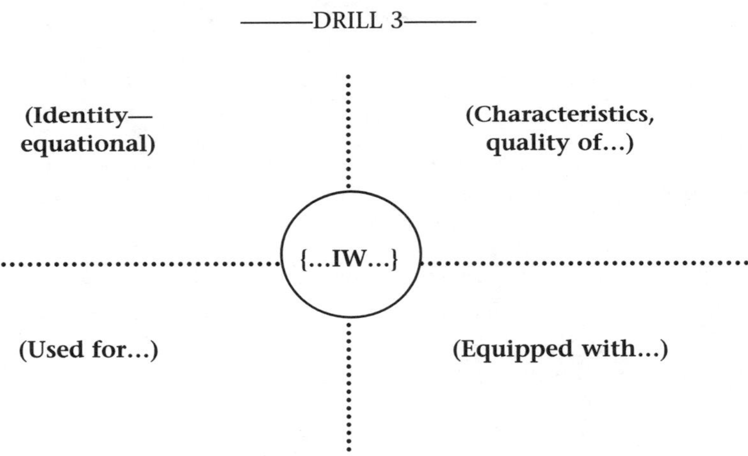

3. Compound Stems with ohci

The use of ohci in a compound stem with the meaning of "from" has already been discussed (Unit 11.B.1.4.i and Unit 14.B.2): *e.g.,* ka-kî-kâhcit-inâw alapîhk - you can catch it from a net. The same construction occurs with expressions of time:

âšay nâ kinwêš kitôchi-ihtân ôta?	Have you been here long?
kêkišêp nâ kitôhci-pêhin?	Have you been waiting for me since this morning?

While the alternative usage: n'tâpatisin kêkišêp ohci, is quite acceptable, the use of ohci as preverb in a compound stem is normal and should be learned.

C. DRILLS

1. Inanimate Intransitive Verbs — VII: 0 and 0p, 0′ and 0′p subjects.

1.1 0 and 0p subjects. Drill down each column, then across each row. If using a recording, mimic the recorded voice as faithfully as you can.

0		0p	
milwâšin	it is nice	milwâšinwa	they are nice
apišâšin	" small	apišâšinwa	" small
pahkihtin	" falling	pahkihtinwa	" falling
ihtakwan	" (at a place)	ihtakwanwa	" (at a place)
wêhtan	" easy	wêhtanwa	" easy
kosikwan	" heavy	kosikwanwa	" heavy
napakâw	" flat	napakâwa	" flat
kâšâw	" sharp	kâšâwa	" sharp
lôskâw	" soft	lôskâwa	" soft
kinwâw	" long	kinwâwa	" long
tahkwâw	" short	tahkwâwa	" short
mišâw	" big	mišâwa	" big
kišitêw	" hot	kišitêwa	" hot
mayêw	" not	mayêwa	" not

1.2 0′ and 0′p subjects. Unlike VAI, VII *do* show a formal difference for singular versus plural subject in the obviative. Drill the following as above.

lâhkašiniliw	it is light	lâhkašiniliwa	they are light (weight)
wîhkašiniliw	" tasty	wîhkašiniliwa	" tasty
pahkihtiniliw	" falling	pahkihtiniliwa	" falling
nipîwaniliw	" wet	nipîwaniliwa	" wet
âlimaniliw	" difficult	âlimaniliwa	" difficult
kosikwaniliw	" heavy	kosikwaniliwa	" heavy
cîpwâliw	" pointed	cîpwâliwa	" pointed
maškawâliw	" hard	maškawâliwa	" hard
kinwâliw	" long	kinwâliwa	" long
tahkwâliw	" short	tahkwâliwa	" short
wâwiyêyâliw	" round disk-like	wâwiyêyâliwa	" round

kišitêliw	" hot	kišitêliwa	" hot
mayêliw	" not	mayêliwa	" not

2.1 Given a VII, produce the corresponding VAI form on the model:

Question: nipîwan nâ wâpwayân?
Is the blanket wet?
Reply: tâpwê, nipîwiw nêsta pahkwêšikan.
It is, and the flour is wet too.[1]

Repeat the question and provide the answer immediately. The recording will check you.

		(Check column)
1.	nipîwan nâ wâpwayân?	tâpwê, nipîwiw nêsta pahkwêšikan.
2.	kosikwan nâ wâpwayân?	kosikwatiw
3.	lâhkašin nâ wâpwayân?	lâhkacišiw
4.	nîskâw [damp] nâ wâpwayân?	nîskisiw
5.	lôskâw nâ wâpwayân?	lôskisiw
6.	pâhkwâw nâ wâpwayân?	pâhkosiw
7.	âliman nâ wâpwayân?	âlimisiw
8.	wêhtan nâ wâpwayân?	wêhtisiw
9.	âlimakihtêw nâ wâpwayân?	âlimakisow
10.	wêhtakihtêw nâ wâpwayân?	wêhtakisow

2.2 Given a VAI, drill as above producing the corresponding VII form on the model:

Question: kinosiw nâ apwoy?
Is the paddle long?
Reply: môla, kinwâw mâka wîla[2] tahkonikan.
No, but the *handle* is long.

		(Check column)
1.	kinosiw nâ apwoy?	môla, kinwâw mâka wîla tahkonikan.
2.	cîposiw nâ apwoy?	cîpwâw
3.	napakisiw nâ apwoy?	napakâw
4.	kâšisiw nâ apwoy?	kâšâw
5.	maškawisiw nâ apwoy?	maškawâw
6.	tahkosiw nâ apwoy?	tahkwâw

[1] A situation which may well arise when a canoe is proceeding through rough water.

[2] wîla here marks emphatic contrast.

7. mišikitiw nâ apwoy? — mišâw
8. apišîšišiw nâ apwoy? — apišâšin
9. wâwiyêsiw nâ apwoy ê-kišipisit? — wâwiyêyâw... ê-kišipâk.

2.3 Drill as in 2.1. above, on the model:

Question: nipîwanwa nâ maskisina?
Are the shoes wet?
Reply: tâpwê, nipîwiwak nêsta ašikanak.
Yes indeed, the socks are wet too.

		(Check column)
1.	nipîwanwa nâ maskisina?	tâpwê, nipîwiwak nêsta ašikanak.
2.	kosikwanwa nâ maskisina?	kosikwatiwak
3.	lâhkašinwa nâ maskisina?	lâhkacišiwak
4.	pâhkwâwa nâ maskisina?	pâhkosiwak
5.	lôskâwa nâ maskisina?	lôskisiwak
6.	nîskâwa nâ maskisina?	nîskisiwak
7.	âlimanwa nâ maskisina?	âlimisiwak
8.	wêhtanwa nâ maskisina?	wêhtisiwak
9.	âlimakihtêwa nâ maskisina?	âlimakisowak
10.	wêhtakihtêwa nâ maskisina?	wêhtakisowak

2.4 Drill as in 2.2 on the model:

Question: kinosiwak nâ âšokanak?
Are the wharves long?
Reply: môla mâškôc nâspic, kinwâwa mâka cîmâna.
Perhaps not very, but the canoes are long.

1.	kinosiwak nâ âšokanak?	môla mâškôc nâspic, kinwâwa mâka cîmâna.
2.	cîposiwak nâ âšokanak?	cîpwâwa
3.	napakisiwak nâ âšokanak?	napakâwa
4.	kâšisiwak nâ âšokanak?	kâšâwa
5.	maškawisiwak nâ âšokanak?	maškawâwa
6.	tahkosiwak nâ âšokanak?	tahkwâwa
7.	mišikitiwak nâ âšokanak?	mišâwa
8.	apišîšišiwak nâ âšokanak?	apišâšinwa
9.	lâhkacišiwak nâ âšokanak?	lâhkašinwa
10.	kosikwatiwak nâ âšokanak?	kosikwanwa
11.	wâwiyêsiwak nâ âšokanak ê-kišipisicik?	wâwiyêyâwa ... ê-kišipâki

2.5 Drill the question-answer exchanges on the pattern:

Question: kî-milwâšiniliw nâ ocîmân?
Was his canoe nice?
Reply: tâpwê, kî-milwâšiniliwa nîšo ocîmâna.
Yes indeed, both his canoes were nice.

		(Check column)
1.	kî-milwâšiniliw nâ ocîmân?	tâpwê, kî-milwâšiniliwa nîšo ocîmâna.
2.	kî-apišâšiniliw nâ ocîmân?	kî-apišâšiniliwa
3.	kî-ihtakwaniliw nâ ocîmân anta?	kî-ihtakwaniliwa... anta.
4	kî-kosikwaniliw nâ ocîmân?	kî-kosikwaniliwa
5.	kî-cîpwâliw nâ ocîmân?	kî-cîpwâliwa
6.	kî-pišišikwâliw [empty] nâ ocîmân?	kî-pišišikwâliwa
7.	kî-tahkwâliw nâ ocîmân?	kî-tahkwâliwa
8.	kî-mišâliw nâ ocîmân?	kî-mišâliwa
9.	kî-kinwâliw nâ ocîmân?	kî-kinwâliwa
10.	kî-kîšponêliw [full] nâ ocîmân?	kî-kîšponêliwa

3. Predication

3.1 Drill down each column, then across each row. If you are using a recording, repeat after the recorded voice. Each item consists of a noun, a verbalizing affix forming an intransitive verb stem, plus the appropriate inflectional ending. The meaning of the verbal affix is *He / it is* or *has the characteristics of* the noun which forms the initial part of the stem. NOTE the variant shapes of the verbal affix as conditioned by the phonemic shape of the noun stem.

namês...iwiw	namês...iwan
acimošiš...iwiw	acimošiš...iwan
natohkolon...iwiw	natohkolon...iwan
	cîmân...iwan
âhkik...owiw [seal]	âhkik...owan
atim...owiw	atim...owan
môs...owiw	môs...owan
okimâw...iw	iškotêw...an
nâpêw...iw	iškotêw...an
iskwêw...iw	pihkotêw...an
ililîwiw	alapîwan
okipahowêsîwiw	nipîwan
pilêsîwiw	ašiškîwan
awâšišîwiw	mêskanâwan

3.2 The verbalizing affix was glossed in the Basic Conversation as *he / it is*. As noted in B.2 above, however, its use and meaning cover a wider semantic area. Here are some further examples of the same affix.

3.2.1 *Manifests characteristics of...*	pahkwêšikan...iwiw	he is covered with flour, it is "floury"
	pihkotêw...an	it is covered with ashes, it is "ashy"
	iškotêw...an	it has fire in it (*said of a stove left untended for a long time*)
	šôliyân...iwiw	it has gold in it (*e.g.,* a stone)
	mîcim...iwan	it has food on it (*e.g.,* a knife)
	cîmân...iwan	it has boat characteristics (*e.g.,* an amphibious aircraft)
	mistik...owiw ...owan	it (a sled) is made of wood (a box)
	âlahkonâw...iw	he is under the species of bread (*said of Christ in Holy Communion*)
3.2.2 *Comes equipped with...*	astotin...iwan	comes with a hat (*as a parka*)
	wâpwayân...iwan	comes with a blanket (*e.g., a sleeping bag*)
	têhtapiwin...iwan	it is furnished with a chair (*e.g., a room*)
	nipêwin...iwan	it is furnished with a bed
	mîcisowinâhtik...owan	it comes with a table
	iškwâhtêm...iwan	it is provided with a door
	mâhkîwan	it has a tent on it (*e.g., a raft*)
	sîpîwan	it has rivers (*e.g., a trapping ground*)
3.2.3 *Is used for...*	âhkosîwikamik...owan	it (*a building*) is used for a hospital
	natohkolonikamik...owan	it is used for a dispensary, it is used for medicine storage
	atâwêwikamik...owan	it is used for a trading post
	ayamihêwikamik...owan	it is used for a church

Read over the discussion of this construction in Section B above. Note uses of this verbal affix in your conversation with Cree speakers and keep a list of examples. You may well discover still further areas of meaning where quite a different English translation from any of those suggested would more faithfully represent the meaning in Cree.

4. More Compound Stems with ohci

4.1 Drill the following question-answer sequence on the pattern:

Question: âšay nâ kinwêš kitôhci-ihtân ôta?
Have you been here (as of) long?
Reply: êhê, nawac kinwêš n'tôhci-ihtân ôta?
Yes, I've been here quite long.

The recording will check you.	**(Check column)**
1. âšay nâ kinwêš kitôhci-ihtân ôta?	n'tôhci-ihtân
2. âšay nâ kinwêš kitôhci-atâwân ôta?	n'tôhci-atâwân
3. âšay nâ kinwêš kitôhci-âpatisin ôta?	n'tôhci-âpatisin
4. âšay nâ kinwêš kitôhci-iskôliwin ôta?	n'tôhci-iskôliwin
5. âšay nâ kinwêš kitôhci-nipân ôta?	n'tôhci-nipân
6. âšay nâ kinwêš kitôhci-apin ôta?	n'tôhci-apin
7. âšay nâ kinwêš kitôhci-kwâškwêpicikân ôta?	n'tôhci-kwâškwêpicikân
8. âšay nâ kinwêš kitôhci-pôsihtâson ôta?	n'tôhci-pôsihtâson

4.2 Repeat the above drill, answering in the negative, on the pattern:

Question: âšay nâ kinwêš kitôhci-ihtân ôta?
Reply: môla nâsic kinwêš n'tôhci-ihtân ôta.
I haven't been here very long.

NOTE: In the negative reply there is only *one* ohci, *not* two as might have been expected.

Redrill if desired, replacing kinwêš with kêkišêp.
The use of ohci in a compound stem as above, with the meaning *have been... -ing,* is a recurrent use in Cree. Quite acceptable, however, is the alternative,

êhê, n'tâpatisin nawac kinwêš ohci,
kêkišêp ohci, etc.

4.3 Drill on the model:

Question: kêkišêp nâ kitôhci-pêhin?
Have you been waiting for me since this morning?
Reply: êhê, kêkišêp kitôhci-pêhitin.
Yes, I've been waiting for you since this morning.

		(Check column)
1.	kêkišêp nâ kitôhci-pêhin?	kitôhci-pêhitin
2.	kêkišêp nâ kitôhci-kanawâpamin?	kitôhci-kanawâpamitin
3.	kêkišêp nâ kitôhci-natawêlimin?	kitôhci-natawêlimitin
4.	kêkišêp nâ kitôhci-nanâtawâpamin?	kitôhci-nanâtawâpamitin
5.	kêkišêp nâ kitôhci-ayamihin?	kitôhci-ayamihitin
6.	kêkišêp nâ kitôhci-itêlimin?	kitôhci-itêlimitin

4.4 Repeat the above drill, answering in the negative:

Question: kêkišêp nâ kitôhci-pêhin?
Reply: môla kitôhci-pêhitin kêkišêp.
I haven't been waiting for you since this morning.

4.5 Drill the following sequence on the model:

Question: ê'kôko nâ ililiwak kâ-kî-ohci-pôsicik môsonîhk?
Are these the people who embarked from Moosonee?
Reply: mayêwak. lawâšîhk ôko kâ-kî-ohci-pôsicik.
They're not. These are the ones who left from Lawashiy.

1. ê'kôko nâ ililiwak kâ-kî-ohci-pôsicik môsonîhk? ... mayêwak. lawâšîhk, etc.
2. ê'kôko nâ ililiwak kâ-kî-ohci-pêci-âpatisicik môsonîhk?
3. ê'kôko nâ ililiwak kâ-kî-ohci-pêci-šwâpihkêcik môsonîhk?
4. ê'kôko nâ ililiwak kâ-kî-ohci-pêci-iskôliwicik môsonîhk?
5. ê'kôko nâ ililiwak kâ-kî-ohci-pêci-atâwêcik môsonîhk?
6. ô'kôko nâ ililiwak kâ-kî-ohci-pêci-pôsihtâsocik môsonîhk?

5. Complete each of the sentences below with the full verb form from the stems listed at the top of each section.

5.1. As your friend, Joe, struggles up the river bank shouldering an apparently heavy load, you offer help and try to guess from the shape of the object what it might be.

wîcih-, wîwaši-, apwêsi-, kosikwan- [twice], pimiwitâ-, ohpin-, lâhkašin-, mâšihtâ-, ihti-.

kišâstaw, mistahi ki... ______________. mâškôc ka-kî- ________________. ______________ nâ? Your friend replies: môla wayêš n'ka- _________. nikaškihtân nîšwâ awasitê 'ci-______________. ______________ piko.

Somewhat unconvinced, you expostulate: šâkoc mâka kit..._________!
išinâkwan ê-_____________. kêkwânihkân? ki...______________ nâ,
nêstapiko ki-kakwê-_____________?

5.2. At this point a curious onlooker joins you and remarks on the parcel's square top, etc.

kahkahkîhkêyâ-, namêsiwan-, wâwiyênâkwan-, natawêliht-,
napakâ-, wâpaht-, cîpwâ-, kospihtatâ-, kihcipalihcikaniwan-,
astâ-, lâsipê-, îkatêsi-.

________________ išpimihk, ____________________ mâka atâmihk
itêhkê. ____________ nêsta pimic itêhkê, ______________ mâka
ê-kišipâk. mâškǒc ___________. tâpwê, mayêw tâpiskôc môs opwâm.
ni..._____________ tahkonikan. mâškôc n'ka-nanâtostahikân:
_________________________ n'titêl'tên.
Wondering whether Joe plans to come back down the bank, you call out:
hêy, côw, âšay nâ ka-_____________? From under his load, he calls down
to both of you: "No, just stay out of the way. I don't need any help."
môla, ____________ nawac; môla ni...______________ 'ci-wîcihikawiyân.
n'ka-__________________ nîla. wakîtatin niwî-iši- ____________.

D. CONVERSATION PRACTICE

1. Review the Basic Conversation as in past units, taking particular care to proceed without stopping to learn the correct forms when you get stuck. Mark problem sections and return to learn them thoroughly. In this way you are less likely to convince yourself that you know something which you have not really learned.

Review the drills on the same plan as above.

2.1 Discuss various objects about the room, or something which you have bought at the store. Use as many describing words as you conveniently can to talk about them, but use words which you *already know.*

2.2 Describe a visit to a member of your family, what his / her village, house, tent, etc., is like, using inanimate intransitive verbs in the obviative and practising the use of both singular and plural forms. Do not go looking for new words, but practise using the words which you *already know*.

2.3 Develop a conversation on a topic of interest to you. Work out a conversation plan ahead of time which will allow you maximum use of words and grammatical forms learned to date. When you have done this you may now like to expand your discourse with some of the following describing words:

kwayaskosi	VAI	be straight	wâkisi-	VAI	be bent
kwayaskwan-	VII		wâkâ-	VII	
			wâwâkisi-	VAI	be crooked
			wâwâkâ-	VII	
kispakisi-	VAI	be thick	papakisi-	VAI	be thin
kispakâ-	VII		papakâ-	VII	
maškawisi-	VAI	be hard	lôskisi-	VAI	be soft
maškawâ-	VII		lôskâ-	VII	

kinosi- kinwâ-	VAI VII	be long	tahkosi- tahkwâ-	VAI VII	be short
kâšisi- kâšâ-	VAI VII	be sharp	pimâtisi- pimâtan-	VAI VII	be living
wâpisi- wâpâ-	VAI VII	be white	mahkatêwisi- mahkatêwâ-	VAI VII	be black
mihkosi- mihkwâ-	VAI VII	be red	apihti-mihkosi- apihti-mihkwâ-	VAI VII	be purple: *i.e.,* "bruised red"
osâwaškosi- osâwaškwâ-	VAI VII	be blue-green:	(includes part of spectrum covered by both English terms. This will be treated further in Unit 28.B.2 (Level II).)		
osâwisi- osâwâ-	VAI VII	be yellow-brown:	(takes in area covered by two English terms as above.)		

NOTE. Do not fall into the error of thinking that Cree speakers cannot distinguish between blue and green, yellow and brown merely because the Cree primary colour terms divide up the spectrum differently. Remember that where speakers of English ordinarily use "round" for both circular and spherical, the Cree speaker always specifies exactly. Distinction between the colour terms in question is made at the next level, somewhat as English keeps shades apart. For the time being, learn to control the basic colour words.

E. LISTENING IN

A Trip to the Trapping Grounds at Kociciy[1]

Côw: âšay wîpac ta-tipiskâw. êko n'tawâc kapâtâ;[2] âšay ka-kapêšinânaw. âšay wêskac itêlihtâkwan kâ-pêci-pôsiyahkopan[3] kêkišêp. nêtê kiyâpac apišîš n'timihk ihtakwan kapêwin.[4] ka-wâpamânaw mistik nêtê pêšoc asinîhk ê-cimasot.[5] ê'kotêni kê-iši-kipihcîyahk.[6]

Cêkap: kayâm! asinîwan ôta n'titêl'tên. pêhkâc piko n'ka-pim'palin.

Côw: êliwêhk n'ka-sikilêsin[7] 'ci-pimišinân 'ci-alwêpiyân mâka. ka-kapatênâsonânaw misiwê kêkwâna.

Cêkap: kê-wâpahk mâškôc ka-mišakânânaw kocicîhk; mâškŏc nêsta pêškiš[8] ka-pakitahwânânaw. milwâšin ê-pakitahwâniwahk ôta; mâškôc nêsta ka-kî-apwânânaw ayawaši-namês. ka-kî-âpacihimânawa nistês otalapiya. atâwêsiw[9] n'kî-ayamihâw otâkošîhk. pêyakošâp môswa kî-wâpamêw otânâhk kâ-kî-tawâstêlik ôta sîpîhk.

Côw: cikêma,—mihcêtiwak ôta! pêyak n'kî-wâpamâw ê-minihkwêt kêkišêp. môla nâspic ohci-milwêlimêw manicôša. têpiskâk nêsta n'kî-pêhtawâwak nôhcimihk ê-pêhtâkosicik.[10]

Cêkap: môla nâspic n'tôsihtân âšay. mâškôc ta-pêci-minihkwêwak môswak kê-otâkošinilik. awasitê môso-wîyâs niwîhkistên[11] ispîš wîla kotak mîcim. hay!—tântê wîla mâhkîw-iškotêhkân?

Côw: atâmihk apahkwâsonihk iši-astêw. kêkât kî-wani-kiskisinânaw âšokanihk, kâ-kî-ohci-pôsihtâsoyahk. awasitê apišâšin ispîš wîla kotak n'kayâš'-iškotêhkân.

1 kocicîy-	NI [place name]	"Outlet" from a lake Cf. Lake Couchiching
2 kapâ-	VAI	go ashore, land; alight from a vehicle
3 wêskac, etc.		"it seems a long time since we came away"
4 kapêwin-	NI	camping site
5 ê-cimasot	VAI 3 conj. indic.	sticking up
6 kê-iši-kipihcîyahk	VAI 21 conj. indic.	"where we will stop"
7 sikilêsi-	VAI	be glad
8 pêškiš	IPC	as well, among other things
9 atâwêsiw-	NA	trader
10 ê-pêhtâkosicik	VAI 3p conj. indic.	"calling"
11 wîhkist-	VTI	enjoy the taste of s.t., savour s.t.

Cêkap:	yâkwâ! pêhkâc! asinîwan ôta! kipihtina[12] kihcipalihcikan, ohpina mâka. n'ka-sêskipitên cîmân; ka-kî-sakahpitênânaw mâka ôta mistikohk ohci.
Côw:	milwâšin ôta. pâhkwatinâw nêsta. pitamâ cimatâtâ kimâhkîminaw. pâtimâ[13] ka-kotawânânaw 'ci-tîwâpohkêyahk. kišâstaw! n'tâhkosin n'cihciy.
Cêkap:	tân' êhkihk?
Côw:	n'kî-oman'côšimin. n'tohkolon-iskwêw kî-mâcišam, kî-wîskwêpitam mâka. otâkošîhk kî-itwêw, "môla kwayask kimîcison; ê'kwâni wêhci-âhkosiyan.[14] ka-cîstohotin." wêsâ mâka wîpac kî-pôsinânaw kêkišêp.
Cêkap:	âh!—wîpac ka-ati-milo-pimâtisin. kwayask piko mîci[15] ayawaši-wîyâs nêsta namês, môla mâka ka-oman'côšimin. yâkwâ! 'kâwila pahkišini,—ašiškîwan anta. kêkât kî-kilišinin. ê, otina ôma kihcipalihcikan; yâkwâ mâka, kosikwan. ôma nîla n'ka-kospihtatân pahkwêšikaniwat.[16] anohc n'tawâc ka-kapatênâsonânaw; êko mâka kê-alwêpiyahk kî-iškwâ.[17] êliwêhk isa kîšponêw cîmân. awasitê ta-wêhtanôpan pitamâ pimic 'ci-ohci-kapatênâsoyahk. nakašik apwoyak anta cîmânihk. môla misawâc awênihkân ta-otinêw.
Côw:	okimâw apišîš kî-pôsihtâsow otâkošîhk. nîšo ocîmâna wêsâ kî-kîšponêliwa. pêyak kêkât kî-kosâpêw pêšoc âšokanihk.
Cêkap:	âtawîla mišâliwa nawac ocîmâna. kêkât nistwâ kišê-mitâhtomitana tipâpêskocikan pôsihtâsômakanwa.[18] pêyak mâka kêkât kî-kwêtapipaliw takwâkohk. awâšišak kî-âpahamwak, okimâšiš mâka kî-wâpamêw. kî-lâsipêpahtâw âšokanihk; kî-pahkišin mâka pîhci cîmânihk. kêkât mâka kî-kwêtipa-wêpiškam,[19] awâšišak mâka kî-pâhpihêwak.

Unfamiliar words in the above selection are of two kinds: new combinations of elements which you have already met in other contexts, and words or constructions which you have not met or which would be difficult to guess at on the basis of what you have learned. Listen to the dialogue several times, consulting the word list, until you understand fully and can follow without the text.

12 kipihtin-	VTI	stop s.t. (by hand)
13 pâtimâ	IPC	later on, by and by
14 ê'kwâni wêhci-âhkosiyan	VAI 2 conj. indic.	"that's why you're ill"
15 mîci-	VAI-T	eat s.t.
16 pahkwêšikaniwat-	NI	flour bag
17 kî-iškwâ	IPC	afterwards
18 pôsihtâsômakanwa	VII 0 pl.	"they hold freight"
19 kwêtipa-wêpišk-	VTI	knock s.t. over

F. REFERENCE LIST

apihti-mihkosi-	VAI	be purple: *i.e.,* be "bruised red"
apihti-mihkwâ-	VII	be purple: *i.e.,* be "bruised red"
apišâšin-	VII	be small
apišîšiši-	VAI	be small
asiniy-	NA	rock, stone
atâwêsiw-	NA	trader *synon.* kâ-atâwêt
âtawîla	IPC	nonetheless, anyway
cêkap-	NA [personal name]	Jacob
cimaso-	VAI	stick up *v.* cimatê-.
[cimatê-	VAI	stick up *v.* cimaso-]
cîposi-	VAI	be pointed
cîpwâ-	VII	be pointed
côw-	NA [personal name]	Joe
ê-kišipâk	VII 0 conj. indic.	in its ending *v.* kišipâ-.
ê-kišipâki	VII 0 pl. conj. indic.	in their ending
ê-kišipisit	VAI 3 conj. indic.	in his ending *v.* kišipisi-.
ê-kišipisicik	VAI 3 pl. conj. indic.	in their ending
išinâkosi-	VAI	appear so, look so
išinâkwan-	VII	appear so, look so
itêlihtâkosi-	VAI	be thought, seem
itêlihtâkwan-	VII	be thought, seem
îkatêsi-	VAI	get out of the way, remove oneself
kahkahkîhkêsi-	VAI	be square
kahkahkîhkêyâ-	VII	be square
kapâ-	VAI	go ashore, land; alight from a vehicle
kapêwin-	NI	campsite
kaških-	VTA	manage s.o.
kaškihtâ-	VAI-T	manage s.t.; be able to, contrive to

kâšâ-	VII	be sharp
kâšisi-	VAI	be sharp
kêkwân wêhci-+ conj. of verb		why (such and such happens *or* is so)
kêkwânihkân-	NI	a sort of thing; what sort of thing?
kihcipalihcikan-	NI	outboard motor, "kicker"
kinosi-	VAI	be long
kinwâ-	VII	be long
kipihtin-	VTA / VTI	stop s.o./ s.t. (by hand)
kipwâm-	NDI	your (2) thigh *v.* mipwâm-.
kispakâ-	VII	be thick
kispakisi-	VAI	be thick
kišipâ-	VII	end, terminate
kišipisi-	VAI	end, terminate
kî-iškwâ	IPC	afterwards: *used alone as adverbial particle*
kocicîy-	NI	outlet (from a lake)
kosikwan-	VII	be heavy
kosikwati-	VAI	be heavy
kospi-	VAI	go up a bank
kospihtah-	VTA	take s.o. up a bank
kospihtatâ-	VAI-T	take s.t. up a bank
kwayaskosi-	VAI	be straight
kwayaskwan-	VII	be straight
kwêtipa-wêpišk-	VTI	knock s.t. over
kwêtipa-wêpiškaw-	VTA	knock s.o. over
lâhkacioši-	VAI	be light (in weight)
lâhkašin-	VII	be light (in weight)
lâsipêhtah-	VTA	carry s.o. down the bank
lâsipêhtatâ-	VAI-T	carry s.t. down the bank
lôskâ-	VII	be soft
lôskisi-	VAI	be soft
mahkatêwâ-	VII	be black
mahkatêwisi-	VAI	be black
maškawâ-	VII	be hard
maškawisi-	VAI	be hard
mayê-	VA / VII	not be
mâših-	VTA	fight s.o.
mâšihtâ-	VAI-T	fight s.t.
mêstahôsi-	VAI	be worn out
mêstahôtê-	VII	be worn out
mihkosi-	VAI	be red
mihkwâ-	VII	be red

minihkwê	VAI	drink
mipwâm-	NDI	thigh, back leg *v.* kipwâm-, nipwâm-, opwâm-, etc.
mîcisowinâhtikw-	NI	table
namêsiwan-	VII	be a fish (*of something inanimate*)
namêsiwi-	VAI	be a fish (*of something animate*)
nanâtoštahikê-	VAI	guess
napakâ-	VII	be flat
napakisi-	VAI	be flat
nipwâm-	NDI	my thigh *v.* mipwâm-.
nôtimâ-	VII	be round (spherical or cylindrical) *v.* wâwiyêyâ-.
nôtimisi-	VAI	be round (spherical or cylindrical) *v.* wâwiyêsi-.
ohpin-	VTA / VTI	lift s.o./ s.t.
opwâm-	NDI	his thigh *v.* mipwâm-.
osâwaškosi-	VAI	be blue-green
osâwaškwâ-	VII	be blue-green
osâwâ-	VII	be yellow-brown
osâwisi-	VAI	be yellow-brown
pahkwêšikaniwat-	NI	flour bag, flour sack
papakâ-	VII	be thin
papakisi-	VAI	be thin
pâtimâ	IPC	later on, by and by
pêhtâkosi-	VAI	be audible, make a sound with the voice
pêškiš	IPC	as well, among other things
pihkotêw-	NI	ash(es)
pimâtan-	VII	be alive, be living
pimâtisi-	VAI	be alive, be living
pôsihtâsômakan-	VII	freight, do freighting; hold freight (*of a canoe*)
sikilêsi-	VAI	be glad, be grateful
tahkonikan-	NI	handle
tahkosi-	VAI	be short
tahkwâ-	VII	be short
wakîc	IPC + loc.	on (top of): *also as* wakic.
wakîtatin	IPC	on top of the bank
wâkâ-	VII	be bent
wâkisi-	VAI	be bent
wâpâ-	VII	be white
wâpisi-	VAI	be white
wâwiyênâkosi-	VAI	appear round, appear circular (disk-like) *v.* nôtimisi-.

wâwiyênâkwan-	VII	appear round, appear circular (disk-like) *v.* nôtimâ-.
wâwiyêsi-	VAI	be round, be circular (disk-like) *v.* nôtimisi-.
wâwiyêyâ-	VII	be round, be circular (disk-like) *v.* nôtimâ-.
wêhtanôpan	VII indep. pret.	(< wêhtan-) it was easy: ta-wêhtanôpan it would be easy
wêskac	IPC	long ago
wîcihikawiyin	VAI 2 conj. indic. passive	(< wîcihikawi- be helped) 'ci-wîcihikawiyin that you be helped (by an unspecified agent)
[wîhkipw-	VTA	savour s.o.]
wîhkist-	VTI	savour s.t.
wîht-	VTI	tell s.t.
wîwaši-	VAI	carry (on the back) *cf.* mîwat-.

G. REVIEW

17.A Kakwêcihkêmôwina—Questions

Formulate reasonably discursive answers to the following questions.

1. wêsâ nâ mistahi wîwašiw?
2. môla nâ ta-kî-ohpinam kihcipalihcikaniliw?
3. awasitê nâ kosikwan ôma walapihcikan nêstapiko kotakiy?
4. ana asiniy, nôtimisiw nâ nêstapiko wâwiyêsiw piko?
5. wîhkašin nâ anima môso-wîyâs?
6. kin'tawêl'tên nâ 'ci-wîcihikawiyin ê-'lilîmoyin?
7. âšay nâ ka-kî-kospihtatân kihcipalihcikan, kititêl'tên?
8. napakâw nâ kîla kicîmân?
9. wîhtamawin: mišikitiwak nâ misiwê namêsak ôta sâkahikanihk?
10. kitâlimisin nâ ê-'lilîmoyin?
11. kistês nâ nêsta kî-n'tawêl'tam cîmâniliw?
12. âšay nâ ka-kî-lâsipêhtatân kititêl'tên?
13. mîna nâ kiwî-kocihtân?
14. išinâkwan kicîmâniwâw apišîš ê-mêstahôtêk [worn out], manâ?
15. ta-mâšihêw nâ okipahowêsiwa nêstapiko ta-kakwê-ayamihêw?
16. kêkwân anima? wakîtatin nâ wî-iši-astâw?
17. âšay nâ n'ka-îkatêsinân?
18. šâkoc mâka nâspic lôskâw ôma wâpwayân, manâ?
19. kiwîhkistên nâ môsostikwân?
20. hay, klêra! namêsiwan nâ? apišîš išinâkwan ê-lôskâk.

17.B Naškwêwašihtwâwina—Answers

Make up questions which may be answered by the statements below.

1. môla n'kiskêl'tên. išinâkwan mâka apišîš ê-kosikwahk.
2. wêhtan kici-kospihtatâyân.
3. môla, awasitê wâwiyêyâw išpimihk.
4. tâpwê wêsâ kosikwan.
5. wakîtatin niwî-iši-astân.
6. môla wîla lâhkašin! nâspic kosikwan.
7. tâpwê n'kî-wâpahtên. kî-kahkahkîhkêyâw ê-kišipâk.
8. awasitê cîpwâw ê-kišipâk ispîš kotakiy.
9. môla nâspic išinâkosiw ê-mišikitit ê-kišipisit.
10. pîkopaliw n'cîmân. misiwê napakâw pimic itêhkê.
11. šâkoc apwêsiw! wêsâ mistahi kakwê-ohpinam.
12. mâškôc ta-kakwê-ayamihêw pitamâ.
13. môla mwêhci n'kiskêl'tên. mâškôc namêsiwan.
14. tâpwê maškawâw wakîc, nâspic nêsta kâšâw capašîš.
15. ê'kwâni tâpwê! ka-kî-wâpahtên apišîš ê-napakâk pimic itêhkê.
16. êhê, âšay niwâpahtên. nawac tahkwâw, manâ?
17. môla, îkatêsik nawac; n'ka-pêci-kospin mâka.
18. ay'hâw, - pimâtan misawâc.
19. n'kaškihtân nîšwâ awasitê 'ci-pimiwitâyân.
20. misawâc, âtawîla mišikitiw nêsta kinosiw.

UNIT EIGHTEEN

A. HISTORY OF THE CREE SYLLABARY

The Reverend James Evans of the Wesleyan Methodist Missionary Society is to be credited with originating the system of Cree syllabic writing. The syllabary was used by him as early as 1840 at Norway House on Lake Winnipeg to print translated materials. It is a composite, developed apparently from Evans's knowledge of the Greek alphabet, the principles of shorthand and some familiarity with the Devanagari syllabic system, used to write Sanskrit. The Cree syllabary displays a clear understanding of the seven vowels of Cree and the fact that voicing is non-distinctive. The resultant "fit", or accuracy in representing the distinctive sounds of the language, is rather better than that of many other writing systems. Evans was literally ana kâ-kî-ayamîmakihtât waškwâliw, "the one who made the birchbark talk". Early Anglican and Roman Catholic missionaries appear first to have transcribed Cree in Roman letters before generally adopting the syllabary.

In 1851 the Reverend John Horden, first Anglican missionary at Moose Factory, made use of the Evans syllabary, with some adaptations, for his extensive production of scriptural and devotional materials in both Cree and Ojibwa. The syllabary as modified by Horden is that used initially in the present text, although the syllabics as used for Plains Cree, in particular the consistent use of the symbol for the aspirate, ", provide a more accurate representation of the distinctive sounds of the language. Variants on the syllabic system are introduced in later sections of the course for specifically Swampy Cree reading passages.

After initial resistance had been overcome, the use of the syllabic system spread quickly; and in 1879 a further adaptation was made by the Reverend E.J. Peck for writing the language of the Eastern Arctic Inuit. Syllabics are widely used today throughout the eastern and central areas of the Northland for a wide variety of purposes: devotional texts, scripture translations, periodicals, anthologies of oral tradition, writing manuals, government reports, public notices, airline timetables, telephone directories, etc. A fuller account of the origin and development of Evans's system may be found in

Boon, Reverend T.C.B., “Use of Catechisms and Syllabics by the Early Missionaries of Rupert’s Land”, *Bulletin of the Canadian Church Historical Society,* October 1960.

Mason, Roger Burford, “The Sound of Innovation—James Evans’ Syllabic Alphabet”, *Queen’s Quarterly* 101(4), 1994; pp. 848–53.

Nichols, John D., “The Cree Syllabary”, in Peter T. Daniels and William Bright, eds., *The World’s Writing Systems*, New York: Oxford University Press, 1996; pp. 599–611.

B. THE CREE SYLLABARY

1. Syllabic Chart

	ê	i	o	a	Finals: Moose	Finals: Plains
Vowel only	ᐁ	ᐃ	ᐅ	ᐊ		
p	ᐯ	ᐱ	ᐳ	ᐸ	ᑉ	ᑊ
t	ᑌ	ᑎ	ᑐ	ᑕ	ᑦ	ᐟ
c	ᒉ	ᒋ	ᒍ	ᒐ	ᒡ	ᐨ
k	ᑫ	ᑭ	ᑯ	ᑲ	ᒃ	ᐠ
m	ᒣ	ᒥ	ᒧ	ᒪ	ᒻ	ᒼ
n	ᓀ	ᓂ	ᓄ	ᓇ	ᓐ	ᐣ
l	ᓓ	ᓕ	ᓗ	ᓚ	ᓪ	≮, ᐪ
r	ᕃ	ᕆ	ᕈ	ᕋ	ᕐ	≯
s	ᓭ	ᓯ	ᓱ	ᓴ	ᔅ ᔉ - sk	ᐢ
š	ᔐ	ᔑ	ᔓ	ᔕ	ᔥ	ᐡ
w	ᐌ	ᐎ	ᐒ	ᐗ	ᐤ	ᐤ
y	ᔦ	ᔨ	ᔪ	ᔭ	ᐤ, ᔾ	ᐤ
h					ᐦ	ᐦ ᕽ - hk

The Syllabary is a so-called "mixed system", partially syllabic, partially alphabetic, as may be seen from the following description.

2. Use of the System

2.1 Vowels

The Cree dialects represented in the text have seven vowels: three short and four long. The writing system provides for four distinctive positions,

ᐁ ê ᐃ i ᐅ o ᐊ a

with a dot written above all but ᐁ, which is always long, to indicate length:

ᐄ î ᐆ ô ᐋ â.

Contrast	ᒫᒋ	mâci *begin to* with	ᒪᒋ	maci *bad*
	ᐹᐦᑳᐣ	pâhkân *presently*	ᐸᐦᑳᐣ	pahkân *separately*
	ᐚᓛᐤ	wâlâw *it is concave*	ᐚᓚᐤ	wâlaw *far off*
	ᓂᒫᐢᑭᓯᐣ	nimâskisin *I am lame*	ᓂᒪᐢᑭᓯᐣ	nimaskisin *my shoe*

Most symbols represent a full syllable consisting of either a vowel, ᐁ ê, ᐃ i or some other, or a consonant and vowel sequence, ᐯ pê, ᐱ pi, ᑌ tê, ᑎ ti, and so on.

2.2 Consonantal Sounds

Other symbols, however, refer to a single, consonantal sound: *e.g.,* ᐦ /h/, ᐧ /w/ before a vowel, ᐤ /w/ in word final position, Plains Cree ᓬ /l/, or ᕑ /r/, finals such as ᐠ /k/, ᒼ /m/, ᐣ /n/ and clusters such as Moose ᐢ /sk/ or Plains Cree ᕽ /hk/. This last is often realised phonetically as [χ]. Clearly, while most unit symbols denote a full syllable, the system is also partially alphabetic in that many signs denote single, vowel or consonant-like sounds. This dual arrangement leads to its classification as a *mixed system* rather than one which is purely syllabic. The following chart illustrates the point:

Syllabic reference only	ᐁ ê	ᐃ i	ᐅ o	ᐊ a
	ᐯ pê	ᐱ pi	ᐳ po	ᐸ pa
	ᑌ tê	ᑎ ti	ᑐ to	ᑕ ta
Partially alphabetic reference (*Plains Cree≠*)	ᐍ wê	ᐏ wi	ᐓ wo	ᐘ wa
	ᐦᐁ hê	ᐦᐃ hi	ᐦᐅ ho	ᐦᐊ ha
	ᓬᐁ lê	ᓬᐃ li	ᓬᐅ lo	ᓬᐊ la

Note also ᐧᐯ pwê ᐧᐱ pwi ᐧᐳ pwo ᐧᐸ pwa.

Western spelling convention places the dot *after* the syllabic to show a pre-vocalic /w/:

ᐯᐧ pwê ᐱᐧ pwi ᐳᐧ pwo ᐸᐧ pwa.

2.3 Initials and Finals

In Moose Cree and the Eastern form of the syllabary generally, /w/ - initial is written before the syllabic: ᐧᐚᑎ wâti *den, lair*; ᐧᐹᑦ Pwât, *a Sioux*.

/w/ in final position is written ᐤ above the line: ᓈᐯᐤ nâpêw *man*.

/y/ - final is written ° immediately above the final syllabic: ᐋᔖ̊ âšay *by now, already*. Note that it is higher, smaller and in a different position than final /w/ ᐤ. For /y/ - final, some writers produce a half-sized, raised ᔾ, on the analogy of other Moose Cree finals.

/l/, /r/. Neither of the sounds normally associated with these letters belongs to Plains Cree, and a symbol to write them was needed only for borrowed terms. ᓬ /l/ and ᕒ /r/ are written either before or after a vowel symbol as required: ᓬᐋᓴᕒᐊᐢ Lazarus. Compare the Moose syllabics, ᓛᓴᕈᔅ.

N-Dialect publications in the James Bay area are often printed with Plains Cree finals, with the exception of /l/-final, which is written ᐪ : *e.g.*,

Plains Cree	Moose Cree	James Bay, N-Dialect
ᐹᐧᓬ	ᐧᐹᓪ	ᐧᐹᐪ

/h/. The aspirate symbol, ᐦ, is usually omitted by Moose Cree writers unless specific emphasis or contrast is desired; but until greater familiarity with the syllabary is developed, it will be used with all features written in full.

/hk/-final is normally written in Moose syllabics simply as ᐠ /k/, but will be presented in the present text as ᐦᐠ : ᐧᐄᑭᐦᐠ wîkihk *in his home*. Western use represents the final cluster, /hk/, with final ᕽ (*v.* 2.2 above.)

/sk/ in final position is written ᔉ : ᐊᒥᔉ amisk *beaver*, but may also be seen in uncontracted form, ᐢᐠ, or by writers of the N-Dialect, ᐢ\.

/f, th/: Two symbols were used by Horden to transcribe "ph" as in <u>Ph</u>ilip or "v" as in Da<u>v</u>id, on the one hand and "th", as in English Timo<u>th</u>y, on the other : ᕔ "fi or vi" and ᖨ "thi", respectively. Since voicing is non-distinctive in Cree, both /f/ and /v/ may be represented by the same symbol. Both /f *or* v/ and /θ/ are sounds foreign to Moose and N-Cree; and Cree speakers most frequently replace ᕔ and ᖨ with ᐱ and ᑎ*: e.g.,* ᑎᒧᑎ Timoti, ᐱᓕᑉ Pilip and ᑌᐱᑦ Têpit.

C. DRILLS

1. Basic Syllabic Drill

Listen to the recording and repeat the syllables after each utterance, reading the syllabics at the same time. The combinations in columns a, b and c are for the most part nonsense syllables. Columns d, e, f, and g comprise Cree forms, each of which is recorded twice.

		a.	b.	c.	d.	e.	f.	g.
ᒥ	1.	ᒪᒥ	ᓂᓇ	ᑭᑲ	ᓃᓇ	ᒪᓈ	ᓃᒥ	ᓃᑳᓐ
		ᒪᒥ	ᓂᓇ	ᑭᑲ	ᑮᓇ	ᒫᓇ	ᓃᑭ	ᒦᓐ
ᓂ		ᒫᒦ	ᓃᓈ	ᑮᑳ	ᒫᑲ	ᓇᒪ	ᒦᓇ	ᑳᒃ
ᑭ		ᒪᒼ	ᓇᓐ	ᑭᒃ				
ᓯ	2.	ᓯᓴ	ᑕᑎ	ᒋᒐ	ᑖᓂ	ᓂᐦᑖ	ᑭᒋ	ᑭᓯᑦ
ᑎ		ᓯᓴ	ᑕᑎ	ᒋᒐ	ᑲᑕ	ᐱᒦ	ᐃᓴ	ᒫᐦᒋᒡ
		ᓰᓵ	ᑖᑏ	ᒌᒑ	ᒪᒋ	ᓰᐲ	ᓂᓯᑦ	ᒫᒪᔅᑳᒡ
ᒋ		ᓴᔅ	ᑕᑦ	ᒐᒡ	ᒫᒋ	ᒌᒫᓐ	ᓂᒥᔅ	ᓃᑎᒼ
ᐱ	3.	ᐸᐱ	ᐊᐃ	ᐧᐃ	ᐊᐧᐊ	ᐲᓯᒼ	ᐋᑕ	ᐧᐄᓇ
		ᐸᐱ	ᐧᐊᐧᐃ	ᐧᐄ	ᐧᐋᐸᒼ	ᐊᑎᒼ	ᐧᐋᐸᓐ	’ᑳᐧᐃᓇ
ᐃ		ᐹᐲ	ᐧᐋᐧᐃ	ᐹ	ᐋᔅᑕᒼ	ᐧᐄᐸᒡ	ᐧᐄᑭ	ᐧᐋᐸᐦᑕᒼ
·		ᐸᑉ	ᐧᐋᐧᐄ	ᐧᐋ	ᐧᐄᐦᑕᒼ	ᐧᐄᐧᐊ	ᐧᐄᔅᑳᒡ	ᐧᐋᐸᐦᑕᐧᒪᒃ
ᔨ	4.	ᑭᓱ	ᑲᔪ	ᔨᒥ	ᑮᔪᑳᐤ	ᐊᐱᐤ	ᐱᑕᒫ	ᓂᐧᐋᐸᒫᐤ
		ᑭᓱ	ᑲᔪ	ᔨᒥ	ᑎᐱᔅᑳᐤ	ᐊᐱᔭᓐ	ᒫᑎᑲ	ᐃᐦᑖᐤ
ᓱ		ᑮᓲ	ᑳᔫ	ᔭᒥ	ᑭᒥᐧᐊᓐ	ᐋᐸᒋᐦᑖᔭᓐ	ᐹᑎᒪ	ᓂᐹᐤ
ᐤ		ᑮᓲᐤ	ᑳᔫᐤ	ᒥᔮᐤ	ᓲᐹᔮᐦᑎᒃ	ᐧᔫᐱᐦᒃ	ᑭᔫᔅᐱᓐ	ᒥᐧᓈᓱᓐ
			ᑳᔾ	ᔪᔾ	ᐋᔩᑎᓯᐤ	ᓲᐲᐤ	ᐊᔭᒥᐤ	ᓂᔫᒼ
ᒧ	5.	ᒣᒧ	ᓀᓄ	ᑫᑯ	ᒧᐦᒋ	ᓅᐦᑖ	ᒣᐧᑳᒡ	
ᓄ		ᒣᒧ	ᓀᓄ	ᑫᑯ	ᒨᓇ	ᓇᒣᔅ	ᐧᒣᐦᒋ	
ᑯ		ᒣᒨ	ᓀᓅ	ᑫᑰ	ᒨᐦᑯᒫᓐ	ᒪᒣᓐ	ᐧᒣᔅᑕᔅ	

ᓱ	6.	ᓴᓱ	ᑐᑌ	ᒍᒉ	ᓂᑑᑌᒻ	ᓇᐧᐊᒡ	ᒦᔅᑯᒡ	
ᑐ		ᓴᓱ	ᑐᑌ	ᒍᒉ	ᑳᓱ	ᒫᐧᐊᒡ	ᑖᐱᐢᑯᒡ	
ᒍ		ᓴᓲ	ᑑᑌ	ᒉᒎ	ᑫᑳᐨ	ᐅᐢᑲᒡ	ᒑᐦᒑᒧ	
ᐳ	7.	ᐁᐯ	ᐅᐳ	ᐳᐳ˚	ᐅᑕ	ᐌᐢᑲᒡ	ᐊᐧᐳ˚	
ᐅ		ᐌᐯ	ᐅᐳ	ᓱᓱ˚	ᐅᓵᒻ	ᐌᐱᓇᒻ	ᐴᔨᐤ	
ᐤ		ᐁᐧᐯ	ᐅ˚ᐳ˚	ᓴᓴ˚	ᐯᐦᑳᒡ	ᐊᐧᐯᔨᐤ	ᐧᐹᐦᑯᒧ	
ᔦ	8.	ᔐᔓ	ᔕᔑ	ᔕ˚	ᐅᔑ˚	ᓂᐹ˚ᐤ	ᒣᐧᑲᔕᔅ	ᑫ ᒦᓂᔥ
ᔓ		ᔐᔓ	ᔭᔦ	ᔦ˚	ᐊᐧᐳ˚	ᓂᐸ˚	ᒪᔕᐤ	ᐃᐢᑲᓂ ᑎᐱᔥ
ᔥ		ᔐᔔ	ᔕᔩ	ᔕ˚	ᓇᑖ˚	ᑮᔒ	ᐧᐹᒧᔑ	ᐅᑖᐹᓈᔥ
		ᔓᔥ	ᒪᔥ	ᔓ˚	ᐋᔕ˚	ᐯᔓᒡ	ᔑᔔᑌᐤ	ᑫ ᐅᑖᒪᐦᐅᔥ

NOTES: 1. ᓓ lê plus ᓕ li, ᓚ la and ᓗ lo, with superscript dots for length, are used in Moose Cree. ᕂ rê, ᕆ ri, ᕋ ra and ᕈ ro are used to transcribe borrowed words.
2. Finals for the consonants differ in Plains Cree syllabics as indicated in the chart and B.2.3 above. ᙾ and ᙿ are used for /l/ and /r/ respectively, followed by the appropriate vowel symbol: *e.g.*, Moose ᓚ = Plains ᙾᐊ. Final /hk/ is represented in Plains Cree syllabics by ˣ above the line. The ᔑ series is not used in Plains Cree.
3. The aspirate, regularly written as ᐦ, in Plains syllabics, is usually omitted in Moose Cree, except for a few fixed forms: *e.g.*, ᐦᐁᕈᐟ Herod.
4. In Scripture and devotional texts the symbol "X" represents the proper name, Christ.

2. Reading Practice

Listen to the following conversation several times, reading the syllabics carefully until you can follow them with ease. From now on, as soon as you control new Conversation or Listening In material (*not before*), follow the syllabics while you listen.

ᐧᒡᓐ:	ᐋᔕ˚ ᓈ ᐯᑖᐸᓐ ?
ᐋᓃ:	ᐁᐦᐁ, ᐋᔕ˚ ᐊᑎ ᑮᔑᑳ˚ᐤᕽ
ᐧᒡᓐ:	ᑭᔖᔅᑕᐤ! ᑖᐧᐯ ᓕᐹᒋ ᑮᔑᑳ˚ᐤ! ᒎᓚ ᑮ ᓂᐹ˚ᐤ ᐊᐧᐁᓂᐦᑳᓐ ᐆᑕᕽ
	ᐅᐦᒋᑲᐧᐃᓐ ᓀᔅᑕ ᑭ ᒫᐦᑮᒥᓈᐤ ᓀᔅᑕ ᒫᑲ ᓂᐚᐧᐊᓐ ᑭ ᐧᐋᐧᐸᔾᓂᓇᐤᕽ
ᐋᓃ:	ᐋᔕ ᒦᓇ ᐧᑲᓐᑕᐤ ᑭ ᐧᐄ ᐊᑎ ᐊᔭᒥᓐᕽ ᑭᐟ ᐊᔮᓈᓇᐤ ᓈ ᒫᑲ ᒥᐦᑕ
	ᑭᒋ ᐃᐢᐸᓕᔭᐦᒃ ᐃᔅᑯᑌᐤ ᐅᐦᒋ ?
ᐧᒡᓐ:	ᑭᐟ ᐊᔮᓈᓇᐤ ᓅᔓ ᒥᐦᑎᑳᓇᕽ ᓂ ᑮ ᐹᐦᐱᓐ ᑌᐱᐢᑳᒃᕽ
ᐋᓃ:	ᑮ ᐧᐄᔭᐧᑖᓈᐧᐋᐤ ᓈ ᒥᔨᐧᐁ ᐋᔓᐧᑲᓂᐦᒃ ?

ᐧᒫᓐ: ᒨᓚ, ᒨᓚ ᐧᑲᓐᑕᐤ ᓂᑦ ᐆᐦᒋ ᐧᐄᔭᐧᑖᓈᓐ᙮ ᓅᓕᔮᓂᑭᒫᐤ ᓀᐢᑕ ᐊᓐᑕ ᑮ ᐃᐦᑖᐤ ᓀᐢᑕ ᒫᑲ ᐅᑭᐸᐦᐅᐧᐁᓯᐤ᙮ ᐯᒋ ᒪᐧᐋᐱᐧᐊᒃ᙮

ᐋᓃ: ᐊᔭᐦᐋᐤ, ᒨᓚ ᓈᐢᐱᐨ ᐧᐄᔭᑌᓕᐦᑖᐧᑲᓐ᙮

ᐧᒫᓐ: ᐁᐦᐁ, ᐅᑭᐸᐦᐅᐧᐁᓯᐤ ᒫᑲ ᑮ ᐃᐧᑌᐤ, "ᐊᐧᐊᓯᑌ ᓂ ᑲ ᓈᑲᒋᐦᑖᓈᓐ ᐧᐊᓚᔕᐧᐁᐧᐃᓐ"᙮

ᐋᓃ: ᒨᓚ ᐧᐊᔦᐢ ᐅᐦᒋ ᐃᔑ ᐊᐧᐁᐸᓕᐤ᙮ ᐅᑭᐸᐦᐅᐧᐁᓯᐧᐊᒃ ᒫᑲ ᓵᑯᒼ ᒨᓚ ᐲᑯᓇᐧᒪᒃ᙮

ᐧᒫᓐ: ᓂ ᑭᐢᑫᓕᐦᑌᓐ᙮ ᐅᑭᐸᐦᐅᐧᐁᓯᐤ ᒫᑲ ᑮ ᐃᐧᑌᐤ, "ᓂ ᑲ ᓈᑲᒋᐦᑖᓐ" ᒫᑲ, ᐃᐢᐲᐢ ᐧᐄᓚ "ᑲ ᓈᑲᒋᐦᑖᓈᓇᐤ"᙮

ᐋᓃ: ᑭ ᑭᐢᑫᓕᐦᑌᓐ ᓈ ᒫᑲ ᑫᐧᑳᓐ ᐅᐦᒋ ? ᐁᒥᐢᑎᑰᔑᐧᐊᒃ ᒫᑲ ᐊᔮᐧᐊᒃ ᐯᔭᒃ ᐱᑯ ᐊᔭᒥᐧᐃᓂᓕᐤ 'ᑮᓚᓈᓇᐤ' ᐅᐦᒋ ᓀᐢᑕ 'ᓃᓚᓈᓐ'᙮

ᐧᒫᓐ: ᐁ'ᑯ ᓈ 'ᓂ ᒫᑲ ᐯᔭᐧᑲᓐ ᐁ ᐧᐁᒥᐢᑎᑰᔒᒧᓈᓂᐧᐊᐦᒃ, 'ᑮᓚᓈᓇᐤ' ᓀᐢᑕ 'ᓃᓚᓈᓐ' ?

ᐋᓃ: ᑭ ᑭᐢᑭᓯᓐ ᓈ ᒫᐦᒋᐟ ᑳ ᑮ ᐊᔭᒥᐦᐁᑮᔑᑳᒃ ᐊᔭᒥᐦᐁᐧᐃᑭᒫᐤ ᑮ ᐧᐄ ᐃᐧᑌᐤ, "ᒥᓯᐧᐁ ᑮ ᑑᑌᓈᓇᐤ ᒪᒋᐦᐧᑖᐧᐃᓐ"᙮ ᑮ ᐃᐧᑌᐤ ᒫᑲ, "ᓂ ᑮ ᑑᑌᓈᓐ", ᐧᐄᓚ ᓀᐢᑕ ᒫᐢᑯᒡ ᑯᑕᑭᔭᒃ ᐊᔭᒥᐦᐁᐧᐃᑭᒫᐧᐊᒃ᙮ ᐋᐢᑲᐤ ᐃᐧᑌᐤ, 'ᓅᐦᑖᐧᐄᓈᓐ'; ᑖᐧᐯ ᒫᑲ ᐧᐄ ᐃᑕᒼ, 'ᑰᐦᑖᐧᐄᓇᐤ'᙮ ᒋᑫᒫᓂᒪ, ᑮ ᐧᐊᓂᑑᑕᒼ᙮

ᐧᒫᓐ: ᒨᓚ ᓈ ᑮ ᐧᐄᐦᑕᐧᒪᒃ ᐲᑐᐢ, 'ᑮᓚᓈᓇᐤ' ᓀᐢᑕ 'ᓃᓚᓈᓐ' ? ᓵᑯᒼ ᐊᔭᒥᐦᐃᑐᐧᐊᒃ᙮ ᑮ ᓂᓯᑐᐦᑖᑐᐧᐊᒃ ᓈ ᒫᑲ ?

ᐋᓃ: ᐁᐦᐁ, ᒫᐢᑯᒡ; ᒨᓚ ᒫᑲ ᓂ ᑫᐦᒋᓈᐦᐅᓐ᙮

D. CONVERSATION PRACTICE

1. Turn back to Unit 5.C.1, Intonation Drill. Cover the right hand column and rewrite the sentences on the left in syllabic spelling. When you have finished, use the right hand column as a check. Here and there in syllabic spelling you may notice slight differences of use: *e.g.,* Sentence #3, where sîpiy is spelled ᓰᐲ rather than ᓰᐱ̊. Pronunciation of either would be identical and, where the diacritics are used, ᓰᐲ represents normal spelling practice.

2. Write a letter to a friend, describing your settlement or an interesting event, and inviting the friend to come and visit you. Use the syllabary chart if you get stuck.

(A letter begins, ᑮᓚ + Name of Addressee, and concludes, ᓃᓚ + Name of Writer.)

3. The following conversation between two students will provide terms with which to discuss the syllabary in Cree.

ᑳ ᐃᓕᓖᐧᐃ ᐊᔭᒥᐦᑖᓂᐧᐊᐦᑭ
Cree Letters

ᐁ ᐊᔭᒥᐦᐃᑐᒋᐠ ᓃᔓ	ê-ayamihitocik nîšo	A Conversation Between
ᑳ ᑭᐢᑭᓄᐦᐊᒫᓱᒋᐠ	kâ-kiskinohamâsocik	Two Students
ᐧᒫᐣ: ᓂ ᓇᑲᒋᐦᑖᐣ	ninakacihtân	I'm used to it
ᒨᓪ ᐁᐡᐧᑳ ᓂ ᓇᑲᒋᐦᑖᐣ	môl' êškwâ ninakacihtân	I'm not used to the Cree
ᑳ ᐃᓕᓖᐧᐃ ᐊᔭᒥᐦᑖᓂᐧᐊᐦᑭ᙮	kâ-ililîwi-ayamihtâniwahki.[1]	letters yet.
ᐋᓕᐠ: ᒥᑌᐦᐃᐦᐠ ᒋ ᐅᐦᒋ ᑭᐢᑫᓕᑕᒫᐦᐠ	mitêhihk 'ci-ohci-kiskêlihtamâhk	to learn by heart
ᑭ ᔕᐧᐁᓕᐦᑖᑯᓯᓈᐧᐋᐤ	kišawêl'tâkosinâwâw	you (pl.) are lucky
ᑮᓚᐧᐋᐤ ᑭ ᔕᐧᐁᓕᐦᑖᑯᓯᓈᐧᐋᐤ᙮	kîlawâw kišawêlihtâkosinâwâw.	*You*'re lucky. We have a
ᓂᐟ ᐊᔮᐧᐋᓈᐣ ᑳ ᑭᐢᑭᓄᐦᐊᒫᑫᐟ	nitayâwânân kâ-kiskinohamâkêt	teacher who makes us
ᑳ ᑭᐢᑭᓄᐦᐊᒪᐧᐃᔭᒥᐦᐟ ᒥᑌᐦᐃᐦᐠ	kâ-kiskinohamawiyamiht mitêhihk	memorize things,—even
ᒋ ᐅᐦᒋ ᑭᐢᑫᓕᐦᑕᒫᐦᐠ, ᐋᑕ ᐁᑳ	'ci-ohci-kiskêlihtamâhk, - âta êkâ	though we don't understand
ᐁ ᓂᓯᑐᐦᑕᒫᐦᐠ᙮	ê-nisitohtamâhk.	them.
ᐧᒫᐣ: ᐁᑯᑌ 'ᓂ ᐯᔭᐧᑲᔦᐠ ᐁ	êkotê 'ni pêyakwayêk	That's one way to learn.
ᐃᔑ ᑭᐢᑭᓄᐦᐊᒫᑳᓂᐧᐊᐦᐠ᙮ ᐲᑐᐡ	ê-iši-kiskinohamâkâniwahk.	There are other ways
ᐃᑌᐦᑫ ᒫᑲ᙮	pîtoš itêhkê mâka.	though.
ᐋᓕᐠ: ᑫᐧᑳᐣ ᐅᓵᒼ ᐧᐁᓈᐦᐃᑯᔨᐣ?	kêkwân osâm wênâhíkoyin?	What's your main problem?
ᒐᐦᑭᐯᐦᐃᑲᓇ ᓈ ?	cahkipêhikana nâ?	The dots?
ᐧᒫᐣ: ᑭᔑᐹᐦᐠ	kišipâhk	at the end
ᑭᔑᐹᐦᐠ ᑳ ᐃᐦᑕᐧᑲᐦᑭ ᒐᐦᑭᐯᐦᐃᑲᓇ	kišipâhk kâ-ihtakwahki	The final dots are easy;
ᐧᐁᐦᑕᐧᓇ;	cahkipêhikana wêhtanwa;	
ᐁ ᐃᔑ ᐧᑫᐢᑭᑌᑭ	ê-iši-kwêskitêki	in their being so turned
ᒨᔕᐠ ᒫᑲ ᓂ ᐧᐊᓃᐦᑳᐣ ᐁ ᐃᔑ	môšak mâka niwanîhkân ê-iši-	But I always forget which
ᐧᑫᐢᑭᑌᑭ ᑯᑕᑭᔭ ᑳ ᐊᔭᒥᐦᑖᓂᐧᐊᐦᑭ᙮	kwêskitêki kâ-ayamihtâniwahki.	way the other letters turn.
ᐋᓕᐠ: ᓀᐧᐊᔦᐠ	nêwayêk	in four ways
ᓀᐧᐊᔦᐠ ᑕ ᑫ ᐃᔑ ᐧᑫᐢᑭᑌᐧᐊ᙮	nêwayêk ta-kî-iši-kwêskitêwa.	They can be turned four ways.
ᑭ ᒐᐦᑭᐯᐦᐁᐣ ᐧᐊᑭᐨ	kicahkipêhên wakic	you dot them on top
ᐁ ᐃᑎᐦᑖᐧᑲᐦᑭ	ê-itihtâkwahki	in their sounding so
ᒋ ᑭᓄᐦᑐᔨᐣ	'ci-kinohtâyin	to make them long
ᒋ ᑭᑲᐦᑖᔨᐣ ᐁ ᐃᑎᐦᑖᐧᑲᐦᑭ	'ci-kinohtâyin ê-itihtâkwahki	To make them sound long
ᑭ ᒐᐦᑭᐯᐦᐁᐣ ᐧᐊᑭᐨ᙮	kicahkipêhên wakic.	you dot them on top.

[1] kâ-akihcikâtêki heard in northern N-Dialect.

ᐧᒫᐣ: ᐁᑯ ᒫᑲ ᐧᑫᐢᑭᐸᓕᐠ	êko mâka kwêskipalik	then it turns, changes
ᐁᑯ ᒫᑲ ᐧᑫᐢᑭᐸᓕᐠ “ᒪ”, “ᒫ” ᒋ ᐃᑎᐦᑖᐧᑲᐦᐠ; ᓀᐢᑕ ᒫᑲ “ᑭ”, “ᑮ” ᒋ ᐃᑎᐦᑖᐧᑲᐦᐠ᙮ ᐁᑯᑌ ᓈ ?	êko mâka kwêskipalik “ma”, “mâ” ’ci-itihtâkwahk; nêsta mâka “ki” “kî” ’ci-itihtâkwahk. êkotê nâ ?	Then “ma” turns to sound like”mâ”; and “ki” becomes “kî”. Is that the way ?
ᐋᓕᐠ: ᐁᑯᑌ ’ᓂ ᒋ ᐲᑐᔑᐦᑖᐧᑲᐦᑭ “ᒪᒋ ᑮᔑᑳᐤ” ᓀᐢᑕ ᒫᑲ “ᒫᒋ ᑮᔑᑳᐤ”, ᓀᐢᑕ “ᑭᔑᑌᐤ” ᐁᑯ ᒫᑲ “ᑮᔑᑌᐤ”᙮	êkotê ’ni ’ci-pîtošihtâkwahki “maci-kîšikâw” nêsta mâka “mâci-kîšikâw”, nêsta “kišitêw”, êko mâka “kîšitêw”.	That’s the difference between “maci-kîšikâw” and “mâci-kîšikâw”, and also between “kišitêw” and “kîšitêw”.
ᒪᓯᓇᐦᐃᑳᑌᐘ ᐘᑭᒡ	masinahikâtêwa wakic	they are written above
ᑳ ᐃᔑ ᐯᔖᐯᐦᑭᐦᑎᐦᐠ	kâ-iši-pêšâpêhkihtihk	the line
ᑳ ᑭᐱᐦᑕᐧᐁᐸᓕᑭ	kâ-kipihtawêpaliki	which stop speaking (*i.e.,* final consonants)
ᑭᔑᐹᐦᐠ ᑳ ᐃᑕᓯᓇᐦᐃᑳᑌᑭ	kišipâhk kâ-itasinahikâtêki	the letters at the end
ᑭᔑᐹᐦᐠ ᑳ ᐃᑕᓯᓇᐦᐃᑳᑌᑭ ᑳ ᐃᔑ ᑭᐱᐦᑕᐧᐁᐸᓕᑭ, ᒪᓯᓇᐦᐃᑳᑌᐘ ᐘᑭᒡ ᑳ ᐃᔑ ᐯᔖᐯᐦᑭᐦᑎᐦᐠ᙮	kišipâhk kâ-itasinahikâtêki kâ-iši-kipihtawêpaliki, masinahikâtêwa wakic kâ-iši-pêšâpêhkihtihk.	The letters at the end, with no sound after them, are written above the line.
ᓇᐢᐱᑕᐧᐁᒪᑲᐧᓇ ᑳ ᐃᓕᓖᐘᐢᑌᑭ “ᐸ, ᑕ, ᒐ, ᑲ, ᒪ, ᓇ”; ᐋᐱᐦᑕᐤ ᐱᑯ ᐃᐢᐱᐦᒑᐘ ᐆᑌ, ᑉ, ᐟ, ᒡ, ᐠ, ᒼ, ᐣ᙮	naspitawêmakanwa kâ-ililîwastêki, “pa, ta, ca, ka, ma, na”; âpihtaw piko ispihcâwa ôtê ……….	They resemble the syllabics for “pa, ta, ca, ka, ma, na”; only they are just half-size: this way, p, t, c, k, m, n.
ᐱᐢᑭᑕᓯᓇᐦᐃᑲᓂᐡ	piskitasinahikaniš [NI]	verse, sentence
ᐁ ’ᑎ ᑭᔑᐱᐸᓕᐠ ᑕᐦᑐ ᐱᐢᑭᑕᓯᓇ… ᐦᐃᑲᓂᐡ, ᐁ ᐊᐱᔖᔑᐦᐠ “᙮” ᑭ ᒪᓯᓇᐦᐁᐣ᙮	ê-’ti-kišipipalik tahto-piskitasina… hikaniš, ê-apišâšihk “x” kimasinahên.	At the end of each sentence, you write a small “x”.
ᐁ ᐧᐁᒥᐢᑎᑰᔒᒧᔨᐣ ᑲ ᒐᐦᑭᐯᐦᐁᐦᑕᐩ᙮	ê-(w)êmistikôšîmoyin, • ka-cahkipêhêhtay	In English you would write a dot.

E. LISTENING AND READING

ᑎᐹᒋᒨᐎᓐ ᐘᐊᐦᑳᓇᒃ ᐅᐦᒋ

A brief reminiscence of his childhood in Wenusk, Ontario, narrated by the late Xavier Sutherland

ᐆᒪ ᑎᐹᒋᒨᐎᓐ ᐘᐊᐦᑳᓇᒃ[1] ᐅᐦᒋ᙮

ᐯᔭᐧᑳ ᐍᔅᑲᐢ ᐁ ’ᐱᔒᔑ’ᔮᐹᓐ[2] ᓂ ᑭᔅᑭᓯᓐ ᐁ ᑮ ’ᔮᐘᑭᐦᑎᐸᓐ[3] ᐊᒥᔥ ᐁ ᐅᑕᐘᐦᑳᓂᔮᐦᒃ [4]᙮ ᒣᐧᑳᒡ ᐁ ᓂᐹᔮᐦᒃ, ᐋᐸᑎᓲᐳᓐ[5] ᑫ’ᓂᑯᐦᒃ [6]᙮ ᒣᐧᑳᒡ ᒫᑲ ᐁ ᑮᔑᑳᓂᒃ, ᓂᐹᐸᓐ ᑫ’ᓂᑯᐦᒃ᙮

ᐁᑯ ᒫᑲ, ᒣᐧᑳᒡ ᐁ ᑎᐱᔅᑳᓂᒃ ᐁ ᓂᐹᔦᐦᒃ ᓅᑮᓈᐦᒃ, ᒦᑭᐚᒥᐦᒃ,[7] ᐃᔥᐧᑳᑌᒥᐦᒃ ᒫᑲ, ᑳ ᐅᐦᒋ ᐘᓇᐧᐋᓈᓂᐘᐦᒃ, ᑫ’ᓂᑯᐦᒃ ᐋᐸᑎᓯᐤ᙮ ᑮᔥᑮᔥᑲᐦᑕᒼ[8] ᓅᐱᓯᔮᐦᑎᐦᑯ[9] ᒥᔅᑎᐧᑲ; ᐁᑯ ᒫᑲ, ᐯᑖᐤ ᐃᔥᐧᑳᑌᒥᐦᒃ᙮

ᐁ ᑫᑭᔐᐹᔮᐦᒃ ᐁ ᐘᓂᔥᑳᔮᐦᒃ, ᒥᑐᓂ ᑮ ᑲᑫᐸᐦᐊᒼ[10] ᓂᑎᔥᐧᑳᑌᒥᓈᓐ᙮ ᒣᐧᑳᒡ ᐁ ᑎᐱᔅᑳᓂᒃ ’ᐧᑳᓐ’ ᐁᐦᑑᑕᐦᒃ: ᐁᓂᑯᐦᒃ ᐋᐸᑎᓯᐤ ᐁ ᑭᐸᐦᐊᐦᒃ ᐃᔥᐧᑳᐦᑌᒼ,[11] ᑖᐱᔅᑯᒼ ᑳ ᐃᐦᑑᑕᐦᒃ ᓲᐲᓂᐤ᙮

ᐁᑯ ᒫᑲ ᐁ ᐘᓂᔥᑳᔮᐦᒃ ᐁ ᑫᑭᔐᐹᔮᓂᒃ ᐋᔖ ᐱᒥᔑᓐ ᐁ ᓂᐹᐟ, ᒣᐧᑳᒡ ᐁ ᑮ ᐋᐸᑎᓯᐟ ᐁ ᑎᐱᔅᑳᓂᒃ᙮

âtalôhkâna nêsta tipâcimôwina / Cree Legends and Narratives from the West Coast of James Bay, Simeon Scott et al., ed., C. Douglas Ellis, Winnipeg: University of Manitoba Press, 1995; p. 158. Reprinted by permission.

1 awahkân-	NA	captive, slave; pet (used here in sense of pet animal)
2 apišîšisi-	VAI	be little: 1 conj. indic. preterit "when I was little"
3 ê-kî-ayâwakihtipan	VTA 1p conj. indic. preterit	"that we used to have"
4 otawahkâni-	VAI	have as a pet
5 âpatisîpan	VAI 3 indep. indic. preterit	"he used to work"
6 k' ênikohk	IPC	"as hard as he could, for all he was worth"
7 mîkiwâmihk < mîkiwâm-	NI	"in the tent"
8 kîškîškaht-	VTI rdpl.	cut s.t. with one's teeth repeatedly, gnaw through s.t.
9 nîpisiyâhtikw-	NI	willow wood
10 kakêpah-	VTI	block s.t. up, obstruct s.t.
11 iškwâhtêm:		iškwâhtêminiw would be expected.

F. REFERENCE LIST

akohp-	NI	dress (*in some areas,* blanket)
alôminâpoy-	NI	oatmeal porridge
awahkân-	NA	captive, slave; pet
awêspiso-	VAI	dress, get dressed
âstawêh-	VTI	extinguish s.t., quench s.t.
cahkipêh-	VTI	dot s.t., make a dot on s.t.
cahkipêhikan-	NI	a dot; *sometimes used to mean* final consonant *in the syllabic system.*
cîstahamawêpon-	NI	fork
cîstêmâw-	NA	tobacco
côcôšinâpoy-	NI	milk: *lit.,* breast liquid
êkôtê	IPC	that (is) the way: *contraction of* êwako ôtê
êmihkwân-	NA	spoon
itasinah-	VTI	write s.t. so
itêh-	VTI	stir s.t.
itihtâkosi-	VAI	sound so
itihtâkwan-	VII	sound so
kawêšimo-	VAI	go to bed, retire for the night
kâ-akihcikâtêki	VII 0p conj. indic.	Cree letters: *lit.,* (things) which are reckoned (*northern N-Dialect*) *Cf. next two terms.*
kâ-ililîw'-astêki	VII 0p conj. indic.	Cree letters: *lit.,* (things) which are set
kâ-ililîwi-ayamihtâniwahki	VAI-T indf. conj. indic.	Cree letters: *lit.,* (things) which are read
kâsîcihcê-	VAI	wash one's hand(s)
kâsîhkwê-	VAI	wash one's face
kâškipâso-	VAI	shave
kêtâspiso-	VAI	undress
kicistâpâwalo-	VAI	wash oneself
kicistâpitêho-	VAI	clean one's teeth

kinoh-	VTA	lengthen s.o.
kinohtâ-	VAI-T	lengthen s.t.
kipihtawê-	VAI	stop speaking; *as an impolite or brusque imperative,* kipihtawê Stop talking!
kišêpânêhkwê-	VAI	have breakfast, breakfast
(kišêpânêhkwêwin-	NI	breakfast)
kišipâhk	NI loc.	at the end: kišipâhk kâ-itasinahikâtêki the finals
kišipâw-	NI	the end: *v.* kišipâhk.
kospâhtawî-	VAI	go upstairs
kotawê-	VAI	build a fire (outside). *Cf.* pôn-.
kwêskipali-	VAI / VII	turn, change (into)
kwêskitê-	VII	be turned
môhkomân-	NI	knife
naspitaw-	VTA	resemble s.o.
nâcipah-	VTA	fetch s.o.
nâcipahtwâ-	VAI-T	fetch s.t.
nêwayêk	IPC	in four ways *v.* pêyakwayêk
nipêwayâna	NI pl.	pyjamas, night clothes
nîšâhtawî-	VAI	go downstairs
osâmihkwâmi-	VAI	sleep in, oversleep
otâkošinêhkwê-	VAI	have supper, have the evening meal
pêšâpêhkihtin-	VII	be a straight line (as in a copy book)
pêyakwayêk	IPC	one way, one means *v.* nêwayêk
piskitasinahikan-	NI	chapter (in a book)
piskitasinahikaniš-	NI diminutive	verse, sentence
pîhtawêskikana	NI pl.	underclothes, underwear
pôn-	VTI	make a fire (in the stove). *Cf.* kotawê-.
pwât-	NA	Sioux
sakipât-	VTA / VTI	button s.o./ s.t.
šawêlihtâkosi-	VAI	be lucky, be blessed
šîkaho-	VAI	comb one's hair
šîwitâkan-	NI	salt
šôkâw-	NI	sugar
tiy-	NI	tea

waniškâ-	VAI	get up (out of bed)
waspitah-	VTI	lace s.t. up: *e.g.,* shoes
wâstên-	VTI	lighten s.t., turn on the light
wât- *sg.,* wâti	NI	den, lair
wêpin-	VTA / VTI	throw s.o./ s.t. out

G. ADDITIONAL DRILL

Daily Routine

Drill this sequence, switching from ni... subject to ki..., to 3 and so on. If possible, use the series as a question-answer drill with someone else. Many of the words you already know. The others you will be more likely to recall when you need them if they have been learned in "chunks" or sequences.

He has supper.	otâkošinêhkwêw.
He goes to bed when it's dark.	kawêšimow ê-tipiskâlik.
He goes upstairs.	kospâhtawîw.
He turns out the light.	âstawêham.
What time do you get up?	tân' êspihcipalik ê-waniškâyan?
He gets up at 7 o'clock.	waniškâw nîswâs ê-ispalilik.
" 7:15 "	šânkwêš awasitê 7 ê-ispalilik.
" 7:30 "	âpihtaw nîšwâs ê-ispalilik.
" 7:45 "	šânkwêš ilikohk niyânânêw.
She sleeps in.	osâmihkwâmiw.
He goes downstairs.	nîšâhtawîw.
He turns on the light.	wâstênam.
He makes a fire (in the stove).	pônam.
He gets washed.	kicistâpâwalow.
He washes his hands.	kâsîcihcêw.
Wash your hands!	kâsîcihcê.
He washes his face.	kâsîhkwêw.
He brushes (*i.e.,* cleans) his teeth.	kicistâpitêhow.
He shaves.	kâškipâsow.
He combs his hair.	šîkahow.
He throws out the ashes.	wêpinam pihkotêliw.
He gets wood.	nâcipahtwâw mihta.
She makes breakfast.	ošihtâw kišêpânêhkwêwiniliw.
He makes tea.	tîwâpohkêw *or* ošihtâw tîliw.
He puts sugar in the tea.	pakitinam šôkâliw tîhk.
Does he put milk in the tea?	pakitinam nâ côcôšinâpôliw tîhk?
Yes. Then he makes porridge.	êhê. êko mâka êti-ošihtât alôminâpôliw.
I put salt in the porridge.	nipakitinên šîwitâkan alôminâpohk.
I stir the porridge.	n'titêhên alôminâpoy.

I eat a good breakfast.	kwayask nikišêpânêhkwân.
I go upstairs again.	mîna nikospâhtawîn.
I get undressed.	nikêtâspison.
I take off my pyjamas.	nikêcikonên ninipêwayâna.
I get dressed.	n'tawêspison.
I put on (my) underwear.	nipohciškên (ni...)pîhtawêskikana.
I put on my socks.	nipohciškawâwak n'tašikanak.
I put on my shirt.	nipohciškên nipakwayân.
I put on my trousers.	nipohciškawâw nipalacîs.
I put on my dress.	nipohciškên n'takohp.
I put on my shoes.	nipohciškên nimaskisina.
I lace up my shoes.	niwaspitahên nimaskisina.
I button up my shirt.	nisakipâtên nipakwayân.
Then I smoke a cigarette.	êko mâka êti-pîhtwâkêyân sikarêt.
Then I begin to work.	êko mâka êti-âpatisiyân.

Additional Words

cîstahamawêpon-	NI	fork
êmihkwân-	NA	spoon
minihkwâkan-	NI	cup, glass: *lit.,* drinking vessel
môhkomân-	NI	knife
olâkan-	NI	dish, plate
cîstêmâw-	NA	tobacco

H. THE CONJUNCT ORDER

A. Résumé

Throughout Units 1 to 17 the independent and imperative orders of the verb have been presented with examples, discussion and paradigms. The conjunct order has been introduced at a less overt level and instances appear throughout the lesson units; but up to this point (except for a handful of forms) only the indicative mode of both independent and conjunct has been introduced. Pending full discussion of the conjunct in Level 2, beginning with Unit 19, a brief overview of some of its main uses will help you as you practise speaking Cree.

1. Occurrences of the Conjunct

The independent and conjunct indicatives may be thought of as two parallel orders of inflectional suffixes: the independent occurring in main clauses, the conjunct set in dependent (*or* subordinate) clauses. The list of examples from 12.B and others which you have added will display a number of common occurrences:

> with the particle <u>ê</u> the most common of all subordinating particles:
> ê-mâtot in her crying, when she cries
> ê-kimiwahk when it rains, as it rains
> ê-oški-kîšikâk on Monday;
>
> or <u>ê</u> in conjunction with another particle,
> mêkwâc ê-tipiskâlik during the night (*v.* E, above.);
>
> with the particle, <u>kâ</u>: kâ-atâwêt (the one) who trades: *i.e.,* the trader
> kâ-iškwâ-nisto-kîšikâk when it finished being three days:
> *i.e.,* three days later
> (*Cf.* kâ-restrictive, 2.2 below.);
>
> with the particle, <u>kici</u> to express purpose:
> kici-kiskêlihtaman (in order) that you know it
> 'ci-iskôliwiyân (so) that I go to school;

with the particle, pwâmoši: pwâmoši pôsiyâhk before we leave,
before we embark;

and in content questions of various kinds, with changed initial vowel on the total verb form:

tân' êhtôtaman? What are you doing?
tân' êšinâkwahk anima? How does that look?
tânt' êtohtêt? Where is she going?
awênihkân wiyâpamat anta? Whom do you see there?
kêkwân nêtawêlihtaman? What do you want?

In Unit 12.B.2 it was suggested that you organise a table of conjunct endings with your own additions to the list of expressions given. These can now be checked against the chart in Appendix 2.

2. kâ Restrictive

In English the function of the relative pronouns is in a sense to link or restrict attention to the person or thing discussed: *who,* alluding to a person, *which,* referring a thing: *e.g.,*

(the person) *who* teaches
(the wood) *which* I am chopping.

When, used in a relative sense, similarly restricts the focus to a particular point in time:

(now) *when* everything is going well
when I called you;

and *where,* as in

(the river) *where* we fish
(the shed) *where* things are put,

restricts the focus of attention to a point in space.

In Cree the particle, kâ, carries out the restrictive, linking function in all three areas: object (animate or inanimate), point in time and, with the addition of iši, point in space. A rough analogy (and no analogy is perfect), the use of the single term, *that,* in English to replace *who/which, when* and *where,* may make this seem less unusual: *e.g.,*

(the one) *that* teaches
(ana) kâ-kiskinohamâkêt
(the wood) *that* I am chopping
(mihta) kâ-cîkahamân

(now) *that* it-days: *i.e.,* today
(anohc) kâ-kîšikâk
(the time) *that* I called you
(   )[1] kâ-kî-têpwâtitân

(the river) *that* we fish (in)
(sîpiy) kâ-iši-nôtamêsêyâhk
(the wharf) *that* things are placed (on)
(âšokwan) kâ-iši-astêki kêkwâna.

Note kâ followed by kî to mark a *completed* action at a point in time: kâ-kî-têpwâtitân when I called you. When pointing to the future, kâ is replaced by kê:

ililiw kê-ayamihtât the person who will read it
mihta kê-cîkahamân the wood which I shall chop
kê-tipiskâk tonight: *lit.,* when it will be night
kê-iši-astêki kêkwâna where things will be placed

[1] No single term for "time" exists in Cree or is required here. See "Cree Grammar" Preference for Verbal Constructions, p. xxxii.

APPENDIX I

General Organisational Scheme of the Cree Verb

The following diagram* presents the general, organisational scheme of the Cree verb. Certain restrictions, for example, that inanimate intransitive verbs (VII) have no imperative forms, are not shown.

TYPE		
TYPE	Intransitive:	Animate Intransitive (VAI) Inanimate Intransitive (VII)
	Transitive:	Transitive Animate (VTA) Transitive Inanimate (VTI)

ORDER	MODE	TENSE	SUBMODE	INFLECTION (VAI, VTI only)
Independent	Indicative	Neutral		Relational
		Preterit		Nonrelational
	Dubitative	*Neutral*		*Relational*
		Preterit		*Nonrelational*
Conjunct	Indicative	Neutral	Simple	*Relational*
		Preterit	Changed	Nonrelational
	Subjunctive	*Neutral*	*Simple*	*Relational*
			Changed	*Nonrelational*
	Dubitative	*Neutral*	*Simple*	*Relational*
		Preterit	*Changed*	*Nonrelational*
Imperative		Immediate (Present)		Relational
		Delayed (Future)		Nonrelational

(Reprinted with permission, from IJAL, 37.2, p. 83.)

* Categories shown in italics occur only incidentally or not at all in Level One and are not represented in the paradigms (Appendix 2).

APPENDIX II

Verbs

Animate Intransitive Verb (VAI)

Table 1—VAI

(Nonrelational)

	Independent Indicative	Conjunct Indicative	Imperative Immediate (Present)
1	...n	...(y)ân	
2	...n	...(y)an, ...(y)in	...Ø
1p	...nân	...(y)âhk	
21	...nânaw	...(y)ahkw̸[1]	...tâ(k) *or* ...tâw
2p	...nâwâw	...(y)êkw̸	...k
3	...w	...t, ~k[2]	
3p	...wak	...cik, ~kik	
3′	...ιliwa[3]	...ιlici[3]	
indef. passive	...(nâ)niwan	...(nâ)niwahk	

1 w̸ denotes /w/ elided when in final position after a consonant. *v.* p. 57.
2 ~ indicates that /n/ of a preceding stem is replaced by /h/: takošin...k > takošihk.
3 ...ιliwa, ...ιlici: after vowel > ...liwa, ...lici.

Table 2—VAI

(Relational)

	Independent Indicative	Imperative Immediate (Present)
1	…w…â…n	
2	…w…â…n	…w
1p	…w…â…nân	
21	…w…â…nânaw	…w…â…tâ(k)
2p	…w…â…nâwâw	…w…â…hk
3	…w…ê…w	
3p	…w…ê…wak	
3′	…ɩliwa*	
indef. passive	*(No separate form in Independent)*	

* …ɩliwa, …ɩlici: after vowel > …liwa, …lici.

Transitive Animate Verb (VTA)

Table 3—VTA

Independent Indicative

Direct	-3	-3p	-3′	-3″*
1-	…âw	…âwak	…ιmâwa	
2-	…âw	…âwak	…ιmâwa	
indef. pass.	…âw	…âwak	…ιmâwa	
1p-	…ânân	…ânânak	…ιmânâna / …ih	
21-	…ânaw	…ânawak	…ιmânawa	
2p-	…âwâw	…âwâwak	…ιmâwâwa	
3-			…êw	…ιmêw
3p-			…êwak	…ιmêwak
3′-				…êliwa

Inverse	3-	3p-	3′-	3″-
-1	…ιkw̸	…ιkwak	…ιkoliwa	
-2	…ιkw̸	…ιkwak	…ιkoliwa	
-1p	…ιkonân	…ιkonânak	…ιkonâna	
-21	…ιkonaw	…ιkonawak	…ιkonawa	
-2p	…ιkowâw	…ιkowâwak	…ιkowâwa	
-3			…ιkow	
-3p			…ιkowak	
-3′				…ιkoliwa

Local

1 - 2	…ιtin	2 - 1	…in
1p - 2	…ιtinân	2 - 1p	…inân
1(p) - 2p	…ιtinâwâw	2p - 1(p)	…inâwâw

* 3″ = further obviative (surobviative)

Table 4—VTA

Conjunct Indicative

Direct	-3	-3p	-3′	-3″
1-	…ak	…akik	…imaki	
2-	…at	…acik	…imaci	
indef. pass.	…ιht	…ιhcik	…ιmιhci	
1p-	…akiht	…akihcik	…imakihci	
21-	…ahkw̸	…ahkok	…imahko	
2p-	…êkw̸	…êkok	…imêko	
3-			…ât	…imât
3p-			…âcik	…imâcik
3′-				…âlici

Inverse	3-	3p-	3′-	3″
-1	…it	…icik	…ιmici	
-2	…ιsk	…ιskik	…ιmιski	
-1p	…iyamiht	…iyamihcik	…(ιm)iyamihci	
-21	…itahkw̸	…itahkok	…imitahko	
-2p	…itâkw̸	…itâkok	…imitâko	
-3			…ikot	
-3p			…ikocik	
-3′				…ikolici

Local

1 - 2	…ιtân	2 - 1	…iyan
1p - 2	…ιtâhk	2 - 1p	…iyâhk
1(p) - 2p	…ιtakok	2p - 1(p)	…iyêk

Table 5—VTA

Immediate (*or* Present) Imperative

(s)*	2 - 1	...in	(s)	-3	...*y > Ø	(s) -3′	...im
(s)	2 - 1p	...inân	(s)	-3p	...ik		
	21 -		(t)	-3	...âtâk	(t) -3′	...imâtânih
	21 -		(t)	-3p	...âtânik *or* ...âtânak		*or*...ιmâtâna
(š)	2p - 1	...ik	(t)	-3	...ιhkw̸	(t) -3′	...ιmâhk
(š)	2p - 1p	...inân	(t)	-3p	...ιhkok		

Jussive (3rd Person Imperative)

3 - 3′	êkoši êkâwila	kata + VTA Stem + ...êw
3p - 3′	êkoši êkâwila	kata + VTA Stem + ...êwak

* (š) above indicates change of stem-final /t/ to /š/: *e.g.*,

têpwât...êw	he calls her
têpwâš	call her (2 - 3 imperative)

Transitive Inanimate Verb (VTI)

Table 6—VTI

(Nonrelational)*

	Independent Indicative	Conjunct Indicative	Imperative (Immediate *or* Present) (Nonrelational)	(Relational)
	-0(p)	-0(p)	-0(p)	
1-	...ên	...amân		
2-	...ên	...aman	...a	...amw̸
1p-	...ênân	...amâhk		
21-	...ênânaw	...amahkw̸	...êtâ(k)	...amwâtâ(k)
2p-	...ênâwâw	...amêkw̸	...amok	...amwâhk
3-	...amw̸	...ahk		
3p-	...amwak	...ahkik		
3′-	...amiliwa	...amilici		
indef. passive	...ikâtêw	...ikâtêk		
0	...amômakanw̸	...amômakahk		
0p	...amômakanwa	...amômakahki		
0′	...amômakaniliw	...amômakanilik		
0′p	...amômakaniliwa	...amômakaniliki		

* VTI stems add ...amw... to form the base for the relational conjugation. Inflectional suffixes are then the same as for Animate Intransitive verbs (VAI). "Pseudo-Transitive"verbs (VAI-T) inflect exactly like VAI.

INTRANSITIVE INANIMATE VERB (VII)

Table 7—VII

	Independent Indicative	Conjunct Indicative
0	... w	~k
0p	...wa	~ki
0′	...ɩliw*	...ɩlik*
0′p	...ɩliwa	...ɩliki

* ...ɩliw, ...ɩlici: after vowel > ...liw, ...lici, &c. *v.* p. 55.

GLOSSARY

Stem-Class Codes and Abbreviations

NA	animate noun	NDA	animate noun, dependent
NI	inanimate noun	NDI	inanimate noun, dependent
Nom. A	nominal animate		
Nom. I	nominal inanimate	IPC	indeclinable particle
		IPN	indeclinable prenoun particle
PR	pronoun	IPP	indeclinable pre-particle
		IPV	indeclinable preverb particle
VAI	animate intransitive verb	VTA	transitive animate verb
VAI-T	animate intransitive verb in form with implied or expressed inanimate object	VTI	transitive inanimate verb
VII	inanimate intransitive verb		
M	medial suffix	F	final suffix
MV	medial suffix with verb only and without related noun form	VAIF	animate intransitive verb final
		VIIF	inanimate intransitive verb final
MF	suffix functioning as medial or final		
anim.	animate	prox.	proximate
conj.	conjunct	rcpr.	reciprocal
dubit.	dubitative	rdpl.	reduplicated
excl.	exclusive	rel.	relative
imv.	imperative	reln.	relational
inan.	inanimate	SC	Swampy Cree (N-Dialect)
incl.	inclusive	sg.	singular
indecl.	indeclinable	s.o.	someone (any animate object of transitive verb)
indf.	indefinite		
indic.	indicative	s.t.	something (inanimate object of transitive verb)
MC	Moose Cree (L-Dialect)		
obv.	obviative	subj.	subjunctive
pl.	plural		

Items in the Glossary are listed by stems, with the hyphen used to indicate the point at which inflectional material may be added: *e.g.*, cîmân- : cîmânihk. Contrary to general practice, dependent stems are not listed separately. Rather, to facilitate reference at Level 1, they have been entered with personal prefixes: *e.g.*, nikosis-, kikosis-, okosisa. Separate listing of dependent stems will occur in the *Cree Learner's Dictionary* and begins at Level 2 with the fuller discussion of word building. Numbers in the rightmost column denote the lesson unit in which each entry first occurs. Alphabetic order of listing is a, â, c, ê, i, k, l, m, n, o, ô, p, s, š, t, w, y.

acimošiš-	NA	puppy *v.* atimw-	[8]
a(h)lapiy	NA	net *v.* alapiy-	
ahtay-	NA	fur; dollar	[10]
akâmihk	IPC	across (the water)	[5]
akiht-	VTI	count s.t.	[6]
akihtâso-	VAI	count, enumerate	[6]
akihtâson-	NI	number, numeral	[6]
akihtâsowin-	NI	number, numbering	[6]
akim-	VTA	count s.o.	[6]
akohp-	NI	dress (*in some areas*, blanket)	[18]
akol-	VTA	hang s.o. up	(15)
akotâ-	VAI-T	hang s.t. up *v.* akol-	[15]
akotê-	VII	hang: kâ-akotêki things which hang	[15]
akwâpasw-	VTA	smoke-dry s.o.	[11]
akwâpicikê-	VAI	fish with a seine net	[11]
al-	VTA	set s.o., place s.o. *v.* astâ-	[12]
alapiy-	NA	(fish) net	[11]
alisipiy-	NI	plain water	[15]
aliwâk	IPC	in excess, over and above : aliwâk ilikohk kâ-natawêlihtahk more than he needs	[11]
alôminaskw-	NA	linseed meal	[16]
alôminâpoy-	NI	oatmeal porridge	[18]
alwêpi-	VAI	take a rest, take a holiday	[12]
amiskokimâw-	NA	Lands and Forests Officer: *lit.*, beaver manager	[3]
ana	PR dem. anim. prox. sg.	that one	[3]
anihi	PR dem. anim. obv.	that (one)	[5]
		those (ones)	[10]
	dem. inan. pl. prox. & obv.	those (ones)	[10]
aniki	PR dem. anim. pl.	those (ones)	[10]
anima	PR dem. inan. prox. sg.	that one	[3]
animêliw	PR dem. inan. obv. sg.	that one	[3]

anohc	IPC	now	[2]
anohcîhkê	IPC	just now, just recently	[11]
anohc kâ-kîšikâk		today (*lit.,* now when-it-is-day)	[2]
anohc kâ-nîpihk		this Summer	[12]
anta	IPC	there [*not as far away as* nêtê]	[1]
antê	IPC	thither	[4]
apahkwâson-	NI	(tent) canvas	[11]
api-	VAI	sit	[3]
apihti-mihkosi-	VAI	be purple: *i.e.,* be "bruised red"	[17]
apihti-mihkwâ-	VII	be purple: *i.e.,* be "bruised red"	[17]
apišâšin-	VII	be small	[17]
apišîš	IPC	a little, a bit	[4]
apišîšiši-	VAI	be small	[17]
apwê-	VAI	roast over an open fire, barbecue	[11]
apwêsi-	VAI	perspire	[14]
apwoy-	NA	paddle	[2]
asiniy-	NI	rock, stone	[17]
askihkw-	NA	kettle, pail	[10]
astâ-	VAI-T	set s.t., place s.t. *v.* al-	[12]
astê-	VII	be set, be placed	[12]
astis-	NA	mitt	[16]
astotin-	NI	hat	[8]
ašam-	VTA	feed s.o.	[8]
ašikan-	NA	sock, stocking	[10]
ašiškiy-	NI	mud	[8]
ašitakimo-	VAI	count oneself in, include oneself	[7]
atâmihk	IPC	underneath, below, at the bottom	[12]
atâwêsiw-	NA	trader *synon.* kâ-atâwêt	[17]
atâwêwikamikw-	NI	trading post, store (*preferred to* šwâp- *by purists*)	[8]
ati	IPV	begin (to) with gradual onset *v.* mâci	[4]
atihkamêkw-	NA	whitefish: *lit.,* caribou fish	[11]
atimw-	NA	dog *v.* otêma	[4], [7]
atôskêlâkan-	NA	servant, assistant	[16]
awa	PR dem. anim. prox. sg.	this one	[2]
awas	IPC	away with you! be off! go away!	[9]
awasitê	IPC	more (*of degree*) *v.* itêhkê	[4]
awasitê itêhkê	IPC	on the far side of, beyond	[4]
awâšiš-	NA	child	[5]
awêna	PR interrogative	who? *Used predicatively:* Who is it?	[15]
awênihkân-	NA	somebody, someone; person	[3]
awênihkân-	PR interrog. anim.	who	[4]
awêspiso-	VAI	dress, get dressed *v.* kêtâspiso-	[18]

awih-	VTA	lend (to) s.o.	[11]
awihâsom-	VTA	borrow (from) s.o.	[12]
awiyâšîš-	NA	animal, beast	[8]
ayami-	VAI	speak	[7]
ayamih-	VTA	speak to s.o., address s.o.	[4]
ayamihê'-kîšikâ-	VII	be Sunday	[7]
ayamihêwikimâw-	NA	clergyman (*normal term for Anglican priest*) *v.* mêhkotêwihkonayêw-	[3]
ayamihito-	VAI rcpr.	speak to each other	
ayamihtâ-	VAI-T	read s.t., *lit.*, address s.t.	[4], [7]
ayamiwin-	NI	word	[7]
ayawiši	IPN	fresh (as of food) *v.* oški; kayâši	[4]
ayâ-	VAI-T	have s.t.	[4]
ayâkwâmisî-	VAI	be careful, be cautious	[15]
ayân-	NI	thing possessed, possession	[8]
ayâw-	VTA	have s.o.	[4]
ayêskosi-	VAI	be tired	[12]
ay'hâw	IPC [pause word]	well, uh... [*contraction of* ayahâw- NI thing]	[2]
aylîn-	NA	Eileen	[9]
aysâya-	NA [personal name]	Isaiah	[8]
âhkikw-	NA	seal (sea mammal)	[8]
âhkoh-	VTA	hurt s.o.	[9]
âhkosi-	VAI	be sick, be ill	[5]
âhkosîwikamikw-	NA	hospital	[5]
âhkwatim-	VTA	freeze s.o.	[11]
âhkwatin-	VII	be freezing	[11]
âhtakwê-	VAI	move camp, move away	[6]
âhtokwê-	VAI	move camp, move away : *less common variant*	[2]
âlahkonâw-	NA	bread	[4]
âlikw-	NA [personal name]	Alec, Alex	[11]
âlimakihtê-	VII	be expensive	[10]
âlimakiso-	VAI	be expensive	[10]
âliman-	VII	be difficult; be expensive	[11]
âlimisi-	VAI	be difficult; be expensive	[11]
âlimôm-	VTA	talk about s.o.	[SUPP. CONV. II]
âlimôt-	VTI	talk about s.t.	(SUPP. CONV. II)
âniy-	NA [personal name]	Annie	[2]
âpacih-	VTA	use s.o.	[11]
âpacihtâ-	VAI-T	use s.t.; âpacihtâtokwê he must be using it	[11], [15]
âpatan-	VII	be useful	[6]
âpatisi-	VAI	work	[2], [3]
âpatisîwin-	NI	work	[12]

âpihko-	VAI	be loose(d), be untethered	[8]
âpihtaw	IPC	half	[10]
âpihtawan-	VII	be Wednesday: *i.e.,* half-way through the week	[12]
âpihtâ	IPV	half	[11]
âskaw	IPC	sometimes	[2]
âstam	IPC	come here, *lit.,* 'facing this way' (*functions as verbal imperative to which* ...ik *may be added to form plural v.* Unit 15.B.2.)	[4]
âstamitê	IPC	to this side (of): *opposite of* awasitê itêhkê	[4]
âstatâpwê	IPC	alas! aw-w!	[SUPP. CONV. I]
âstawêh-	VTI	extinguish s.t., quench s.t.	[18]
âšay	IPC	now, by now; already	[1]
âšokan-	NA	wharf, dock, jetty [regional variant of âšokwan-]	[2]
âšokwan-	NA	wharf, dock, jetty [regional variant of âšokan-]	[1], [2]
âšowah-	VTI	cross s.t. (*e.g.,* a river)	[15]
âtawîla	IPC	nonetheless, anyway	[17]
âwêpali-	VAI	*w. neg.,* môla âwêpaliw he doesn't talk sense	[7]
cahkipêh-	VTI	dot s.t., make a dot on s.t.	[18]
cahkipêhikan-	NI	dot: *sometimes used to mean* final consonant *in the syllabic system*	[18]
cahkišim-	VTA	stub s.o. (a cigarette); *v.* pišošimiko-	[16]
cakawâšiši-	VAI	be few	[13]
capašîš	IPC	low, low down; below	[8]
câhcâmo-	VAI	sneeze	[2]
câlis-	NA [personal name]	Charles	[14]
cêkap-	NA [personal name]	Jacob	[17]
ci	IPC	if you wouldn't mind	[SUPP. CONV. I]
cikêmânima	IPC	why, naturally! of course!	[7]
cim-	NA [personal name]	Jim	[14]
cimaso-	VAI	stick up *v.* cimatê-	[17]
cimatâ-	VAI-T	erect s.t., pitch it (a tent), build it (a house)	[6], [14]
cimatê-	VII	stick up (UNIT 17) *v.* cimaso-	
cîhkêliht-	VTI	be interested in s.t. *v.* kišišawêliht-, kistêliht-	[14]
cîhkêlim-	VTA	be interested in s.o. *v.* kišišawêlim-. kistêlim-	[14]
cîkah-	VTI	chop s.t.	[11]
cîkahw-	VTA	chop s.o.	[11]
cîkic	IPC + loc.	beside	[14]
cîmân-	NI	canoe, boat	[2]
cîmis-	NA [personal name]	James	[8]
cîpayâhtiko-kîšikâ-	VII	be Friday	[12]
cîpâš-	NA	scamp, rascal	[9]

cîposi-	VAI	be pointed	[17]
cîpwâ-	VII	be pointed	[17]
cîstah-	VTI	prick s.t., puncture s.t.	[16]
cîstahamawêpon-	NI	fork	[18]
cîstahw-	VTA	prick s.o., puncture s.o.; give an injection to s.o.	[9]
cîstêmâw-	NA	tobacco	[16]
côcôšinâpoy-	NI	milk: *lit.*, breast liquid	[18]
côsipîn-	NA [personal name]	Josephine	[7]
côw-	NA [personal name]	Joe	[17]
cwân-	NA [personal name]	John	[1]
ê	IPV	as (doing), in (doing): *subordinating particle used with conjunct order of the verb: e.g.,* ê-ililîmonâniwahk in (one's) speaking Cree, as one speaks Cree	[4]
êhê	IPC	yes	[1]
êkâ	IPV	not (*with imperative and conjunct*)	[9]
êko	IPC	so, well then *v.* êkwa	[3]
ê'ko	PR intens. anim.	the very one, the selfsame one: *contraction of* êwako (*marked as indeclinable, but occurs in obviative form* êwakwêliw)	[4]
êko isa	IPC phrase	So then…! Well, then…! (Conversation concluder)	[8]
êkoši	IPC	so then (*used as polite introduction to a directive*)	[15]
êkotê	IPC	that very way, that (is) the way	[1]
		contr. of êwako ôtê	[18]
êko wâs' âni	IPC phrase	well, that's that (*at conclusion of conversation*)	[3]
êkôma	PR intensive	this very one [inan. singular]: *contr. of* êwako ôma	[1]
êkwa	IPC	so, well then (*inland, to the west of James Bay coast*) *v.* êko	[3]
ê'kwân' êkoši	IPC phrase	Never mind!	[8]
ê'kwâni	PR dem. inan. intensive	that (is it): *contraction of* êwako ani	[3]
ê'kwânima	PR dem. inan. prox.	that very one	[3]
êlikohk	IPC	vigorously, strenuously, a great deal *v.* sohki	[7]
êliwêhk	IPC	especially, very much so, ever so!	[3]
êmihkwân-	NA	spoon	[18]
êmiliy-	NA [personal name]	Emily	[2]
êmistikôšiw-	NA	Englishman, White-man *v.* wêmistikôšiw-	[7]
êmwayêš	IPC + conj. indic.	before (Lake Winnipeg area) *v.* pwâmoši	[12]
êncini-pimiy-	NI	gasoline	[12]
êškwâ	IPC	yet	[7]
ê-takwâkihk	VII conj. indic.	in the Fall *v.* takwâkin-	[8]
êtiy-	NA [personal name]	Eddie	[5]
êwako	PR intensive	the very one, the selfsame one	[5], [7]

ihkin-	VII	happen; fare, ail	[8]
ihtâ-	VAI	be (at a place *as opposed to* be, exist)	[1]
ihtâwin-	NI	village	[1]
ihti-	VAI	fare, be in such-and-such a state, ail; happen	[2], [8]
ihtôt-	VTI	so do (it)	[5]
iko	IPC	only *v.* piko	[13]
ilâpatan-	VII	be good for, be useful for	[16]
ilikohk	IPC	as much as, up to: tânîlikohk how much?	[9]
ililiw-	NA	person, *usually* Indian person	[1]
ililîmo-	VAI	speak Cree	[4]
isa	IPC	to be sure, of course	[2]
iskali	IPN	whole, entire, all	[11]
iskali-kîšik	IPC	all day	[11]
iskali-tipisk	IPC	all night	[11]
iskonikan-	NI	(Indian) reservation: *lit.*, leftover (land)	[Supp. Conv. II]
iskôliwi-	VAI	go to school, attend school	[9]
iskwêw-	NA	woman	[2]
ispakocin-	VAI	fly high: *lit.*, hang high	[8]
ispali-	VAI / VII	get along so, go so, go thus; last	[7], [9], [10]
ispêlohkê-	VAI	take a short rest from work, take a "spell"	[12]
ispî	IPC	when	[16]
ispihcâ-	VII	be so large, be of such a size *v.* ispîhcâ-	[10]
ispîhcâ-	VII	be so large, be of such a size *v.* ispihcâ-	[10]
ispîhcikiti-	VAI	be so large, be of such a size	[10]
ispîš	IPC	than	[4]
iši	IPV	so, thus	[2]
išicišahamaw-	VTA	send (s.t.) to s.o.	[11]
išicišahikan-	NI	parcel (to be sent) *v.* walahpicikan-	(10)
išinâkosi-	VAI	appear so	(12), (17)
išinâkwan-	VII	appear so	[12]
išinihkâso-	VAI	be so named, be called	[1], [4]
išinihkâtê-	VII	be called, be named	[4]
išiwil-	VTA	take s.o. (somewhere)	[6]
išiwitâ-	VAI-T	take s.t. (somewhere)	[6]
iškotêhkân-	NI	stove	[12]
iškotêw-	NI	fire	[7]
iškwâ	IPV	finish, complete: ê-kî-iškwâ-âpihtâ-kîšikâk after noon-hour, in the afternoon	[11]
iškwâhtêm-	NI	door	[15]
iš̌pimihk	IPC	above, aloft; upstairs	[3]
itakihtê-	VII	cost so much	[10]
itakiso-	VAI	cost so much	[10]
itamahciho-	VAI	feel so (health-wise)	[3]

itasinah-	VTI	write s.t. so	[18]
itasinâso-	VAI	be marked, be listed	[SUPP. CONV. I]
itaši-	VAI (in pl.)	be so many	[SUPP. CONV. II]
itâpi-	VAI	look there, look about	[15]
itâpicî-	VAI	be away, be absent	[4]
itêh-	VTI	stir s.t.	[18]
itêhkê	IPC	...wards, on the... side	[1], [7]
itêliht-	VTI	think s.t.	[2]
itêlihtâkosi-	VAI	be so thought, be considered, seem	[17]
itêlihtâkwan-	VII	be so thought, be considered, seem	[17]
itêlim-	VTA	think s.o.	[3]
itihtâkosi-	VAI	sound so	[18]
itihtâkwan-	VII	sound so	[18]
itikiti-	VAI	be so big	[10]
itin-	VTA / VTI	hold s.o./ s.t. so, hold s.o./ s.t. in such a way	[11]
itohtê-	VAI	go (to a given place)	[1]
itwê-	VAI	say	[1]
itwêwin-	NI	something said, word, utterance	[8]
...îk-	NDI	home, dwelling *v.* kîki, nîki, wîki	[6]
îkatên-	VTA / VTI	put s.o./ s.t. aside, store s.o./ s.t. away (for a short time)	[12]
îkatêsi-	VAI	get out of the way, remove oneself	[17]
ka	IPV future marker with ni... and ki... subject prefixes	shall, will	[2]
kahkahkîhkêsi-	VAI	be square	[17]
kahkahkîhkêyâ-	VII	be square	[17]
kakêpâtisi-	VAI	be stupid *v.* kisisawisî-	[9]
kakwê	IPV	try (to)	[11], [15]
kakwêcim-	VTA	ask s.o. (about s.t.) *v.* natotamaw-	[11]
kanawâpaht-	VTI	look at s.t.	[8]
kanawâpam-	VTA	look at s.o.	[8]
kanawêliht-	VTI	keep s.t.	[8]
kanwêlim-	VTA	keep s.o.	[8]
kapatênâso-	VAI	unload (a boat), put (things) ashore	[12]
kapâ-	VAI	go ashore, land; alight from a vehicle	[17]
kapêši-	VAI	camp	[11]
kapêwin-	NI	campsite	[17]
kaških-	VTA	manage s.o.	[17]
kaškihtâ-	VAI-T	manage s.t.; be able to, contrive to	[17]
kata	IPV future marker	shall, will: with 3 and 3' subjects *v.* ta	[16]
kawah-	VTI	take *or* knock s.t. down with an instrument	[10]

kawahw-	VTA	take *or* knock s.o. down with an instrument	[10]
kawêšimo-	VAI	go to bed, retire for the night	[18]
kawin-	VTA / VTI	knock s.o./ s.t. down; *with* mâhkiy- break camp	[6]
kawipit-	VTA / VTI	pull s.o./ s.t. down	[10]
kawišk-	VTI	bring *or* knock s.t. down by body action	[10]
kawiškaw-	VTA	bring *or* knock s.o. down by body action	[10]
kayâm	IPC	quietly, tranquilly; all right!	[10]
kayâši	IPN	old, stale *v.* ayawiši, oški	[4]
kâ	IPV restrictive, rel. + conj. indic.	who (*of persons*), which (*of things*), when (*of time*), *with conj. indic.* where (*with* iši, *of place*)	[7], [18]
kâ-akihcikâtêki	VII 0p conj. indic.	Cree letters: *lit.,* (things) which are reckoned (*northern N-Dialect*) *v.* kâ-ililîw'-astêki, kâ-ililîwi-ayamihtâniwahki	[18]
kâ-atâwêt	Nom. A [VAI conj.]	trader: *lit.,* (one) who trades	[8]
kââ	IPC	Oh! So, that's it!	[1]
kâhci	IPV	shove, push	[9]
kâhcitin-	VTA / VTI	catch s.o./ s.t.	[8]
kâhci-wêpin-	VTA / VTI	shove s.o./ s.t., push s.o./ s.t.	[9]
kâhtin-	VTA / VTI	push s.o./ s.t.	[15]
kâ-ililîw'-astêki	VII 0p conj. indic.	Cree letters: *lit.,* (things) which are set	[18]
kâ-ililîwi-ayamihtâniwahki	VAI-T indf. conj. indic.	Cree letters: *lit.,*(things) which one reads, (things) which are read	[18]
kâ-kiskinohamâkêt	Nom. A	teacher *v.* kiskinohamâkê-	[9]
kâ-pîsisicik šôliyânak	Nom. A	small change	[10]
kâsîcihcê-	VAI	wash one's hand(s)	[18]
kâsîhkwê-	VAI	wash one's face	[18]
kâsîp-	NA	boil (swelling on skin) *v.* omanicôšimi-, sîkihp-	[16]
kâšâ-	VII	be sharp	[17]
kâšisi-	VAI	be sharp	[17]
kâškipâso-	VAI	shave	[18]
kêhcinâho-	VAI	be sure, be certain	[7]
kêkât	IPC	almost, nearly	[11]
kêkišêp	IPC	this morning	[9]
kêkišêpâyâkê	VII conj. subj.	in the morning (looking forward) *v.* kišêpâyâkê	(12)
kêko	PR interrog.	which (one)?	[3]
kêkwân	PR interrog.	what (thing)?	[2]
kêkwân-	NI	thing	[3]
kêkwânihkân-	NI	a sort of thing; what sort of thing?	[17]
kê-otâkošihk	VII (fut. ptcl. prefix + conj. indic.)	(late) this afternoon, early this evening	[11]
kêposkâw-	NI	Kapiskau (place name): *lit.,* reeds abundant	[11]

kêšîciwanw-	NI	Kashechewan, formerly Albany Post, Ontario: *lit.*, Swift Flow, Swift Current	[11]
kêtâspiso-	VAI	undress *v.* awêspiso-	[18]
kê-tipiskâk	VII (fut. ptcl. prefix + conj. indic.)	tonight (looking forward)	[12]
kê-wâpahk	VII (fut. ptcl. prefix + conj. indic.)	tomorrow: *lit.*, when it will dawn	[8]
kêyâpac	IPC	still, yet; more *v.* kiyâpic	[3]
ki(t)...	Prefix	2nd person possessor *or* subject marker: your, you	[1]
kicêmišiš-	NDA	your puppy. *v.* nicêmišiš-, ocêmišiša	[8]
kici	IPV + conj. indic.	so that, in order that	[6]
kicin-	NI [loanword]	kitchen	[14]
kicistâpâwacikê-	VAI	wash	[15]
kicistâpâwatâ-	VAI-T	wash s.t.	[11]
kicistâpâwal-	VTA	wash s.o.	[11]
kicistâpâwalo-	VAI	wash (oneself)	[18]
kicistâpitêho-	VAI	clean one's teeth	[18]
kihci	IPN / IPV	great, big, greatly	[2]
kihciniskîhk	IPC	on the right *v.* namatiniskîhk	[14]
kihcipalihcikan-	NI	outboard motor, "kicker"	[17]
kihciwil-	VTA	carry s.o. off, carry s.o. away	[13]
kihciwitâ-	VAI-T	carry s.t. off, carry s.t. away	(13)
kihtimi-	VAI	be lazy	[12]
kihtohtê-	VAI	go away	[1]
kikâwiy-	NDA	your (2) mother *v.* nikâwiy-, okâwiya	[2]
kikosis-	NDA	your (2) son *v.* nikosis-, okosisa	[2]
kilihtin-	VII	slip	[12]
kilišin-	VAI	slip	[12]
kimis-	NDA	your (2) older sister *v.* nimis-, omisa	[2]
kimiwan-	VII	rain	[3], [14]
kimiwanâpoy-	NI	rain water	[15]
kimošôm-	NDA	your (2) grandfather *v.* nimošôm-, omošôma	[13]
kinahâhkaniskwêm-	NDA	your (2) daughter-in-law *v.* ninahâhkaniskwêm-, onahâhkaniskwêma	[13]
kinahâhkišîm-	NDA	your (2) son-in-law *v.* ninahâhkišîm-, onahâhkišîma	[13]
kinîkihikwak	NDA	your (2) parents *v.* ninîkihikwak, onîkihikwa	[13]
kinoh-	VTA	lengthen s.o.	[18]
kinohtâ-	VAI-T	lengthen s.t.	[18]
kinosi-	VAI	be long	[17]
kinošêw-	NA	pike, jackfish *v.* 11.B.2.2, Dialect Variation	[11]
kinwâ-	VII	be long	[17]
kinwêš	IPC	a long time	[4]

kipah-	VTI	close s.t., shut (off) s.t. *v.* okipahowêsiw-	[15]
kipahw-	VTA	close s.o., shut (off) s.o.	(15)
kipihcî-	VAI	stop, come to a standstill, halt	[15], [17]
kipihtawê-	VAI	stop speaking: *as impolite or brusque imperative,* kipihtawê! Stop talking! *v.* kito-	[18]
kipihtin-	VTA / VTI	stop s.o./ s.t. (by hand)	[17]
kisikos-	NDA	your (2) aunt, your (2) mother-in-law *v.* nisikos-, osikosa	[Supp. Conv. II]
kisis-	NDA	your (2) uncle, your(2) father-in-law *v.* nisis-, osisa	[Supp. Conv. II]
kisisawisî-	VAI	be smart, be clever *v.* kakêpâtisi-	[9]
kisiso-	VAI	be warm (over-warm), have a fever	[16]
kisiwâsi-	VAI	be angry	[9]
kisiwâsîstaw-	VTA	become angry at s.o. *v.* kišiwâh-	[9]
kiskêliht-	VTI	know s.t.	[4]
kiskêlihtamoh-	VTA	inform s.o., *lit.,* make s.o. to know	[16]
kiskêlim-	VTA	know s.o.	[3]
kiskinohamaw-	VTA	teach s.o.	[22]
kiskinohamâkê-	VAI	teach	[9]
kiskinohamâso-	VAI	learn	[4], [Supp. Conv. I]
kiskinohamâtôwikamikw-	NI	school	[9]
kiskisi-	VAI	remember	[8]
kispakâ-	VII	be thick	[17]
kispakisi-	VAI	be thick	[17]
kistêliht-	VTI	be interested in s.t., respect s.t., esteem s.t. *v.* cîhkêliht-, kišišawêliht-	[14]
kistêlim-	VTA	be interested in s.o., respect s.o., esteem s.o. *v.* cîhkêlim-, kišišawêlim-	[14]
kistês	NDA	your older brother, *v.* nistês, ostêsa	
kišâstaw	IPC	Gosh! My, but...!	[7]
kišê-ililiw-	NA	old person (*contraction:* kišê-'liliw-)	[13]
kišê-ililîwi-	VAI	be an old person	[13]
kišêpânêhkwê-	VAI	have breakfast, breakfast	[18]
kišêpânêhkwêwin-	NI	breakfast	(18)
kišêpâyâkê	VII 0 conj. subj.	in the morning (looking forward) *v.* kêkišêpâyâkê	[12]
kišipâ-	VII	end, terminate	[17]
kišipâw-	NI	end: kišipâhk at the end	[18]
kišipisi-	VAI	end, terminate	[17]
kišišawêliht-	VTI	be interested in s.t. *v.* cîhkêliht-, kistêliht- (N.W. James Bay)	[14]
kišišawêlim-	VTA	be interested in s.o. *v.* cîhkêlim-, kistêlim- (N.W. James Bay)	[14]

kišitê-	VII	be hot	[3]
kišiwâh-	VTA	anger s.o. *v.* kisiwâsîstaw-	[9]
kišk-	VTI	wear s.t.	[14]
kiškaw-	VTA	wear s.o.	[14]
kitânis-	NDA	your (2) daughter *v.* nitânis-, otânisa	[2]
kitêhi	NDI	your (2) heart *v.* mitêh-	[18]
kitêm-	NDA	your dog *v.* nitêm-, otêma; atimw-	[8]
kitimâkisi-	VAI	be poor, be pitiable *v.* mîšakisî-	[14]
kito-	VAI	bellow: 'kâ kito keep quiet! shut up! *v.* kipihtawê-	[9]
kitohcikan-	NI	musical instrument, fiddle	[14]
kitohcikê-	VAI	make music, play music	[Supp. Conv. I]
kitot-	VTA	scold s.o. severely, bawl s.o. out *v.* kîhkâm-.	[9]
kitôsim-	NDA	your (2) stepson *v.* nitôsim-, otôsima	[Supp. Conv. II]
kitôsimiskwêm-	NDA	your (2) stepdaughter *v.* nitôsimiskwêm-, otôsimiskwêma	[Supp. Conv. II]
kitôsis-	NDA	your (2) aunt, stepmother *v.* nitôsis-, otôsisa	[Supp. Conv. II]
kitôtêm-	NDA	your (2) friend *v.* nitôtêm-, otôtêma	[6]
kiyâpic	IPC	more, more of; still, yet *v.* kêyâpac	[3]
kiyâskw-	NA	seagull	[11]
kî[1]	IPV	*completed action or past time marker w. affirmative*	[6]
kî[2]	IPV	potential prefex, can, be able to	[3]
kîcišân-	NDA	your (2) kinsman	[Supp. Conv. II]
kîhkâm-	VTA	scold s.o. mildly, chide s.o. *v.* kitot-	[9]
kîhkêhtakâhk	IPC	in the corner	[10]
kî-iškwâ	IPC	afterwards: *used alone as adverbial particle* *v.* pâtimâ	[17]
kîki	NDI	your (2) home *v.* nîki, wîki, ...îk-	[6]
kîla	PR [2nd pers. sing.]	you	[1]
kîlanânaw	PR [21 pers.] *MC*	we (*inclusive*) *v.* kînânaw	[7]
kîlawâw	PR [2nd pers. pl.]	you	[6]
kînânaw	PR [21 pers.] *SC*	*we* (inclusive) *v.* kîlanânaw	[7]
kîsis-	VTI	cook s.t., bake s.t.	[4]
kîsisw-	VTA	cook s.o., bake s.o.	[4]
kîsôsi-	VAI	be (snug) warm	[16]
kîstâw-	NDA	your (2) brother-in-law *v.* nîstâw-, wîstâwa	[13]
kîšikâ-	VII	be day	[3]
kišowâ	VII	be warm	[15]
kîšôh-	VTA	keep s.o. warm (as with a blanket)	[16]
kîšôn-	VTA	keep s.o. warm (by holding him)	[16]
kîšponê-	VII	be full	[12]
kîtimw-	NDA	your (2) sister-in-law *v.* nîtimw-, wîtimwa	[13]
kîwat-	NDI	your (2) hunting bag *v.* mîwat-, nîwat-, wîwat-	[14]

kîwê-	VAI	return, go home	[9]
kocicîy-	NI	outlet (from a lake)	[17]
kocišk-	VTI	try s.t. on (clothing)	[10]
kociškaw-	VTA	try s.o. on (clothing)	[10]
kosâpê-	VAI / VII	sink	[12]
kosikwan-	VII	be heavy	[12]
kosikwati-	VAI	be heavy	(12), [17]
kosisim-	NDA	your (2) grandchild *v.* nosisim-, osisima	[13]
kospâhtawî-	VAI	go upstairs	[18]
kospi-	VAI	go up a bank	[17]
kospihtah-	VTA	take s.o. up a bank	(17)
kospihtatâ-	VAI-T	take s.t. up a bank	[17]
kostâci-	VAI	be afraid	[8]
koškwêliht-	VTI	be surprised (at s.t.)	[8]
kotak-	PR anim. / inan. prox. sg.	other, another one (*pl.* kotakiyak/kotakiya)	[4]
kotakiy-	PR anim. / inan.	the other, the other one *v.* kotakîliw.	[4]
kotakîliw	PR inan. obv. sg.	another (one), the other (one)	[4]
kotawê-	VAI	kindle a(n open) fire	[15]
kotikošin-	VAI	sprain oneself	[12]
kotin-	VTA / VTI	test s.o./ s.t. by hand	[16]
kôhkomis-	NDA	your (2) uncle / stepfather *v.* nôhkomis-, ôhkomisa	[SUPP. CONV. II]
kôskawâtapi-	VAI	sit quietly	[16]
kôskawâtêlihtâkwan-	VII	be quiet, be tranquil	[11]
kwantaw	IPC	to no purpose, idly, at random; offhand, not seriously;] *contraction of* pakwantaw	[7]
kwatapipali-	VAI / VII	capsize	[12]
kwayask	IPC	properly, correctly	[3]
kwayaskosi-	VAI	be straight	[17]
kwayaskwan-	VII	be straight	[17]
kwâpahipân-	NI	dipper, jug	[15]
kwâškwêpicikê-	VAI	fish with a hook, angle	[11]
kwêskah-	VTA / VTI	turn s.o./ s.t. (*e.g.* a canoe) using a paddle	[15]
kwêskipali-	VAI / VII	turn, change (into)	[18]
kwêskitê-	VII	be turned	[18]
kwêtipa-wêpišk-	VTI	knock s.t. over	[17]
kwêtipa-wêpiškaw-	VTA	knock s.o. over	(17)
lâhkaciši-	VAI	be light (in weight)	[17]
lâhkašin-	VII	be light (in weight)	[17]
lâlatin	IPC	on the bank (near water level) *v.* nanâmatin	[6]
lâlih	IPC + loc.	beside, alongside	[14]

lâlihtak	IPC	along the wall	[15]
lâsipêhtah-	VTA	carry s.o. down the bank	[17]
lâsipêhtatâ-	VAI-T	carry s.t. down the bank	[17]
lâsipêtimihk	IPC	down the bank	[13]
lipâci-kîsikâ-	VII	be a drizzly day	[7]
lîsamawi-natohkoliy-	NI	bicarbonate of soda	[16]
lôskâ-	VII	be soft	[17]
lôskisi-	VAI	be soft	[17]
maci	IPN / V	bad: *e.g.*, maci-kîšikâw, maci-manitôw	[3]
macihtwâwin-	NI	sin	[7]
maci-kîšikâ-	VII	be a bad day	[3]
mahkatêwâ-	VII	be black	[17]
mahkatêwisi-	VAI	be black	[17]
manâ	IPC	is it not? n'est-ce pas? [nama not + nâ]	[3]
masinahikan-	NI	book	[3]
masinahikê-	VAI	write, get "debt" (*i.e.*, credit) at the store	[10]
masinahwânêkinwân-	NI	paper	[9]
maskisin-	NI	shoe, boot, moccasin	[10]
maskw-	NA	bear: *sg.* maskwa, *pl.* maskwak	[8]
maškawâ-	VII	be hard	[17]
maškawisi-	VAI	be hard	[17]
maškawisî-	VAI	be healthy	[16]
maškawîmakan-	VII	be powerful	[14]
maškwašiy-	NI	grass; *pl.* vegetables	[4]
matakwan-	VII	not be (at a place) *v.* matê-	[4]
matay-	NDI	belly, stomach *v.* katay-, natay-, watay-, *etc.*	[16]
matê-	VAI	not be (at a place) *v.* matakwan-	[4]
mat(w)ê	IPV	at a distance, just discernible (either by hearing or sight)	[14]
matwêhcicikê-	VAI	ring the bell	[9]
matwêhiskohkwê-	VAI	drum, play the drum	[Supp. Conv. I]
mawâpi-	VAI	visit	[1]
mawâpîstaw-	VTA	visit s.o.	[12]
mayâšk-	VTI	pass s.t. (walking)	[14]
mayâškaw-	VTA	pass s.o. (walking)	[13]
mayâwahw-	VTA	pass s.o. (by water)	[13]
mayê-	VAI / VII	not be	[3]
mâci	IPV	begin (to) with immediate onset *v.* ati	[11]
mâcik'	IPC	lo, behold; look!	[3]
mâciš-	VTI	cut s.t.	(13), [16]
mâcišw-	VTA	cut s.o., operate (surgically) on s.o.	[13], [16]
mâhcic	IPC	at last, last	[7]

mâhkîw'-iškotêhkân-	NI	camp stove: *lit.,*tent stove	[12]
mâhkiy-	NI	tent (rectangular base)	[4]
mâka	IPC	but, however; and	[1]
mâkwahpit-	VTA / VTI	tie s.o./ s.t. up	[10]
mâmaw	IPC	together, altogether	[10]
mâmihk	IPC	down river	[5]
mâmišâ-	VII rdpl.	be large (collectively), be large all over *v.* mišâ-	[13]
mâmitonêliht-	VTI	think about s.t., ponder s.t.	[12]
mâmîšah-	VTI	mend s.t. all over, mend s.t. here and there *v.* mîšah-	[13]
mâmîšahw-	VTA rdpl.	mend s.o. all over, mend s.o. here and there *v.* mîšahw-	[13]
mâna	IPC	repeatedly, frequently	[9]
mâsamêkos-	NA	(speckled) trout *v.* 11.B.2.2, Dialect Variation	[11]
mâših-	VTA	fight s.o.	(17)
mâšihtâ-	VAI-T	fight s.t.	[17]
mâškôc	IPC	perhaps, maybe	[1]
mâtih	IPC	see then! look then!	[15]
mâtika	IPC	behold, look	[15]
mâtinamâkê-	VAI	distribute, apportion, allot	[12]
mâtinawê-	VAI	distribute, apportion, allot	[12]
mâtinawê-kîšikâ-	VII	be Saturday	[12]
mâtinawê-kîšikâšin-	VII	be Friday	[12]
mâto-	VAI	cry *v.* môh-	[9]
mâwac	IPC	most (*of degree*)	[4]
mâwisikostâ-	VAI-T	pile s.t. together, stack s.t. *v.* piskwastâ-	[15]
mêkwayâhtikw	IPC	among the trees (on land)	[15]
mêkwayêš	IPC + loc.	among	[15]
mêriy-	NA [personal name]	Mary	[14]
mêscipali-	VAI / VII	be worn out	[8]
mêskanaw-	NI	path, trail, road	[1]
mêstahôsi-	VAI	be worn out	(17)
mêstahôtê-	VII	be worn out	[17]
mêšakwani-piponw	IPC	every year, *lit.,* every Winter	[15]
mêtawê-	VAI	play	[Supp. Conv. I]
micihciy-	NDI	a / the hand *v.* kicihciy-, nicihciy-, ocihciy-	[15]
mihcêt	IPC	many, much	[8]
mihcêti-	VAI (in pl.)	be many	[Supp. Conv. II], [15]
mihcêtwâ	IPC	many times	[13]
mihcilawêsi-	VAI	be sorry	[3]
mihkosi-	VAI	be red	[17]
mihkwâ-	VII	be red	[17]
miht-	NI	log of wood, firewood (*sg.* mihti, *pl.* mihta)	[7]

mihtihkân-	NI	woodpile, cord (of wood)	[7]
mikisimo-	VAI	bark	[8]
mihkwacakâš-	NA	(red horse) sucker *v.* 11.B.2.2 Dialect Variation	[11]
mikwaškâtêliht-	VTI	worry about s.t.	[10]
mikwaškâtêlim-	VTA	worry about s.o.	[10]
milihkw-	NDA	tonsil: kilihkw-, nilihkw-, olihkwa	[16]
milo	IPN / V	good: *e.g.,* milo-kîšikâw	[3]
milo-kîšikâ-	VII	be a fine day	[3]
milomahciho-	VAI	feel well	[3]
milomâtisi-	VAI	be well	[12]
milonâkosi-	VAI	look nice	[10]
milonâkwan-	VII	look nice	[10]
milo-pimâtisi-	VAI	be well, be in good health	[3]
milopali-	VAI / VII	go well, get along well	[2]
mil'-otâkošin-	VII	be a fine evening *or* late afternoon	[3]
milotêpo-	VAI	be a good cook, be good at cooking	[10]
milo-tipiskâ-	VII	be a fine night	[3]
milo-wâhkom-	VTA	get on well with s.o.	[13]
milwâšin-	VII	be nice, be fine, be pleasant	[1]
milwâšiši-	VAI	be good, be fine	[3]
milwêliht-	VTI	like s.t.	[2]
milwêlim-	VTA	like s.o.	[4]
minawê-	VAI	cook	[Supp. Conv. I]
minihkwâkan-	NI	drinking vessel, cup, glass	[15]
minihkwê	VAI	drink	[17]
ministikw-	NI	island	[13]
mipwâm-	NDI	thigh, back leg *v.* kipwâm-, nipwâm-, opwâm-	[17]
misawâc	IPC	anyway, anyhow	[8]
misit-	NDI	foot *v.* kisit-, nisit-, osit-, *etc.*	[16]
misiwê	IPC	all	[6]
misk-	VTI	find s.t.	[9]
miskaw-	VTA	find s.o.	[9]
miskât-	NDI	leg *v.* kiskât-, niskât-, oskât-, *etc.*	[16]
mispiton-	NDI	arm *v.* kispiton-, nispiton-, ospiton-, *etc.*	[16]
mistahi	IPC	much	[13]
mistikw-	NI	stick	[11]
mistikwân-	NDI	head *v.* kistikwân-, nistikwân-, ostikwân-, *etc.*	[16]
mistikwâni-natohkoliy-	NI	aspirin: *lit.,* head-medicine; *possessed:* nimistikwâni-natohkolîm, *etc.*	[16]
mišakâ-	VAI	land, come to shore	[11]
mišâ-	VII	be big *v.* mâmišâ	[12]
mišikiti-	VAI	be big	(12)
mitâhtw-	IPC	ten	[6]

mitâhtomitana	IPC	one hundred	[10]
mitêh-	NDI	heart *sg.* mitêhi *v.* kitêhi-, nitêhi-, otêhi-, *etc.*	[16]
mitêhiyâpiy-	NDI	artery *v.* otêhiyâpiy-	[16]
mitoni	IPC	entirely, very much so, altogether	[9]
mitôn-	NDI	mouth: nitôn-, kitôn-, otôn-, *etc.*	[11], [16]
mîci-	VAI-T	eat s.t. *v.* mow-	[9]
mîcim-	NI	food	[4]
mîcisôwikamikw-	NI	restaurant: *lit.*, eating building	[Supp. Conv. I]
mîcisowinâhtikw-	NI	table	[17]
mîcisôwipaliho-	VAI	have a quick snack	[Supp. Conv. I]
mîkiwâm-	NI and NDI	wigwam-type tent *v.* Unit 14.F, mîkiwâm-	[14]
mîkwêc	IPC	thank you	[2]
mîl-	VTA	give (to) s.o.: mîlêw he gives him	[7]
mîna	IPC	again	[1]
mîpit-	NDI	tooth *v.* nîpit-, kîpit-, wîpit-, *etc.*	(9)
mîpiti-natohkolon-	NA	dentist	[9]
mîsî-	VAI	defecate	[9]
mîsîwikamikw-	NI	outdoor toilet *v.* walawîwikamikw-.	[9]
mîsîwi-natohkoliy-	NI	castor oil *v.* walawîwi-natohkoliy-	[16]
mîskaw	IPC	by way of a change, for a change	[13]
mîšah-	VTI	mend s.t., fix s.t., repair s.t. *v.* mâmîšah-	[4]
mîšahw-	VTA	mend s.o., fix s.o., repair s.o. *v.* mâmîšahw-	[4]
mîšakisî-	VAI	be rich, be well off *v.* kitimâkisi-	[14]
mîwat-	NDI	(hunting) bag *v.* kîwat-, nîwat-, wîwat-	[14]
mohcihtak	IPC	on the floor	[16]
mow-	VTA	eat s.o. *v.* mîci-	[9]
môh-	VTA	make s.o. cry *v.* mâto-	[9]
môhkomân-	NI	knife	[18]
môla	IPC	no; not	[1]
môla wîlâhpahk		that's too bad, that's a pity	[3]
môsoniy-	NI	Moosonee: townsite eight km. up Moose River at SW corner of James Bay, Ontario	[2]
môso-wîyâs-	NI	moose meat	[4]
môsw-	NA	moose	[4]
môšihtâ-	VAI-T	feel s.t., experience sense of s.t.	[16]
môšak	IPC	always	[4]
mwêhci	IPC	exactly *v.* mwêhci anohc	[5]
mwêhci anohc		right now	[5]
nahêlim-	VTA	be fond of s.o.	[13]
nahišk-	VTI	fit s.t.	[10]
nahiškaw-	VTA	fit s.o. (*i.e.*, a garment represented by an NA)	[10]
nakat-	VTA / VTI	leave s.o./ s.t. behind	[6]

nakiskaw	IPC	a little while	[4]
nakiškaw-	VTA	meet s.o.	[13]
namatiniskîhk	IPC	on the left *v.* kihciniskîhk	[14]
namês-	NA	fish	[6]
nanâmatin	IPC	on the bank (near water level) *Lake Winnipeg, N Dialect: v.* lâlâtin	[6]
nanâskom-	VTA	be obliged to s.o., thank s.o.	[9]
nanâtawâpaht-	VTI	look for s.t., search for s.t. *Cf.* nânatawâpaht-	[10]
nanâtawâpam-	VTA	look for s.o., search for s.o. *Cf.* nânatawâpam-	[10]
nanâtawim-	VTA rdpl.	examine s.o. *v.* 'nâtawim-, 'nâtawicikan-	[16]
nanâtoštahikê-	VAI	guess, take a blind shot at	[17]
napakâ-	VII	be flat	[17]
napakisi-	VAI	be flat	[17]
naspâc	IPC	back to front, wrong way to, wrongly	[7]
naspitaw-	VTA	resemble s.o.	[18]
naškwêwašihikaniyâpiy-	NI	telephone answer taking machine	[SUPP. CONV. I]
naškwêwašihtwâwiniyâpiy-	NI	telephone answering machine	[SUPP. CONV. I]
natawaho-	VAI	hunt	[13]
natawâpaht-	VTI	go to see s.t., go to fetch s.t.	[8]
natawâpam-	VTA	go to see s.o., go to fetch s.o.	[8]
natawê	IPV	go to (do s.t.): *variant of* natawi	[SUPP. CONV. I]
natawêliht-	VTI	want s.t., desire s.t.	[3]
natawêlim-	VTA	want s.o., desire s.o.	[3]
natawi-	IPV	go to (do s.t.)	[8]
natawi-ašam-	VTA	go to feed s.o.	[8]
natawi-kanawâpaht-	VTI	go to look at s.t.	[8]
natawi-kanawâpam-	VTA	go to look at s.o.	[8]
natawi-kapêši-	VAI	go to pitch camp	[11]
natimihk	IPC	upstream, upriver *v.* mâmihk	[5]
natohkoliy-	NI	medicine *MC*	(3)
natohkolon-	NA	doctor	[3]
natohkolon-	NI	medicine (*at* Kêšîciwan). *v.* natohkoliy-	[3]
natohkolonikamikw-	NI	dispensary	[5]
natohkolon-iskwêw-	NA	nurse	[2]
natoht-	VTI	listen to s.t.	[8]
natohta	VTI 2 imperative	listen (to s.t.)	[8]
natohtaw-	VTA	listen to s.o.	[16]
natom-	VTA	call s.o., invite s.o., "beckon to " s.o.	[16]
natotamaw-	VTA	ask s.o. for s.t., request s.t. of s.o.*v.* kakwêcim-	[11]
nawac	IPC	quite, pretty much	[2]
nâ	IPC	question marker	[1]
nâcipah-	VTA	fetch s.o.	[14]
nâcipahtâ-	VAI-T	fetch s.t.	(14)

nâcipahtwâ-	VAI-T	fetch s.t.	[18]
nâha	PR dem. anim. prox. sg.	that one (more distant), yonder one *v.* nêma	[8]
nâkacihtâ-	VAI-T	attend to s.t., observe s.t.	[7]
nâkê	IPC	later, later on	[5]
nânatawâpaht-	VTI	*variant of* nanâtawâpaht-, *q.v.*	[10]
nânatawâpam-	VTA	*variant of* nanâtawâpam-, *q.v.*	[10]
nâpêšiš-	NA	boy	[9]
nâpêw-	NA	man	[2]
nâsic	IPC	very, very much *synon. for* nâspic, *q.v.*	[10]
nâspic	IPC	very, very much	[1]
nâspitoht-	VTI	imitate s.t.	[6]
nâspitohtaw-	VTA	imitate s.o.	[6]
nâtahw-	VTA	approach s.o. (by water)	[13]
nâtakah-	VTI	bring s.t. to shore (by instrument, *i.e.,* a paddle)	[15]
'nâtawicikan-	NI [contraction]	thermometre *v.* 'nâtawim- *below*	[16]
'nâtawim-	VTA [contraction]	examine s.o. *v.* nanâtawim- *above*	[16]
nêma	PR dem. inan. prox. sg.	yonder one, yon one (*more distant than* anima) *v.* nâha	[6]
nêmitana	IPC	forty	[10]
nêmitanawêhtay-	NA	forty dollars	[10]
nêsta	IPC	and; also, too	[1]
nêta	IPC	over yonder, yonder thereabouts	[6]
nêtê	IPC	yonder, over there [*more distant than* anta]	[1]
nêw	IPC	four	[6]
nêw-ahtay-	NA	four dollars	[10]
nêwayêk	IPC	in four ways	[18]
nêw'-kîšikâ-	VII	be Thursday	[12]
nêw'šâpw	IPC	fourteen	[10]
ni(t)...	Prefix	1st person possessor *or* subject marker: my, I	[1]
nicêmišiš-	NA	my puppy *v.* kicêmišiš-, ocêmišiša	[8]
nihtâ	IPV	be good at (doing) s.t., be given to (doing) s.t.	[9]
nikamo-	VAI	sing	[SUPP. CONV. I]
nikâwiy-	NDA	my mother *v.* kikâwiy-, okâwiya	[2]
nikosis-	NDA	my son *v.* kikosis-, okosisa	[2]
nikotwâsw	IPC	six	[6]
nikotwâsomitana	IPC	sixty	[10]
nikotwâsošâpw	IPC	sixteen	[10]
nimis-	NDA	my older sister *v.* kimis-, omisa	[2]
nimošôm-	NDA	my grandfather *v.* kimošôm-, omošôma	[13]
ninahâhkaniskwêm-	NDA	my daughter-in-law *v.* kinahâhkaniskwêm-, onahâhkaniskwêma	[13]
ninahâhkišîm-	NDA	my son-in-law *v.* kinahâhkišîm-, onahâhkišîma	[13]

ninîkihikwak	NDA	my parents *v.* kinîkihikwak, onîkihikwa	[13]
nipah-	VTA	kill s.o.	[8]
nipâ-	VAI	sleep	[3]
nipêwayâna	NI pl.	pyjamas, night clothes	[18]
nipêwin-	NI	bed, bunk	[15]
nipiy-	NI	water	[6]
nipîwan-	VII	be wet	[7]
nisikos-	NDA	my aunt, my mother-in-law *v.* kisikos-, osikosa	[SUPP. CONV. II]
nisis-	NDA	my uncle, my father-in-law *v.* kisis-, osisa	[SUPP. CONV. II]
nisitoht-	VTI	understand s.t.	[1]
nisitohtaw	VTA	understand s.o	[1]
nisk-	NA	goose: *sg.* niska, *pl.* niskak	[8]
nistês	NDA	my older brother, *v.* kistês, ostêsa	[2]
nisto	IPC	three	[6]
nistomitana	IPC	thirty	[10]
nistošâpw	IPC	thirteen	[10]
nistwâ	IPC	three times	[10]
ništam	IPC	first	[11]
nitânis-	NDA	my daughter *v.* kitânis-, otânisa	[2]
nitêm-	NDA	my dog *v.* nitêm-, kitêm-	[8]
nitôsim-	NDA	my stepson *v.* kitôsim-, ôsima	[SUPP. CONV. II]
nitôsimiskwêm-	NDA	my stepdaughter *v.* kitôsimiskwêm-, otôsimiskwêma	[SUPP. CONV. II]
nitôsis-	NDA	my aunt / stepmother *v.* kitôsis-, otôsisa	[SUPP. CONV. II]
nitôtêm-	NDA	my friend *v.* kitôtêm-, otôtêma	[6]
niyâlanw	IPC	five	[6]
niyâlano-kîšikâ-	VII	be Friday	[12]
niyâlomitana	IPC	fifty	[10]
niyâlošâpw	IPC	fifteen	[10]
niyânânêw	IPC	eight	[6]
niyânânêw'šâpw	IPC	eighteen	[10]
niyânânêyamitana	IPC	eighty	[10]
nîhci	IPC	below; downstairs	[3]
nîhtin-	VTA / VTI	hand s.o./ s.t. down	[15]
nîkânî-	VAI	go ahead, go in lead position	[15]
nîki	NDI	my home *v.* kîki, wîki, ...îk-	[6]
nîla	PR [1st pers. sing.]	I	[1]
nîmi-	VAI	dance	[SUPP. CONV. I]
nîmin-	VTA / VTI	hold s.o./s.t. up (by hand)	[13]
nîpawi-	VAI	stand	[14]

nîpin-	VII	be Summer *v.* anohc kâ-nîpihk this Summer	[11]
nîstâw-	NDA	my brother-in-law *v.* kîstâw-, wîstâwa	[13]
nîswâsomitana	IPC	seventy	[10]
nîswâsošâpw	IPC	seventeen	[10]
nîswâsw	IPC	seven	[6]
nîšâhtawî-	VAI	go downstairs	[18]
nîši-	VAI	be two	[13]
nîšo	IPC	two	[6]
nîšo-kîšikâ-	VII	be Tuesday	[12]
nîšošâpw	IPC	twelve	[10]
nîšwâ	IPC	twice	[10]
nîšitana	IPC	twenty	[10]
nîtimw-	NDA	sister-in-law *v.* kîtimw-, wîtimwa	[13]
nîwat-	NDI	my (hunting) bag *v.* kîwat-, mîwat-, wîwat-	[14]
nôcih-	VTA	work at s.o.	[9]
nôcihtâ-	VAI-T	work at s.t.	[9]
nôhcimihk	IPC	in the bush, inland	[6]
nôhkomis-	NDA	my uncle / stepfather *v.* kôhkomis-, ôhkomisa	[Supp. Conv. II]
nôkosi-	VAI	appear, be visible	[2], [14]
nôsisim-	NDA	my grandchild *v.* kôsisim-, ôsisima	[13]
nôtamêsê-	VAI	fish	[11]
nôtimâ-	VII	be round (spherical or cylindrical) *v.* wâwiyêyâ-	[17]
nôtimisi-	VAI	be round (spherical or cylindrical) *v.* wâwiyêsi-	[17]
n'tawâc	IPC	just as well	[8]
o(t)...	Pers. infl. prefix	3rd person possessor: his, her	[1]
ocawâšimiši-	VAI	have child(ren)	[Supp. Conv. II]
ocâpânišîš-	NI	snowmobile	[9]
ocêmišiša	NDA	his puppy *v.* nicêmišiš-, kicêmišiš-	[8]
ocipit-	VTA / VTI	pull s.o./ s.t.	[15]
ohci	IPC	for	[4]
ohci	IPV	from: kinwêš ohci-ihtakwan it's been (there) as of a long time (ago)	[5]
ohci	IPV	*contraction of* kî-ohci: *completed action or past time marker with negative v.* kî *and* ohci	[6], [4]
ohcikawin-	VII	drip, leak (as a tent *or* house)	[7]
ohci-kâhcitin-	VTA / VTI	catch s.o./ s.t.from...	[11]
ohcipici-	VAI	move (with family and belongings) from, move camp from	[15]
ohcistin-	VII	leak, let in water	[3]

ohcitaw	IPC	purposely	[9]
ohcî-	VAI	originate, come from, *v.* ohtêhtê-	—
ohpaho-	VAI	fly up	[16]
ohpiki-	VAI	grow up	[Supp. Conv. II]
ohpikih-	VTA	bring up, raise (*i.e.*, children)	[Supp. Conv. II]
ohpin-	VTA / VTI	lift s.o./ s.t.	[17]
ohtê-	VII	boil *v.* oso-	[16]
ohtohtê-	VAI	come from (*i.e.*, be on way from: not in sense of originate) *v.* ohcî-	[2]
okâsîpimi-	VAI	have a boil *v.* omanicôšimi-, osîkihpimi-	[16]
okâwiya	NDA	his / her mother *v.* kikâwiy-, nikâwiy-	[2]
okimâhkân-	NA	chief	[4]
okimâw-	NA	manager, boss	[1]
okimâwi-	VAI	be manager	[2]
okipahowêsiw-	NA	policeman: *lit.*, the one who shuts away *v.* kipah–	[7]
okosisa	NDA	his / her son *v.* kikosis-, nikosis-	[2]
olâkan-	NI	dish, plate; basin	[15]
omanicôšimi-	VAI	have a boil: *lit.*, have an insect *v.* kâsîp-, sîkihp-	[16]
omisa	NDA	his / her older sister *v.* kimis-, nimis-	[2]
omošôma	NDA	his / her grandfather *v.* kimošôm-, nimošôm-	[13]
onahâhkaniskwêma	NDA	his / her daughter-in-law *v.* kinahâhkaniskwêm-, ninahâhkaniskwêm-	[13]
onahâhkišîma	NDA	his / her son-in-law *v.* kinahâhkišîm-, ninahâhkišîm-	[13]
onîkihikwa	NDA	his / her parents *v.* ninîkihikwak, kinîkihikwak	[13]
opahipê-	VII	float	[12]
opiskoni	IPC + loc.	(at the) back of *v. also* otânâhk	[15]
osâmihkwâmi-	VAI	sleep in, oversleep	[9]
osâwaškosi-	VAI	be blue-green	[17]
osâwaškwâ-	VII	be blue-green	[17]
osâwâ-	VII	be yellow-brown, be tawny coloured	[17]
osâwisi-	VAI	be yellow-brown, be tawny coloured	[17]
osihtê-	VAI	hear: *used with negative,* be hard of hearing, be deaf	[13]
osikosa	NDA	his / her aunt, his / her father-in-law *v.* kisikos-, nisikos-	[Supp. Conv. II]
osisa	NDA	his / her uncle, his / her father-in-law *v.* kisis-, nisis-	[Supp. Conv. II]
oskac	IPC	at first	[7]
oso-	VAI	boil *v.* ohtê-	[16]
ostêsa	NDA	his / her older brother *v.* kistês, nistês	[2]
ostêsi-	VAI	have an older brother	[Supp. Conv. II]

ostostot-	VTI	cough	[5]
ostostocikanâpoy-	NI	cough syrup, cough medicine	[3]
ošîma	NDA	his / her younger sibling (no distinction as to sex) *v.* kišîm-, nišîm-	[2]
ošîmi-	NDA	have a younger sibling	[SUPP. CONV. II]
oški	IPC / IPV	new, fresh *v.* ayawiši; kayâši	[4]
oški-kîšikâ-	VII	be Monday	[11]
otakikomi-	VAI	have a cold, *lit.*, have mucus	[3]
otamî-	VAI	be busy	[2]
otâkošin-	VII	be evening	[3]
otâkošinêhkwê-	VAI	have supper, have the evening meal	[18]
otâkošîhk	IPC	yesterday	[8]
otâmah-	VTI	hit s.t.	[9]
otâmahw-	VTA	hit s.o.	[9]
otânâhk	IPC	back, behind; otânâhk itêhkê towards the backside, behind; backwards;	[7]
		otânâhk kâ-tawâstêk last week	[11]
		otânâhk wâskâhikanihk behind the house *v.* opiskoni	[15]
otânisa	NDA	his / her daughter *v.* kitânis-, nitânis-	[2]
otâpânâskw-	NA	sled	[9]
otâpê-	VAI	haul (wood)	[11]
otêhiyâpiy-	NI	his artery: *lit.*, heart-line *v.* mitêhiyâpiy-	[16]
otêma	NDA	his dog. *v.* atimw-; nitêm-, kitêm-	[4]
otihtah-	VII	come up to s.t., reach s.t.	[12]
otin-	VTA / VTI	take s.o./ s.t.	[8]
otôn-	NDI	his / her mouth: nitôn-, kitôn-, etc. *v.* mitôn-	[11]
otôsima	NDA	his / her stepson *v.* kitôsim-, nitôsim-	[SUPP. CONV. II]
otôsimiskwêma	NDA	his / her stepdaughter *v.* kitôsimiskwêm-, nitôsimiskwêm-	[SUPP. CONV. II]
otôsisa	NDA	his / her aunt / stepmother *v.* kitôsis-, otôsisa	[SUPP. CONV. II]
otôtêma	NDA	his / her friend: *cf.* nitôtêm, kitôtêm, *etc.*	[6]
otôtêmimâw-	NDA	friend	[5]
otwâwê-	VAI	have hiccoughs	[16]
ô	IPC	reference to immediate vicinity: *e.g.*, nîla ô it's me, *lit.*, me here; tânta ô? where (right around here)?	[15]
ôhkoma	NDA	his / her grandmother *v.* kôhkom-, nôhkom-	[13]
ôhkomisa	NDA	his / her uncle / stepfather *v.* kôhkomis-, nôhkomis-	[SUPP. CONV. II]

ôho	PR dem. anim. obv.	this (one)	[2], [5]
		these (ones)	[10]
	inan. prox & obv. pl.	these (ones)	[10]
ôhtâwi-	VAI	have a father	[Supp. Conv. II]
ôko	PR dem. anim. prox. pl.	these (ones)	[10]
ôlo-	VAI	howl	[8]
ôma	PR dem. inan. prox.	this one	[2]
ômêliw	PR dem. inan. obv.	this one	[2], [5]
ôsisima	NDA	his / her grandchild *v.* kôsisim-, nôsisim-	[13]
ôta	IPC	here	[1]
ôtê	IPC	hither, to here, this way, in this direction	[1]
ôtênaw-	NI	dwelling group *v.* pêyak ôtênaw	[Supp. Conv. II]
pahkân	IPC	separately	[12]
pahkihtin-	VII	fall	[12]
pahkišin-	VAI	fall; have a rupture	[12], [16]
pahkwêšikan-	NA	flour	[12]
pahkwêšikaniwat-	NI	flour bag, flour sack	[17]
pakitahwâ-	VAI	set out nets	[11]
pakitin-	VTA / VTI	put s.o./ s.t., let s.o./ s.t.	[12]
pakwantaw	IPC	to no purpose, idly, at random *v.* kwantaw	(7)
pakwayân-	NI	shirt	[10]
palacis-	NA	trousers, pants (*from English* breeches)	[8]
'pâmipali-	VAI / VII	travel about, move about: *contraction of* papâmipali-	[15]
papakâ-	VII	be thin	[17]
papakisi-	VAI	be thin	[17]
papâmipali-	VAI / VII	travel about, move about	[15]
papâmohtah-	VTA	take s.o. for a walk	[9]
papâmohtê-	VAI	walk about	[9]
papâ-wîcêw-	VTA	accompany s.o. around	[9]
pâhkân	IPC	presently, shortly	[10]
pâhkwatinâ-	VII	be dry ground, be a dry bank	[6]
pâhkwâ-	VII	be dry	[6]
pâhkwâhk	IPC	on the dry (part)	[6]
pâhpi-	VAI	laugh	[7]
pâhpih-	VTA	laugh at s.o.	[9]
pâhpitâ-	VAI-T	laugh at s.t.	(16)
pâkisê-	VII	be swollen	[16]
pâmâšakwê-	VAI	go for a stroll around	[Supp. Conv. I]
pâpawahikê-	VAI	knock, rap	[15]
pâpihlâ-	VAI	fly hither	[8]

pâs-	VTI	dry s.t. out	[11]
pâsitêniko-	VAI	have heartburn, have stomach distress	[16]
pâskis-	VTI	shoot s.t.: *lit.,* burst s.t. by heat, explode s.t. by heat	[8]
pâskisikan-	NI	gun	[8]
pâskisw-	VTA	shoot s.o.	[8]
pâstê-	VII	dry	[15]
pâsw-	VTA	dry s.o. out	[11]
pâtimâ	IPC	later on, by and by	[17]
pâtniy-	NA [personal name]	Evadney	[14]
pêci	IPV	in this direction, towards speaker	[2]
pêcicišahamaw-	VTA	send s.t. hither (to) s.o.	[11]
pêci-kîwê-	VAI	come back home, return	[11]
pêci-nôkosi-	VAI	come into view, appear	[7]
pêci-pêyako-	VAI	come alone	[15]
pêh-	VTA	wait for s.o., await s.o.	[16]
pêho-	VAI	wait	[2]
pêhkâc	IPC	slowly, carefully	[1]
pêht-	VTI	hear s.t.	[8]
pêhtaw-	VTA	hear s.o.	[8]
pêhtâ-	VAI-T	wait for s.t., await s.t. (Not to be confused with pêtâ-.)	[16]
pêhtâkosi-	VAI	be audible, make a sound with the voice	[17]
pêkatê-	VAI	belch	[16]
pêšâpêhkihtin-	VII	be a straight line (as in a copy book)	[18]
pêšiw-	VTA	bring s.o.	[8]
pêškiš	IPC	as well, among other things	[17]
pêšoc	IPC	near to (*w. loc.*), nearby	[11]
pêtâ-	VAI-T	bring s.t. (*Cf.* pêhtâ-.)	[8]
pêtâpan-	VII	be daybreak, be dawn, come the dawn	[7]
pêyakw	IPC	one, a certain…	[6], [8]
pêyako-	VAI	be one, be alone *v.* pêci-pêyako-	[Supp. Conv. II]
pêyakošâpw	IPC	eleven	[10]
pêyako-tipisk	IPC	period of one night, overnight	[13]
pêyak ôtênaw		as one family v. ôtênaw	[Supp. Conv. II]
pêyakwayêk	IPC	one way, one means	[18]
pêyakwâ	IPC	once	[11]
pihci	IPV	accidentally *Cf.* root pist…, in pistahw-.	[9]
pihcišitiso-	VAI	cut oneself accidentally	[16]
pihkotêw-	NI	ash(es)	[17]
pikiwaskisin-	NI	rubber boot, gum boot	[12]
piko	IPC	only	[1]
pilêsiw-	NA	bird	[8]

pimâskošin-	VAI	lie lengthwise (on a solid surface)	[11]
pimâtan-	VII	be alive, be living	[17]
pimâtisi-	VAI	live, be living	[3]
pimicihtakâhk	IPC	on the wall (*MC*) *v.* pimihtakâhk	[15]
pimihlâ-	VAI	fly	[8]
pimihtakâhk	IPC	on the wall *v.* pimicihtakâhk	[15]
pimihtin-	VII	lie	[12]
pimipali-	VAI	go along	[9]
pimipalih-	VTA	make s.o. go, drive s.o.	[9]
pimipalihtwâ-	VAI-T	make s.t. go, drive s.t.	[9]
pimišin-	VAI	lie	[12]
pimiwil-	VTA	carry s.o. (general word for carrying in the arms) *v.* išiwil-	[14]
pimiwitâ-	VAI-T	carry s.t. (general word for carrying in the arms) *v.* išiwitâ-	[14]
pimiy-	NI	oil, grease: *i.e.,* fuel	[11]
pimîwi-kân-	NI	oil can	[12]
pimot-	VTA	throw (s.t.) at s.o.	[16]
piponohk	NI loc. / IPC	last Winter	[13]
piponw-	NI	Winter	[13]
pisci	IPV	accidentally: *alternate form of* pihci, *q.v*	
pisiskâpaht-	VTI	notice s.t.	[9]
pisiskâpam-	VTA	notice s.o.	[9]
piskihcâ-	VII	be separate, be segregated, be distinct [SUPP. CONV. II]	
piskitasinahikan-	NI	chapter (in a book)	[18]
piskitasinahikaniš-	NI dim.	verse, sentence	[18]
piskwastâ-	VAI-T	pile s.t. into a heap *v.* mâwisikostâ-	[15]
pistah-	VTI	hit s.t. accidentally *v.* otâmah-	[9]
pistahw-	VTA	hit s.o. accidentally, *v.* otâmahw-	[9]
pišišik	IPC	consistently, throughout	[12]
pišišikosi-	VAI	be empty	(12)
pišišikwâ-	VII	be empty	[12]
pišošim-	VTA	trip s.o., cause s.o. to stumble	(12)
pišošimiko-	VTI inv. [like VAI]	be tripped by s.t., stumble	[16)
pišošin-	VAI	stumble	[12]
pitamâ	IPC	first (before doing anything else)	[4]
pîhcihtin-	VII	be inside, be contained inside	[15]
pîhcišin-	VAI	lie inside, be inside	(15)
pîhtawêskikana	NI pl.	underclothes, underwear	[18]
pîhtokah-	VTA	bring s.o. in	[16]
pîhtokwah-	VTA	bring s.o. in	[16]
pîhtokê-	VAI	enter *v.* pîhtokwê-	[3]
pîhtokwamihk	IPC	indoors, inside	[3]

pîhtokwê-	VAI	enter *v.* pîhtokê-	[3]
pîkoh-	VTI	break s.t. by instrument	[10]
pîkohw-	VTA	break s.o. by instrument	[10]
pîkon-	VTA / VTI	break s.o./ s.t.	[7]
pîkopali-	VAI / VII	be broken	[5]
pîkošk-	VTI	break s.t. by body action	[10]
pîkoškaw-	VTA	break s.o. by body action	[10]
pîliš	IPC	up to, until	[12]
pîsikah-	VTI	split s.t.	[11]
pîsikahw-	VTA	split s.o.	[11]
pîsimohkân-	NA	clock	(SUPP. CONV. I)
pîsisi-	VAI	be in bits, be in pieces	[10]
pîsiskâkan-	NI	coat, jacket *v.* pîskâkan-	[10]
pîskâkan-	NI	jacket: *contraction of* pîsiskâkan-	[8]
pîtoš	IPC	differently, different	[12]
pîtoš wayêš	IPC	somewhere else, elsewhere	[12]
pîwâpiskw-	NI	metal; motor	[13]
plâstiko-têhamân-	NA	credit card	[10]
pohcišk-	VTI	put s.t. on (as clothing)	[10]
pohciškaw-	VTA	put s.o. on (as clothing)	[10]
pôn-	VTI	make a fire (in the stove) *v.* kotawê-	[18]
pônihkâkê-	VAI	make a fire out of s.t., use s.t. to make a fire	[7]
pônihkê-	VAI	make a fire (in a stove)	[7]
pôsi-	VAI	depart by vehicle, embark	[4]
pôsihtâso-	VAI	load (freight on a canoe), do freighting	[12]
pôsihtâsômakan-	VII	freight, do freighting, hold freight	[17]
pôtâcikan-	NI	bugle, trumpet, blowing instrument (of music)	[10]
pwâkit-	NI	pocket	[10]
pwâmoši	IPC + conj. indic.	before: *v.* êmwayêš	[12]
pwâstaw	IPC	late	[9]
pwâstawi	IPV	late	[9]
pwât-	NA	Sioux	[18]
sakahikan-	NI	screw	[14]
sakahpit-	VTA / VTI	tie s.o./s.t. (to s.t.), tether s.o.	[8]
sakipât-	VTA / VTI	button s.o./ s.t.	[18]
saylas-	NA [personal name]	Silas	[5]
sâkahikan-	NI	lake	[8]
sâmin-	VTA / VTI	touch s.o./ s.t.	[16]
sâpêliht-	VTI	*with negative:* not be keen about s.t.	[6]
sâpêlim-	VTA	*with negative:* not be keen about s.o.	[6]
sêns-	NA	cent	[10]
sêskipalihtwâ-	VAI-T	bring s.t. to shore (using a motor) *v.* nâtkah-	[15]

sêskipit-	VTA / VTI	pull s.o./ s.t. ashore, beach s.o./ s.t.	[6]
sikalêt-	NA	cigarette	[10], [16]
sikilêsi-	VAI	be glad; be grateful	[17]
sîhcâ-	VII	be tight-packed, be tight fitting; be crowded	[12]
sîhcisi-	VAI	be tight-packed, be tight fitting	(12)
sîhkaci-	VAI	be cold	[14]
sîkihp-	NI	boil (swelling on skin) *v.* omanicôšimi-, kâsîp-	[16]
sîkin-	VTA / VTI	pour s.o./ s.t.	[15]
sîmiyan-	NA [personal name]	Simeon	[9]
sîpîwâpoy-	NI	river water	[15]
sîpiy-	NI	river	[1]
sîtwahpicikan-	NI	bandage, binding	[16]
sîtwahpit-	VTA / VTI	bandage s.o., bind up s.t.	[16]
sôp-	NA	soap	[16]

šawêlihtâkosi-	VAI	be lucky, be blessed	[18]
šâ	IPC	tch, tch!, tsk, tsk!	[5]
šâkitâtw	IPC	nine *MC. v.* šânkw.	[6]
šâkoc	IPC	sure thing! certainly!	[4]
šânkw	IPC	nine *SC. v.* šâkitât	[6]
šânkomitana	IPC	ninety	[10]
šânkošâpw	IPC	nineteen	[10]
šânkw-ahtay-	NA	nine dollars	[10]
šânkwêš-	NA	quarter; twenty-five cents	[10]
šâpopali-	VAI / VII	go through	[14]
šâpopêkan-	VII	be soaking (of the ground)	[7]
šihkipiš-	NA	diver duck: hooded merganser, coot *v.* šinkipiš- and UNIT 11.B.2.2	[11]
šiki-	VAI	urinate	[9]
šinkipiš-	NA	diver duck, probably the small or hooded merganser *v.* UNIT 11.B.2.2	[11]
šîkaho-	VAI	comb one's hair	[18]
šîpâ	IPC	under	[12]
šîpâstêwayân-	NI	sweater	[14]
šîpâyâhtikohk	IPC	under a / the tree (s)	[12]
šîšîp-	NA	duck	[8]
šišôtêw	NI and IPC	the shore, at the shore; edge of a plain	[6]
šîwah-	VTI	salt s.t. down	[11]
šîwahw-	VTA	salt s.o. down	[11]
šîwitâkan-	NI	salt	[18]
šôkâw-	NI	sugar	[18]
šwâp-	NI	shop, store	[1]
šwâpihkê-	VAI	buy, shop	[10]

ta	IPV future marker with 3 and 3′ subjects	shall, will: contraction of kata	[2]
tahkâyâ-	VII	be cold	[3]
tahkisi-	VAI	grow cool, cool off	[16]
tahkon-	VTA / VTI	hold s.o./ s.t. by hand	[10]
tahkonikan-	NI	handle	[17]
tahkosi-	VAI	be short	[17]
tahkoskât-	VTA / VTI	step on s.o./ s.t.	[15]
tahkošk-	VTI	hold s.t. by leg *or* body action	[10]
tahkoškaw-	VTA	hold s.o. by leg *or* body action	[10]
tahkwah-	VTI	hold s.t. by instrument; steer s.t. *Also as* tahkoh-	[10]
tahkwahw-	VTA	hold s.o. by instrument *Also as* tahkohw-	(10)
tahkwatêht-	VTI	hold s.t. in the mouth (with the teeth)	[10]
tahkwatêm-	VTA	hold s.o. in the mouth (with the teeth)	[10]
tahkwâ-	VII	be short	[17]
tahtw-ahtay-	NA	so many dollars *v.* tân'tahto- how many?	[10]
takošin-	VAI	arrive	[11]
takošinômakan-	VII	arrive	[12]
takwâkin-	VII	be Autumn, be Fall *v.* ê-takwâkihk	[8]
tašinê	IPC	all the time, continually, incessantly	[14]
tašîhkê-	VAI	dwell, live	[1]
tawâ-	VII	be room (for s.t.)	[12]
tawâstê-	VII	be a week	[11]
tawâstêw-	NI	week	[11]
tâni	IPC	how?	[2]
tânîlikohk	IPC	(up to) how much, to what extent; also as tânilikohk	[10]
tântahto	IPC	how many...? tân'tahto-cîmâna how many canoes?	[6]
tântê	IPC	where?	[1]
tâpask	IPC + indep. indic.	it is unlikely that, probably not	[9]
tâpiskôc	IPC	as, like	[7]
tâpišah-	VTI	string s.t., thread s.t.	[11]
tâpišahw-	VTA	string s.o., thread s.o.	[11]
tâpitâw	IPC	regularly	[16]
tâpwê	IPC	truly, really, seriously	[1]
tâpwêwin-	NI	truth	[13]
têhamân-	NA	card	[10]
têhtal-	VTA	set s.o. upon, place s.o. upon	[16]
têhtapiwin-	NI	seat, chair	[16]
têhtastâ-	VAI-T	set s.t. upon, place s.t. upon	[16]
têhtêpahipê-	VII	float (upon the surface)	[13]
têpiskâk	VII changed conj.	last night	[7]

têpit-	NA [personal name]	David	[9]
têpwât-	VTA	call s.o.	[7]
têpwê-	VAI	shout, proclaim	[8]
têwistikwânê-	VAI	have a headache	[16]
tik-	NA [personal name]	Dick	[8]
tipah-	VTI	pay for s.t., measure s.t.	[10]
tipahamaw-	VTA	pay s.o. (for s.t.)	[11]
tipahw-	VTA	pay for s.o., measure s.o.	[10]
tipâpêskocikan-	NI	pound	[12]
tipiskâ-	VII	be night, be dark	[3]
tîwâpohkê-	VAI	make tea	[13]
tîy-	NI	tea	[18]
tôt-	VTI	do s.t.	[9]
tôtaw-	VTA	do to s.o., do for s.o.	[9]
tôwi	IPN	kind of..., sort of...	[3], [11]
tôwihkân-	NI	kind, type, sort	[3]
twâmas-	NA [personal name]	Thomas	[8]
twoyêhk	IPC	immediately	[16]
wakîc	IPC + loc.	on (top of): *also as* wakic	[17]
wakîtatin	IPC	on top of the bank	[17]
walahpicikan-	NI	(wrapped) parcel *Cf.* parcel to be sent: išicišahikan-	[10]
walahpit-	VTA / VTI	wrap s.o./ s.t. up	[10]
walašawêwin-	NI	law	[7]
walawî-	VAI	go outside	[3]
walawîtimihk	IPC	outside	[3]
walawîwikamikw-	NI	outhouse (more polite term) *v.* mîsîwikamikw-	[9]
walawîwi-natohkoliy-	NI	milk of magnesia *v.* mîsîwi-natohkoliy-	[16]
wanâh-	VTA	disturb s.o., interrupt s.o., confuse s.o. *v.* niwanâhikon I get mixed up (9.A.3)	[9]
wani-kiskisi	VAI	misremember, forget, have a slip of mind	[8]
waniškâ-	VAI	get up (out of bed)	[9]
wani-tôt-	VII	do s.t. wrongly, misdo s.t.	[7]
wanîhkê-	VAI	forget	[7]
waspitah-	VTI	lace s.t. up: *e.g.*, shoes	[18]
wayêš	IPC	about, approximately	[3]
wâciyê	IPC	Hello; Good-bye	[1]
wâhtâkan-	NI	barrel: *contraction of* wiyâhtâkan-	[13]
wâkâ-	VII	be bent	[17]
wâkisi-	VAI	be bent	[17]
wâlaw	IPC	far away	[5]
wâlâ	VII	be concave	[18]

wâpaht	VTI	see s.t.	[4]
wâpahtil-	VTA	show (to) s.o.	[12]
wâpam-	VTA	see s.o.	[3]
wâpâ-	VII	be white	[17]
wâpisi-	VAI	be white	[17]
wâpwayân-	NI	blanket	[7]
wâskâhikan-	NI	house (*originally* stockade, palisade)	[7]
wâstên-	VTI	lighten s.t., turn on the light	[18]
wâšakâm	IPC + loc.	around: wâšakâm iškotêhk around the fire	[11]
wâšêyâkamin-	VII	be clear (liquid)	[15]
wât-	NI	den, lair *sg.* wâti	[18]
wâwâc	IPC	even	[12]
wâwiyênâkosi-	VAI	appear round, appear circular (disk-like) *v.* nôtimisi-	[17]
wâwiyênâkwan-	VII	appear round, appear circular (disk-like) *v.* nôtimâ-	[17]
wâwiyêsi-	VAI	be round, be circular (disk-like) *v.* nôtimisi-	[17]
wâwiyêyâ-	VII	be round, be circular (disk-like) *v.* nôtimâ-	[17]
wêhtakiht-	VTI	be inexpensive, be cheap	[10]
wêhtakiso-	VTA	be inexpensive, be cheap	[10]
wêhtan-	VII	be cheap, be inexpensive: *i.e.,* be easy	[11]
wêhtisi-	VAI	be cheap, be inexpensive: *i.e.,* be easy	[11]
wêmistikôšiw-	NA	Englishman, White-man: *often as* êmistikôšiw-	[7]
wêmistikôšîmo-	VAI	speak English	[4]
wêpâstan-	VII	drift	[5]
wêpâši-	VAI	drift	(5)
wêpin-	VTA / VTI	throw s.o./ s.t. out *v.* kâhci-wêpin-	[9]
wêsâ	IPC	too (much)	[8]
wêskac	IPC	long ago	[17]
wî	IPV	want (to) be going (to)	[4], [7]
wîcêw-	VTA	accompany s.o., be with s.o.	[13]
wîci	IPV	together with, co-	[13]
wîcih-	VTA	help s.o.	[16]
wîci-mêtawêm-	VTA	play together with s.o. *v.* mêtawê-	[13]
wîci-natawahom-	VTA	hunt with s.o. *v.* natawaho-	[13]
wîci-tašîhkêm-	VTA	dwell together with s.o.	[13]
wîhcêkinâkosi-	VAI	appear dirty	[15]
wîhcêkinâkwan-	VII	appear dirty	[15]
wîhkaciši-	VAI	taste good, be delicious	[4]
wîhkašin-	VII	taste good, be delicious	[4]
wîhkipw-	VTA	savour s.o.	(17)
wîhkist-	VTI	savour s.t.	[17]
wîht-	VTI	tell s.t.	[17]

wîhtamaw-	VTA	tell s.o.	
wîki-	VAI	dwell (in), live (in)	[SUPP. CONV. II]
wîki-	NDI	his / her home *v.* nîki-, kîki-, ...îk-	[6]
wîkimâkan-	NA	wife	[4]
wîkito-	VAI reciprocal	marry, marry each other	[13]
wîkitôwin-	NI	wedding	[14]
wîla	PR [3rd pers sg.]	he, she; it	[2]
wîla	IPC intensive	*e.g.,* môla wîla anohc not *now*	[6]
wîlawâw	PR [3rd pers. pl.]	they	[6]
wîlâhcikan-	NI	a wearable, article of clothing: *usu. in pl.* wîlâhcikana	[8]
wîlâht-	VTI	wear s.t.	[8]
wîlâm-	VTA	wear anim. obj., *e,g.,* palacîs-	[8]
wîlâta	IPC	nonetheless	[7]
wîliy-	NA [personal name]	Willie	[9]
wîpac	IPC	soon, shortly	[2]
wîsakêliht-	VTI	have a pain	[16]
wîsakikohtaskwê-	VAI	have a sore throat	[16]
wîskâc	IPC	ever, at any time	[6]
wîstâsihtâkosi-	VAI	be noisy	[8]
wîstâsihtâkwan-	VII	be noisy	[8]
wîstâwa	NDA	his brother-in-law *v.* kîstâw-, nîstâw-	[13]
wîtapim-	VTA	sit with s.o.	[13]
wîtimwa	NDA	his sister-in-law *v.* kîtimw-, nîtimw-	[13]
wîwaši-	VAI	carry (on back) *cf.* mîwat-	[17]
wîwat-	NDI	his (hunting) bag *v.* kîwat-, mîwat-, nîwat-	[2], [14]
wîyatêlihtâkosi-	VAI	be funny	[7]
wîyatêlihtâkwan-	VII	be funny	[7]
wîyatwê-	VAI	joke	[7]
wîyâs-	NI	flesh, meat	[4]
'yâkwâ	IPC [interjection]	Look out!	

SELECTED BIBLIOGRAPHY

Bloomfield, Leonard. 1927. "The Word-Stems of Central Algonquian", in *Festschrift Meinhof*, pp. 393–402. Hamburg.

________. 1933. *Language*. New York.

________. 1946. "Algonquian", in *Linguistic Structures of Native America*, Viking Fund Publications in Anthropology 6; pp. 85–129. New York. Republished in *A Leonard Bloomfield Anthology*, ed. C.F. Hockett, pp. 440–88. Bloomington, Ind.: Indiana University Press, 1970.

Boon, T.C.B. 1960. "Use of Catechisms and Syllabics by the Early Missionaries of Rupert's Land, 1820–1880." The Canadian Church Historical Society, Offprint No. 21. Toronto.

Campbell, Lyle and Marianne Mithun. 1979. *The Languages of Native America*. Austin: University of Texas Press.

Ellis, C.D. 1971. "Cree Verb Paradigms". *International Journal of American Linguistics* 37, no. 2; pp. 119–24.

________. 1995. *âtalôhkâna nêsta tipâcimôwina / Cree Legends and Narratives from the West Coast of James Bay*. Winnipeg: University of Manitoba Press.

Faries, Richard. 1938. *A Dictionary of the Cree Language*. Toronto.

Goddard, Ives. 1967. "The Algonquian Independent Indicative." National Museum of Canada, Bulletin 214; pp. 66–106.

Haas, Mary R. 1967. "The Development of Proto-Algonkian *-awe-". In *Studies in Historical Linguistics in Honor of George Sherman Lane*, University of North Carolina Studies in the Germanic Languages and Literatures, 58; pp. 137–45. Chapel Hill.

Hockett, Charles F. 1958. *A Course in Modern Linguistics*. New York.

________. 1966."What Algonquian is Really Like", *International Journal of American Linguistics* 32, no. 1; pp. 59–73.

Horden, John. 1881. *A Grammar of the Cree Language*, Society for the Promotion of Christian Knowledge. London.

________. 1927. (Translation, with others) ᐅᐢᑭ ᑌᐢᑕᒣᓐᑦ (*misprinted as* ᑎᐢᑌᒥᓐᑦ), *New Testament*; British and Foreign Bible Society. London. Reprint, 1991, in larger type with section headings, by Canadian Bible Society, Toronto.

Lacombe, Albert. 1874. *Dictionnaire de la langue des Cris*. Montréal.

LeClaire, Nancy and George Cardinal. 1998. *Alberta Elders' Cree Dictionary/alperta ohci kehtehayak nehiyaw otwestamâkewasinahikan.* Edited by Earle Waugh. University of Alberta Press.

Mason, Roger Burford. 1994. "The Sound of Innovation—James Evans' Syllabic Alphabet", *Queen's Quarterly* 101, no. 4; pp. 848–53.

McNulty, G.E. 1971. *Petite grammaire du parler montagnais en Tš - N*, Collection Notes de cours, No. 4; Centre d'Etudes Nordiques, Université Laval, Québec.

Minde, Emma. 1997. *kwayask ê-kî-pê-kiskinowâpahtihicik / Their Example Showed Me the Way.* Ahenakew, Freda and H.C. Wolfart, eds. Edmonton: University of Alberta Press.

Nida, Eugene A. 1952. *God's Word in Man's Language*. New York: Harper and Brothers.

_________. 1954. *Customs and Cultures*. New York: Harper and Brothers.

_________. 1960. *Message and Mission*. New York: Harper and Brothers.

Nichols, John D. 1996. "The Cree Syllabary", in Peter T. Daniels and William Bright, eds., *The World's Writing Systems*, pp. 599–611. New York: Oxford University Press.

Pentland, D.H. 1978. "A Historical Overview of Cree Dialects", Papers of the Ninth Algonquian Conference, ed. W. Cowan; pp. 104–26. Ottawa: Carleton University Press.

Piggott, G.L., and A. Grafstein. 1983. *An Ojibwa Lexicon*. Ottawa: National Museums of Canada.

Sapir, Edward. 1921. *Language*. New York.

Teeter, K.V. 1967. "Genetic Classification in Algonquian", National Museum of Canada, Bulletin 214; pp. 1–6. Ottawa.

Todd, Evelyn. 1970. *A Grammar of the Ojibwa Language*. Ann Arbor, Michigan: University Microfilms, Inc.

Wesley, A. 1974. (*Translation under supervision of Jules Leguerrier, O.M.I.*) *The Four Gospels* / ᒥᓄ·ᐊᒋᒧ·ᐃ ᒪᓯᓇᐃᑲᓇ. (R.C.) Diocese of Moosonee.

_________. 1976. (*Translation under supervision of Jules Leguerrier, O.M.I.*) Acts of the Apostles, Letters of Saint Paul, Letters to all Christians, Book of Revelation / ᐃᔑᑎᓴ·ᐊᑲᓇᐠ ᐅᐟ ᐃᔑᒋᑫ·ᐃᓂ·ᐊ·ᐊ, ᐅ ᒪᓯᓇᐊᒪᑫ·ᐃᓇ ᒥᓄ·ᑕ ·ᐸᐪ, ᐁ ᒪᓯᓇᐊᒪᒋᐠ ᒥᓯ·ᐁ ᑲ ᐊᔭᒥᐊᒋᐠ, ᑭᐢᑫᓂᑕᒧ·ᐃ·ᐁ·ᐃ ᒪᓯᓇᐃᑲᐣ. (R.C.) Diocese of Moosonee.

Wolfart, H.C. 1973. *Plains Cree: A Grammatical Study*, Transactions of the American Philosophical Society, n.s. 63, no. 5. Philadelphia.

Wolfart, H.C. and J.F. Carroll. 1973; 2nd edit., 1981. *Meet Cree*. Edmonton: University of Alberta Press.

Wolfart, H.C. and Freda Ahenakew. 1998. *The Student's Dictionary of Literary Plains Cree*; Memoir 15, Algonquian and Iroquoian Linguistics, University of Manitoba Press.

TOPICAL INDEX

ABOUT THE AUTHOR

C. Douglas Ellis has made Cree the focal point of his studies since 1954. He first taught linguistics in the Department of Anthropology at the University of Toronto, then in the Department of Classics at McGill University, Montreal, where he became one of the founding members, and later, Chairman of the Department of Linguistics. He has done extensive field work in Cree speaking country and has taught courses in Cree. He is Emeritus Professor of Linguistics at McGill and currently Adjunct Research Professor in the School of Linguistics and Applied Language Studies at Carleton University, Ottawa.